WILLIAM CONGREVE: THE CRITICAL HERITAGE

THE CRITICAL HERITAGE SERIES

GENERAL EDITOR: B.C. SOUTHAM, M.A., B.LITT. (OXON.)
*Formerly Department of English, Westfield College,
University of London*

WILLIAM CONGREVE

THE CRITICAL HERITAGE

Edited by
ALEXANDER LINDSAY
and
HOWARD ERSKINE-HILL

ROUTLEDGE
LONDON AND NEW YORK

First published in 1989 by
Routledge
11 New Fetter Lane, London EC4P 4EE
29 West 35th Street, New York, NY 10001

Set in 10/12pt Bembo
by Thomson Press (India) Limited
New Delhi
and printed in Great Britain
by TJ Press (Padstow) Ltd
Padstow, Cornwall

British Library Cataloguing in Publication Data

William Congreve: the critical heritage.
(The Critical heritage series)
1. Drama in English. Congreve, William,
1670–1729 — Critical studies
I. Lindsay, Alexander   II. Erskine-Hill,
Howard   III. Series
822'.4

ISBN 0–415–02535–4

Library of Congress Cataloging in Publication Data

William Congreve: the critical heritage / edited by Alexander Lindsay
and Howard Erskine-Hill.
p.   cm.—(The Critical heritage series)
Includes index.
ISBN 0–415–02535–4
1.   Congreve, William, 1670–1729—Criticism and interpretation.
I Lindsay, Alexander. II. Erskine-Hill, Howard.
III. Series
PR3367.W47 1989
822'.4–dc19   88–32176

General Editor's Preface

The reception given to a writer by his contemporaries and near-contemporaries is evidence of considerable value to the student of literature. On one side we learn a great deal about the state of criticism at large and in particular about the development of critical attitudes towards a single writer; at the same time, through private comments in letters, journals or marginalia, we gain an insight upon the tastes and literary thought of individual readers of the period. Evidence of this kind helps us to understand the writer's historical situation, the nature of his immediate reading-public, and his response to these pressures.

The separate volumes in the *Critical Heritage Series* present a record of this early criticism. Clearly, for many of the highly productive and lengthily reviewed nineteenth- and twentieth-century writers, there exists an enormous body of material; and in these cases the volume editors have made a selection of the most important views, significant for their intrinsic critical worth or for their representative quality – perhaps even registering incomprehension!

For earlier writers, notably pre-eighteenth century, the materials are much scarcer and the historical period has been extended, sometimes far beyond the writer's lifetime, in order to show the inception and growth of critical views which were initially slow to appear.

In each volume the documents are headed by an Introduction, discussing the material assembled and relating the early stages of the author's reception to what we have come to identify as the critical tradition. The volumes will make available much material which would otherwise be difficult of access and it is hoped that the modern reader will be thereby helped towards an informed understanding of the ways in which literature has been read and judged.

B.C.S.

Contents

Preface

There are one or two features of this collection which may require comment. Some readers will be surprised at the amount of space given to comments on *The Mourning Bride*, and even Congreve's non-dramatic verse. But it is by no means uncommon for the history of a writer's critical reputation to reveal that his contemporaries and their immediate successors valued highly works quite other than those on which that reputation rests today. We have simply presented Congreve's critical record as we found it. We have tried also to preserve an awareness that Congreve's plays belong primarily in the theatre, and that except for the latter half of the last century they have maintained their place in the repertory; their performance demands a special kind of critical response on the part of both actors and audience. To this end we have included a selection of dramatic reviews from the eighteenth and nineteenth centuries, especially those which contain critical comment of a more general nature.

The texts are given in their earliest form, where available. The original spelling and punctuation have been preserved, apart from the customary modernization of 'long s', and the transposing of Roman and italic type in a few cases. A few obvious printing errors have been silently corrected. Occasionally, where a modern edition answered our requirements, we have used it. Choice of an accessible edition of Congreve for references has been difficult because the *Works* of 1710 introduces not only readings which differ from the quartos, especially in *The Mourning Bride*, but scene divisions after the French manner. Congreve's *Amendments of Mr. Collier's False and Imperfect Citations* shows that even before 1710 he had begun to think in terms of French-style scene divisions; but even there the references which he gives do not correspond with the *Works*. Our solution has been to provide references for material prior to 1710 from the *Complete Plays*, ed. Herbert Davis, Chicago, University of Chicago Press, 1966, which is based on the quartos. References to the poems, and to the plays *post* 1710, have been taken from the twin World's Classics volumes edited by Bonamy Dobrée and published by the Oxford University Press, *The*

Mourning Bride and Miscellanies (1928) and *Comedies* (1925).

As regards the degree of collaboration between the editors, the introduction was drafted by Howard Erskine-Hill; the items were edited and their headnotes drafted by Alexander Lindsay. We have extensively revised and commented upon each other's work, however, and share responsibility for the volume as a whole.

Acknowledgements

The editors wish to thank the following for their permission to use copyright material: the Clarendon Press, Oxford, for items 8, 44 (c), 48, 49, 52 (a) and (b), 64, and 73; John Murray Ltd for 85 (a) and (b); Duke University Press for 10 (b); Yale University Press for 43; and Johns Hopkins University Press for 45.

Our thanks are also due to the staff of Cambridge University Library, of the British Library, of the Library, Trinity College, Dublin, and of the Dublin Public Libraries' Gilbert Library. Finally, we owe a special debt to Professor Donald McKenzie of Pembroke College, Oxford, for his encouragement and for copies of some rare items; and to Professor Kathleen Tillotson for her expert help with an allusion to Dickens.

It would be impossible to acknowledge individually our debts to Congreve scholarship, but two exceptions should perhaps be made. Arthur Freeman's prefaces to the Garland Publishing series of facsimiles, 'The English Stage: Attack and Defense 1557–1730', provided up-to-date details of dating and authorship for items belonging to the Collier controversy; while Emmet L. Avery's *Congreve's Plays on the Eighteenth-Century Stage*, New York, Modern Languages Association of America, 1951, guided us to several valuable newspaper reviews of performances.

THE CRITICAL HERITAGE SERIES

GENERAL EDITOR: B.C. SOUTHAM

Volumes published and forthcoming

ADDISON AND STEELE	Edward A. Bloom and Lillian D. Bloom
MATTHEW ARNOLD: THE POETRY	Carl Dawson
MATTHEW ARNOLD: PROSE WRITINGS	Carl Dawson and John Pfordresher
W.H. AUDEN	John Haffenden
JANE AUSTEN 1811–1870	B.C. Southam
JANE AUSTEN 1870–1940	B.C. Southam
SAMUEL BECKETT	L. Graver and R. Federman
ARNOLD BENNETT	James Hepburn
WILLIAM BLAKE	G.E. Bentley Jr
THE BRONTËS	Miriam Allott
BROWNING	Boyd Litzinger and Donald Smalley
ROBERT BURNS	Donald A. Low
BYRON	Andrew Rutherford
THOMAS CARLYLE	Jules Paul Seigel
CHAUCER 1385–1837	Derek Brewer
CHAUCER 1837–1933	Derek Brewer
CHEKHOV	Victor Emeljanow
CLARE	Mark Storey
CLOUGH	Michael Thorpe
COLERIDGE	J.R. de J. Jackson
WILKIE COLLINS	Norman Page
WILLIAM CONGREVE	Alexander Lindsay and Howard Erskine-Hill
CONRAD	Norman Sherry
FENIMORE COOPER	George Dekker and John P. McWilliams
CRABBE	Arthur Pollard
STEPHEN CRANE	Richard M. Weatherford
DANTE	Michael Caesar
DEFOE	Pat Rogers
DICKENS	Philip Collins
JOHN DONNE	A.J. Smith
DOS PASSOS	Barry Maine
DRYDEN	James and Helen Kinsley
GEORGE ELIOT	David Carroll
T.S. ELIOT	Michael Grant
WILLIAM FAULKNER	John Bassett
HENRY FIELDING	Ronald Paulson and Thomas Lockwood
FORD MADOX FORD	Frank MacShane

Introduction

Congreve has been generally judged the finest dramatist of later seventeenth-century England. Further, he has come to seem the essence of the drama of that time. In a diminishing perspective upon the period its comedy alone seemed excellent, and Congreve its most sophisticated spirit. As Charles Cowden Clarke put it in 1871, *The Way of the World* (1700) 'comprises the most quintessentialised combination of qualities requisite to compound an artificially legitimate comedy to be found in the whole range of our dramatic literature' (No. 93). Equally, when we turn to the tragedy of the period, Congreve's *The Mourning Bride* (1697), long a theatrical success, will seem a fair representation of the strengths and weaknesses of its form in that age.

Many would now challenge this distillation of later seventeenth-century drama to a Congrevian essence. A nearer investigation of the period shows that not only the versatile Dryden, not only the well-remembered Etherege and Wycherley, but Shadwell, Southerne, Otway, Vanbrugh, Farquhar, Crowne, and Rowe, at least, had something to admire. Yet the image of Congreve still holds its troubling brilliance, challenging reader and theatre-goer alike to praise, exorcize, or understand. This has long been so. Congreve's critical heritage is a cloud of witnesses that could scarcely be more distinguished or diverse: Dryden, Swift, Addison, Collier, Pope, Fielding, Voltaire, Horace Walpole, Burke, Johnson, Fanny Burney, Hazlitt, Coleridge, Lamb, Macaulay, Thackeray, Edmund Gosse, and William Archer, to name but a few. Several, including Johnson's friend Thomas Davies, and the brilliant Hazlitt, respond not only to the text but the presentation of Congreve on the stage, affording us valuable reminiscences and clues to his relative theatrical success in the century following the performance of his final and most famous play.

THE EARLY RESPONSE

'"Aye, Mr. Tonson, he was Ultimus Romanorum!" (with a sigh, speaking of poor Mr. Congreve, who died a year or two before)':

Pope's comment of 28 or 29 November 1730, together with his other brief remarks, sums up a great deal in the early reception of Congreve. Pope paid tribute to Congreve's wit but questioned if it were always true to nature; he defended his superiority to Colley Cibber's best comedy, *The Careless Husband*, while affirming that Molière and Jonson's *Silent Woman* were better still. But it is Pope's remark to Tonson that is most interesting, bringing to the fore as it does the question of a line or succession of the best authors.

When in 1692 Thomas Southerne drew to the attention of Dryden the work of an unknown young playwright it was the chance Dryden had been looking for. Deposed from his laureateship by the revolution of the Prince of Orange, Dryden had little reason to admire his successor, and none to expect kindnesses from him. His pride as well as his sense of his own worth prompted him to name his own heir in the realm of letters. He needed someone of the younger generation whom he could himself recognize and assist; one whose talent, with assistance, could not fail to win applause; and one, not of Dryden's own religion and loyalty, who would be acceptable to the new Orange establishment. This heir might then protect his 'father' and mentor, and defend his reputation after death. Such an heir might have been John Oldham, 'too little and too lately known' as Dryden said in his great elegy. Congreve, a young poet already known to him, now promised to be the candidate for fame he sought. Certainly various remarks on the times, hit off in dialogue in the earliest text of *The Old Batchelour* (1693), gave promise of a wit that was able to override the tragic religious and political divisions of the period – 'Every Man, now, changes his Mistress and his Religion, as his Humour varies or his Interest' (II, ii, 148–9); 'Undoubtedly 'tis impossible to be a Pimp and not a Man of parts. That is, without being politick, diligent, secret, wary and so forth – And to all this, valiant as Hercules – That is, passively valiant and actively obedient' (III, i, 149–52). Probably it was the wit and diction of the dialogue which impressed Dryden, and Southerne's letter to Birch describing Dryden's reaction suggests that it was in the order and shaping of the play that Congreve was judged to need help: 'the stuff was rich indeed, it wanted only the fashionable cutt of the town' (No. 2). Thus refashioned and with a strong cast, Betterton playing Heartwell, Dogget Fondlewife, Mrs Bracegirdle Araminta and Mrs

Barry Laetitia, the first play of the new young author had 'extraordinary' success in the theatre, not less so, perhaps, for including some broad farce of an easy and standard kind. Early reactions stressed the wit of the piece, and welcomed a new author. Significantly it was Dryden's colleague Southerne who raised, in his prefatory poem to *The Old Batchelour*, the question of a literary successor to Dryden (No. 3a). The town was being prepared, but for the moment Dryden held back his commendation. In his dedication to *Examen Poeticum* (1693) (No. 6) he might publicly praise his protégé's skill as a translator of Homer, but he did not yet consider Congreve a rival to the greatest of Elizabethan dramatists.

When, however, he read, prior to its performance in late 1693, Congreve's next play, *The Double-Dealer*, Dryden made up his mind. He composed a verse-letter to Congreve that is as great a short poem as the 'To the Memory of Mr. Oldham': a commentary on the times, a piece of cultural criticism, and (picking up the theme from Southerne's poem on *The Old Batchelour*) the dramatic declaration of Congreve as his literary heir. In a letter to his friend Walsh (No. 10b) Dryden makes it clear that his poem was written before the rather cool early reception of *The Double-Dealer* in the theatre. He stood by his judgement and had the satisfaction of seeing opinion come round. The play's reputation was powerfully assisted by the honour of a command performance from Mary II herself, to whom Congreve penned a special complimentary prologue.[1]

It is a mistake to read a poem such as 'To my Dear Friend Mr. Congreve, On His Comedy, call'd, The Double-Dealer' as literary criticism alone. It is in many ways a veiled apologia and vindication of Dryden himself, in which the political judgement of the non-juring ex-laureate is affirmed, as well as his literary judgement. Indeed there is a special cunning in the way in which the literary merit of the politically acceptable young Congreve is seen in implied analogy with the significance of the exiled Prince of Wales:

> Oh that your Brows my Lawrel had sustain'd,
> Well had I been Depos'd, if You had reign'd!
> The Father had descended for the Son;
> For only You are lineal to the Throne.
> Thus when the State one *Edward* did depose;
> A Greater *Edward* in his room arose.
>
> (No. 10a, ll. 41–6)

The same judgement, Dryden is saying, recognizes the right heir, whether in the political or the poetic kingdom. Appropriately for a poem the object of which is the recognition of a successor, its literary mode is panegyric.[2] As in straightforward political panegyric, such as Dryden's own *Astraea Redux* (1660), its praise is enlarged in order to display an ideal and express a hope.

This must be borne in mind when the modern reader seeks the stratum of literary criticism in Dryden's complex poem. It is the direction rather than the degree of the praise which is of most significance. What emerges from the poem, as reason for Dryden's recognition of Congreve, is the importance he attaches to the right balance between strength and grace. A number of terms are associated in this polarity: with strength, genius and wit; with grace, judgement, ease, and sweetness of manners. Dryden thinks of these opposites temporally and spatially. Historically speaking, he sees literature before the Civil War, 'the Gyant Race, before the Flood', as that of strength, wit, genius, and crude vigour. Literature since the Restoration has by and large enjoyed the other set of qualities. In these terms Congreve can be seen in relation to Jonson and Fletcher on the one hand, to Etherege, Southerne, and Wycherley on the other. Dryden does not wish to express a preference for one set of qualities rather than the other. The melancholy thing about this historical evolution is that one set of virtues is lost as another is gained – and the former, no doubt, the more fundamental. 'Our Age was cultivated thus at length; / But what we gain'd in skill we lost in strength.'

When Dryden considers Congreve as a writer who has managed to transcend this sad pattern of historical gain-with-loss he offers a spatial rather than a temporal perspective, for in his new drama, as in a well-designed work of architecture, strength and grace can there be seen simultaneously combined:

> Firm *Dorique* Pillars found Your solid Base:
> The Fair *Corinthian* Crowns the higher Space;
> Thus all below is Strength, and all above is Grace.
>
> (ll. 17–19)

These lines allude to classical architectural teaching, going back to the Augustan architect Vitruvius, that where the different architectural orders are combined in one edifice the plainer and stronger Doric should be used below, the more elaborate and delicate Corinthian above. Dryden's skill and learning can be seen from the fact that in Vitruvius the Doric, Ionic, and Corinthian orders themselves have a historical significance, marking an evolution from relatively simple to sophisticated and luxurious stages of social development. Congreve is 'the best *Vitruvius*' (in Dryden's compliment) because he collects and combines the various merits of those evolving cycles of civilization which compose history itself.[3] This is Dryden's vision of the great writer, and true literary successor.

Explained in this way Dryden's poem may seem more expressive of the old poet's hope than the young playwright's achievement. Yet *The Double-Dealer*, in comparison with the popular *Old Batchelour*, is a strikingly stronger play, completely in the author's command, with nothing added for easy entertainment alone. Furthermore its roots seem to reach back through Wycherley's *Plain Dealer* (which Congreve's title recalls) to the tragicomedy of Fletcher's era and the last years of Shakespeare. The vigour and intelligence of 'Maskwell, a Villain', a psychologically simple but dramatically powerful conception, owe something to figures such as Iachimo, Iago, and Don John. In Maskwell and Lady Touchwood, Congreve has taken something from the drama of 'the Gyant Race, before the Flood' though he has shaped and dressed it in (Southerne's phrase) 'the fashionable cutt of the town'. There is something 'tremendous' in Maskwell, as Bonamy Dobrée remarked,[4] but Congreve's combination of Doric and Corinthian in one bold plot has troubled critics, who have sometimes reached for the word 'melodrama' to describe the effect. Macaulay said that 'there is something strangely revolting in the way in which a group that seems to belong to the house of Laius or of Pelops, is introduced into the midst of the Brisks, Froths, Carelesses, and Plyants' (No. 90). It may be so; yet both Elizabethan and Restoration drama have strikingly transgressed that neoclassical frontier. Congreve may have achieved his aim in this respect better in *The Way of the World*, but he knew what he was doing in *The Double-Dealer*, as his epigraph from Horace, '*Interdum tamen, et vocem Comeodia tollit*' ('Nevertheless, sometimes even comedy exalts her voice'), shows. Dryden's Vitruvian compliment, in the context of his exposition of the history of early and late Renaissance English drama, brings out what a Roman ambition might have meant for Congreve in the 1690s, and what Pope perceived when he called him, sighing to Jacob Tonson, 'Ultimus Romanorum'.

Congreve's Roman reputation gained a new side to it when, on the death of Mary II on 28 December 1694, he composed his best-known poem, 'The Mourning Muse of *Alexis*. A Pastoral. Lamenting the death of our late gracious Queen Mary' (1695). It was at once rewarded by £100 from the king.[5] The death and state funeral of the queen were, of course, great public events, a communal drama that far eclipsed the favourable or unfavourable reception of a new play in the theatre. Adopting the form of the Virgilian pastoral eclogue, Congreve mourned the death of the queen, and thus gave himself a part in the great national drama. In his own lifetime, at least, the poem was as much remembered as anything he wrote, and in the year it came out he was favourably compared to Virgil in a slightly muddled tribute by the Hon. Edward Howard (No. 15). Discussion of Congreve as a poet may begin with Addison's praise, in 1694, of '*Harmonious Congreve*' (No. 12) and continues through many a compliment and, more rarely, attack (Nos 14, 15, 20, 21, 29, 40). By a nice judgement of his own public emotion, the right moment, and an appropriate literary form, Congreve had now attached his rising literary reputation firmly to the House of Orange. This would be seen even more clearly from his 'Pindarique Ode, Humbly Offer'd to the King On His Taking *Namure*' (1695), the political and dynastic implications of which were noted by William Pittis in his 'Epistolary Poem to N. Tate' (at the end of No. 17). This was what now seems to have struck public attention: Congreve was writing as if he were poet laureate, though Dryden as 'abdicated laureate' and now Nahum Tate as official Poet Laureate were both very much alive. In this year, it is also relevant to note, Congreve was given a government 'place': that of commissioner for licensing hackney coaches. It is, at all events, a remarkable comment on what captured the literary imagination in 1695 that there is virtually no commentary on the phenomenal success of Congreve's third and greatest theatrical comedy, *Love for Love*, when it was acted at the new theatre at Lincoln's Inn Fields on 30 April. The original triumph of *Love for Love* is widely attested, as many later items in the present collection show, but the literary record in 1695 is far more concerned with Congreve's response to the death of the queen.

In due course the remarkable features of *Love for Love* (whose title as tellingly recalls Dryden's *All for Love* and D'Urfey's *Love for Money* as *The Double-Dealer* had *The Plain Dealer*) come through. It is notable that in Daniel Kenrick's sceptical if not hostile review of Congreve in *A New Session of the Poets, Occasion'd by the Death of Mr. Dryden* (1700) the still young playwright's demand for divine recognition is supported, before all else, by the two most popular low-life figures from *Love for Love*:

> Stiff, as his Works, th'elab'rate *Cong—ve* came,
> Who could so soon Preferment get, and Fame.
> And with him brought the Product of his Pen,
> Miss *Prue* before, behind his Back stood *Ben*.
> (No. 39)

It really is an unconscious tribute to 'th'elab'rate *Cong—ve*' that his claims should be supported first and foremost by the least stiff and elaborate characters in his drama, characters who in their linguistic and theatrical expression, their articulate humanity, can match comparably important figures in the greatest Elizabethan or Jacobean comedies. It is not only in these respects that *Love for Love* fulfils Dryden's prediction that Congreve combined the merits of earlier and later seventeenth-century drama. The comedy is Congreve's most theatrically imaginative work. The character of Foresight the astrologer is fully Jonsonian: it partakes of the world of *The Alchymist*. We not only laugh at him as (in the words of the Dramatis Personae) 'An illiterate Old Fellow, peevish and positive, superstitious, and pretending to understand Astrology', but we are made to see the world as he sees it, and share (though not identify with) the habit of his mind. Greater still than these features of the play are the mad scenes of Valentine, the bankrupt lover, scenes which, though inexplicable in terms of a comedy of manners, express a moral and human concern that is deeper by far, and one may think come as near to a direct revelation of Congreve's vision of the world as any part of one of his plays can do.

Angelica. Do you know me, *Valentine?*
Valentine. Oh very well.
Angelica. Whom am I?
Valentine. You're a Woman, – One to whom Heav'n gave Beauty, when it grafted Roses on a Briar. You are the reflection of Heav'n in a Pond, and he that leaps at you is sunk. You are all white, a sheet of lovely spotless Paper, when you first are Born; but you are to be scrawl'd and blotted by every Goose's Quill. I know you; for I liv'd a Woman,

7

and lov'd her so long, that I found out a strange thing: I found out what a
Woman was good for.

    Tattle. Aye, prithee, what's that?

    Valentine. Why to keep a Secret.

(IV, i, 631–43)

Here are Plato, Shakespeare, and Locke; here is the vividness of
proverbial wisdom; here is knowledge of the ways of the world.
Here, rarer still, is an oracular voice through feigned madness
which briefly breaks through the idiom of manners to declare what
must otherwise be constructed from the implications of what is said
by the sane characters of Congreve's drama.

    The next inflection in the reputation of Congreve occurs not
with the reception of this great comedy, but with the public
response to his only tragedy, *The Mourning Bride*, first performed
on 27 February 1697, and when published, in the same year,
dedicated to the Princess Anne. With Mrs Bracegirdle playing
Almeria, Mrs Barry Zara, and Verbruggen the King, it was
acclaimed and played for thirteen nights. Particularly notable must
have been Bracegirdle's beautiful delivery of her lines as she and
Leonora enter the temple aisles in Act II, Scene 1, 51–69, a passage
later to become famous through Samuel Johnson's praise, and
which is certainly a poetic and theatrical effect far different from
anything Congreve had attempted before. Though similar in its
setting and period to the two parts of Dryden's *Conquest of Granada*,
The Mourning Bride belongs to that long trajectory of Restoration
tragedy from the hyperbole of the 1660s through Lee's and
Dryden's adoption of blank verse to the chaste and restrained form
of Addison's *Cato* (1713). Congreve's tragedy was to remain
popular in the theatre throughout the eighteenth century. Its
appearance in 1697 signalled that its author had now mastered the
only remaining area of literary achievement necessary to make his
fame complete. As Catharine Trotter put it in her poem 'To Mr.
Congreve, on his Tragedy, the *Mourning Bride*':

> This only part was wanting to thy name,
> That wit's whole empire thou mightst justly claim.

(No. 18)

The praise of this young poet was endorsed by the very
well-known and prolific poet of that period, Sir Richard Blackmore, in the preface to his epic *King Arthur* (1697). Blackmore

8

wrote that *The Mourning Bride* had won 'Universal Applause' and was 'look'd on as the most perfect *Tragedy* that has been wrote in this Age'. This was praise indeed; but Blackmore went on to strike a new note in the critical reception of Congreve, one that would echo and re-echo through what is perhaps the most remarkable public controversy about drama that England has known. Blackmore noted that despite its popular reception *The Mourning Bride* was, save 'some few Exceptions', 'Chast, Just, and Decent'. Congreve's most recent success, Blackmore argued, showed that there was no need for playwrights to write 'in that leud Manner, that has been of late years introduc'd, and too long Encourag'd' (No. 19). These remarks heralded a revolution in theatrical taste. Blackmore was commending *The Mourning Bride* as an honourable exception to the libertinism which prevailed upon the London stage. Nor was the preface to *King Arthur* the first of his denunciations of the contemporary drama; he had made a similar attack two years previously in the preface to his earlier epic *Prince Arthur*. J. E. Spingarn may have overstated his case when he claimed that 'the victory had been achieved before Collier wrote';[6] but Blackmore had certainly prepared the way. During the Collier controversy he continued to wage his own war against the evils which for him were summed up under the head of 'wit' (No. 35), and he was still campaigning with scarcely diminished zeal in the preface to *Creation* (1712) and *Essays on Several Subjects* (1716).

THE COLLIER CONTROVERSY

In the autumn of 1693 Congreve's old schoolfellow and fellow-student, Jonathan Swift, in a long and somewhat self-serving poem designed to have been printed with *The Double-Dealer* if that play were well received, had declared:

> Thus I look with mercy on the age,
> By hopes my CONGREVE will reform the stage;
> For never did poetic mine before
> Produce a richer vein or cleaner ore.
> (No. 8, ll. 49–52)

Swift was doubtless well informed as to the nature of *The Old Batchelour*, and it is improbable that the reformation of the stage

9

that he had in mind in 1693 was the simple moral reformation desired by Blackmore. More likely Swift is thinking of a more regular classical drama for England, though this would also imply a less licentious muse; indeed, 'cleaner ore' may ambiguously hint at this. What is clear is that Swift saw the desired reformation of the stage as within reach because of Congreve's wit, and the word is no doubt used in its more comprehensive sense.

The opinion that under Charles II both court and theatre had grown licentious is to be noticed in the next reign, 1685–8. James II's queen, Mary of Modena was devout as well as beautiful: change came slowly, but the new court was much more decent than the old. In this reign Dryden wrote *The Hind and the Panther* with its two confessional passages, in Parts I and III; and it was in this reign that he wrote his 'Ode to the Pious Memory of Anne Killigrew', a poem in which he speaks with loathing of his own part in a morally corrupt theatre. Hostility to libertine comedy, however, had existed long before the 1690s, occasionally among the dramatists themselves. As early as 1668, in the preface to his first play, *The Sullen Lovers*, Thomas Shadwell had complained:

in the *Playes* which have been wrote of late, there is no such thing as perfect Character, but the two chief persons are most commonly a Swearing, Drinking, Whoring, Ruffian for a Lover, and an impudent ill-bred tom-rig for a Mistress, and these are the fine people of the *Play*; and there is that Latitude in this, that almost anything is proper for them to say; but their chief subject is bawdy, and profaneness, which they call *brisk writing*, when the most dissolute of Men, that rellish these things well enough in private, are *chok'd* at 'em in publick; and methinks, if there were nothing but the ill Manners of it, it should make Poets avoid that Indecent way of Writing.

There was towards the end of the century a slow but widespread reaction by the moral and religious majority against what must often have appeared a merely shallow laxity and profanity which seemed to have been flowing from court and theatre. The attitude of the new House of Orange towards this swell of opinion was classically divided. On the one hand Mary II had honoured Congreve with a command performance of *The Double-Dealer*, probably on 13 January 1694; on the other hand on 4 June 1697 and again on 18 February 1699, William III made public 'His Majesty's Pleasure, That you do not hereafter presume to act anything in any Play, contrary to Religion or good Manners, as you shall answer it at your utmost Peril'.[8] Charles II's documents concerning the theatre had been equally moral, but the reiteration of the king's wishes is noteworthy here. The drama could not be changed overnight, however. Few dramatists indeed would have owned up to a desire to offend religion or good manners, but they often appear to be trying how far they can go with their audiences; licence had come to be so taken for granted as to seem inoffensive. Again, Blackmore's preface is evidence for the opinion that a play could hardly succeed in the theatre without some measure of licence.

Blackmore's general denunciation of the drama had not precluded generous praise of the young Congreve, his fellow-Whig. No such encouragement was to be found in Jeremy Collier's *A Short View of the Immorality, and Profaneness of the English Stage, Together With the Sense of Antiquity upon this Argument*, which appeared in the spring of 1698. Detecting, one may well suppose, the movement of opinion his way, Collier wrote a root-and-branch attack on the English theatre, especially drama since the Restoration, most especially drama since the Bloodless Revolution. The attacker was as remarkable a man as Congreve himself. A clergyman of principle and eloquence, a courageous non-juror and Jacobite, he was after the revolution the author of a series of pamphlets which asserted the right of James II under the legal hereditary monarchy, and assailed the claims of William and Mary to the throne. He was especially effective against those who urged that a successful revolution must mean the blessing of providence upon it, resolving 'all Title into Force and Success' and thus making 'the Devil, if he should prevail, the Lord's Anointed'.[9] He gave up his benefice rather than take the new oaths, was twice imprisoned for his politics, and attended to Tyburn as priest Sir John Friend and Sir William Parkins who had (rightly or wrongly) been convicted of plotting to assassinate William III. A learned ecclesiastical historian, as well as a political pamphleteer and public moralist, Collier ended his career as a bishop of the non-juring Anglican Church.

Given the consistency of Collier's political allegiance one may wonder how far there was political motivation in his assault on the stage. In his magnanimous tribute to a man of radically different politics from his own Macaulay says that Collier here lays aside his political prejudices. 'He has forgotten that he is a Jacobite, and remembers only that he is a citizen and a Christian' (No. 90). This is certainly the impression one has reading *A Short View*, and one can hardly doubt Collier's religious sincerity. Above all he does not hesitate to attack, and prominently, the drama of Dryden, himself a non-juror and Jacobite. All this granted, however, it may still have struck Collier that a broad moral sweep through the drama would in the end embarrass the flourishing 'Orange comedies' (Edmund Gosse's term) of Congreve and Vanbrugh most of all. Colley Cibber would go on record in 1740 as thinking that 'The authors of the "Old Batchelour" and of "The Relapse" were those whom Collier most labour'd to convict of immorality.'[10] As for Dryden, he was a Catholic convert who, having confessed his part in a licentious theatre, had later written as profanely as ever. With *Love Triumphant* (1694), however, he had finally withdrawn from the stage. In Dryden's case, at least, the reproof Collier considered he had deserved 'would not strike him down in mid-career. To a hostile political commentator of the time Collier seemed to soften towards Dryden: 'he can change his Opinion, and be more complaisant if he pleases; witness his soft Usage of Mr. *Dryden*; in the Defence he ranks him amongst the best Criticks; allows him a good Judge in Language, and mentions him, quite contrary to his Custom, with much decency and respect; nay, I believe, shou'd the Old Gentleman become Poet Laureat again, Mr. *Collier* wou'd afford him a Panegyrick' (No. 28). For Dryden to have become 'Poet Laureat' again would have meant, what both Dryden and Collier wished, a restoration of James II. Congreve, on the other hand, was linked to the House of Orange by his public poetry, and was now a Williamite placeman. That he was in his way as much concerned with inheritance and succession as Dryden or Collier *The Double-Dealer* and *Love for Love* demonstrate, but this was consistent with some markedly Whig moments. When Valentine resists his father's plan to disinherit him, Sir Sampson exclaims: 'What, I warrant my Son thought nothing belong'd to a Father, but Forgiveness and Affection; no Authority, no Correction, no Arbitrary Power; nothing to be done, but for him to offend, and me to pardon.' Later in the same scene Sir Sampson confronts Valentine with the angry questions: 'Are you not my Slave? Did I not beget you.... Did you come a Voluntier into the World?' (*Love for Love*, II, i, 175–8, 324–30). This is brilliant mockery of the patriarchal theory of kingship[11] which in the form of Sir Robert

Filmer's *Patriarcha* had been the chief theoretical defence of the monarchy in the exclusion crisis of 1680, and which was consistently ridiculed by Locke in his *Two Treatises of Government*, written around the same time, but only able to be published after the revolution.

It is not hard to hear the political resonances in the exchanges of Collier and Congreve on Valentine and Sir Sampson. To Collier Valentine is 'a prodigal Debauchee, unnatural, and Profane, Obscene, Sawcy, and undutiful, and yet this Libertine is crown'd for the Man of Merit' (*A Short View*, pp. 142–3). Congreve responds: 'That he is unnatural and undutiful, I don't understand: He has indeed a very unnatural Father; and if he does not very passively submit to his Tyranny and barbarous Usage, I conceive there is a Moral to be apply'd from thence to such Fathers' (No. 24 iv). Passive obedience to lawful princes even when they behaved tyrannously was a key point in the Anglican non-juror creed. Congreve fights back even more *ad hominem* when, commenting on Maskwell's plot in *The Double-Dealer*, he says: 'many damnable Plots have miscarried, wherein Priests have been concern'd' (No. 24 iii). This hinted at a greater involvement by Collier in the recent plot to assassinate William than attending the condemned to the scaffold. Collier, unmoved, responds that Valentine is not only indecent and profane, but 'Undutiful' (No. 27 iv).

If this exchange illustrates the political undercurrents in the Collier controversy, it remains clear that the major issues between Congreve and the others who joined in the debate were literary critical, moral, and religious. For Collier these spheres, and the political too, were intimately connected. Congreve is inclined to insist on the autonomy of the drama, though perhaps only as a defensive strategy. Collier is well versed in literary criticism. He is hardly the pedantic parson, described by Leslie Stephen (No. 101), who blunders into a sphere he knows nothing of. 'The business of *Plays*', he writes, 'is to recommend Virtue, and discountenance Vice; To shew the Uncertainty of Humane Greatness, the suddain Turns of Fate, and the Unhappy Conclusions of Violence and Injustice: 'Tis to expose the Singularities of Pride and Fancy, to make Folly and Falshood contemptible, and to bring every Thing that is Ill under Infamy, and Neglect' (*A Short View*, p. 1). This is close to the neoclassicism of Sidney in his *Defence of Poetry*. Collier quotes from Jonson's *Discoveries* that '*The excess of Feasts and Apparel*, *are the Notes of a Sick State, and the Wantonness of Language of a sick Mind'* and also Jonson's later condemnation of the 'Insolent and obscene Speeches' of the Old Comedy (*A Short View*, p. 51). He does not hesitate to invoke the views of Socrates on Athenian drama, as represented by Plato, and of course to condemn the representation of Socrates in Aristophanes. He surveys Greek and Roman drama, and in showing its greater decency and greater reverence for the divine than seventeenth-century English drama, he cannot be said to show insensitivity to the ancient theatre. He has read Corneille, Molière, and Racine, and is sufficiently up-to-date, and up to the mark critically, to cite Racine's *Athalie* (1691) as a drama that treats the loyal High Priest with respect (though not the priest Mathan, who belongs to the faction of the usurping Athaliah) (*A Short View*, p. 124). Congreve accused him of using the '*Pedantical Cant*' of criticism: Collier responds: 'He means the *Pedantical Cant* of *Aristotle* and *Horace*, of *Bossu* and *Corneille*, of *Rapin*, and Mr *Dryden*; that is of the best Criticks, both Ancient and Modern, upon the Subject' (*A Defence*, p. 80). His plea is well made. We may not agree with Collier's judgements, but by the literary critical standards of the time they are neither ignorant nor stupid.

The conventions of literary criticisms did not, however, constitute for Collier a self-sufficient realm of discourse. Collier took it for granted that the moral tradition concerning drama that descended from Plato, Aristotle, and Horace, meant, when applied to the theatre of his own Christian and late Renaissance era, that modern plays should support the ethos of a Christian society. A Christian society, in his view, could live devoutly under God only through the ministry of the Church, and the holy office of its priests, ordained by apostolic succession from Christ himself. Yet when Collier looked at the drama of his time and country he found priests treated as an easy and almost invariable jest: political time-servers like the Mufti in Dryden's *Don Sebastian*, or mere functionaries brought on to hitch a couple and tie up a plot. When he turned to contemporary France, however, he found in Racine's *Athalie* a drama in which the priesthood played an altogether more elevated part. Hence a whole chapter of *A Short View* is devoted to the abuse of the clergy by the stage. His chapters on the immodesty, the immorality, and the profanity of the stage, and the remaining chapters devoted to specific plays, stem from this central religious concern. Collier is not, therefore, a modern literary critic

14

whose concern begins and ends with literature. He begins with man's relation to the divine, and deduces his social and literary values from that. His method is detailed and practical. He combs his texts for instances of profanity, immorality, or immodesty, paying special attention to the uttered sentiment. His concern is relentlessly literal; for him a publicly uttered profanity was three-quarters of the offence, and he was less attentive to the question of who uttered the profanity, in what situation, and in what kind of play. To any modern critical judgement, therefore, Congreve's strongest plea in his own defence is that Collier takes objectionable remarks out of their context. This is not wholly true, however. Collier does note that many of those who express objectionable sentiments are of high rank and find happiness and fortune at the end of the action. This, Collier thinks, means that Congreve cannot be sincere in any profession to expose and ridicule vice in his plays. But, in any case, Collier considers that Congreve's drama is so crammed with immorality and profanity that considerations of literary context melt into insignificance.

The conflict between the playwright and the religious moralist can best be focused, perhaps, by turning again to *Love for Love*, and to the mad scene in Act IV. '*Love for Love*', says Collier in his chapter on 'The Profaneness of the Stage', 'will give us a farther account of this Authors Proficiency in the *Scriptures*. Our Blessed Saviour affirms himself *to be the Way, the Truth, and the Light* [later corrected to 'Life'], *that he came to bear witness to the Truth, and that His Word is Truth*. These expressions were remembered to good purpose. For *Valentine* in his pretended Madness tells *Buckram* the Lawyer; *I am Truth,* — I am Truth. — *Who's that, that's out of his way, I am Truth, and can set him right*. Now a *Poet* that had not been smitten with the pleasure of Blasphemy, would never have furnish'd Frenzy with Inspiration; nor put our Saviours Words in the Mouth of a Madman' (No. 22 iv) (John xiv, 6, 17; viii, 32; xvii, 17, 18). Collier alerts the modern reader to a specific verbal echo of John's gospel: the question is how Congreve uses this echo. In his *Amendments of Mr. Collier's False and Imperfect Citations* (1698), Congreve responds by explaining why Valentine 'counterfeits madness':

One reason of his Counterfeiting in that manner, is, that it conduces somewhat to the design and end of the Play. Another reason is, that it makes a Variation of the Character; and has the same effect in the Dialogue of the Play, as if a new Character were introduc'd. A third use of this pretended madness is, that it gives a Liberty to Satire; and authorises a Bluntness which would otherwise have been a Breach in the Manners of the Character. Mad-men have generally some one Expression which they use more frequently than any other. *Valentine* to prepare his Satire, fixes on one which may give us to understand, that he will speak nothing but Truth....

I had at first made him say, I am *Tom-tell-troth*; but the sound and meanness of the Expression displeas'd me: and I alter'd it for one shorter, that might signifie the same thing. What a Charitable and Christian-like Construction my dear Friend Mr. *Collier* has given to this Expression, is fit only to be seen in his own Book... a Priest who was not himself furnish'd with Frenzy instead of Inspiration, would never have mistaken one for the other.

(No. 24 iii)

Congreve's explanation is both illuminating and evasive. His reasons for having Valentine counterfeit madness are entirely convincing. Collier's challenge, on the other hand, is why Congreve has a counterfeit madman quote the words of Christ. (That this really was a quotation is sufficiently shown by the collocation of the words: 'I am Truth' and 'way' – Collier's other citations from John are explanatory of the significance of these words.) This Congreve omits directly to explain. Yet he could not be more revealing than when he discloses why he rejected the more obviously popular and proverbial '*Tom-tell-troth*': it is not sufficient for Valentine to speak like a madman; his madness must have no meanness of expression. Congreve wanted the apparently mad Valentine to sound impressive, the 'Liberty' of his 'Satire' to have power. Finally, he accuses Collier of an uncharitable and un-Christian interpretation. This may imply something more than that Collier is putting the worst construction on Congreve's scene. It suggests that Congreve himself had set some kind of Christian construction on Valentine's words. True, as a general *postulatum*, Congreve had already attempted to lay down the distinction, 'That when Words are apply'd to sacred things, and with a purpose to treat of sacred things; they ought to be understood accordingly: But when they are otherwise apply'd, the Diversity of the Subject gives a Diversity of Signification' (No. 24 i). But this was intended to apply to the innumerable examples of profane wit in Congreve's plays; here he does not deny Valentine's quotation from the New Testament; it was, no doubt, what raised Valentine's tone from that of a babbling lunatic to the solemn and oracular manner desired. In short, a more Christian interpretation by Collier could have recognized a certainly daring but unblasphemous example of Christian satire in Act IV of *Love for Love*. Valentine is, after all, no unsuitable spokesman for such judgement. As Congreve emphasizes in his *Amendments*, Valentine has been a prodigal but is so no longer; he is the repentant prodigal, the libertine who seeks to redeem himself by and for love.

In his *Defence of a Short View* (1698) Collier fails to engage with these possibilities. To make someone mad 'for the sake of Variety' strikes him as totally absurd: 'without doubt, Raving and Incoherence are wonderfully taking'. As for the argument about giving liberty to satire, Collier says 'it gives *Valentine* a Commission to talk Smut, and abuse his Father. But Mr. *Congreve* needed not to have given himself this trouble about *Valentine*; For *Valentine* when he was in his Wits, and under the Character of a fine Gentleman, had Breeding enough to be Smutty, and Undutiful.' Collier then proceeds to prove the quotation from Christ in John's Gospel even more clearly, showing how it works through the whole scene (ll. 164–490). 'And is this not horrible Stuff?', he concludes after quoting ll. 486–90. 'What can be more intolerable Boldness, than thus to usurp the Regal Stile, to prostitute the Language of Heaven, and apply it to Drollery and Distraction?' (No. 27 iv). At this point the two writers seem to be talking past one another. Each has said things of real interest. But Congreve neither accepts nor denies that Valentine has used the words of Christ, while Collier considers he has clinched his case by establishing the quotation. The excluded middle case, that Valentine's quotation might serve a moral and religious purpose of the play, never emerges in their dispute.

From this exchange the larger outlines of the controversy may be discerned. At its heart is the question of profanity and blasphemy. Congreve argues that sacred words can be separated from their original source and function, to be used on the stage in imitation of nature, for entertainment and instruction. This 'Diversity of Signification' can be seen, in retrospect, as a plea for an independent and more secular drama. Collier will have none of this. Words cannot be cut off from their primary meanings, he thinks, any more than if 'a Man applies his Money to an ill Purpose' this transmutes 'the Metal' and makes it 'none of the Kings Coin'.

'Thus 'tis impossible to Travestie a Book, and *Virgil* was never burlesqu'd by *Ausonius* or Mr. *Cotton*!' (No. 27 i). As this telling literary analogy suggests, it was in any case disingenuous to claim that the dramatists were uninterested in the original meaning of sacred words. As Collier had earlier observed, 'to some People an Atheistical Rant is as good as a Flourish of Trumpets' (*A Short View*, p. 65). As in the poetry of Rochester, so in the drama of Congreve, libertine wit gains its sharpness, its shock, its derisory view of the world, its very sense of liberty, from the ways in which it transgresses the line between the modest and the immodest, the religious and the profane. Neither Rochester nor Congreve could dispense with religious language, and a great part of the value of Collier for modern readers is that he sharpens our sense of this aspect of Congreve's literary practice.[12]

It is perhaps because Congreve's comedies live on this frontier between sacred and profane, moral and immoral, that he seems at times so maladroit in his self-defence. An all-out secular and rationalistic defence, which could challenge all Collier's assumptions, might have seemed a good deal more convincing to the modern reader. But Congreve was of Collier's age, not our own. He accepted most of the clergyman's assumptions and allowed him to lay down the terms of the debate. On even some of the smallest blemishes discovered by Collier, such as calling a clergyman Mr Prig, and a coachman Jehu after the fast-driving King of Israel, Congreve seriously repudiates the charge of profanity, which even Macaulay, Collier's most favourable commentator, recognizes as flimsy in this case (No. 90). Again, Congreve tries to vindicate the moral direction of his comedies by reference to their concluding verses. In the case of *The Old Batchelour* and *Love for Love* these are some of the most cynical observations of the plays in which they are found, and it is hardly surprising that Collier is not impressed. Congreve makes a better case for *The Double-Dealer*.

That there is a strong moral case in favour of Congreve's comedies most readers and theatre-goers will concede. His vision of the ways of the world discloses ruthless self-interest and cold-hearted treachery. We have no difficulty in distinguishing these qualities from the vanity of witty fops, still less from the generosity of the imperfect hero such as Valentine or Mirabel. His comedy is in no way amoral, and it is intelligently rather than routinely licentious. The nearest Congreve comes to asserting the moral outlook of his drama is in his stated *postulatum* that comedy, according to Aristotle, 'is an Imitation of the worst sort of People... in respect to their Manners' (No. 24 i), that is, their moral behaviour; and in his judgement of Valentine: 'the Character is a mix'd Character; his Faults are fewer than his good Qualities; and, as the World goes, he may pass well enough for the best Character in a Comedy; where even the best must be shewn to have Faults' (No. 24 vi). On the first count Collier disputes Congreve's understanding of Aristotle's Greek, arguing that instead of 'the worst sort of People' we should read the 'Common' sort, 'the ordinary Rank of Mankind' (No. 27 i). On the second, Collier is altogether too simple a moralist, at least where drama is concerned, to be convinced by an argument which, in any case, Congreve has not put very powerfully or directly. In the difference between Congreve's dramatic practice and Collier's moral argument we have a relatively early example of the perennial dispute between the artist who seeks to show things as he considers they are, and the social moralist who demands that art should be strongly and obviously edifying.

If Collier was a less subtle moralist than Congreve, he was a more effective controversialist. Congreve was too much the gentleman to make the most of his best points in a controversy; and he often wrote condescendingly, sometimes sneeringly, occasionally with downright menace. Collier by contrast blends humour with moral indignation, as Macaulay saw (No. 90). In some respects he shares the strengths and weaknesses of the earlier English critic Thomas Rymer, whose judgements were sharpened with satire, and whose plain, downright prose style could make short work of high-flown rhetoric and fine distinctions. Commenting on a remarkable sequence of expressions in *The Mourning Bride*, '*Soothing Softness, Sinking Ease, Wafting Air, thrilling Fears, and incessant scalding Rain*', Collier says: 'to talk a little in the way of the Stage, This Litter of Epithetes makes the *Poem* look like a Bitch overstock'd with Puppies, and sucks the Sence almost to skin and Bone. But all this may pass in a *Playhouse*: False Rhetorick and false Jewells, do well together' (No. 22 i). Here Collier has seized on libertine wit, coarsened it, and turned it back on the playhouse: his second comparison is the expression of his own thought. He is very severe on *The Mourning Bride*, but critical opinion was to agree with his view in the end.

At other times Collier's humour is allowed to play on his own argument. Here is his summary of Sophocles's *Philoctetes*:

> Philoctetes calls the Gods Kakòs [evil], and Libells
> their Administration. This Officer we must
> understand was left upon a Solitary Island, ill
> used by his Friends, and harrass'd with Poverty
> and Ulcers, for Ten Years together. These, under
> the Ignorance of Paganism, were trying Circumstances,
> and take off somewhat of the Malignity of the
> Complaint. Afterwards he seems to repent, and
> declares his Assurance that the Gods will do
> Justice, and prays frequently to them. The
> Conclusion of this Play is remarkably Moral.
>
> (*A Short View*, p. 93)

This dry humour seems to mitigate Collier's examination. Yet he makes no real concession: indeed *Philoctetes* is a telling example against the smart profanity with which Collier charged the Restoration and the Orange theatre. Of course, Collier's humour is not always merely dry: it can run to the sarcastic and brutal. In the end it is the strength of Collier's convictions, what Macaulay calls 'that peculiar eloquence which comes from the heart, and goes to the heart', that makes him so 'inspiriting' to read. This carries us through his multitude of minor instances; indeed we pass through impatience as their sheer accumulation convinces us that the dramatists had a case to answer in regard to what Collier, at least, regarded as the corruption of the stage.

To stress that Collier has a coherent and serious point of view is not to claim that he is faultless. 'Perhaps the Parson stretch'd a point too far' wrote Dryden in his epilogue to *The Pilgrim*. Collier is not above arguing for victory and exaggerating the evidence on his own side of the case. Earlier seventeenth-century drama was less decent than he admitted, or perhaps knew. He praises Fletcher's *The Faithful Shepherdess* (*A Short View*, p. 53) but it was again Dryden who pointed out that 'There is more Baudry in one play of *Fletcher*'s, call'd *The Custom of the Country*, than in all ours together.' Other criticisms were to be levelled at him, with varying degrees of justice. In his zeal to defend the Church, which he was not alone in considering to be in danger, Collier had even challenged the mocking representation on the stage of Muslim and pagan priesthoods. To some this seemed to typify a lack of sense of proportion, but the particular instance is consonant with Collier's premisses. His basic principle was that the divine should be reverently treated in drama; it is exemplified by his examination of how the gods are spoken of in *Philoctetes*. He was also as aware as any that the stage could work through innuendo, and that mockery of other religions carried often an anti-Christian and anti-ecclesiastical implication. In a further charge, Dryden in his induction to 'Cymon and Iphigenia' in the *Fables* (1700) accused Collier of prurience:

> The World will think that what we loosly write,
> Tho' now arraign'd, he read with some delight;
> Because he seems to chew the Cud again,
> When his broad Comment makes the Text too plain:
> And teaches more in one explaining Page,
> Than all the double Meanings of the Stage.
>
> (ll. 15–20)

The world might well think so; but the impression one has reading Collier is hardly one of prurience, if only because of his rough humour. If Dryden had said that Collier often seems determined to present the drama in the worst possible light, he would have been nearer the mark.

It is often said that Collier turned the tide of public opinion against licence in the theatre. The written record in the years following the publication of *A Short View of the Stage* does not, so far as it concerns Congreve, show a violent swing of opinion; it seems rather to be evenly divided. As we have seen, Collier quickened rather than created the moral reaction; King William's declaration of June 1697 was known; James I's statute against the abuse of God's name in the theatre (3 Jac. I, 21), recited in *A Short View* (pp. 58–9), was still in force; under this statute prosecutions began, often brought by members of the Society for Reformation of Manners. On 12 May 1698, according to Narcissus Luttrell's diary, Congreve was prosecuted for writing *The Double-Dealer*, part of a movement by the Middlesex Justices of the Peace against several dramatists, and against the playhouses. Several further prosecutions followed, and information was laid against the players in May 1701 for the performance of *Love for Love* the previous June.[13]

From this point on, the texts of Congreve's plays in performance are unlikely to correspond to those originally performed – at least until the theatre club productions in the early twentieth century.[14] Considerable liberties were taken with Congreve's text in eighteenth-century productions, going even to the omission of scenes and alteration of the names of characters. This must always be borne in mind when considering eighteenth-century reactions to Congreve. In his *Collected Works* (1710) Congreve himself introduced a series of revisions designed to produce more decent texts, and less frequent resort to the divine name.[15] But perhaps the clearest sign that the Collier controversy had altered the relation of playwright and public is the text of Congreve's final comedy, *The Way of the World*, first performed early in March 1700 in the Lincoln's Inn Fields theatre, with Betterton playing Fainall, Verbruggen Mirabel, Underhill Sir Wilfull Witwoud, Mrs Leigh Lady Wishfort, Mrs Bracegirdle Mrs Millamant, Mrs Barry Mrs Marwood, and Mrs Bowman Mrs Fainall. Congreve's vision of the world in this play is more intelligently bleak than ever – there is no easy obvious edification here – but the language is less immoral and less profane than that of his earlier comedies.[16] The point is made obliquely in the prologue:

> Satire, he thinks, you ought not to expect,
> For so Reform'd a Town, who dares Correct?
>
> (p. 393)

At the same time Congreve makes his best reply to Jeremy Collier: Lady Wishfort tells Mrs Marwood she will find, over the chimney in the closet, '*Quarles* and *Pryn*, and the *Short View of the Stage*, with *Bunyan*'s Works to entertain you' (III, i, 64–7). Collier is here associated with low Puritan piety.[17]

CONGREVE IN THE EIGHTEENTH CENTURY

With *The Way of the World* Congreve set the crown on his dramatic achievement in the last year of the seventeenth century. Less easy to appreciate at first sight than *Love for Love*, it did not at first enjoy the same success in the theatre. It is more deeply worked, more sophisticated, and, though it has no obsessed astrologer, no sailor Ben, and no mad scene to give liberty to satire, it has as much richness and variety as the earlier play. Despite its profusion of wit, its characters all achieve their individual expression, drawn together though they are at different times and to different degrees by a shared social idiom. As in *The Double-Dealer*, though less obviously at first, evil moves coldly behind the play of wit, the froth of absurdity and the 'True and Distinct Humour'.[18] There are more than a few moments in the play when we are made aware of pain, resentment, and danger, though, as in *The Double-Dealer*, the threat at the heart of society, of the family, can be outwitted in the ways of the world. Tragedy is checked: the comedy shows that men and women need not fall prey to the world; they can sometimes manage their destinies, sometimes win and hold happiness. The world of this play is a game of skill and fortune, and in the middle of it, vulnerable to each hope as to each disappointment, torn between her *amour propre* and her care for her family, is Lady Wishfort, a comic creation in the same league as Jonson's Face, Shakespeare's Falstaff and Cervantes' Don Quixote, like Face held within the frame of a regular comedy. Like these earlier comic figures she is far from being just a collection of idiosyncrasies, though this is what strikes us at first sight; her language conveys a mental idiom, a fantasy, that can transform the world, and yet be capable of complete realism:

> Let me see the Glass——Cracks, say'st thou?
> Why I am arrantly flea'd—I look like an old
> peel'd Wall. Thou must repair me *Foible*, before
> Sir *Rowland* comes; or I shall never keep up to my
> Picture.... Tenderness becomes me best—A
> sort of dyingness—.... A swimminess in the
> Eyes—Yes, I'll look so—My Niece affects it;
> but she wants Features.
>
> (III, i, 146–50, 167–70)

If Congreve was disappointed at the immediate reception of *The Way of the World* it did his reputation no harm to enjoy a *succès d'estime*. In his 'Epistle to Mr. Congreve, occasion'd by his Comedy call'd *The Way of the World*' (1700), Richard Steele expressed the situation in fulsome couplets:

> How could, Great Author, thy Aspiring mind
> Dare to Write only to the few refin'd!
> Yet tho' that Nice Ambition you pursue,

> 'Tis not in *Congreve*'s power to please but few,
> Implicitly devoted to his fame,
> Well-dress't Barbarians know his awful Name.
>
> (No. 41)

Steele praised his poetry, and his tragedy, indeed said everything
Congreve wanted to hear, but his lines on comedy are his most
intelligent tribute:

> By thy selected Scenes and handsome Choice,
> Ennobled Comedy exalts her Voice;
> You check unjust Esteem and fond desire,
> And teach to Scorn, where else we should Admire;
> The just Impression taught by thee we hear,
> The Player Acts the World, the World the Player.
>
> (No. 41)

Steele has remembered Witwoud's exclamation at the end of Act V
of *The Way of the World*:

> Hey day! what are you all got together like
> Players at the end of the last Act?
>
> (ll. 521–2)

He has also remembered the Horatian epigraph to *The Double-
Dealer* (see p. 5 above). These lines are attuned to Congreve's aims
and achievement.

Congreve rested on his laurels for the rest of his life, twenty-
eight years. He did not abruptly stop writing, but his literary
activities soon died away. He had a hand in the translation of
Molière's *Monsieur de Pourceaugnac; or Squire Trelooby*, performed at
Lincoln's Inn Fields in March 1704, but makes no claims for its
importance (*Letters and Documents*, p. 29). Three years earlier his
interest in music, evidenced by the settings of the songs in his
plays, found satisfaction in the performance at the Queen's
Theatre, Dorset Garden, of his masque *The Judgement of Paris*
(1701). It is possible that Congreve, having seemed to master
comedy, tragedy, elegy, and ode, now proposed to turn seriously
towards music, and write for the composers. An opera, *Semele*,
was first printed with his *Works* (1710) but was not acted in his
lifetime. Set to music magnificently by Handel it was first
performed in February 1744. Congreve had now no need to write
more to make a living. He may have been appalled to see a man of
Dryden's genius and fame forced to write for the theatre in his later

INTRODUCTION

years, and to enter into toughly negotiated contracts with a publisher to produce such a Herculean work as the translation of Virgil. At the end of 1705 Congreve's small place as one of five commissioners for licensing hackney and stage coaches was relinquished for the more profitable one of commissioner for licensing wines, which carried the salary of £200 a year. Always seen as a Whig placeman he evidently expected to lose this office when the Tories gained power in the last years of Queen Anne, but the efforts of Swift and Lord Halifax, together with Harley's respect for his literary fame, preserved the office for him. In 1714 when the queen died, the Tories fell, and George I acceded to the throne, the Whig Congreve received substantial reward: he was now appointed Undersearcher of Customs for the Port of London, and Secretary of Jamaica.[19] These offices sometimes involved Congreve in business and trouble, but they made him comfortable financially for the rest of his life. Congreve never married; the famous actress Anne Bracegirdle was probably his mistress for a time; and his situation in 1704 as it appeared to an unimpressed and perhaps malicious contemporary can be seen in the anonymous *Tryal of Skill*, possibly by William Pittis:

> When *Congreve* brim full of his Mistresses Charms,
>   Who had likewise made bold with *Molier*,
> Came in piping hot from his *Bracegirdle*'s Arms.
>
> (No. 43)

The other great female attachment of Congreve's life, his long and tender friendship with Lady Henrietta Churchill, eldest daughter of the first Duke of Marlborough, dominated his later years. He thus came to be associated with the Marlborough family and their Whig grandeur. Though his poems and plays were so carefully worked, perhaps because they were, Congreve never saw himself as a professional writer. Though doubtless proud of his achievement at heart, he deprecated it to the surprised Voltaire, when visited by that ambitious *philosophe*, and asked to be approached just as an English gentleman.

On Congreve's death on 19 January 1729, the finest of several verse tributes to him was a poem inscribed to Henrietta, Duchess of Marlborough, by David Mallet. Long thought to be the work of James Thomson, this extended meditation on Congreve's death in Thomsonian blank verse belongs in its form and idiom to a later

25

and very different age from that of the Orange theatre where Congreve found his fame. There is little or no wit in this poem; its style is that of perceptive sensibility. Mallet was evidently sure that it showed enough understanding of the young duchess's dead friend to please her and he was surely right. It is interesting to compare it with Dryden's poem to Congreve: for the union of strength with grace is again important in the later tribute:

> Nature was his,
> Bold, sprightly, various: and superiour Art,
> Curious to chuse each better grace, unseen
> Of vulgar eyes; with delicacy free,
> Tho' labour'd happy, and tho' strong refin'd.
> Judgement, severely cool, o'erlooked his toil,
> And patient finish'd all: each fair design
> With freedom regular, correctly great,
> A Master's skilful daring.

Dryden's poem, of course, had known only *The Double-Dealer* and *The Old Batchelour*; Mallet's following lines comprehend the later drama:

> Closely wrought
> His meaning Fable, with deep art perplex'd,
> With striking ease unravel'd: no thin plot
> Seen thro' at once and scorn'd; or ill conceal'd
> By borrow'd aids of mimickry and farce.
> His Characters strong-featur'd, equal, just,
> From finer nature drawn: and all the mind
> Thro' all her mazes trac'd: each darker vice,
> And darling folly, under each disguise,
> By either Sex assum'd, of study'd ease,
> False friendship, loose severity, vain wit,
> Dull briskness, shallow depth, or coward-rage.

Congreve's concern with the nature of humour is remembered:

> Of the whole Muse possess'd, his piercing eye
> Discern'd each richer vein of genuine mirth,
> Humour or wit; where differing, where agreed;
> How counterfeited, or by folly's grin,
> Or affectation's air: and what their force
> To please, to move, to shake the ravish'd scene
> With laughter unreprov'd.
>
> (No. 50, ll. 26–52)

26

Few tributes have done such justice to Congreve's best work, its pervasive intelligence and perfect art. Justice too is done to his private virtues; a reading of his personal letters shows the 'easy goodness, open truth' (l. 62) of which Mallet speaks.

After his death, Congreve's eighteenth-century reception displays several concerns. There is still interest in his non-dramatic poetry. His tragedy *The Mourning Bride*, though much performed, seems slowly to lose favour. The moral argument against his comedies appears, if anything, to gain support. But the comedies also give rise to questions which interested Congreve himself concerning wit and humour. Finally, a number of notices of exceptional quality focus on the fortunes of Congreve's plays on the stage. Samuel Johnson's 'Life' in his *Prefaces, Biographical and Critical, to the Works of the English Poets (1779–81)*, here printed from the first edition, touches on all these aspects of Congreve. We shall consider each in turn.

Congreve's poems had been praised throughout his life. Steele at the start of the eighteenth century, and Mallet on Congreve's death, had paid tribute to them. The first negative voice is that of William Melmoth, writing in 1750 as Sir Thomas Fitzosborne, on Congreve as a poetic translator of Homer. Comparing Congreve and Pope he contrasts 'the lowest and most unaffecting prose' of the former's verse, its 'heavy and tasteless rhimes' and 'usual flatness of numbers' with 'the highest possible perfection of strength and harmony' of the latter. Pope, he says, can show 'a vein of poetry much superior even to the original' (No. 59). Pope certainly thought of Congreve's Homer versions when he dedicated his Iliad translation to the older man. Melmoth now dethroned the dedicatee quite abruptly. Another index of change is to be found in the different editions of the *Biographia Britannica* which, on the publication of its large-scale earlier volumes in 1750, contained a lengthy review of Congreve's work by John Campbell, including an appreciative discussion of his original poems and translations. This is one of the few notices to mention Congreve's 'fine taste for Musick' and his collaboration with John Eccles, 'his great friend, and one of the most elegant Composers our nation has produced' (No. 60a). In the revised version of the *Biographia* Andrew Kippis contrasts Campbell's 'indiscriminate praise' of the poems with the fastidious and severe judgement which Samuel Johnson had in the meantime published in his

Prefaces, Biographical and Critical (The Lives of the Poets). 'Impotence and poverty' are the words Johnson uses of Congreve's miscellaneous poems. The pastoral elegy on Mary II is called 'a despicable effusion' and condemned in terms similar to Johnson's well-known condemnation of Milton's *Lycidas.* Johnson's method in this part of his *Preface* is to give lengthy extracts followed up by brief sarcasms. Various specific faults are briskly mentioned, and the whole discussion is wrapped up with the statement that this 'tissue of poetry' is now 'totally neglected' (No. 74). Patient exploratory criticism might have something more to say in favour of the poems, but is not to be expected from Johnson. His method of dismissal could hardly have been more effective, and the case for Congreve as a non-dramatic poet has never been reopened.

Among Johnson's lengthy extracts, however, is that passage from *The Mourning Bride* which, according to Boswell, Johnson praised to Garrick, Arthur Murphy, and Thomas Davies, on 16 October 1769, as 'the finest poetical passage he had ever read', in certain carefully defined respects better than anything in Shakespeare (No. 67). Boswell's account hints at some mischievousness on Johnson's part, but he holds to this opinion in the 'Life of Congreve': indeed the most telling of his quotations are the contrasting opening pair, Almeria's description of the temple in the second act of *The Mourning Bride* with ll. 139–58 of 'The Mourning Muse of *Alexis*'. They surely do show the difference between a graceful artificial tribute, the elegy on the queen, and an individual expression of the emotion of awe. This might seem to justify what Johnson says in a fine simile elsewhere in the Life: 'The powers of Congreve seem to desert him when he leaves the stage, as Antaeus was no longer strong than he could touch the ground.' Almeria's speech is in the highest sense theatrical expression. Johnson's view of *The Mourning Bride* as a whole is much more reserved. While Congreve is admitted to have revised the numbers into greater regularity, the play still has 'more bustle than sentiment; the plot is busy and intricate, and the events take hold on the attention; but, except a very few passages, we are rather amused with noise, and perplexed with stratagem, than entertained with any true delineation of natural characters'. Johnson's testimony that *The Mourning Bride* continued to be 'acted and applauded' at the end of the 1780s is interesting evidence of theatrical taste at that time. Thirty years earlier a reviewer who may have been Johnson's friend, Arthur

Murphy, had commented on 'a kind of Fatality in the literary World, that Fashion seems to govern, what should only be directed by the Standard of Nature'. He sees the play as pleasing in 'Trick, Incident, and Business, without Character, Fable, or Language' and lacking 'the Simplicity always natural to Emotions of the Heart' (No. 63a). Four years later the satirist Charles Churchill, in a review of the theatrical profession, called the play 'Congreve's favour'd pantomime', a term to be found again in reviews of later performances of *The Mourning Bride* (No. 64). The word 'pantomime' aptly conveys a steadily increasing conviction of the extravagance and unnaturalness of Congreve's tragedy, and, taken together, the remarks of Lord Kames (No. 66), Francis Gentleman (No. 68), and Hugh Blair (No. 75) confirm the same impression. Gentleman, writing in 1770, calls *The Mourning Bride* 'one of the worst living tragedies'. It may seem that in this case the critics were leading the fashion while the theatre lagged behind.

The moral argument against Congreve is strikingly endorsed in the spring of 1748 by the young Edmund Burke, then 18 and in his last year as undergraduate at Trinity College, Dublin. In his survey of drama then popular in Dublin, Congreve figures as one 'who seems to have shared the Gifts of Nature as largely as he has abused them' and 'who, to the Charms of a lively Wit, solid Judgment and rich Invention, has added such Obscenity, as none can, without the greatest Danger to Virtue, listen to; the very texture and groundwork of some of his Plays is Lewdness, which poisons the surer, as it is set off with the Advantage of Wit'. Burke will have no truck with the argument that Congreve merely 'copied' the morals of his age. Angelica in *Love for Love* was plainly 'meant for a perfect Character', he thinks, and yet the 'Rankness' of her ideas and expressions in her scene with Foresight (II, iii), is consistent with neither male nor female modesty (No. 58). Ten years later Arthur Murphy could call the same play 'the best comedy either antient or modern, that ever was written to please upon the stage' though Congreve gave in to the notion that 'vicious persons' are proper to comedy (No. 63b). Four years later again Murphy considered that Fielding had developed a 'vicious turn' from copying Wycherley and Congreve. A more equal balance between virtue and vice, Murphy argued, would have given a closer imitation of nature (No. 65). Lord Kames, in his *Elements of Criticism* (1762–3), says that if the comedies of Congreve 'did not rack him with remorse in his last moments, he must have been lost to all sense of virtue'. Congreve had spread infection through his country, yet comedy need not be impure to be entertaining, as Shakespeare's *Merry Wives of Windsor* showed (No. 66). Fanny Burney, in her lively account of a visit to the theatre to see *Love for Love*, in Letter XX of *Evelina* (1778), has her heroine 'hope I shall never see it represented again; for it is so extremely indelicate, – to use the softest word I can, – that Miss Mirvan and I were perpetually out of countenance, and could neither make any observations ourselves, nor venture to listen to those of others'. Collier himself had remarked on the dilemma in which such comedies placed women: "tis almost a Fault for them to Understand they are ill Used. They can't discover their Disgust without disadvantage, nor Blush without disservice to their Modesty' (*A Short View*, pp. 7–8). Fanny Burney's ladies manage very well in the circumstances. 'Want of entertainment', says Mrs Mirvan, is the play's 'least fault; but I own there are objections to it, which I should be glad to see removed.' When Sir Clement praises Angelica as 'a noble girl', Mrs Mirvan objects not to her 'Rankness' in the scene with Foresight (to which she has perhaps already obliquely alluded) but, more interestingly, to her 'too much consciousness of her power' (No. 73). Short notices of performances of Congreve, from the 1730s to the 1780s, regularly warn against the immorality of the plays. This is perhaps the clearest sign that Collier's message had struck home and was remembered.

Johnson's handling of the issue of immorality in Congreve is, in the circumstances, admirably deft. He does not thunder against the comedies; he hardly expresses a direct reproof. As is often the case in the *Lives* he uses his material to convey his own view. Thus he writes appreciatively and perceptively of the plays prior to Collier's attack, saying that any objection must be lost 'in the blaze of admiration' at Congreve's precocious achievement. Collier is then allowed to make Johnson's case for him, with Johnson free to qualify, assess, and endorse. He correctly notes the importance of Collier's accumulative method; he also notes that 'contest was his delight'. At the end of his graphic account of the Collier controversy, Johnson can simply say that 'The cause of Congreve was not tenable ... the general tenour and tendency of his plays must always be condemned ... their ultimate effect is to represent pleasure in alliance with vice, and to relax those obligations by which life ought to be regulated' (No. 74). Blair, following hard upon the *Lives* with his *Lectures on Rhetoric and Belles Lettres* (1783), makes similar points with less skill.

Johnson is a good example of a mind in whom moral disapproval did not extinguish critical appreciation of Congreve's comedies. They were still found entertaining, he knew, and readers and playgoers alike continued to be interested in their wit and humour. The actor-dramatist Samuel Foote, in his *Roman and English Comedy Consider'd and Compar'd* (1747), is one of many to consider that Congreve was too prodigal with his own wit. 'Wit is not... the Essence of Comedy', he declares, and is 'of no Use, but as it is subservient to Character' (No. 57). Foote, himself an actor of Congreve, here opens up the opportunity for a more radical argument against the comedies, which Joseph Warton takes in his *Adventurer* paper of 12 February 1754: 'Will it be deemed a paradox', he asks, 'to assert that CONGREVE has not drawn a single character? His FONDLEWIFE and FORESIGHT are but faint portraits of common characters, and BEN is a forced and unnatural caricatura. His plays appear not to be legitimate comedies, but strings of repartees, and sallies of wit, the most poignant and polite indeed, but unnatural and ill placed' (No. 61). Joseph Warton was often at the forefront of changing taste, as his book on Pope shows. At such a point as this Congreve's comedies might have been conclusively condemned, the moral argument bolstering the aesthetic objection, and gone the way of *The Mourning Bride* and the miscellaneous poetry. But taste cannot be changed overnight, and enjoyment forgotten. The *London Chronicle* reviewer who may have been Arthur Murphy insisted that *Love for Love* enjoyed a 'variety of characters and incidents', that if it had too much wit so rare a fault might be forgiven, and that behind the rich freight of wit Congreve had still taken care never to violate Nature (No. 63b). Responding later to Joseph Warton's *Adventurer* argument, Murphy is inclined to yield to his strictures, though he sees the Old Bachelor, Sir Sampson Legend, and Foresight as exceptions, and continues to insist on Congreve's liveliness. Francis Gentleman, the Dubliner who so firmly rejected *The Mourning Bride* in 1770, could in the same work say of Congreve that 'no man who ever wrote for the stage has shewn more capital, more correct, or more pleasing delineations of life; his characters are beautifully contrasted, his language pointed, his wit brilliant, his plots amazingly regular and pleasingly intricate, his scenes variegated, and his disposition of the whole masterly'. After such praise, the two faults of too much wit and bad morals seem unlikely to check Congreve's fame. This was nevertheless a time when the comedies were coming to be less and less performed.[20] In 1775–6 William Mason and Horace Walpole had occasion to touch on Congreve's humour. In the first of these two excellent passages Mason denies '*pure* humour' to Gray and Congreve; it was too blended with wit, fancy, and singularity. Addison had pure humour, and 'we know where one person relishes my Lady Wishfort, there are thousands that admire Sir Roger de Coverley' (No. 70). Mason does justice to Lady Wishfort, however, who has 'so much folly and affection, and at the same time so much wit and fancy': take the wit and fancy away and she would cease to entertain, becoming more insipid as she became more natural. Mason ends by distinguishing humour that pleases, humour that pleases and makes us smile, and that (found in Shakespeare, Swift, Congreve, and Prior) which pleases and makes us laugh (No. 70). Horace Walpole, for his part, 'can scarce allow Congreve's to be true comedies'. They are 'something more'; and in the tour of praise Walpole makes to bring us to this conclusion he effectively reconciles wit with character and nature, so far as Congreve is concerned (No. 71).

Thomas Davies, in his remarkable *Dramatic Miscellanies* (1784), resembles Horace Walpole in prizing laughter: 'the *risus* of the antients, which is the same as our hearty laugh'. 'A genuine laugh is as difficult, I believe, to be had, as a generous tear.' Entering into the most difficult critical distinctions to which Congreve's comedy gives rise, Davies designates Foresight 'a character of humour' while Ben, though 'calculated to excite much laughter, and to carry on the fable with comic spirit', is 'not a humourist; he is, what Angelica terms him, an absolute sea-wit; his being a sailor is a matter of accident'. At a later point in his discussions Davies is at a loss whether to think Petulant 'a character of humour'; quoting Congreve's own distinction of humour from habit and affectation, he shrewdly cites Locke's opinion 'that we have no innate principles' to suggest that a humour cannot be natural in the sense of originally innate: our physical constitution, conditioning our perceptions, must affect the growth of humour, and from this one may think that habit and affectation may after all enter into the definition (No. 76, p. 284).

Davies, like Foote and Arthur Murphy, had experience as an actor. Indeed, he had played in Congreve.[21] He and Murphy have an intelligent interest in the actors and actresses who performed Congreve's plays. Their reviews and recollections afford a few glimpses of that aspect of the critical heritage of Congreve which is now most difficult to retrieve: the manner of his reception in theatrical performance. The whole question of the early acting of Congreve is as interesting as it is elusive, but a few details may be noted concerning the original performances. Congreve was first performed by the company of which Betterton was the most celebrated member. Alan S. Downer has called their 'school' 'a school of nature, insofar as the drama of the time allowed'.[22] Betterton himself, a great tragic actor famous for his Hamlet, played in every Congreve drama: Heartwell in *The Old Batchelour*, Maskwell in *The Double-Dealer*, Valentine in *Love for Love*, Osmyn in *The Mourning Bride*, and Fainall in *The Way of the World*.[23] He had tremendous presence, fine delivery of his lines, and was measured, grave, and restrained, though capable of youthful energy when the part required it. It will be noticed that he has the most feeling part in *The Old Batchelour*, the two coldly evil parts in *The Double-Dealer* and *The Way of the World*, while his 'grave action' was not thought too dignified for the vigorous and varied Valentine in *Love for Love*.[24] Of the great actresses of the company, Mrs Barry played Laetitia in *The Old Batchelour*, and Mrs Bracegirdle Araminta. In *The Double-Dealer* they played Lady Touchwood and Cynthia respectively, in *Love for Love* Mrs Frail and Angelica, in *The Mourning Bride* Zara and Almeria, in *The Way of the World* Mrs Marwood and Mrs Millamant. Mrs Barry was a tragic actress known for her power, tenderness, and pity. She had also some sexual notoriety, which must have added piquancy for audiences who watched her take the roles of Laetitia, Lady Touchwood, Zara, and Mrs Marwood. Mrs Bracegirdle was a younger beauty of the company: 'her youth, and lively aspect, threw out such a glow of health and cheerfulness, that ... few spectators ... could behold her without desire.' She too could command tragedy and comedy, but it was 'when she acted Millamant all the faults, follies and affectations of that agreeable tyrant were venially melted down into so many charms and attractions of a conscious beauty'.[25] At a time when, to a great extent, parts were written with particular actors and actresses in mind, it is notable that these players, skilled in both tragedy and comedy, were most famous for their tragic roles.[26] This may tell us something of how they played in Congreve. They must have sometimes seemed to suggest concealed depth and power in reserve; they certainly had occasion to show dignity and presence.

A very different kind of actor was Thomas Dogget, recently arrived from Dublin, who played Fondlewife in *The Old Batchelour*, Sir Paul Plyant in *The Double-Dealer*, and Ben in *Love for Love*. He specialized in low parts and even despised tragedy as unnatural (and expensive). He was described as 'the best face-player' of the company, not only a master of facial expression but of imitative make-up.[27] His 'dry and closely-natural manner of acting', as Cibber described it,[28] won him tremendous theatrical successes with Fondlewife and Ben – indeed some attributed to him chiefly the success of the plays themselves. Another more specialized player was Mrs Leigh who had the parts of Betty in *The Old Batchelour*, Lady Plyant in *The Double-Dealer*, the Nurse in *Love for Love*, and Lady Wishfort in *The Way of the World*. 'She had a very droll way of dressing the pretty foibles of superannuated beauties. She had, in herself, a good deal of humour, and knew how to infuse it into the affected mothers, aunts and modest stale maids, that had miss'd their market.' Cibber instances several such parts, ending with 'the languishing Lady Wishfort', where she was 'extremely entertaining, and painted in a lively manner the blind side of nature'.[29] It seems probable that Congreve created the part of Lady Wishfort for her.

What stands out in all this is the range of different acting effect in a Congreve comedy as it was originally acted. The contrast between Betterton's Valentine and Dogget's Ben is comparable to that between Hamlet and the gravedigger, with all the gradations between in each case. The stress upon natural playing is also of great importance. This too had its gradations, from Betterton's restraint, through Mrs Bracegirdle's 'charms and attractions of a conscious beauty', to the performances such as those of Dogget and Mrs Leigh which were confidently expected to make the theatre rock with laughter. Even the two last players relied on a meticulous study of appearance and behaviour.

Davies's reminiscences seem to record some casting errors in relation to lower and high styles. Harper, 'a good low comedian', was not up to the 'sarcastic poignancy of expression, the whimsical struggles of amorous passion, or the violent rage of discovered folly' necessary for Heartwell in *The Old Batchelour*, 'all which Quin perfectly conceived'. Colley Cibber was justly admired as Fondle-wife, 'though some greatly preferred Dogget's portrait of old doting impotence to his'. Cibber was a 'finished Tattle' but when, past 60, he played Ben, he lacked 'the rough animation of a sailor'. In other cases adequate castings and performances seem to have been achieved. Murphy praised the gentility of Ross's Valentine, and Davies praised Wilks's performance, in old age, of the same part 'with all the spirit and fire of youth'. A succession of skilful actresses, Mrs Cibber, Mrs Clive, and Mrs Abington, played Prue, capturing her life, 'romping spirit', 'childish simplicity and playful aukwardness'. Mrs Younger's Millamant 'was spritely' but evidently Mrs Oldfield's 'fine figure, attractive manner, harmonious voice, and elegance in dress' came closer to Mrs Bracegirdle (No. 76). Mrs Pritchard, according to Churchill, impressed as an actress in *The Mourning Bride* even when this play seemed no better than 'Congreve's favour'd pantomime' (No. 64). Perhaps the most significant record of all these is Murphy's discussion of Lady Wishfort in performance:

The author has invented a language on purpose for her; forged new manners, and in short left nothing wanting but what can only be given by such an actress as Mrs. Clive. Lady Wishfor't is indeed a ridiculous character, but she shews a ridiculous woman of quality; whereas all the actresses that have hitherto performed the part have dressed themselves like mad women, and acted in the strain of an old nurse. A high fruze tower, a gaudy petticoat of one sort, and a gown of another, was sure to create a laugh; but Mrs. Clive is not obliged to have recourse to any such pityful expedients. Accordingly she dresses the part in the pink of the present mode, and makes more of it than any actress ever did.

(No. 63c)

One wonders if Murphy remembered that the original Lady Wishfort had played the old nurse in *Love for Love*. Whether Mrs Clive were really superior to Mrs Leigh or not, Murphy is correct to see how ridiculous external detail and a playing for easy laughter could and still can spoil this part. Lady Wishfort is both a ridiculous and a serious character; if once she is put down as a mad woman she is written off. Dressing her in the height of fashion was a way of taking her seriously, suspending judgement while the art of the actress herself supplied the only life lacking to what the dramatist had created.

By the end of the eighteenth century, if the critical record here assembled can be accepted as a guide, Congreve had, just about, survived. Much in which he had taken pleasure and pride had now been dismissed or forgotten. Interest in the wit, humour, and morality of his comedies remained.[30]

THE NINETEENTH-CENTURY RECEPTION OF CONGREVE

In the second decade of the next century Congreve was fortunate to find a critic exceptionally responsive to the pleasures which the comedies characteristically convey, and able to express his response in a lively and sympathetic way. This was William Hazlitt. It is significant that his discussion grew out of a review of a theatrical performance: *Love for Love* at Drury Lane in January 1816, and that what he subsequently wrote on Congreve is literary and theatrical criticism at one and the same time.

In this *Examiner* review, 28 January 1816, Hazlitt praised the character of Foresight as played by Munden: 'We hardly ever saw a richer or more powerful piece of comic acting. It was done to the life, and indeed somewhat over; but the effect was irresistible. His look was planet-struck, his dress and appearance like one of the signs of the Zodiac taken down. We never saw any thing more bewildered' (No. 83a). Hazlitt has here perceived that crucial balance between the mind of the character and the appearance of the player: his dress is like a sign of the Zodiac, but his look is planet-struck: he is bewildered. A similar observation is made when Hazlitt praises Mrs Harlow's Mrs Frail, 'with all her airs of mincing affectation, and want of principle. The character was seen quite in dishabille' (ibid.). Here an external term is used to describe an internal condition. And, it may be noted, a moral condition. The word 'dishabille' following on 'want of principle' makes that point clearly. A final point concerned the scene between Mrs Frail, Mrs Foresight, and the bodkin (II, i, 450–72). It was 'managed', said Hazlitt, 'with as much coolness as any thing of this sort that ever happened in real life' (ibid.).

When in 1819 Hazlitt, in his *Lectures on the English Comic Writers*, returned to the subject of Congreve, he built on his *Examiner* review. Munden's Foresight is again praised, but the remark on the bodkin scene is developed: 'Mrs. Frail and Mrs. Foresight are "sisters every way;" and the bodkin which Mrs. Foresight brings as a proof of her sister's levity of conduct, and which is so convincingly turned against her as a demonstration of her own – "Nay, if you come to that, where did you find that bodkin?" – is one of the trophies of the moral justice of the comic drama.' Here is an example of how to discuss what William Archer, in 1912, was to call 'the endless question of Congreve's morality' (*William Congreve* (1912), p. 34). This is the intelligent and appropriate way to bring out the morality of Congreve's comic world. Nor is this an isolated example in the few brilliant pages of his lecture which Hazlitt devotes to Congreve. The scene in which Valentine invites his father to '"divest him, along with his inheritance, of his reason, thoughts, passions, inclinations, affections, appetites, senses, and the huge train of attendants which he brought into the world with him", with his valet's accompanying comments, is', says Hazlitt, 'one of the most eloquent and spirited specimens of wit, pathos, and morality, that is to be found'. Such dealing with morality does not seem heavy-handed, as the word seems here naturally allied with 'wit' and 'pathos', knowledge and feeling.

Hazlitt had a wonderful appreciation of Congreve's shining comic intelligence: 'The short scene with Trapland, the money-broker, is of the first water. What a picture is here drawn of Tattle! "More misfortunes, Sir!" says Jeremy. *Valentine*. "What, another dun?" *Jeremy*. "No, Sir, but Mr. Tattle is come to wait upon you." What an introduction to give of an honest gentleman in the shape of a misfortune!' Or again: 'What can be more enchanting than Millamant and her morning thoughts, her *doux sommeils*? What more provoking than her reproach to her lover, who proposes to rise early, "Ah! idle creature!"'

Striking too in Hazlitt's discussion is the attention he pays to Mrs Millamant, who is not considered so much as one might have expected in the eighteenth-century critical record. His enjoyment, his appreciation of Millamant, need no quotation to demonstrate; more surprising, this being the case, is his clear recognition that she is 'the reflection of an artificial character. The springs of nature... are but feebly touched.' In his eloquent comparison of Millamant with Rosalind, Perdita, and Imogen (significantly all women who display their true nature in rural surroundings: would not Beatrice have afforded a different view?) he concludes that Congreve's heroine is 'nothing but a fine lady'. Yet this is not the regular degrading of the artificial below the natural, for here the life of the theatre comes to the rescue of Congreve's and Millamant's artifice. 'For that reason I think the character better adapted for the stage: it is more artificial, more theatrical, more meretricious. I would rather have seen Mrs. Abington's Millamant, than any Rosalind that ever appeared on the stage.' One need not assent to all that Hazlitt implies about Rosalind on the stage to agree that a great part of human experience is of the artificial, and that the artificial Millamant is a native, even a genius, of the theatrical space.

A final feature of Hazlitt's appreciation of Congreve concerns the language of the comedies. He comments on Sir Sampson Legend's 'Shakespearian cast of language' and, following an amusing and valuably ambiguous statement, 'The description of Lady Wishfort's face is a perfect piece of painting', he can declare: 'The force of style in this author at times amounts to poetry' (No. 83b). This appears to be a real critical breakthrough. It is hard to find in the more formulaic praise of the eighteenth century so clear an acknowledgement of the richness and power of Congreve's dramatic prose.

Hazlitt's response to Congreve is in many respects a good introduction to the nineteenth-century reception. Congreve on the stage or in the closet, 'the endless question of Congreve's morality', his wit, his presentation of women, and the quality of his comic language are all themes that arise in significant ways. These will demand comment as we move through the nineteenth century, but it would give a deceptive impression of order if they were to be considered in thematic sequence. Equally, there are themes other than those just introduced, which have real interest. For example, Hazlitt himself is only one of those who continue to discuss, if not recommend, *The Mourning Bride*.

Charles Lamb's consideration of Congreve in his essay on 'The Old Actors' (*The London Magazine*, April 1822) confronts the question of Congreve's morality in a quite different way from Hazlitt. Hazlitt would say that Congreve's morality was everywhere implicitly present, sometimes, though comparatively rarely, explicit. Lamb, on the other hand, will have it that Congreve's comic world is simply amoral. His characters 'seem engaged in their proper element. They break through no laws, or conscientious restraints. They know of none. They have got out of Christendom into the land – what shall I call it? – of cuckoldry – the Utopia of gallantry, where pleasure is duty, and the manners perfect freedom.' This is an intelligent, paradoxical, and erroneous position. His reason for his contention is surprisingly close to Collier: 'every character in these plays – the few exceptions only are *mistakes* – is alike essentially vain and worthless.' Lamb does not attend to the shades of moral life, and because he finds nobody strikingly virtuous, and this state of affairs taken quite for granted within the comedies, he concludes that Congreve has 'spread a privation of moral light... over his creations'. We need only read Collier, and what he made of Valentine's mad scene in *Love for Love*, to see how little 'out of Christendom' Valentine, and Congreve, had really got. Yet in another way Lamb is right. For him Congreve's world is an escape, a liberty, from 'the all-devouring drama of common life; where the moral point is everything'. Returning from reading, or watching Congreve, 'I wear my shackles more contentedly for having respired the breath of an imaginary freedom' (No. 86). This sense of freedom is a real part of the experience of Congreve, and arises from his and his characters' repeated transgression of moral and religious frontiers. There is in Congreve's vision a strain of cold realism, a knowledge of how people behave whatever they profess, of what it is like to act, or to see another person act, without regard for morality. In failing to realize that such knowledge is by definition moral, however, Lamb oversimplified his case. One consequence followed from this, concerning nomenclature. Lamb's essay began with the terms: 'The artificial Comedy, or Comedy of manners', which he applied to Wycherley, Congreve, and others. 'Manners' was a word that, in the eighteenth century and earlier, comprehended morals as well as, and usually before, social forms. 'General way of life; morals; habits' is the most relevant sense in Johnson's *Dictionary*, and what William III meant when, quoting the act of James I, he forbade the theatres to perform anything 'contrary to religion and good manners' (see p. 10 above). Lamb's use of the term 'Comedy of manners', combined with his case for a 'privation of moral light' in Congreve, empties it of moral meaning, leaving only what Lamb saw: a comedy of social forms. In so far as this narrowed sense of the term has become current, it has done a disservice to Congreve's reputation and indeed to Restoration comedy as a whole.

'*Wickedness* is no subject for comedy. This was Congreve's great error, and almost peculiar to him.' Coleridge's judgement, almost the opposite view to Lamb's, was prompted by his son Hartley's comment on *The Double-Dealer*, that 'There are degrees of wickedness too bad to laugh at, however they may be mingled with folly, affectation, or absurdity.' One of several annotations in Hartley Coleridge's *Biographia Borealis* (1833) (No. 88), it forms part of Coleridge's decisive view of comedy, morality, and religion prompted by his son's account of Congreve and the Collier controversy. Responding to Hartley's view that *The Way of the World* 'has no moral interest' because it contains nobody good enough for us to care about, Coleridge writes: 'Virtue and wickedness are *sub eodem genere*. The absence of *Virtue* is no deficiency in a genuine comedy, but the presence of wickedness a great defect.' This accords with Coleridge's further view that 'Genuine Comedy is, I fear, almost incompatible with Christianity, as it exists among the many, who neither can, nor will *abstract*. Now Comedy *is* an abstraction.' Lamb's image of Congreve's comedy, an imaginary realm abstracted from the moral issues and contingencies of the real world, is then what Coleridge thinks comedy should be. It is not, as Coleridge correctly sees, what Congreve actually produced. Though Coleridge saw it as a great error, he correctly recognized that Congreve had been pressing at the frontiers of the comic form.

A different though related theme emerges from Hartley Coleridge's discussion. He takes for granted an improvement in public taste for diversion since the age of Congreve, and ascribes it to 'the general good education of females, the purifying influences of female society, the higher value set upon the domestic affections, the greater freedom of choice in marriage, and the more frequent intercourse between the religious and the fashionable world'. Collier would have rejoiced to hear this. Perhaps the author of the contract scene in *The Way of the World* (IV, i) would have also. Coleridge himself added: 'And more than all, the attendance of all classes on the theatres, except the gloomier sects; at least till of late.'

The essays of Hazlitt and Lamb were made more widely known

by the extended quotations, and discussion of them, that appeared in Leigh Hunt's Introduction to *The Dramatic Works of Wycherley, Congreve, Vanbrugh, and Farquhar* (1840) (No. 89). His reservations with regard to Lamb's view of Congreve are generously expressed; so is his endorsement of Hazlitt. Where he expresses his own views he is more conventional than either, and claims only to have provided 'a more pains-taking set of memoirs than, we believe, has yet appeared' (No. 89). The whole production now elicited a lengthy and powerful discussion by Macaulay in the *Edinburgh Review* the influence of which must be thought to have reached well into the twentieth century. Leigh Hunt, inclined to prefer the qualified moral analysis of Hazlitt to Lamb's case for amorality, nevertheless expressed a certain amount of moral disapproval on his own account. This is roundly condemned by Macaulay as 'exceeding lenity'; shifting the centre of debate decisively towards the moral end of the critical spectrum Macaulay associates Leigh Hunt with the 'easy style of Lucio' in *Measure for Measure* and demands not 'the merciless rigour of Lord Angelo' but 'the gentle rebuke of Escalus'. This he himself seeks to provide when he declares that 'this part of our literature is a disgrace to our language and our national character.... We find ourselves in a world, in which the ladies are like very profligate, impudent, and unfeeling men, and in which the men are too bad for any place but Pandaemonium or Norfolk Island.' It is not coarseness of expression to which Macaulay chiefly objects, for the standard of acceptable expression changes from age to age. It is the 'systematic attempt to associate vice with those things which men value most and desire most, and virtue with everything ridiculous and degrading'. Macaulay thus takes his stand firmly with Jeremy Collier, of whom he gives an on the whole admiring account, and firmly against Lamb. The code of Congreve's characters, Macaulay says, is obeyed by great numbers of people. 'We need not go to Utopia or Fairyland to find them. They are near at hand. Every night some of them play at the "hells" in the Quadrant, and others pace the Piazza in Covent-Garden' (No. 90 i). At such a moment the great Whig historian of the reign of William III, Congreve's creative decade, seems to concede the relevance of Congreve to the early Victorian era. 'The Comic Dramatists of the Restoration' is a memorable lay sermon adopting a classical moral position concerning man's proneness to corruption through imitation of bad example. His moralism is less useful for an understanding of Congreve than that of Collier, however, because he lacks the latter's detailed interest in the texts of the plays. It is also unfortunate that Macaulay's moral thunderbolt should have deflected attention from Hazlitt's subtler moral response to Congreve, an example from which we have, arguably, still much to learn.

Something of what these attitudes to Congreve meant for the practical performance of his plays may be seen from two *Times* reviews of Congreve productions in 1842: of *Love for Love* at Drury Lane, published 21 November, and of *The Way of the World* at the Haymarket, published on 19 December. Neither review sees Congreve as 'a disgrace to our language and national character', but the first, noting that the author of the version of *Love for Love* performed, 'could have modified Ben Jonson's *Bartholomew Fair* so as to suit even the Barebones Parliament', congratulates this author 'for having so well succeeded in turning a mass of licentiousness into a very proper sort of piece'. It is hard not to hear some faint irony behind this approval. The expurgations consisted of Scandal's intrigue with Mrs Foresight, Angelica's 'coarse dialogue with her uncle' in II, i, and 'a softening to the catastrophe of Miss Prue's love-scene with Tattle'. The reviewer then complains of substitutions such as 'gentlemen' for 'fellows'.

Love for Love is here praised as 'a magnificent specimen' not of the national poetic and ideal drama, but of the later 'real drama' in prose, designed to display a knowledge of the world. '"Knowledge of the world," says Mr. Dickens in one of his novels, "means the knowledge of every rascal in it," and it was in that knowledge that Congreve, Wycherley, and Vanbrugh loved to display their proficiency.' This, surely, is a striking moment in the Victorian reception of Congreve. What the reviewer most admires however, is the wit of the play, and he advises audiences to close their hearts and keep their heads clear. Amidst much intelligent praise of the actors and actresses, what stands out is his remark that Mr Anderson, playing Valentine 'with great spirit', 'by his tricks in the mad scene kept up the most violent laughter' (No. 91a). It does not sound as if the right note was struck there.

Such a conclusion is, perhaps, strengthened by the review of *The Way of the World* which, by way of drawing a contrast with *Love for Love*, describes the latter's characters as 'a roaring lot: without

42

principle or chastity they kick the world before them like a foot-ball'.

In *The Way of the World*, on the other hand, 'the most artificial of artificial comedies', 'men are quiet, smooth-spoken, well-behaved scoundrels, who say their good things cautiously, who glide about noiselessly in their laced coats and dress swords, and who having studied "the way of the world", as they call it, are calmly resolved to make a practical use of their knowledge'. They hatch 'plots worthy of an Iago, and bide their time.... Certain it is, that your neighbour will make a thrust at you, if you are not sharp enough to anticipate the event by a thrust at him.' It seems probable that these two reviews are by the same person, for the theme of an appeal to the head rather than the heart runs through each of them. His judgement of Congreve is obviously affected by the performance he has just seen, and this has the effect of exaggerating the rumbustiousness of *Love for Love* and, in turn, underestimating the humour and emotion of *The Way of the World*. This having been said, however, the following passage is the most perceptive criticism of Congreve since Hazlitt:

A calm quiet knowledge of a state of society in which heart has no place, in which unclouded intellect reigns alone, is fully displayed in this wonderful production. That constant fire of epigrams which is kept up in *Love for Love* is not to be found here; indeed, by making Witwould, the utterer of epigrams, and those often good, a ridiculous character, by holding up to ridicule the construction of a repartee, it would almost seem as if Congreve had wished to discharge himself once for all of that kind of writing which is so great in *Love for Love*. Throughout the whole of *The Way of the World* the springs of a sophisticated life are inspected with the utmost acuteness; little truthful pictures find their way into it, which we may vainly seek for elsewhere; and in one dialogue, the celebrated treaty of marriage between Mirabell and Millamant, all the vices and foibles of the fair sex are condensed into a few speeches with wonderful fulness. Then, while we call *The Way of the World* the most artificial of comedies, we ought to define our meaning. *Love for Love* is artificial, because it is a thing of imagination. The characters are a set of impossible wits, who start full armed from the brain of their author, but he enjoys the joke, and halloos them on to the sport; so that they have a kind of spurious reality, from the manifest heartiness of their creator. On the other hand, *The Way of the World* gives a picture which is more true to life, but it is more artificial because the life represented is completely artificial, and the author has tamed himself down to the cool observer.

(No. 91b)

The contrast between the summarizing lay sermon and the more particular insights of the theatre review is even more obvious when we turn to Thackeray, a lecture first given between May and July 1851. Thackeray's lay sermon is not just, like Macaulay's, against an era of English drama. It is not even a meditation on the *memento mori* of the skull of Congreve's muse ('We gaze at the skeleton, and wonder at the life which once revelled in its mad veins'). It is a sub-Shakespearian tirade on the mutability of experiences more general than that of the Orange comedies: of youth, beauty, strength, and pleasure. It is a strange performance for the author of *Vanity Fair* and *The History of Henry Esmond*, for if there is any Victorian author who should have appreciated Congreve's moral vision, and known his world, it is Thackeray. Nevertheless, what comes over to the reader is not Macaulay's lofty moral disapproval: it is a more intense, and lurid, sermon, and if it seems to convey contempt for Congreve's vanished world, there seems also to be a measure of envy for the spirit of youth and pleasure, what Thackeray sees as a pagan spirit, which had animated Congreve's lost world (No. 92).

Charles Cowden Clarke (No. 93, pp. 393–401) is another of those nineteenth-century commentators on Congreve who feel obliged to open with a moral denunciation, only to be drawn into praise once they begin to give a specific account of the four comedies. It is the steady development of Congreve's art which compels respect; and it proves possible to give a thoroughly disgusted opinion of *The Old Batchelour* (Cowden Clarke does so) while recognizing finer qualities in the later comedies. Thus Cowden Clarke can praise Ben in *Love for Love*: 'How finely his straightforward conduct comes in relief against the manoeuvring and insincerity of all the others', he notes, thus making a substantial qualification to his overall view of the utter heartlessness and hoar-frost glitter of the age of William III, focused in Congreve. He describes *The Way of the World* as 'this admirable collection of wit, raillery, sarcasm, and repartee... the most natural in plot, and the least offensive in language and arrangement'. As Cowden Clarke returns to his overall moral view, at the end of his essay, he again expresses his preference for Restoration over Orange comedy. Obscene and coarse as the former was, it carried with it 'some soul of redemption'. However curious it may be to see the friend of Keats and Leigh Hunt prefer Wycherley to Congreve, and on grounds which perhaps the Romantics might approve, Cowden Clarke's essay belongs with an earlier phase in the reception of Congreve.

Meredith strikes a newer note, though only picking up themes already touched on by Hazlitt, when he writes of the connected matters of language and female portrayal. To Meredith, Millamant is 'an admirable, almost a loveable heroine' so presumably he thinks she has 'some soul of redemption'. 'It is a piece of genius in a writer', Meredith continues, 'to make a woman's manner of speech portray her. You feel sensible of her presence in every line of her speaking.' Meredith is happy in his own choice of words when he writes of the creation of Lady Wishfort in language: 'The flow of boudoir Billingsgate in Lady Wishfort is unmatched for the vigour and pointedness of the tongue. It spins along with a final ring, like the voice of Nature in a fury, and is, indeed, racy eloquence of the elevated fishwife.' To find in so stylized a comedy 'the voice of Nature in a fury' is not only at first sight surprising: this remark is a tribute to the extraordinary blend of nature and art in this character of the play. It is Meredith's best tribute, as a critic, for it is upon the relatively equal position of woman in society that he considers the success of comedy to rest, and of course the comic dramatist can enter into the diversity of female awareness through language itself. Here, though with a measure of qualification, Meredith finds Congreve a master:

He hits the mean of a fine style and a natural in dialogue. He is at once precise and voluble. If you have ever thought upon style, you will acknowledge it to be a signal accomplishment. In this he is a classic, and is worthy of treading a measure with Molière. *The Way of the World* may be read out currently at a first glance, so sure are the accents of the emphatic meaning to strike the eye, perforce of the crispness and cunning polish of the sentences.

(No. 94, p. 404)

Comparison with Molière links the Victorian novelist's assessment of Congreve with that of a Victorian poet, Algernon Charles Swinburne. As befits an encyclopaedia article, Swinburne's discussion is comprehensive and balanced. Congreve's fame as 'our greatest comic dramatist' (he writes) rests on three out of five plays, *The Old Batchelour* being little more than a brilliant study, and *The Mourning Bride* a work of ambition rather than genius. *Love for Love* is 'the crowning triumph of his art and life' while *The Way of the World* is 'the crowning work of his genius, – the unequalled and unapproached master-piece of English comedy. The one play in our language which may fairly claim a place beside or but just beneath the mightiest work of Molière is *The Way of the World*.' It is at this point that Swinburne touches on the tragic strain in the greatest comedy. While Congreve lacks the 'deepest and subtlest quality' of Molière's mind, 'ce moqueur pensif comme un apôtre', his tragedy 'appears rouged and wrinkled, in the patches and powder of Lady Wishfort':

> Only perhaps in a single part has Congreve half consciously touched a note of almost tragic depth and suggestion; there is almost something well-nigh akin to the grotesque and piteous figure of Arnolphe himself in the unvenerable old age of Lady Wishfort, set off and relieved as it is, with grace and art worthy of the supreme French master, against the only figure on any stage which need not shun comparison even with that of Célimène.
>
> (No. 95, p. 409)

With the assessments by Meredith and Swinburne behind us, it is appropriate to pause for a moment to consider the changing forms of criticism. A number are employed repeatedly: in the seventeenth and eighteenth centuries the poem for tribute, in the nineteenth century the essay or lecture, often on the English comic dramatists, comedy itself, or a similar topic. The theatre review is the third, running alongside the poem and essay, and providing an indispensable standard of comparison whenever it is to be found. The lay sermon, exemplified by Collier and Macaulay, is a fourth. With the publication in 1888 of Edmund Gosse's *Life of William Congreve* we encounter academic criticism for the first time in this collection. Academic, first, because Gosse's book was published when he was delivering the Clark lectures at Trinity College, Cambridge, and thus an academic at that time; but, more important, the capacious book-length study devoted to a single author was to become, along with the learned article on the specialized topic, one of the two typical forms of academic criticism during the century of institutionalized and vocational study of literature to come.

Gosse's critical biography makes good use of its greater space. It can afford to be meticulous in detail, noting, for example, that *The Double-Dealer* was published on 4 December 1693, with the date 1694 on the title-page (*The Life of William Congreve*, p. 56). It has a detailed knowledge of the literary scene in the 1690s, mentioning that Robert Gould, George Granville (later Lord

Lansdowne), Colley Cibber, Mrs Pix, Mrs Manley, and Mrs Trotter all had new plays performed in 1696. It displays a proper interest in all the circumstances of theatrical performance in Congreve's time, and laments that more information cannot be found. Each of the five plays is fully discussed, and several valuable but neglected points of interest are made. Thus in his judicious account of *The Mourning Bride* Gosse examines the metrics of Congreve's blank verse, concluding that his model was Milton rather than Shakespeare, and his follower Edward Young in his tragedies and *Night Thoughts*. Again, Gosse recognizes Congreve's reliance on soliloquy in *The Double-Dealer*, noticing how this marks him off from Restoration comedy, and brings him closer to Molière. Neither of these aspects of Congreve had been much remarked before. Gosse naturally attends to the Collier controversy, treating it, as his reviewer W.E. Henley was to point out, fully and fairly. All this is sober gain over what one could have expected to find in an essay on, say, the English comic writers. It is not even a question of judiciousness and comprehensiveness on the part of the book, and personal appreciation on the part of the essay, for Gosse, as it happens, feels an enthusiasm for Congreve, and manages to be lavish in praise and balanced in judgement at the same time. Yet this is not like Hazlitt's enthusiasm: it is not a response to a specific quality or moment, as when Hazlitt says that the introduction of Tattle in *Love for Love* is 'of the first water', but more like that positive commitment to a subject which grows from the very writing of a book-length study. Ever since Pope opined that Congreve was inferior to Molière comparisons between the two playwrights had been made, but it is in the first book devoted wholly to Congreve that a critic finds Molière in several respects inferior to him (No. 97, pp. 412–14).

In his review of this book Henley perceived that Gosse had gone further in his admiration of Congreve than any recent commentator. In response the review gathers together all the most hostile attitudes to the playwright, especially from the lay sermon tradition going back through Thackeray and Macaulay to Collier. 'His enthusiasm is so large', Henley says of Gosse, that he is able 'to ignore the ineradicable turpitude of his author's view of life'. For Henley Congreve is merely a master of style, 'uneasy, self-conscious, intrusive, even offensive, the very reverse of dramatic': it is here that the contemptuous attitude of this reviewer betrays him. He repeatedly seeks to clinch his argument by observing that Congreve's plays have 'dropped out of the *répertoire*, and the truth is they are worthy of no better fate' (No. 98, p. 422). Had he recalled the basis of Hazlitt's essay, or known the two *Times* reviews of Congreve productions in 1842, he might have hesitated in his confident assumption that lack of performance meant that the comedies must now be deemed stage failures. Only a few more years were to prove him wrong.

Evidence of that proof, in a further theatre review, is the exception in our remaining selection of materials on the reception of Congreve, which is now to a greater or lesser degree academic. It is not a matter of the author's profession for most of them belong to that late Victorian and Edwardian category, the 'man of letters'; but their criticisms may be described as academic in approach and flavour. Leslie Stephen's *English Literature and Society in the Eighteenth Century* (1904) (No. 101, pp. 438–43) (his Ford lectures at Oxford the previous year), true to its ambitious subject, concentrates on the moral argument about Restoration and Orange comedy and the Collier controversy, because the question of public taste is what allows him to consider the relations between literature and society. A series of good comments on Addison, Lamb, Hazlitt, and on Meredith's view that only an equality of the sexes would allow feminine refinement to improve society and thus produce a finer comedy, leads Stephen to the conclusion that society prevented Congreve from writing more refined comedy than he did. G. S. Street, in his introduction to his edition of *The Comedies of William Congreve* (1895), is academic in his shrewd review of the opinions of his predecessors, something of value being found in almost all, none fully endorsed, and in the way his appreciation of Congreve is based on a kind of literary common sense, an understanding of the chosen genre. 'The great primal fallacy', he says, reviewing the moral arguments about Congreve, 'comes from a habit of expecting everything in everything.' Satiric comedy, comedy of manners, is selective in choice of material and manner of presentation. Rules of art compel it to do what it does, and what it does cannot be to present the whole truth of human life, or to do strict moral justice to its most sacred values, as the writers of the lay sermon tradition required. The evolution of an age of criticism, says Street, affords 'modern methods' which can teach 'quite humble critics to discriminate between issues, and to deal with such a matter as this with some mental detachment' (No. 100, pp. 427–38). Here again is the hallmark of academic criticism though Street was not a professional academic. His diagnosis is the readiest way to refute Collier and his followers, but it carries with it a constraint upon the appreciative criticism of Congreve which, in more recent times, has seen in his comedies of family betrayal and survival a wider vision of the world.

Our three remaining academic critics, William Archer, Charles Whibley, and John Palmer, are distinguished in several ways. Archer is the strongest and most memorable, in that he pursues singlemindedly his concept of the well-made play and plot, seeing drama as a structure which 'technical considerations' (No. 103, pp. 447–63) can enable us to understand. The friend of Shaw and Granville Barker, and translator of Ibsen, might well see himself as a specialist in drama. Congreve had long been a sitting target for such a critic. Praised by Dryden for his architectural structure, concerned seriously as we know he was about the fable of his plays, Congreve had nevertheless been criticized more than once for his lack of plot. Archer's *examen* of *The Double-Dealer*, arguably the strongest plotted comedy, was therefore a critical ordeal Congreve had to undergo, and from which he does not emerge entirely unscathed. Charles Whibley, by contrast, writing in the *Cambridge History of English Literature* (1912), is academic in an opposite way: he is catholic and assimilative; in his clear, open, and appreciative discussion Hazlitt, Lamb, Meredith, and others mingle their rays in his light. Severe criticisms are touched on; but Whibley's palpable enjoyment of Congreve in the manner of Hazlitt is there on every page. Sometimes, indeed, he builds on Hazlitt. Hazlitt had written of the wit, pathos, and morality of Valentine's encounter with his father in *Love for Love*. Whibley finds in it 'a nobility of phrase and thought ... which may be called Shakespearean in no mere spirit of adulation ... Congreve rises to a height of eloquent argument, which gives a tragic force to his work' (No. 104, p. 468). Whibley's running title at this point in the *Cambridge History*, 'The Comedy of Manners', is that of Palmer's book published a year later. It is now used loosely to indicate a phase of comedy between Elizabethan and modern. It is 'artificial' but also in some measure realist comedy in the tradition of Menander and Terence, comedy that painted the ways of its world. The problems of the term, as already seen in its use by Lamb, is that 'manners' are thought to refer only to the social forms of a bygone age. Palmer does little to make good this weak sense of the term, and in his discussion of Congreve himself allows it to lapse almost completely. Though the book itself has been commonly accounted a landmark in the criticism of later seventeenth-century comedy, and thus earns its place as the final item in the present collection, it cannot be pretended that Palmer greatly advances our understanding of Congreve, unless perhaps to those unready to see or read the playwright himself. Palmer quotes copiously, following up with brief remarks of his own. In one respect, however, Palmer stands out from his predecessors. While *The Way of the World* had been steadily gaining in prestige among those who admired Congreve, *Love for Love* had held its place as a comic masterpiece. Palmer considers it inferior to *The Double-Dealer* and 'so obviously a backwater of the authentic stream, that it scarcely pays to dwell on it very particularly'. Granted *Love for Love* had long been a stage success, the qualities that made it so (strong plot, good 'character' parts) are, Palmer argues, simply stage qualities. *The Way of the World*, on the other hand, sought to educate audiences to expect something different. There is something disturbing about the way Palmer here reduces theatrical success to an audience being taught what to expect. Insufficient attention is being paid to the character of theatrical presentation, the three hours 'traffic of the stage', and the direct visual nature of the medium. In writing of *Love for Love* as 'of the stage' Palmer is in his own terms slighting qualities in which Charles Whibley, for one, had recognized a Shakespearian character. To distinguish, with Swinburne, between *Love for Love* as the triumph of Congreve's life and art, and *The Way of the World* as the triumph of his genius, is one thing, to strike Palmer's rather lofty attitude to the theatre is another (No. 105, p. 482).

It is telling that only one of the last three writers about Congreve, William Archer, makes so much as a passing reference to the Mermaid Society's revival of *The Way of the World* in the spring of 1904. Archer's friend A. B. Walkley reviewed it for the *Times Literary Supplement*, the review being republished in his *Drama and Life* (1907). Congreve had been so long out of production, it would seem, that he had grown into a kind of intellectual classic, a fine stylist from the library shelf, emancipated from the theatre which gave him birth. The natural process by which Hazlitt's appreciation of Congreve grew out of a review of a performance seems not to have been easily available to

Archer, Whibley, or Palmer. The 1904 *Way of the World*, however, ended the longest period in which Congreve had been absent from the stage; since then he has never been long out of production. It is appropriate to end this introductory survey of the critical heritage of Congreve with A. B. Walkley's 1904 *Times Literary Supplement* review.

Walkley opens with a fighting defence of the importance of the live theatre for an old classic. Congreve, he finds, 'is still capable of giving you a vivid sense of reality' and 'it is only through the Mermaid Society that you know it for certain. And how have they enabled you to know it? Through the quite straightforward and familiar, yet magical and inscrutable, influence of flesh and blood.' This, he argues, is the chief element of an acted drama, something 'infinitely more important' than costume, scenery, and acting skill,

something which marks off an acted drama from every other work of art, and something with which art has nothing to do – flesh and blood, their bodies, gestures, glance and voices.... The curious psychical influence of bodily presence, the invisible currents that pass between one human being and another .... There is all the difference in the world between certain lines of printed dialogue headed 'Millamant,' supplemented by the reader's imagination, and the same words spoken by a real woman, with a certain smile, a certain toss of the head, a certain gait. It is a difference not of degree but of kind. What Congreve has done for an imaginary woman called Millamant suddenly springs into life through everything that nature has done for a real woman called Ethel Irving.

Put to this test of flesh and blood what might pass muster in print would 'stand forth' as false or inadequate in performance, but Congreve's characters survive this test. 'Therefore *The Way of the World* is still a "live" classic.'

Walkley shows the 'flesh and blood' effect working in two ways. The more permanent features of human nature in the play will have their reality deepened. 'Such a scene, for instance, as that between Fainall and Mrs. Marwood in the Mall, when the guilty lovers fall out, taste something of the bitterness of a clandestine *amour* with its eternal hovering on the edge of hate, and then kiss again with tears, gains enormously in reality, though it was real enough in the printed page. It was real enough, but now it becomes "modern".' The play will also disclose 'temporary transitory features, manners, or language now obsolete'. Here, we may note, is that attenuated sense of 'manners' which for Palmer seemed the heart of Congreve.

The 'flesh and blood' element is now found 'not deepening the impression but transforming it. What was "historical" now becomes "actual".' Walkley concludes his argument about Congreve in performance by turning back to Lamb. The revival of *The Way of the World*, he says, 'has knocked the bottom out of Lamb's plea for Congreve's immoral world as something conventional and fantastic. So soon as the characters are put solidly before you by living men and women you are absolutely appalled by their grim reality. To say that you are appalled is only another way of saying that you are pleased; you snatch a fearful joy' (No. 102, p. 446). This is better than most of the academic critics included here. This is as good as Hazlitt. Here humanity, drama, and theatre are seen to be joined in their challenge to other minds.

A word of summary. Time, the general wisdom runs, weeds out the works of famous authors, leaving only the best and sturdiest blooms for the satisfaction of a discriminating posterity. The critical heritage of Congreve presents an uncomfortably extreme case of this process – indeed the readers who have traced the reception of Congreve from Thomas Southerne to John Palmer's slighting of *Love for Love* will want to retrieve the weeds. To simplify an already selective introduction, it may be said that the eighteenth century discarded the non-dramatic poems and forgot the works for music. The early nineteenth century discarded *The Mourning Bride*, despite a stubborn rearguard action by those in or close to the theatre. Gosse's critical biography showed the capacity of academic criticism to explore this discarded work, and Sir Walter Raleigh (No. 99, pp. 425–6) discussed Congreve's interesting earliest text, the novel *Incognita*, whose previous critical heritage consisted largely of people confessing they had not read it.[31] But Palmer used the capacity of academic criticism in the opposite way, to expedite the process of discarding so as to be left only with that fine essence of Congreve, *The Way of the World*. The relentless logic of this process could end only by the retention of the Mirabel/Millamant contract scene, alone, in an anthology. Fortunately, academic criticism has also fostered a more liberal and adventurous approach to Congreve.

Academic criticism, however, hardly seems the high point of Congreve's critical heritage. Of the various forms which conveyed a critical response to him, the poems in tribute may seem the most memorable and impressive, though not for their critical content alone. Dryden and Mallet deal with the general qualities of Congreve's life and art, yet the more their judgements are applied to the specific features of Congreve's practice, in the perspective of his time, the more persuasive they seem. Another form, the lay sermon running from Collier through Macaulay and Thackeray into Henley's review of Gosse, and influencing much other criticism on the way, appears to degenerate. Despite his faults the critical value of Collier is high, while the moral outlook of the lay sermon tradition can only be ignored at the risk of too easy a separation between art and life, such as we have found in Charles Lamb. Critics as different as Macaulay and A. B. Walkley have attested to the 'grim reality' of Congreve's vision. It is Hazlitt who shows how to combine an appreciation of moral issues with an appropriate response to stage comedy, and it will have become clear that in the opinion of the present editors Hazlitt has a fair claim to be the finest critic of Congreve. His chosen form of the lecture, close to the essay as it came down to him from Addison and Montaigne, so short as to go quickly to the heart of the matter, so light as to allow a personal style, must seem hard to rival. Yet at its best the theatre review can attain to this form and we have no hesitation in recommending the two 1842 *Times* reviews, and A. B. Walkley in the *Times Literary Supplement* in 1904, as in the same league of criticism. Like Hazlitt and several earlier critics they bring the eloquent and indispensable testimony of the theatre to bear upon the critical reputation. The last word of praise must go to Charles Whibley, who shows that life and enjoyment no less than intelligence and learning can find a place in academic criticism. The humour to appreciate the absurd and the moral intelligence to recognize a grim reality, in constantly surprising combination, are what Congreve continues to demand of his audiences and readers.

H. H. E. H.
W. A. L.

NOTES

1 Colley Cibber, *An Apology for the Life of Colley Cibber* (1740), ed. R. W. Lowe (*Beaux and Belles of England*, 2 vols, London: Grolier Society, 1889), Vol. I, p. 245.

2 On the form and its implications at this time, see James D. Garrison, *Dryden and the Tradition of Panegyric* (London: University of California Press, 1975).

3 Dryden's architectural allusion in this poem, not fully explained by either the Oxford or California editions of Dryden, is discussed by Howard Erskine-Hill in 'Heirs of Vitruvius: Pope and the idea of architecture', in *The Art of Alexander Pope*, ed. Howard Erskine-Hill and Anne Smith (London: Vision Press, 1978), pp. 144–8.

4 Bonamy Dobrée, 'Congreve', in *Restoration Drama: Modern Essays in Criticism*, ed. John Loftis (Oxford: Oxford University Press, 1966), p. 102.

5 Harold Love, *Congreve* (Oxford: Basil Blackwell, 1974), p. 122.

6 J. E. Spingarn (ed.), *Critical Essays of the Seventeenth Century*, 3 vols (Oxford: Clarendon Press, 1908), Vol. I, p. lxxxv.

7 Thomas Shadwell, *Works*, ed. Montague Summers, 5 vols (London: Fortune Press, 1927), Vol. I, p. 11. For a discussion of Shadwell's importance as a writer of 'reform' or 'exemplary' comedy, see John Harrington Smith, *The Gay Couple in Restoration Comedy* (Cambridge, Mass.: Harvard University Press, 1948), pp. 120–31.

8 John C. Hodges (ed.), *William Congreve: Letters and Documents* (London: Macmillan, 1964), pp. 102–3.

9 Jeremy Collier, *Animadversions on 11 Henry 7 Cap. 1. Or, a King De Facto* (London, n.d.), p. 8. For the context of Collier's political pamphleteering, see J. P. Kenyon, *Revolution Principles: The Politics of Party, 1689–1720* (Cambridge: Cambridge University Press, 1977) and Howard Erskine-Hill, 'Literature and the Jacobite cause', in Eveline Cruickshanks (ed.), *Ideology and Conspiracy: Aspects of Jacobitism, 1688–1759* (Edinburgh: John Donald, 1982), pp. 49–53. It is unfortunate that the institutionalized division of studies has led to Collier's attack on the stage being known only to literary scholars, and his attack on the Revolution Settlement only to historical scholars. We shall not have a satisfactory picture of Collier until his political and literary writing, together with his essays on manners and society, are seen in relation to one another.

10 Cibber, *An Apology for the Life of Colley Cibber*, edn cit., Vol. I, pp. 334–5.

11 This is pointed out by William Myers in 'Plot and meaning in Congreve's comedies', in Brian Morris (ed.), *William Congreve* (London: Ernest Benn, *Mermaid Critical Commentaries*, 1972), pp. 78–80.

12 Indeed Collier's comments ought to be generously represented in the explanatory notes of modern scholarly editions of Congreve. Recent research on the eighteenth century, for example, J. C. D. Clark's *English Society, 1688–1832: Ideology, social structure and political*

practice during the ancien regime (Cambridge: Cambridge University Press, 1985) suggests that Collier was a widely representative figure, though he may have over-articulated general views.

13 This development is described by Montague Summers in his introduction to his edition of *The Complete Works of William Congreve*, 4 vols (London: Nonesuch Press, 1923), Vol. I, pp. 48–9.

14 The fortunes of Congreve on the eighteenth-century stage are studied by Emmett L. Avery, *Congreve's Plays on the Eighteenth-Century Stage* (New York: Modern Language Association of America, 1951).

15 See *The Complete Plays of William Congreve*, ed. Herbert Davis (London: University of Chicago Press, 1967), pp. 480–500.

16 ibid., pp. 501–3.

17 ibid., p. 426.

18 See No. 16 below, pp. 90–8.

19 Hodges, *William Congreve: Letters and Documents*, pp. 83–6.

20 See Avery, *Congreve's Plays on the Eighteenth-Century Stage*, p. 120.

21 Avery, *Congreve's Plays on the Eighteenth-Century Stage*, pp. 135–6.

22 Alan S. Downer, 'Nature to advantage dressed: eighteenth-century acting', in John Loftis (ed.), *Restoration Drama: Modern Essays in Criticism* (New York: Oxford University Press, 1966), p. 332. This essay also considers late seventeenth-century acting.

23 Herbert Davis, in his excellent edition of *The Complete Plays of William Congreve*, gives the cast list for the original performance of each play.

24 For an account of Betterton, see Cibber, *An Apology for the Life of Colley Cibber*, edn cit., Vol. I, pp. 157–77.

25 Cibber, *An Apology*, edn cit., Vol. I, p. 232

26 Love, *Congreve*, pp. 5–7; Peter Holland, *The Ornament of Action: Text and Performance in Restoration Comedy* (Cambridge: Cambridge University Press, 1979), pp. 55–98.

27 Downer, 'Nature to advantage dressed', *Restoration Drama*, p. 333.

28 Cibber, *An Apology*, edn cit., Vol. I, p. 290.

29 ibid., Vol. I, p. 222.

30 Avery, *Congreve's Plays on the Eighteenth-Century Stage*, gives a fuller and less generalized account.

31 On *Incognita*, see I. M. Westcott, 'The role of the narrator in Congreve's *Incognita*', *Trivium*, 1976, Vol. II, pp. 40–8; and Paul Salzman, *English Prose Fiction, 1558–1700: A Critical History* (Oxford: Clarendon Press, 1985), pp. 328–37.

1. William Congreve, Preface to *Incognita*

1691

From *Incognita: or, Love and Duty Reconcil'd* (London: 1692), sig. A5r–A8r.

Incognita was licensed on 22 December 1691, and its publication advertised in the *London Gazette*, no. 2742, for 18 to 22 February 1691/2.

THE
PREFACE
TO THE
READER.

Reader,

SOME Authors are so fond of a Preface, that they will write one tho' there be nothing more in it than an Apology for its self. But to show thee that I am not one of those, I will make no Apology for this, but do tell thee that I think it necessary to be prefix'd to this Trifle, to prevent thy overlooking some little pains which I have taken in the Composition of the following Story. Romances are generally composed of the Constant Loves and invincible Courages of Hero's, Heroins, Kings and Queens, Mortals of the first Rank, and so forth; where lofty Language, miraculous Contingencies and impossible Performances, elevate and surprize the Reader into a giddy Delight, which leaves him flat upon the Ground whenever he gives of, and vexes him to think how he has suffer'd himself to be pleased and transported, concern'd and afflicted at the several Passages which he has Read, *viz.* these Knights Success to their Damosels Misfortunes, and such like, when he is forced to be very well convinced that 'tis all a lye. Novels are of a more familiar nature; Come near us, and represent to us Intrigues in practice, delight us with Accidents and odd Events, but not such as are wholly unusual or unpresidented, such which not being so distant from our Belief bring also the pleasure nearer us. Romances give more of Wonder, Novels more Delight. And with reverence be it spoken, and the Parallel kept at due distance, there is something of equality in the Proportion which they bear in reference to one another, with that between Comedy and Tragedy; but the *Drama* is the long extracted from Romance and History: 'tis the Midwife to Industry, and brings forth alive the Conceptions of the Brain. *Minerva* walks upon the Stage before us, and we are more assured of the real presence of Wit when it is delivered *viva voce*—

> *Segnius irritant animos demissa per aurem,*
> *Quam quae sunt oculis subjecta fidelibus, & quae*
> *Ipse sibi tradit spectator.*—[1]
>
> Horace.

Since all Traditions must indisputably give place to the *Drama*, and since there is no possibility of giving that life to the Writing or Repetition of a Story which it has in the Action, I resolved in another beauty to imitate *Dramatick* Writing, namely, in the Design, Contexture and Result of the Plot. I have not observed it before in a Novel. Some I have seen begin with an unexpected accident, which has been the only surprizing part of the Story, cause enough to make the Sequel look flat, tedious and insipid; for 'tis but reasonable the Reader should expect it not to rise, at least to keep upon a level in the entertainment; for so he may be kept on in hopes that at some time or other it may mend; but the 'tother is such a balk to a Man, 'tis carrying him up stairs to show him the Dining-Room, and after forcing him to make a Meal in the Kitchin. This I have not only endeavoured to avoid, but also have used a method for the contrary purpose. The design of the Novel is obvious, after the first meeting of *Aurelian* and *Hippolito* with *Incognita* and *Leonora*, and the difficulty is in bringing it to pass, maugre all apparent obstacles, within the compass of two days. How many probable Casualties intervene in opposition to the main Design, *viz.* of marrying two Couple so oddly engaged in an intricate Amour, I leave the Reader at his leisure to consider: As also whether every Obstacle does not in the progress of the Story act as subservient to that purpose, which at first it seems to oppose. In a Comedy this would be called the

Unity of Action; here it may pretend to no more than an Unity of Contrivance. The Scene is continued in *Florence* from the commencement of the Amour; and the time from first to last is but three days. If there be any thing more in particular resembling the Copy which I imitate (as the Curious Reader will soon perceive) I leave it to show it self, being very well satisfy'd how much more proper it had been for him to have found out this himself, than for me to prepossess him with an Opinion of something extraordinary in an Essay began and finished in the idler hours of a fortnight's time: for I can only esteem it a laborious idleness, which is Parent to so inconsiderable a Birth. I have gratified the Bookseller in pretending an occasion for a Preface; the other two Persons concern'd are the Reader and my self, and if he be but pleased with what was produced for that end, my satisfaction follows of course, since it will be proportion'd to his Approbation or Dislike.

NOTE

1 *Ars Poetica*, ll. 180–2. 'Things which have sunk in through the ear move our minds more slowly than those which have been exposed to our faithful eyes, and which the onlooker records for himself.'

2. John Dryden on *The Old Batchelour*

1692

From B.L. Add. MS. 4221, fol. 341.

The following extract is from a letter written by the dramatist Thomas Southerne to Thomas Birch, one of the editors of *A General Dictionary, Historical and Critical* published 1734–41. The letter, endorsed 12 January 1735/6, was to supply biographical information for an entry on Congreve. The 'friend' who engaged Dryden on Congreve's behalf was almost certainly Southerne himself.

Mr Congreve was of the Middle temple, his first performance was a Novel, calld incognita, then he began his Play the old Batchelor having little Acquaintance withe the traders in that way, his Cozens recommended him to a friend of theirs, who was very usefull to him in the whole course of his play, he engaged Mr. Dryden in its favour, who upon reading it sayd he never saw such a first play in his life, but the Author not being acquainted with the stage or the town, it would be pity to have it miscarry for want of a little Assistance: the stuff was rich indeed, it wanted only the fashionable cutt of the town. to help that Mr Dryden, Mr Arthur Manwayring, and Mr Southern red it with great care, and Mr Dryden putt it in the order it was playd, Mr Southerne obtaind of Mr Tho: Davenant who then governd the Playhouse, that Mr Congreve shoud have the privilege of the Playhouse half a year before his play was playd, wch I never knew allowd any one before: it was playd with great success.

3. Prefatory poems to *The Old Batchelour*

1693

From *The Old Batchelour* (London: 1693), sig. A3r–ar.

Congreve's first play was printed almost immediately after its opening early in March.

Of the authors of these three poems, Thomas Southerne (1660–1746) had preceded Congreve at Trinity College, Dublin, and the Middle Temple. He began his career as a playwright in 1682, with a short spell in the army during the reign of James II. Congreve had supplied a song, 'Tell me no more I am deceiv'd', for Southerne's comedy *The Maid's Last Prayer*, which may have been first acted in late February 1693.

Jeremiah Marsh (1667–1734) was the son of Francis Marsh, Archbishop of Dublin, and on his mother's side grandson of Jeremy Taylor. He graduated at Trinity College, Dublin, four years ahead of Congreve, and subsequently became Dean of Kilmore in 1700.

Bevil Higgins (1670–1735) was a nephew of George Granville, later Lord Lansdowne. The family were Jacobite in
sympathy, and after the revolution of 1688 Higgons spent
some time in France. In 1693 he contributed five poems to
Examen Poeticum: being the Third Part of Miscellany Poems,
including 'To Mr. *Dryden*, on his Translation of Persius'. His
unsuccessful tragedy, *The Generous Conqueror* of 1702, was
alleged to contain Jacobite allusions; it was dedicated to John
Sheffield, Marquis of Normanby and Earl of Mulgrave,
former patron of Dryden and a leader of the Tory opposition
under William III.

(a)

TO MR. *CONGREVE.*

When Vertue in pursuit of Fame appears,
And forward shoots the growth beyond the Years:
We timely court the rising Hero's Cause;
And on his side, the Poet wisely draws;
Bespeaking him hereafter, by Applause.
The days will come, when we shall all receive,
Returning Interest from what now we give:
Instructed, and supported by that Praise,
And Reputation, which we strive to raise.
Nature so coy, so hardly to be Woo'd
Flies, like a Mistress, but to be pursu'd.
O *CONGREVE*! boldly follow on the Chase;
She looks behind, and wants thy strong Embrace:
She yields, she yields, surrenders all her Charms,
Do you but force her gently to your Arms:
Such Nerves, such Graces, in your Lines appear,
As you were made to be her Ravisher.
DRYDEN has long extended his Command,
By Right divine, quite through the Muses Land,
Absolute Lord; and holding now from none,
But great *Apollo*, his undoubted Crown:
(That Empire settled, and grown old in Pow'r)
Can wish for nothing, but a Successor:
Not to enlarge his Limits, but maintain
Those Provinces, which he alone could gain.
His eldest *Wicherly*, in wise Retreat,
Thought it not worth his quiet to be great.

Loose, wandring, *Etherege*, in wild Pleasures tost,
And foreign Int'rests, to his hopes long lost:
Poor *Lee* and *Otway* dead! *CONGREVE* appears,
The Darling, and last Comfort of his Years:
May'st thou live long in thy great Masters smiles,
And growing under him, adorn these Isles:
But when—when part of him (be that but late)
His Body yielding must submit to Fate,
Leaving his deathless Works, and thee behind,
(The natural Successor of his Mind)
Then may'st thou finish what he has begun:
Heir to his Merit, be in Fame his Son.
What thou hast done, shews all is in thy Power;
And to Write better, only must Write more.
'Tis something to be willing to commend;
But my best Praise, is, that I am your Friend.
THO. SOUTHERNE.

(b)

TO MR. CONGREVE.

The Danger's great in these censorious days,
When Criticks are so rife, to venture Praise:
When the infectious and ill-natured Brood
Behold, and damn the Work, because 'tis good;
And with a proud, ungenerous Spight would try
To pass an Ostrocism on Poetry.
But you, my Friend, your Worth does safely bear
Above their Spleen; you have no cause for fear;
Like a well-metled Hawk, you took your flight
Quite out of reach, and almost out of sight.
As the strong Sun, in a fair Summers day,
You rise, and drive the Mists and Clowds away, }
The Owls and Bats, and all the Birds of Prey. }
Each Line of yours, like polisht Steel's so hard,
In Beauty safe, it wants no other guard.
Nature her self's beholden to your Dress,
Which tho' still like, much fairer you express.
Some vainly striving Honour to obtain,
Leave to their Heirs the Traffick of their Brain;
Like *China* under Ground, the ripening Ware,
In a long time, perhaps grows worth our Care:
But you now reap the Fame, so well you've sown;
The Planter tasts his Fruit to ripeness grown.

As a fair Orange-tree at once is seen,
Big with what's ripe, yet springing still with Green:
So at one time, my worthy Friend appears,
With all the sap of Youth, and weight of Years.
  Accept my pious Love, as forward Zeal,
Which tho' it ruins me I can't conceal:
Expos'd to Censure for my weak Applause,
I'm pleas'd to suffer in so just a Cause:
And tho' my Offering may unworthy prove,
Take as a Friend the Wishes of my Love.

J.D. MARSH.

(c)

TO MR. *CONGREVE*, ON HIS PLAY, CALLED, THE *OLD BATCHELOR*

Wit, like true Gold, refin'd from all Allay,
Immortal is, and never can decay:
'Tis in all Times and Languages the same;
Nor can an ill Translation quench the Flame:
For, tho' the Form and Fashion don't remain,
Th' intrinsick value still it will retain.
Then let each studied Scene be writ with Art;
And Judgment sweat to form the labour'd Part:
Each Character be just, and Nature seem;
Without th' Ingredient, Wit, 'tis all but Phlegm:
For that's the Soul, which all the Mass must move,
And wake our Passions into Grief, or Love.
But you, too Bounteous, sow your Wit so thick,
We are surpriz'd, and know not where to pick:
And while our Clapping does you Justice do,
Our selves we injure, and lose something new.
What may'nt we then, great Youth, of thee presage,
Whose Art and Wit so much transcend thy Age?
How wilt thou shine at thy Meridian height?
Who, at thy rising, give so vast a Light.
When *DRYDEN* dying, shall the World deceive,
Whom we Immortal, as his Works, believe;
Thou shalt succeed, the Glory of the Stage,
Adorn and entertain the coming Age.

BEVIL HIGGINS.

4. Peter Motteux in *The Gentleman's Journal*

1693

From *The Gentleman's Journal: or the Monthly Miscellany* (February 1693), 2: 61.

Peter Motteux (1663–1718) was a Huguenot who had come to England after the revocation of the edict of Nantes in 1685. Besides the writing or adapting of plays and operas, he completed Sir Thomas Urquhart's translation of Rabelais and in collaboration with others translated *Don Quixote*. *The Gentleman's Journal* was a literary periodical which Motteux edited between 1692 and 1693; its issues appeared two or three months late, and the following extract from the February number must have appeared at the end of March after the publication of *The Old Batchelour*. See John C. Hodges, 'The composition of Congreve's first play' (*PMLA*: 1943), 58: 971–6. Motteux had announced the imminent performance of the play in his January number (p. 28), actually published in early March.

The success of Mr. *Congreve*'s *Old Batchelor* has been so extraordinary, that I can tell you nothing new of that Comedy; you have doubtless read it before this, since it has been already printed thrice. And indeed the Wit which is diffus'd through it, makes it lose but few of those Charms in the Perusal, which yield such pleasure in the Representation. Mr. *Congreve* will in some time give us another Play; you may judge by this how acceptable it will be.

5. Henry Higden in the Preface to *The Wary Widdow*

1693

From *The Wary Widdow: or, Sir Noisy Parrat* (London: 1693), sig. A3r–A3v.

Henry Higden was a minor wit and a member of the Middle Temple. He published translations of Juvenal's thirteenth and tenth satires in octosyllabic couplets in 1686 and 1687 respectively; the latter was accompanied by commendatory poems by Dryden, Settle, and Aphra Behn. Higden's comedy *The Wary Widdow* succeeded *The Old Batchelour* at the Theatre Royal, Drury Lane; by his own admission it was badly produced, and met a hostile reception from a rowdy audience. The following extract was written by a jealous and disgruntled man.

I am not Ignorant a just Cause may suffer under the prejudice of an *Ignoramus Jury*, or an unjust Judge may stop his Ears against the voice of the Charmer, and harden his heart to the severest Judgment; or that an incensed *Mob* may be wrought up to break thro' all Laws, and commit the highest outrages, and Barbarities. But after the fury of their military Execution is over they may relent of their rigour, and have some reserve of compassion for the unfortunate Martyr, that suffered their indignities with all constancy and Patience. Had our unlucky Authour been worthy to have known they were absolutely bent to damn his Play, unsight unseen, his caution would have withdrawn him from the Thunder of their displeasure. But now we are convinc'd by the surprising success of the Baudy Batchelour, that the nicest Ladies may be brought (by good mannagment) to stand the fire of a smutty Jest, and never flintch for the matter. They are the sensible Judges that family duties can not proceed without the creature comfort: Nor Nature be well instructed without the help of a feskue. These Camelion Ladies cannot like the Spanish Jennets conceive by the ayr, or grow big with such a Timpany.

64

Tanquam conjugibus suis Mariti,
Non possunt sine Mentula placere.
What Sot can thinke to please a Beauty.
That wants wherewith to do his duty.

But I must beg the Ladies pardon that I introduce a Forreign Tongue, that can make use of their Mothers to a better advantage, but in a Preface it is necessary to sprinkle a little Latin, to shew our Breeding. The Authours are now convinc'd the Batchelour has touch'd upon the true string, to please and tickle: They are now grown more generous then to deny their sentiments and Inclinations, and scorn any such bashfull pretence, but openly avow and countenance that Poet, that seasons his Scenes with salt and good humour, to please the haut-gousts of their fancies: and make their Eares glow with licentious Farce, which they are resolv'd to stand by and justify: What though the Plots are old, and stale, they are so prettily jumbled and blended together they can never fail of being well receiv'd. Tho some nicer Ladies are of an opinion, that an impure Idea, that is obscene in the first conception (though never so cleanly wrapt up) can no way be made passable: But these are squeamish pallats that strain at a gnat in publick, and after make no bones of a Camel on occasion. What does it import if *Parson Spintext* have a wicked design on the Alderman's wife? What harm was it if his agreable Impudence revenged the City cheats upon the Aldermans head, and exalted his horns above the rest of his Brethren? There cannot be a taking Play without some Limberham or fumbling Alderman, or keeper to expose. Let the fair Gilt ingage her Gallant like a Spider in her own cobweb, before her own Nickapoops face, unbar the sluces, that her kindness may run down in a mighty stream; let the lightening of Courtship melt his Daughters maidenhead in the scaboard, or chopping of that *Hidra's* Head of barren Virginity, let twins sprout up in their stead and let the Family of love be propigated quite through the City.

6. John Dryden in the dedication to *Examen Poeticum*

1693

From *Examen Poeticum: being the Third Part of Miscellany Poems* (London: 1693).

Examen Poeticum was dedicated to Edward, Lord Radclyffe. The Homeric episodes translated by Congreve were 'Priam's Lamentation and Petition to *Achilles*, For the Body of his Son *Hector*' and 'The Lamentations of *Hecuba, Andromache,* and *Helen,* Over the Dead Body of *Hector*'. Dryden contributed 'The Last parting of *Hector* and *Andromache*'.

(i)

Notwithstanding my haste, I cannot forbear to tell your Lordship, that there are two fragments of *Homer* Translated in this *Miscellany*; one by Mr. *Congreve* (whom I cannot mention without the Honour which is due to his excellent Parts, and that entire Affection which I bear him;) and the other by my self. Both the Subjects are pathetical; and I am sure my Friend has added to the Tenderness which he found in the Original; and, without Flattery, surpass'd his Author.

(sig. B4v)

(ii)

But let *Homer* and *Virgil* contend for the Prize of Honour, betwixt themselves, I am satisfied they will never have a third Concurrent. I wish Mr. *Congreve* had the leisure to Translate him, and the World the good Nature and Justice, to Encourage him in that Notable Design, of which he is more capable than any Man I know. The Earl of *Mulgrave*, and Mr. *Waller*, two the best Judges of our Age, have assur'd me, that they cou'd never Read over the Translation of *Chapman*, without incredible Pleasure, and extreme Transport. This Admiration of theirs, must needs proceed from the Author himself: For the Translator has thrown him down as low, as harsh Numbers, improper *English*, and a monstrous length of Verse/

66

cou'd carry him. What then wou'd he appear in the Harmonious
Version, of one of the best Writers, Living in a much better Age
than was the last? I mean for versification, and the Art of Numbers;
for in the *Drama* we have not arriv'd to the pitch of *Shakespear* and
Ben Johnson.

(sig. B6r – v)

7. Thomas Yalden, 'To Mr. Congreve. An Epistolary Ode Occasion'd by his late Play'

1693

From *Examen Poeticum: being the Third Part of Miscellany Poems*
(London: 1693), pp. 343–8.

Thomas Yalden (1670–1763) was a high-church clergyman
and minor poet. He was a contemporary of Addison at
Magdalen College, Oxford; both men, like Congreve,
contributed to the third and fourth parts of *Miscellany Poems*.
Yalden's verse remained uncollected until his inclusion, at
Samuel Johnson's insistence, in *The English Poets*.

TO MR. *CONGREVE.*

AN

EPISTOLARY ODE.

OCCASION'D BY HIS LATE PLAY.

FROM MR. *YALDEN.*

I.

Fam'd *Wits* and *Beauties*, share this common fate,
    To stand expos'd to publick Love and Hate,
    In ev'ry *Breast* They diff'rent Passions raise,
    At once provoke our Envy, and our Praise.

67

For when, like you, some noble Youth appears,
For Wit and Humour fam'd above his Years:
Each emulous Muse, that views the Laurel won,
Must praise the worth so much transcends their own,
And, while his Fame they envy, add to his renown.
    But sure like you, no youth, cou'd please,
Nor at his first attempt boast such success:
Where all Mankind have fail'd, you glories won:
    Triumphant are in this alone,
In this, have all the *Bards* of old outdone.

II.

Then may'st thou rule our Stage in triumph long,
    May'st Thou it's injur'd Fame revive,
And matchless proofs of Wit, and Humour, give,
Reforming with thy Scenes, and Charming with thy Song.
And tho' a Curse ill-fated Wit persues,
And waits the Fatal Dowry of a Muse:
    Yet may thy rising Fortunes be
Secure from all the blasts of Poetry;
As thy own Laurels flourishing appear,
Unsully'd still with Cares, nor clog'd with Hope and Fear.
As from its want's be from its Vices free,
    From nauseous servil Flattery:
Nor to a Patron prostitute the Mind,
Tho' like *Augustus* Great, as Fam'd *Mæcenas* kind.

III.

Tho' great in Fame! believe me generous Youth,
    Believe this oft experienc'd Truth,
From him that knows thy Virtues, and admires their worth.
Tho' Thou'rt above what vulgar Poets fear,
    Trust not the ungrateful World too far;
Trust not the Smiles of the inconstant Town:
Trust not the Plaudits of a Theater,
(Which *D[ur]fy* shall, with *Thee*, and *Dryden* share)
Nor to a Stages int'rest Sacrifice thy own.
Thy *Genius*, that's for Nobler things design'd,
    May at loose Hours oblige Mankind:
Then great as is thy Fame, thy Fortunes raise,
Joyn thriving int'rest to thy barren *Bays*,
And teach the World to envy, as thou do'st to praise.

The *World*, that does like *common Whores* embrace,
Injurious still to those it does caress:
Injurious as the *tainted Breath* of Fame,
That *blasts* a Poet's *Fortunes*, while it *sounds* his *Name*.

IV.

When first a *Muse* inflames some Youthful *Breast*,
Like an unpractis'd Virgin, still she's kind:
Adorn'd with Graces then, and *Beauties* blest,
She *charms* the *Ear* with *Fame*, with *Raptures* fills the *Mind*.
    Then from all *Cares* the *happy Youth* is free,
        But those of Love and Poetry:
    Cares, still allay'd with pleasing Charms,
That *Crown* the Head with *Bays*, with *Beauty* fill the *Arms*.
    But all a Woman's Frailties soon she shows,
    Too soon a stale domestick Creature grows:
    Then wedded to a Muse that's nauseous grown,
We loath what we enjoy, druge when the Pleasure's gon.
    For tempted with imaginary *Bays*,,
    Fed with immortal Hopes, and empty Praise:
    He Fame pursues, that fair, but treacherous, bait,
Grows wise, when he's undone, repents when 'tis too late.

V.

Small are the Trophies of his boasted *Bays*,
The Great Man's promise, for his flattering Toyl,
Fame in reversion, and the publick smile,
All vainer than his Hopes, uncertain as his Praise.
    'Twas thus in Mournful Numbers heretofore,
    Neglected *Spencer* did his Fate deplore:
        Long did his injur'd Muse complain,
Admir'd in midst of *Wants*, and *Charming* still in vain.
        Long did the Generous *Cowley* Mourn,
    And long oblig'd the *Age* without return:
    Deny'd what every Wretch obtains of Fate,
        An humble Roof, and an obscure retreat,
Condemn'd to *needy Fame*, and to be *miserably* great.
    Thus did the World thy great Fore-Fathers use,
        Thus all the inspir'd *Bards* before,
    Did their hereditary Ills deplore:
From tuneful *Chaucer*'s, down to thy own *Dryden*'s Muse.

VI.

Yet pleas'd with gaudy ruin Youth will on,
As proud by publick Fame to be undone:
Pleas'd tho' he does the worst of Labours chuse,
To serve a *Barb'rous Age*, and an ungrateful *Muse*.
Since *Dryden*'s self, to Wit's great Empire born,
    Whose Genius and exalted Name,
  Triumph with all the *Spoils* of *Wit* and *Fame*;
Must midst the loud *Applause* his barren *Laurels* mourn
  Even that Fam'd *Man* whom all the *World* admires,
  Whom every Grace adorns, and Muse inspires:
    Like the great injur'd *Tasso* shows,
    Triumphant in the midst of Woes;
In all his Wants Majestick still appears,
Charming the *Age* to which he ows his Cares,
And cherishing that *Muse* whose *fatal Curse* he bears.

From Mag. Col. Oxon.

8. Jonathan Swift, 'To Mr. Congreve'

1693

From *The Poems of Jonathan Swift*, ed. Harold Williams, 2nd edn, 3 vols (Oxford: Clarendon Press, 1958), I, pp. 43–50.

Swift was an elder contemporary of Congreve at Kilkenny College and at Trinity College, Dublin, but their friendship seems to have begun at the latter where both were tutorial pupils of St George Ashe.

Swift appears to have hoped that his poem might be printed with *The Double-Dealer*, only just performed in London. Sir Harold Williams cites a letter of 6 December 1693, to his cousin Thomas Swift:

I desire You would inform yr self what you mean by bidding me keep my Verses for Will Congreve's next Play, for I tell You they were calculated for any of his, and if it were but acted when you say,

THE CRITICAL HERITAGE

it is as early as ever I intended, since I onely design they should be
printed before it, So I desire you will send me word immediatly,
how it succeeded, whether well, ill, or indifferently, because my
sending them to Mr Congreve depends upon knowing the issue.
(*Correspondence of Jonathan Swift*, ed. Harold Williams, 5 vols
(Oxford: Clarendon Press, 1963–5), I, pp. 13–14.)

If Swift did have *The Double-Dealer* in mind, its prompt
publication forestalled him. His poem was first printed in
1789 by John Nichols in a gathering of material omitted from
Sheridan's edition of Swift.

TO MR. CONGREVE.
WRITTEN NOVEMBER 1693.

Thrice, with a prophet's voice and prophet's pow'r,
The Muse was call'd in a poetic hour,
And insolently thrice, the slighted Maid
Dar'd to suspend her unregarded aid;
Then with that grief we form in spirits divine,
Pleads for her own neglect, and thus reproaches mine:
   Once highly honour'd! False is the pretence
You make to truth, retreat, and innocence;
Who, to pollute my shades, bring'st with thee down
The most ungen'rous vices of the town;   10
Ne'er sprang a youth from out this isle before
I once esteem'd, and lov'd, and favour'd more,
Nor ever maid endur'd such court-like scorn,
So much in mode, so very city-born;
'Tis with a foul design the muse you send,
Like a cast mistress to your wicked friend;
But find some new address, some fresh deceit,
Nor practise such an antiquated cheat;
These are the beaten methods of the stews,
Stale forms of course, all mean deceivers use,   20
Who barbarously think to 'scape reproach,
By prostituting her they first debauch.
   Thus did the Muse severe unkindly blame
This off'ring long design'd to CONGREVE's fame;
First chid the zeal as unpoetic fire,
Which soon his merit forc'd her to inspire;
Then call this verse, that speaks her largest aid,

71

The greatest compliment she ever made,
And wisely judge, no pow'r beneath divine
Could leap the bounds which part your world and mine;   30
For, youth, believe, to you unseen, is fix'd
A mighty gulph unpassable betwixt.
    Nor tax the goddess of a mean design
To praise your parts by publishing of mine;
That be my thought when some large bulky writ
Shews in the front the ambition of my wit;
There to surmount what bears me up, and sing
Like the victorious wren perch'd on the eagle's wing;
This could I do, and proudly o'er him tow'r,
Were my desires but heighten'd to my pow'r.   40
    Godlike the force of my young CONGREVE's bays,
Soft'ning the muse's thunder into praise;
Sent to assist an old unvanquish'd pride
That looks with scorn on half mankind beside;
A pride that well suspends poor mortals fate,
Gets between them and my resentment's weight,
Stands in the gap 'twixt me and wretched men,
T'avert th'impending judgments of my pen.
    Thus I look down with mercy on the age,
By hopes my CONGREVE will reform the stage;   50
For never did poetic mine before
Produce a richer vein or cleaner ore;
The bullion stampt in your refining mind
Serves by retail to furnish half mankind.
With indignation I behold your wit
Forc'd on me, crack'd, and clipp'd, and counterfeit,
By vile pretenders, who a stock maintain
From broken scraps and filings of your brain.
Through native dross your share is hardly known,
And by short views mistook for all their own;   60
So small the gain those from your wit do reap,
Who blend it into folly's larger heap,
Like the sun's scatter'd beams which loosely pass,
When some rough hand breaks the assembling-glass.
    Yet want your critics no just cause to rail,
Since knaves are ne'er oblig'd for what they steal.
These pad on wit's high road, and suits maintain
With those they rob, by what their trade does gain.
Thus censure seems that fiery froth which breeds
O'er the sun's face, and from his heat proceeds,   70

Crusts o'er the day, shadowing its parent beam
As antient nature's modern masters dream;
This bids some curious praters here below
Call Titan sick, because their sight is so;
And well, methinks, does this allusion fit
To scribblers, and the god of light and wit;
Those who by wild delusions entertain
A lust of rhiming for a poet's vein,
Raise envy's clouds to leave themselves in night,
But can no more obscure my CONGREVE's light   80
Than swarms of gnats, that wanton in a ray
Which gave them birth, can rob the world of day.
   What northern hive pour'd out these foes to wit?
Whence came these Goths to overrun the pit?
How would you blush the shameful birth to hear
Of those you so ignobly stoop to fear;
For, ill to them, long have I travell'd since
Round all the circles of impertinence,
Search'd in the nest where every worm did lie
Before it grew a city butterfly;   90
I'm sure I found them other kind of things
Than those with backs of silk and golden wings;
A search, no doubt, as curious and as wise
As virtuosoes' in dissecting flies;
For, could you think? the fiercest foes you dread,
And court in prologues, all are country-bred;
Bred in my scene, and for the poet's sins
Adjourn'd from tops and grammar to the inns;
Those beds of dung, where schoolboys sprout up beaus
Far sooner than the nobler mushroom grows: 100
These are the lords of the poetic schools,
Who preach the saucy pedantry of rules;
Those pow'rs the criticks, who may boast the odds
O'er Nile, with all its wilderness of gods;
Nor could the nations kneel to viler shapes,
Which worship'd cats, and sacrific'd to apes;
And can you think the wise forbear to laugh
At the warm zeal that breeds this golden calf?
   Haply you judge these lines severely writ
Against the proud usurpers of the pit;   110
Stay while I tell my story, short, and true;
To draw conclusions shall be left to you;
Nor need I ramble far to force a rule,

But lay the scene just here at Farnham school.
   Last year, a lad hence by his parents sent
With other cattle to the city went;
Where having cast his coat, and well pursu'd
The methods most in fashion to be lewd,
Return'd a finish'd spark this summer down,
Stock'd with the freshest gibberish of the town;   120
A jargon form'd from the lost language, wit,
Confounded in that Babel of the pit;
Form'd by diseas'd conceptions, weak, and wild,
Sick lust of souls, and an abortive child;
Born between whores and fops, by lewd compacts,
Before the play, or else between the acts:
Nor wonder, if from such polluted minds
Should spring such short and transitory kinds,
Or crazy rules to make us wits by rote
Last just as long as ev'ry cuckow's note: 130
What bungling, rusty tools, are us'd by fate!
'Twas in an evil hour to urge my hate,
My hate, whose lash just heaven has long decreed
Shall on a day make sin and folly bleed;
When man's ill genius to my presence sent
This wretch, to rouse my wrath, for ruin meant;
Who in his idiom vile, with Gray's-inn grace,
Squander'd his noisy talents to my face;
Nam'd ev'ry player on his fingers ends,
Swore all the wits were his peculiar friends;   140
Talk'd with that saucy and familiar ease
Of Wycherly, and you, and Mr. Bays;
Said, how a late report your friends had vex'd,
Who heard you meant to write heroics next;
For, tragedy, he knew, would lose you quite,
And told you so at Will's but t'other night.
   Thus are the lives of fools a sort of dreams,
Rend'ring shades, things, and substances of names;
Such high companions may delusion keep,
Lords are a footboy's cronies in his sleep.   150
As a fresh miss, by fancy, face, and gown,
Render'd the topping beauty of the town,
Draws ev'ry rhyming, prating, dressing sot,
To boast of favours that he never got;
Of which, whoe'er lacks confidence to prate,
Brings his good parts and breeding in debate;

And not the meanest coxcomb you can find,
But thanks his stars, that Phyllis has been kind;
Thus prostitute my CONGREVE's name is grown
To ev'ry lew'd pretender of the town.   160
'Troth I could pity you; but this is it,
You find, to be the fashionable wit;
These are the slaves whom reputation chains,
Whose maintenance requires no help from brains.
For, should the vilest scribbler to the pit,
Whom sin and want e'er furnish'd out a wit;
Whose name must not within my lines be shewn,
Lest here it live, when perish'd with his own;
Should such a wretch usurp my CONGREVE's place,
And chuse out wits who ne'er have seen his face;   170
I'll be my life but the dull cheat would pass,
Nor need the lion's skin conceal the ass;
Yes, that beau's look, that voice, those critic ears,
Must needs be right, so well resembling theirs.
    Perish the Muse's hour, thus vainly spent
In satire, to my CONGREVE's praises meant;
In how ill season her resentments rule,
What's that to her if mankind be a fool?
Happy beyond a private muse's fate,
In pleasing *all that's good among the great,*   180
Where tho' her elder sisters crowding throng,
She still is welcome with her inn'cent song;
Whom were my CONGREVE blest to see and know,
What poor regards would merit all below!
How proudly would he haste the joy to meet,
And drop his laurel at *Apollo*'s feet.
    Here by a mountain's side, a reverend cave
Gives murmuring passage to a lasting wave;
'Tis the world's wat'ry hour-glass streaming fast,
Time is no more when th'utmost drop is past;   190
Here, on a better day, some druid dwelt,
And the young Muse's early favour felt;
Druid, a name she does with pride repeat,
Confessing Albion once her darling seat;
Far in this primitive cell might we pursue
Our predecessors foot-steps, still in view;
Here would we sing—But, ah! you think I dream,
And the bad world may well believe the same;
Yes; you are all malicious standers-by,

While two fond lovers prate, the Muse and I.   200
   Since thus I wander from my first intent,
Nor am that grave adviser which I meant;
Take this short lesson from the god of bayes,
And let my friend apply it as he please:

Beat not the dirty paths where vulgar feet have trod,
   But give the vigorous fancy room.
For when like stupid alchymists you try
   To fix this nimble god,
   This volatile mercury,
The subtil spirit all flies up in fume;   210
   Nor shall the bubbl'd virtuoso find
More than a fade insipid mixture left behind.

   Whilst thus I write, vast shoals of critics come,
And on my verse pronounce their saucy doom;
The Muse, like some bright country virgin, shows,
Fall'n by mishap amongst a knot of beaux;
They, in their lewd and fashionable prate,
Rally her dress, her language, and her gait;
Spend their base coin before the bashful maid,
Current like copper, and as often paid: 220
She, who on shady banks has joy'd to sleep
Near better animals, her father's sheep;
Sham'd and amaz'd, beholds the chatt'ring throng,
To think what cattle she has got among;
But with the odious smell and sight annoy'd,
In haste she does th'offensive herd avoid.
   'Tis time to bid my friend a long farewell,
The muse retreats far in yon chrystal cell;
Faint inspiration sickens as she flies,
Like distant echo spent, the spirit dies.   230
   In this descending sheet you'll haply find
Some short refreshment for your weary mind,
Nought it contains is common or unclean,
And once drawn up, is ne'er let down again.

9. William Congreve, Epistle Dedicatory to *The Double-Dealer*

1693

From *The Double-Dealer* (London: 1694), sig. A2r–av.

Congreve's second play was not an initial success, and his resentment is apparent in the dedication. Some of the more acrimonious passages were toned down or omitted in the second quarto of 1706.

Congreve's patron Charles Montagu (1661–1715) had been an early supporter of the 1688 Revolution. First appointed to the Treasury in 1692, he proved a brilliant financier, establishing the Bank of England and the National Debt. He was created Baron Halifax in 1700, and became an earl the year before his death. In 1687 Montagu had joined Matthew Prior in a skit on Dryden, *The Hind and the Panther Transvers'd to the Story of the Country Mouse and the City-Mouse*, but his real contribution to literature was his patronage of Whig writers. In 1695 he secured for Congreve the post of Commissioner for Licensing Hackney Coaches.

TO THE RIGHT HONOURABLE

CHARLES MOUNTAGUE,

ONE OF THE

LORDS OF THE *TREASURY*.

SIR,

I Heartily wish this Play were as perfect as I intended it, that it might be more worthy your acceptance; and that my Dedication of it to you, might be more becoming that Honour and Esteem which I, with every Body, who are so fortunate as to know you, have for you. It had your Countenance when yet unknown; and now it is made publick, it wants your Protection.

    And give me leave, without any Flattery to you, or Vanity in my self, to tell my Illiterate Criticks, as an answer to their Impotent Objections, that they have found fault with that, which has been pleasing to you. This Play in relation to my concern for its Reputation, succeeded before it was Acted, for thro' your early Patronage it had an audience of several Persons of the first Rank both in Wit and Quality; and their allowance of it, was a Consequence of your approbation. Therefore if I really wish it might have had a more popular reception; it is not at all in consideration of my self; but because I wish well, and would gladly contribute to the benefit of the Stage, and diversion of the Town. They were (not long since) so kind to a very imperfect Comedy of mine, that I thought my self justly indebted to them all my endeavours for an entertainment that might merit some little of that Applause, which they were so lavish of, when I thought I had no Title to it. But I find they are to be treated cheaply, and I have been at an unnecessary expence.

I would not have any Body imagine, that I think this Play without its Faults, for I am Conscious of several, and ready to own 'em; but it shall be to those who are able to find 'em out. I confess I design'd (whatever Vanity or Ambition occasion'd that design) to have written a true and regular Comedy, but I found it an undertaking which put me in mind of—*Sudet multum, frustraque laboret ausus idem.* And now to make amends for the vanity of such a design, I do confess both the attempt, and the imperfect performance. Yet I must take the boldness to say, I have not miscarried in the whole; for the Mechanical part of it is perfect. That, I may say with as little vanity, as a Builder may say he has built a House according to the Model laid down before him; or a Gardiner that he has set his Flowers in a knot of such or such a Figure. I design'd the Moral first, and to that Moral I invented the Fable, and do not know that I have borrow'd one hint of it any where. I made the Plot as strong as I could, because it was single, and I made it single, because I would avoid confusion, and was resolved to preserve the three Unities of the Drama, which I have visibly done to the utmost severity. This is what I ought not to observe upon my self; but the Ignorance and Malice of the greater part of the Audience is such, that they would make a Man turn Herauld to his own Play, and Blazon every Character. However, Sir, this Discourse is very impertinent to you, whose Judgment, much better can discern the Faults, than I can excuse them; and whose good Nature, like that of a Lover, will find out those hidden Beauties (if there are any such) which it would be great immodesty in me to discover. I think I don't speak improperly when I call you a *Lover* of Poetry; for it is very well known she has been a kind Mistress to you; she has not deny'd you the last Favour; you have injoy'd her, and she has been fruitful in a most Beautiful Issue——If I break off abruptly here, I hope every Body will understand that it is to avoid a Commendation, which, as it is your due, would be most easie for me to pay, and too troublesome for you to receive.

I have since the Acting of this Play hearkned after the Objections which have been made to it; for I was Conscious where a true Critick might have put me upon my defence. I was prepared for their Attack; and am pretty confident I could have vindicated some parts, and excused others; and where there were any plain Miscarriages, I would most ingenuously have confess'd 'em. But I have not heard any thing said sufficient to provoke an Answer. Some little snarling and barking there has been, but I don't know one well-mouth'd Curr that has opened at all. That, which looks most like an Objection, does not relate in particular to this Play, but to all or most that ever have been written; and that is Soliloquy. Therefore I will answer it, not only for my own sake, but to save others the trouble, to whom it may hereafter be Objected.

I grant, that for a Man to Talk to himself, appears absurd and unnatural; and indeed it is so in most Cases; but the circumstances which may attend the occasion, make great alteration. It oftentimes happens to a Man, to have designs which require him to himself, and in their Nature, cannot admit of a Confident. Such, for certain, is all Villany; and other less mischievous intentions may be very improper to be Communicated to a second Person. In such a case therefore the Audience must observe, whether the Person upon the Stage takes any notice of them at all, or no. For if he supposes any one to be by, when he talks to himself, it is monstrous and ridiculous to the last degree. Nay, not only in this case, but in any part of a Play, if there is expressed any knowledge of an Audience, it is insufferable. But otherwise when a Man is Soliloquy reasons with himself, and *Pro's* and *Con's*, and weighs all his Designs: We ought not to imagine that this Man either talks to us, or to himself; he is only thinking, and thinking such Matter, as were inexcusable Folly in him to speak. But because we are conceal'd Spectators of the Plot in agitation, and the Poet finds it necessary to let us know

79

the whole Mystery of his Contrivance; he is willing to inform us of this Persons Thoughts, and to that end is forced to make use of the expedient of Speech, no other better way being yet invented for the Communication of Thought.

Another very wrong Objection has been made by some who have not taken leisure to distinguish the Characters. The Hero of the Play as they are pleas'd to call him, (meaning *Mellefont*) is a Gull, and made a Fool, and cheated. Is every Man a Gull and a Fool that is deceived? At that rate I'm afraid the two Classes of Men, will be reduc'd to one, and the Knaves themselves be at a loss to justifie their Title: But if an Open-hearted Honest Man, who has an entire Confidence in one whom he takes to be his Friend, and whom he has obliged to be so; and who (to confirm him in his Opinion) in all appearance, and upon several tryals has been so: If this Man be deceived by the Treachery of the other; must he of necessity commence Fool immediately, only because the other has proved a Villain? Ay, but there was Caution given to *Mellefont* in the first Act by his Friend *Careless*. Of what Nature was that Caution? Only to give the Audience some light into the Character of *Maskwell*, before his appearance; and not to convince *Mellefont* of his Treachery; for that was more than *Careless* was then able to do: He never knew *Maskwell* guilty of any Villany; he was only a sort of Man which he did not like. As for his suspecting his Familiarity with my Lady *Touchwood*: Let 'em examine the answer that *Mellefont* makes him, and compare it with the Conduct of *Maskwell*'s Character through the Play.

I would have 'em again look into the Character of *Maskwell*, before they accuse any Body of weakness for being deceiv'd by him. For upon summing up the enquiry into this Objection, find they have only mistaken Cunning in one Character, for Folly in another.

But there is one thing, at which I am more concerned than all the false Criticisms that are made upon me; and that is, some of the Ladies are offended: I am heartily sorry for it, for I declare I would rather disoblige all the Criticks in the World, than one of the Fair Sex. They are concerned that I have represented some Women Vicious and Affected: How can I help it? It is the Business of a Comick Poet to paint the Vices and Follies of Humane kind; and there are but two Sexes that I know, *viz. Men*, and *Women*, which have a Title to Humanity: And if I leave one half of them out, the

Work will be imperfect. I should be very glad of an opportunity to make my Complement to those Ladies who are offended: But they can no more expect it in a Comedy, than to be Tickled by a Surgeon, when he's letting 'em Blood. They who are Virtuous or Discreet, I'm sure cannot be offended, for such Characters as these distinguish them, and make their Beauties more shining and observ'd: And they who are of the other kind, may nevertheless pass for such, by seeming not to be displeased, or touched with the Satyr of this *Comedy.* Thus have they also wrongfully accused me of doing them a prejudice, when I have in reality done them a Service.

I have heard some whispering, as if they intended to accuse this Play of Smuttiness and Bawdy: But I declare I took a particular care to avoid it, and if they find any in it, it is of their own making, for I did not design it to be so understood. But to avoid my saying any thing upon a Subject, which has been so admirably handled before, and for their better instruction, I earnestly recommend to their perusal, the Epistle Dedicatory before the *Plain-Dealer.*

You will pardon me, Sir, for the freedom I take of making Answers to other People, in an Epistle which ought wholly to be sacred to you: But since I intend the Play to be so too, I hope I may take the more liberty of Justifying it, where it is in the right. I hear a great many of the Fools are angry at me, and I am glad of it; for I Writ at them, not to 'em. This is a bold confession, and yet I don't think I shall disoblige one Person by it; for no Body can take it to himself, without owning the *Character.*

I must now, Sir, declare to the World, how kind you have been to my Endeavours; for in regard of what was well meant, you have excused what was ill perform'd, I beg you would continue the same Method in your acceptance of this Dedication. I know no other way of making a return to that *Charity* you shew'd, in protecting an Infant, but by Enrolling it in your Service, now that it is of Age and come into the World. Therefore be pleased to accept of this as an Acknowledgement of the Favour you have shewn me, and an earnest of the real Service and Gratitude of,

SIR,

Your Most Obliged
Humble Servant
William Congreve.

10. John Dryden on *The Double-Dealer*

1693

From (a) *The Double-Dealer* (London: 1694), sig. a2r–a3v; (b) *The Letters of John Dryden*, ed. Charles E. Ward (Durham, NC: Duke University Press, 1942), pp. 62–3.

TO MY DEAR FRIEND

MR. CONGREVE,

ON HIS COMEDY, CALL'D,

THE DOUBLE-DEALER.

Well then; the promis'd hour is come at last;
The present Age of Wit obscures the past:
Strong were our Syres; and as they Fought they Writ,
Conqu'ring with force of Arms, and dint of Wit;
Theirs was the Gyant Race, before the Flood;
And thus, when *Charles* Return'd, our Empire stood.
Like *Janus* he the stubborn Soil manur'd,
With Rules of Husbandry the rankness cur'd:
Tam'd us to manners, when the Stage was rude;
And boistrous *English* Wit, with Art indu'd.
Our Age was cultivated thus at length;
But what we gain'd in skill we lost in strength.
Our Builders were, with want of Genius, curst;
The second Temple was not like the first:
Till You, the best *Vitruvius*, come at length;
Our Beauties equal; but excel our strength.
Firm *Dorique* Pillars found Your solid Base: ⎫
The Fair *Corinthian* Crowns the higher Space; ⎬
Thus all below is Strength, and all above is Grace. ⎭
In easie Dialogue is *Fletcher*'s Praise:
He mov'd the mind, but had not power to raise.
Great *Johnson* did by strength of Judgment please:
Yet doubling *Fletcher*'s Force, he wants his Ease.
In differing Tallents both adorn'd their Age;
One for the Study, t'other for the Stage.
But both to *Congreve* justly shall submit,

One match'd in Judgment, both o'er-match'd in Wit.
In Him all Beauties of this Age we see; }
Etherege his Courtship, *Southern*'s Purity; }
The Satire, Wit, and Strength of Manly *Witcherly*. }
All this in blooming Youth you have Atchiev'd;
Now are your foil'd Contemporaries griev'd;
So much the sweetness of your manners move,
We cannot envy you because we Love.
Fabius might joy in *Scipio*, when he saw
A Beardless Consul made against the Law,
And joyn his Suffrage to the Votes of *Rome*;
Though He with *Hannibal* was overcome.
Thus old *Romano* bow'd to *Raphel*'s Fame;
And Scholar to the Youth he taught, became.

   Oh that your Brows my Lawrel had sustain'd,
Well had I been Depos'd, if You had reign'd!
The Father had descended for the Son;
For only You are lineal to the Throne.
Thus when the State one *Edward* did depose;
A Greater *Edward* in his room arose.
But now, not I, but Poetry is curs'd;
For *Tom* the Second reigns like *Tom* the first.
But let 'em not mistake my Patron's part;
Nor call his Charity their own desert.
Yet this I Prophecy; Thou shalt be seen,
(Tho' with some short Parenthesis between:)
High on the Throne of Wit; and seated there,
Not mine (that's little) but thy Lawrel wear.
Thy first attempt an early promise made;
That early promise this has more than paid.
So bold, yet so judiciously you dare,
That Your least Praise, is to be Regular.
Time, Place, and Action, may with pains be wrought,
But Genius must be born; and never can be taught.
This is Your Portion; this Your Native Store; }
Heav'n that but once was Prodigal before, }
To *Shakespeare* gave as much; she cou'd not give him more. }

   Maintain Your Post: That's all the Fame You need;
For 'tis impossible you shou'd proceed.
Already I am worn with Cares and Age;
And just abandoning th' Ungrateful Stage:
Unprofitably kept at Heav'ns expence,

I live a Rent-charge on his Providence:
But You, whom ev'ry Muse and Grace adorn,
Whom I foresee to better Fortune born,
Be kind to my Remains; and oh defend,
Against Your Judgment Your departed Friend!
Let not the Insulting Foe my Fame pursue;
But shade those Lawrels which descend to You:
And take for Tribute what these Lines express:
You merit more; nor cou'd my Love do less.

John Dryden.

(b)

I have rememberd you to all your friends; and in particular to
Congreve; who sends you his play, as a present from him selfe, by
this conveyance; & much desires the honour of being better known
to you. His Double Dealer is much censurd by the greater part of
the Town: and is defended onely by the best Judges, who, you
know, are commonly the fewest. Yet it gets ground daily, and has
already been acted Eight times. The women thinke he has exposd
their Bitchery too much; & the Gentlemen, are offended with him;
for the discovery of their follyes: & the way of their Intrigues,
under the notion of Friendship to their Ladyes Husbands. My
verses, which you will find before it, were written before the play
was acted. But I neither alterd them nor do I alter my opinion of the
play.

11. William Dove, 'To Mr. Congreve'

1693

From *The Gentleman's Journal: or the Monthly Miscellany*
(November 1693), 2: 374.

I need not say any thing of Mr. *Congreve*'s *Double-Dealer*, (the only
new Play since my last) after the Character which Mr. *Dryden* has
given of it: Yet my Respect for its Author will not suffer me to
omit the following Lines.

TO MR. *CONGREVE*: BY MR. *WILLIAM DOVE*.

Since Inspiration's ceas'd, I fain would know
To whom thy wond'rous store of Wit we owe?
'Tis more than e're Philosophy could teach,
How Imperfection should Perfection reach;
Yet while thy Works with native Glory shine,
And sprightly Phrazes render them divine,
We think thou'rt sprung from the Prophetic Line.
How smooth the Current of thy Fancy glides!
It never ebbs, and knows no boist'rous Tides;
No lofty nonsence in thy Play appears,
With shew of Wit to please unskilfull Ears.
Thus we with pleasure, and with wonder view,
That charming Landskip which thy Fancy drew.
There, there, thy Genius revels in each Part,
And lavish Nature is improv'd by Art.
There's in thy Satire, as in Music, found
Something that's pleasing in the sharpest Sound.
Sure thy Soul acts in a divided State,
Free from the Body, and exempt from Fate!
Go on, great Youth, but as thou hast begun,
The Prize thou'lt merit e're the Race is run.
Thus fledg'd with honour, let thy Muse expand
Her infant Wings, and her swift Flight extend,
So far, till at the Last she may come nigh
Wycherly's Fame, and with his Glory vye.

12. Joseph Addison in 'An Account of the Greatest English Poets'

1694

From *The Annual Miscellany: for the year 1694, being the fourth part of Miscellany Poems* (London: 1694), pp. 325–6.

Addison's poem is dated 3 April 1694, and addressed 'To Mr.

H.S.'. The latter is usually identified with Henry Sacheverell, the controversial high-church preacher of Queen Anne's reign, who was Addison's contemporary at Magdalen College, Oxford.

But see where artful *Dryden* next appears,
Grown old in Rhime, but Charming ev'n in Years.
Great Dryden next! who's Tuneful Muse affords
The sweetest Numbers, and the fittest words.
Whether in *Comick* sounds or *Tragick* Airs
She form's her voice, she moves our Smiles or Tears.
If *Satire* or *Heroick Strains* she writes,
Her *Heroe* pleases, and her *Satire* Bites.
From her no harsh, unartful Numbers fall,
She wears all Dresses, and she Charms in all:
How might we fear our *English* Poetry,
That long has flourish'd, shou'd decay with Thee;
Did not the Muses other Hope appear,
Harmonious Congreve, and forbid our Fear.
Congreve! who's Fancies unexhausted Store
Has given already much, and promis'd more.
Congreve shall still preserve thy Fame alive,
And *Dryden's* Muse shall in his Friend survive.

13. Charles Hopkins in 'To Walter Moyle, Esq.'

1694

From *Epistolary Poems; on Several Occasions* (London: 1694), p. 7.

Charles Hopkins, son of Ezekiel Hopkins, Bishop of Derry, was born in Dublin and educated at Trinity College before transferring to Queens' College, Cambridge. See Alice E. Jones, 'A note on Charles Hopkins (*c.* 1671–1700)', *MLN*

(1940), vol. 55, pp. 191–4, which corrects the *DNB* entry. Hopkins's addressee, Walter Moyle (1672–1721), was like Congreve a Templar and a member of the literary circle of Dryden and John Dennis. Between 1695 and 1698 he enjoyed a short career as an MP and Whig pamphleteer before retiring to his native Cornwall to lead the life of a private scholar.

> In full delights, let sprightly *Southern* live,
> With all that Women, and that Wine, can give.
> May generous *Wicherly*, all Sufferings past,
> Enjoy a well-deserv'd Estate, at last.
> Fortune, with Merit, and with Wit, be Friends,
> And sure, tho' slowly, make a large amends.
> Late, very late, may the Great *Dryden* dye,
> But when deceas'd, may *Congreve* rise as high.
> To him, my Service, and my Love commend,
> The greatest Wit, and yet the truest Friend.

14. Anon. in *The Mourning Poets*

1695

From *The Mourning Poets: or, an Account of the Poems on the Death of the Queen* (London: 1695), sig. Aiiv – Br.

This poem is a composite review of the funeral elegies for Queen Mary II, who died on 28 December 1694. Congreve had written what was to become one of his most admired poems, 'The Mourning Muse of *Alexis*. A Pastoral. Lamenting the death of our late gracious Queen Mary'. In the latter the queen is commemorated under the name of 'Pastora'.

> In *Congreve Dryden*'s ours, to Him we owe
> The tuneful Notes which from *Alexis* flow:
> He chose out *Congreve*, and inspir'd his Flame;
> *Congreve*, his best belov'd, and next in Fame:

Whose Beams the unexpecting World surprise,
As when unseen the Sun in Clouds does rise,
Then breaking through, at once attracts our Eyes.
Unlike in this, no Night succeeds his Day,
But still he shines with one continued Ray.
When in full Glory *Congreve* first appear'd,
We saw, we wonder'd, and confest the Bard:
Dryden by Thee All own these Wonders done,
Thou taught'st this Eagle to approach the Sun.

He to the Swains *Pastora*'s Fate bemoans,
Sighs to the Winds, and fills the Vales with Groans.
The Vales return his Groans, the Winds his Sighs;
And ev'ry Swain repeats the tuneful Crys.
Not so lamented *Græcian Bion* fell,
Nor *Venus* mourn'd the lovely Boy so well;
Poets unborn shall make his Lays their Theme,
And future *Rapins* take their Rules from him.

15. Edward Howard in the Proem to *An Essay upon Pastoral*

1695

From *An Essay upon Pastoral* (London: 1695), sig. Br – Bv.

The Hon. Edward Howard (1624–1712) was the younger brother of Sir Robert Howard and Dryden's brother-in-law. 'Ned' Howard's persistent attempts to establish himself as a poet and dramatist failed repeatedly, with the exception of *The Change of Crownes*, acted in April 1667. He was caricatured as the poet Ninny in Shadwell's *The Sullen Lovers* (1668), and his heroic poem *The British Princes* (1669) only made him the butt of the wits.

Virgil, in the Ninth Eclogue of his *Bucolicks*, makes a heavy Complaint, that his Muse cou'd not please two great Wits of *Rome*, namely, *Varus* and *Cinna*, saying in this sad Ditty,

Nam neque adhuc Varo *videor nec dicere* Cinna
Digna, sed argutos inter strepere anser olores.[1]

Where *Virgil* jests pretty freely with himself: and in good truth, how well soever he might think of the Issues of his Brain, yet that *Virgil* was a Poet altogether unblameable, and without fault, is what no Man can believe that shall read *Monsieur Rapin's* Comparison between *Him* and *Homer*. What are all the *Georgicks* of *Virgil* but a meer heap of Earth and Dung, fit only to be read by *Drovers* and *Ploughmen*? It is true indeed, here and there one may meet with a curious Thought, or fine Saying; but I should be glad to know what Relation those things he there makes such a puther and stir about, have to the *Muses*, or to *Poetry*. I speak not this to lessen the Reputation of *Virgil* in the least, for there is no one more ready to render Tribute where it is due, than my self; and I often make mention of *Virgil* in this following *Essay*, as an Ornament to my Discourse. I say, it is not with any Design to detract from his just Worth, that makes me here thus to speak of him, (for undoubtedly he was a Celebrated Wit amongst the *Romans*, and may pass for a considerable Poet now-a-days) but only with an intention that Men should not talk so unbecomingly fond of the Shadow and Image of a dead Poet, and to make *Virgil* the Standard of Wit, when we have two such Favourites of the *Muses* continually before our eyes; I mean, a *Dryden* and a *Congreve*: And how much soever some People may be enamour'd with this *Mantuan* Poet, I will here be bold to affirm, that that Great Youngman (*Mr. Congreve*) has in his Pastoral *Alexis* upon the Death of the Late *Queen*, evidenced himself to the World, to have a sufficient degree and quantity of unmingled Fire and pure Rapture of the Poet (as well as a Correctness of Thought and Felicity of Expression) to constitute Ten *Virgils*, nay, and enough to spare to furnish out a *Theocritus*.

NOTE

1 *Eclogues*, ix. 35–6: 'For still I seem to recite things worthy neither of Varius nor of Cinna, but make a noise like a goose among tuneful swans.'

16. William Congreve, 'Concerning Humour in Comedy'

1695

From *Letters upon several Occasions*, Published by Mr. Dennis (London: 1696), pp. 80–96.

Congreve's discussion of humour, in the Jonsonian sense, was written at the invitation of the critic John Dennis (1657–1734), who published it in a collection of his correspondence with Dryden, Congreve, Wycherley, and others. The volume was dedicated to Charles Montagu. A staunch defender of Restoration comedy, Dennis contributed to the Collier controversy with *The Usefulness of the Stage, to the Happiness of Mankind. To Government, and to Religion* (1698) and *The Person of Quality's Answer to Mr. Collier's Letter, Being a Disswasive from the Play-House* (1704).

MR. CONGREVE, *TO MR*. DENNIS.
CONCERNING HUMOUR IN COMEDY.

Dear Sir,

You write to me, that you have Entertained your self two or three days, with reading several Comedies, of several Authors; and your Observation is, that there is more of *Humour* in our English Writers, than in any of the other Comick Poets, Ancient or Modern. You desire to know my Opinion, and at the same time my Thought, of that which is generally call'd *Humour* in Comedy.

I agree with you, in an Impartial Preference of our English Writers, in that Particular. But if I tell you my Thoughts of *Humour*, I must at the same time confess, that what I take for true *Humour*, has not been so often written even by them, as is generally believed: And some who have valued themselves, and have been esteem'd by others, for that kind of Writing, have seldom touch'd upon it. To make this appear to the World, would require a long and labour'd Discourse, and such as I neither am able nor willing to undertake. But such little Remarks, as may be continued within the Compass of a Letter, and such unpremediated Thoughts, as may be Communicated between Friend and Friend, without incurring the Censure of the World, or setting up for a *Dictator*, you shall have from me, since you have enjoyn'd it.

To Define *Humour*, perhaps, were as difficult, as to Define *Wit*; for like that, it is of infinite variety. To Enumerate the several *Humours* of Men, were a Work as endless, as to sum up their several Opinions. And in my mind the *Quot homines tot Sententiae*, might have been more properly interpreted of *Humour*; since there are many Men, of the same Opinion in many things, who are yet quite different in Humours. But thô we cannot certainly tell what *Wit* is, or, what *Humour* is, yet we may go near to shew something, which is not *Wit* or not *Humour*; and yet often mistaken for both. And since I have mentioned *Wit* and *Humour* together, let me make the first Distinction between them, and observe to you that *Wit is often mistaken for Humour.*

I have observed, that when a few things have been Wittily and Pleasantly spoken by any Character in a Comedy; it has been very usual for those, who make their Remarks on a Play, while it is acting, to say, *Such a thing is very Humorously spoken: There is a great Deal of Humour in that Part.* Thus the Character of the Person speaking, may be, Surprizingly and Pleasantly, is mistaken for a Character of *Humour*; which indeed is a Character of *Wit*. But there is a great Difference between a Comedy, wherein there are many things *Humorously*, as they call it, which is *Pleasantly* spoken; and one, where there are several Characters of *Humour*, distinguish'd by the Particular and Different Humours, appropriated to the several Persons represented, and which naturally arise, from the different Constitutions, Complexions, and Dispositions of Men. The saying of Humorous Things, does not distinguish Characters; For every Person in a Comedy may be allow'd to speak them. From a Witty Man they are expected; and even a *Fool* may be permitted to stumble on 'em by chance. Thô I make a Difference betwixt *Wit* and *Humour*; yet I do not think that Humorous Characters exclude Wit: No, but the Manner of *Wit* should be adapted to the *Humour*. As for Instance, a Character of a Splenetick and Peevish *Humour*, should have a Satyrical Wit. A Jolly and Sanguine *Humour*, should have a Facetious Wit. The Former should speak Positively; the Latter, Carelesly: For the former Observes, and shews things as they are; the latter, rather overlooks Nature, and speaks things as he would have them; and his *Wit* and *Humour* have both of them a less Alloy of Judgment than the others.

As *Wit*, so, its opposite, *Folly, is sometimes mistaken for Humour.*

When a Poet brings a *Character* on the Stage, committing a thousand Absurdities, and talking Impertinencies, roaring Aloud, and Laughing immoderately, on every, or rather upon no occasion; this is Character of Humour.

Is any thing more common, than to have a pretended Comedy, stuff d with such Grotesques, Figures, and Farce Fools? Things, that either are not in Nature, or if they are, are Monsters, and Births of Mischance; and consequently as such, should be stifled, and huddled out of the way, like *Sooterkins*; that Mankind may not be shock'd with an appearing Possibility of the Degeneration of a God-like *Species*. For my part, I am as willing to Laugh, as any body, and as easily diverted with an Object truly ridiculous: but at the same time, I can never care for seeing things, that force me to entertain low thoughts of my Nature. I dont know how it is with others, but I confess freely to you, I could never look long upon a Monkey, without very Mortifying Reflections; thô I never heard any thing to the Contrary, why that Creature is not Originally of a Distinct *Species*. As I dont think *Humour* exclusive of *Wit*, neither do I think it inconsistent with *Folly*; but I think the Follies should be only such, as Mens Humours may incline 'em to; and not Follies intirely abstracted from both Humour and Nature.

Sometimes, *Personal Defects are misrepresented for Humours.*

I mean, sometimes Characters are barbarously exposed on the Stage, ridiculing Natural Deformities, Casual Defects in the Senses, and Infirmities of Age. Sure the Poet must both be very Ill-natur'd himself, and think his Audience so, when he proposes by shewing a Man Deform'd, or Deaf, or Blind, to give them an agreeable Entertainment; and hopes to raise their Mirth, by what is truly an object of Compassion. But much need not be said upon this Head to any body, especially to you, who in one of your Letters to me concerning Mr. *Johnson*'s *Fox*, have justly excepted against this Immoral part of *Ridicule* in *Corbaccio*'s Character; and there I must agree with you to blame him, whom otherwise I cannot enough admire, for his great Mastery of true Humour in Comedy.

External Habit of Body is often mistaken for Humour.

By *External Habit*, I do not mean the Ridiculous Dress or

Cloathing of a Character, thô that goes a good way in some received Characters. (But undoubtedly a Man's Humour may incline him to dress differently from other People) But I mean a Singularity of Manners, Speech, and Behaviour, peculiar to all, or most of the same Country, Trade, Profession, or Education. I cannot think, that a *Humour*, which is only a Habit, or Disposition contracted by Use or Custom; for by a Disuse, or Complyance with other Customs, it may be worn off, or diversify'd.

Affectation is generally mistaken for Humour.

These are indeed so much alike, that at a Distance, they may be mistaken one for the other. For what is *Humour* in one, may be *Affectation* in another; and nothing is more common, than for some to affect particular ways of saying, and doing things, peculiar to others, whom they admire and would imitate. *Humour* is the Life, *Affectation* the Picture. He that draws a Character of *Affectation*, shews *Humour* at the Second Hand; he at best but publishes a Translation, and his Pictures are but Copies.

But as these two last distinctions are the Nicest, so it may be most proper to Explain them, by Particular Instances from some Author of Reputation. *Humour* I take, either to be born with us, and so of a Natural Growth; or else to be grafted into us, by some accidental change in the Constitution, or revolution of the Internal Habit of Body; by which it becomes, if I may so call it, Naturaliz'd.

Humour is from Nature, *Habit* from Custom; and *Affectation* from Industry.

Humour, shews us as we *are*.

Habit, shews us, as we appear, under a forcible Impression.

Affectation, shews what we would be, under a Voluntary Disguise.

Thô here I would observe by the way, that a continued Affectation, may in time become a Habit.

The Character of *Morose* in the *Silent Woman*, I take to be a Character of Humour. And I choose to Instance this Character to you, from many others of the same Author, because I know it has been Condemn'd by many as Unnatural and Farce: And you have your self hinted some dislike of it, for the same Reason, in a Letter to me, concerning some of *Johnson*'s Plays.

Let us suppose *Morose* to be a Man Naturally Splenetick and Melancholly; is there any thing more offensive to one of such a Disposition, than Noise and Clamour? Let any Man that has the

Spleen (and there are enough in *England*) be Judge. We see common Examples of this Humour in little every day. 'Tis ten to one, but three parts in four of the Company that you dine with, are Discompos'd and Startled at the Cutting of a Cork, or Scratching a Plate with a Knife: It is a Proportion of the same Humour, that makes such or any other Noise offensive to the Person that hears it; for there are others who will not be disturb'd at all by it. Well; But *Morose* you will say, is so Extravagant, he cannot bear any Discourse or Conversation, above a Whisper. Why, It is his excess of this Humour, that makes him become Ridiculous, and qualifies his Character for Comedy. If the Poet had given him, but a Moderate proportion of that Humour, 'tis odds but half the Audience, would have sided with the Character, and have Condemn'd the Author, for Exposing a Humour which was neither Remarkable nor Ridiculous. Besides, the distance of the Stage requires the Figure represented, to be something larger than the Life; and sure a Picture may have Features larger in Proportion, and yet be very like the Original. If this Exactness of Quantity, were to be observed in Wit, as some would have it in Humour; what would become of those Characters that are design'd for Men of Wit? I believe if a Poet should steal a Dialogue of any length, from the *Extempore* Discourse of the two Wittiest Men upon Earth, he would find the Scene but coldly receiv'd by the Town. But to the purpose.

The Character of Sir *John Daw* in the same Play, is a Character of Affectation. He every where discovers an Affectation of Learning; when he is not only Conscious to himself, but the Audience also plainly perceives that he is Ignorant. Of this kind are the Characters of *Thraso* in the Eunuch of *Terence*, ad *Pyrgopolinices* in the *Miles Gloriosus* of *Plautus*. They affect to be thought Valiant, when both themselves and the Audience know they are not. Now such a boasting of Valour in Men who were really Valiant, would undoubtedly be a *Humour*; for a Fiery Disposition might naturally throw a Man into the same Extravagance, which is only affected in the Characters I have mentioned.

The Character of *Cob* in *Every Man in his Humour*, and most of the under Characters in *Bartholomew-Fair*, discover only a Singularity of Manners, appropriated to the several Educations and Professions of the Persons represented. They are not Humours but Habits contracted by Custom. Under this Head may be ranged all

Country-Clowns, Sailers, Tradesmen, Jockeys, Gamesters and such like, who make use of *Cants* or peculiar *Dialects* in their several Arts and Vocations. One may almost give a Receipt for the Composition of such a Character: For the Poet has nothing to do, but to collect a few proper Phrases and terms of Art, and to make the Person apply them by ridiculous Metaphors in his Conversation, with Characters of different Natures. Some late Characters of this kind have been very successful; but in my mind they may be Painted without much Art or Labour; since they require little more, than a good Memory and Superficial Observation. But true *Humour* cannot be shewn, without a Dissection of Nature, and a Narrow Search, to discover the first Seeds, from whence it has its Root and growth.

If I were to write to the World, I should be obliged to dwell longer, upon each of these Distinctions and Examples, for I know that they would not be plain enough to all Readers. But a bare hint is sufficient to inform you of the Notions which I have on this Subject: And I hope by this time you are of my Opinion, that Humour is neither Wit, nor Folly, nor Personal defect; nor Affectation, nor Habit; and yet, that each, and all of these, have been both written and received for Humour.

I should be unwilling to venture even on a bare Description of Humour, much more, to make a Definition of it, but now my hand is in, Ile tell you what serves me instead of either. I take it to be, *A singular and unavoidable manner of doing, or saying any thing, Peculiar and Natural to one Man only; by which his Speech and Actions are distinguish'd from those of other Men.*

Our *Humour* has relation to us, and to what proceeds from us, as the Accidents have to a Substance; it is a Colour, Taste, and Smell, Diffused through all; thô our Actions are never so many, and different in Form, they are all Splinters of the same Wood, and have Naturally one Complexion; which thô it may be disguised by Art, yet cannot be wholly changed: We may Paint it with other Colours, but we cannot change the Grain. So the Natural sound of an Instrument will be distinguish'd, thô the Notes expressed by it, are never so various, and the Divisions never so many. Dissimulation, may by Degrees, become more easy to our practice; but it can never absolutely Transubstantiate us into what we would seem: It will always be in some proportion a Violence upon Nature.

A Man may change his Opinion, but I believe he will find it a

Difficulty, to part with his *Humour*, and there is nothing more provoking, than the being made sensible of that difficulty. Sometimes, one shall meet with those, who perhaps, Innocently enough, but at the same time impertinently, will ask the Question; *Why are you not Merry? Why are you not Gay, Pleasant, and Cheerful?* then instead of answering, could I ask such one; *Why are you not handsome? Why have you not Black Eyes, and a better Complexion?* Nature abhors to be forced.

The two Famous Philosophers of *Ephesus* and *Abdera*, have their different Sects at this day. Some Weep, and others Laugh at one and the same thing.

I dont doubt, but you have observed several Men Laugh when they are Angry; others who are Silent; some that are Loud: Yet I cannot suppose that it is the passion of *Anger* which is in it self different, or more or less in one than t'other; but that it is the *Humour* of the Man that is Predominant, and urges him to express it in that manner. Demonstrations of pleasure are as Various; one Man has a Humour of retiring from all Company, when any thing has happen'd to please him beyond expectation; he hugs himself alone, and thinks it an Addition to the pleasure to keep it Secret. Another is upon Thorns till he has made Proclamation of it; and must make other people sensible of his happiness, before he can be so himself. So it is in Grief, and other Passions. Demonstrations of Love and the Effects of that Passion upon several Humours, are infinitely different; but here the Ladies who abound in Servants are the best Judges. Talking of the Ladies, methinks something should be observed of the Humour of the Fair Sex; since they are sometimes so kind as to furnish out a Character for Comedy. But I must confess I have never made any observation of what I Apprehend to be true Humour in Women. Perhaps Passions are too powerful in that Sex, to let Humour have its Course; or may be by Reason of their Natural Coldness, Humour cannot Exert it self to that extravagant Degree, which it often does in the Male Sex. For if ever any thing does appear Comical or Ridiculous in a Woman, I think it is little more than an acquir'd Folly, or an Affectation. We may call them the weaker Sex, but I think the true Reason is, because our Follies are Stronger, and our Faults are more prevailing.

One might think that the Diversity of Humour, which must be allowed to be diffused throughout Mankind, might afford endless matter, for the support of Comedies. But when we come closely to consider that point, and nicely to distinguish the Difference of Humours, I believe we shall find the contrary. For thô we allow every Man something of his own, and a peculiar Humour; yet every Man has it not in quantity, to become Remarkable by it: Or, if many do become Remarkable by their Humours; yet all those Humours may not be Diverting. Nor is it only requisite to distinguish what Humour will be diverting, but also how much of it, what part of it to shew in Light, and what to cast in Shades; how to set it off by preparatory Scenes, and by opposing other humours to it in the same Scene. Thrô a wrong Judgment, sometimes, Mens Humours may be opposed when there is really no specific Difference between them; only a greater proportion of the same, in one than t'other; occasion'd by his having more Flegm, or Choller, or whatever the Constitution is, from whence their Humours derive their Source.

There is infinitely more to be said on this Subject; thô perhaps I have already said to much; but I have said it to a Friend, who I am sure will not expose it, if he does not approve of it. I believe the Subject is intirely new, and was never touch'd upon before; and if I would have any one to see this private Essay, it should be some one, who might be provoked by my Errors in it, to Publish a more Judicious Treatise on the Subject. Indeed I wish it were done, that the World being a little acquainted with the scarcity of true Humour, and the difficulty of finding and shewing it, might look a little more favourably on the Labours of them, who endeavour to search into Nature for it, and lay it open to the Publick View.

I dont say but that very entertaining and useful Characters, and proper for Comedy, may be drawn from Affectations, and those other Qualities, which I have endeavoured to distinguish from Humour: but I would not have such imposed on the World, for Humour, nor esteem'd of Equal value with it. It were perhaps, the Work of a long Life to make one Comedy true in all its Parts, and to give every Character in it a True and Distinct Humour. Therefore, every Poet must be beholding to other helps, to make out his Number of ridiculous Characters. But I think such a One deserves to be broke, who makes all false Musters; who does not shew one true Humour in a Comedy, but entertains his Audience to the end of the Play with every thing out of Nature.

I will make but one Observation to you more, and have done; and that is grounded upon an Observation of your own, and which

97

I mention'd at the beginning of my Letter, *viz*, That there is more of Humour in our English Comick Writers than in any others. I do not at all wonder at it, for I look upon Humour to be almost of English Growth; at least, it does not seem to have found such Encrease on any other Soil. And what appears to me to be the reason of it, is the great Freedom, Privilege, and Liberty which the Common People of *England* enjoy. Any Man that has a Humour, is under no restraint, or fear of giving it Vent; they have a Proverb among them, which, may be, will shew the Bent and Genius of the People, as well as a longer Discourse: *He that will have a May-pole, shall have a May-pole.* This is a Maxim with them, and their Practice is agreeable to it. I believe something Considerable too may be ascribed to their feeding so much on Flesh, and the Grossness of their Diet in general. But I have done, let the Physicians agree that. Thus you have my Thoughts of *Humour*, to my Power of Expressing them in so little Time and Compass. You will be kind to shew me wherein I have Err'd; and as you are very Capable of giving me Instruction, so, I think I have a very just title to demand it from you; being without Reserve,

July 10, 1695.

Your real Friend,
and humble Servant,
W. Congreve.

17. William Pittis in *An Epistolary Poem to N. Tate, Esquire*

1696

From *An Epistolary Poem to N. Tate, Esquire: and Poet Laureat to his Majesty: Occasioned by the taking of Namur* (London: 1696).

William Pittis (1674–1724) was a friend of Tom Brown and Peter Motteux, and an acquaintance of Dryden. He contri-

buted some poems to *The Gentleman's Journal* in 1692 while still
an undergraduate at New College, Oxford. Three years later
Pittis relinquished a Fellowship at his college and took up
residence in the Inner Temple with the aim of studying
medicine. Instead he became a pamphleteer and journalist.
The present poem invites the Whig laureate Nahum Tate to
surpass Congreve's 'A Pindarique Ode, Humbly Offer'd to
the King On His Taking *Namure*'; it refers closely to the
second and eighth strophes of Congreve's ode.

(i) From the Preface
As for my taking notice of Mr. *C[ongreve]*'s Ode, I have this to say
for my self, that as every Man is Master of his own Sentiments, so
he may vent 'em when they are agreeable to truth and good-
manners. And I can't see why Mr. *C[ongreve]* should take it amiss,
that he is not counted the best Pindarick Writer, when he has so
large a share of Reputation in Pastoral. A standerby often see's
things a Gamester himself does not perceive, and I may tell him his
faults, when perhaps I am so fond of my self as not to discern my
own. I am so far from using a Gentleman of his Character
ungenteely, that tho I can't say of his Ode, as Mr. *Norris*[1] said of
Mr. *Lock*'s *Humane Understanding*, (viz.) *that he would not after all its
faults part with it for a* Vatican; yet I can't but tell the World I have an
extraordinary value for it. I can't see why the same liberty may not
be taken with a Gentleman of *Will*'s, as those Gentlemen took with
Dr. *Blackmore*, and that they who would have Christened a certain
Poem *Arthur of Bradly*,[2] should have their own examin'd by the
Friends of *Prince Arthur*. If I have misinterpreted any of his
Beauties, I beg his pardon, but if I have found out his faults, I think
I may have the liberty to show them.

(sig. A2r)

(ii)

> Lo! *C[ongreve]*'s *Dairy-Muse* forgets her charge,
> Tricks up her self, and roams about at large,
> And thinks in Flights and Raptures to excell
> Because she tun'd the *lowly reed* so well!
> As at some Wake, where *Joan* or *Nell* appear,
> And represent the Queen in Sundays Gear,
> With hobbling steps the Rabble Rout advance,

And trample round, and form a kind of Dance:
Susan amidst the rest, with awkward Mien
Capers, and shows her feet, and will be seen,
Thinks what she does, deserves the most esteem,
Because she makes good Cheese, and skim's the better Cream.
On *Pindar*'s Wings she takes her aery Course,
But *Pindar*'s judgment's wanting to his Force.
Up to the head of Fame She boldly flies,
(And + Fames a mischief, or the Poet lies.)

Fama malum-Virg. Aen. appears to the left of the last three lines.

O Youth take heed, let *Virgill*'s hallow'd Page
Escape thy fury, and avoid thy rage,
With holy dread approach the Reverend Bard,
Nor play with Wit, when Sense should be prefer'd,
A fine digression, and with Judgment wrote,
Is more esteem'd a Beauty than a fau't,
But when a Muse impatient of delay,
Leaps o're the bounds, and frollicks all the way,
Forces through *oppositions self*, and climbs
With all the tinckling chime of Pack-horse Rhimes;
We damn the Muse, and justly blame her skill,
Who leaves good beaten ways, and chuses ill,
And sweats and drudges upward with her load,
When She might go beneath, and keep the Road.
But above all (for he that Verse endites
Shou'd know his Sense and meaning as he writes)
Thy Verse shou'd speak Thee Loyal, not compare
The Siege of *Namure* to the *Gyants War*:
Nor make *Mars tumble* from the *Empyreal-skie*.
Those whom their + Author never brought so high:
Thy *Pow'r unseen*, and boundless force restrain,
Nor make those *Rebells* who deserve to Reign.

Ovid. appears to the left near the line "Those whom their + Author never brought so high:".

(pp. 1–2)

NOTES

1 John Norris (1657–1711), rector of Bemerton, poet and philosopher. His reply to Locke was appended to his *Christian Blessedness*, published in 1690.
2 A doggerel ballad.

18. Catharine Trotter, 'To Mr. Congreve, on his Tragedy, the *Mourning Bride*'

1697

From *The Works of Mrs. Catharine Cockburn, Theological, Moral, Dramatic, and Poetical*, 2 vols (London: 1751), II, pp. 564–5.

Catharine Trotter's verse epistle to Congreve was published posthumously, but its date can be ascertained by his reply which was written *c.* 15 March, 1697. See John C. Hodges (ed.), *William Congreve: Letters and Documents* (London: Macmillan, 1964), pp. 198–200. Sir Edmund Gosse suggested that she met Congreve through Bevil Higgons; see his 'Catharine Trotter, the precursor of the bluestockings', *Transactions of the Royal Society of Literature* (1916), 34: 92. In 1703 Catharine Trotter submitted a draft of her final play, the tragedy *The Revolution in Sweden*, to Congreve; his reply contains concise but acute advice (*Letters and Documents*, pp. 212–13).

TO MR. CONGREVE, ON HIS TRAGEDY, THE MOURNING BRIDE.

> Had heav'n bestow'd on me half *Sappho's* flame,
> This noble theme had gain'd me larger fame;
> For none can think great *Congreve's* to extend,
> Or praising thee, ought but their own intend.
> Boundless thy fame does as thy genius flow,
> Which spread thus far, can now no limits know:
> This only part was wanting to thy name,
> That wit's whole empire thou mightst justly claim:
> On which so many vain attempts were made,
> Numbers pretending right their strength assay'd,
> But all alike unfit for the command,
> Only defac'd and spoil'd the sacred land;

Which thou, as its undoubted native lord,
Has to its ancient beauty thus restor'd;
Where with amazement we at once may see
Nature preserv'd pure, unconstrain'd, and free,
And yet throughout, each beauty, ev'ry part,
Drest to the strictest forms of gracing art:
Thus perfected, on such a finish'd piece,
Where can my praise begin, or admiration cease!
Sublime thy thoughts, easy thy numbers flow,
Yet to comport with them, majestic too!
But to express how thou our souls do'st move,
How at thy will, we rage, we grieve, we love,
Requires a lofty, almost equal flight,
Nor dare I aim at such a dang'rous height,
A task, which well might *Dryden's* muse engage,
Worthy the first, best poet of the age;
Whose long retreat that we might less bemoan, ⎫
He left us thee, his greatest darling son, ⎬
Possessor of the stage, once his alone. ⎭
Tho' even he gain'd not thy height so soon,
And but the young great *Macedonian*, none;
Alike in youth you both sought early fame,
Both sure to vanquish too where'er you came;
But he by others aid his conquests gain'd,
By others too the fame of them remain'd;
Thou sov'reign o'er the vast poetic land,
Unaided, as unrival'd, do'st command,
And not oblig'd for fame, which records give,
In thy own works thou shalt for ever live.

19. Sir Richard Blackmore in the Preface to *King Arthur*

1697

From *King Arthur: An Heroic Poem* (London: 1697), pp. vii – viii.

The second of Blackmore's Arthurian epics was entered in the Term Catalogues for June 1697. The preface renews the general attack on the stage begun in its predecessor of two years before, *Prince Arthur*, but singles out for praise *The Mourning Bride*, first acted in February.

Since the writing of this, I have seen a *Tragedy* call'd the *Mourning Bride*; which I think my self oblig'd to take notice of in this place. This *Poem* has receiv'd, and in my Opinion very justly, Universal Applause; being look'd on as the most perfect *Tragedy* that has been wrote in this Age. The *Fable*, as far as I can judge at first sight, is a very Artful and Masterly Contrivance. The *Characters* are well chosen, and well delineated. That of *Zara* is admirable. The *Passions* are well touch'd, and skillfully wrought up. The *Diction* is Proper, Clear, Beautiful, Noble, and diversify'd agreeably to the variety of the Subject. Vice, as it ought to be, is punish'd, and Opprest Innocence at last Rewarded. Nature appears very happily imitated, excepting one or two doubtful Instances, thro' the whole Piece, in all which there are no immodest Images or Expressions, no wild, unnatural Rants, but some few Exceptions being allow'd, all things are Chast, Just, and Decent. This *Tragedy*, as I said before, has mightily obtain'd; and that without the unnatural and foolish mixture of *Farce* and *Buffoonry*, without so much as a Song, or Dance to make it more agreeable. By this it appears, that as a sufficient *Genius* can recommend it self, and furnish out abundant matter of Pleasure and Admiration without the paultry helps above nam'd, so likewise that the Tast of the Nation is not so far deprav'd, but that a Regular and Chast Play will not only be forgiven, but highly Applauded. And now there is some reason to hope that our *Poets* will follow this excellent Example, and that hereafter no slovenly Writer will be so hardy as to offer to our Publick Audiences his obscene and prophane Pollutions, to the great Offence of all Persons of Vertue and good Sense. The common pretence that the Audience will not be otherwise pleas'd, is now wholly remov'd; for here is a notorious Instance to the contrary. And it must be look'd on hereafter as the *Poet*'s fault, and not the *People*'s, if we have not better Performances. All men must now conclude that 'tis for want of Wit and Judgment to support them, that our *Poets* for the Stage apply themselves to such low and unworthy ways to recommend their Writings; and therefore I cannot but conceive Great Hopes that every good *Genius* for the future will look on it self debas'd by condescending to Write in that leud Manner, that has been of late years introduc'd, and too long Encourag'd. And if this comes to pass the Writers in the late Reigns will be asham'd of their own Works, and wish they had their *Plays* in again, as well as their fulsome Dedications.

20. Charles Hopkins, dedication of *Boadicea, Queen of Britain*

1697

From *Boadicea, Queen of Britain. A Tragedy* (London: 1697), sig. A2r–A3r.

Boadicea was possibly given its first performance in November and published soon after. It was the second of Hopkins's three tragedies, which were all performed at Lincoln's Inn Fields by Betterton's company. Congreve had written a prologue for Hopkins's first play, *Pyrrhus, King of Epirus*, acted in 1695.

TO

MR. CONGREVE.

Let other Poets other Patrons Chuse,
Get their best Price, and prostitute their Muse.
With flattering hopes, and fruitless labour wait,
And Court the slippery Friendship of the Great:
Some trifling Present by my Lord is made,
And then the Patron thinks the Poet paid.
On you, my surer, nobler Hopes depend,
For you are all I wish; you are a Friend.
From you, my Muse her Inspiration drew,
All she performs, I Consecrate to you.
You taught me first my Genius and my Power,

Taught me to know my own, but gave me more,
Others may sparingly their Wealth impart,
But he gives Noblest, who bestows an Art.
Nature, and you alone, can that confer,
And I owe you, what you your self owe her.
O! *Congreve*, could I write in Verse like thine,
Then in each Page, in every Charming Line,
Should Gratitude, and Sacred Friendship shine.
Your Lines run all on easie, even Feet;
Clear is your Sense, and your Expression sweet.
Rich is your Fancy, and your Numbers go
Serene and smooth, as Crystal Waters flow.
Smooth as a peaceful Sea, which never rolls,
And soft, as kind, consenting Virgins Souls.
Nor does your Verse alone our Passions move,
Beyond the Poet, we the Person Love.
In you, and almost only you; we find
Sublimity of Wit, and Candour of the Mind.
Both have their Charms, and both give that delight,
'Tis pity that you should, or should not Write;
But your strong Genius Fortune's power defies,
And in despight of Poetry, you rise.
To you the Favour of the World is shown;
Enough for any Merit, but your own.
Your Fortune rises equal with your Fame,
The best of Poets, but above the Name.
O! may you never miss deserv'd success,
But raise your Fortunes 'till I wish them less.

   Here should I, not to tire your patience, end,
But who can part so soon, with such a Friend.
You know my Soul, like yours, without design,
You know me yours, and I too know you mine.
I owe you all I am, and needs must mourn,
My want of Power to make you some return.
Since you gave all, do not a part refuse,
But take this slender Offering of the Muse.
Friendship, from servile Interest free, secures
My Love, sincerely, and entirely, yours,

                    CHARLES HOPKINS

21. Anon. in *The Justice of Peace*
1697

From *The Justice of Peace: Or a Vindication of Peace from Several Late Pamphlets, Written by Mr. Congreve, Dennis, &c.* (London: 1697), pp. 1–4.

The following are the opening verse paragraphs of a poem on the Peace of Ryswick, which was concluded in September 1697. As its title page makes clear, it is a retort to poems by Congreve and John Dennis, 'The Birth of the Muse' and 'The Nuptials of Britain's Genius and Fame. A Pindaric Poem on the Peace' respectively.

A
POEM
ON THE PEACE.

Dedicated to a Young LADY.

Assist me Muse, who oft has been
Kind Midwife to my Teeming Brain;
Who to its Pangs no sooner didst
Apply thy gentle Artful Fist,
But out came Bantling, Scan'd by Finger,
And soon as Born turn'd Ballad-singer;
And as 'twould crack its tender Weazon,
In Rhyme 'gan Squawling without Reason.
Assist me Muse in this last Issue;
For which may ever Gown of Tissue
Grace thy fair Corps, and double *Nancy*
Fill *Helicon* to Inspire thy Fancy:
And *Thou*, First-Cousin to the *Nine*,
In whom both Wit and Beauty shine,
Bright Nymph, my kind Inspiring Guide,
Oh, sit down gently by my Side;

Make tuneful *Crambo* thy Pastime,
And help thy Slave to pump for Rhyme;
That in lewd Doggrel I may fall at
Making of Peace, so quaint a Ballad,
That may, as Simple as my Pen is,
Congreve out-Rhyme, and out Rage *Dennis*.
    Instead of saying what we want,   *Dennis.*
One Banters us with rumbling Cant;
Talks of deep *Pindar*'s sounding Lyre,
Of *Rapture, Fury, Flame* and *Fire*:
As if no Peace cou'd e'er be had,
But Hairbrain'd Poet must run Mad.
Another writes such soothing Number,   *Congreve.*
'Twoud almost lull one to a Slumber;
In Frontispiece stands *Birth of Muse*,
A *Porch* too big for such a *House*:
In gentle Strains he tells a Tale
Of *Heavenly Orb*, and *Earthly Ball*;
By dint of Rhyme he proves it clear,
That the *World hangs in Ambient Air*;[1]
Sings of *Creation*, and rehearses
Good Prose of *Moses* in bad Verses.
But sure Transported Bard forgot,
Peace was the thing he shou'd be at;
For what is *Genesis* pray to it,
More than Religion to a Poet?
But I shan't *Moses* filch, nor *Pindar*;
Since nought my honest Heart can hinder,
But in a plain unborrow'd Dress,
I'll treat of nothing but *meer Peace*.

NOTE

1 cf. 'The Birth of the Muse', l. 272: 'He launch'd the World to float in ambient Air.'

22. Jeremy Collier in *A Short View of the Immorality, and Profaneness of the English Stage*

1698

From *A Short View of the Immorality, and Profaneness of the English Stage* (London: 1698).

On Jeremy Collier, see the introduction, pp. 11–21. The preface to *A Short View* is dated 5 March, and it was advertised in *The Post Boy* for 16 to 18 April, and in *The Flying Post* for 19 to 21 April.

(i) From Chapter 1, 'The Immodesty of the Stage' (Collier has been discussing Euripides.)

Menelaus and *Helen* after a long Absence manage the surprize of their good Fortune handsomely. The Most tender Expression stands clear of ill Meaning. Had *Osmin* parted with *Almeria* as civilly as these Two met, it had been much better. That Rant of smut and profainness might have been spared. The *Reader* shall have some of it.

> *O my* Almeria;
> *What do the Damn'd endure but to despair,*
> *But knowing Heaven, to know it lost for ever.*
> [III, i, 364–6]

Were it not for the *Creed*, these *Poets* would be crampt in their Courtship, and Mightily at a loss for a Simile! But *Osmin* is in a wonderful Passion. And truly I think his Wits, are in some danger, as well as his Patience. You shall hear.

> *What are all Wracks, and Whips, and Wheels to this;*
> *Are they not soothing softness, sinking Ease,*
> *And wasting Air to this?*
> [ibid., ll. 362–4]

Sinking Ease, and Wasting Air, I confess are strange comforts; This Comparison is somewhat oddly equip'd, but Lovers like sick People may say what they please! *Almeria* takes this Speech for a Pattern, and suits it exactly in her return.

> *O I am struck, thy words are Bolts of Ice?*
> *Which shot into my Breast now melt and chill me.*
> [ibid., ll. 367–8]

Bolts of Ice? Yes most certainly! For the Cold is struck up into her Head, as you may perceive by what follows.

> *I chatter, shake, and faint with thrilling Fears.*
> [ibid., l. 369]

By the way 'tis a mighty wonder to hear a Woman Chatter! But there is no jesting, for the Lady is very bad. She won't be held up by any Means, but Crys out.

> ——*lower yet, down down;*

One would think she was learning a Spanel to *Sett*. But there's something behind.

> ——*no more we'll lift our Eyes,*
> *But prone and dumb, Rot the firm Face of Earth,*
> *With Rivers of incessant scalding Rain.*
> [ibid., ll. 372–4]

These Figures are some of them as stiff as Statues, and put me in mind of *Sylvesters Dubartas*.[1]

> *Now when the Winters keener breath began*
> *To Crystallize, the Baltick Ocean,*
> *To glaze the Lakes, to bridle up the Floods,*
> *And periwig with Snow the bald pate woods.*

I take it, the other Verses are somewhat of Kin to These, and shall leave them to Mr. *Dryden's* Reflection. But then as for *Soothing Softness, Sinking Ease, Wasting Air, thrilling Fears, and incessant scalding Rain*; It puts me to another stand. For to talk a little in the way of the *Stage*. This Litter of *Epithetes* makes the *Poem* look like a Bitch overstock'd with Puppies, and sucks the Sence almost to skin and Bone. But all this may pass in a *Play-house*: False Rhetorick and false Jewells, do well together.

(pp. 32–4)

(ii) From Chapter 2, 'The Profaness of the Stage'
In the *Old Batchelour*, *Vain-love* asks *Belmour, could you be content to go to Heaven?*

 Bell. Hum, not immediatly in my Conscence, not heartily—[III, i, 105–8]. This is playing I take it with Edge-Tools. To go to Heaven in jeast, is the way to go to Hell in earnest. In the Fourth *Act*, Lewdness is represented with that Gaity, as if the Crime was purely imaginary, and lay only in ignorance and preciseness. *Have you throughly consider'd (says Fondlewife) how detestable, how Heinous, and how crying a Sin the Sin of Adultery is? have you weighed I say? For it is a very weighty Sin: and altho' it may lie—yet thy Husband must also bear his part; For thy iniquity will fall on his Head* [IV, i, 67–72]. I suppose this fit of Buffoonry and profaness, was to settle the Conscience of young Beginners, and to make the Terrors of Religion insignificant. *Bellmour* desires *Lætitia to give him leave to swear by her Eyes and her Lips*: He kisses the Strumpet, and tells her, *Eternity was in that Moment* [IV, ii, 72 ff.]. *Lætitia* is horibly profane in her Apology to her Husband; but having the *Stage-Protection* of Smut for her Guard, we must let her alone. *Fondlewife* stalks under the same shelter, and abuses a plain Text of Scripture to an impudent Meaning. A little before, *Lætitia* when her Intrigue with *Bellmour* was almost discover'd, supports her self with this Consideration. *All my comfort lies in his impudence, and Heaven be prais'd, he has a Considerable Portion* [IV, iv, 202–4]. This is the *Play-house* Grace, and thus Lewdness is made a part of Devotion! Ther's another Instance still behind: 'Tis that of *Sharper* to *Vain-Love*, and lies thus.

 I have been a kind of God Father to you, yonder: I have promis'd and vow'd something in your Name, which I think you are bound to Perform [V, ii, 81–3]. For Christians to droll upon their Baptism is somewhat extraordinary. But since the *Bible* can't escape, 'tis the less wonder to make bold with the *Catechisme*.

 In the *Double Dealer*, Lady *Plyant* cries out *Jesu* and talks Smut in the same Sentence. Sr. *Paul Plyant* whom the Poet dub'd a Fool when he made him a Knight, talks very Piously! *Blessed be Providence, a Poor unworthy Sinner, I am mightily beholden to Providence* [III, i, 413–15]: And the same word is thrice repeated upon an odd occasion. The meaning must be that *Providence* is a ridiculous supposition, and that none but Blockheads pretend to Religion. But the Poet can discover himself farther if need be. Lady

Froth is pleas'd to call *Jehu a Hackney Coachman*. Upon this, *Brisk* replies, *If Jehu was a Hackney Coachman, I am answer'd—you may put that into the Marginal Notes tho', to prevent Criticisms—only mark it with a small Asterisme and say,—Jehu was formerly a Hackney Coachman* [III, i, 549–53]. This for a heavy Piece of Profaness, is no doubt thought a lucky one, because it burlesques the Text, and the Comment, all under one. I could go on with the *Double Dealer* but he'll come in my way afterwards, and so I shall part with him at present.

(pp. 62–4)

(iii) ibid.

Love for Love has a Strain like this, and therefore I shall put them together: *Scandal* solicits Mrs. *Foresight*; She threatens to tell her Husband. He replys, *He will die a Martyr rather then disclaim his Passion* [III, i, 595–6]. Here we have Adultery dignified with the stile of Martyrdom: As if 'twas as Honourable to perish in Defence of Whoring, as to dye for the Faith of Christianity. But these *Martyrs* will be a great while in burning, And therefore let no body strive to grace the Adventure, or encrease the Number. And now I am in this *Play* the Reader shall have more. *Jeremy* who was bred at the University, calls the Natural Inclinations to Eating and Drinking, *Whoreson Appetites*. This is strange Language! The *Manicheans* who made Creation the work of the Devil, could scarcely have been thus Coarse. But the *Poet* was *Jeremy's* Tutor, and so that Mystery is at an end. Sr. *Samson* carries on the Expostulation, rails at the Structure of Human Bodies, and says, *Nature has been Provident only to Bears, and Spiders* [II, i, 391–2]; This is the Authors Paraphrase on the 139 *Psalm*; And thus he gives God thanks for the Advantage of his Being! The *Play* advances from one wickedness to another, from the *Works* of God, to the Abuse of his Word. Foresight *confesses 'tis Natural for Men to mistake*. Scandal replies, *You say true, Man will err, meer Man will err—but you are something more——There have been wise Men; but they were such as you—Men who consulted the Stars, and were observers of Omens—* Solomon *was wise but how?—by his Judgment in Astrology* [III, i, 524–31]. 'Tis very well! *Solomon* and *Foresight* had their Understandings qualified alike. And pray what was *Foresight*? Why an *Illiterate Fellow. A pretender to Dreams, Astrology, Palmistry* &c. This is the *Poets* account of *Solomon's* Supernatural Knowledge! Thus the wisest Prince is dwindled into a Gypsie! And the Glorious Miracle resolved into Dotage, and Figure-flinging! *Scandal* continues his Banter, and says, the *wise Men of the East owed their Instruction to a Star; which is rightly observ'd by* Gregory *the Great in favour of Astrology* [ibid., ll. 535–7]. This was the Star which shone at our Saviour's Birth. Now who could imagine by the Levity of the occasion, that the Author thought it any better than an *Ignis Fatuus*, or *Sydrophel*'s Kite in *Hudibras*? Sr. *Sampson* and the fine *Angelica*, after some lewd raillery continue the Allegory, and drive it up into Profaness. For this reason the Citation must be imperfect.

Sr. Samps. Sampson's *a very good Name for—your* Sampsons *were strong Dogs from the Beginning.*

Angel. *Have a care——If you remember the strongest* Sampson *of your Name, pull'd an old House over his Head at last* [V, i, 155–9]. Here you have the Sacred History burlesqu'd, and *Sampson* once more brought into the House of *Dagon*, to make sport for the *Philistines!* To draw towards an end of this *Play*. *Tattle* would have carried off *Valentine*'s Mistress. This later, expresses his Resentment in a most Divine manner! Tattle *I thank you, you would have interposed between me and Heaven, but Providence has laid Purgatory in your way* [V, i, 595–7]. Thus Heaven is debas'd into an Amour, and Providence brought in to direct the Paultry concerns of the *Stage!* *Angelica* concludes much in the same strain. *Men are generally Hypocrites and Infidels, they pretend to Worship, but have neither Zeal, nor Faith; How few like* Valentine *would persevere unto Martyrdom? &c.* [ibid., l. 634ff.]. Here you have the Language of the *Scriptures*, and the most solemn Instances of Religion, prostituted to Courtship and Romance! Here you have a Mistress made God Almighty, Ador'd with Zeal and Faith, and Worship'd up to Martyrdom! This if 'twere only for the Modesty, is strange stuff for a Lady to say of her self. And had it not been for the profane Allusion, would have been cold enough in all Conscience.

(pp. 74–7)

(iv) ibid.

The *Double Dealer* to say the least of him, follows his Master in this Road, *Passibus æquis*. Sr. *Paul Plyant* one would think had done his part: But the ridiculing *Providence* won't satisfie all People: And therefore the next attempt is somewhat bolder.

Sr. Paul. *Hold your self contented my Lady* Plyant,—*I find Passion coming upon me by Inspiration* [II, i, 206–7]. In *Love Triumphant*,

Carlos is by the Constitution of the *Play* a Christian; and therefore must be construed in the sense of his Religion. This Man blunders out this horrible expression. *Nature has given me my Portion in Sense with a P——to her. &c.* The *Reader* may see the Hellish Syllable at Length if he pleases. This Curse is borrow'd for *Young Fashion* in the *Relapse*. The *Double Dealer* is not yet exhausted. *Cynthia the Top Lady grows Thoughtful.* Upon the question she relates her Contemplation. *Cynth. I am thinking (says she) that tho' Marriage makes Man and Wife one Flesh, it leaves them two Fools* [ibid., ll. 155–6]. This Jest is made upon a Text in *Genesis*, and afterwards applyed by our Saviour to the case of Divorse (Gen. 2. St Math. 19.). *Love for Love* will give us a farther account of this Authors Proficiency in the *Scriptures*. Our Blessed Saviour affirms himself *to be the Way, the Truth, and the Light, that he came to bear witness to the Truth, and that his Word is Truth.* These expressions were remember'd to good purpose. For *Valentine* in his pretended Madness tells *Buckram* the Lawyer; *I am Truth,—I am Truth.—Who's that, that's out of his way, I am Truth, and can set him right* [IV, i, 251–2]. Now a *Poet* that had not been smitten with the pleasure of Blasphemy, would never have furnish'd Frensy with Inspiration; nor put our Saviours Words in the Mouth of a Madman.

(pp. 82–3)

(v) From Chapter 3, 'The Clergy Abused by the Stage'
The *Old Batchelour* has a Throw at the *Dissenting Ministers*. The *Pimp Setter* provides their Habit for *Bellmour* to Debauch *Lætitia*. The Dialogue runs thus.

Bell. *And hast thou Provided Necessaries?*

Setter. *All, all Sir, the large Sanctified Hat, and the little precise Band, with a Swingeing long Spiritual Cloak, to cover Carnal Knavery,—not forgetting the black Patch which Tribulation* Spintext *wears as I'm inform'd upon one Eye, as a penal Mourning for the—Offences of his Youth* &c. [III, i, 122–8].

Barnaby calls another of that Character Mr. *Prig*, and *Fondlewife* carrys on the Humour lewdly in *Play-house Cant*; And to hook the *Church* of *England* into the Abuse, he tacks a *Chaplain* to the End of the Description.

Lucy gives an other Proof of the *Poets* good Will, but all little Scurilities are not worth repeating.

In the *Double Dealer* the discourse between *Maskwell* and *Saygrace* is very notable. *Maskwell* had a design to cheat *Mellifont* of his Mistress, and engages the Chaplain in the Intrigue: There must be a *Levite* in the case; *For without one of them have a finger in't, no Plot publick, or private, can expect to prosper.*

To go on in the order of the *Play*.

Maskwell calls out at *Saygraces door*, Mr. *Saygrace* Mr. *Saygrace*.

The other answers, *Sweet sir I will but pen the last line of an Acrostick, and be with you in the twingling of an Ejaculation, in the pronouncing of an* Amen. *&c.*

Mask. *Nay good Mr.* Saygrace *do not prolong the time*, &c.

Saygrace. *You shall prevail, I would break off in the middle of a Sermon to do you Pleasure.*

Mask. *You could not do me a greater—except—the business in hand—have you provided a Habit for Mellifont?*

Saygr. *I have*, &c.

Mask. *have you stich'd the Gownsleeve, that he may be puzled and wast time in putting it on?*

Saygr. *I have; the Gown will not be indued without Perplexity* [V, i, 267ff.]. There is a little more profane, and abusive stuff behind, but let that pass.

(pp. 101–3)

NOTE

1 From *The Divine Weeks and Works of Guillaume de Saluste, sieur du Bartas,* translated by Joshua Sylvester, first printed 1605–6. This particular passage from the III Part of the I Day of the II Week, ll. 173–6, had been cited by Dryden in his dedication of *The Spanish Friar* (1681) as an example of 'abominable fustian' (see *Of Dramatic Poesy and other Critical Essays,* ed. George Watson, 2 vols (London: Dent, 1962), I, p. 277). The inaccuracy of the quotation shows that Collier has taken it from Dryden rather than the original.

23. Elkanah Settle in *A Defence of Dramatick Poetry*

1698

From *A Defence of Dramatick Poetry* (London: 1698), pp. 88–9.

For much of his life Elkanah Settle (1648-1724) was indeed, in Samuel Johnson's phrase, 'the Rival and Antagonist of Dryden'. In the years of the Popish Plot and the Exclusion Bill crisis Settle initially took the Whig side, answering Dryden's *Absalom and Achitophel* with *Absalom Senior, or Achitophel Transpros'd* (1682). But their rivalry went back nearly fifteen years, when Dryden was writing heroic plays for the King's Company, and Settle likewise for the Duke's Company. *A Defence of Dramatick Poetry* was one of the earliest replies to Collier, and Settle's authorship was established comparatively recently; its publication was announced for 31 May/2 June, and *A Farther Defence*... followed on 23 June.

Nay, I dare be so bold, as to tell this angry Gentleman, as highly as he Resents the Cuckolding of Aldermen and Quality in our Comedies, that I could find him Matter of very good Instruction, from a Character of this kind, in a very Ingenious Author, though not much in Mr. *Colliers* Favour. For Example, If the Reverend Gentlemen of the Fur would be but half as kind to a *Play-house* as a *Pin-makers-Hall*, and step for Edification, but so far towards *Westminster*, as to see the *Old Batchelor*; I doubt not but an *Isaac Fondlewife* would be a very seasonable Monitor to Reverend City Sixty, to warn against the Marrying to Sixteen. Nor can I think it such a scandalous part of the Dramatick Poet; but rather a true Poetick Justice, to expose the unreasonableness of such Superannuated Dotage, that can blindly think or hope, that a bare Chain of Gold has Magick enough in the Circle to bind the Fidelity of so unequal a Match, a Match so contrary to the Holy Ordinance of Matrimony; and an Itch at those Years that deserves the severest

Lash of the Stage. And if an Author would pick out such a Character for a little Stage Satyr, where can he meet with it but amongst the City or Court Quality? Such Inequality of Marriages are rarely to be found, but under the Roofs of Honour, for so Antiquated a Lover, (the least he can do) must bring a Coach and Six, to carry off such a Young Bride.

One thing mightily offends this Divine Author, *viz.* That our Modern Plays make our Libertines of both Sexes, Persons of Figure and Quality, Fine Gentlemen and Ladies of Fashion, a fault utterly unpractis'd by the Ancient Poets: *For* Terence *and* Plautus *his Strumpets are little People.*

Now this is so far from a fault in our Comedies, that there's a necessity of those Characters, and a Vertue in that Choice. For as the greatest and best part of our Audience are Quality, if we would make our Comedies Instructive in the exposing of Vice, we must not lash the Vices at *Wapping* to mend the Faults at *Westminster.*

24. William Congreve in *Amendments of Mr. Collier's False and Imperfect Citations*

1698

From *Amendments of Mr. Collier's False and Imperfect Citations* (London: 1698).

Congreve's reply to Collier was prompt, in spite of the show of reluctance and indifference in its opening pages. It was advertised in *The Post Man* for 9 to 12 July.

(i) Congreve's *Postulata*

Before I proceed, for methods sake, I must premise some few things to the Reader, which if he thinks in his Conscience are too much to be granted me, I desire he would proceed no further in his Perusal of these Animadversions, but return to Mr. *Collier's Short View,* &c.

First, I desire that I may lay down *Aristotle's* Definition of Comedy; which has been the Compass by which all the Comick Poets, since his time, have steer'd their Course. I mean them whom Mr. *Collier* so very frequently calls *Comedians;* for the Distinction between *Comicus* and *Comædus,* and *Tragicus* and *Tragædus* is what he has not met with in the long Progress of his Reading.

Comedy (says *Aristotle*) is an Imitation of the worst sort of People. Μίμησις φαυλοτέρων, *imitatio pejorum.* He does not mean the worse sort of People in respect to their Quality, but in respect to their Manners. This is plain, from his telling you immediately after, that he does not mean Κατὰ Πᾶσαν κακίαν, relating to all kinds of Vice: there are Crimes too daring and too horrid for Comedy. But the Vices most frequent, and which are the common Practice of the looser sort of Livers, are the subject Matter of Comedy. He tells us farther, that they must be exposed after a ridiculous manner: For Men are to be laugh'd out of their Vices in Comedy; the Business of Comedy is to delight, as well as to instruct: And as vicious People are made asham'd of their Follies or Faults, by seeing them expos'd in a ridiculous manner, so are good People at once both warn'd and diverted at their Expence.

Thus much I thought necessary to premise, that by shewing the Nature and End of Comedy, we may be prepared to expect Characters agreeable to it.

Secondly, Since Comick Poets are oblig'd by the Laws of Comedy, and to the intent that Comedy may answer its true end and purpose above-mentioned, to represent vicious and foolish Characters: In Consideration of this, I desire that it may not be imputed to the Perswasion or private Sentiments of the Author, if at any time one of these vicious Characters in any of his Plays shall behave himself foolishly, or immorally in Word or Deed. I hope I am not yet unreasonable; it were very hard that a Painter should be believ'd to resemble all the ugly Faces that he draws.

Thirdly, I must desire the impartial Reader, not to consider any Expression or Passage cited from any Play, as it appears in Mr. *Collier's* Book; nor to pass any Sentence or Censure upon it, out of its proper Scene, or alienated from the Character by which it is spoken; for in that place alone, and in his Mouth alone, can it have its proper and true Signification.

I cannot think it reasonable, because Mr. *Collier* is pleas'd to write one Chapter of *Immodesty,* and another of *Profaneness,* that therefore every Expression traduc'd by him under those Heads, shall be condemn'd as obscene and profane immediately, and without any further Enquiry. Perhaps Mr. *Collier* is acquainted with the *deceptio visus*, and presents Objects to the View through a stain'd Glass; things may appear seemingly profane, when in reality they are only seen through a profane *Medium,* and the true Colour is dissembled by the help of a Sophistical Varnish: Therefore, I demand the Privilege of the *habeas Corpus* Act, that the Prisoners may have Liberty to remove, and to appear before a just Judge in an open and an uncounterfeit light.

Fourthly, Because Mr. *Collier* in his Chapter of the Profaneness of the Stage, has founded great part of his Accusation upon the Liberty which Poets take of using some Words in their Plays, which have been sometimes employed by the Translators of the Holy Scriptures: I desire that the following Distinction may be admitted, *viz*. That when Words are apply'd to sacred things, and with a purpose to treat of sacred things; they ought to be understood accordingly: But when they are otherwise apply'd, the Diversity of the Subject gives a Diversity of Signification. And in truth, he might as well except against the common use of the Alphabet in Poetry, because the same Letters are necessary to the spelling of Words which are mention'd in sacred Writ.

(pp. 7–11)

(ii) The alleged immodesty of *The Double-Dealer and The Mourning Bride*

The *Double-dealer* (he says) *runs riot* upon some occasion or other, *and gives Lord* Touchwood *a Mixture of Smut and Pedantry to conclude with*: For Proof of this, he directs the Reader in his Margin to the 79*th* Page, which is the last of the Play. He has made no Quotation, therefore I will do it for him, and transcribe what Lord *Touchwood* says in that place, being the concluding Lines and Moral of the whole Comedy. *Mellefont* and *Cynthia* are to be married, the Villainies of *Maskwell* having been detected; Lord *Touchwood* gives 'em Joy, and then concludes the Play as follows.

Lord *Touch—be each others Comfort;—let me join your hands.— unwearied nights, and wishing Days attend you both; mutual Love, lasting Health, and circling Joys tread round each happy Year of your long lives.*

Let secret Villany from hence be warn'd;
Howe'er in private, mischiefs are conceiv'd,
Torture and Shame attend their open Birth:
Like Vipers in the Womb base treachery lies, ⎫
Still gnawing that whence first it did arise; ⎬
No sooner born but the vile parent dies. ⎭

[V, i, 586–96]

This in Mr. *Collier's* polite Phrase, *is running riot upon Smut and Pedantry.* I hope this is some reason for my having laid down my third Proposition; where the Reader is desired not to rely upon Mr. *Collier's* bare word, but to consult the Original, before he passes his Censure on the Author.

Before he finishes his Chapter of Immodesty, he taxes the *Mourning-Bride* with *Smut* and *Profaness*; if he can prove it, I must of necessity give up the Cause. If there be Immodesty in that Tragedy, I must confess my self incapable of ever writing any thing with Modesty or Decency.

Had Osmin (says he) *parted with* Almeria *civilly, it had been much better, that rant of* Smut *and* Profaness *might have been spared.* What he means by *civilly* I know not, unless he means *dully* and *insensibly*; neither Civility nor Incivility have any thing to do with Passion; where a Scene is wrought to an Excess of Tenderness and Grief, there is no room for either Rudeness or Complaisance. Mr. *Collier* is pleas'd to condemn the parting of *Osmin* and *Almeria*, by comparing it with the meeting of *Menelaus* and *Helen*; but I must take the Liberty to tell him, that meeting and parting are two things, and especially between two Lovers. Now for the rant of *Smut* and *Profaness.*

> *Osm. O my* Almeria.
> *What do the damn'd endure but to despair,*
> *But knowing Heav'n to know it lost for ever.*
> [III, i, 364–6]

I will not here so much as refer my self to my third Proposition, nor desire the Reader to trouble himself so far, as to look on these Lines in their proper Scene and Place, tho' most of the foregoing Incidents in the Poem were contrived so as to prepare the Violence of this Scene; and all the foregoing part of this Scene was laid as a Gradation of Passion, to prepare the violence of these Expressions,

119

the last and most extream of the whole, in *Osmin*'s Part.

For once I will let these Lines remain as they are set by Mr. *Collier*, with his own filthy Foil beneath, hem'd in and sullied over with his own *Smut*. And still what is there either of Profaness or Immodesty in the Expression? Is not the Reflection rather moral and religious than otherwise? Does not the Allusion set forth the terrors of Damnation? I dare affirm that Mr. *Collier* himself, cannot so transpose those words as to make 'em signifie any thing either *smutty* or *profane*: What he may be able to do with the Letters if they were disjointed, I know not; I will not dispute his Skill in *Anagram*; and if the truth were known, I believe there lies the Stress of his Proof. Well, Mr. *Saygrace*, in the *Double-dealer*, is beholding to him for his new Amusement, for the future he shall renounce Acrosticks and pursue *Anagrams*.

As to what he says after, that these Verses are a similitude drawn from the Creed; I no more understand it, than he himself would bclieve it, tho' he should affirm it.

In the rest of his Remarks upon this Scene, his *Zeal* gives way to his *Criticism*; he had but an ill hold of *Profaness*, and was reduc'd to catch at the *Poetry*. The corruption of a rotten Divine is the Generation of a sowr Critick.

He is very merry, and as he supposes with me; in laughing at *wasting Air*. *Wasting* he thinks is a senseless *Epithet* for *Air*, truly I think so too. I will not lose this occasion of consenting with him, because he will not afford me many more: But where does he meet with *wasting Air*? not in the *Mourning-bride*; for in that Play it is printed *wafting Air*, so that all his awkard Railery about this word, reflects alone upon himself: To say nothing of his Honesty in making a false Quotation, or of his becoming assurance in charging me with his own Nonsense.

He proceeds in his unlucky and satirical Strain, and ridicules half a dozen Epithets, and about as many Figures, which follow in the same Scene, with much Delicacy of fine Railery, Excellence of good Manners, and Elegancy of Expression.

Almeria, in the Play, oppress'd and sinking beneath her Grief, adapts her words to her Posture, and says to *Osmin*—

> —*O let us not support,*
> *But sink each other lower yet, down, down,*
> *Where levell'd low, &c.*
>   [ibid., ll. 370–2]

One would think (says Mr. *Collier) she was learning a Spaniel to set.*

Learning a Spaniel to set! *Delectus verborum est Origo eloquentiæ,* is an Aphorism of *Julius Cæsar,* and Mr. *Collier* makes it plain. This poor Man does not so much as understand even his own Dog-language, when he says *learning,* I suppose he means *teaching a Spaniel to set,* a dainty Critick, indeed!

A little before, *Almeria* is cold, faint and trembling in her Agony, and says,

—I chatter, shake and faint with thrilling fears.

[ibid., l. 369]

By the way (says Mr. *Collier,* for now he is Mr. *Collier* emphatically) *'tis a mighty wonder to hear a Woman chatter! but there is no Jesting,* &c.

Jesting quotha! What, does he take the letting a Pun to be the breaking of a Jest? a Whip and a Bell, and away with him to Kennel again immediately.

Ay, now he's in his Element, as you shall hear.

This litter of Epithets makes the Poem look like a Bitch over-stock'd with Puppies, and sucks the Sence almost to skin and bone. The Comparison is handsome, I must needs say; but I desire the Reader to consider that it is Mr. *Collier* the Critick, that talks at this odd rate; not Mr. *Collier* the Divine: I would not, by any means, that he should mistake one for the other.

If it is necessary for me to give any reason in this place, why I have used Epithets and Figures in this Scene, I will do it in few words. First I desire the Reader to remove my Verses from amongst Mr. *Collier*'s Interlineations of sad Drollery; and reinstate 'em in the Scene of the Play from whence they were torn. If there is found Passion in those parts of the Scene where those Epithets and Figures are used, they will stand in need of no Vindication; for every body knows that Discourses of men in Passion, naturally abound in Epithets and Figures, in Agravations and Hyperboles. To this I add, That the Diction of Poetry consists of Figures; by the frequent use of bold and daring Figures, it is distinguish'd from Prose and Oratory. Epithets are beautiful in Poetry, but make Prose languishing and cold; and the frequent use of them in Prose, makes it pretend too much and approach too near to Poetry (*Arist. Rhet.* L. 3. C. 3.). If Figures and Epithets are natural to Passion, and if they compose the Diction of Poetry, certainly Tragedy, which is of the sublime and first-rate Poetry, and which ought every where to abound in *Passion*, may very well be allow'd to use Epithets and Figures, more especially in a Scene consisting entirely of Passion, and still more particularly in the most violent part of that Scene. Thus much, to justifie the use and frequency of Epithets and Figures in the Scene abovemention'd. Ay, but Mr. *Collier* says some of the Figures there are *Stiff:* He says so, I confess; but what then? Why in answer, I say they are not, and so leave it to be determin'd by better Judges.

(pp. 21–31)

(iii) Alleged profanity and contempt for the clergy

Mr. *Collier* in his second Chapter, Charges the Stage with Profaness. Almost all the Quotations which he has made from my Plays in this Chapter are represented falsly, or by halves; so that I have very little to do in their Vindication, but to represent 'em as they are in the Original, fairly and at length; and to fill up the Blanks which this worthy honest Gentleman has left.

In the Old Batchelour (says he) *Vain-love asks* Bellmour, *Could you be content to go to Heav'n?*

Bell. *Hum, not immediately, in my Conscience not Heartily*—[III, i, 105–8].

Here Mr. *Collier* concludes this Quotation with a dash, as if both the Sense and the Words of the whole Sentence, were at an end. But the remainder of it in the Play *Act. 3. Scene 2.* is in these words—*I would do a little more good in my generation first, in order to deserve it.*

I think the meaning of the whole is very different from the meaning of the first half of this Expression. 'Tis one thing for a Man to say positively, he will not go to Heaven; and another to say, that he does not think himself worthy, till he is better prepared. But Mr. *Collier* undoubtedly was in the right, to take just as much as would serve his own turn. The Stile of this Expression is Light, and suitable to Comedy, and the Character of a wild Debauchee of the Town; but there is a Moral meaning contain'd in it, when it is not represented by halves.

From Scene 3. of the 4th Act of the same Comedy, he makes the following Quotation. *Fondlewife* a Jealous Puritan is obliged for some time to be absent from his Wife:

Fond. *Have you throughly consider'd how detestable, how heinous, and*

*how Crying a Sin the sin of Adultery is? Have you weigh'd it, I say? for it
is a very weighty sin: and although it may lie—yet thy Husband must also
bear his part; for thy Iniquity will fall upon his Head* [IV, i, 67–72].
Here is another Dash in this Quotation, I refer the Reader to the
Play to see what words Mr. *Collier* has Omitted; and from thence
he may guess at the Strength of his Imagination.

For this Quotation, the Reader sees it in the same Condition that
Mr. *Collier* thinks fit to shew it: His Notes upon it are as follow.
*This fit of Buffoonry and Profaneness, was to settle the Conscience of
Young Beginners, and to make the Terrors of Religion insignificant.*

Indeed I cannot hold Laughing, when I compare his dreadful
Comment with such poor silly words as are in the Text: especially
when I reflect how *young a beginner,* and how very much a Boy I
was when that Comedy was Written; which several know was
some years before it was Acted: When I wrote it I had little
thoughts of the Stage; but did it to amuse my self in a slow
Recovery from a Fit of Sickness. Afterwards through my Indiscretion it was seen; and in some little time more it was Acted: And I
through the remainder of my Indiscretion, suffer'd my self to be
drawn in, to the prosecution of a difficult and thankless Study; and
to be involved in a perpetual War with Knaves and Fools. Which
reflection makes me return to the Subject in hand.

Bellmour desires Lætitia *to give him leave to Swear by her Eyes and
her Lips.* Well, I am very glad Mr. *Collier* has so much Devotion for
the Lips and Eyes of a Pretty Woman, that he thinks it Profanation
to Swear by 'em. I'll give him up this, if he pleases. To the
next.

He kisses the Strumpet, and tells her—Eternity was in that Moment
[IV, ii, 77].

To say *Eternity is in a Moment,* is neither Profane nor Sacred, nor
good nor bad. With Reverence of my Friend the Author be it
spoken, I take it to be stark Nonsense; and I had not cared if Mr.
Collier had discover'd it.

Something or other he saw amiss in it, and Writing a Chapter of
Profaneness at that time, like little *Bays,* he popt it down for his
own.

Lætitia when her Intrigue was like to be discover'd, says of her
Lover,

*All my Comfort lies in his Impudence, and Heav'n be prais'd, he has a considerable
Portion.* [IV, iv, 202–4]

This Mr. *Collier* calls the *Play-house Grace*. It is the expression of a wanton and a vicious Character, in the Distress and Confusion of her Guilt. She is discover'd in her Lewdness, and suffer'd to come no more upon the Stage.

In the end of the last Act *Sharper* says to *Vain-love*:

I have been a kind of Godfather to you yonder: I have promis'd and vow'd some things in your name, which I think you are bound to perform. [V, ii, 81–3]

I meant no ill by this Allegory, nor do I perceive any in it now. Mr. *Collier* says it was meant for Drollery on the Catechism; but he has a way of discovering Drollery where it never was intended; and of intending Drollery where it can never be discovered. So much for the *Old Batchelour*.

In the *Double-Dealer* (he says) *Lady Plyant cries out Jesu, and talks Smut in the same Sentence*. That Exclamation I give him up freely. I had my self long since condemn'd it, and resolv'd to strike it out in the next Impression. I will not urge the *folly*, viciousness, or affectation of the Character to excuse it. Here I think my self oblig'd to make my Acknowledgments for a Letter which I receiv'd after the Publication of this Play, relating to this very Passage. It came from an Old Gentlewoman and a Widow, as she said, and very well to pass: It contain'd very good Advice, and requir'd an Answer, but the Direction for the Superscription was forgot. If the good Gentlewoman is yet in being, I desire her to receive my Thanks for her good Counsel, and for her Approbation of all the Comedy, that Word alone excepted.

That Lady *Plyant* talks *Smut* in the same Sentence, lies yet upon Mr. *Collier* to prove. His bare Assertion without an Instance, is not sufficient. If he can prove that there is downright *Smut* in it, why e'en let him take it for his pains: I am willing to part with it.

His next Objection is, that Sir *Paul*, who he observes bears the Character of a Fool, makes mention too often of the word *Providence*; for says Mr. *Collier*, *the meaning must be* (by the way, that *must* is a little hard upon me) *that Providence is a ridiculous Supposition; and that none but Blockheads pretend to Religion.* What will it avail me in this place to signifie my own meaning, when this modest Gentleman says, I *must mean* quite contrary?

Lady Froth is pleased to call Jehu a Hackney Coachman.

Lady *Froth*'s words are as follow—*Our Jehu was a Hackney Coachman when my Lord took him* [III, i, 547–8]. Which is as much as to say, that the Coachman's Name is *Jehu*: And why might it not be *Jehu* as well as *Jeremy*, or *Abraham*, or *Joseph*, or any other Jewish or Christian Name? *Brisk* desires that this may be put into a Marginal Note in Lady Froth's Poem.

This Mr. *Collier* says, is meant to *burlesque the Text, and Comment under one*. What Text, or what Comment, or what other earthly Thing he can mean, I cannot possibly imagine. These Remarks are very Wise; therefore I shall not Fool away any time about them.

Sir *Paul* tells his Wife, *he finds Passion coming upon him by Inspiration* [II, i, 207].

The poor Man is troubled with the *Flatus*, his Spleen is pufft up with Wind; and he is likely to grow very angry and peevish on the suddain; and desires the privilege to Scold and give it Vent. The word *Inspiration* when it has *Divine* prefix'd to it, bears a particular and known signification: But otherwise, to *inspire* is no more than to *Breath into*; and a Man without profaneness may truly say, that a Trumpet, a Fife, or a Flute, deliver a Musical Sound, by the help of Inspiration. I refer the Reader to my fourth Proposition, in this Case. For a Dispute about this word, would be very like the Controversie in *Ben. Johnson's Barthol. Fair*, between the *Rabbi* and the *Puppet*; it *is* profane, and it *is not* profane, is all the Argument the thing will admit of on either side.

The Double-dealer is not yet exhausted.ib.

That is, Mr. *Collier* is not yet exhausted; for to give double Interpretations to single Expressions, with a design only to lay hold of the worst, is double dealing in a great degree.

Cynthia the top Lady grows thoughtful. Cynthia it seems is the Top Lady now; not long since, the other Three were the three *biggest*. Perhaps the Gentleman speaks as to personal proportion, *Cynthia* is the Tallest, and the other Three are the Fattest of the Four.

Well. *Cynthia is thoughtful, and upon the question relates her Contemplation.*

Cyn. *I am thinking, that though Marriage makes Man and Wife one Flesh, it leaves them two Fools.* [II, i, 155–6]

Here he has filch'd out a little word so slily, 'tis hardly to be miss'd; and yet without it, the words bear a very different signification. The Sentence in the Play is Printed thus—*Though Marriage makes Man and Wife one Flesh, it leaves 'em STILL two Fools.* Which by means of that little word *still*, signifies no more, than that if two People were Fools, before or when they were married, they would continue in all probability to be Fools still, and after they were married. *Ben. Johnson* is much bolder in the first Scene of his *Bartholomew Fair*. There he makes Littlewit say to his Wife—*Man and Wife make one Fool*; and yet I don't think he design'd even that, for a Jest either upon *Genesis* 2. or St. *Matthew* 19. I have said nothing comparable to that, and yet Mr. *Collier* in his penetration has thought fit to accuse me of nothing less.

Thus I have summ'd up his Evidence against the *Double-dealer*. I have not thought it worth while to Cross-examine his Witnesses very much, because they are generally silly enough to detect themselves.

In *Love for Love*, *Scandal* tells Mrs. *Foresight*, he will *die a Martyr rather than disclaim his Passion* [III, i, 595–6]. The word Martyr is here used Metaphorically to imply Perseverance. *Martyr* is a Greek word, and signifies in plain English, no more than a *Witness*. A holy Martyr, or a Martyr for Religion is one thing; a wicked Martyr, or Martyr for the Devil is another: A Man may be a Martyr that is a Witness to Folly, to Error, or Impiety. *Mr. Collier* is a Martyr to Scandal and Falshood quite through his Book. This Expression he says, is *dignifying Adultery with the Stile of Martyrdom*; as if any word could dignifie Vice. These are very trifling Cavils, and I think all of this kind may reasonably be referr'd to my Fourth Proposition.

Jeremy who was bred at the University, calls the natural Inclinations to Eating and Drinking, Whoreson Appetites.

Jeremy bred at the University! Who told him so? What *Jeremy* does he mean, *Jeremy Collier*, or *Jeremy Fetch*? The last does not any where pretend to have been bred there. And if the t'other would but keep his own Counsel, and not Print *M.A.* on the Title Page of his Book, he would be no more suspected of such an Education than his Name-sake. *Jeremy* in the *Play*, banters the Coxcomb *Tattle*, and tells him he has been at *Cambridge*: Whereupon *Tattle* replies—

'Tis well enough for a Servant to be bred at an University. [V, i, 186–7]

Which is said to expose the impudence of illiterate Fops, who speak with Contempt of Learning and Universities. For the word *Whoreson*, I had it from *Shakespear* and *Johnson*, who have it very often in their Low Comedies; and sometimes their Characters of some Rank use it. I have put it into the Mouth of a Footman. 'Tis not worth speaking of. But Mr. *Collier* makes a terrible thing of it, and compares it to the *Language of Manicheans, who made the Creation to be the Work of the Devil.* After which he civilly solves all by saying, *the Poet was* Jeremy's *Tutor, and so the Mystery is at an end.* This by a Periphrasis is calling me *Manichean*; well let him call me what he pleases, he cannot call me *Jeremy Collier.*

His next Quotation is of one line taken out of the middle of eight more in a Speech of Sir *Sampson* in the second Act of this Comedy: he represents it as an Aphorism by it self, and without any regard to what either preceeds or follows it. I desire to be excused from transcribing the whole Scene or Speech. I refer to my third Proposition, and desire the Reader to view it in its place. Mr. *Collier's* Citation is—*Nature has been provident only to Bears and Spiders* [II, 1, 391–2]. I beg the Reader to peruse that Scene, and than to look into the 139 *Psalm*, because Mr. *Collier* says it is paraphrased by me in this Place. I wonder how such remote Wickedness can enter into a Man's Head. I dare affirm the Scene has no more resemblance of the *Psalm*, than Mr. *Collier* has of the Character of a Christian Priest, which he gives us in page 127, 128. of his own Book. Towards the end of the third Act, *Scandal* has occasion to flatter Old *Foresight.* He talks to him, and humours him in the Cant of his own Character, recites Quotations in favour of Astrology, and tells him the wisest Men have been beholding to that Science—

Solomon (says he) *was Wise, but how? By his Judgment in Astrology.* So *says* Pineda *in his third Book and eight Chap* [III, i, 530–2][1]. But the Quotation of the Authority is omitted by Mr. *Collier*, either because he would represent it as my own Observation to ridicule the Wisdom of *Solomon*, or else because he was indeed Ignorant that it belong'd to any Body else.

The Words which gave me the Hint are as above cited. *Pin. de rebus Salom.*

—*Illum Judiciariam Astrologiam calluisse circa naturalia, circa inclinationes hominum,* &c.

Do's Mr. *Collier* believe in Prognostications from Judicial Astrology? Do's he think that *Solomon* had his Wisdom only from thence? If he does not, why will he not permit the Superstitions growing from that Science to be expos'd? Why will he not understand that the exposing them in this Place and Manner, does not ridicule the Wisdom of *Solomon*, but the Folly of *Foresight?*

Scandal he says, continues his Banter, and says, *The Wise Men of the East ow'd their Instruction to a Star, which is rightly observ'd by* Gregory *the Great, in favour of Astrology* [ibid., ll. 534 ff.].

Scandal indeed Banters *Foresight*, but he does not banter the Audience, in mentioning *Gregory* the Great: Take his own Words.

Deus accommodate ad eorum scientiam docuit, ut qui in Stellarum Observatione versabantur ex stellis Christum discerent.

The rest of the Banter is what *Scandal* relates from *Albertus Magnus*, who makes it the most *valuable Science, because it teaches us to consider the Causation of Causes in the Causes of things.*

I am but a bare Translator in this place; for example:

—*Nos habemus unam scientiam mathematicam, quæ docet nos in rerum causis Causationem causarum Considerare.* [Albert. Mag. Tom. 5. p. 659]

Is not all this stuff, and fit to be exposed; yet these and some other like Sayings, have I sometimes met with as Authorities in Vindication of Judicial Astrology.

In Page 76. Mr. *Collier* is very angry that Sir *Sampson* has not another Name; because *Sampson* is a Name in the Old Testament.

He says it is Burlesquing the Sacred History, for Sir *Sampson* to boast of his Strength; because *Sampson* in the Testament is said to be very strong. The rest that he quarrels at is a metaphorical expression or two, of less Consideration if possible, than any of his former Cavils.

I refer the Reader to the Scene, which is the last in the Play: And for an Answer, to what has before been said on the word *Martyr*. When I read in this page these words of *Mr. Collier*—*to draw towards an end of this Play*, I thought he had no more to say to it; but his method is so admirable, that he never knows where to begin, nor when to make an end. Five or six pages farther I find another of his Remarks.

In *Love for Love, Valentine* says, *I am Truth.*

If the Reader pleases to consult the Fourth Act of that Comedy, he will there find a Scene, wherein *Valentine* counterfeits madness.

One reason of his Counterfeiting in that manner, is, that it conduces somewhat to the design and end of the Play. Another reason is, that it makes a Variation of the Character; and has the same effect in the Dialogue of the Play, as if a new Character were introduc'd. A third use of this pretended madness is, that it gives a Liberty to Satire; and authorises a Bluntness, which would otherwise have been a Breach in the Manners of the Character. Mad-men have generally some one Expression which they use more frequently than any other. *Valentine* to prepare his Satire, fixes on one which may give us to understand, that he will speak nothing but Truth; and so before and after most of his Observations says—*I am Truth*. For example. *Foresight* asks him

—*What will be done at Court?*
    Val. *Scandal will tell you—I am Truth, I never come there.* [IV, i, 496–8]

I had at first made him say, *I am Tom-tell-troth*; but the sound and meanness of the Expression displeas'd me: and I alter'd it for one shorter, that might signifie the same thing. What a Charitable and Christian-like Construction my dear Friend *Mr. Collier* has given to this Expression, is fit only to be seen in his own Book; and thither I refer the Reader: I will only repeat his Remark as it personally aims at me—*Now a Poet that had not been smitten with the pleasure of Blasphemy, would not have furnish'd Frenzy with Inspiration, &c.* Now I say, a Priest who was not himself furnish'd with Frenzy instead of Inspiration, would never have mistaken one for the other.

In his next Chapter he Charges the Stage with the Abuse of the Clergy. He quotes me so little in this Chapter, and has so little reason even for that little, that it is hardly worth examining.

The *Old Batchelour* has a *Throw* (as he calls it) at the dissenting Ministers.

Now this *Throw*, in his own Words, amounts to no more than that a Pimp provides the Habit of a dissenting Minister, as the safest Disguise to conceal a Whoremaster: Which is rather a Complement than an Affront to the Habit.

Barnaby calls another of that Character Mr. Prig. Calls him Mr. *Prig?* Why what if his Name were Mr. *Prig?* Or what if it were not? This is furiously simple! *Fondlewife to hook in the Church of* England *into the Abuse, tacks a Chaplain to the End of the Description.*

How this pretty little Reasoner has (as he calls it) hook't in the Church of *England?* Can't a Man be a Chaplain unless he is of the Church of *England?*

Father *Dominick* the 2d. he's for bringing in Heav'n and the Church by hook or crook into his Quarrel. If a *Mufti* had been tack'd to the Description, he would have been equally offended; for

Mufti in the Language of the Theater, he says, signifies *Bishop*.

Maskwell in the *Double Dealer*, has a Plot, and is for engaging *Saygrace* in it. He is for *instructing the Levite*, and says, *without one of them have a Finger in't, no Plot, publick or private, can expect to prosper.*

Perhaps that is a Mistake; many damnable Plots have miscarried, wherein Priests have been concern'd.[2]

After this, he has transcrib'd a broken Piece of a Dialogue between *Maskwell* and *Saygrace*, which I leave to shift for it self; having nothing in it worth an Accusation, or needing a Defence.

Mr. *Collier* is very florid in this Chapter; but it is very hard to know what he would be at. He seems to be apprehensive of being brought upon the Stage, and in some Places endeavours to prove, that as he is a Priest, he should be exempted from the Correction of the *Drama*.

(pp. 36–59)

(iv)   Alleged immorality of *Love for Love* and *The Old Batchelour*

I come now to his Chapter of the Immorality of the Stage.

His Objections here are rather Objections against Comedy in general, than against mine, or any bodies Comedies in particular. He says the Sparks that *marry up the Top-Ladies,* and are rewarded with Wives and Fortunes in the last *Acts,* are generally debauch'd Characters. In answer to this, I refer to my first and second Proposition. He is a little particular in his Remarks upon *Valentine,* in *Love for Love.* He says,

This Spark, the Poet would pass for a Person of Vertue; but he speaks too late.

I know who, and what he is, that always speaks too soon. Why is he to be pass'd for a Person of Vertue? Or where is it said that his Character makes extraordinary Pretensions to it! *Valentine* is in *Debt,* and in *Love*; he has honesty enough to close with a hard Bargain, rather than not pay his Debts, in the first *Act*; and he has Generosity and Sincerity enough, in the last *Act,* to sacrifice every thing to his Love; and when he is in danger of losing his Mistress, thinks every thing else of little worth. This, I hope, may be allow'd a Reason for the Lady to say, *He has Vertues*: They are such in respect to her; and her once saying so, in the last *Act,* is all the notice that is taken of his *Vertue* quite thro' the Play.

Mr. *Collier* says, he *is Prodigal*. He was prodigal, and is shewn, in the first *Act* under hard Circumstances, which are the Effects of his

Prodigality. That he is unnatural and undutiful, I don't understand: He has indeed a very unnatural Father; and if he does not very passively submit to his Tyranny and barbarous Usage, I conceive there is a Moral to be apply'd from thence to such Fathers. That he is *profane* and *obscene*, is a false Accusation, and without any Evidence. In short, the Character is a mix'd Character; his Faults are fewer than his good Qualities; and, as the World goes, he may pass well enough for the best Character in a Comedy; where even the best must be shewn to have Faults, that the best Spectators may be warn'd not to think too well of themselves.

He quotes the *Old Batchelor* twice in this Chapter. His first Quotation is made with his usual assurance and fair dealing.

If any one would understand what the Curse of all tender-hearted Women is, Bellmour *will inform him. What is it then? 'Tis the Pox.*

Here he makes a Flourish upon ill Nature's being recommended as a Guard of Vertue and of Health, *&c.*

The whole Matter of Fact is no more than this.

Lucy to Belmour, Act 5. Scene 2. If you do deceive me, the Curse of all kind tender-hearted Women light upon you.

Bell. *That's as much as to say, The Pox take me.* [V, i, 76–8]

It is his Interpretation; and it is agreeable to his Character. He is a Debauchee, and he thinks there is but one way for Women to be kind and tender-hearted; and, I think, his threat'ning them with such a Curse as the consequence of too much easiness, does not seem to recommend the Vice at all, but rather to forbid it: His very Leudness, in this place, is made moral and instructive.

I am very glad our Author is in such Circumstances, in this Chapter, that he can bear the sight of that *Hellish Syllable, Pox*; and prevail with himself to write it at its full length. *Non ita pridem.* In Page 82. he loves his Love with a P—but no naming: That is not like a Cavalier. What *Ermin* was ever an Instance of superfine Nicety comparable to Mr. *Collier*? I will not say, what *Cat*? Tho' if I should, I can quote a *Spanish* Proverb to justifie the Comparison.

El gato scaldado tiene miedo de agua fria.[3]

He makes one Quotation more, to what purpose indeed I know not; but I will repeat it, in Justice to him, because it is the last that he has made, and the first fair one. *Old Batch.* Act 4.

Belinda to *Sharp.—Where did you get this excellent Talent of Railing?*
Sharp.—Madam, the Talent was born with me.—I confess I have taken care to
improve it, to qualifie me for the Society of Ladies.   [IV, iii, 196–200]

These are the Words just as the Gentleman quotes 'em; but why, or wherefore, he is not pleas'd to discover; for he says not one Syllable, for, nor against 'em: I suppose he thinks the Proof plain, and the Evidence firm without a Coroborator.

I hope the Reader will not forget, that these Instances are produc'd, to prove that I have encourag'd Immorality in my Plays. I thought the Expression, above-mentioned, had been a gentle Reproof to the Ladies that are addicted to railing; and since Mr. *Collier* has not said that it *must* mean the contrary, I don't see why it may not be understood so still?

I have now gone thorough with all Mr. *Collier*'s Quotations; I have been as short as I could possibly in their Vindication; I have avoided all Recriminations, and have not so much as made one Citation from any of my Plays in favour of them: Whatever they contain of Morality, or Invectives against Folly and Vice, is no more than what ought to be in them; therefore I do not urge it as a Merit.

My Business was not to paint, but to wash; not to shew Beauties, but to wipe off Stains.

Mr. *Collier* has indeed given me an opportunity of reforming many Errors, by obliging me to a review of my own Plays.

(pp. 87–93)

NOTES

1 The authorities whom Scandal cites are the Spanish Jesuit, Juan de Pineda of Seville, author of a commentary on Solomon, and the scholastic Albertus Magnus, teacher of St Thomas Aquinas.
2 Possibly a veiled allusion to Collier's attending to the scaffold two of those found guilty in the 1696 plot to assassinate William III.
3 'The scalded cat fears cold water.'

25. Anon. in *A Letter to Mr. Congreve*

1698

From *A Letter to Mr. Congreve on his Pretended Amendments, &c. of Mr. Collier's Short View of the* Immorality *and* Prophaneness *of the* English Stage (London: 1698), pp. 9–19.

This acrimonious rejoinder to Congreve's *Amendments* was advertised in *The Post Man* for 30 August to 1 September 1698.

I am now come to your *Postulata*.

The first I grant you, because 'tis *Aristotles*, and a Just one. The second I must refuse you, that is your own, and Unreasonable: You ought not to represent any Immoralities upon the Stage, either in Word, or Deed, that will give offence to chaste and sober Ears, no, tho you pretend to punish them afterwards: You might as well argue, it would be of use to have idle Fellows Swear and Curse in the Streets, purely for the sake of giving sober Men, an opportunity to Chide them: We are offended much at such things from the Persons themselves; and much more, when we have them represented to us, with advantages at second hand. You say, *it were very hard, a Painter should be thought to resemble all the the ugly Faces he draws*; [remember here again your Doctrine of *Ideas*.] But what if a *Painter* chooses to draw Obscene, and Baudy Pieces, and exposes them to the Publick, for their Diversion; is it hard that such a one should be Censured? Or, can we think, his Thoughts were altogether so chastly taken up, and employ'd, when they were directing the Pencil?

Your Third I grant you, tho your own; nor do I expect Thanks for the favour, because I think 'tis very indifferent, whether your *Passages* are read in *Collier* or your self: There are but two words odds that I can find, and they are *wasting*, for *wafting*; and the little word, *still*, omitted: Only, if we must needs look back *into the Field of Nature, from whence they were transplanted*; we shall have a larger *Field* of Debauchery to walk in, and a great deal of worse Stuff, than Mr. *Collier* has Collected still in view.

If you demand the priviledge of the *Habeas Corpus Act*, to remove your offensive Plays, from the *Quarter-Sessions of Middlesex*, to the *King's-Bench Bar*; and appeal from the *Presentment of the Grand Jury*, to a *just Judge*; I believe the thing may be practicable enough, but I question whether it would do you any Service.

I must differ with you a little again, about your fourth *Postulatum*. [You should be advised, Mr. *Congreve*, when you chose this odd way of vindicating Poems Mathematically; to see that your Principles be self-evident: But you shew your self so needy, and ask such unreasonable things, and with that Confidence, that you will be taken notice of, by all the *Philomaths in and about* London, for a sturdy Beggar in their way.] *When words*, you say, *are applied to Sacred things, and with a purpose to treat of Sacred things, they ought to be understood accordingly*: Right! and so they ought. *But when they are otherwise applied, the diversity of the Subject, gives them a diversity of signification*: Right again! That is to say, in the former case, they are *sacredly* used; but when the same peculiar words are taken, and used in this latter case, which is yours, they are used *Prophanely*; and is the Sin that is commonly express'd by that Phrase, *ludere cum Sacris*: And now, what service can you expect from a Proposition, that is already Revolted from you? I must tell you, there is a great deal of difference, between using the same common *Alphabet*, with that in Scripture; and the borrowing of some peculiar Words, or Phrases, from it, that are *spelt out of that Alphabet*. For Example, our Saviour has this peculiar Expression of himself, 𝕴 𝖆𝖒 𝖙𝖍𝖊 𝕿𝖗𝖚𝖙𝖍; which is so emphatical, and remarkable, in relation to his Person, that the whole tenor of the Gospel depends upon it: When this Expression therefore is put familiarly into the Mouth of a Mad-man upon the Stage, and made as it were, the distinguishing Catch, and Bob of his Frenzy; this I think, is something more, than spelling out of the *Alphabet*. I do assure you, it had that ill effect, that I never met with any one, who came from that Play, but confest, it gave them Offence; and minded them from whom the expression was taken. Wou'd you had been contented with your first thought, I am *Tom tell troth*! for that had been harmless, and foolish enough, and fit for a Mad-man.

Having ended your *Postulata*, and made such an Apology, as was necessary, for the *latitude* they be speak: you proceed to subjoin a sort of *Hypothesis*, of the *moral instruction of Plays*, to this purpose: That when the *Play is over*, we have all the moral of it, summ'd up in a few lines to the Audience, *in Rhyme, to be more engaging upon the memory*: for example, *In Love for Love*; the moral of it is summ'd up very briefly in that Distick, at the close.

> The mistery this day is, that we find,
> A Lover true; not that a Womans kind.

[V, i, 636–7]

here, you have the whole Moral of a long Play, wrapt up at last, in a *mistery*, for the better instruction of the Audience.

I see no great occasion of moderating distinctly, between you both, in relation to all the particular matters in dispute, from your Plays: Your *Tragedy* is a very good one, and Answers Sir *Rich. Blackmores* Character of it, who recommends it, for an admirable one; but still with this reserve, *some few things only excepted*: for instance; when you make King *Manuel*, in the fury of his resentment, say, of *Osmyns pleading audacious Love* to his Mistress;

> Better for him, to tempt the rage of Heaven,
> And wrench the bolt red-hissing, from the hand
> Of him that thunders,——
> 'Tis daring for a God.——

[II, ii, 368–71]

Thats a bold stroke indeed! I protest, if I had been the Author of it, I should have trembled at the *Gigantick* insolence of my fancy: afterward, the attempt is likened to *Ixions Embracing Divinity*: Bless me! you Poets do frequently make so bold with God Almighty, and his Divinity; that if he had not declared himself, from his own mouth, to be a God of Patience and long suffering; I should wonder how he does bear it of you.

Then again, you make this blustering King pay his, and your respects, to the Character, and Office of a Clergyman, very handsomely.

> I'll have a Priest shall preach her from her faith,
> And make it sin, not to renounce that vow,
> Which I'd have broken.

[I, i, 354–6]

But when you make so very bold with God's honour, his Priests may contentedly take any thing, in the same Play: *The Disciple is not above his Master, nor the Servant above his Lord, &c.* vid Matt. 10. 24, 25, 26.

I would fain bestow one note more upon the *Mourning Bride*, tho'
I am sure to incur the Censure of ill nature, and the *Splene* for it:
This I know is your Darling Off-spring, and therefore I would be
very tender of it; you have been at the expence of more Education
than ordinary upon it, and therefore you say, p. 23, *If Smut, and
Prophaneness, can be prov'd against this, you must give up the Cause.* I
am not now upon charging it with *Smut*; but when I have dropt this
one remark more to the two former, I will leave it to your self to
judge, whether it is not now and then a little *Prophane*: Methinks
you seem somewhat Conscious of it already, when immediately
after, in that same Paragraph, you silently let fall the word
Prophaneness; and cry out, *if there be immodesty in that Tragedy, I
must confess my self incapable of ever writing any thing with modesty, or
decency.*

But to convince you farther (if you are not yet convinc't) that
there is *Prophaneness* in that Play, let me prevail with you to weigh
that violent rapture of *Osmyn* to his *Bride* over again. *Mourn. Bride*,
p. 35.

> *My all of bliss, my everlasting Life,*
> *Soul of my soul, and end of all my wishes.* [III, i, 304–5]

Osmyn, or *Alphonso*, is your *Hero*; and design'd for the Character
of a very good, and brave Person; and therefore, when it comes to
his turn to speak, we expect a great deal of the *Poets* mind, and
Principles from him; for the Honourable Mr. *Granville*, makes it *a
pretty true observation of Poets, that in the frame of their Heroes, they
commonly draw their own Pictures* (Preface to Heroick Love): But now,
when *your All of bliss, Your everlasting life, Your very Soul,* and *the
end of all your wishes*, are all wrapt up together, and consummated in
the enjoyment of one Woman; What is become of your *Heaven?* Or
what farther business, or interest can you have depending in that
eternal state, where *they neither Marry, nor are given in Marriage?* I am
clearly for your encouraging Men to Love their Wives; but there is
no necessity of representing a Good Husband so very *uxorious*, as to
make him declare himself possest of *Heaven*, and the *eternal rewards
of Religion*, when he has his *Spouse* in his Arms.——But some
grains of allowance must be made here, since

> *This was an Off'ring to the sex design'd.* Epil. [l. 31]

After all, allowing your Adversary has been a little too angry with that Celebrated Tragedy of yours; Would you have your Comedies pass without exception too? What think you of your *Prologue* to the *Double Dealer?* where you would insinuate, by the allusion of a *Moorish Custom*, that there's hardly a Husband in all the City of *London*, but what's a *Cuckold*: and, the better to grace them in that Character, you are pleas'd to give them the venerable Epethite of, *Christian Cuckolds*.

> *I'th Good Man's Arms, the Chopping bastard thrives,*
> *For he thinks all his own, that is his Wives.*
>
> [ll. 29–30]

I am sure it ought to be so, and to insinuate the contrary, is to stir up Jealousie; which is evidently the design of the whole Play that follows. On this occasion, be so kind to lend me the two first Verses of your *Prologue* to the old *Batchelour*.

> *How this vile World is chang'd! in former days,*
> *Prologues, were serious Speeches, before Plays;*
> *Grave solemn things,——*

There is your own Confession, to one great part of Mr. *Collier's* Book, how infinitely the *Antients* exceeded our *Modern* pretenders to Poetry, in the *Gravity*, and *Morality* of their performances.

In short, if *Belinda*, and *Letitia*, in the old *Batch.* If *the three biggest*, of the four Women in the *Double Dealer*, have their Characters, and Cues, contrived for the advancement of Modesty, and Virtue; If, in *Love for Love*, *Tattle's* instructing of *Miss Prue*, and her saying her *Catechism* after him, wherein she is taught a little of Mr. *Congreve's Court breeding*; To give up her Virtue, *and to lye, to be angry, and yet more complying; to fall back, when she should run away; and to hold her tongue, when she should cry out*; And, if Mrs. *Foresights* leaving them together, to do their worst, in that juncture, were intended *out of good morality*; then some well meaning People have been very much mistaken, that's all.

26. Anon. in *Animadversions on Mr. Congreve's Late Answer to Mr. Collier*

1698

From *Animadversions on Mr. Congreve's Late Answer to Mr. Collier* (London: 1698), pp. 36–8.

Cast in the form of a 'Dialogue between Mr. *Smith* and Mr. *Johnson*', this attack on Congreve was advertised for the 3–8 September. Sir Edmund Gosse suggested as a possible author the actor and minor dramatist George Powell. Most of the piece is vulgar abuse, interesting only for its repeated charges of plagiarism. The following is a representative sample.

Smith. No truly, I can't commend a dull thing, if I know it to be such; I can't forbear falling a-sleep over the *Double Dealer*, tho' *Dryden* has writ a fine Commendatory Copy before it: Where the paint's lay'd on so very thick, 'tis a sign the Face is a very scurvy one; and as for *Dryden*, why he'd give *Du[rfe]y* a Copy of Verses if he would cringe to him, pray did he not write one to'ther day, prefix'd to as wretched a piece of Stuff of a Play, as ever a *Tennis-Court Theatre* tost into the World?

Here in page 38. he musters up a Speech *of the crying Sin of Adultery*. Shows us that Mr. *Collier* has left a rank broken and imperfect, and refers us to the Play, as the main body to make the breach up from thence. A pretty sort of an Answer this; Is Mr. *Congreve* so assur'd that every Body has his foolish Plays by them? Or does he think those that have, will take the pains? Pray, whose Business is it? 'tis they that Answer Mr. *Collier*, if they do, not he——Ah! poor Man! *Indeed I cannot forbear Laughing when I compare his dreadful Comment with such poor silly words as are in the Text.*——But hold, what's here? is our *Democritus* turn'd *Heraclytus* already? Alas!

Let sable Clouds her chalky Cliffs adorn.[1]

138

Which with his foregoing Line, which makes up the burthen of the Song, is Stol'n from a Poem written on the Death of *General Monk*; but I need not detect him in Particulars, what has he publish'd that is not Stol'n?

NOTE

1 The second line of the refrain in 'The Mourning Muse of *Alexis*'.

27. Jeremy Collier in *A Defence of the Short View*

1698

From *A Defence of the Short View of the Profaneness and Immorality of the English Stage, &c. being a reply to Mr. Congreve's Amendments* (London: 1699).

Collier's rejoinder to Congreve was advertised for 8–10 November, although dated 1699 on the title page. The volume also included his reply to Vanbrugh's *Short Vindication of the Relapse and the Provok'd Wife*.

(i) On Congreve's *Postulata*

Mr. *Congreve* is now making *Outworks* to fortify the Garison. He lays down four Rules as the Test of Criticism and Comedy. These He calls *Postulata*, as if they were Principles of *Science*, and carried the Evidence of an *Axiom*. And after he has spent some *Pages* in setting down these Demonstrative Things, he frankly tells us, they *seem at first Sight* to *comprehend a Latitude*. Do they so? Then they are not Self-evident; They are unqualifyed for the Post he has put them in; and prove nothing but Sophistry and Legerdemain. Well! What tho' these Rules are false in themselves, Mr. *Congreve* promises to make them True before he has done with them. For they shall be so *limited*, and *restrain'd*, and used with such Discretion; that the *Reader* shall be perfectly indemnifyed. However, I can't help suspecting these fair Words: For if He intends to deal clearly, why does he make the Touchstone faulty, and the Standard uncertain? For these reasons, I must examine for my Self; And since he owns his *Propositions* not evidently true, I'll try if I can't prove the greatest part of them evidently false.

To begin with him. His Latitude of *Comedy* upon *Aristotle's* Definition; as he Explains it, wont pass without Limitation. For

1*st*. His Construction of Μίμησις Φαυλοτέρων is very questionable. These Words may as properly be Translated the *Common,* as *the worst Sort of People.* And thus *Hesychius* interprets Φαυλος by εὐτελής

2*ly*. *Comedy* is distinguish'd from *Tragedy* by the Quality of the Persons, as well as by other Circumstances. *Aristotle* informs us that the Appearance, Characters, or Persons are greater in *Tragedy,* than in *Comedy* (Lib. de Poet cap. 4.). Τὰ σχήματα μείζω καὶ εντιμότερα. And to this Sense *Petitus* interprets the Words Βελτίονας ἢ χείρονας, affirming they ought to relate to Quality, as well as Manners (In not. ad Lib. *Arist.* de Poet. cap. 2.).

Now as the Business of *Tragedy* is to represent Princes and Persons of Quality; so by the Laws of Distinction, *Comedy* ought to be confin'd to the ordinary Rank of Mankind. And that *Aristotle* ought to be thus interpreted appears from the Form of *New Comedy,* set up in the Time of this Philosopher. And tho' we have none of these *Comedies* extant, 'tis agreed by the Criticks that they did not meddle with Government and Great People; The *Old Comedy* being put down upon this Score. And tho' *Menander* and the rest of that Set are lost, we may guess at their Conduct from the Plays of *Plautus* and *Terence,* in all which there is not so much as one Person of Quality represented.

Farther, Mr. *Congreve's* Reason why *Aristotle* should be interpreted by *Manners,* and not *Quality* is inconclusive. His remark on κατὰ πάσαν κακίαν will serve as well the other way. Lets try it a little: *Aristotle* shall say then that *Comedy* is an imitation of the ordinary, and middle sort of People, but not κατὰ πάσαν κακίαν, *in every branch and aggravation of Vice*; for as Mr. *Congreve* observes, *there are Crimes too daring and too horrid for Comedy.* Now I desire to know, if this Sense is not clear and unembarrass'd, if it does not distinguish *Comedy* from *Tragedy,* and bring down the Definition to Matter of Fact?

But granting Mr. *Congreve* his Definition; all Blemishes and Instances of Scandal are not fit to make sport with. Covetousness, and Profusion; Cowardize, Spleen, and Singularity, well managed, might possibly do. But some Vices Mr. *Congreve* confesses *are too daring for Comedy*. Yes and for *Tragedy* too. And among these I'll venture to say Profaneness is one. This Liberty even *Aristotle* durst not allow: He knew the Government of *Athens* would not endure it. And that some of the *Poets* had been call'd to account upon this Score.

2ly. Immodesty and lewd Talking, is another part of Vice which ought not to appear in *Comedy. Aristotle* blames the *Old Comedians* for this sort of Mismanagement; and adds, that intemperate Rallying ought to lie under publick Restraint. And therefore Mr. *Congreve* is mistaken in his Consequence if he makes it general. For *the looser sort of Livers*, as to the Foulness of Conversation, are no proper *Subject of Comedy.*

But supposing *Aristotle* more liberal to Mr. *Congreve*, what service would it do him? Does not Christianity refine the Pleasures, and abridge the Liberties of *Heathenism?* St. *Paul* bids us *put away all filthyness and foolish talking* (*Ephes.* 5.4.), and that such things *ought not so much as to be named amongst Christians* (*Colȯs.* 3.8.). And when *Revelation* says one thing, and *Paganism* another, how are we to determine? Is not an *Apostle*'s Testimony more cogent than that of a Philosopher, and the *New Testament* above all the Rules of *Aristotle* and *Horace?*

Thus we see his first *Postulatum* is far from being true in the Generality stated by him.

Before I part with him on this Head, I can't but take notice of his saying, that *the Business of Comedy is to delight, as well as instruct*: If he means as much, by *as well*, he is mistaken. For Delight is but the secondary End of *Comedy*, as I have prov'd at large. And to satisfy him farther, I'll give him one Testimony more of Mr. *Dryden's*. 'Tis in his *Preface* to *Fresnoy's Art of Painting*. Here he informs us that as to Delight *the parallel of the* (two) *Arts holds true; with this difference; That the principal End of Painting is to please, and the chief design of Poetry is to instruct.*

Thus Mr. *Congreve*'s first Rule signifies little; And therefore his *Second* being, but a consequence of it, must fall of Course. *Pleasure*, especially the Pleasure of *Libertines*, is not the Supreme *Law of Comedy*. Vice must be under Discipline and Discountenance, and

Folly shown with great Caution and Reserve. Lussious Descriptions, and Common Places of Lewdness are unpardonable. They affront the virtuous, and debauch the unwary, and are a scandal to the Country where they are suffer'd. The pretence of *Nature*, and *Imitation*, is a lamentable Plea. Without doubt there's a great deal of *Nature* in the most brutal Practices. The infamous *Stews* 'tis likely talk in their own way, and keep up to their Character. But what Person of probity would visit them for their Propriety, or take Poyson because 'tis true in its kind? All Characters of Immodesty (if there must be any such) should only be hinted in remote Language, and thrown off in Generals.

If there must be Strumpets, let *Bridewell* be the *Scene*. Let them come not to Prate, but to be Punish'd. To give Success, and Reputation to a *Stage Libertine*, is a sign either of Ignorance, of Lewdness, or Atheism, or altogether. Even those Instances which will bear the relating ought to be punish'd. But as for Smut and Profaneness, 'tis every way Criminal and Infectious, and no Discipline can atone for the Representation: When a *Poet* will venture on these Liberties, his *Perswasion* must suffer, and his *private Sentiments* fall under Censure. For as Mr. *Dryden* rightly observes, *vita proba est*, is no excuse: For *'twill scarcely be admitted that either a Poet or a Painter can be chast, who give us the contrary Examples in their Writings, and their Pictures.* I agree with Mr. *Congreve it would be very hard a Painter should be believ'd to resemble all the ugly Faces he draws.* But if he suffers his Pencil to grow Licentious, if he gives us Obscenities, the Merits of *Raphael* won't excuse him: No, To do an ill Thing well, doubles the Fault. The Mischief rises with the Art, and the Man ought to smart in proportion to his Excellency: 'Tis one of the Rules in Painting according to Mr. *Dryden* and *Fresnoy*; To *avoid every Thing that's immoral and filthy, unseemly, impudent, and obscene.* And Mr. *Dryden* continues, that a Poet is bound up to the same Restraint, and ought neither to *Design*, or *Colour* an offensive Piece.

Mr. *Congreve*'s 4th Proposition relates to the *Holy Scriptures*; And here he endeavours to fence against the Censure of Profaneness. He desires the following Distinction *may be admitted*, viz. *when Words are applied to sacred Things, they ought to be understood accordingly: But when they are otherwise applied, the Diversity of the Subject gives a Diversity of Signification*: By his favour this Distinction is loose, and nothing to the Purpose. The inspired Text is appropriated to *Sacred Things*, and never to be used but upon serious Occasions. The Weight of the Matter, and the Dignity of the Author, challenge our utmost regard. 'Tis only for the Service of the *Sanctuary*, and Privileged from common Use. But Mr. *Congreve* says *when they* (the Words of Scripture) *are otherwise applied, the Diversity of the Subject gives a Diversity of Signification.* This is strange Stuff! Has Application so transforming a Quality, and does bare use enter so far into the Nature of Things? If a Man applies his Money to an ill Purpose, does this transmute the Metal, and make it none of the Kings Coin? To wrest an Author, and turn his Words into Jest, is it seems to have nothing to do with him. The meer Ridicule destroys the Quotation; and makes it belong to another Person. Thus 'tis impossible to Travestie a Book, and *Virgil* was never burlesqu'd by *Ausonius* or Mr. *Cotton*! Not at all! They only made use of the 24 Letters, and happen'd to chop exactly upon *Virgil*'s Subject, his Words and Versification. But 'tis plain they never intended to quote him: For *Virgil* is always grave, and serious, but these Gentlemen apply, or translate the Words in the most different manner imaginable: And run always upon Buffoon-ry and Drolling. This is Mr. *Congreve*'s Logick, and to abuse an Author is to have nothing to do with him. The Injury it seems destroys the Relation, and makes the Action perfectly foreign. And by this Reasoning one would think my Book had never been cited by Mr. *Congreve*. ...

I shall now go back to his 3*d*, which I think would have stood as well in the last place. He *desires the impartial Reader, not to consider any Expression or Passage, cited from any Play, as it appears in* my Book; *nor to pass any Sentence upon it out of its proper Scene*, &c. For it must not be medled with *when 'tis alienated from its Character*. Well! Let the *Reader* compare his *Plays* with the *View*, &c. as much as he pleases. However, there's no necessity of passing through all his Forms, and Methods of prescribing. For if the Passage be truly cited, if the Sentence be full, and determin'd, why mayn't we understand it where'ere 'tis met with? Why must we read a Page for a Period? Can't a Plant be known without the History of the Garden? Besides, He may remember I have frequently hinted his *Characters*, touched upon their Quality and Fortune, and made them an Aggravation of his Fault.

But to silence this Plea, I had told him before that no pretence of Character, or Punishment, could justify Profaneness on the *Stage*. I gave him my Reasons for't too, which he is not pleas'd to take notice of.

(pp. 5–15)

(ii) The concluding moral of *The Old Batchelour* and of *Love for Love*

Mr. *Congreve* proceeds to acquaint us how careful the *Stage* is for the *Instruction* of the *Audience*. That *the Moral of the whole is generally summ'd in the concluding Lines of the Poem, and put into Rhyme that it may be easy and engaging to the Memory.* To this I answer,

1st. That this *Expedient* is not always made use of. And not to trouble the *Reader* with *many* Instances, we have nothing of it in *Love in a Nunnery*, and the *Relapse*, both which *Plays* are in my Opinion not a little dangerous.

2*ly*. Sometimes these Comprehensive Lines do more harm than good: They do so in *the Souldiers Fortune*: They do so likewise in the *Old Batchelour*; which instructs us to admirable purpose in these Words;

> But oh—
> *What rugged ways attend the Noon of Life?*
> *(Our sun declines) and with what anxious strife,*
> *What pain we tug that galling Load a Wife?*
> [V, ii, 190–3]

This Moral is uncourtly, and vitious, it encourages Lewdness, and agrees extreamly well with the *Fable*. *Love for Love* may have somewhat a better Farewel, but would do a Man little Service should he remember it to his dying Day. Here *Angelica* after a fit of Profane Vanity in *Prose*, takes her Leave as follows;

> *The Miracle to Day is that we find*
> *A Lover true: Not that a Woman's kind.*
> [V, i, 636–7]

This last Word is somewhat ambiguous, and with a little help may strike off into a light Sense. But take it at the best, 'tis not overloaden with Weight and Apothegme. A *Ballad* is every jot as sententious.

3*dly*. Supposing the Moral grave, and unexceptionable, it amounts to little in the present Case. Alas! The Doctor comes too late for the Disease, and the Antidote is much too weak for the Poyson. When a *Poet* has flourished on an ill Subject for some

Hours: When he has Larded his *Scenes* with Smut, and play'd his Jests on Religion; and exhausted himself upon Vice; what can a dry Line or two of good Counsel signify? The Tincture is taken, the Fancy is preingaged, and the Man is gone off into another Interest. Profane Wit, Luscious Expressions, and the handsome Appearance of a *Libertine*, solicit strongly for Debauchery. These Things are mighty Recruits to Folly, and make the Will too hard for the Understanding. A taste of Philosophy has a very flat relish, after so full an Entertainment. An agreeable Impression is not easily defaced by a single Stroak, especially when 'tis worn deep by Force, and Repetition. And as the *Audience* are not secur'd, so neither are the Poets this way. A Moral Sentence at the Close of a Lewd Play, is much like a pious Expression in the Mouth of a dying Man, who has been Wicked all his Life time. This some ignorant People call making a good End, as if one wise Word would attone for an Age of Folly. To return to the *Stage*. I suppose other parts of a Discourse besides the Conclusion, ought to be free from Infection. If a Man was Sound only at his Fingers Ends, he would have little comfort in his Constitution. *Bonum fit ex integra causa*; A good Action must have nothing bad. The Quality must be uniform, and reach to every Circumstance. In short. This Expedient of Mr. *Congreve*'s as 'tis insignificant to the purpose 'tis brought, so it looks very like a piece of formal Hypocricy: And seems to be made use of to conceal the Immorality of the *Play*, and cover the *Poet* from Censure.

(pp. 19–21)

(iii) Profanity in *The Mourning Bride*

We are now come to the *Mourning-Bride*, and Mr. *Congreve* seems so well assur'd of the Decency of this *Play*, that he casts the whole Cause upon it. *If there be Immodesty in this Tragedy* (says he) *I must confess my self incapable of ever writing any thing with Modesty.* It may be so: An ill Custom is very hard to Conquer, with some People. But setting this matter aside; I still charge Mr. *Congreve* with Immodesty; 'tis in *Osmin*'s last Speech in the *Page* above-mentioned. Indeed I did not Cite the words because I am not willing to furnish the Reader with a Collection of Indecencies, to shew I design nothing but fair dealing: I always refer to the *Play*, and generally to the Character, and *Page*, where such Entertainment is to be met with. This is pressing the Charge as far as the Case will bear; But because the Passages are unfit to be shown, Mr.

Congreve and his Brethren deny the Fact: A great Instance of their Modesty in another Sense. Is it Innocence then to be guilty of things too bad to be nam'd? What sort of Faults must those be, which won't endure the Light, tho only to punish them.

This Gentleman quarrels with me because I would have had *Almeria* and *Osmin* parted *Civilly*; as if it was not proper for Lovers to do so; But *Civility*, and *Incivility have nothing to do with Passion*. I deny that, *Incivility* and *Passion*, are often concern'd together; And I suppose his *Amendments* may make an Instance.

By *Civilly*, I meant only decently, as any one might easily imagine. And as for *Tenderness*, when it grows Rank, and Nauseous, 'tis Rudeness, I take it.

Mr. *Congreve* would excuse *Osmin*'s Rant, by saying, *That most of the Incidents of the Poem of this Scene and the former, were laid to prepare for the Violence of these Expressions*. If it be so, I think the Play was not worth the Candle. 'Tis much as Wise as it would be for a Man to make a long Preparation to get out of his Wits, and qualifie himself for *Bedlam*. For nothing can be more distracted than *Osmin*. He is for *riving his clotted Hair, Smearing the Walls with his Blood, and dashing his disfigured Face against* something [III, i, 350–2]. And a great deal more such stuff, as a Man may go to all the Mad-Houses in Town, and scarcely hear of. Was it worth *Osmin*'s while to be thus Crazy, and are all Lovers to take a Pattern from this *Hero*? I am sorry Mr. *Congreve* was at all this trouble for a Prophane Allusion; but he is positive there's nothing *either of Prophaneness or Immodesty in the Expression*. With *Immodesty* I did not Charge it: But is there nothing of *Profaneness* in bringing the most solemn Things in Religion upon the *Stage*; In making a Mad-man Rave about *Heaven*, and in comparing the disappointments of Love, with *Damnation?* The Lines shall appear once again.

> *O my* Almeria;
> *What do the Damn'd endure but to despair;*
> *But knowing Heaven to know it lost for ever!*
> [ibid., 364–6]

Mr. *Congreve* does not know how *these Verses are a Similitude drawn from the Creed*: I can't help it. I thought the Eternal Punishment of the Damned had been part of the *Creed*. I shan't untie such knots as these are for the future. He tells me *I had but an ill hold of Profaneness in his Play, and was reduced to catch at the Poetry*;

And then makes a miserable jest about *Corruption* and *Generation*. *I had but ill hold of Profaneness!* As ill as 'twas, he has not yet wrested it from me. 'Twas in my Power besides to have taken better, and since he complains of gentle usage, I shall do it.

In the first place, here's frequent Swearing *by Heaven*; I suppose the *Poets* think this nothing, their *Plays* are so much larded with it. But our *Saviour* has given us an other Notion of this Liberty; He charges us *not to Swear at all.* And tells us expressly, that *He that swears by Heaven, swears by the Throne of God, and by him that sits thereon* (St. Mat. 5.34. xxiii. 22.).

To go on to another Branch of his *Irreligion.* The Scene of this *Play* lies in Christendom, as is evident from the History, or Fable; and to mention nothing more from *Osmin*'s Rant: Let us see then how *Osmin* accosts *Almeria*, when he found her safe on Shore: Truly I think their *Meeting* is as extravagant, as their *Parting*, tho Mr. *Congreve* won't allow it should be so. The Ceremony runs thus.

> *Thou Excellence, thou Joy, thou Heaven of Love.*
> [II, ii, 109]

Thus the little successes of a pair of Lovers, are equall'd with the Glories of Heaven; And a Paultry Passion strain'd up to the Beatifick Vision. I say Paltry, for so 'tis upon the Comparison. To go on. *Almeria* having somewhat of the *Play-House* Breeding, is resolved not to be wanting in the return of these Civilities. She therefore makes him a Glorified Saint for the first piece of Gratitude, and then gives him a sort of Power Paramount to *Omnipotence*, and tells him that God Almighty could not make her happy without him.

> I *pray'd* to *thee* as to *a Saint.*
> And *thou* hast *heard* my *Prayer*, for *thou* art *come*
> *To my Distress, to my Despair; which Heaven*
> *Without thee could not Cure.*
> [ibid., ll. 131–4]

Almeria has another Flight, and shews the Rankness of her Wing every jot as much as in the former.

> *'Tis more than Recompence to see thy Face,*
> *If Heaven is greater Joy, it is no Happiness.*
> [ibid., ll. 147–8]

This is Mrs. *Brides* Complement, which both for the Religion and Decency is somewhat Extraordinary.

Manuel, a Christian Prince, upon the news of a Rival, Swaggers at a most Impious rate, *Paganism* was never bolder with *Idols*, nor *Jupiter* more brav'd by the Gyants. It runs thus.

> *Better for him to tempt the Rage of Heaven,*
> *And wrench the Bold red hissing from the Hand*
> *Of him that Thunders, than but think such Insolence,*
> *'Tis daring for a God.*
>
> [ibid., ll. 368–71]

And to make the matter worse, Mr. *Congreve* does not seem to think this Atheistical Sally a fault in *Manuel*. He lets us know he has punish'd him for his Tyranny, but not a word of his Profaneness.

Once more and I have done. *Osmin*'s Caresses of *Almeria* are an Original in their kind.

> *My all of Bliss, my everlasting Life,*
> *Soul of my Soul, and End of all my Wishes.*
>
> [III, i, 304–5]

Here's Ceremony to Adoration; He makes her his Supreme Happiness, and gives her Sovereign Worship: In short, This Respect is the Prerogative of Heaven. 'Tis flaming Wickedness to speak it to any thing less than God Almighty: And to set the Profaneness in the better Light, it runs all in devout Language, and Christian Transport.

I come now to the Vindication of his Poetry: Where in the first place, he Complains extreamly; because I Misquoted *Wasting Air*, for *Wafting Air*. Now to my Mind, the restoring of the Text is a very poor relief. For this later *Epithete* is perfectly expletive and foreign to the matter in hand; there's neither Antithesis nor Perspicuity in't. It neither clears the Sense, nor gives Spirit to the Expression: Besides, the word is almost worn out of use, and were it otherwise, 'twould rather belong to the *Water*; For to *waft* a *Fleet* of *Merchants* is to Convoy them, but not, I suppose, through the Air: So that the *Poët* at best, seems to have mistaken his Element. However, I ask his Pardon for Transcribing an *s*, for an *f*, and expect he should ask mine; for putting *Superstition* upon me, and commenting upon his own Blunder, when 'twas Printed *Supposition* in all the three *Editions* of my Book.

Mr. *Congreve* is now Cruizing for Reprisals, and bears down boldly upon a whole *Period. This litter of Epithets*, &c. He says *this Comparison* of mine *is handsome*. Why, so it may be for all his Disproof: Unless the standing of it in his Book is enough to make it ridiculous. I confess there may be something in that, for bad Company is often a disadvantage; besides, I was Illustrating his fine Sentences, and showing his *Buckram* to the *Reader*: Upon this occasion a little singularity in the Expression was not unseasonable: However I was sensible of it, and introduced it with Qualifying, and Caution.

Mr. *Congreve* in defence of some Lines of his Cited by me, Answers, that the *Diction of Poetry consists of Figures, and the frequent use of Epithets*. I agree with him, but then the *Figures* should be unforc'd, drawn with Proportion, and allyed to the matter in hand. The *Epithets* likewise must be Smooth, Natural and Significant. But when they are lean, and remote from the business, when they look hard and stiff, when they clog and incumber the Sense, they are no great Ornaments. Whether Mr. *Congreve*'s are of this later kind, or not, I shall leave it to the *Reader* to determine!

(pp. 31–8)

(iv) Profaneness in *The Double-Dealer* and *Love for Love*

Mr. *Congreve* perceiving himself press'd retires with all Speed to his Fourth Proposition. But that I have disabled already. If he is poison'd with his Profaneness, and finds himself Sick, he must take what follows; for his Antidote is gone. To return to Sir *Paul*.

I find Passion (says he) *coming upon me by Inspiration, and I cannot submit as formerly*. [*The Double-Dealer*, II, i, 206–8]

You see what an admirable reason he urges in Defence of his Folly, from the extraordinary Circumstances of it! No *Prophet* could have justified his Resentments from a higher pretence.

The fine Lady *Cynthia* out of her pious Education acquaints us, That *though Marriage makes Man and Wife one Flesh, it leaves them still two Fools*. But the little word STILL is left out in the Quotation; which like the Fly on the *Coach-Wheel*, raises a mighty Dust. I grant I have by Chance omitted the word STILL; and if he had done so too, the Sense had been perfectly the same, only better expressed. For *Still* is plainly useless, and comprehended in the Verb *Leaves*. For if *Marriage leaves 'em two Fools*, they are Fools after Marriage, and then they are Fools *Still*, I think; Nothing can be clearer than this. But besides, *Cynthia* her self won't allow of Mr. *Congreve's* excuse. For after she has deliver'd that remarkable Sentence of *leaving 'em two Fools*, &c. *Mellifont* answers, *That's only when two Fools meet*, which is exactly Mr. *Congreve* in his *Amendments*. This *Cynthia* denies to be her meaning. *Cynth. Nay* (says she) *I have known two Wits meet, and by the opposition of their Wits render themselves as ridiculous as Fools*. And therefore after she has given Matrimony an odd Name, she advises him to Court no farther, to *draw Stakes, and give over in time* [ibid., l. 155 ff.]. So that besides Burlesquing the Bible, the Satyr is pointed against Marriage. And the Folly is made to lye in the State, as well as in the Persons. Upon the whole, we see the *Double Dealer*, and the *Amendments* can't agree; and thus two Blemishes, as well as two Beauties, are sometimes unlike to each other. Mr. *Congreve* says, *Ben. Johnson is much bolder in the first Scene of his Bartholomew Fair*. Suppose all that. Is it an excuse to follow an ill Example, and continue an Atheistical practice? I thought Mr. *Congreve in his penetration* might have seen through this Question. *Ben. Johnson* (as he goes on) *makes Littlewit say, Man and Wife make one Fool. I have said nothing comparable to that.* Nothing comparable! Truly in the usual sense of that Phrase, Mr. *Congreve*, 'tis possible, has said nothing comparable to *Ben. Johnson*, nor it may be never will: But in his new Propriety he has said something more than comparable, that is a great deal worse. For though *Littlewit's* Allusion is profane, the words of the *Bible* are spared. He does not Droll directly upon *Genesis*, or St. *Matthew*; Upon God the Son, or God the Holy Ghost: Whereas Mr. *Congreve* has done that which amounts to both. And since he endeavours to excuse himself upon the Authority of *Ben. Johnson*, I shall just mention what Thoughts this Poet had of his profane Liberties, at a time when we have reason to believe him most in earnest. Now Mr. *Wood* reports from the Testimony of a great Prelate then present. 'That when *Ben. Johnson* was in his last Sickness, he was often heard to repent of his profaning the Scriptures in his Plays, and that with Horrour' (Athen. Oxoniens. Vol. 1. p. 519).

Now as far as I can perceive, the Smut and Profaneness of Mr. *Congreve's* Four Plays out-swell the Bulk of *Ben. Johnson's* Folio. I heartily wish this Relation may be serviceable to Mr. *Congreve*, and that as his Faults are greater, his Repentance may come sooner.

Quem secutus es peccantem, sequere pænitentem. (S. Ambro.)

The *Double Dealer* is now done with, and Mr. *Congreve* concludes his Vindication in his usual Strain of Triumph and Assurance.

Love for Love comes at last upon the Board. In this *Play* I blamed him for making a *Martyr* of a Whoremaster: Upon this, he flies immediately for Succour to *Scapula*, and the *Greek Grammar*. He very learnedly tells us, that Martyr is a Greek *word, and signifies in plain English no more than a Witness*. Right! these two words are the same; and when a Cause comes on in *Westminster-Hall*, the *Martyrs* are call'd immediately! But *Martyr* is but bare *Witness* in the Greek. Not always: Christian Writers often use it in a sense appropriated. And were it otherwise, there's no arguing from one Language to another. *Tyrant* was once an Honourable Name in *Greek*, but always a Reproach in *English*. But to dilate upon these Cavils, is throwing away time. If the Reader desires more, he may please to look back on my Answer to his Objection about *Inspiration*.

This *Poet's* way of understanding *English*, puts me in mind of a late Misfortune which happen'd to a Country Apothecary. The Dr. had prescrib'd a Lady Physick to be taken in something Liquid, which the Bill according to Custom call'd a *Vehicle*. The Apothecary being at a Stand about the word, applies, as Mr. *Congreve* might have done, to *Littleton's Dictionary*. And there he finds *Vehiculum* signified several considerable Things. He makes up the *Bill*, and away he goes to the Lady, where upon the Question, how the Physick was to be taken? He answers very innocently; Madam, says he, You may take it in a *Cart*, or a *Waggon*, but not to give your Ladyship too much trouble, I think a *Wheelbarrow* may do; for the word *Vehicle* in the Bill, will carry that sense. In short, This Direction was comply'd with, and the *Footman* drove the *Wheelbarrow* about the Chamber. To return to Mr. *Congreve*. I had said that this Libertine Application of his, was dignifying Adultery with the Stile of Martyrdom; As if (says Mr. *Congreve*) *any word could dignifie Vice*. And pray why not? Does not the Varnish hide the Coarseness underneath, and the Pill go down the better for the Guilding? Whether he knows it or not, there's a great deal of Charm and Imposture in *Words*; and an ill practice is often comply'd with upon the Strength of a Fashionable Name.

He asks, who told me Jeremy Fetch was bred at the University? Why *Jeremy* says so himself pretty plainly, and *Tattle* says so, and I suppose Mr. *Congreve* says as much as that comes to in his

Reflection immediately following. But this notable question was put to introduce another Business of greater Consequence. For upon this occasion, out of *his excellence* of *good Manners*, he is pleased to observe, That *I should not have been suspected of an University Education any more than his Jeremy in the Play, if I had not Printed* M.A. *on the Title Page.* Here the Poor Man has shewn his Will, and his Weakness sufficiently! I'm almost sorry 'tis so low with him. When a Poet is so extreamly well inclin'd to be Witty, 'tis pity he has no more in his power. Mr. *Congreve* goes on Manfully in his Defence and says, *For the word Whoreson, I had it from* Shakespear *and* Johnson. Not unlikely. People are apt to learn what they should not. Mr. *Congreve*'s Memory, or his Invention, is very considerable this way. Indeed one would almost think by his Writings, that he had digested ill Language into a Common Place. But it was not only *Whoreson*, but *Jeremy*'s saying He was Born with *Whoreson Appetites*, which I complain'd of; and which I take to be Blaspheming the Creation.

He pretends I have wrong'd him strangely in a Rant of Sir *Sampson*'s: And would make the Reader believe I charge him literally with Paraphrasing the 139th Psalm. I'm sorry I'm forced to explain my self in so clear a case.

We may observe then, that the Psalmist in Contemplation of the astonishing Beauty and Serviceableness of Humane Bodies, breaks out in a Rapture of Gratitude, *I will give thanks unto thee, for I am fearfully and wonderfully made, marvellous are thy works, and that my Soul knows right well.* Let us now hear Sir *Sampson*. This Gentleman after having railed a Lecture over *Jeremy*'s Body, for being born with Necessities too big for his Condition; he crys, *These things are unacountable, and unreasonable; Why was not I a Bear?—Nature has been provident only to Bears and Spiders* [II, i, 388–92]: Thus we see what a Harmony of Thought there is between *David* and our Author. The one Adores while the other Reproaches. The one Admires, the other Burlesques the wonders of Providence. And this was all the *Paraphrasing* I meant, as any one might easily Imagine.

The Dialogue of *Scandal* and *Foresight* lies next in our way, I shall once more Transcribe it from *Love for Love.*

Fore. Alas Mr. *Scandal*, Humanum est errare.

Scand. You say true, Man *will err; meer* Man *will err—but you are something more—There have been wise Men, but they were such as you—Men who consulted the Stars, and were observers of Omens—* Solomon *was wise, but how? By his Judgment in Astrology,—So says* Pineda in his Third Book and eighth Chap [III, i, 526–32]. But (says Mr. *Congreve*) the *Quotation* of the *Authority* is *omitted* by Mr. Collier, *either because he would* represent *it as my own Observation to ridicule the Wisdom* of Solomon *or else because he was indeed Ignorant that it belong'd to any body else.* To this I answer,

1. That Mr. *Congreve* yields *Solomon's* Wisdom ridiculed by *this Observation*, therefore by his own confession, if 'tis none of his Authors, he must Answer for't himself. Now *Pineda* gives us a quite different account of the Cause of *Solomon's* Wisdom, and which is perfectly inconsistent with *Congreve's* Banter. '*Pineda* affirms that *Solomon's* Wisdom was given him by God in a supernatural Dream mentioned in Scripture. And that after the Dream, he found an unusual Light in his Understanding; his Ideas were brighten'd, and the extent of his Knowledge strangly enlarged (Pined. Lib. 3. Cap. 8. P. 142, 147. Ed. Mogunt.). 'Tis true, *Pineda* believed that *Solomon* understood *Astronomy* in Perfection, and that he had skill in *Prognosticks* which he calls *Astronomia judiciaria* (Lib. 3. C. 18). He continues, that he could in a great measure reach the Inclinations and Reasonings of Men, where they did not depend purely upon choice, and the turn of the *Will*. But then he does not say that *Solomon's* Skill in *Prognosticks* was that which made him *wise*. No: This Tallent was only a Branch, but not the Cause of his Wisdom. For as *Pineda* speaks elsewhere, *Solomon* had a Universal Knowledge of Nature, but then this Excellency was no result of Natural parts, or Humane Industry; 'Twas an immediate Bounty from Heaven; And both the Thing, and the Conveyance, were extraordinary.'

Mr. *Congreve* agrees with *Pineda* at least in a jesting way, *Solomon was wise, but how? By his Judgment in Astrology.* That is, his distinguishing Attainments were gained this way. There was nothing in the case, but that he had looked into a Star somewhat farther than other people: He Learned his Wisdom it seems from the *Caldeans*, or *Ægyptians*, or from some such Book as *Lillies Almanack*. This is *Scandal's* Solution of the Mystery; and the best that I can make on it. For 'tis one thing to say that a Man is *wise* by *Astrology*, and another that *Astrology* or *Astronomy* was only a part of his Wisdom. The one Implies the Cause, and the other but a Branch of the Effect. The one excludes the Miracle, and the other affirms it. Upon the whole matter, Mr. *Congreve*, and *Pineda*, are not to be reconciled, so that by his own confession he has *ridiculed the Wisdom of Solomon*, and falsifyed his Author into the Bargain.

2ly. Supposing *Pineda* had been fairly reported by Mr. *Congreve*, the *Poet* had been much to blame; For then the Case had stood thus; *Pineda* as Mr. *Congreve* observes had ridiculed *Solomon*, and himself had done no less, by Citing him without Censure, and upon a Drolling Occasion. For this reason I waved the consulting of *Pineda*, as well knowing that should the Testimony have been right, the *Play* was certainly in the wrong. Besides, 'tis somewhat to be suspected Mr. *Congreve* never saw *Pineda*; My reason is, because he falls twice into the same Mistake, he Quotes the *Eighteenth* Chapter for the *Eighth*, and to make it appear the more gross, 'tis done in words of Length, and not in Figures. I hope for the future Mr. *Congreve* wont bring in *Solomon* to divert the *Play-House*, nor compare him with Fools and Fortunetellers.

Scandal's telling *Foresight* he was *more than meer Man*, and secure from Mistake upon that Score, is likewise a profane expression. To affirm this of any person, is as much as to say, he is either our *Saviour*, or a *Prophet*, or under some Miraculous Influence.

Scandal goes on with *Foresight*, 'and sayes the Wise Men of the East ow'd their Instruction to a Star, which is rightly observed by *Gregory* the Great in favour of *Astrology*' [ibid., ll. 534–7].

Mr. *Congreve* vindicates this passage by saying, that *Scandal Banters Foresight*, but *not the Audience*. Not Banter the Audience! He affronts the Audience I'm sure, if they have any Christianity in them, by drolling upon a Miracle at our Saviour's Birth: He banters St. *Matthew* too, who has recorded the Miracle, and *Gregory* the Great, who discourses upon it.

Mr. *Congreve* is pleased to say that *I am very angry that Sir Sampson has not another Name*, because *Sampson is a Name in the Old Testament*. This is false in every syllable, as the Reader may see by consulting my Book. But this I say, that Mr. *Congreve* has burlesqu'd the History of *Sampson*, and wrested the *Scripture* into Smut.

There are two other profane Passages Censur'd by me in the same Page: These he leaves as it were to shift for themselves, and has not as yet, made them worse by defending them: Excepting that he comes up with his old Cavil about the Word *Martyr*, which I have answer'd already.

The next Place Mr. *Congreve* leads us to is *Bedlam*: And here he gives us three Reasons for *Valentine*'s pretended Madness. The two later are somewhat extraordinary. He makes him Mad it seems *for a variation of the Character.* A shrewd Contrivance, to put a Man out of his Wits for the sake of Variety? For without doubt, Raving and Incoherence are wonderfully taking. I suppose Mr. *Congreve* made *Bellmour* talk Nonsense for this wise reason. For 'tis a dull thing for a Man to be always tyed up to Sense, and confin'd to his Understanding. His third reason for taking away Reason, is *because Madness gives a liberty to Satyr, and authorises a Bluntness, &c. which would otherwise have been a Breach of Manners in the Character.* That is, it gives *Valentine* a Commission to talk Smut, and abuse his Father. But Mr. *Congreve* needed not to have given himself this trouble about *Valentine*; For *Valentine* when he was in his Wits, and under the Character of a fine Gentleman, had Breeding enough to be Smutty, and Undutiful. Mr. *Congreve* would perswade the Reader that I interpret him with too much Rigour, for making *Valentine* in his Lunacy say, *I am Truth,* &c. If this Point needs any farther Disputing, we may take notice that our Blessed Saviour mentions the word *Truth* in a solemn and peculiar manner. He sometimes applies it to Himself, sometimes to the Holy Ghost, and sometimes to the Revelation of the Gospel. In short, 'tis as it were appropriated to the greatest Persons, and Things, mark'd as the Prerogative of God; and used in a sense of Emphasis and Distinction. Let us compare St. *John*, and Mr. *Congreve* a little, and then we may easily judge where the Fault lies.

St. *Thomas* answers our Blessed Saviour, *Lord we know now not whither thou goest, and how can we know the way? Jesus saith unto him, I am the Way, and the Truth, and the Life* (Joh. 14.6.). Sir *Sampson* is at a loss, Swears, and cries out, *I know not which way to go.* Valentine enquires, *Who's that, that's out of his Way? I am Truth, and can set him right* [IV, 1, 251–2].

Our Saviour assures his Disciples, That he will send them the *Comforter.* And that *when he the Spirit of Truth is come, he will guide you into all Truth, and he will shew you things to come* (Joh. 16.13.).

The execrable *Valentine* says, *Interrupt me not—I'll whisper Prediction to thee, and thou shalt Prophesie. I am Truth, and can teach thy Tongue a new Trick: I am Truth, and come to give the World the Lie* [ibid., ll. 486–8].

And is not this horrible Stuff? What can be more intolerable

Boldness, than thus to usurp the Regal Stile, to prostitute the Language of Heaven, and apply it to Drollery and Distraction?

(pp. 51-64)

(v) Contempt of the clergy in *The Old Batchelour*
Mr. *Congreve* is advanced to my 3*d* Chapter, concerning the Abuse of the Clergy. As for the Dissenting *Ministers*, he says I charge him with nothing more than *Setter's*, procuring their Habit for *Bellmour*. Under favour, this is a great Mistake. The Pimp reads a Lecture of Abuse upon the Habit, exposes *Spintext* from Head to Foot, makes him both a Knave and a Libertine, and his Wife a Whore into the bargain. The *View*, &c. has remark'd, *that Barnaby calls another of that Character Mr. Prig*. He does so. And *Fondlewife* represents him lewd in a luscious Description. Mr. *Congreve* replies, *What if his Name were Mr.* Prig, *or what if it were not?* Now 'tis possible he'll not like it, if I don't consider these weighty Questions. I say then, If his Name was so, he has misbehaved himself by putting him in his *Play*. If 'twere not so, He has used the Dissenting Ministers ill, by representing one of their Order in a contemptuous Manner. For as he himself confesses, a Mr. *Prig, and a Mr. Smirk, are Names implying Characters worthy of Aversion and Contempt*. Now for a Man not to understand his own ill Language, and contradict himself in a few Pages, is, in his own decent expression, *furiously simple*.

Mr. *Congreve* pretends that a Reflection on a *Lord's Chaplain* is no Reflection on a Parson of the Church of *England*. That's somewhat strange. The *Roman* Catholick Lords have no *Chaplains*; the Law does not allow it. And as for the Dissenters, there are very few Lords of their Perswasion. I desire therefore to know upon what Party the Abuse must stick? In earnest, I'm almost tired with answering these things. To strike the Air, does but make a Man's Arm ake.

(pp. 65-6)

(vi) On the language of *The Mourning Bride*
Now though I have examined Mr. *Congreve*'s Writings but loosely upon this Head, yet in return to his Civilities, I shall present the Reader with some Proprieties of His in Phraseology and Sense. In his Amendments we have, To *Savour of Utterance*, &c. And in the *Mourning Bride*, we have all the Delicacies of Language and Rhetorick, and the very Spring it self upon Paper. Here's *Respiring Lips, ample Roof, and ample Knowledge, the Noon of Night, fear'd,* for

frighted, the *pageantry of Souls, Eyes rain Blood*, and what not. To go on a little with the *Mourning Bride*, with reference to Sense and Character.

King *Manuell* asks his Daughter *Almeria*, why she wears Mourning at his Triumph. She tells him, *She mourns for her deliverance from a Wreck*. This was a wise Answer, and a very natural way of expressing her Gratitude for coming safe on Shore.

Gonsalez relates *Manuall*'s Victorious Entry after his Success against the Moors. The Cavalcade is wonderfully Splendid and Pompous: But the Story goes off somewhat unluckily.

> The swarming Populace spread every Wall,
> And cling as if with Claws they did enforce
> Their Hold through clifted Stones stretching and staring.
>
> [I, i, 238–40]

Here he Struts to purpose in *Sophocles*'s Buskins! *Cling* and *Claws* are extreamly magnificent in solemn Description, and strangely proper for Tragedy and Triumph. To give him his due, I think these two Lines are the best Image of a parcel of Cats running up a Wall, that I have met with. That which follows is worth the remembring.

> As they were all of Eyes, and every Limb,
> Would feed his faculty of Admiration.
>
> [ibid., ll. 241–2]

A Limb of an Eye, I confess, is a great Curiosity; And one would think if the *Poet* had any of these Limbs in his Head, he might have discover'd it. We must not forget *Osmin*'s Talent in Arithmetick, who let us understand that

> Heaven can continue to bestow,
> When scanty Numbers shall be spent in telling.
>
> [II, ii, 188–190]

As Scanty as they are, I *fancy Telling* will be spent much sooner than *Numbers*: But Sense in a Tragedy is cold and unaffecting. To go on. *Zarah* makes *Osmin* a high Compliment upon his Air and Complexion: She tells him when she first saw him,

> Pale and expiring, drenched in briny Waves,
>
> [ibid., l. 276]

That he was

God-like even then. [ibid., ll. 280–1]

Death and Paleness are strong Resemblances of a Deity! But I perceive, to some People, a Seraphim, and a drown'd Rat, are just alike. King *Manuell* is giving Sentence upon the Rebels: Let us see how he supports his Character:

> *Bear to the Dungeon those Rebellious Slaves,*
> *The ignoble Curs that Yelp to fill the Cry,*
> *And spend their Mouths in barking Tyranny.*
> [IV, i, 62–4]

And a little after, he calls the Noble *Osmin, that foreign Dog.* Here's Majestick Passion, Royal Vengeance, and magnificent Railing for ye! A Common Hunt could not have done it better! This, as Mr. *Congreve* has it, is *Dog-Language* with a Witness; and never made for a Monarch's Mouth.

Zara has another Flight very remarkable, and with that I shall conclude. This Princess, we must know, was strangely smitten with *Osmin,* and finding her Amour cross'd, was resolv'd, out of stark Love and Kindness, to Poison him: 'Tis true, she intended to be so just, as to dispose of her self the same way. Now coming to the Prison she spies a Body without a Head, and imagining it *Osmin's,* grows distracted upon't. And why so? Was it because she was prevented, and had not the satisfaction of dispatching her Spark her self? Or was it because she had a mind to convince *Osmin* of the strength of her Affection by murthering him? That's somewhat odd. Was it then to shew how willing she was to dye with him? She says so; but presently rejects this reason as frivolous and unnecessary. For if you'll believe her, *Osmin* was capable of knowing her Passion, without so barbarous an Expedient.

> *His Soul still sees, and knows each purpose,*
> *And fixt event of my persisting Faith.*
> [V, ii, 196–7]

Well, Let the reason of her Disorder be what it will, for we can't agree about it, she falls into a most terrible Fit of Fustian, upon the sight of the Body.

> *Ha! prostrate! bloody! headless! O,—start Eyes,*
> *Split heart, burst every Vein at this dire object;*

At once dissolve and flow; meet Blood with Blood,
Dash your encountring Streams with mutual Violence,
Till Surges roll, and foaming Billows rise,
And curle their Crimson Heads to kiss the Clouds!
[ibid., ll. 162–7]

One would think by this Rant, that *Zara* had Bloud enough in her Veins to fill the *Bay* of *Biscay*, or the *Gulph* of *Lions*. At this rate a Man may let the *Thames* out of his little Finger! This is monstrous Impropriety of Thought! Never were Things and Words, joyn'd more unluckily. Call you this Poetry! The Figures and Flights of Poetry are Bold; but then the Fancy should be Natural, the Figures Just, and the Effects hold some proportion with the Cause. *Zara* rises in her Rumbling, if 'tis possible, rails bitterly on the King, in *Astronomy;* And, as far as I can discover, she goes somewhat upon the System of *Copernicus.*

Rain, rain, ye Stars spout from your burning Orbs,
Precipitated Fires, and pour in Sheets,
The blazing Torrent on the Tyrant's Head.
[ibid., ll. 168–70]

Well. Tho this Lady has not much Wit in her Anger, she has a great deal of Learning: I must own, this is a very Scholar-like piece of Distraction. If Mr. *Congreve* replies, the Occasion was extraordinary; and that the fight of *Osmin*'s Murther must mightily affect her. Granting all this, the old Saying will hold good against him: *Curæ leves loquntur, ingentes stupent:* Here *Almeria*'s Fit of Fainting, and a good Swoon at the end on't, would have look'd like Business, and been very Natural upon the occasion. I could have been somewhat larger upon the *Mourning Bride,* but this may suffice at present.

(pp. 91–5)

28. Anon. in *Some Remarks upon Mr. Collier's Defence*

1698

From *Some Remarks upon Mr.* Collier's *Defence of his Short View of the* English *Stage, &c. In Vindication of Mr.* Congreve, *&c. In a letter to a Friend* (London: 1698).

(i)

Mr. *Collier's* Reproofs to me seem inveterate; he writes with Animosity, as if he had an Aversion to the Man as well as his Faults, and appears only pleas'd when he has found a Miscarriage. Who, but Mr. *Collier,* wou'd have ransack'd the *Mourning Bride,* to charge it with Smut and Prophaneness, when he might have sate down with so many Scenes wherein even his malicious Chymistry cou'd have extracted neither? But against this Play, as if the Spirit of Contradiction were his delight, he musters all his Forces; and having passed Sentence as the Divine, commences Critick, and brings the Poetry to his severe Scrutiny, transcribes half Speeches, puts the beginning and end together, as in *Page* 92.

> *Drenched in briny Waves, pale and expiring,*
> *Yet God-like even then.*
>
> [II, ii, 277–81]

His own charming Simile comes next, of a Seraphim and a drown'd Rat: So on the other Leaf he is got to the Image of Cats running up a Wall: Truly (*Frank*) I cannot but impute these abject Thoughts to his own reptile Mind; for I have read the *Mourning Bride* often, and it always inspired me with the noblest Ideas: Then he cavils at *Almeria's* Answer, That she mourns for a Deliverance from the Wreck: This too is a Line taken out of a very probable and modest Reply. And here I conceive Mr. *Collier,* as indeed he has sometimes done before, seems to change his own Opinion; for I shou'd have thought he wou'd have liked *Almeria* better for commemorating her Deliverance in Mourning and Humiliation,

than if she had enjoined Mirth and Revelling, nay, perhaps Plays.
Well, since Mr. *Collier* by his good-will shows nothing but what he
thinks bad in the Play, pray give me leave to transcribe one Speech
amongst many, which sure will stand Mr. *Collier's* Test.

> *I've been too blame, and question'd within piety*
> *The Care of Heaven; not so my Father bore*
> *More anxious Grief; this shou'd have better taught me*
> *This Lesson, in some hour of Inspiration*
> *By him set down, when his pure Thoughts were born*
> *Like Fumes of Sacred Incense o're the Clouds,*
> *And wafted thence on Angels Wings through Ways*
> *Of Light to the bright Source of all. There in*
> *The Book of Prescience he beheld this Day,*
> *And waking to the World and mortal Sense,*
> *Left this Example of his Resignation;*
> *This his last Legacy to me, which I*
> *Will treasure here, more worth than Diadems,*
> *Or all extended Rule of Regal Power.*
>
> [III, i, 125–38]

Now I can pick Instruction and Delight out of this, and rest
satisfied, if in a Tragedy the Passions rise either Love, Anger or
Madness; I can behold them without one Thought of Imitation. It
appears Mr. *Collier* has a very mean Opinion of the Capacity of the
Audience, when he conceives all the Poets Flights will so far affect
them as to practice the same; like *Don Quixote*, who cou'd not read
Romances, but he must turn Knight-Errant. So several Characters
in Comedy, which Mr. *Collier* has fell foul upon, I dare venture to
affirm, the Poet never design'd for Examples; the fulsome *Belinda*
in the *Old Batchellor* (as the cleanly-mouth'd Mr. *Collier* is pleas'd to
call her) is shown full of Affectation; but I find it no where in the
Play commended; and I always thought the Vanity was design'd to
be exposed, not promoted; and if at last she's married to a Libertine
she likes, where's the mighty Happiness? Doth not Fortune daily
produce the same in the World? Are not Fools, and Knaves, and
Villains, often rich, and great, and in appearance happy? Yet this
real Example doth not, I hope, tempt the good Man to forsake his
Vertue for Preferment. What think ye now, dear *Frank*, of the
Viewer? Do ye imagine he had any design to ingratiate himself
with the severer Clergy when he chose this Subject, or to Cajole
the Dissenting Ministers, when he took up their Quarrel, or make

his Court yet higher? Since Plays are not in vogue, as they were the two last Reigns; truly I shrowdly suspect he has a mind to tack about; he can change his Opinion, and be more complaisant if he pleases; witness his soft Usage of Mr. *Dryden*; in the Defence he ranks him amongst the best Criticks; allows him a good Judge in Language, and mentions him, quite contrary to his Custom, with much decency and respect; nay, I believe, shou'd the Old Gentleman become Poet Laureat again, Mr. *Collier* wou'd afford him a Panegyrick, notwithstanding he tells the Author of the *Relapse* he is not very full of them.

No, there I think he is in the right, railing is properly his talent, and that he does with a gust the Christian Religion never inspired; no plea of Youth, no acknowledgment appeases him; thus he makes himself a tinkling Cymbol, who whilst he gingles with his Wit, and joins the Fathers and the Poets in his Citations, forgets the noblest gift of Heaven, *Charity*; proudly Judges and Condemns, finds Guilty or Absolves by his own Authority.

(pp. 6–11)

(ii)

All my Acquaintance that discourse this Matter, are convinced Mr. *Collier* has a particular Pique against Mr. *Congreve*; nay, some will go farther, and guess the Cause; perhaps there may be Lines of that Author's that vex the *Non-Juror* more than all the smutty Jests he has pickt up; Lines that Mourn the Royal *Pastora*; Heroick Lines, that sound the Glory of our Monarch. From this sweet Poetry they judge his Gall is raised; which being gorged and full, overflows, nor spares the dead or living, Friends and Foes, the bitter Deluge reaches and bespatters all.

(p. 17)

29. Charles Gildon in *A Letter to Mr. Congreve, Occasion'd by the Death of the Countess Dowager of Manchester*

1698

From *A Letter to Mr. Congreve, Occasion'd by the Death of the Countess Dowager of Manchester, Late Wife to his Excellency the Right Honourable Charles Montague* (London: 1698).

Charles Montagu had married the widow of his cousin Robert Montagu, Earl of Manchester, in 1688. She died in July 1698. The following extracts invite Congreve to attempt a pastoral elegy emulating his own achievement in 'The Mourning Muse of *Alexis*', written on the death of Queen Mary II. The printed folio is anonymous, but in a manuscript copy, Bodleian MS. Rawlinson Poet. 99, the title page dedication to Montagu is signed by Charles Gildon. The manuscript is undated, and there are minor verbal variants.

Charles Gildon (1665–1724) was himself the author of five plays, and Congreve had contributed five poems to Gildon's *Miscellany Poems on Several Occasions* in 1692. Friend and literary executor to the freethinker Charles Blount, Gildon himself subscribed to deism for some years. In 1714 he attacked Pope as 'Sawney Dapper' in *A new Rehearsal, or Bays the Younger,* which earned him dishonourable mention in *The Dunciad* and An Epistle *To Dr. Arbuthnot.*

(i)

> O *Congreve!* sound again your tuneful Reed,
> To which you sung the great *Pastora* dead.
> How, on thy Verse the Mourning Shepherds hung!
> How blest the Poet! how ador'd his Song!
> Not the *Sicilian*, or the *Mantuan* Bard,
> With juster Wonder, and Delight was heard.
> Thy charming Voice, O *Congreve!* once more raise,
> Another MARY challenges thy Lays.

Again thro' Woods and Vales thy sorrow spread,
Another *Hero* mourns, another *Heroine* dead.

(p. 2)

(ii)

O *Congreve!* here, draw o're an awful Veil, ⎫
No Art can Paint, no mighty Poet tell   ⎬
The *Hero*'s Pangs, and Tortures when she fell. ⎭
From hateful Throngs, and ev'n from Friends he flies,
To lonely Shades, and there, a living Death he dies!
Miser in only this, he hugs his Care,
And with strange Avarice of Woe, denys his Friends a share.

(p. 9)

(iii)

O *Congreve!*———
Now raise thy Voice, now tow'r above the height
Of the *Moeonian*, or the *Mantuan* Flight.
Like *Milton* Soar, like *Milton* too declare
Amazing things, that Man's unus'd to hear,   ⎫
That Ecstasie the ravish'd Soul, through the glad listning Ear. ⎭

(p. 10)

30. Anon. in 'A Session of the Poets'

1698

From *Poems on Affairs of State: From Oliver Cromwell, to this present time. Part III. With other Miscellany Poems; And a new Session of the present POETS. The whole never before Printed* (London: 1698), pp. 307–8.

The 'sessions of the poets', where rivals laid claim to the bays in the presence of Apollo, were a useful vehicle for satire on literary affairs during the Restoration period. The precursor of the form was a poem by Sir John Suckling, which itself derives from Traiano Boccalini's *Ragguagli di Parnasso*.

The next Thought without pleading the Laurel to get
Since by most he'd been told he was *the best Wit*.
The greatest Young Man, rising Sun of the Age,

164

But *Apollo* the Gentleman's heat to asswage,
Proclaim'd if his Writing the Laurel shou'd wear,
Of the Garland he'd have but a very small share.
Since by his Plays, he most plainly descry'd,
He did not much in his own Noddle confide;
But yet him, for one of the Tribe he wou'd own,
If in his next play for his Thefts to attone,
He'd Write a whole Leafe that was truly his own:
But to show he cou'd Write, and recover his Cause,
An Elegy out of his Pocket he draws.
Where he hop'd he shou'd purchase the Bays for this Flight,
  Lost is the Day which had from her its Light,
  For ever lost with her in endless Night:
  In endless Night and Arms of Death she lies,
  Death in Eternal Shades has shut Pastoras *Eyes*.[1]
Concern so Passionate who ever read,
That Dictates nothing, but she's Dead, Dead, Dead![2]
But still of all that fell upon the Queen,
He's least injurious to her Ashes been.
For what he has of Dread *Pastora* Sung,
To *Cloris, Cynthia, Cisly* may belong.

NOTES

1 'The mourning muse of *Alexis*', ll. 73–6.
2 *Romeo and Juliet*, IV, v, l. 24.

31. John Oldmixon in *Reflections on the Stage*

1699

From *Reflections on the Stage, and Mr Collyer's Defence of the Short View* (London: 1699), pp. 14–16.

Reflections on the Stage consists of four critical dialogues; the extract below comes from the first of these. The book was

advertised in *The Post Man* for 2 to 4 May, and dedicated to
Charles Montagu. Its author, John Oldmixon (1673–1742),
had just commenced the first phase of his literary career, as an
undistinguished poet and dramatist; he would later become a
journalist, pamphleteer, and historian, serving the Whig
interest.

A Poet is permitted to shew an *Achilles* or a *Mezentius*, as well as an
Ulysses or an *Æneas*. He may represent Prodigality and Avarice, as
Lawfully as Liberality, and the just oeconomy of a good Husband,
or an honest Citizen. But whatever he does, whether for Virtue or
Vice, or any other indifferent quality, he must know what he is
about, not only because 'tis scandalous for him not to know it, but
because this knowledge will make him manage himself with much
more justness. Thus we see *Bossu*[1] would not have been displeas'd
with *Dorax*'s Rant in *Don Sebastian*.

> Shall I trust Heaven
> With my revenge, then where's my satisfaction?
> No, it must be my own, I scorn a Proxy.
>
> [I, i, 254–6]

He would have consider'd this Bully was a Renegado and a
Mezentius in point of Principles, tho this is not so outrageous as
what that Atheist says in the last Moment of his Life.

> Nec mortem horremus, nec divum parcimus ulli,
> Nor fear I fate, but all the Gods defy.
>
> Vir. Eneid. Dryd. transl.

This judicious Critick, tho a Christian and a Divine, is not so
scrupulous as to throw such lines as these out of a Poem, When he
knows the Character of the man that spake 'em. *Manuel* in the
Mourning Bride is a wicked Prince, and as Mr *Collier* says, swaggers
in these Heroick lines.

> Better for him to tempt the rage of Heaven,
> And wrench the Bolt red hissing from the hand
> Of him that Thunders, than but think such Insolence,
> 'Tis daring for a God.
>
> [II, ii, 368–71]

But *Bossu* wou'd have excus'd this Sally when he found him
punish'd; 'tis true, 'tis not immediately for this, but 'tis for his

Crimes in general, and his Lust and Pride being two of the greatest, our Adversary ought not to have imputed his punishment only to his Tyranny. There are worse passages in *Milton*'s *Paradice lost* than any Mr *Collier* has quoted from the Stage Writers, yet none ever pretended to blame *Milton* for Profaneness.

NOTE

1 René le Bossu, author of *Traité du Poëme épique* (1675).

32. James Drake in *The Ancient and Modern Stages Survey'd*

1699

From *The Ancient and Modern Stages Survey'd* (London: 1699), pp. 214–17.

Dr James Drake (1667–1707) was a Tory controversialist during the reign of Anne, and the author of some medical works. In company with Samuel Garth, Tom Brown, and other wits, he contributed to *Commendatory Verses, on the Author of the Two Arthurs, and the Satyr Against Wit* (1700), a riposte to Blackmore. The work from which the following extract comes is one of the most learned of the replies to Collier. As Drake makes clear, he had already made brief reference to *The Mourning Bride* in his discussion of poetic justice on pp. 108–9.

The next and last Tragedy I shall instance in is the *Mourning Bride*. I have had occasion already to say something of the Observation of Poetick Justice in this Play, but this being the proper place, I shall take it a little more particularly into consideration.

167

The Fable of this Play is one of the most just, and regular that the Stage, either Antient or Modern, can boast of. I mean, for the distribution of Rewards, and Punishments. For no virtuous person misses his Recompence, and no vitious one escapes Vengeance. *Manuel* in the prosecution and exercise of his Cruelty and Tyranny, is taken in a Trap of his own laying, and falls himself a Sacrifice in the room of him, whom he in his rage had devoted. *Gonsalez* villanous cunning returns upon his own head, and makes him by mistake kill the King his Master, and in that cut off, not only all his hopes, but his only Prop and Support, and make sure of his own Destruction. *Alonzo*, his Creature and Instrument, acts by his instructions, and shares his Fate. *Zara*'s furious Temper and impetuous ungovernable Passion, urge her to frequent violences, and conclude at last in a fatal mistake. Thus every one's own Wickedness or Miscarriage determines his Fate, without shedding any Malignity upon the Persons and Fortunes of others. *Alphonso* in reward of his Virtue receives the Crowns of *Valentia* and *Granada*, and is happy in his Love; all which he acknowledges to be the Gift of Providence, which protects the Innocent, and rewards the Virtuous. *Almeria*, whose Virtues are much of the same kind, and who Sympathiz'd with him in his afflictions, becomes a joynt Partner of his Happiness. And *Garcia*, tho a Servant of the Tyrant, and Son of the treacherous, ambitious Statesman, yet executing only his Soveraigns lawful Commands, and being untainted with his Fathers guilt, and his Principles undebauch'd, is receiv'd into *Alphonso*'s favour.

All this as well as the *Moral* is summ'd up so fully, and so concisely in *Alphonso*'s last speech, that 'twere injustice not to give it in the Poets own words.

(*To* Alm.) *Thy Father fell, where he design'd my Death.*
Gonsalez *and* Alonzo, *both of Wounds*
Expiring, have with their last Breath Confest
The just Decrees of Heaven, in turning on
Themselves their own most bloody Purposes...
(*To* Garcia——*O* Garcia
Seest thou, how just the hand of Heaven has been?
Let us, that thro our Innocence survive,
Still in the Paths of Honour persevere,
And not for past, or present ills despair.

For Blessings ever wait on virtuous deeds;
And tho a late, a sure Reward succeeds.

[V, ii, 304–22]

These I think are all the *English* Tragedies, which Mr *Collier* has by name excepted against. Taking therefore our View of the Modern Tragedy from that quarter, which he has alotted to draw a Prospect of it in, I shall leave it to the Reader to judge, whether have raised the more beautiful structures. But if we can with these Forces, which our Enemies have raised for us, make head, and maintain our ground against the united strength of all Antiquity, what might have been done, had we had the listing, and sizing 'em our selves.

33. Charles Hopkins in 'An Epistle from Mr. *Charles Hopkins* to Mr. *Yalden* in Oxon.'

1699

From *Poetical Miscellanies: The Fifth Part* (London: 1704), pp. 185–7.

On Hopkins and Yalden see Nos 13 and 7 above. This poem appeared posthumously but is dated '*From* London-Derry, August 3. 1699'.

Methinks I see the tuneful Sisters ride,
Mounted like Sea-Nymphs on the swelling Tide,
The Silver Swans are silent while they play,
Augusta hears their Notes, and puts to Sea,
Dryden and *Congreve* meet them half the way.
All wafted by their own sweet Voices move,
And all is Harmony—
And all that's Harmony, is Joy and Love.

All are in all the tuneful Numbers skill'd,
And now *Apollo* boasts his Consort fill'd.

Here listen while our *English Maro* sings,
Born like the *Mantuan* Swan on equal Wings:
Mark the great Numbers, mind the lofty Song,
The Sense as clear and just, the Lines as strong.

Hark yonder where the *Mourning Bride* complains,
And melt with pity at the moving Strains:
Wait the Conclusion, then allay your Grief,
Vice meets with Ruin, Virtue with Relief.

34. Charles Gildon in *Lives and Characters of the English Dramatick Poets*

1699?

From *Lives and Characters of the English Dramatick Poets* (London: 1699), pp. 21–5.

On Charles Gildon, see No. 29 above. The following comes from what is both an abridgement and a chronological continuation of Gerard Langbaine's *An Account of the English Dramatick Poets*, which had appeared in 1691.

WILLIAM CONGREVE.

A Gentleman now living, who derives himself from an Ancient Family in *Staffordshire* of that Name. His Politer Knowledge he owes to *Dublin* Colledge, from whence being returned to *England*, his first Applications were to the *Law*. But Mr. *Congreve* was of too delicate a Taste, had a Wit of too fine a turn, to be long pleas'd with that crabbed, unpalatable Study; in which the laborious dull plodding Fellow, generally excells the more sprightly and vivacious Wit; for the Law is something like Preferment at Court, won by Assurance and Assiduity; this concurring with his Natural

Inclinations to Poetry, diverted him from the Bar to the declining Stage, which then stood in need of such a Support; and from whence the Town justly receiv'd him as *Rome's other Hope*.

Rochfoucault truly observes, that Merit alone will never make a Heroe, without the friendly Assistance of Fortune; and therefore Mr. *Congreve* must be said to be as much oblig'd to her for his *Success*, as to Nature for his *Wit*, which truly deserv'd it, and of which all those that read his Plays, must allow him a more than ordinary Share. And indeed he took the most certain way to make sure of *Fortune*, by the Intimacy he contracted with the most active part of the *establish'd* and *receiv'd* Wits and Poets of the Age, before he ventur'd his Reputation to the Publick. For as a celebrated French Writer has observ'd, an Author should never expect to raise his Fame in the World, from an unknown State, by the Single Force of his own Genius, and without the Help and Concurrence of the Men of Wit, that have an Influence over the Opinion of the World in things of that Nature. But then on the other side, it must be confess'd, that his Merit was certainly of more than ordinary Power, to oblige them to forget their habitual *Ill-Nature*; and criminal Emulation or Jealousy (to give it no worse Name) of all those, whom they have any Cause to fear, will once prove any considerable Rivals in their Fickle Mistress, *Fame*. Mr. *Congreve* has already given us Four Plays, of which in their Alphabetical Order.

The Double Dealer, a Comedy, Acted at the Theatre Royal by their Majesties Servants, 1694. *4to.* and Dedicated to the Right Honourable *Charles Montague*, Esq. one of the Lords of the Treasury. This Play not meeting with that Success as was expected, the Author, as Poets are generally apt to do, engages a little too violently in a Defence of his Comedy. The Character of *Maskwell* I take to be an Image of *Vernish* in *The Plain Dealer*.

Love for Love, a Comedy, Acted at the Theatre in *Little Lincolns-Inn-Fields*, by his Majesty's Servants, 1695. *4to.* and Dedicated to the Right Honourable *Charles*, Earl of *Dorset* and *Middlesex*. This Play, tho' a very good Comedy in it self, had this Advantage, that it was Acted at the Opening of the New House, when the Town was so prepossess'd in Favour of the very Actors, that before a Word was spoke, each Actor was Clapt for a considerable Time. And yet all this got it not more Applause than it really deserv'd: For there is abundance of Wit in it, and a great deal of diverting Humour. The Characters are justly distinguish'd, and the Manners well marked. Yet in the Plot he has not given himself the Pains of avoiding that so often repeated Improbability of Marrying in Masques and Disguises, which Mr. *Tattle*, nor Mrs. *Frail* had Sense enough to avoid, if we may judge by the rest of their Characters; yet it must be own'd, that he has much better prepar'd this Incident to gain it, at least some shew of Probability, than in the *Old Batchelor*, or than I have generally met with in other Plays. I leave the nicer Criticks to decide whether the unravelling of the Plot, and the Conduct of *Angelica* in it, be extreamly just or no: I shall only say it pleas'd, and that is a considerable Defence, whatever some may think to the contrary.

The Mourning Bride, a Tragedy, Acted at the Theatre in *Little Lincolns-Inn-Fields*, by His Majesty's Servants, and Dedicated to her Royal Highness the Princess *ANN* of *Denmark*, 1697. *4to* This Play had the greatest Success, not only of all Mr. *Congreve's*, but indeed of all the Plays that ever I can remember on the English Stage, excepting none of the incomparable *Otway's*; and if what Dr. *Blackmore* says of it be true, it deserved even greater than it met with; for the learned Doctor in the Seventh Page of his Preface to *King Arthur*, says thus:

[Quotes no. 19 above.]

Thus far the Learned Doctor, of whom I will not say, as the *Plain Dealer* says of my Lord *Plausible*, That *rather than not Flatter, he will Flatter the Poets of the Age*, &c. Yet I must needs say, so very great a Commendation, will make some of the Censorious Criticks imagine what it was that oblig'd him to take such particular Notice of this Play; which, tho' I should be never so willing to allow a Place in the first Form, yet I can never prefer it to the *All for Love* of Mr. *Dryden*, *The Orphan*, and *Venice Preserv'd* of Mr. *Otway*, or the *Lucius Junius Brutus* of Mr. *Lee*, either in true Art in the Contrivance and Conduct of the Plot; or the Choice and Delineation of the Characters for the true End of Tragedy, *Pitty* and *Terror*; or the *true* and *natural Movement* of the Passions, in which Particular, none of the Ancients (I was going to say equal'd, but I will boldly say) surpass'd our English dead Bards in those Plays, and our living Poet in this of his that I have mention'd. Or the *Diction*, either in regard to its *Propriety, Clearness, Beauty, Nobleness*, or *Variety*. Let any impartial Judge read but *All for Love*, and tell me if there is or can be a Style more Pure, or more Sublime, more adapted to the

Subject in all its Parts: And I believe, notwithstanding all that some Gentlemen have urg'd against the Language in *Otway*'s Plays, it seldom wants any of those Qualities that are necessary to the Perfection of the Piece he has undertaken; he has seldom given us any Persons of Kings or Princes, and if his Stile swell not so much in the Mouths of those of a Lower Degree, whom he has chosen, it was because he had too much regard to the Nature of the Person he introduces. And in *Lee* (with the *Critick's* permission let me speak it) you find always something Wildly Noble, and Irregularly Great; and I am unwilling, with some, to think his Stile puffie or tumid; I'm sure in his Play of *Lucius Junius Brutus* he is generally Just, both in his Thoughts and his Expressions; and it is rather for want of a true Taste of him, than his want of Merit, that he is condemn'd in that Play, I mean, if there be any that do not exempt that from the Faults of his other Plays.

I urge not this as any Reflection on Mr. *Congreve*'s Performance, for which I have all the just Value the Merit of the Play commands; but to do Justice to his great Predecessors on the Stage, at the depressing whose Praise, the Doctor, both in this and his former Preface, seems rather to aim, than at the raising that of Mr. *Congreve*. No, had I a mind to exert the *Critick*, I might, like many other of that Denomination, urge those Defects that either the Malice, or too nice Palate of others have descover'd in the Play it self. But I think 'tis a very ungenerous Office (and not to be excus'd by any thing but some extraordinary Provocation) to dissect the Works of a Man of Mr. *Congreve*'s undoubted Merit, when he has done his Endeavour to please the Town, and so notoriously obtain'd his End; and when the Faults that may perhaps be found in 'em, are of a Nature that makes them very disputable, and in which both his Predecessors and Contemporaries have offended; and I suppose he does not pretend to infallibility in Poetry. But tho' I purposely omit all Critical Reflections, yet the Duty of this Undertaking, and the Foundation I build on, obliges me to examine what he may have borrowed from others; which indeed is not much, tho' the Incident of the Tomb, seems to be taken from the Meeting of *Artaban* and Eliza, at the Tombe of *Tyridates*, in the Romance of *Cleopatra*. And *Zara* has many Features resembling *Nourmahal* in *Aurenge Zebe*, and *Almeria* in the *Indian Emperor*; I know some will have the whole Play a kind of a Copy of that; but I confess I cannot discover likeness enough to justify their Opinion:

unless it be *Zara*'s coming to the Prison to *Osmin*, as *Almeria* does to *Cortez*. I believe our Poet had the *Bajazet* of *Racine* in view, when he formed his Design, at least there is as much Ground for this as the former Opinion. *Perez* resenting the Blow the King gave him, is like an Incident in *Cæsar Borgia*; but the *Spaniard*'s Revenge is more generous, and less cruel than that of the *Italian*.

Thus much for the *Mourning Bride*, of which, if I may be allow'd to speak my impartial Sense, I must needs say, that in spite of its *Excellence*, it discovers Mr. *Congreve*'s *Genius* more inclin'd and turn'd to Comedy, than Tragedy, tho' he has gain'd an uncommon Praise for both; however, it being his first Poem of that Kind, it promises more perfect Products hereafter; and for which all Lovers of Poetry long with Impatience.

Old Batchelor, a Comedy, Acted at the Theatre Royal by their Majesties Servants, and Dedicated to the Right Honourable *Charles* Lord *Clifford*, of *Lanesborough*, 1693. 4*to*. This Comedy was Acted with so general an Applause, that it gave both Fame and Fortune to our Author; at once made him known to the Town, and to an Honourable *Mecænas*; who, to the Satisfaction of all Lovers of Learning, Wit, and Poetry, has ever since prov'd a generous Friend to our Poet. The *Old Batchelor* was usher'd into the World with several Copies of Verses of his Friends, and which the Merit of the Play abundantly justifies: For there's a genteel and sprightly Wit in the Dialogue, where it ought to be; and the humorous Characters are generally within the Compass of Nature, which can scarce be truly said of those of several Poets, who have met with Success enough on the Stage. *Bluff* seems an Imitation of the *Miles Gloriosus* of *Plautus*; of *Bounce* in *Greenwich Park*; and *Hackum* in the *Squire of Alsatia*, &c. The Incident of Sir *Joseph Wittoll*'s Marrying *Sylvia*, and Captain *Bluff*, *Lucy*, in Masques, has been too often an Incident on the Stage, since I'm confident it was scarce ever done in reality. Some other Characters are not entirely new, but that is very excusable in a Young Poet, especially in a Play, which I have been assur'd was writ, when our Author was but Nineteen Years Old, and in nothing alter'd, but in the Length, which being consider'd, I believe few Men that have writ, can shew one half so good at so unripe an Age.

35. Sir Richard Blackmore in *A Satyr* *against Wit*

1699

From *A Satyr against Wit* (London: 1700).

Published in late November with '1700' on the title page, Blackmore's poem was an attack on the wits in general, and an answer to the ridiculing of his poetry in Samuel Garth's *Dispensary*, which had appeared in May the same year. Both men were Whigs, but Blackmore had sided with the apothecaries against Garth and other physicians who wished to open a dispensary to provide medicines for the poor. As the first of the following passages makes clear, a central metaphor of *A Satyr* is the establishment of a mint or exchequer to assay the currency of wit.

(i)

Set forth your Edict, let it be enjoyn'd
That all defective Species be recoyn'd.
St. E[vre]m[on]t and *R[yme]r* both are fit
To oversee the Coining of our Wit.
Let these be made the Masters of Essay,
They'll every Piece of Metal touch and weigh,
And tell which is too light, which has too much Allay.
'Tis true when that the course and worthless Dross
Is purg'd away, there will be mighty Loss.
Ev'n *C[ongrev]e, S[outher]n, Manly W[ycher]ly,*
When thus refin'd will grievous Suff'rers be.

(sig. Cr)

(ii)

V[anbrugh]e and *C[ongrev]e* both are Wealthy, they
Have Funds of Standard-Sense, need no Allay,
And yet mix'd Metal oft they pass away.
The Bank may safely their Subscriptions take,
But let 'em for their Reputation's sake,
Take care their Payments they in Sterling make.

(sig. Ciir)

36. William Congreve, dedication of *The Way of the World*

1700

From *The Way of the World* (London: 1700), sig. A3r–av.

Congreve's dedicatee, Ralph, Earl of Montagu (1638–1709), was second cousin to Charles Montagu. A diplomat and politician, his changes of side during the reigns of Charles and James were remarkable even by the standards of those times. His support for the revolution had secured him his earldom in 1689.

TO THE RIGHT HONOURABLE

RALPH

EARL OF *MOUNTAGUE*, &C

My LORD,

Whether the World will arraign me of Vanity, or not, that I have presum'd to Dedicate this Comedy to your Lordship, I am yet in doubt: Tho' it may be it is some degree of Vanity even to doubt of it. One who has at any time had the Honour of your Lordship's Conversation, cannot be suppos'd to think very meanly of that which he would prefer to your Perusal: Yet it were to incur the Imputation of too much Sufficiency, to pretend to such a Merit as might abide the Test of your Lordship's Censure.

Whatever Value may be wanting to this Play while yet it is mine, will be sufficiently made up to it, when it is once become your Lordship's; and it is my Security, that I cannot have overrated it more by my Dedication, than your Lordship will dignifie it by your Patronage.

That it succeeded on the Stage, was almost beyond my Expectation; for but little of it was prepar'd for that general Taste which seems now to be predominant in the Pallats of our Audience.

Those Characters which are meant to be ridiculous in most of our Comedies, are of Fools so gross, that in my humble Opinion, they should rather disturb than divert the well-natur'd and reflecting part of an Audience; they are rather Objects of Charity than Contempt; and instead of moving our Mirth, they ought very often to excite our Compassion.

This Reflection mov'd me to design some Characters, which should appear ridiculous not so much thro' a natural Folly (which is incorrigible, and therefore not proper for the Stage) as thro' an affected Wit; a Wit, which at the same time that it is affected, is also false. As there is some Difficulty in the formation of a Character of this Nature, so there is some Hazard which attends the progress of its Success, upon the Stage: For many come to a Play, so over-charg'd with Criticism, that they very often let fly their Censure, when through their rashness they have mistaken their Aim. This I had occasion lately to observe: For this Play had been Acted two or three Days, before some of these hasty Judges cou'd find the leisure to distinguish betwixt the Character of a *Witwoud* and a *Truewit*.

I must beg your Lordship's Pardon for this Digression from the true Course of this Epistle; but that it may not seem altogether impertinent, I beg, that I may plead the occasion of it, in part of that Excuse of which I stand in need, for recommending this Comedy to your Protection. It is only by the Countenance of your Lordship, and the *Few* so qualified, that such who write with Care and Pains can hope to be distinguish'd: For the Prostituted Name of *Poet* promiscuously levels all that bear it.

Terence, the most correct Writer in the World, had a *Scipio* and a *Lelius* if not to assist him, at least to support him in his Reputation: And notwithstanding his extraordinary Merit, it may be, their Countenance was not more than necessary.

The Purity of his Stile, the Delicacy of his Turns, and the Justness of his Characters, were all of them Beauties, which the greater part of his Audience were incapable of Tasting: Some of the coursest Strokes of *Plautus*, so severely censured by *Horace*, were more likely to affect the Multitude; such, who come with expectation to Laugh out the last Act of a Play, and are better entertained with two or three unseasonable Jests, than with the artful Solution of the *Fable*.

As *Terence* excell'd in his Performances, so had he great Advantages to encourage his Undertakings; for he built most on the Foundations of *Menander*: His Plots were generally modell'd, and his Characters ready drawn to his Hand. He, copied *Menander*;

and *Menander* had no less Light in the Formation of his Characters, from the Observations of *Theophrastus*, of whom he was a Disciple; and *Theophrastus* it is known was not only the Disciple, but the immediate Successor of *Aristotle*, the first and greatest Judge of Poetry. These were great Models to design by; and the further Advantage which *Terence* possess'd, towards giving his Plays the due Ornaments of Purity of Stile, and Justness of Manners, was not less considerable, from the freedom of Conversation, which was permitted him with *Lelius* and *Scipio*, two of the greatest and most polite Men of his Age. And indeed, the Privilege of such a Conversation, is the only certain Means of attaining to the Perfection of Dialogue.

If it has hapned in any part of this Comedy, that I have gain'd a Turn of Stile, or Expression more Correct, or at least more Corrigible than in those which I have formerly written, I must, with equal Pride and Gratitude, ascribe it to the Honour of your Lordship's admitting me into your Conversation, and that of a Society where every-body else was so well worthy of you, in your Retirement last Summer from the Town: For it was immediately after, that this Comedy was written. If I have fail'd in my Performance, it is only to be regretted, where there were so many, not inferiour either to a *Scipio* or *a Lelius*, that there should be one wanting equal to the Capacity of a *Terence*.

If I am not mistaken, Poetry is almost the only Art, which has not yet laid claim to your Lordship's Patronage. Architecture, and Painting, to the great Honour of our Country, have flourish'd under your Influence and Protection. In the mean time, Poetry, the eldest Sister of all Arts, and Parent of most, seems to have resign'd her Birth-right, by having neglected to pay her Duty to your Lordship; and by permitting others of a later Extraction, to prepossess that Place in your Esteem, to which none can pretend a better Title. Poetry, in its Nature, is sacred to the Good and Great; the relation between them is reciprocal, and they are ever propitious to it. It is the Privilege of Poetry to address to them, and it is their Prerogative alone to give it Protection.

This receiv'd Maxim, is a general Apology for all Writers who Consecrate their Labours to great Men: But I could wish at this time, that this Address were exempted from the common pretence of all Dedications; and that as I can distinguish your Lordship even among the most Deserving, so this Offering might become

remarkable by some particular Instance of Respect, which shou'd
assure your Lordship, that I am, with all due Sense of your extream
Worthiness and Humanity,

My LORD,
Your Lordship's most obedient
and most oblig'd humble Servant,
Will. Congreve.

37. Samuel Wesley in *An Epistle to a Friend concerning Poetry*

1700

From *An Epistle to a Friend concerning Poetry* (London: 1700),
p. 19.

Samuel Wesley (1662–1735) was the father of John, the
founder of Methodism. His family intended him for the
independent ministry and he was sent to a dissenting
academy, but his admiration for John Tillotson led him to
take orders in the established church. Wesley's poetic *magnum
opus* was a heroic poem in ten books on the life of Christ,
published in 1693. *An Epistle* is interesting in that it combines
praise of Blackmore with qualified admiration for Congreve
and Dryden, who are both censured for the immoral
tendencies of their writings.

> CONGREVE from *Ireland* wond'ring we receive,
> Would he the *Town's loose way* of Writing leave,
> More Worth than all their Forfeit Lands will give:
> *Justness* of *Thought*, a *Courtly Style*, and clear,
> And well-wrought *Passions* in his *Works* appear:
> None knows with *finer Strokes* our Souls to move,
> And as he please we *smile*, or *weep*, or *love*.
> When *Dryden* goes, 'tis he must fill the *Chair*,
> With Congreve *only* Congreve *can compare*.

179

Yet, tho he *natural* is as untaught Loves,
His *Style* as *smooth* as *Cytherea*'s Doves,
When e'er unbyass'd *Judges* read him o'er,
He sometimes *nodds*, as *Homer* did before:
Some Lines his most *Admirers* scarce would please,
Nor B[*lackmore*]s Verse alone could *raise Disease*.

38. Samuel Cobb in *Poetae Britannici*

1700

From *Poetae Britannici. A Poem* (London: 1700), p. 22.

A prolific translator and poet, Samuel Cobb (1675–1713) was
orphaned young and educated at Christ's Hospital. After
graduating from Trinity College, Cambridge, he returned to
the school as an 'under grammar master' in 1702 and remained
there until his death. A revised version of *Poetae Britannici*,
retitled 'Of Poetry. A Poem', was included in Cobb's *Poems
on several Occasions* of 1707.

This *Congreve* follows in his deathless Line,
And the tenth hand is put to the Design.
The happy boldness in his finish'd toil,
Smells more than *Sh[akespea]r*'s Wit, or *J[ohnso]n*'s Oil.
Sing, sing, harmonious Swan, in weeping Strains,
And tell *Pastora*'s Death to mournful Swains:
Or with more pleasing Charms, with softer Airs,
Sweeten our Passions, and delude our Cares.
To Noble *D[orse]t* bear thy Lyrick Song,
D[orse]t, round whom the crouding Muses throng.
Or let thy Satyr grin with half a smile,
And jeer in easie *Eth[ere]ge*'s style.
Let manly *W[ycher]ly* chalk out the way,
While Art directs where Nature goes astray.
'Tis not for Thee to write of conquering Kings,
The noise of Arms will break thy Peaceful Strings.
The *Teian* Muse invites Thee from above,
To lay thy Trumpet down, and sing of Love.

39. Daniel Kenrick in *A New Session of the Poets, Occasion'd by the Death of Mr. Dryden*

1700

From *A New Session of the Poets, Occasion'd by the Death of Mr. Dryden* (London: 1700), pp. 6–8.

This poem first appeared in an anonymous folio edition in September 1700. It was reprinted in 1721 in *The Grove; or, a Collection of Original Poems, Translations, &c.*, edited by Lewis Theobald, as one of several 'Posthumous Pieces' by 'Dr. Kenrick'. Theobald's preface (p. iv) describes Kenrick as being essentially an amateur in poetry, and as holding degrees in both medicine and divinity. Not much else is known about him, except that he was born *c.* 1652, was educated at Christ Church, Oxford, and for a time at least practised medicine at Worcester.

> Stiff, as his Works, th' elab'rate *Cong[re]ve* came,
> Who could so soon Preferment get, and Fame.
> And with him brought the Product of his Pen,
> Miss *Prue* before, behind his Back stood *Ben*:
> Who quickly found the *Foible* of the Town,
> When ev'ry thing that *Dogget*[1] did went down.
> His *Double Dealer* at a distance stood,
> At once extreamly regular, and lew'd.
> While in Procession by their Parent's Side
> March't the *Old Batchelour* and *Mourning Bride*.
> Then, at *Apollo*'s Feet his Labours laid,
> Thus to his Sire with good assurance said:
> If, bright *Apollo*, Young to gain renown,
> And please each Palate in this Ticklish Town,
> Has been my Talent still, and mine alone;
> Your Godship must the Laurel needs allow
> Of all your Sons, the best to suit my Brow:
> This Truth the Under-Graduates all confess

181

Of both the Famous Universities.
And who so fit to be great *Dryden*'s Heir,
As he, who living did his Empire share?
This said, he bow'd, and bluffishly sate down;
Whilst thus the God harangu'd his hopeful Son.
How can you from those Bards expect the Bays,
Who him that wore 'em, could so sadly praise?
Those Princes Titles justly we suspect,
Whom the unthinking, giddy Mob elect.
If on you headlong hurry with the Herd,
Arthur to *Absolom*, will be preferr'd:
All-pleasing *Garth*, to *Milbourn* must give place,
And Med'cine leave the Throne of Wit, for Grace.
E're at the Wreath you reach, all else excell:
You write correct, but *Southern* writes as well.
Avoid Bombast, still the Sublime pursue,
By Merit rise, and not by *Mon[ta]gue*:
Take Nature for your Guide; and when I see
You up to *Otway* come, or *Wicherly*,
You'll find your pretty Parts may be preferr'd,
And time, the Bays may get you, and a Beard.

NOTE

1 Thomas Dogget, the famous comic actor who played the original
Fondlewife in *The Old Batchelour*, and Ben in *Love for Love*.

40. Anon. in *An Epistle to Sir Richard Blackmore*

1700

From *An Epistle to Sr. Richard Blackmore, Occasion'd by* The
New Session of the Poets (London: 1700), p. 7.

This poem is a riposte to No. 39 above. It begins with praise
of Blackmore and, rather strikingly because a dozen years

before the publication of his *Creation*, the divinely made natural world as a theme for poetry. There follows an unrestrained attack on the author of *The New Session*, Dryden, and his followers; Samuel Garth and Congreve's patron Montagu are special targets for abuse. The poem ends with an appeal for further reform of the stage and Collier receives a brief but highly favourable mention.

His mighty *Dr[yde]n* to the Shades is gone,
And *Con[gre]ve* leaves Successor of his Throne:
Tho long before his final *Exit* hence
He was himself an abdicated Prince,
Disrob'd of all Regalities of State,
Drawn by a *Hind* and *Panther* from his Seat:
Heir to his Plays, his Fables and his Tales,
Con[greve] is the *Poetick Prince of Wales*;
Not at *St. Germains*, but at *Will*'s his Court,
Whither the Subjects of his Dad resort;
Where Plots are hatch'd, and Councils yet unknown,
How young *Ascanius* may ascend the Throne,
That in despite of all the *Muses* Laws
He may revenge his injur'd Father's Cause.

41. Richard Steele, 'Epistle to Mr. Congreve, occasion'd by his Comedy call'd *The Way of the World*'

1701

From *A New Collection of Poems*, ed. Charles Gildon (London: 1701), pp. 335–9.

The following is the original version of a poem written between the production of Congreve's play in early March 1700, and early 1701 when it was printed in a miscellany of poems compiled by Charles Gildon, *A New Collection of Poems on Several Occasions*. It next appeared in Abel Boyer's *Letters of Wit, Politicks and Morality*. The final version of the poem appeared in Congreve's collected *Works* of 1710, and again in Steele's *Poetical Miscellanies* of 1714, which carried a dedication to Congreve. It may be found in *The Occasional Verse of Richard Steele*, ed. Rae Blanchard (Oxford: Clarendon Press, 1952), pp. 77–8.

EPISTLE

TO

MR. CONGREVE,

OCCASION'D BY HIS

COMEDY

CALL'D,

THE WAY OF THE WORLD.

BY MR. *STEELE.*

When Pleasure is fallen to the low delight,
In the vain Joys of the uncertain Sight,

No sense of Wit when rude Spectators know,
But in distorted Gesture, Farce and Show;
How could, Great Author, thy Aspiring mind
Dare to Write only to the few refin'd!
Yet tho' that Nice Ambition you pursue,
'Tis not in *Congreve*'s power to please but few,
Implicitly devoted to his fame,
Well-dress't Barbarians know his awful Name;
Tho' senseless they're of Mirth, but when they Laugh,
As they feel Wine, but when till Drunk they Quaff.

    Forgotten Author's, who have lately Writ,
Despair now to revive their fame of Wit;
Hard fate, that all Poetick hopes are fled,
Spite of that help to Glory being Dead;
On thee from fate, a lavish portion fell
In ev'ry way of Writing to excell.
Thy Muse applause to *Arabella* brings,
In Notes as sweet as *Arabella* Sings.[1]
When e're you sigh an undissembled Woe,
With sweet distress your rural Numbers flow,
Pastora's the Complaint of ev'ry Swain,
Pastora still the Eccho of the plain!
Or if thy Muse describe with warming force,
The Wounded French-man falling from his Horse;
And her own *William* glorious in the strife,
Bestowing on the prostrate Foe his Life.[2]
You the great Act as generously rehearse,
And all the English fire is in thy Verse:
By thy selected Scenes and handsome Choice,
Ennobled Comedy exalts her Voice;
You check unjust Esteem and fond desire,
And teach to Scorn, where else we should Admire;
The just Impression taught by thee we hear,
The Player Acts the World, the World the Player,
Whom still the World, unjustly disesteems,
Tho' he, alone, professes what he seems;
But when thy Muse assumes her Tragick part,
She Conquers and she Reigns in ev'ry Heart;
To mourn with her Men cheat their private Woe,
And generous pity's all the Grief they know;
The Widow, who impatient of delay,
From the Town-joys must Mask it to the Play,
Joyns with thy Mourning-Bride's resistless moan,

And Weeps a loss she slighted, when her own;
You give us Torment, and you give us Ease,
And vary our Afflictions as you please;
Is not a Heart so kind as yours in pain,
To load your Friends with care you only feign;
Your Friends in Grief, compos'd your self to leave,
But 'tis the only way you'll e're deceive?
Then still great Sir, your moving power employ,
To lull our Sorrow and Correct our Joy.

NOTES

1 Congreve's poem 'Upon a Lady's Singing. Pindarick Ode', which first
appeared in Charles Gildon's *Miscellany* in 1692. It was reprinted the
following year in Dryden's *Examen Poeticum: being the Third Part of
Miscellany Poems*, retitled 'On Mrs. Arabella Hunt Singing. A Pindarique
Ode'.
2 See 'A Pindarique Ode, Humbly Offer'd to the King On His Taking
Namure' (1695).

42. Anon. in *A Comparison between the Two Stages*

1702

From *A Comparison between the Two Stages* (London: 1702).

This lively critical dialogue takes place between two gentlemen, Ramble and Sullen, and a critic named Chagrin. The
two stages of the title are the Theatre Royal in Drury Lane
and the rival house in Lincoln's Inn Fields which had been
established by Thomas Betterton and other dissatisfied
players. The latter had opened in the spring of 1695 with
Congreve's *Love for Love*, and its survival was due in no small
measure to his subsequent plays. *A Comparison* is a wide-
ranging piece, although nearly a third of it is taken up with an

'Examen' of Bevil Higgons's *The Generous Conqueror*. The attribution to Charles Gildon is no longer accepted; for a discussion of the authorship, see Staring B. Wells, 'An eighteenth century attribution', *Journal of English and Germanic Philology* (1939), 38: 239–46.

(i)

Sull. I can't directly charge that on *Dryden*, because as some say, that was a trick of his to suppress Mr. *Creech*'s growing Reputation; so for ought I know, it may be their envy to suppress *Dryden*'s; but this I know, that he has publickly Panegyrick'd one Author with the *Old Batchelor*, another with the *Relapse*, and Mr. *Southern* very frequently and on all occasions; and yet I have seen him bite his Nails for Vexation that they came so near him.

Crit. Two of those three you've nam'd have oblig'd us with better Comedies than any of his; and tho' Mr. *Congreve*'s Reputation arises from his first, third and fourth Play, yet I must needs say, that according to my taste, his second is the best he ever writ.

Ramb. If you mean the *double Dealer*, you go against the Opinion of all the Town.

Crit. I can't help that; I'll follow my own Judgment as far as it will carry me, and if I differ from the Voice of the crowd, I shall value my self the more for my Sincerity: But you're mistaken, all the Town was not of that Opinion; some good Judges were of another; but without being byass'd or prejudic'd, I do take the *Double Dealer* to be among the most correct and regular Comedies: Mr. *C.* intended it so, and it cost him unusual Labour to do't; but as he says, he has been at a needless Expence, and the Town is to be treated at a cheaper rate: But with all Mr. *Congreve*'s Merit, I don't take his Characters to be always natural; even in the *Double Dealer* some are out of probability, one in his *Old Batchelor*, and several in *Love for Love* obsolete.

Sull. We shall be glad you'll convince us of that; for as yet I have not heard that objected.

Crit. Whenever you please Gentlemen.

Ramb. Why not now?

Crit. My time's expir'd; I have an Appointment at Four in a Ladies Chamber; and I love to be punctual in such a Case.

Sull. Methinks you'll carry but little good Humour with you to the Lady; this discourse has put you into a kind of ferment.

Crit. Then I'll go and work it off there; at six I'll meet you at *Lincolns-Inn-fields* Play-House.

Sull. What Play is't?

Ramb. The way of the World, with the new wonder *Madam D'Subligny*.

(pp. 65–7)

(ii)

Sull. You forget what we propos'd at our first meeting.

Crit. What's that?

Sull. To consider some things of the Author's who writ the *Mourning Bride*: How d'ee stand inclin'd to that now?

Crit. I am tir'd with the Drudgery of my Office: Besides my Forces are so weaken'd already, I have not strength enough left to incounter such a gigantick Author.

Ramb. What, not *The way o' the World*? as weak as I am, I dare appear against that.

Sull. 'Tis not so easy a matter as you imagine: That Comedy cost Mr. *Congreve* (as some say) two Years study.

Ramb. I have known a better writ in a Month; *Ben's Fox* was begun and finish'd in that time: *Shadwel's Libertine* was writ in One and twenty Days; nay, I have seen a very modern Comedy which the Author says he writ in ten Days.

(pp. 195–6)

43. Anon. in *The Tryal of Skill*

1704

From *Poems on Affairs of State: Augustan Satirical Verse, 1660–1714*, ed. George deF. Lord and others, 7 vols (New Haven, Conn.: Yale University Press, 1963–75), VI, *1697–1704*, ed. Frank H. Ellis, 1970, pp. 705–6.

The full title of this poem reads *The Tryal of Skill: or, A New Session of the Poets. Calculated for the Meridian of Parnassus, In the Year, MDCCIV.* The extract below jibes at Congreve's intimacy with the celebrated actress Anne Bracegirdle, and his share in the writing of *Squire Trelooby*, a play now lost but acted early in 1704. It was an adaptation of Molière's *Monsieur de Pourceaugnac*, Congreve's collaborators being Vanbrugh and Dryden's former protégé, William Walsh. The Yale editor suggests as a possible author of *The Tryal of Skill* William Pittis.

When *Congreve* brim full of his Mistresses Charms,
  Who had likewise made bold with *Molier*,
Came in piping hot from his *Bracegirdle*'s Arms,
  And would have it his Title was clear.

What he rendred in English, was nothing like *Smut*;
  For he wisely had taken his Choice;
And though the first Act in this Version might not,
  Yet his Prudence should give him their Voice.

Said *Apollo*, You did most discreetly to take
  A Part that was easiest and best;
Though the Rules of Behaviour Distinction should make,
  And you'd not done amiss to chuse last.

But never pretend to be Modest or Chast,
  Th' Old Batchelor speaks you Obscene,
And *Love for Love* shews, notwithstanding your hast,
  That your Thoughts are Impure and Unclean.

That meaning's Lascivious your Dialogues bear,
  Fit to grace the foul Language of *Stews*,
And though you are said to make a Wife of a Play'r,
  You in those make a Whore of your Muse.

                  (ll. 481–500)

44. Richard Steele on *The Old Batchelour* and 'Doris'

1709–13

The two extracts from *The Tatler* are quoted from *The Lucubrations of Isaac Bickerstaff Esq;*, 4 vols (London: 1710–11): (a) I, p. 76, misnumbered 68; (b) IV, p. 20. Extract (c) is quoted from *The Spectator*, ed. Donald F. Bond, 5 vols (Oxford: Clarendon Press, 1965), III, pp. 585–6. The text of (d) is taken from *Poetical Miscellanies.* (London: 1714), sig. A2r–A5v. The latter was actually published on 29 December 1713.

(a) From *The Tatler* No. 9, Thursday 28 April to Saturday 30 April 1709.

This Evening we were entertained with *The Old Batchelor*, a Comedy of deserved Reputation. In the Character which gives Name to the Play, there is excellently represented the Reluctance of a battered Debauchee to come into the Trammels of Order and Decency: He neither languishes nor burns, but frets for Love. The Gentlemen of more regular Behaviour are drawn with much Spirit and Wit, and the *Drama* introduced by the Dialogue of the first Scene with uncommon, yet natural, Conversation. The Part of *Fondlewife* is a lively Image of the unseasonable Fondness of Age and Impotence. But instead of such agreeable Works as these, the Town has this half Age been tormented with Insects called *Easie Writers*, whose Abilities Mr. *Wycherly* one Day described excellently well in one Word: *That*, said he, *among these Fellows is called* Easy Writing, *which any one may easily write.*

(b) From *The Tatler* No. 193, Saturday 1 July to Tuesday 4 July 1710.

I had hardly entered the Room, when I was accosted by Mr. *Thomas Dogget*, who desired my Favour in Relation to the Play which was to be acted for his Benefit on *Thursday*. He pleased me in saying it was *The Old Batchelor*, in which Comedy there is a necessary Circumstance observed by the Author, which most other

Poets either overlook or do not understand, that is to say, the Distinction of Characters. It is very ordinary with Writers to indulge a certain Modesty of believing all Men as witty as themselves, and making all the Persons of the Play speak the Sentiments of the Author, without any manner of Respect to the Age, Fortune, or Quality, of him that is on the Stage. Ladies talk like Rakes, and Footmen make Similes: But this Writer knows Men, which makes his Plays reasonable Entertainments, while the Scenes of most others are like the Tunes between the Acts. They are perhaps agreeable Sounds, but they have no Idea's affixed to them.

(c) From *The Spectator* No. 422, Friday 4 July 1712.

After these several Characters of Men who succeed or fail in Raillery, it may not be amiss to reflect a little further what one takes to be the most agreeable Kind of it; and that to me appears when the Satyr is directed against Vice, with an Air of Contempt of the Fault, but no ill Will to the Criminal. Mr. *Congreve's Doris* is a Master-piece in this Kind. It is the Character of a Woman utterly abandoned, but her Impudence by the finest Piece of Raillery is made only Generosity.

> *Peculiar therefore is her Way,*
> *Whether by Nature taught,*
> *I shall not undertake to say,*
> *Or by Experience bought.*
>
> *For who o'er Night obtain'd her Grace,*
> *She can next Day disown,*
> *And stare upon the strange Man's Face,*
> *As one she ne'er had known.*
>
> *So well she can the Truth disguise,*
> *Such artful Wonder frame,*
> *The Lover or distrusts his Eyes,*
> *Or thinks 'twas all a Dream.*
>
> *Some censure this as lewd or low,*
> *Who are to Bounty blind;*
> *But to forget what we bestow,*
> *Bespeaks a noble Mind.*

['Doris', ll. 49–64]

(d) Dedication of *Poetical Miscellanies*

TO

MR. *CONGREVE*.

SIR,

MY Name, as Publisher of the following Miscellanies, I am sensible, is but a slight Recommendation of them to the Publick; but the Town's Opinion of them will be raised, when it sees them address'd to Mr. *Congreve*. If the Patron is but known to have a Taste for what is presented to him, it gives an hopeful Idea of the Work; how much more, when He is an acknowledg'd Master of the Art He is desired to Favour? Your just Success in the various Parts of Poetry, will make Your Approbation of the following Sheets a Favour to many Ingenious Gentlemen, whose Modesty wants the Sanction of such an Authority. Men of your Talents oblige the World, when they are studious to produce in others the Similitude of their Excellencies. Your great Discerning in distinguishing the Characters of Mankind, which is manifested in Your Comedies, renders Your good Opinion a just Foundation for the Esteem of other Men. I know, indeed, no Argument against these Collections, in Comparison of any other *Tonson* has heretofore Printed; but that there are in it no Verses of Yours: That gentle, free, and easie Faculty, which also in Songs, and short Poems, You possess above all others, distinguishes it self where-ever it appears. I cannot but instance Your inimitable *DORIS*, which excels, for Politeness, fine Raillery, and courtly Satyr, any Thing we can meet with in any Language.

Give me leave to tell You, that when I consider Your Capacity this Way, I cannot enough Applaud the Goodness of Your Mind, that has given so few Examples of these Severities, under the Temptation of so great Applause, as the ill-natured World bestows on them, tho' addressed without any Mixture of Your Delicacy.

I cannot leave my Favourite *DORIS*, without taking Notice how much that short Performance discovers a True Knowledge of Life. *DORIS* is the Character of a Libertine Woman of Condition, and the Satyr is work'd up accordingly: For People of Quality are seldom touched with any Representation of their Vices, but in a Light which makes them Ridiculous.

As much as I Esteem You for Your Excellent Writings, by which You are an Honour to our Nation; I chuse rather, as one that has passed many Happy Hours with You, to celebrate that easie

Condescention of Mind, and Command of a pleasant Imagination, which give You the uncommon Praise of a Man of Wit, always to please, and never to offend. No one, after a joyful Evening, can reflect upon an Expression of Mr. *Congreve*'s, that dwells upon him with Pain.

In a Man capable of Exerting himself any Way, this (whatever the Vain and Ill-natured may think of the Matter) is an Excellence above the brightest Sallies of Imagination.

The Reflection upon this most equal, amiable, and correct Behaviour, which can be observed only by your intimate Acquaintance, has quite diverted me from acknowledging your several Excellencies as a Writer; but to dwell particularly on those Subjects, would have no very good Effect upon the following Performances of my Self and Friends: Thus I confess to You, your Modesty is spared only by my Vanity, and yet I Hope You will give me leave to indulge it yet further, in telling all the World, I am, with great Truth,

SIR,

Your most Obedient, and
most Humble Servant,

RICHARD STEELE.

45. John Dennis in *Remarks upon Mr. Pope's Translation of Homer*

1717

From *The Critical Works of John Dennis*, ed. E.N. Hooker, 2 vols (Baltimore, Md: Johns Hopkins University Press, 1943), II, pp. 121–2.

The following tribute occurs in Dennis's hostile critique of Pope's Homer, which, perhaps not coincidentally, had been dedicated to Congreve. Dennis's animosity towards Pope does not seem to have soured his relations with Congreve, who for his part remained on good terms with both men.

There is a Gentleman, the living Ornament of the Comick Scene, who after he had for several Years entertain'd the Town, with that Wit and Humour, and Art and Vivacity, which are so becoming of the Comick Stage, produc'd at last a Play, which besides that it was equal to most of the former in those pleasant Humours which the Laughers so much require, had some certain Scenes in it, which were writ with so much Grace and Delicacy, that they alone were worth an entire Comedy. What was the Event? The Play was hiss'd by Barbarous Fools in the Acting; and an impertinent Trifle was brought on after it, which was acted with vast Applause. Which rais'd so much Indignation in the foresaid Writer, that he quitted the Stage in Disdain, and Comedy left it with him. And those nice great Persons, whose squeamish Palates rejected Quails and Partridges, have pin'd ever since in such a Dearth, that they greedily feed upon Bull-Beef.

Thus have I set before the Readers Eyes, in as short a Method as I could, the cruel Treatment that so many extraordinary Men have received from their Countrymen for these last hundred Years. If I should now shift the Scene, and show all that Penury, and that Avarice chang'd all at once to Riot and Profuseness, and more squander'd away upon one Object, than would have satisfied the greater part of those extraordinary Men, the Reader to whom this one Creature should be altogether unknown, would fancy him a Prodigy of Art and Nature, would believe that all the great Qualities of those extraordinary Persons were centred in him alone; that he had the Capacity and Profoundness of BACON, the fine Painting of SPENSER, the Force and Sublimity, and Elevation of MILTON; the fine Thinking and Elegance, and Versification of DRYDEN; the Fire and Enthusiasm of LEE; the moving melting Tenderness of OTWAY; the Pleasantry of BUTLER; the Wit and Satire of WYCHERLEY; and the Humour and Spirit, and Art and Grace of C——.

46. Richardson Pack in '*Of* STUDY'

1719

From *Miscellanies in Verse and Prose* (London: 1719), p. 95.

Major Richardson Pack (1682–1728) was a veteran of the War of the Spanish Succession. His *Miscellanies* were published by Edmund Curll. The 'Essays on *Study* and *Conversation*' are in the form of letters addressed to 'D.C.', his friend Captain David Campbell.

CONGREVE of all the Moderns, seems to me, to have the rightest Turn for *Comedy*. In all his Plays there is a great deal of Lively and Uncommon Humour, and such as yet, for the most part, is a Picture of true Life. Besides, he hath raised the Vein of *Ridicule*, and made the Stage, which had been too much prostituted to the Mob, *edifying* to Persons of the first Condition. And as his Fable is Diverting, so is it wrought according to the strictest Rules.

47. Giles Jacob in *The Poetical Register*

1719

From *The Poetical Register: or, the Lives and Characters of the English Dramatick Poets. With an Account of their Writings*, 2 vols (London: 1719–20), I, pp. 41–6.

Giles Jacob (1686–1744) was a prolific compiler of books, mostly legal works. Consequently he was lampooned as 'mighty *J——b* Blunderbus of Law' in the 1728 *Dunciad*, III, 157, after provoking Pope by adverse comments on *Three Hours after Marriage*. The Preface to *The Poetical Register* acknowledges Congreve's 'free and early Communication of what relates to himself, as well as his kind Directions for the Composing of this Work' (sig. A7r).

Mr. *Congreve*, notwithstanding he has justly acquir'd the greatest Reputation in Dramatick Writings, is so far from being puff'd up with Vanity (a Failing in most Authors of Excellency) that he abounds with Humility and good Nature. He does not shew so much the Poet as the Gentleman; he is ambitious of few Praises, tho' he deserves numerous Encomiums; he is genteel and regular in Oeconomy, unaffected in Behaviour, pleasing and informing in his Conversation, and respectful to all. And as for his Talents in Dramatick Poetry, I shall omit a Description of the Beauty of his Dialogue, Fineness of his Humour, and other particulars; and confine what I have to say in the smallest Compass of Poetical Expression.

> *As rising Sparkles in each Draught of Wine,*
> *So Force of Wit appears in ev'ry Line.*

Mr. *Congreve* has oblig'd the World with the following Plays.

I. *The Old Batchelor*, a Comedy, acted at the Theatre Royal, in the Year 1693. Dedicated to the Right Honourable *Charles* Lord *Clifford*. This Comedy was acted with a general Applause, and was introduc'd into the World with several Copies of Verses, which it justly merited, tho' the Author was then not above nineteen Years of Age; and it not only made him known to the Town, and a noble *Mecaenas,* but was honour'd with the Presence of the beautiful and virtuous Queen *Mary*: And Mr. *Congreve*, in return of Gratitude, wrote one of the finest Pastorals we have in the *English* Language, on the lamented Death of that incomparable Princess. There's a genteel and sprightly Wit in the Dialogue of this Play; and the humorous Characters are agreeable to Nature, which can be said of few other Dramatick Performances; yet the Criticks attack him for the Incidents of Marriages in Masks, as being scarce ever done in reality.

II. *The Double Dealer*, a Comedy, acted at the Theatre Royal, 1694. Dedicated to the Right Honourable *Charles Montague*, Esq; one of the Lords of the Treasury. This Play did not meet with the Encouragement as the former; neither had it equal Success with any of Mr. *Congreve's* latter Dramatick Pieces; but I never saw any particular Criticism on its Defects; which gives me leave to think its ill Reception proceeded more from a capricious Humour of the Town, than any considerable Errors in the Composure of the Play.

III. *Love for Love*; a Comedy, acted at the Theatre in Little *Lincolns-Inn-Fields*, by his Majesty's Servants, 1695. Dedicated to the Right Honourable *Charles* Earl of *Dorset* and *Middlesex*. This Play was acted with very great Applause, at the opening of the New House. There is abundance of Wit in it, and a great deal of fine and diverting Humour; the Characters are justly distinguish'd, and the Manners well mark'd. Some of the nicer Criticks find Fault with the unravelling of the Plot, and the Conduct of *Angelica* in it: But in spite of Envy, this Play must be allow'd to be one of the best of our modern Comedies.

IV. *The Mourning Bride*; a Tragedy, acted at the Theatre in *Little Lincolns-Inn-Fields*, by his Majesty's Servants, 1697. Dedicated to her Royal Highness the Princess *Anne* of *Denmark*. This Play had the greatest Success of all Mr. *Congreve's* Performances; and indeed met with Encouragement inferior to no Dramatick piece, that has at any time appear'd on the *English* Stage. The Excellency of this Tragedy can in nothing be more particularly describ'd, than in Sir *Richard Blackmore's* Preface to his Poem, entitled, *King Arthur*; which runs thus:

[Quotes No. 19 above.]

This is the Character given by the learned Doctor of Mr. *Congreve's Mourning Bride*; and I can, by no means, be of Opinion with some pretending Criticks, that Sir *Richard's* Aim, in this Commendation, was more to depress the Praises of Mr. *Congreve's* Predecessors, Mr. *Dryden*, Mr. *Otway*, and Mr. *Lee*, than the raising of Mr. *Congreve*; I look upon it to be meerly a Debt due to Merit, and pursu'd without any further protracted Views.

V. *The Way of the World*; a Comedy acted at the Theatre in Little *Lincolns-Inn-Fields*, by his Majesty's Servants, Dedicated to the Right Honourable *Ralph* Earl of *Mountague*. This Play, equal to, if not the best of Mr. *Congreve's* Comedies, unless it be his *Love for Love*, had not the Success of most of his other Performances; which shews there is still an uncertainty in hitting the Humour of the Town: But tho' at first it seem'd to be rejected, it has been lately reviv'd at the Theatre in *Drury-lane*, and acted several Nights with very great Applause.

VI. SEMELE; an Opera. This Performance was never represented on the Theatre.

VII. *The Judgment of* PARIS; a Masque.

These Dramatick Performances of Mr. *Congreve*, were publish'd with his other Poetical Writings, in three Volumes *Octavo*, 1710. and the Criticks do him the Justice to confess, that the Faults which may be found in them, are of a Nature that makes them very disputable; and in which both his Predecessors and Cotemporaries have offended. Whatever small Errors there may be in Mr. *Congreve*'s Dramatick Pieces, he may be justly excus'd, when 'tis consider'd, that he both began and left off to write when he was very Young; he quitted writing at the Age of seven and twenty: And what might not the World have expected from him, if he had continu'ed his Dramatical Studies, when he was capable of writing an *Old Batchelor* at Nineteen? and the great Mr. *Dryden* did not compleat his first Performance till he was above the Age of Thirty.

He is the only Dramatick Poet now living, excellent for both Comedy and Tragedy; the Plays he has written in both ways, being very much applauded: And what Mr. *Dennis* has lately observ'd of Mr. *Congreve*, is esteem'd, by most Persons, very just; That he left the Stage early, and Comedy has quitted it with him.

48. Lady Mary Wortley Montagu, 'To the Memory of Mr. Congreve'

1729

From *Essays and Poems and* Simplicity, *A Comedy*, ed. Robert Halsband and Isobel Grundy (Oxford: Clarendon Press, 1977), pp. 246–7.

Congreve died on 19 January 1729, and Lady Mary's poem was probably written very soon after. She was 8 years old when she first met Congreve; both he and her father were members of the Kit-Cat Club. Spence's *Anecdotes* No. 744 records Lady Mary's opinion that Congreve was the wittiest man she had ever known.

Farewell the best and loveliest of Mankind
Where Nature with a happy hand had joyn'd
The softest temper with the strongest mind,
In pain could counsel and could charm when blind.

In this Lewd Age when Honor is a Jest
He found a refuge in his Congreve's breast,
Superior there, unsully'd, and entire;
And only could with the last breath expire.

His wit was never by his Malice stain'd,
No rival writer of his Verse complain'd,
For neither party drew a venal pen
To praise bad measures or to blast good men.

A Queen indeed he mourn'd, but such a Queen
Where Virtue mix'd with royal Blood was seen,
With equal merit grac'd each Scene of Life
An Humble Regent and Obedient Wife.

If in a Distant State blest Spirits know
The Scenes of Sorrow of a World below,
This little Tribute to thy Fame approve,
A Triffling Instance of a boundless Love.

49. Jonathan Swift in a letter to Viscount Bolingbroke and Alexander Pope

1729

From *The Correspondence of Jonathan Swift*, ed. Sir Harold Williams, 5 vols (Oxford: Clarendon Press, 1963), III, p. 329.

Dublin, April 5, 1729

I have read my friend Congreve's verses to Lord Cobham, which end with a vile and false moral, and I remember is not in Horace to Tibullus, which he imitates, 'that all times are equally virtuous and vicious' wherein he differs from all Poets, Philosophers, and Christians that ever writ.[1] It is more probable that there may be an equal quantity of virtues always in the world, but sometimes there may be a pack of it in Asia, and hardly a thimble-full in Europe.

NOTE

1 'Of Improving the Present Time', ll. 79–82, first printed in 1729 with the title, 'A Letter from Mr. Congreve to the Right Honourable the Lord Viscount Cobham'.

50. David Mallet, 'A Poem to the Memory of Mr. Congreve'

1729

From *A Poem to the Memory of Mr. Congreve* (London: 1729).

The authorship of this poem, which first appeared anonymously, has been long disputed. It was edited for the Percy Society in 1843 by Peter Cunningham who attributed it to James Thomson on the suggestion of H. F. Cary. In 1908 James Logie Robertson included the poem in his Oxford Standard Authors edition of Thomson but with a strong caveat that Thomson's friend and fellow Scot David Mallet was more likely the author. George G. Williams defended the attribution to Thomson on internal evidence: see 'Did Thomson write the poem "To the Memory of Mr. Congreve"?', *PMLA* (1930), 45: 1010–13. But in 'The authorship of "A Poem to the Memory of Mr. Congreve"', *MLN*

(1939), 54: 599, Alan D. McKillop drew attention to two
advertisements for the poem by the publisher John Millan;
both assign it to the author of poems known to have been
written by Mallet.

Advertisement

THE author of the following Poem, not having had the happiness of
a personal acquaintance with Mr. CONGREVE, is sensible that he has
drawn his private character very imperfectly. This all his friends
will readily discover: and therefore, if any one of them had thought
fit to do justice to those amiable qualifications, which made him the
love and admiration of all that knew him, these verses had never
seen the light.

A

POEM

TO THE MEMORY OF

MR. *CONGREVE.*

INSCRIBED TO HER GRACE,

HENRIETTA,

DUTCHESS OF *MARLBOROUGH.*

OFT has the muse, with mean attempt, employ'd
Her heaven-born voice to flatter prosperous guilt,
Or trivial greatness: often stoop'd her song
To sooth ambition in his frantick rage,
The dire destroyer, while a bleeding world
Wept o'er his crimes. Of this pernicious skill
Unknowing I, these voluntary lays
To genuine worth devote; to worth, by all
Confess'd and mourn'd; to CONGREVE now no more.
   First of the fairer kind! by heaven adorn'd   10
With every nobler praise; whose smile can lift
The MUSE unknown to fame, indulgent now
Permit HER strain, ennobled by a name,
To all the better few, and chief to thee,
Bright MARLBRO', ever sacred, ever dear.
   Lamented Shade! in him the comic Muse,
Parent of gay instruction, lost her lov'd,
Her last remaining hope; and pensive now
Resigns to Folly, and his mimic rout,
Her throne usurp'd: presage of darker times,   20

201

And deeper woes to come! with taste declin'd
Fallen vertue droops; and o'er th' ill-omen'd age,
Unseen, unfear'd, impend the thousand ills
That wait on ignorance: no CONGREVE now
To scourge our crimes, or laugh to scorn our fools,
A new and nameless herd. Nature was his,
Bold, sprightly, various: and superiour Art,
Curious to chuse each better grace, unseen
Of vulgar eyes; with delicacy free,
Tho' labour'd happy, and tho' strong refin'd.   30
Judgment, severely cool, o'erlooked his toil,
And patient finish'd all: each fair design
With freedom regular, correctly great,
A Master's skilful daring. Closely wrought
His meaning Fable, with deep art perplex'd,
With striking ease unravel'd: no thin plot
Seen thro' at once and scorned; or ill conceal'd
By borrow'd aids of mimickry and farce.
His Characters strong-featur'd, equal, just,
From finer nature drawn: and all the mind   40
Thro' all her mazes trac'd; each darker vice,
And darling folly, under each disguise,
By either Sex assum'd, of study'd ease,
False friendship, loose severity, vain wit,
Dull briskness, shallow depth, or coward-rage.
Of the whole Muse possess'd, his piercing eye
Discern'd each richer vein of genuine mirth,
Humour or wit; where differing, where agreed;
How counterfeited, or by folly's grin,
Or affectation's air: and what their force   50
To please, to move, to shake the ravish'd scene
With laughter unreprov'd. To him the Soul,
In all her higher workings, too was known:
What passions tumult there; whence their prompt spring,
Their sudden flood of rage, and gradual fall;
Infinite motion! source supreme of bliss,
Or woe to man; our heaven, or hell, below!
   Such was his public name; nor less allow'd
His private worth: by nature made for praise.
A pleasing form; a soul sincere and clear,   60
Where all the human graces mix'd their charms,
Pure candor, easy goodness, open truth,
Spontaneous all: where strength and beauty join'd.

With wit indulgent; humble in the height
Of envy'd honours: and, but rarely found,
Th' unjealous friend of every rival-worth.
Adorn'd for social life: each talent his
To win each heart; the charm of happy ease,
Free mirth, gay learning, ever-smiling wit,
To all endear'd, a pleasure without pain: 70
What HALLIFAX approv'd, and MARLBRO' mourns.
   Not so th' illiberal mind, where knowledge dwells,
Uncouth and harsh, with her attendant, Pride,
Impatient of attention, prone to blame,
Disdaining to be pleas'd; condemning all,
By all condemn'd; for social joys unfit,
In solitude self-curst, the child of spleen.
Oblig'd, ungrateful; unoblig'd, a foe;
Poor, vitious, old: such fierce-ey'd ASPER was.[1]
Now meaner CENUS, trivial with design,   80
Courts poor applause by levity of face,
And scorn of serious thought; to mischief prompt,
Tho' impotent to wound; profuse of wealth,
Yet friendless and unlov'd; vain, fluttering, false:
A vacant head, and an ungenerous heart.
   But slighting these ignobler names, the Muse
Pursues her favourite SON, and sees him now,
From this dim spot enlarg'd, triumphant soar
Beyond the walk of Time to better worlds,
Where all is new, all wonderous, and all blest!   90
What art thou, death! by mankind poorly fear'd,
Yet period of their ills. On thy near shore,
Trembling they stand, and see thro' dreaded mists
Th' eternal port, irresolute to leave
This various misery, these air-fed dreams
Which men call life, and fame. Mistaken minds!
'Tis reason's prime aspiring, greatly just;
'Tis happiness supreme, to venture forth
In quest of nobler worlds; to try the deeps
Of dark futurity, with HEAVEN our guide,   100
Th' unerring HAND that led us safe thro' time:
That planted in the soul this powerful hope,
This infinite ambition of new life,
And endless joys, still rising, ever new.
   These CONGREVE tastes, safe on th' ethereal coast,
Join'd to the numberless, immortal quire

Of spirits blest. High-seated among these,
He sees the public Fathers of mankind,
The greatly Good, those universal Minds,
Who drew the sword, or plan'd the holy scheme,   110
For liberty and right; to cheque the rage
Of blood-stain'd tyranny, and save a world.
Such, high-born MARLBRO', be thy Sire divine
With wonder nam'd; fair freedom's champion he,
By heaven approv'd, a conqueror without guilt.
And such, on earth his friend, and join'd on high
By deathless love, GODOLPHIN's patriot-worth,
Just to his country's fame, yet of her wealth
With honour frugal; above interest great.
Hail men immortal! social VERTUES hail!   120
First heirs of praise!—But I, with weak essay,
Wrong the superiour theme: while heavenly quires,
In strains high-warbled to celestial harps,
Resound your names; and CONGREVE's added voice
In heaven exalts what he admir'd below.

    With these he mixes, now no more to swerve
From reason's purest law; no more to please,
Borne by the torrent down, a sensual age.
Pardon, lov'd shade, that I with friendly blame
Slight-note thy error; not to wrong thy worth,   130
Or shade thy memory (far from my soul
Be that base aim) but haply to deter,
From flattering the gross vulgar, future pens,
Powerful like thine in every grace, and skill'd
To win the listening soul with vertuous charms.

    If manly thought and wit refin'd may hope
To please an age, in aimless folly sunk,
And sliding swift into the depth of vice.
Consuming Pleasure leads the gay and young
Thro' their vain round; and venal Faith the old,   140
Or Avarice, mean of soul: instructive arts
Pursu'd no more: the general taste extinct,
Or all-debas'd: even sacred liberty
The great man's jest, and BRITAIN's welfare nam'd,
By her degenerate Sons, the Poets dream,
Or fancy's air-built vision, gaily vain.
Such the lost age: yet still the Muse can find,
Superiour and apart, a sacred band,
Heroic vertues, who ne'er bow'd the knee

To sordid Interest: who dare greatly claim 150
The Priviledge of men, unfearing truth,
And freedom, heaven's first gift; th' ennobling bliss
That renders life of price, and cheaply sav'd
At life's expence; our sum of happiness.
On these the drooping Muses fix their eyes;
From these expect their ancient fame restor'd.
Nor will the hope be vain: the public Weal
With theirs fast-link'd: a generous truth conceal'd
From narrow-thoughted power, and known alone
To souls of highest rank. With these, the Fair 160
Be join'd in just applause; the brighter few,
Who rais'd above gay folly, and the whirl
Of fond amusements, emulate thy praise,
Illustrious MARLBRO'; pleas'd, like thee, to shine
Propitious on the Muse; whose charms inspire
Her noblest raptures, and whose goodness crowns.

NOTE

1 Asper was a Roman grammarian of the second century A.D. Cunningham suggested that the name is here applied to John Dennis. Cenus has
not been identified.

51. Anon. in *An Epistle to Lord Viscount Cobham*

1730

From *Cobham and Congreve. An Epistle to Lord Viscount Cobham, In Memory of his Friend, The late Mr. Congreve* (London: 1730).

The poem from which the following passages are taken was published by the unscrupulous and opportunist Edmund Curll. It is addressed to Richard Temple, Viscount Cobham, who had served under Marlborough during the War of the Spanish Succession, and whose circle included Pope and James Thomson as well as Congreve. Cobham was a staunch Whig, but in the 1730s he became a leader of the anti-Walpole faction within that party. As the notes make clear, there is close reference to Congreve's 'A Pindarique Ode, Humbly Offer'd to the Queen, On the Victorious Progress of Her Majesty's Arms, under the Conduct of the Duke of Marlborough' and his own poems addressed to Cobham.

(i)

TO

LORD VISCOUNT *COBHAM*

IN MEMORY OF HIS FRIEND

THE LATE MR. CONGREVE.

Primâ dicte mihi, summâ dicende Camoenâ. Hor.
['You of whom my first Muse told, and of whom my last must tell.' *Ep.* I.i.l]

SINCE my weak Voice in *Congreve*'s Praise preferr'd,
Will, thro' a *Virgil*, be by *Pollio* heard;*
Low Rhimes made sacred, to his name I join,
Fix'd to such Fame they'll make great Glories mine;
Such humblest Swains deserve for *saying* Hymns divine.†
    Far from these Lines, all low-Lamentings be!
His Soul sprung, glad, to Immortality!
That, first from Heav'n commission'd, for our sake,
Men happier, wiser, better, came to make.
This Task long try'd, in each divinest Strain,
Call'd Home, It Heav'nwards took its flight again;
But first his Dirge he makes, and Fun'ral Rites,‡
And, just at Death, as all thro' Life, Delights:
To Dust gives Dust, his Corps, pale Ashy-Pile!
Then upwards flies the *Phoenix* of our Isle.
    Now what vain Poet, what poor Rhiming Elf,
Shall mend what *Congreve* sung upon himself;
Sung in sweet Notes, o'er dying *Swans*, admir'd,
Which he, like them, just ended, and expir'd?
When they can drop such Tears upon the Dead
As *Amaryllis* for *Amintas* shed,§

Or with *Alexis'*¶ mourning Muse can vye,
Then, nor till then, let vainest Voices try,
To tune in Verse, a *Congreve*'s Elegy—
   No, let us rather decent Feasts prepare,
And Off'rings on his annual Day, now near,‖·
Sing round his Shrine his Songs, and mend the *British* Ear:
Nor mend their Ear alone, but, thro' that part,
Sound, in good Sense, each Soul, and honest make each Heart.**
   Might, 'mong these sweet memorials so prepar'd
By Nymphs and Heroes, my mean Voice be heard;
While Nymphs to sing his fair *Cecilia* chuse,
Heroes the *Birth* immortal of his *Muse*;
To whom were my Memorial justly due,
But you alone, O *Cobham*, only you?
   Thee early, and thee last his tuneful Breath,**
Addrest with grateful Notes—till stopt by Death.
   Your *Art of Pleasing*,†† in his earlier days
He writ and gain'd, as you gain'd, all Men's praise:
That hardest Art he paints with greatest ease,
In Lines so proper, that they'll ever please.
   By Friendship more, tho' vastly much by Wit,
That Art of pleasing, oft I've thought was writ;
From Him *it*'s Master, to *it*'s Master You,
By Sympathy‡‡ the charming Poem grew.
   Your Ways were One; Wits of congenial Parts!
That sure had Consanguinity of Hearts;
Both, of Delighting all Mankind, could boast,
But, knowing best that Art, each other most.
   'Twas fit it should be so—what other Two
Could be by Nature match'd more near than you?
A Bard that Sieges, Battles, Conquests writes,
And a young Hero fam'd at fifty Fights,§§
That of his *Marlbro*'s Toils had Sharer been,
And War's whole Art as much as *Julius* seen.
   Thus *Horace* lov'd *Augustus*, thus was lov'd,¶¶
Wit rais'd War's Glory, Glory Wit improv'd.
In all Heroic Times 'tis Wit's Reward,
That War's chief Champions love the noblest Bard.‖·‖·
That this was, is, and will, nay must be *so*,
Witness the *Bard* your Friend, and your Friend *Marlborough*.***

(pp. 3–7)

(ii)

Say, *Cobham*, now,^{†††} where's now thy Hero's Soul?
Can he his Passions for true Fame controul?
Does he not read, rise raptur'd, sit again,
Then read, till fir'd afresh by some new Strain,
He makes, with well-pleas'd Mind, each past Campaign? }
So, when his Harp divine^{‡‡‡} *Timotheus* strung,
And play'd, by *Dryden*'s Mouth, what *Phoebus* sung,
Warm'd into Flights of War young *Ammon* flew,
And fought, in Thought, his Battles o'er a-new.
  He read; new Life felt rising, while he read,
His Deeds compar'd, with those most mighty Dead,
Whose Names, in Fame's immortal List, enroll'd,
Their Glories date from Years, by thousands told.
And found in *Congreve*'s like Prophetic Song,
His soar'd as high, and sure to last as long.
But when to those warm well-judg'd Lines he came,
That *Churchill*'s justly fix'd o'er^{§§§} *Caesar*'s Fame;
Able no longer to contain, he said,
'I own my Toils and Hazards all repaid.
How short the Verse, that so great Truths displays!
They, like collected^{¶¶¶} Beams thro' Crystals blaze! }
He, with the Lustre, gives the Fire of Praise!
Matchless as *Pindar*'s is my *Congreve*'s Rage,
That can contract an *Iliad* to a Page;
Yet so judicious, while he sings with Flame,
That where he heightens most, he most secures my Fame,
Caesar's *Pharsalia* (true!) made Slaves,^{‖‖‖} but I
Fought at *Ramillia*'s Plain for precious Liberty.
Perish that mean-born Pride, that Bastard State,
Which aims to grow, by Men's Misfortunes, Great.
Sooner might I be beat,—myself made Slave,
Than subdue Realms, to ruin, not to save.
More Curses on such Chiefs than Blessings wait,
Those that their Triumphs love, the Traytors hate.
The Laurels *Congreve* brings me, I approve,
Sprung from, and nourish'd by my Country's Love.
My End, Man's Freedom gain'd; to crown the Scene
The Muse applauds me, and the World's best Queen.'

(pp. 16–18)

(iii)

Yet this^{****} *Moeonian*, and the *Mantuan* Flame,
And *Congreve*'s Modern Fire are all the same; }
All from one Source, in diff'rent Ages came.

'Twas hard, indeed, thus coming last, to climb,
Against their advantageous Hill of Time;
Yet still we find Priority of Days
No Birth-right to Priority of Praise.
Change but each Age, when these three Poets shone,
Their Persons, to impartial Eyes, are ONE.
Congreve had *Homer* been, in *Homer's* Time;
Homer been *Congreve*, now, and wrote such *British* Rhime.
Both could, with Magic Arts of Verse, alike,
Rouze Souls to Arms, and warlike Passions strike.
   Cobham, if Poesy's Persuasive Parts,
Thus move (best Martial†††† Musick!) Heroes Hearts;
'Tis hard to say, we, rather of the two,
To You owe Poets, or to Poets You.
If your brave Acts make their bright Numbers shine,
They fire you to those Acts by Verse divine.
Pleas'd with both Song and Subject, Thus we know, ⎫
Arms and the Man (like *Virgil's* sung) we owe,   ⎬
Alike to *Congreve* and to *Marlborough*.   ⎭

   When his brave *Stilicho*‡‡‡ bright *Claudian* sung,
Rome with the Poet's Praise and Hero's, rung:
Senates and Emperors, by Statutes wise,
Bad to their *Claudian* Bay-crown'd Statues rise.
Greater our Chief, sublimer was our Bard;
And shall more Merit meet with less Reward?
Shall it in *Britain* be the Poet's Doom,
To fall neglected for excelling *Rome*?
Forbid *That* Monarchs, Senates, Heroes, all,
Whom we can Brave, Great, Wise, and Noble call:
All, whose Deeds claim *that Verse*, which never dies, ⎫
Those Deeds, their Glories to immortalize;   ⎬
Else, may those Poems cease, they cease to prize!   ⎭

(pp. 27–8)

NOTES

* Intimating that the same Friendship subsisting between Lord *Cobham* and Mr. *Congreve*, as there was between the Noble *Pollio* and *Virgil*; any thing in the Praise of such a Poet, must be acceptable to such a Nobleman's Ear.
† These Hymns (as they are called by the Ancients) were usually sung, but sometimes only recited; and as I pretend not to write of these sublime Poems in a Style, beyond that, which consists of

Rhimes, that are *Sermoni propiora*, I pretend to call it only *saying a Hymn*; to which *Pliny*, in the beginning of his Panegyric to the Emperor *Trajan* gives, methinks, sufficient Commendation for a *less modest Man* than myself, that is but an Epistolary Writer, to be contented with. He represents these bare Reciters as acceptable to the Gods as the sublimest Poets; they were reckoned by many of the Ancients as much inspired as the Poets themselves, whose Works they recited, as *Spondanus* tells us.

‡ Alluding to the last Poem Mr. *Congreve* wrote not long before he died to the Lord *Cobham*, on the Improvement of Time, in which are these Preparatory remarkable Lines on Death, in Imitation of *Horace*'s Epistle to *Alb. Tibullus*.

> *Still think the present Day the last of Life.*
> *Who thus can think, and who such Thoughts pursues,*
> *Content may keep his Life, or calmly lose.*
> *All Proofs of this thou mayst thy self receive:*
> *When Leisure from Affairs will give thee leave,*
> *Come see thy Friend,* &c.

§¶ These two Verses refer to those two Patterns for *Elegy* Writing, Mr. *Congreve*'s Pastorals on the Death of Q. *Mary*, and the Marquis of *Blandford*.

‖ Alludes to the Custom of the Ancients, by Annual Celebrations of their Poets and Heroes.

**†† Alludes to Mr. *Congreve's Art of Pleasing*, and his last Copy of Verses, both address'd to Lord *Cobham*.

‡‡ The Sympathy here mentioned, and in some following Verses, representing the Friendships Great Personages naturally take to one another, makes a fine Chapter in *Gracian*'s Hero, and is delicately handled by several eminent Writers, quoted in the Notes upon that Chapter.

§§ *Fifty Fights*, &c. meaning a great Number, or near the Number, which is true.

¶¶‖.‖.*** This is manifest by many Parts of *Horace*'s Works, particularly from the Esteem *Augustus* had for him. Herein also the Friendship of Mr. *Congreve*, Lord *Cobham* and the Duke of *Marlborough* are represented.

††† This appeal to Lord *Cobham* is to shew the Power of Poetry, and refers still to Mr. *Congreve*'s Ode, on the Success of the Victorious Duke of *Marlborough*'s Arms.

‡‡‡ Mr. *Dryden*, in his *Alexander*'s Feast, very finely describes the Power of Music and Poetry over the Passions.

§§§ All this Passage shews, that, in this Praise attributed to the Duke by

Mr. *Congreve*, the principal Regard is, that the highest Parts of it are carried no farther, than what are truly, exactly, and religiously *just*.

¶¶¶ Alluding to Mr. *Congreve*'s Ode, *ut supra*.

‖.‖.‖. Here is given a very just Reason for preferring the Victories of *Marlborough* to those of *Caesar*.

**** Refers to the beginning of Mr. *Congreve*'s *Ode*, &c. viz.

> O well-known Sounds! O Melody the same,
> That kindled *Mantuan* Fire, and rais'd *Moeonian* Flame.

†††† *Poesy best Martial Musick*, &c. Many are the fine Descriptions of the *Power of Music*; such is that with which Mr. *Congreve* opens his Tragedy of the *Mourning Bride*.

‡‡‡‡ See *Claudian*'s Praise of *Stilico*. [In the panegyric *De Consolatu Stilichonis*.]

52. Alexander Pope, miscellaneous comments

From (a) Joseph Spence, *Observations, Anecdotes, and Characters of Books and Men*, ed. James M. Osborn, 2 vols (Oxford: Clarendon Press, 1966), I, p. 207; (b) ibid., I, p. 208; (c) Alexander Pope, *Imitations of Horace*, ed. John Butt (London: Methuen, 1939, rev. 1961), p. 219; (d) Owen Ruffhead, *The Life of Alexander Pope, Esq.* (London: 1769), p. 493 n.

Pope's comments on his friend Congreve are disappointingly sparse. The following are the more substantial of those recorded.

(a) From Spence's *Anecdotes* 486
Corneille, Racine, and Molière better than any of ours. [The] *Careless Husband* not our best comedy; Congreve has one or two better: [The] *Silent Woman* our best.

(1733 or 1734)

(b) ibid. 488

Aye, Mr. Tonson, he was Ultimus Romanorum! (with a sigh, speaking of poor Mr. Congreve, who died a year or two before).

(28 or 29 November 1730)

(c) From Pope's Epistle *To Augustus* (l. 287)
Tell me if Congreve's Fools are Fools indeed?

(d) From Owen Ruffhead's *Life of Alexander Pope, Esq.*
Mr. POPE esteemed Congreve for the manners of a gentleman and a man of honour, and the sagest of the poetic tribe. He thought nothing wanting in his Comedies but the simplicity and truth of nature.

53. François-Marie Arouet de Voltaire in *Letters Concerning the English Nation*

1733

From *Letters Concerning the English Nation* (London: 1733), pp. 188–9.

Voltaire's *Lettres philosophiques* were the product of his sojourn in England between 1726 and 1729. An English version, translated by John Lockman, actually preceded the French into print by a year. The following extract is taken from Letter XIX, 'On Comedy'.

THE late Mr. *Congreve* rais'd the Glory of Comedy to a greater Height than any English Writer before or since his Time. He wrote only a few Plays, but they are all excellent in their kind. The Laws of the Drama are strictly observ'd in them; they abound with Characters all which are shadow'd with the utmost Delicacy, and we don't meet with so much as one low, or coarse Jest. The Language is every where that of Men of Honour, but their Actions are those of Knaves; a Proof that he was perfectly well acquainted with human Nature, and frequented what we call polite Company. He was infirm, and come to the Verge of Life when I knew him. Mr. *Congreve* had one Defect, which was, his entertaining too mean an Idea of his first Profession, (that of a Writer) tho' 'twas to this he ow'd his Fame and Fortune. He spoke of his Works as of Trifles that were beneath him; and hinted to me in our first Conversation, that I should visit him upon no other Foot than that of a Gentleman, who led a Life of Plainness and Simplicity. I answer'd, that had he been so unfortunate as to be a mere Gentleman I should never have come to see him; and I was very much disgusted at so unseasonable a Piece of Vanity.

MR. *Congreve*'s Comedies are the most witty and regular, those of Sir *John Vanbrugh* most gay and humourous, and those of Mr. *Wycherley* have the greatest Force and Spirit. It may be proper to observe, that these fine Genius's never spoke disadvantageously of *Moliere*; and that none but the contemptible Writers among the *English* have endeavour'd to lessen the Character of that great comic Poet.

54. William Popple in *The Prompter*

1735

From *The Prompter,* 11 November 1735.

William Popple (1701–64) was author of two comedies and a translation of Horace's *Ars Poetica.* He became governor of the Bermudas in 1745. His discussion of *The Double-Dealer,* occasioned by a revival at Drury Lane, appeared in No. 105 of *The Prompter,* a theatrical periodical written by Aaron Hill with Popple's assistance.

I SHALL now take a cursory View of a Comedy revived at the other Theatre.

THE *Double Dealer*, like all *Congreve's* Plays, abounds in *Wit*: It has, besides, the Advantage of a Plot, which, tho' very *intricate*, is not in the least *confused*, and is conducted in so masterly a Manner, that it *thickens* naturally from the Circumstances in which the Characters of the Drama are placed, and is *unravelled* by the same happy Intervention of *probable* and *expected* Incidents. Each *Light Character* has likewise a pleasing Vein of Humour running through it, strongly *distinguished*, yet theatrically PLAYING into each other.

NEVERTHELESS, with all this Merit, the Play is *fundamentally bad*, because its Fable, like that of *Alexander*,[1] is *ill-chosen*; and a *Play*, where the *Fable* is *ill-chosen*, can never be *good*.

THE principal Character, that of *Maskwell*, or the *Double Dealer*, is out of the Province of Comedy: No *Vice* can be introduced there, that does not result from some *Passion*—*A cold, deliberate, thinking* Villain, *that preponderates every Stroke, and consults his Understanding, how best to perpetrate it*, and laughs at the very Notion of Virtue, is only to be corrected by TYBURN.—*Maskwell* is the most consummate Villain that can be painted, without one single Passion that might soften his original Deformity.—'*He is kept by his Patron's Wife, whom he loves not—Not content with receiving, each Day, fresh Proofs of his increasing Friendship, and aggravating his Villainy by fresh Wrongs, in Proportion as his Patron's Confidence in him administers fresh Occasions to do it, he is under-hand at work to make him disinherit his Nephew, (who is his Bosom-Friend, and by whom he is employed, as a trusty Agent, for very contrary Purposes) and settle his Estate upon him, with his Niece*, whom his Friend is in love with.—*He sticks at nothing, and is so* base-principled, *that the* very Woman *that* maintains him *is not only* deceived *in her Turn, but by him who was privy to her Passion for her Husband's Nephew (a fine Character for Comedy, by the bye, that of a Woman who* wrongs *her Husband with* one Man, *at the same time that she is* in love *with* another,) *put upon endeavouring to gratify that Passion, and, in case of Disappointment,* presented with a Dagger to MURTHER *him!*' In short, these two Characters are so *deformed* and *diabolical*, and the *Whole* such *a Complication of Villainy*, and the lighter Characters so *obscene*, that Comedy blushes to have received, with a *Stain* not to be *washed out*, a *mortal stab* from one of her favourite Sons. To sum up the Contents of the principal Characters—in a few Words—

IN *Maskwell* we have, (besides his Proneness to *Murther*) *Adultery*, *Ingratitude* to his Patron, *Treachery* to his Bosom-Friend, *Deceit* to the Woman who (in the Grossness of his Ideas) *keeps him*, and to the young Lady whom he proposes to marry;—with (not a *bare Want*, but) an *argumented Rejection* of all the Principles of common *Honour* and *Honesty*, as well as *Humanity*.

IN Lady *Touchwood*, (but in her Vice is made an Effect of strong Passions) the same *murtherous* Disposition, together with the *actual Commission* of *Adultery* with one Man through *Intemperance*, and a strong Desire to *commit* it with *another*, through (what she calls) *Love*.

OF Four Ladies in the Drama, *Two more* treat the *Audience* with *Adultery*; but their Characters are so drawn, that their *Adultery* seems less than *Simple Fornication* in another, not being of Weight enough to give any of their Actions the Stamp of *Virtue* or *Vice*.—But there may be some Alleviation to their Case, for the Poet claims a Right of *Prescription* in behalf of Cuckoldom, where-ever he introduces a *Coxcomb*, a *Fool*, or an *Old Man, Married*.

WHAT then could justify the Revival of this Comedy? Nothing *critically* or *morally*. What apologize for it? The infinite *Humour* that shoots, like a Porcupine's Quills, *from every Part of every one of the Comick Characters!* Lord and Lady *Froth*, Sir *Paul Plyant* and his Lady, together with Mr. *Brisk*, are Characters (abstracted from their *moral* and *obscene* Failings) such as Comedy derives, with *Beauty* and *Propriety*, its greatest Power of *Pleasing* from. In favour therefore of the TRULY COMICK Genius of the Play, we'll suppose the *Manager* that revived it rather weighing in his Judgment, whether the *Bad* might not be tolerated on account of the *Good*, than ignorant of the *Bad*, and led into the Mistake of *Reviving it*, from the Approbation given too commonly to *loose* and *immoral* Scenes by the Generality of Audiences, when *heightened* by *Wit, Humour*, or *Action*.

THE *Word* therefore to be *given him*, is, henceforward not to *represent Vicious Characters* because they may be *indulged* by the *Corruption* of the *Times*, but to reform the *Corruption* of the *Times* by Scenes adapted to that Purpose. Now the Stage is not to punish such Vices as are *cognizable* by Course of Law, and *punitively terminable* at *Tyburn*: Poetical Justice extends only to such as the Law cannot lay hold off, such as are to be tried in FORO CONSCIEENTIAE, where the Delinquent, being strongly touched by a Resemblance of Himself, may amend.

NOTE

1 Nathaniel Lee's tragedy, *The Rival Queens*, which had just been revived at Covent Garden and is discussed in the first half of Popple's review.

55. Anon. in *The Daily Gazetteer*

1737

From *The Daily Gazetteer, Saturday* 16 July 1737.

The following attack upon *The Way of the World* occurs in the pro-Walpole paper's defence of the Licensing Act, introduced in May 1737 to muzzle dramatic satire upon the government. 'Caleb D'Anvers', the pseudonymous conductor of *The Craftsman*, the journal run by Bolingbroke, had opposed the Act and asserted that the English drama was less licentious than the Old Comedy of ancient Greece.

As a Proof of Mr. *D'Anvers's* singular Honesty and Judgment, where he says, that no such Liberties have been taken on the *British* Stage, as in the *Old Comedy* of the *Greeks*, I have made an *Examen* of the *Way of the World*. I chose that Play for two Reasons, the one, because the author wrote it after he had been disciplined by Mr. Collier for former Transgressions against Religion, Morality and Modesty; the other, because it has lately been play'd several Times, and the Ladies have not forborn shewing themselves in the Front-Boxes, while Mrs. *Fainall* and Mrs. *Marwood*, two of the Top Characters, two Women living and glorying in Adultery, were inculcating the Practice of it on the Stage. All the Characters in that Play are immoral, immodest, and shocking in Sobriety of Thinking, as is proved in the *Examen*, which shall be forth coming when this Assertion is call'd in Question, together with a Word or two on the Wit of it, which perhaps is not so marvellous as it is said to be by the smaller Judges. The Traps laid for Jests in it, are like the Traps laid for Claps in Tragedy, *Rants* and *Rhimes* at the *Exit* of the Player, which Mrs. *Barry* said she taught *Row*, and that sort of Trap-Wit being forced and affected, and consequently out of Nature, loses its Character in a Species of Poetry, which is the Posture of human Life, and raises Laughter without Pleasure. However some of these smaller Judges pretend that the Wit of the *Way of the World* excuses the Lewdness. The last Expression discovers them, for common Understanding, I dare not use the Term *Common Sense*, since it has been so scandalously abused, teaches us that the Tickling a Man's Ear is no Excuse for corrupting his Mind.

56. Henry Fielding in *The Champion*

1739

From *The Champion: Containing A Series of Papers, Humourous, Moral, Political, and Critical,* 2 vols (London: 1741), I, pp. 15–16.

The Champion was a periodical which commenced publication on 15 November 1739, and until the following June was largely written by Fielding, its part owner. Thereafter the bulk of the writing passed to James Ralph, who finally acquired Fielding's shares in 1742. The extract below comes from the third number, for Tuesday 20 November 1739. The essay is unsigned, which is common practice in the early issues of this paper; it has been attributed to Fielding on internal evidence. See J. E. Wells, 'The "Champion" and some unclaimed essays by Henry Fielding', *Englische Studien* (1913), 46: 355–66.

Wycherly, whom I have always esteemed one of the best of our comic Writers, left the *Drama*, where he had acquired so great and so just an Applause, to write some of the worst Poems that any Age hath produced; and *Congreve*, who will always be esteemed by those who have a polite Taste in Comedy, could not forbear attempting Reputation, in a Manner for which he was so disqualified, that he produced a Tragedy (notwithstanding its Success) little superior to those of our worst Writers.

57. Samuel Foote in *The Roman and English Comedy Consider'd and Compar'd*

1747

From *The Roman and English Comedy Consider'd and Compar'd* (London: 1747).

Samuel Foote (1720–77) was a successful actor-dramatist, and in his later years owner of the Haymarket Theatre.

(i)
No Writer more abounds with Characters of this Cast, than *Congreve*; and had his Execution been equal to his Imagination, he would have had a just Title to be rank'd with the foremost of our Comic Poets. All his Humourists are well sketch'd, and generally well begun, but ill conducted. The Author, from an Impatience to show his own Wit, throws it into the Mouths of Characters, who are not, in Propriety, entitled to an Atom.

And this is, indeed, the Failing of all young Writers: They jump at the Shadow, and lose the Substance: The main Article is neglected, and their Pursuit directed after Point, Antithesis, and, what is called, fine Writing.

Wit is not what it has been by many imagined to be, the Essence of Comedy; so far from it, that it is of no Use, but as it is subservient to Character.

And from this Mistake it happens, that the Quality which chiefly recommends the Works of Mr. *Congreve*, to the Observation of the

Million, is the very Circumstance that diminishes his Excellence with the Judicious.

(pp. 23–4)

(ii)

Ben Johnson is most successful in his Plots, *Congreeve* in his Characters, and *Vanburgh* in his Dialogue. The former possessed most Knowledge and Judgment, the second most Fancy and Fire, the last most Propriety, Ease, and Elegance. The first, in order to preserve Correctness, was often flat; *Congreeve*, too roving and unconfin'd; and, *Vanburgh*, too immoral. Divest this last Writer of this Failing, and his Comedies are unexceptionably the best in the Language.

(p. 26)

58. Edmund Burke in *The Reformer*

1748

From *The Reformer*, No. 2, Thursday 4 February 1748, pp. 2–3.

The Reformer was a weekly periodical published in Dublin between 28 January and 21 April 1748. Its thirteen numbers were edited and largely written by Burke, then 18 years old and a final year undergraduate at Trinity College, Dublin. The essay from which this extract is taken begins with a complaint that the manager of the Theatre Royal in Smock Alley, Thomas Sheridan, has failed to improve the morality of the plays produced there.

But he who seems to have shared the Gifts of Nature as largely as he has abused them, was the celebrated Mr. *Congreve*, who, to the Charms of a lively Wit, solid Judgment and rich Invention, has added such Obscenity, as none can, without the greatest Danger to Virtue, listen to; the very texture and groundwork of some of his Plays is Lewdness, which poisons the surer, as it is set off with the

Advantage of Wit. I know 'tis said in his Excuse, that he drew his Pictures after the times; but whoever examines his Plays will find, that he not only copied the ill Morals of the Age, but approved them, as may be seen in such Characters as he plainly proposes for Imitation; thus his *Angelica* in *Love for Love*, (the chastest of all his Plays) he meant for a perfect Character, and such perhaps as he would have wished his own Mistress to have been; but the Rankness of her Ideas, and Expressions, in the Scene between her and old *Foresight*, (as well as in other Parts of the Play) are scarce consistent with any *Male*, much less *Female* Modesty. Much of that Respect we pay the Sex is owing to the Opinion we have of their Innocence; but if the Lady lets her Lover understand she is as knowing as himself, a great Part of it must necessarily vanish.

59. William Melmoth on Congreve's translations of Homer

1750

From *The Letters of Sir Thomas Fitzosborne, on Several Subjects*, 3rd edn (London: 1750), pp. 270–5.

William Melmoth (1710–99), later known as a translator of Pliny the Younger, won himself a high reputation with his first book, *The Letters of Sir Thomas Fitzosborne*. It was first published in 1742 and went through ten editions in his own lifetime. Letter LII, 'Some passages in Mr. Pope's translation of the Iliad, compared with the versions of Denham, Dryden, Congreve, and Tickel', was included first in the third edition of 1750. It develops the judiciously admiring criticism of Pope's translation in Letters XX and XLIII. Melmoth considered Pope's Homer to have surpassed all rivals, and Congreve's '*Priam*'s Lamentation and Petition to *Achilles*' and

'The Lamentations of *Hecuba*, *Andromache*, and *Helen*' are roughly handled.

I shall close this review with Mr. Congreve; who has translated the petition of Priam to Achilles for the body of his son Hector, together with the lamentations of Andromache, Hecuba, and Helen.

HOMER represents the unfortunate king of Troy, as entering unobserved into the tent of Achilles; and illustrates the surprize which arose in that chief and his attendants, upon the first discovery of Priam, by the following simile:

Ὡς δ' οταν ανδρ' ατη πυκινη λαβῃ, ος' ενι πατρη
Φωτα κατακτεινας αλλον εξικετο δημον,
Ανδρος ες αθνειου, θαμβος δ'εχει εισοροωντας·
Ὡς Αχιλευς θαμβησεν, ιδων Πριαμον θεοειδεα.
                                                        xxiv. 480.[1]

Nothing can be more languid and inelegant than the manner in which Congreve has rendered this passage:

> *But as a wretch, who has a murder done,*
> *And seeking refuge, does from justice run;*
> *Entring some house, in haste, where he's unknown,*
> *Creates amazement in the lookers on:*
> *So did Achilles gaze, surpriz'd to see*
> *The godlike Priam's royal misery.*
>   CONG.
> ['*Priam*'s lamentation etc.', ll. 20–5]

But Pope has raised the same thought with his usual grace and spirit:

> *As when a wretch, who, conscious of his crime,*
> *Pursu'd for murder, flies his native clime,*
> *Just gains some frontier, breathless, pale, amaz'd!*
> *All gaze, all wonder: thus Achilles gaz'd.*
>   POPE.
>   [xxiv, ll. 590–3]

THE Speech of Priam is wonderfully pathetic and affecting. He tells Achilles, that out of fifty sons he had one only remaining; and of him he was now unhappily bereaved by his sword. He conjures him by his tenderness for his own father to commiserate the most wretched of parents, who, by an uncommon severity of fate, was thus obliged to kiss those hands which were imbrued in the blood of his children:

> του νυν εινεχ' ικανω νηας Αχαιων,
> Λυσομενος παρα σειο, φερω δ' απερεισι' αποινα.
> Αλλ' αιδειο θεους, Αχιλευ, αυτον τ' ελεησον,
> Μνησαμενος σου πατρος· εγω δ' ελεεινοτερος περ,
> Ετλην δ', οι ουπω τις επιχθονιος βροτος αλλος,
> Ανδρος παιδοφονοιο ποτι στομα χειρ' ορεγεσθαι.
> X 501.[2]

THESE moving lines Mr. Congreve has debased into the lowest and most unaffecting prose:

> *For his sake only I am hither come;*
> *Rich gifts I bring, and wealth, an endless sum;*
> *All to redeem that fatal prize you won,*
> *A worthless ransom for so brave a son.*
> *Fear the just gods, Achilles, and on me*
> *With pity look, think, you your father see:*
> *Such as I am, he is; alone in this*
> *I can no equal have in miseries;*
> *Of all mankind most wretched and forlorn,*
> *Bow'd with such weight as never has been borne;*
> *Reduc'd to kneel and pray to you, from whom*
> *The spring and source of all my sorrows come;*
> *With gifts to court mine and my country's bane,*
> *And kiss those hands which have my children slain.*
>
> CONGREVE.
> [ibid., ll. 64–77]

Nothing could compensate the trouble of laboring thro these heavy and tasteless rhimes, but the pleasure of being relieved at the end of them with a more lively prospect of poetry:

> *For him thro hostile camps I bent my way,*
> *For him thus prostrate at thy feet I lay;*
> *Large gifts proportion'd to thy wrath I bear;*
> *O hear the wretched, and the gods revere!*
> *Think of thy father, and this face behold!*
> *See him in me, as helpless and as old!*
> *Tho not so wretched: there he yields to me,*

The first of men in sov'reign misery;
Thus forc'd to kneel, thus grov'ling to embrace
The scourge and ruin of my realm and race:
Suppliant my children's murd'rer to implore,
And kiss those hands yet reeking with their gore.

POPE.

[XXIV, ll. 622–33]

ACHILLES having at length consented to restore the dead body of Hector, Priam conducts it to his palace. It is there placed in funeral pomp, at the same time that mournful dirges are sung over the corpse, intermingled with the lamentations of Andromache, Hecuba, and Helen:

τον μεν επειτα
Τρητοις εν λεχεεσσι θεσαν, παρα δ' εισαν αοιδους,
Θρηνων εξαρχους, οιτε στονοεσσαν αοιδην
Οι μεν αρ' εθρηνεον, επι δε στεναχοντο γυναικες.
                                                         X 719.[3]

There is something extremely solemn and affecting, in Homer's description of this scene of sorrow: a translator, who was touched with the least spark of poetry, could not, one should imagine, but rise beyond himself, in copying after so noble an original. It has not, however, been able to elevate Mr. Congreve above his usual flatness of numbers:

then laid
With care the body on a sumptuous bed,
And round about were skilful singers plac'd,
Who wept and sigh'd, and in sad notes express'd
Their moan: All in a chorus did agree
Of universal, mournful harmony.

CONGREVE.

['The Lamentations of *Hecuba*, etc.', ll. 41–6]

IT would be the highest injustice to the following lines to quote them in opposition to those of Mr. Congreve: I produce them, as marked with a vein of poetry much superior even to the original:

They weep, and place him on a bed of state.
A melancholy choir attend around
With plaintive sighs and music's solemn sound:
Alternately they sing, alternate flow
Th'obedient tears, melodious in their woe;

While deeper sorrows groan from each full heart,
And nature speaks at ev'ry pause of art.

POPE.

[XXIV, ll. 899–905]

THUS, Euphronius, I have brought before you some of the most renowned of our British bards, contending, as it were, for the prize of poetry: And there can be no debate to whom it justly belongs. Mr. Pope seems, indeed, to have raised our numbers to the highest possible perfection of strength and harmony: And, I fear, all the praise that the best succeeding poets can expect, as to their versification, will be, that they have happily imitated his manner. Farewel. I am, &c.

NOTES

1 'As when overpowering blindness of mind seizes a man, who killing a person in his homeland flies to another country, to a rich man, wonder holds them who see him; so Achilles wondered when he saw godlike Priam.'

2 'For the sake of his being restored from you, I am now come to the ships of the Achaeans, and I carry a ransom not to be reckoned. Stand in awe of the gods, Achilles, take pity on me, remembering your father; I am indeed more pitiable, and have endured what never yet any man on earth endured, to stretch out my hand to the mouth of the man who is the killer of my sons.'

3 'Then they put him on an inlaid bedstead, and placed beside him singers, the leaders of the funeral-song, who wailed a mournful lament, and the women moaned in response.'

60. John Campbell and Andrew Kippis in *Biographia Britannica*

1750 and 1789

From (a) *Biographia Britannica; or, The Lives of the Most Eminent Persons who have flourished in Great Britain and Ireland*, 6 vols

(London: 1747–66); (b) 2nd edition, With Corrections by Andrew Kippis, 5 vols (London: 1778–93).

The 'Congreve' entry for the original *Biographia Britannica* was written by the Scotsman John Campbell (1708–85), a writer of historical and topographical works. The revised edition by Andrew Kippis (1725–95), a nonconformist minister and tutor, adds notes upon Campbell's article. A comparison clearly illustrates the decline of Congreve's reputation as a non-dramatic poet during the eighteenth century (see the Introduction, pp. 27–8).

(a)

He had a fine taste for Musick as well as Poetry, which sufficiently appears in his 'Hymn to Harmony in honour of St Cecilia's day 1701', set by Mr John Eccles, his great friend, and one of the most elegant Composers our nation has produced. To him also our author was obliged, for setting several of his songs, which are very beautiful in their kind, and have all that vivacity of wit which can give life and lustre to such performances. His early acquaintance with the Great, had promised him not an easy only, but a happy station in life, to which it is very rare that either true genius, or any kind of literary merit, recommends any man. This freed him from all obligations of courting any longer publick favour, though it still left him under the tie of gratitude to his illustrious friends. He acted in a manner suitable to his situation, he very seldom risked the character he had obtained for the sake of exalting it: but he never missed any opportunity of paying his complements to his high patrons, in a manner worthy of himself and of them. The death of the Marquis of Blandford, only son to the Duke of Marlborough, which happened Feb. 20, 1705, afforded him a melancholy occasion of endeavouring to soften, by celebrating, the distress of that illustrious family, which he did in a most beautiful Pastoral, inscribed to the Lord Godolphin, Lord High-Treasurer of England. The glorious successes of the British arms, under the invincible Duke beforementioned, supplied a glorious theme for an Ode to the late Queen Anne, in which he celebrates victories most honourable to this nation, in numbers that justly entitle their author to unfading reputation, as they cannot fail of preserving the memory of those victories, as long as our memory shall last, or a true taste in poetry remains. In another pindarick Ode he celebrated that great Statesman, and true Patriot, the Lord High-Treasurer Godolphin, taking occasion from that Nobleman's great delight in horse-racing, to imitate, or rather to emulate, the Greek Poet, in his favourite manner of writing, by a truly elegant and exquisite digression. We owe to him not only these two pieces in a kind of poetry almost before unknown to our language, but also a very learned and judicious Dissertation upon this species of poesy, which contains a solid and just criticism on those sort of irregular pieces, that hitherto have passed, though very undeservedly, for Pindaricks. The clearness and candour of his criticism, ought to give him as high a character in the Republick of Letters, as even his fine performances in so many different kinds of poetry. His *Birth of the Muse*, and his *Dedication* in verse of his poems when collected, both addressed to his old patron Charles Lord Halifax, are equally grateful and pleasing, though as different in their composition as any two pieces can be; the former is solemn and sublime, the latter easy and familiar. We see in one, how able the Poet was to rise to the greatest heights without the least mixture of bombast or fustian; and in the other, how finely he could unite the becoming liberty of a friend, with that respect which was nevertheless due to his patron's superior rank and dignity. But as, in the earlier part of his life, Mr Congreve had received obligations from persons of less exalted station, so of these he was highly sensible, and never let slip any favourable opportunity of returning. He wrote an Epilogue for his old friend Mr Southerne's fine tragedy of *Oroonoko*, and we learn from Mr Dryden himself, how much he owed to his assistance in the translation of Virgil. He contributed by translating the eleventh Satire to the translation of Juvenal published by that great poet, and wrote an admirable copy of verses on the version of Perseus performed by Mr Dryden alone. He wrote likewise a Prologue for a Play of Mr Charles Dryden's, full of kindness for that young gentleman, and of respect for his father. But the noblest testimony he gave of his filial reverence for that exalted genius, was in that inimitable panegyrick upon his writings, contained in the Dedication of his Plays to his Grace the Duke of Newcastle, a monument that will for ever express, in the most lively colours, the worth of him to whose honour it is consecrated, and the capacity, candour, and critical justice, of the hand that raised it. His translations have done him the greatest honour, in the sentiments of those who were the best judges, and who have taken pains to compare them with their originals. The *Hymn to Venus*, and some of the most moving passages in the *Iliad*, appear with all the spirit and dignity of Homer in the English version, and as it is impossible for a learned writer to peruse them without confessing his accuracy, so whoever has a true taste for poetry must feel the effects of that art and force, with which all the emotions naturally rising from the passions of the human mind, are expressed in these nervous pieces. His imitations of Horace have as much the air of that Poet as our times or language will permit, that is, the same strength, vivacity, and delicacy, for which, through a long series of years, they have been admired in the original. The third book of Ovid's *Art of Love* appears in our tongue with all the sweetness and softness peculiar to that author, who was perfectly acquainted with the passion, and knew how to describe it with all the masterly graces of a great Poet, and what was admired in the Augustan age, becomes excellent in ours, from the skill of Mr Congreve, and the happy union of the most distant excellencies in a translator, ease and exactness. He was the better qualified for an undertaking of this kind, from the natural turn of his own temper, for his Poem to, and his excellent epigram on, Mrs Arabella Hunt, are entirely in the Ovidian strain, and are as pleasingly pathetick as any Poems in their kind, in our own, or perhaps in any other language. There is a strength and solemnity in his verses to the memory of Lady Gethins, and in his Epitaph upon the two Huntingtons, that makes one scarce conceive it possible that he should succeed as well in lighter compositions, and yet the tales that he has told after a celebrated French author, are so unaffected and natural, that if we were not apprised of it we should never have suspected they were translations; but there is one piece of his which ought to be particularly distinguished, as being so truly an original, that though it seems to be written with the utmost facility, yet we may despair of ever seeing it copied; this is his *DORIS*, so highly and so justly commended by Sir Richard Steele, as the sharpest and most delicate satire he had ever met with. We must not omit, in this free catalogue of his works, two pieces of the dramatick kind, which do him equal honour as a Poet, and as a lover of Musick, *viz.* the *Judgment of Paris*, a *Masque*, and the *Opera of Semele*. Of these, the former was acted with great applause, and the latter finely set to musick by Mr Eccles. In respect to both it is but bare justice to say, that they have the same stamp of excellency borne by the rest of Mr. Congreve's works, were considered as master-pieces when published, and may serve as models to posterity. We have now almost finished the list of his poetical labours, in which we have been the more particular, because it was peculiar to Mr Congreve to have written and excelled, not barely in every kind of dramatick poetry, but almost in every kind of poetry. The last to which he turned his genius was that of familiar epistles, of these that on the *Art of Pleasing*, addressed to Sir Richard Temple, now the Field Marshal Viscount Cobham, is the only one inserted in his works, and is so truly admirable, that the publick has just reason to regret some others that are still said to be preserved in the cabinets of his friends to whom they were addressed, and which it is hoped will one day see the light. Another epistle of his to the same noble person, as it is not to be found in his works, we have, as one of it's brightest ornaments, inserted in ours, from a copy that appeared to be very correct.

(III, pp. 1444–7)

(b)

On *Incognita*:

It has merit, considering the age of the author. What it is chiefly distinguished by, is that intricacy of plot which he afterwards so much displayed in his dramatic writings; and something may be traced in the dialogue parts, of his succeeding coruscations of wit. The story, however, is very unnatural. We shall not read it again.

(IV, p. 79)

On Congreve's poems:

In our Predecessor's article, the most extravagant encomiums are bestowed upon Mr. Congreve's Miscellaneous Poems. Such exuberant and indiscriminate praise is seldom the result of judgment, and certainly is not so in the present case. Our Author's Dramatic Works excepted, few readers will now be able to go through his poetical productions with any great degree of pleasure. Dr. Johnson's criticism upon them affords a fine contrast to the loud applauses of the text; and, indeed, in every view, deserves to be inserted. Perhaps, in the fastidiousness of his taste, he may sometimes be thought too severe: but if he have erred in this respect, with regard to the instance before us, his error is very trifling.

(ibid., p. 81)

61. Joseph Warton in *The Adventurer*

1754

From *The Adventurer*, 2 vols (London: 1753–4), II, pp. 375–6.

Joseph Warton (1722–1800), critic and poet, is now best remembered for his *Essay on the Genius and Writings of Pope*, of which the first volume appeared in 1756, and the second in 1782. The success of his Latin and English edition of Virgil, published in 1753, led to Samuel Johnson's inviting him to write for *The Adventurer*. It was anticipated that Warton's contributions would belong to the 'Province of Criticism and Literature'. See No. 46 in *The Letters of Samuel Johnson*, ed. R. W. Chapman, 3 vols (Oxford: Clarendon Press, 1952), I, pp. 44–5. The extract below comes from an essay discussing the superiority of the moderns to the ancients in the field of humour and ridicule; it appeared in No. cxxxiii, for Tuesday 12 February 1754.

WILL it be deemed a paradox to assert that CONGREVE has not drawn a single character? His FONDLEWIFE and FORESIGHT are but faint portraits of common characters, and BEN is a forced and unnatural caricatura. His plays appear not to be legitimate comedies, but strings of repartees, and sallies of wit, the most poignant and polite indeed, but unnatural and ill placed. The trite and trivial character of a fop hath strangely engrossed the English stage, and given an insipid familiarity to our best comic pieces. Originals can never be wanting in such a kingdom as this, where each man follows his natural inclinations and propensities, if our writers would really contemplate nature, and endeavour to open those mines of humour which have been so long and so unaccountably neglected.

62. Arthur Murphy in *The Gray's Inn Journal*

1754

From *The Gray's Inn Journal*, No. 49, Saturday, 31 August 1754, p. 293.

Arthur Murphy (1727–1805), an Irishman, began his career as a merchant's clerk, and became a journalist, an actor, a dramatist, and barrister by turns. Many of his plays are adaptations, usually from French sources. Murphy supplied an 'Essay on the Life and Genius of Samuel Johnson' for the 1792 edition of Johnson's *Works*; consequently this has come to be known, albeit inaccurately, as 'Murphy's edition'.

The publishing history of *The Gray's Inn Journal* is complex. It began in October 1752 as a series of weekly essays which Murphy wrote for *The Craftsman* under the pseudonym of 'Charles Ranger'; the originals of these are now lost. From September 1753 until September 1754, it appeared as a separate paper which ran to fifty-two numbers. The two-volume collection of 1756 incorporates both the 1753–4 series and the forty-nine *Craftsman* essays, with additional material and considerable rewriting. There was a further revision of the *Journal* for Murphy's collection of his *Works* in 1786. The extract below is taken from an essay in the original 1753–4 series.

In producing Portraits of Mankind it is not enough to display Foibles and Oddities; a fine Vein of Ridicule must run through the whole, to urge the Mind to frequent Emotions of Laughter; otherwise there will be Danger of exhibiting disagreeable Characters without affording the proper Entertainment. I think *Ben Johnson* extremely apt to err in this Point; His *Morose*, is a surly, ill-natured, absurd Humourist, whom we can hardly laugh at, and he soon becomes very bad Company. Many of *Johnson*'s Characters are of the same Cast, while in *Shakespear*'s *Falstaff*, the ridiculous

Ideas are placed in such an artful Point of View, that our Merriment can never be restrained, whenever Sir *John* appears. *Congreve* in my Opinion had a great Deal of the same Talent, and what I have somewhere seen objected to him, that many of his Characters are obvious in human Life, is with me a strong Proof of his superior Genius. An Old *Batchelor*, for Instance, is very common, but he must pass thro' such an Imagination as *Congreve*'s to support several Scenes in the Drama with the most exquisite Pleasantry. Though the Character was not new, yet his Management of it has all the Graces of Novelty, and the Situations in which we see him are all exquisitely ridiculous. Personages of this Class, unless artfully conducted, may very soon tire an Audience, but in this excellent Poet's Hands nothing suffers a Diminution. The same, I think, appears in his Sir *Paul Plyant*, in which Character there is perhaps as much Comic Force as in any one Piece on the Stage.

63. Arthur Murphy (?), three reviews in *The London Chronicle*

1757–8

From (a) *The London Chronicle, or, Universal Evening Post* (1757), 1 (12): 96; (b) ibid. (1758), 4 (280): 367; (c) ibid. (1758), 4 (294): 479.

The following notices of performances of Congreve's plays are from 'The Theatre', a review column in Robert Dodsley's *London Chronicle*. 'The Theatre' appeared intermittently over two years between January 1757 and December 1758, and forms four distinct series. Scholarship has gradually established that the column was very probably instigated and written by Arthur Murphy. For a discussion of the authorship which conveniently summarizes earlier findings see *New Essays by Arthur Murphy*, ed. Arthur Sherbo (East Lansing, Mich.: Michigan State University Press, 1963), pp. 75–8.

(a) From TUESDAY, JANUARY 25, to THURSDAY, JANUARY 27, 1757
The Theatre. No. 3 DRURY–LANE, Jan. 25, 1757.

MR. *Congreve*'s Tragedy called the *Mourning Bride*, produced for the
first Time in Lincoln's-Inn-Fields, in the Year 1696, was exhibited
here this Evening. The Success of this Piece was, in all Probability,
chiefly owing to the great Reputation of its Author, and the false
Taste, which prevailed in those Days. It seems a kind of Fatality in
the literary World, that Fashion seems to govern, what should only
be directed by the Standard of Nature. One may reasonably
imagine that Audiences, when the *Mourning Bride* was wrote, were
chiefly fond of being elevated and surprized, and indeed the same
vicious Relish seems to re-commence at present; otherwise we
should not see Plays received with Applause, when their chief
Merit consists in Trick, Incident, and Business, without Character,
Fable, or Language. The *Mourning Bride* is not entirely defective in
the three last-mentioned Particulars: *Zara* is a commanding
Character; the Vicissitudes of her Rage and Love; her noble
Propensities, and the Vehemence of her Passions, *which tear her
Virtues up*, are all drawn in very fine Proportions. *Osmyn* is likewise
a Character well conceived: The first Introduction of him is very
striking, and his Exit in the Close of the first Act leaves the Mind in
a Pause of Suspence. His filial Piety very properly leads him to visit
his Father's Tomb; the Discovery that he is *Alphonso*, when he
comes out of the Vault, is very artificial, and is succeeded by a
recognizing Scene between him and *Almeria*, in which Joy and
Tenderness are affectingly mingled. After this, the Remainder of
Osmyn's Part is all Rant and wild Poetry, the Ideas and Expressions
being drawn from the Stores of Imagination, without the Simplicity always natural to Emotions of the Heart. The rest of the Piece
is a Succession of Miracles, unnatural and improbable Turns of
Fortune, and we are every Moment surprized with some new
Discovery to make us stare, but not reach our Hearts. However,
upon the Whole, this Tragedy is on the Side of Virtue, and in that
Respect, and that only, it is the best of all Mr. *Congreve*'s Plays.

(b) From THURSDAY, October 12, to SATURDAY, October 14, 1758
Saturday, October 14. Postscript. The Theatre COVENT-GARDEN

Yesterday evening was performed at the above theatre, the comedy
of *Love for Love*.

Were I to give my own opinion, I should say, that this is the best comedy either antient or modern, that ever was written to please upon the stage; for while the most superficial judges admire it, it is impossible but the nicest, and most accurate, must approve.

It is written strictly up to the rules of the drama; yet it has all that variety of characters and incidents, which is pleaded in their excuse by those who deviate from them. What fault then can we find in it? Oh, says somebody, it has too much Wit. Well, that is a fault so seldom committed, I should think we might overlook it for once; but even in this case we can only say of Congreve, what Addison has already said of Cowley,

He'd pleas'd us more if he had pleas'd us less.

and it must be confessed indeed that Congreve was richer in wit, I mean in wit of the true sterling kind, than any man whatsoever; and in this particular he puts me in mind of a certain Dutch Jewess I once heard of, who had so many jewels that she stuck them in the heels of her shoes, for he has made all the personages in his comedies Wits, from the highest to the lowest; and in particular the character of Jeremy, in this play, is one of the wittiest that ever was writ. But, I don't know how it is, he has still taken care never to violate Nature; for tho' he has shewn her every where loaded with finery, it may be rather said to set her off to advantage, than disguise her; since her acquaintance might distinguish her at first sight.

Nor is there any Writer that has marked his characters so strongly, or so highly finished them, as Congreve. He seems indeed to have given into the notion that vicious persons are the proper representations for a comic writer to make: and I remember Voltaire mentions it as an instance of his consummate knowledge in human nature that he has made all his characters speak the language of honest men, but commit the actions of knaves. I will not say that he copied his manners from the Great among whom he lived.

It is with great pleasure that I take this opportunity of doing justice to the merit of Mr. Ross, who performs Valentine better, than I ever saw it done by any one else. Indeed genteel comedy seems to be his *fort*: not that I would be thought to insinuate as if he had it not in his power to make himself considerable in any part which he thought proper to take pains with; but he has so much of the gentleman about him in every respect, that he appears to more immediate advantage in those, because this appears more like himself.

Collins takes the superstitious, credulous old fool upon him, in the character of *Foresight*, with great justness; and no body can see Shuter in the part of *Ben*, without being put in a good humour.

I am at a loss how to reconcile the little notice which is taken of this excellent play, by a certain manager, with the ideas which I have conceived of his judgment in other respects. Nor can I be of any other way of thinking, than if that Love for Love were represented on Drury-lane stage, the actor who made such a figure in the prologue to Britannia, might give a pleasure in the part of *Ben*, which would more than recompence for the loss of the ballad about *a Soldier and a Sailor*.

(c) From TUESDAY, NOVEMBER 14, to THURSDAY, NOVEMBER 16, 1758. The THEATRE. No. 10

DRURY-LANE, *Nov.* 14. Yesterday evening at the above theatre was presented *The Way of the World*, a comedy, which for poignancy of wit; delicacy of humour; regularity of conduct; propriety of manners; and continuity of character; may (if ever work might) be reckoned a finished piece.

Mr. Congreve had too intimate an acquaintance with human nature not to know that the generality of mankind have a much greater share of vices, than virtues, in their composition; and it is the business of a comic poet to turn the most glaring side outward. To this we owe his Fainal and Mirabel: two parts, the justness of which, Mr. Havard and Mr. Palmer make us conscious of; and yet all that can be said in their favour is that they are a couple of well-bred rascals. Mirabel indeed seems to be immoral in principle; his vices are shewn as an ornament to his character. Fainal is vicious, but in a grosser way.

It was at two characters in this comedy (Witwou'd and Petulant) that Mr. Pope seems to have levelled these lines,

> Observe how seldom even the best succeed,
> Tell me if Congreve's fools be fools indeed?[1]

because the abovementioned gentlemen happen to say as many good things as any in the piece. But if they cannot properly be called fools, in which light the author intended to shew them, they must certainly be called coxcombs, which are but a degree above them. And since the best things degenerated become the worst, why may we not say that an impertinent wit is the most disagreeable of fools.

Mr. Obrien has a peculiar tone of voice very fit for doing justice to a part of this kind; and the significancy of his looks and gestures add not a little to the pleasure of the spectators. However the quickness of his parts does not seem to slacken his industry, and if he continues to mind his business, I think there is no doubt of his making a great actor.

It may not be universally known, perhaps, as he has not thought proper to give any intimation of the thing, that Mr. Congreve took the plot of his *Way of the World* from the French. Yet the most unobserving reader will easily perceive upon looking over the *Amorous Widow*, a comedy translated from Dancourt, by Mr. Betterton, that both those plays have taken their rise from the same original. However Mr. Congreve was too great a Genius to submit to a servile copy; he has therefore by his refinement, additions, and alterations, given the thing quite a different air. How much superior is Lady Wishfor't to Lady Laycock? The author has invented a language on purpose for her; forged new manners, and in short left nothing wanting but what can only be given by such an actress as Mrs. Clive. Lady Wishfor't is indeed a ridiculous character, but she shews a ridiculous woman of quality; whereas all the actresses that have hitherto performed the part have dressed themselves like mad women, and acted in the strain of an old nurse. A high fruze tower, a gaudy petticoat of one sort, and a gown of another, was sure to create a laugh; but Mrs. Clive is not obliged to have recourse to any such pityful expedients. Accordingly she dresses the part in the pink of the present mode, and makes more of it than any actress ever did.

There is a strong tincture of affectation in the character of Millemant; which is so foreign to Mrs. Pritchard's disposition, one of whose chief beauties is ease, and a close attention to nature, that it is not strange if this part should appear less becoming upon her than many others. Notwithstanding which, her life and spirit is such, that, since Mrs. Woffington's retirement from the stage, I do not see any actress, besides herself, in any degree equal to it. Mrs. Yates does the part of Marwood incomparably well, and gives us great reason to regret that we have not the pleasure of seeing her oftener.

This is the last play that Mr. Congreve ever writ; and it is said, that the cold reception which it met with from the public, on its first appearance, was the reason why he would never write another: but since that, they have acquired a juster notion of its value; and it gave me great pleasure to see such a crouded pit and boxes last night. Yates, in the character of Sir Wilful, hardly ever opened his mouth, but he set the house in a roar; and from the great satisfaction they expressed at the whole performance, it is evident, that however fond the town may be of those fantastical representations (which old Cibber aptly enough compares to dram-drinking) it is evident I say that their tastes are not yet so vitiated, but they have still a relish for some wholesome entertainments.

NOTE

1 *Imitations of Horace*, Ep.II.i, 'To Augustus', ll. 286–7.

64. Charles Churchill in *The Rosciad*

1761

From *The Poetical Works of Charles Churchill*, ed. Douglas Grant (Oxford: Clarendon Press, 1956), p. 26.

Churchill's poem is concerned with the theatrical profession rather than the drama, but it contains the following lines on Mrs Hannah Pritchard (1711–68) in the role of Zara in *The Mourning Bride*. Contemporary opinion of Mrs Pritchard's acting varied widely; cf. Davies in No. 76 below.

> PRITCHARD, by Nature for the stage design'd,
> In person graceful, and in sense refin'd;

Her Art as much as Nature's friend became,
Her voice as free from blemish as her fame.
Who knows so well in majesty to please,
Attemper'd with the graceful charms of ease?

    When Congreve's favour'd pantomime to grace,
She comes a captive queen of Moorish race;
When Love, Hate, Jealousy, Despair and Rage,
With wildest tumults in her breast engage;
Still equal to herself is Zara seen;
Her passions are the passions of a Queen.

(ll. 803–14)

65. Arthur Murphy in 'An Essay on the Life and Genius of Henry Fielding, Esq;'

1762

From *The Works of Henry Fielding, Esq;*, 4 vols (London: 1762), I, pp. 24–5.

Perhaps the asperity of Fielding's muse was not a little encouraged by the practice of two great wits, who had fallen into the same vein before him; I mean *Wycherley* and *Congreve*, who were in general painters of harsh features, attached more to subjects of deformity than grace; whose drawings of women are ever a sort of *Harlot's Progress*, and whose men for the most part lay violent hands upon deeds and settlements, and generally deserve informations in the king's bench. These two celebrated writers were not fond of copying the amiable part of human life; they had not learned the secret of giving the softer graces of composition to their tablature, by contrasting the fair and beautiful in characters and manners to the vicious and irregular, and thereby rendering their pieces more exact imitations of nature. By making Congreve his model, it is no wonder that our author contracted this vicious turn, and became

237

faulty in that part of his art, which the painters would call DESIGN. In his style, he derived an error from the same source: he sometimes forgot that humour and ridicule were the two principal ingredients of comedy; and, like his master, he frequently aimed at decorations of wit, which do not appear to make part of the *ground*, but seem rather to be embroidered upon it. It has been observed*, that the plays of *Congreve appear not to be legitimate comedies, but strings of repartees and sallies of wit, the most poignant and polite indeed, but unnatural and ill-placed*. If we except the *Old Batchelor, Foresight*, and Sir *Sampson Legend*, there will hardly, perhaps, be found a character in this lively writer exempt from this general censure. The frequent surprises of allusion, and the quickness and vivacity of those sudden turns, which abound in Mr. Congreve, breaking out where you least expected them, as if a train of wit had been laid all around, put one in mind of those fire-works in a water-piece, which used formerly to be played off at *Cuper's Gardens*; no sooner one tube, charged with powder, raised itself above the surface, and vented itself in various forms and evolutions of fire, but instantly another and another was lighted up; and the pleasure of the spectators arose from seeing secret artificial mines blazing out of an element, in which such a machinery could not be expected. The same kind of entertainment our author aimed at, too frequently, in his comedies; and as in this he bore a similitude to *Wycherley* and *Congreve*, so he also frequently resembled them in the indelicacy, and sometimes the downright obscenity of his raillery; a vice introduced, or, at least, pampered by the wits of Charles II: the dregs of it, till very lately, not being quite purged away.

NOTE

* See the Adventurer [i.e. No. 61 above].

66. Henry Home, Lord Kames in *Elements of Criticism*

1762–3

From *Elements of Criticism*, 3 vols (Edinburgh: 1762; 2nd edition, 1763).

Henry Home (1696–1782) took the title Lord Kames when he became lord of session in the Scots judiciary in 1752. A distinguished figure in the eighteenth-century Scottish Enlightenment, he engaged in controversy with Hume on the subject of natural religion. *Elements of Criticism* first appeared in 1762 and went through five editions in the author's lifetime; additions and corrections were made frequently, right up to the posthumous sixth edition of 1785.

(i) From Chap. XVI, 'Sentiments'

So much in general upon the genuine sentiments of passion. I proceed to particular observations. And, first, passions are seldom uniform any considerable time: they generally fluctuate, swelling and subsiding by turns, often in a quick succession. This fluctuation, in the case of a real passion, will be expressed externally by proper sentiments; and ought to be imitated in writing and acting. Accordingly, a climax shows never better than in expressing a swelling passion. The following passages may suffice for an illustration.

> *Oroonoko.*——Can you raise the dead?
> Pursue and overtake the wings of time?
> And bring about again, the hours, the days,
> The years, that made me happy?
> *Oroonoko*, II, ii, 36–9

> *Almeria.*——How hast thou charm'd
> The wildness of the waves and rocks to this?
> That thus relenting they have giv'n thee back
> To earth, to light and life, to love and me?
> *Mourning Bride*, II, vii, 26–9

> I would not be the villain that thou think'st
> For the whole space that's in the tyrant's grasp,
> And the rich earth to boot.
>
> *Macbeth*, IV, iii, 35−7

The following passage expresses finely the progress of conviction.

> Let me not stir, nor breathe, lest I dissolve
> That tender, lovely form, of painted air,
> So like Almeria. Ha! it sinks, it falls;
> I'll catch it ere it goes, and grasp her shade.
> 'Tis life! 'tis warm! 'tis she! 'tis she herself!
> It is Almeria! 'tis, it is my wife!
>
> *Mourning Bride*, II, vi, 12−18

In the progress of thought, our resolutions become more vigorous as well as our passions.

> If ever I do yield or give consent,
> By any action, word, or thought, to wed
> Another Lord; may then just Heav'n show'r down, etc.
>
> *Mourning Bride*, I, i, 173−5

(II, pp. 163−5)

(ii) ibid.

Congreve shows a fine taste in the sentiments of the *Mourning Bride*. But in the following passage the picture is too artful to be suggested by severe grief:

> *Almeria*. O no! Time gives increase to my afflictions.
> The circling hours, that gather all the woes
> Which are diffus'd through the revolving year,
> Come heavy-laden with th' oppressing weight
> To me; with me, successively they leave
> The sighs, the tears, the groans, the restless cares,
> And all the damps of grief, that did retard their flight:
> They shake their downy wings, and scatter all
> The dire collected dews on my poor head;
> Then fly with joy and swiftness from me.
>
> (I, i, 144−53)

In the same play, Almeria seeing a dead body, which she took to be Alphonso's, expresses sentiments strained and artificial, which nature suggests not to any person upon such an occasion:

Had they, or hearts, or eyes, that did this deed?
Could eyes endure to guide such cruel hands?
Are not my eyes guilty alike with theirs,
That thus can gaze, and yet not turn to stone?
—I do not weep! The springs of tears are dry'd,
And of a sudden I am calm, as if
All things were well; and yet my husband's murder'd!
Yes, yes, I know to mourn! I'll sluice this heart,
The source of wo, and let the torrent loose.

V, xi, 21–9

(II, pp. 180–1)

(iii) ibid.

When the fable is of human affairs, every event, every incident, and every circumstance, ought to be natural, otherwise the imitation is imperfect. But an imperfect imitation is a venial fault, compared with that of running cross to nature. In the *Hippolytus* of Euripides★, Hippolytus, wishing for another self in his own situation, How much (says he) should I be touched with his misfortune! as if it were natural to grieve more for the misfortunes of another than for one's own.

> *Osmyn.* Yet I behold her—yet—and now no more.
> Turn your lights inward, Eyes, and view my thought,
> So shall you still behold her—'twill not be.
> O impotence of sight! mechanic sense
> Which to exterior objects ow'st thy faculty,
> Not seeing of election, but necessity.
> Thus do our eyes, as do all common mirrors,
> Successively reflect succeeding images.
> Nor what they would, but must; a star or toad;
> Just as the hand of Chance administers!
>
> *Mourning Bride*, II, viii, 1–10

No man, in his senses, ever thought of applying his eyes to discover what passes in his mind; far less of blaming his eyes for not seeing a thought or idea.

(II, pp. 196–8)

(iv) From Chap. XVII, 'Language of Passion'

AMONG the particulars that compose the social part of our nature, a propensity to communicate our opinions, our emotions, and every thing that affects us, is remarkable. Bad fortune and injustice affect every one greatly; and of these we are so prone to complain, that if we have no friend or acquaintance to take part in our sufferings, we

sometimes utter our complaints aloud even where there are none to
listen.

But this propensity, though natural, operates not in every state
of mind. A man immoderately grieved, seeks to afflict himself; and
self-affliction is the gratification of the passion. Immoderate grief is
therefore mute; because complaining is struggling for relief:

> It is the wretch's comfort still to have
> Some small reserve of near and inward wo,
> Some unsuspected hoard of inward grief,
> Which they unseen may wail, and weep, and mourn,
> And glutton-like alone devour.
>
> *Mourning Bride*, I, i, 78–82
>
> (II, pp. 204–5)

(v) ibid.

The next class of the grosser errors which all writers ought to
avoid, shall be of language elevated above the tone of the
sentiment; of which take the following instances.

> *Zara.* Swift as occasion, I
> Myself will fly; and earlier than the morn
> Wake thee to freedom. Now 'tis late; and yet
> Some news few minutes past arriv'd, which seem'd
> To shake the temper of the King—Who knows
> What racking cares disease a monarch's bed?
> Or love, that late at night still lights his lamp,
> And strikes his rays through dusk, and folded lids,
> Forbidding rest, may stretch his eyes awake,
> And force their balls abroad at this dead hour.
> I'll try.
>
> *Mourning Bride*, III, iv, 53–63

The language here is undoubtedly too pompous and laboured for
describing so simple a circumstance as absence of sleep.

> (II, pp. 224–5)

(vi) From Chap. XXIII 'The three Unities'

A play analyzed, is a chain of connected facts, of which each scene
makes a link. Each scene, accordingly, ought to produce some
incident relative to the catastrophe or ultimate event, by advancing
or retarding it. If no incident be produced, such a scene, which may
be termed barren, ought not to be indulged, because it breaks the
unity of action. A barren scene can never be intitled to a place,

because the chain is complete without it. In the *Old Bachelor*, the 3d scene of act 2. and all that follow to the end of that act, are mere conversation-pieces, without any consequence. The 10th and 11th scenes, act 3. *Double Dealer*, the 10th, 11th, 12th, 13th, and 14th scenes, act 1. *Love for Love*, are of the same kind. Neither is *The Way of the World* entirely guiltless of such scenes. It will be no justification, that they help to display characters. It were better, like Dryden, in his *dramatis personae*, to describe characters beforehand, which would not break the chain of action. But a writer of genius has no occasion for such artifice: he can display the characters of his personages much more to the life in sentiment and action. How successfully is this done by Shakespear! in whose works there is not to be found a single barren scene.   (III, pp. 266–7)

(vii) ibid.

Further, music, though it cannot of itself raise a passion, prepares us for the passion that follows: by making chearful, tender, melancholy, or animated impressions, music has power to dispose the heart to various passions. Of this power, the first scene of the *Mourning Bride* is a shining instance: without the preparation of soft music in a melancholy strain, it would be extremely difficult to enter all at once into Almeria's deep distress. In this manner, music and representation support each other delightfully: the impression made upon the audience by the representation, is a fine preparation for the music that succeeds; and the impression made by the music is a fine preparation for the representation that succeeds.

(III, p. 284)

(viii) ibid.

French writers, generally speaking, are extremely correct in this particular: the English, on the contrary, are so irregular as scarce to deserve a criticism: actors not only succeed each other in the same place without connection; but what is still worse, they frequently succeed each other in different places. This change of place in the same act, ought never to be indulged; for, beside breaking the unity of the act, it has a disagreeable effect. After an interval, the mind can readily accommodate itself to any place that is necessary, just as readily as at the commencement of the play; but during the representation, the mind rejects change of place. From the foregoing censure must be excepted the *Mourning Bride* of Congreve, where regularity concurs with the beauty of sentiment and of language, to make it one of the most complete pieces England has to boast of. I must acknowledge, however, that in point of regularity, this elegant performance is not altogether unexceptionable. In the first four acts, the unities of place and time are strictly observed: but in the last act, there is a capital error with respect to unity of place. In the first three scenes of that act, the place of action is a room of state, which is changed to a prison in the fourth scene: the chain of the actors withal is broken; for the persons introduced in the prison, are different from those who made their appearance in the room of state. This remarkable interruption of the representation, makes in effect two acts instead of one: and therefore, if it be a rule, that a play ought not to consist of more acts than five, this performance is so far defective in point of regularity. I may add, that even admitting six acts, the irregularity would not be altogether removed, without a longer pause in the representation than is allowed in the acting; for it requires more than a momentary interruption, to enable the imagination readily to accommodate itself to a new place, or to prorogation of time. In *The Way of the World*, of the same author, unity of place is preserved during every act, and a stricter unity of time during the whole play than is necessary.

(III, pp. 292–3)

(ix) From Chap. XXIV, 'Gardening and Architecture'

How odious ought those writers to be, who thus spread infection through their country, employing the talents they have from their Maker most ungratefully against himself, by endeavouring to corrupt and disfigure his creatures! If the comedies of Congreve did not rack him with remorse in his last moments, he must have been lost to all sense of virtue. Nor will it afford any excuse to such writers, that their comedies are entertaining, unless it could be maintained, that wit, sprightliness, and other such qualifications, are better suited to a vicious than a virtuous character: the direct contrary of which holds true in theory; and is exemplified in practice from the *Merry Wives of Windsor*, where we are highly entertained with the conduct of two ladies, not more remarkable for mirth and spirit than for the strictest purity of manners.

(2nd edn, III, p. 400)

NOTE

* ll. 1078–9.

67. Samuel Johnson in *The Life of Samuel Johnson, L.L.D.*, by James Boswell

1769

From *The Life of Samuel Johnson, L.L.D.*, 2 vols (London: 1791), I, pp. 317–18.

Johnson's praise of *The Mourning Bride*, II, iii, 1–17, occurs in a conversation which, according to Boswell, took place after dinner at the latter's lodgings on 16 October 1769. The other guests included Arthur Murphy and Thomas Davies, the authors of Nos 62 and 76 respectively.

Johnson said, that the description of the temple, in *The Mourning Bride*, was the finest poetical passage he had ever read; he recollected none in Shakspeare equal to it.—'But, (said Garrick, all alarmed for 'the god of his idolatry,') we know not the extent and variety of his powers. We are to suppose there are such passages in his works. Shakspeare must not suffer from the badness of our memories.' Johnson, diverted by this enthusiastick jealousy, went on with greater ardour: 'No, Sir; Congreve has *nature*,' (smiling on the tragick eagerness of Garrick;) but composing himself, he added, 'Sir, this is not comparing Congreve on the whole, with Shakspeare on the whole; but only maintaining that Congreve has one finer passage than any that can be found in Shakspeare. Sir, a man may have no more than ten guineas in the world, but he may have those ten guineas in one piece; and so may have a finer piece than a man who has ten thousand pounds: but then he has only one ten-guinea piece.—What I mean is, that you can shew me no passage where there is simply a description of material objects, without any intermixture of moral notions, which produces such an effect.' Mr. Murphy mentioned Shakspeare's description of the night before the battle of Agincourt; but it was observed, it had *men* in it. Mr. Davies suggested the speech of Juliet, in which she figures herself awaking in the tomb of her ancestors. Some one mentioned the description of Dover Cliff. JOHNSON. 'No, Sir, it should be all

precipice,—all vacuum. The crows impede your fall. The diminished appearance of the boats, and other circumstances, are all
very good description; but do not impress the mind at once with
the horrible idea of immense height. The impression is divided;
you pass on by computation, from one stage of the tremendous
space to another. Had the girl in *The Mourning Bride* said, she could
not cast her shoe to the top of one of the pillars in the temple, it
would not have aided the idea, but weakened it.'

68. Francis Gentleman in *The Dramatic Censor*

1770

From *The Dramatic Censor; or Critical Companion*, 2 vols
(London: 1770).

Francis Gentleman was born in Dublin in 1728, and died there
in 1784 having spent most of his adult life in England. After a
short spell in the army, he turned actor and playwright. Much
of his output consists of adaptations from earlier dramatists,
especially Ben Jonson. *The Dramatic Censor* was published
anonymously, the first volume being dedicated to Garrick,
with whom Gentleman had a rather uneasy friendship, and
the second to Samuel Foote. It consists of essays on forty-nine
plays, Shakespearean and post-Restoration. The usual format
is a detailed summary of the plot followed by a short general
assessment including remarks on the performance of the
leading roles by well-known actors. The first of the two
extracts given below comes from the notice of *The Mourning
Bride*, omitting the acrimoniously written résumé; the second
from 'A Summary View of the Most Known Dramatic
Writers', one of three general essays which conclude the
work.

(i)

The conclusion of this play draws a very moral inference, justly observing, that though virtue may labour under occasional chastisement, yet perseverance in rectitude cannot fail of reward. The MOURNING BRIDE has been, at different times, supported by very able performance, and has drawn many brilliant audiences, yet we cannot help thinking it one of the worst living tragedies: it is apparently laboured, the sentiments in general strained, the versification in many places monotonous, and the plot equivocal.

In point of characters, we find the King a weak, blustering, tyrannical object; a credulous lover, and a harsh father. His passions, especially in the fourth act, are laughable, and the device which occasions his death, farcical; he is altogether the most ungracious load that ever lay heavy on the shoulders of a performer. The highest merit that can be attained is to pass through him inoffensively, and in this view we have seen Mr. SPARKS. Mr. BERRY rumbled him out in a most disgusting manner: why he should be imposed upon Mr. J. AICKIN, we cannot conceive, unless to prejudice his merit in public opinion; his brother's general cast and stile of acting, should have royalized him in this play.

Osmyn is described to us as a hero, but appears in no other light than that of an affectionate, constant husband. His situations and embarrassments raise sensations of pity, but being totally out of the fourth act, and so immaterially concerned in the first and fifth, he becomes a very imperfect hero for representation.

We have seen Mr. SHERIDAN make Gothic attempts upon this part, for which he had not a single requisite: an insufficiency of figure, dissonance of expression, and limitation of voice, conjoined to overshadow every trace of merit. Mr. BARRY was happy enough to be the very reverse of the forementioned gentleman; his love, grief and rage, were all expressed by very adequate powers. Mr. GARRICK, we think, in the soliloquies, and the scene with Heli, outstripped every competitor; but the Moorish habit proved rather too much for his figure, and the amorous passages did not flow from him with that natural sincerity, of which Mr. BARRY gave us an ample and very pleasing idea. Mr. MOSSOP is much too mechanical and boisterous, he cannot shake off the bashaw; he should never attempt any thing in the amorous stile, but that sultanic hint of dropping the handkerchief. Mr. HOLLAND stiffened his deportment into a degree of aukwardness, and tortured the tones of his voice into an irksome degree of dissonance. Mr. INCHBALD has presented himself in Osmyn this season with a very slender degree of credit, being in every respect much worse than any we have named, except Mr. SHERIDAN. Gonzales, like most statesmen, of all ages, moves upon that ruling principle self-interest, and aggrandisement of his family. As a part he stands in a state of mediocrity, neither for or against the actor: we remember to have seen him well done by Mr. HAVARD; and Mr. PACKER, who may be stiled the *Pack-horse* of DRURY LANE, does him sufficiently well. Mr. HULL has abilities, if required, to render the part respectable. As to all the other male characters, we shall leave them to their own insignificancy.

Almeria, who gives name to the play, is amiable in her principles, and pitiable in her circumstances; the author has run her a little into the romantic strain, but she has the happiness of opening the play with two of the best lines in the whole piece.There is a variety of acting in this part, yet her royal highness is undoubtedly too much upon the whine: no person whom we have seen had equal capabilities to Mrs. CIBBER for this part; Mrs. BELLAMY, though inferior in requisites, must not be placed far behind; her painting of distraction was more faint, but love and tenderness she always expressed with admirable feeling. Miss MACKLIN, about seventeen years ago, by the instruction of, and playing with Mr. GARRICK, supported Almeria through a considerable run, with much credit, and really struck out several beauties; but her feelings, though correct in tragedy, always wanted the animation of expression; her voice was too thin and contracted. Miss YOUNG, whom we consider as a rising actress, has shewn ability in the part, but we object to this lady's frequent attempts at what she can't execute; striving to excel is, no doubt, a laudable ambition, but as a performer should not overstep the *modesty* of nature, no more should he or she strain the *powers* of nature; it is better to be a little below, than above the point of rectitude.

Zara is, beyond dispute, the most indelicate Queen that can well be imagined; she is vicious and mean, gross in sentiment, and vulgar in expression. Had she been more delicate in the former, and more reserved in the latter, she might have attracted some degree of humane concern; but, as she is, good sense and decorum must frown through the four first acts, while ridicule attends her and the head-shaking ministers of death in the fifth. The author's peculiar unhappiness in the catastrophe of this leading character, is plainly evinced by an observation we have repeatedly made, that scarce any degree of merit can save expiring Zara and her dismal attendants from being laughed at.

Mrs. WOFFINGTON's figure and deportment were well adapted to the captive Queen; but the violent, as well as tender passions, grated abominably in her dissonant voice. Mrs. PRITCHARD was majestic, but rather too corpulent; in speaking and acting the part, she shewed correct and fine preservation of character. The amorous passages were indeed not so harmonious as might be wished, but in the jealousy she made ample amends.

We remember to have seen Mrs. CLIVE make a laughable assault upon Zara, which was nearer burlesque than could well be imagined. Had it not been to excite curiosity upon her night, it would have been one of the most unpardonable attempts that ever was made: exclusive of a voice dreadfully unfit for serious speaking, her person rendered all the King's amorous compliments ludicrous; and justified Osmyn's coldness, admitting he had no other engagement to warp his inclination.

It is amazing that a principle of selfishness should cause people of great merit and good circumstances, for the sake of a few pounds, to exhibit themselves in a contemptible point of view. Mrs. HOPKINS, who now apologizes for most of the above excellent comedian's parts, makes rather a better figure in Zara, yet is bad enough, heaven knows. We have now got to the end of our remarks upon this laborious tragedy, and, without any hesitation, venture to pronounce it, though capable of drawing tears when well acted, the worst composition that any man of equal genius to Mr. CONGREVE ever produced.

(II, pp. 413–17)

(ii)
We now come to authors who have chiefly professed themselves votaries of the comic muse, and first mention CONGREVE, not only in point of time, but, as we think, of merit; no man who ever wrote for the stage has shewn more capital, more correct, or more pleasing delineations of life; his characters are beautifully contrasted, his language pointed, his wit brilliant, his plots amazingly regular and pleasingly intricate, his scenes variegated, and his disposition of the whole masterly; two faults, one of a very heavy

nature, countervail his extensive merit, his flashes of wit are too frequent, often too much for the person who utters them, his dialogue rather profuse, and a most abominable vein of licentious-ness runs through the whole; virtue reluctantly peeps in, while vice with brazen front bolts forward unblushing, unrestrained: Had this author written under the commendable restrictions of this age, his luxuriousness would have been brought within better bounds. His pieces must give great pleasure either in action or perusal, but are like the sweet scented rose, with prickles beneath, which while it gratifies one sense wounds another; it is with reluctance we pronounce the sentence of moral justice which condemns his four comedies to oblivion, as pernicious; but we doom his tragedy to contempt, with the full satisfaction of critical propriety.

(II, pp. 467–8)

69. Anon., review of *The Way of the World* in *The Gazetteer and New Daily Advertiser*

1775

From *The Gazetteer and New Daily Advertiser*, Monday 9 October 1775.

This review appeared simultaneously in *The Middlesex Journal, and Evening Advertiser* for 7–10 October.

THEATRICAL INTELLIGENCE

Drury-lane

Sentimental Comedy has so vitiated the taste of the town, that it ceases to be matter of surprise why Congreve's pieces are not more frequently laid before the public. This great Master of the Drama, were he to rise, and take a view of our modern *sermon-like pieces*, would blush for his countrymen and scarcely desire to exist (if not to reform) among the playmakers that infested the stage since Murphy's abdication. *The Way of the World,* though confessedly replete with wit and character, is not the most entertaining play in representation. It is so full of plot and intrigue, that it demands an unusual degree of attention in the *performers* and *audience* to excite admiration: on Saturday they both seemed averse to assist the author. Mr. King in Witwou'd was as entertaining and full of spirit as usual. Mr. Jefferson, in the gay admired Mirabel, (independent of the antique mode of his wig, and formal cut of his cloaths, which surely were both uncharacteristic) seemed, in attempting to be *quite natural*, to keep the entire plot of the play in his own bosom, looked more like the father than the Mirabel of Congreve. Mr. Reddish [Fainall] was a contrast to his friend Mirabel: he seemed attentive, nervous, and played the latter part of his character well; and had he but a little more the ease of comedy in the former part, and the address of a gentleman through the whole, he would have appeared to considerable advantage. Mr. Yates was well received, and in his performance of Sir Wilful met with much judicious applause. Mr. Baddeley's Petulant could not possibly offend. Mr. Parson's humour [as Waitwell] is strong and pleasant, but so much the same, that whoever has seen him play any other laughable character (whether young or old) may judge of his merit in this. Mrs. Abington's person, manner, and dress [as Millamant] were fashionable and elegant; but though the character was certainly a fine one, there was a want of *that spirit* best calculated to call her powers into action: her delivery was tediously formal: and had the audience been deprived of their sight, they would conclud that Capt. Bobadil had got into petticoats. Mrs. Hopkins [as Judy Wishfort] was sometimes tediously affected: surely the idea is false to dress old ladies of fashion who would appear young, in antiquated figured silks, &c. they certainly would follow the present taste. Miss Sherry played Marwood extremely well. Miss Dawes's Foible would have received much addition if she had spoke slower and louder. Mrs. Greville [as Mrs. Fainall], to convince the town that she could keep a secret, whispered it only to a few friends in the pit: this lady behaves as if she were a Princess in disguise, that had been ousted of her dominions, and took up with her present profession until she was restored: her indifference is intollerable, and should be noticed by her employers.

70. William Mason in 'Memoirs of the Life and Writings of Mr. Gray'

1775

From *The Poems of Mr. Gray*. To which are prefixed Memoirs of his Life and Writings by W. Mason, M.A., 1st edn (York: 1775), pp. 212–13.

William Mason (1724–97), friend and poetic disciple of Thomas Gray, was the latter's literary executor and biographer.

Mr. Gray had not (in my opinion) either in his conversation or writing much of what is called *pure* humour; it was always so much blended either with wit, fancy, or his own peculiar character, that it became equivocal, and hence not adapted to please generally: It had more of the manner of Congreve than Addison; and we know where one person relishes my Lady Wishfort, there are thousands that admire Sir Roger de Coverley: It will not however from hence follow, that Lady Wishfort is ill drawn; for my own part I think it one of the most entertaining characters that ever was written. I know, however, that it is commonly thought extravagant and unnatural; and I believe it is true, that no woman ever existed who had so much folly and affectation, and at the same time so much wit and fancy; yet every one sees that were this fancy and wit taken away, her character would become insipid, in proportion as it became more natural; so that, in this and other instances, *if Congreve's fools were fools indeed*, they would, by being *true* characters, cease to be *entertaining* ones. It may be further observed on the subject of humour, that it may and ought to be divided into several species: there is one sort, that of Terence's, which simply pleases without forcing a smile; another, like Mr. Addison's, which not only pleases, but makes us smile into the bargain. Shakespear's, Swift's, Congreve's and Prior's usually goes further, and makes us laugh: I infer not from hence that this latter sort is the best: I only assert, that howsoever it may be mixt with other ingredients, it ought also to be called Humour. The critic, however, who judges by rule, and who will not be pleased unless legitimately, will be apt to condemn this species of mixt humour; and the common reader will not always have either wit or imagination enough to comprehend or taste it.

71. Horace Walpole in 'Thoughts on Comedy'

1775–6

From *The Works of Horatio Walpole, Earl of Orford*, 4 vols (London: 1798), II, pp. 315–17.

Horace Walpole (1717–97) was the fourth son of Sir Robert Walpole, the great Whig Prime Minister. At his home at Strawberry Hill, Twickenham, he pursued his interests in landscape-gardening and printing; Walpole's own Gothic novel, *The Castle of Otranto*, and the 1757 *Odes* by his friend Thomas Gray were among the most notable productions of his private press. His famous and voluminous correspondence was published in 1857–9. 'Thoughts on Comedy', from which the following extract is taken, was published in a posthumous collection of his works, but is dated 'Written in 1775 and 1776'.

Plot, the vital principle of Spanish and female plays, ought to be little laboured; nor is scarcely more necessary than to put the personages into action and to release them. Vanbrugh's plays, *The Man of Mode*, and *The Careless Husband*, have no more intrigue than accounts for the meeting of the characters, as a passion or an intended marriage may do. *The Double Dealer*, the ground-work of which is almost serious enough for tragedy in private life, perplexes the attention; and the wit of the subordinate characters is necessary to enliven the darkness of the back ground.

253

Congreve is undoubtedly the most witty author that ever existed. Though sometimes his wit seems the effort of intention, and, though an effort, never failed; it was so natural, that, if he split it into ever so many characters, it was a polypus that soon grew perfect in each individual. We may blame the universality of wit in all his personages, but nobody can say which ought to have less. It assimilated with whatever character it was poured into: and, as Congreve would certainly have had wit in whatever station of life he had been born; as he would have made as witty a footman or old lady, as a fine gentleman; his gentlemen, ladies old or young, his footmen, nay his coxcombs (for they are not fools but puppies) have as much wit, and wit as much their own, as his men of most parts and best understandings. No character drops a sentence that would be proper in any other mouth. Not only Lady Wishfor't and Ben are characteristically marked, but Scandal, Mrs. Frail, and every fainter personage, are peculiarly distinct from each other. Sir Wilful Witwoud is unlike Sir Joseph Wittol. Witwoud is different from Tattle, Valentine from Mellefont, and Cynthia from Angelica. That still each play is unnatural, is only because four assemblages of different persons could never have so much wit as Congreve has bestowed on them. We want breath or attention to follow their repartees; and are so charmed with what every body says, that we have not leisure to be interested in what any body does. We are so pleased with each person, that we wish success to all; and our approbation is so occupied, that our passions cannot be engaged. We even do not believe that a company who seem to meet only to show their wit, can have any other object in view. Their very vices seem affected, only to furnish subject for gaiety: thus the intrigue of Careless and Lady Pliant does not strike us more than a story that we know is invented to set off the talents of the relator. For these reasons, though they are something more, I can scarce allow Congreve's to be true comedies. No man would be corrected, if sure that his wit would make his vices or ridicules overlooked.

72. Anon., review of *The Way of the World* in *The Morning Chronicle*

1776

From *The Morning Chronicle, and London Advertiser*, Monday 4 November 1776.

THEATRICAL INTELLIGENCE

The Way of the World, like the rest of Congreve's Comedies, exhibits a variety of strong marked characters, many good situations, and a superabundance of wit in the dialogue. All the plays of this able writer labour under a similar defect,—that of a want of a well constructed fable; perhaps *Love for Love*, and *The Way of the World*, are the two least deficient in this essential particular. However, with all due respect to, and acknowledgement of, Congreve's genius, we may warrantably observe, that the line in Dr. Johnson's famous Prologue, spoken by Mr. Garrick, on opening Drury-lane Theatre in 1747, is particularly applicable to Congreve's pieces,

> Intrigue was plot, obscenity was wit.

Congreve certainly is less to blame on this score than the bad taste of the age he lived in. Writers, especially writers for the stage, must accommodate their dramatic manners to the prevailing dramatic taste. Hence we find the brilliant productions of Congreve, Wycherly, and Farquhar, almost inadmissable, from the prudish coyness of modern audiences. Each of these writers gave the 'living manners as they rose;' if the manners were then as really gross as they are now professedly pious, what wonder is it, that the dramatic productions of that day should teem with *doubles entendres*, indecent allusions, and downright obscenity.

The Way of the World, on Saturday evening, was tolerably well performed at Covent-garden Theatre. Mr. Lewis in Mirabel, Mr. Woodward in Petulant, Mr. Wroughton in Fainall, and Mr. Lee Lewes in Witwoud, were equal to their respective characters. Mr.

Dunstall did Sir Willfull so much justice, that, now Shuter is dead, we place him second to Yates in that character. Mr. Wilson over-acted Waitwell, particularly while he personated Sir Rowland; why did he then dress himself like Justice Midas? No serious character (and we mean by the word *serious* a copy of real life,) ever wore such a wig.

Mrs. Barry never comes before us without deserving our praise; she played Millemant in such a stile, as to defy censure; but she did not excite that involuntary applause which in tragedy she generally extorts. In fact, there is a better Millemant now on the stage. Mrs. Barry has too much sense, and too much knowledge of her profession, to fail entirely, but there are parts in which she falls short of herself; Millemant is one of these parts.

Mrs. Mattocks in Mrs. Marwood, looked and spoke the very character Congreve drew. We have not lately seen her with more satisfaction.

Mrs. Pitt *bawled* out Lady Wishfor't with more applause than she deserved, while Mrs. Whitefield was content with *whispering* the words of Mrs. Fainall. If these ladies would consent to put their respective stage manners into the scale, and made an equal composition, it would be better for both; Mrs. Pitt is always loud and vulgar; Mrs. Whitefield generally soft, gracefull, and gentle-womanlike. A *melange* might produce a good effect. Mrs. Green was excellent in Foible.

73. Fanny Burney in *Evelina*

1778

From *Evelina*, ed. Edward A. Bloom (London: Oxford University Press, 1968), pp. 78 and 80–2.

Fanny Burney (1752–1840) was the daughter of Dr Charles Burney, musician and friend of Samuel Johnson. *Evelina* was her first novel, published in January 1778. It was a pronounced success and won her entry into London literary circles. The following passages come from Letter XX. The heroine is recounting a visit to the theatre in the company of friends. There they are joined first by Lord Orville, whom Evelina will marry at the end of the novel, and then by Mr Lovel, an impudent fop.

The play was *Love for Love*, and tho' it is fraught with wit and entertainment, I hope I shall never see it represented again; for it is so extremely indelicate,—to use the softest word I can,—that Miss Mirvan and I were perpetually out of countenance, and could neither make any observations ourselves, nor venture to listen to those of others. This was the more provoking, as Lord Orville was in excellent spirits, and exceedingly entertaining.

When the Play was over, I flattered myself I should be able to look about me with less restraint, as we intended to stay the Farce; but the curtain had hardly dropped when the box-door opened, and in came Mr. Lovel, the man by whose foppery and impertinence I was so much teazed at the ball where I first saw Lord Orville.

'Pr'ythee a truce with all this palavering,' cried the Captain, 'the women are vain enough already; no need for to puff 'em up more.'

'We must all submit to the commanding officer,' said Sir Clement, 'therefore let us call another subject. Pray, Ladies, how have you been entertained with the play?'

'Want of entertainment,' said Mrs. Mirvan, 'is its least fault; but I own there are objections to it, which I should be glad to see removed.'

'I could have ventured to answer for the Ladies,' said Lord Orville, 'since I am sure this is not a play that can be honoured with their approbation.'

'What, I suppose it is not sentimental enough!' cried the Captain, 'or else it's too good for them; for I'll maintain it's one of the best comedies in the language, and has more wit in one scene, than there is in all the new plays put together.'

'For my part,' said Mr. Lovel, 'I confess I seldom listen to the players: one has so much to do, in looking about, and finding out one's acquaintance, that, really, one has no time to mind the stage. Pray,—(most affectedly fixing his eyes upon a diamond-ring on his little finger) pray—what was the play to-night?'

'Why, what the D——l,' cried the Captain, 'do you come to the play, without knowing what it is?'

'O yes, Sir, yes, very frequently; I have no time to read play-bills; one merely comes to meet one's friends, and shew that one's alive.'

'Ha, ha, ha!—and so,' cried the Captain, 'it costs you five shillings a night, just to shew that you're alive! Well, faith, my friends should all think me dead and under ground, before I'd be at that expence for 'em. Howsomever, this here you may take from me;—they'll find you out fast enough, if you've any thing to give 'em. And so you've been here all this time, and don't know what the play was?'

'Why, really, Sir, a play requires so much attention,—it is scarce possible to keep awake, if one listens;—for, indeed, by the time it is evening, one has been so fatigued, with dining,—or wine,—or the house,—or studying,—that it is—it is perfectly an impossibility. But, now I think of it, I believe I have a bill in my pocket; O, ay, here it is—*Love for Love*, ay,—true,—ha, ha,—how could I be so stupid!'

'O, easily enough as to that, I warrant you,' said the Captain; 'but, by my soul, this is one of the best jokes I ever heard! Come to a play, and not know what it is!—Why, I suppose you would n't have found it out, if they had *fob'd* you off with a scraping of fidlers, or an opera?—Ha! ha! ha!—why now, I should have thought you might have taken some notice of one Mr. *Tattle* that is in this play!'

This sarcasm, which caused a general smile, made him colour: but, turning to the Captain with a look of conceit, which implied that he had a retort ready, he said, 'Pray, Sir, give me leave to ask,—what do *you* think of *one Mr. Ben*, who is also in this play?'

The Captain, regarding him with the utmost contempt, answered in a loud voice, 'Think of him!—why I think he's a *man!*' And then, staring full in his face, he struck his cane on the ground, with a violence that made him start. He did not, however, chuse to take any notice of this; but, having bit his nails some time, in manifest confusion, he turned very quick to me, and, in a sneering tone of voice, said, 'For my part, I was most struck with the *country* young lady, Miss Prue; pray what do *you* think of her, Ma'am?'

'Indeed, Sir,' cried I, very much provoked, 'I think—that is, I do not think any thing about her.'

'Well, really, Ma'am, you prodigiously surprise me!—*mais, apparement ce n'est qu'un façon à parler?*—though I should beg your pardon, for probably you do not understand French?'

I made no answer, for I thought his rudeness intolerable; but Sir Clement, with great warmth, said, 'I am surprised that you can suppose such an object as Miss Prue would engage the attention of Miss Anville even for a moment.'

'O Sir,' returned this fop, ''tis the first character in the piece!—so well drawn,—so much the thing!—such true country-breeding,—such rural ignorance!—ha! ha! ha!—'tis most admirably hit off, 'pon honour!'

I could almost have cried, that such impertinence should be levelled at me; and yet, chagrined as I was, I could never behold Lord Orville and this man at the same time, and feel any regret for the cause I had given of displeasure.

'The only character in the play,' said Lord Orville, 'worthy of being mentioned to these ladies, is Angelica.'

'Angelica,' cried Sir Clement, 'is a noble girl; she tries her lover severely, but she rewards him generously.'

'Yet, in a trial so long,' said Mrs. Mirvan, 'there seems rather too much consciousness of her power.'

'Since my opinion has the sanction of Mrs. Mirvan's,' added Lord Orville, 'I will venture to say, that Angelica bestows her hand rather with the air of a benefactress, than with the tenderness of a mistress. Generosity without delicacy, like wit without judgment, generally give as much pain as pleasure. The uncertainty in which she keeps Valentine, and her manner of trifling with his temper, give no very favourable idea of her own.'

'Well, my Lord,' said Mr. Lovel, 'it must, however, be owned, that uncertainty is not the *ton* among our ladies at present; nay, indeed, I think they say, though, faith,' taking a pinch of snuff, 'I hope it is not true—but they say, that *we* now are most shy and backward.'

The curtain then drew up, and our conversation ceased. Mr. Lovel finding we chose to attend to the players, left the box. How strange it is, Sir, that this man, not contented with the large share of foppery and nonsense which he has from nature, should think proper to affect yet more! for what he said of Tattle and of Miss Prue, convinced me that he really had listened to the play, though he was so ridiculous and foolish as to pretend ignorance.

259

74. Samuel Johnson, 'Congreve'

1781

From *Prefaces, Biographical and Critical, to the Works of the English Poets*, 10 vols (London: 1779–81), VI, pp. 1–38 (separately paginated).

WILLIAM CONGREVE, descended from a family in Staffordshire, of so great antiquity that it claims a place among the few that extend their line beyond the Norman Conquest; and was the son of William Congreve, second son of Richard Congreve of Congreve and Stratton. He visited, once at least, the residence of his ancestors; and, I believe, more places than one are still shewn, in groves and gardens, where he is related to have written his *Old Batchelor*.

Neither the time nor place of his birth are certainly known: if the inscription upon his monument be true, he was born in 1672. For the place; it was said by himself that he owed his nativity to England, and by every body else that he was born in Ireland. Southerne mentioned him with sharp censure, as a man that meanly disowned his native country. The biographers assign his nativity to Bardsa, near Leeds in Yorkshire, from the account given by himself, as they suppose, to Jacob.

To doubt whether a man of eminence has told the truth about his own birth, is, in appearance, to be very deficient in candour; yet nobody can live long without knowing that falsehoods of convenience or vanity, falsehoods from which no evil immediately visible ensues except the general degradation of human testimony, are very lightly uttered, and once uttered, are sullenly supported. Boileau, who desired to be thought a rigorous and steady moralist, having told a petty lie to Lewis XIV. continued it afterwards by false dates; thinking himself obliged *in honour*, says his admirer, to maintain what, when he said it, was so well received.

Wherever Congreve was born, he was educated first at Kilkenny, and afterwards at Dublin, his father having some military employment that stationed him in Ireland: but after having passed

260

through the usual preparatory studies, as may be reasonably supposed with great celerity and success, his father thought it proper to assign him a profession, by which something might be gotten; and about the time of the Revolution sent him, at the age of sixteen, to study law in the Middle Temple, where he lived for several years, but with very little attention to Statutes or Reports.

His disposition to become an author appeared very early, as he very early felt that force of imagination, and possessed that copiousness of sentiment, by which intellectual pleasure can be given. His first performance was a novel, called *Incognita, or Love and Duty reconciled*: It is praised by the biographers, who quote some part of the preface, that is indeed, for such a time of life, uncommonly judicious. I would rather praise it than read it.

His first dramatick labour was the *Old Batchelor*; of which he says, in his defence against Collier, 'that comedy was written, as several know, some years before it was acted. When I wrote it, I had little thoughts of the stage; but did it, to amuse myself, in a slow recovery from a fit of sickness. Afterwards through my indiscretion it was seen, and in some little time more it was acted; and I, through the remainder of my indiscretion, suffered myself to be drawn in, to the prosecution of a difficult and thankless study, and to be involved in a perpetual war with knaves and fools.'

There seems to be a strange affectation in authors of appearing to have done every thing by chance. The *Old Batchelor* was written for amusement, in the languor of convalescence. Yet it is apparently composed with great elaborateness of dialogue, and incessant ambition of wit. The age of the writer considered, it is indeed a very wonderful performance; for, whenever written, it was acted (1693) when he was not more than twenty-one years old; and was then recommended by Mr. Dryden, Mr. Southerne, and Mr. Maynwaring. Dryden said that he never had seen such a first play; but they found it deficient in some things requisite to the success of its exhibition, and by their greater experience fitted it for the stage. Southerne used to relate of one comedy, probably of this, that when Congreve read it to the players, he pronounced it so wretchedly that they had almost rejected it; but they were afterwards so well persuaded of its excellence, that, for half a year before it was acted, the manager allowed its author the privilege of the house.

Few plays have ever been so beneficial to the writer; for it procured him the patronage of Halifax, who immediately made him one of the commissioners for licensing coaches, and soon after gave him a place in the pipe-office, and another in the customs of six hundred pounds a year. Congreve's conversation must surely have been at least equally pleasing with his writings.

Such a comedy, written at such an age, requires some consideration. As the lighter species of dramatick poetry professes the imitation of common life, of real manners, and daily incidents, it apparently presupposes a familiar knowledge of many characters, and exact observation of the passing world; the difficulty therefore is to conceive how this knowledge can be obtained by a boy.

But if the *Old Batchelor* be more nearly examined, it will be found to be one of those comedies which may be made by a mind vigorous and acute, and furnished with comick characters by the perusal of other poets, without much actual commerce with mankind. The dialogue is one constant reciprocation of conceits, or clash of wit, in which nothing flows necessarily from the occasion, or is dictated by nature. The characters both of men and women are either fictitious and artificial, as those of *Heartwell* and the Ladies; or easy and common, as *Wittol* a tame idiot, *Bluff* a swaggering coward, and *Fondlewife* a jealous puritan; and the catastrophe arises from a mistake not very probably produced, by marrying a woman in a mask.

Yet this gay comedy, when all these deductions are made, will still remain the work of a very powerful and fertile mind: the dialogue is quick and sparkling, the incidents such as seize the attention, and the wit so exuberant that it *o'er-informs its tenement*.

Next year he gave another specimen of his abilities in *The Double Dealer*, which was not received with equal kindness. He writes to his patron the lord Halifax a dedication, in which he endeavours to reconcile the reader to that which found few friends among the audience. These apologies are always useless; *de gustibus non est disputandum*; men may be convinced, but they cannot be pleased, against their will. But though taste is obstinate, it is very variable, and time often prevails when arguments have failed.

Queen Mary conferred upon both those plays the honour of her presence; and when she died, soon after, Congreve testified his gratitude by a despicable effusion of elegiac pastoral; a composition in which all is unnatural, and yet nothing is new.

In another year (1695) his prolifick pen produced *Love for Love*; a comedy of nearer alliance to life, and exhibiting more real manners, than either of the former. The character of *Foresight* was then common. Dryden calculated nativities; both Cromwell and king William had their lucky days; and Shaftesbury himself, though he had no religion, was said to regard predictions. The *Sailor* is not accounted very natural, but he is very pleasant.

With this play was opened the New Theatre, under the direction of Betterton the tragedian; where he exhibited, two years afterwards (1697), *The Mourning Bride*, a tragedy, so written as to shew him sufficiently qualified for either kind of dramatick poetry.

In this play, of which, when he afterwards revised it, he reduced the versification to greater regularity, there is more bustle than sentiment; the plot is busy and intricate, and the events take hold on the attention; but, except a very few passages, we are rather amused with noise, and perplexed with stratagem, than entertained with any true delineation of natural characters. This, however, was received with more benevolence than any other of his works, and still continues to be acted and applauded.

But whatever objections may be made either to his comick or tragick excellence, they are lost at once in the blaze of admiration, when it is remembered that he had produced these four plays before he had passed his twenty-fifth year; before other men, even such as are some time to shine in eminence, have passed their probation of literature, or presume to hope for any other notice than such as is bestowed on diligence and inquiry. Among all the efforts of early genius which literary history records, I doubt whether any one can be produced that more surpasses the common limits of nature than the plays of Congreve.

About this time began the long-continued controversy between Collier and the poets. In the reign of Charles the First the Puritans had raised a violent clamour against the drama, which they considered as an entertainment not lawful to Christians, an opinion held by them in common with the church of Rome; and Prynne published *Histrio-mastix*, a huge volume, in which stage-plays were censured. The outrages and crimes of the Puritans brought afterwards their whole system of doctrine into disrepute, and from the Restoration the poets and the players were left at quiet; for to have molested them would have had the appearance of tendency to puritanical malignity.

This danger, however, was worn away by time; and Collier, a fierce and implacable Nonjuror, knew that an attack upon the theatre would never make him suspected for a Puritan; he therefore (1698) published *A short View of the Immorality and Profaneness of the English Stage*, I believe with no other motive than religious zeal and honest indignation. He was formed for a controvertist; with sufficient learning; with diction vehement and pointed, though often vulgar and incorrect; with unconquerable pertinacity; with wit in the highest degree keen and sarcastick; and with all those powers exalted and invigorated by just confidence in his cause.

Thus qualified, and thus incited, he walked out to battle, and assailed at once most of the living writers, from Dryden to Durfey. His onset was violent: those passages, which while they stood single had passed with little notice, when they were accumulated and exposed together, excited horror; the wise and the pious caught the alarm, and the nation wondered why it had so long suffered irreligion and licentiousness to be openly taught at the publick charge.

Nothing now remained for the poets but to resist or fly. Dryden's conscience, or his prudence, angry as he was, withheld him from the conflict; Congreve and Vanbrug attempted answers. Congreve, a very young man, elated with success, and impatient of censure, assumed an air of confidence and security. His chief artifice of controversy is to retort upon his adversary his own words: he is very angry, and, hoping to conquer Collier with his own weapons, allows himself in the use of every term of contumely and contempt; but he has the sword without the arm of Scanderbeg; he has his antagonist's coarseness, but not his strength. Collier replied; for contest was his delight, he was not to be frighted from his purpose or his prey.

The cause of Congreve was not tenable: whatever glosses he might use for the defence or palliation of single passages, the general tenour and tendency of his plays must always be condemned. It is acknowledged, with universal conviction, that the perusal of his works will make no man better; and that their ultimate effect is to represent pleasure in alliance with vice, and to relax those obligations by which life ought to be regulated.

The stage found other advocates, and the dispute was protracted through ten years; but at last Comedy grew more modest, and

Collier lived to see the reward of his labour in the reformation of the theatre.

Of the powers by which this important victory was atchieved, a quotation from *Love for Love*, and the remark upon it, may afford a specimen.

Sir Samps. *Sampson's a very good name; for your Sampsons were strong dogs from the beginning.*

Angel. *Have a care——If you remember, the strongest Sampson of your name pull'd an old house over his head at last.*

'Here you have the Sacred History burlesqued, and Sampson once more brought into the house of Dagon, to make sport for the Philistines!' (*A Short View*, p. 76).

Congreve's last play was *The Way of the World*; which, though, as he hints in his dedication, it was written with great labour and much thought, was received with so little favour, that, being in a high degree offended and disgusted, he resolved to commit his quiet and his fame no more to the caprices of an audience.

From this time his life ceased to be publick: he lived for himself, and for his friends; and among his friends was able to name every man of his time whom wit and elegance had raised to reputation. It may be therefore reasonably supposed that his manners were polite, and his conversation pleasing.

He seems not to have taken much pleasure in writing, as he contributed nothing to the *Spectator*, and only one paper to the *Tatler*, though published by men with whom he might be supposed willing to associate; and though he lived many years after the publication of his Miscellaneous Poems, yet he added nothing to them, but lived on in literary indolence; engaged in no controversy, contending with no rival, neither soliciting flattery by publick commendations, nor provoking enmity by malignant criticism, but passing his time among the great and splendid, in the placid enjoyment of his fame and fortune.

Having owed his fortune to Halifax, he continued always of his patron's party, but, as it seems, without violence or acrimony; and his firmness was naturally esteemed, as his abilities were reverenced. His security therefore was never violated; and when, upon the extrusion of the Whigs, some intercession was used lest Congreve should be displaced, the earl of Oxford made this answer:

Non obtusa adeo gestamus pectora Poeni,
Nec tam aversus equos Tyriâ sol jungit ab urbe.[1]

He that was thus honoured by the adverse party, might naturally expect to be advanced when his friends returned to power, and he was made secretary for the island of Jamaica; a place, I suppose, without trust or care, but which, with his post in the customs, is said to have afforded him twelve hundred pounds a year.

His honours were yet far greater than his profits. Every writer mentioned him with respect; and, among other testimonies to his merit, Steele made him the patron of his Miscellany, and Pope inscribed to him his translation of the Iliad.

But he treated the Muses with ingratitude; for having long conversed familiarly with the great, he wished to be considered rather as a man of fashion than of wit; and when he received a visit from Voltaire, disgusted him by the despicable foppery of desiring to be considered not as an author but a gentleman; to which the Frenchman replied, 'that, if he had been only a gentleman, he should not have come to visit him.'

In his retirement he may be supposed to have applied himself to books; for he discovers more literature than the poets have commonly attained. But his studies were in his latter days obstructed by cataracts in his eyes, which at last terminated in blindness. This melancholy state was aggravated by the gout, for which he sought relief by a journey to Bath; but being overturned in his chariot, complained from that time of a pain in his side, and died at his house in Surrey-street in the Strand Jan. 29, 1728–9. Having lain in state in the Jerusalem-chamber, he was buried in Westminster-abbey, where a monument is erected to his memory by Henrietta dutchess of Marlborough, to whom, for reasons either not known or not mentioned, he bequeathed a legacy of about ten thousand pounds; the accumulation of attentive parcimony, which, though to her superfluous and useless, might have given great assistance to the ancient family from which he descended, at that time by the imprudence of his relation reduced to difficulties and distress.

Congreve has merit of the highest kind; he is an original writer, who borrowed neither the models of his plot, nor the manner of his dialogue. Of his plays I cannot speak distinctly; for since I inspected them many years have passed; but what remains upon my memory is, that his characters are commonly fictitious and artificial, with very little of nature, and not much of life. He formed a peculiar idea of comick excellence, which he supposed to consist in gay remarks and unexpected answers; but that which he endeavoured, he seldom failed of performing. His scenes exhibit not much of humour, imagery, or passion: his personages are a kind of intellectual gladiators; every sentence is to ward or strike; the contest of smartness is never intermitted; his wit is a meteor playing to and fro with alternate coruscations. His comedies have therefore, in some degree, the operation of tragedies; they surprise rather than divert, and raise admiration oftener than merriment. But they are the works of a mind replete with images, and quick in combination.

Of his miscellaneous poetry, which this collection has admitted, I cannot say any thing very favourable. The powers of Congreve seem to desert him when he leaves the stage, as Antaeus was no longer strong than he could touch the ground. It cannot be observed without wonder, that a mind so vigorous and fertile in dramatick compositions should on any other occasion discover nothing but impotence and poverty. He has in these little pieces neither elevation of fancy, selection of language, nor skill in versification: yet if I were required to select from the whole mass of English poetry the most poetical paragraph, I know not what I could prefer to an exclamation in *The Mourning Bride*:

ALMERIA.
It was a fancy'd noise; for all is hush'd.
LEONORA.
It bore the accent of a human voice.
ALMERIA.
It was thy fear, or else some transient wind
Whistling thro' hollows of this vaulted isle:
We'll listen—
LEONORA.
Hark!
ALMERIA.
No, all is hush'd, and still as death.—'Tis dreadful!
How reverend is the face of this tall pile;
Whose ancient pillars rear their marble heads,
To bear aloft its arch'd and pond'rous roof,
By its own weight made stedfast and immoveable,
Looking tranquillity! It strikes an awe

And terror on my aching sight; the tombs
And monumental caves of death look cold,
And shoot a chilness to my trembling heart.
Give me thy hand, and let me hear thy voice;
Nay, quickly speak to me, and let me hear
Thy voice—my own affrights me with its echoes.

[II, iii, 1–17]

He who reads those lines enjoys for a moment the powers of a poet; he feels what he remembers to have felt before, but he feels it with great increase of sensibility; he recognizes a familiar image, but meets it again amplified and expanded, embellished with beauty, and enlarged with majesty.

Yet could the author, who appears here to have enjoyed the confidence of Nature, lament the death of queen Mary in lines like these:

> The rocks are cleft, and new-descending rills
> Furrow the brows of all th' impending hills.
> The water-gods to floods their rivulets turn,
> And each, with streaming eyes, supplies his wanting urn.
> The Fawns forsake the woods, the Nymphs the grove,
> And round the plain in sad distractions rove;
> In prickly brakes their tender limbs they tear,
> And leave on thorns their locks of golden hair.
> With their sharp nails, themselves the Satyrs wound,
> And tug their shaggy beards, and bite with grief the ground.
> Lo Pan himself, beneath a blasted oak,
> Dejected lies, his pipe in pieces broke.
> See Pales weeping too, in wild despair,
> And to the piercing winds her bosom bare.
> And see yon fading myrtle, where appears
> The Queen of Love, all bath'd in flowing tears;
> See how she wrings her hands, and beats her breast,
> And tears her useless girdle from her waist:
> Hear the sad murmurs of her sighing doves!
> For grief they sigh, forgetful of their loves.

'The Mourning Muse of *Alexis*', ll. 139–58

And many years after he gave no proof that time had improved his wisdom or his wit; for on the death of the marquis of Blandford this was his song:

> And now the winds, which had so long been still,
> Began the swelling air with sighs to fill:

268

The water-nymphs, who motionless remain'd,
Like images of ice, while she complain'd,
Now loos'd their streams; as when descending rains
Roll the steep torrents headlong o'er the plains.
The prone creation, who so long had gaz'd,
Charm'd with her cries, and at her griefs amaz'd,
Began to roar and howl with horrid yell,
Dismal to hear, and terrible to tell;
Nothing but groans and sighs were heard around,
And Echo multiplied each mournful sound.
        'The Tears of *Amaryllis* for *Amytas*', ll. 134–45

In both these funeral poems, when he has *yelled* out many *syllables* of senseless *dolour*, he dismisses his reader with senseless consolation: from the grave of Pastora rises a light that forms a star; and where Amaryllis wept for Amyntas, from every tear sprung up a violet.

But William is his hero, and of William he will sing:

The hovering winds on downy wings shall wait around,
And catch, and waft to foreign lands, the flying sound.
        'To the King, On the Taking of *Namure*', ll. 18–19

It cannot but be proper to shew what they shall have to catch and carry:

'Twas now, when flowery lawns the prospect made,
And flowing brooks beneath a forest shade,
A lowing heifer, loveliest of the herd,
Stood feeding by; while two fierce bulls prepar'd
Their armed heads for fight; by fate of war to prove
The victor worthy of the fair-one's love.
Unthought presage of what met next my view;
For soon the shady scene withdrew.
And now, for woods, and fields, and springing flowers,
Behold a town arise, bulwark'd with walls and lofty towers;
Two rival armies all the plain o'erspread,
Each in battalia rang'd, and shining arms array'd;
With eager eyes beholding both from far,
Namur, the prize and mistress of the war.
        ibid., ll. 44–57

The *Birth of the Muse* is a miserable fiction. One good line it has, which was borrowed from Dryden. The concluding verses are these:

This said, no more remain'd. Th' ethereal host
Again impatient crowd the crystal coast.
The father, now, within his spacious hands,
Encompass'd all the mingled mass of seas and lands;
And, having heav'd aloft the ponderous sphere,
He launch'd the world to float in ambient air.

ll. 267–72

Of his irregular poems, that to Mrs. Arabella Hunt seems to be the best: his ode for Cecilia's Day, however, has some lines which Pope had in his mind when he wrote his own.

His Imitations of Horace are feebly paraphrastical, and the additions which he makes are of little value. He sometimes retains what were more properly omitted, as when he talks of *vervain* and *gums* to propitiate Venus.

Of his Translations the satire of Juvenal was written very early, and may therefore be forgiven, though it have not the massyness and vigour of the original. In all his versions strength and sprightliness are wanting: his hymn to Venus, from Homer, is perhaps the best. His lines are weakened with expletives, and his rhymes are frequently imperfect.

His petty poems are seldom worth the cost of criticism: sometimes the thoughts are false, and sometimes common. In his verses on lady Gethin, the latter part is an imitation of Dryden's ode on Mrs. Killigrew; and Doris, that has been so lavishly flattered by Steele, has indeed some lively stanzas, but the expression might be mended; and the most striking part of the character had been already shewn in *Love for Love*. His *Art of Pleasing* is founded on a vulgar but perhaps impracticable principle, and the staleness of the sense is not concealed by any novelty of illustration or elegance of diction.

This tissue of poetry, from which he seems to have hoped a lasting name, is totally neglected, and known only as it is appended to his plays.

While comedy or while tragedy is regarded, his plays are likely to be read; but, except what relates to the stage, I know not that he has ever written a stanza that is sung, or a couplet that is quoted. The general character of his Miscellanies is, that they shew little wit, and little virtue.

Yet to him it must be confessed that we are indebted for the correction of a national error, and for the cure of our Pindarick madness. He first taught the English writers that Pindar's odes were regular; and though certainly he had not the fire requisite for the higher species of lyrick poetry, he has shewn us that enthusiasm has its rules, and that in mere confusion there is neither grace nor greatness.

NOTE

1 *Aeneid*, I, 567–8. 'We Carthaginians do not have such insensible hearts, nor does the sun yoke his horses so distant from the Tyrian city.'

75. Hugh Blair in *Lectures on Rhetoric and Belles Lettres*

1783

From *Lectures on Rhetoric and Belles Lettres*, 2 vols (London: 1783).

Hugh Blair (1718–1800) was a fashionable preacher and the first Regius Professor of Rhetoric and Belles Lettres in the University of Edinburgh. His circle of friends included Hume, Lord Kames, and Adam Smith. Blair acknowledged that he had taken some ideas for his lectures from a manuscript treatise by the latter. Blair's criticism was highly admired in its day, but rapidly declined in value.

(i) From Lecture XLV, 'Tragedy'

AMONG the Moderns, much greater variety of events has been admitted into Tragedy. It has become more the theatre of passion than it was among the Ancients. A greater display of characters is attempted; more intrigue and action are carried on; our curiosity is more awakened, and more interesting situations arise. This variety is, upon the whole, an improvement on Tragedy; it renders the entertainment both more animated, and more instructive; and when kept within due bounds, may be perfectly consistent with unity of subject. But the Poet must, at the same time, beware of not deviating too far from Simplicity, in the construction of his Fable. For if he overcharges it with Action and Intrigue, it becomes perplexed and embarrassed; and, by consequence, loses much of its effect. Congreve's *Mourning Bride*, a Tragedy, otherwise far from being void of merit, fails in this respect; and may be given as an instance of one standing in perfect opposition to the simplicity of the ancient Plots. The incidents succeed one another too rapidly. The Play is too full of business. It is difficult for the mind to follow and comprehend the whole series of events; and, what is the greatest fault of all, the catastrophe, which ought always to be plain and simple, is brought about in a manner too artificial and intricate.

(II, pp. 489–90)

(ii) From Lecture XLVI, 'English Tragedy'

In Congreve's *Mourning Bride*, there are some fine situations, and much good Poetry. The two first Acts are admirable. The meeting of Almeria with her husband Osmyn, in the tomb of Anselmo, is one of the most solemn and striking situations to be found in any Tragedy. The defects in the catastrophe, I pointed out in the last Lecture.

(II, p. 526)

(iii) From Lecture XLVII, 'English Comedy'

Congreve is, unquestionably, a Writer of genius. He is lively, witty, and sparkling; full of character, and full of action. His chief fault as a Comic Writer, is, that he overflows with wit. It is often introduced unseasonably; and, almost every where, there is too great a proportion of it for natural well-bred conversation. Farquhar is a light and gay Writer; less correct, and less sparkling than Congreve; but he has more ease, and, perhaps, fully as great a share of the Vis Comica. The two best, and least exceptionable of his Plays, are the *Recruiting Officer*, and the *Beaux Stratagem*. I say the least exceptionable; for, in general, the tendency of both Congreve and Farquhar's Plays is immoral. Throughout them all, the Rake, the loose intrigue, and the life of licentiousness, are the objects continually held up to view; as if the assemblies of a great and polished nation could be amused with none but vitious objects. The indelicacy of these Writers, in the female characters which they introduce, is particularly remarkable. Nothing can be more awkward than their representations of a woman of virtue and honour. Indeed, there are hardly any female characters in their Plays except two; women of loose principles, or women of affected manners, when they attempt to draw a character of virtue.

(II, pp. 545–6)

76. Thomas Davies in *Dramatic Miscellanies*

1784

From *Dramatic Miscellanies*, 3 vols (London: 1783–4).

Thomas Davies (1712–85) spent his career alternating between acting and bookselling; the abandonment of the former profession is said to have been caused by a jibe in Churchill's *The Rosciad*, ll. 319–22. Davies dedicated his edition of Massinger to Johnson, who in his turn encouraged and helped Davies to write a biography of Garrick which appeared the following year, 1780. Its success emboldened Davies to proceed with *Dramatic Miscellanies*, where he makes good use of his first-hand theatrical experience. Much of the book's interest lies in its accounts of particular productions, and portrayals by distinguished actors and actresses of the period.

(i)
Congreve formed himself upon Wycherly; but his wit is more flowing, his fancy more exuberant, his knowledge more extensive, and his judgement more profound; though he is by no means a strict observer of the unities, the conduct of his fables is well studied, and sometimes exact; his catastrophes are generally perplexed and sometimes improbable.

When Congreve began to write, the licentious manners, introduced by Charles II. were in full vigour; the passion to establish popery, in the reign of his successor, had not diminished the immorality of the people. The great view of James was the converting his subjects to his own superstition; to which, I believe, he was the more devoted, as he fancied their imbibing his religious creed would render them more submissive to his government. Papists, like other dissenters, when in a state of persecution, or deprived of benefits which they ought to enjoy, will endeavour to gain a mitigation of their hardships by contributing to support every scheme of government with their utmost weight and interest: remove the clogs that separate them from the rest of the people, and papists will be as staunch friends to liberty as any other subjects.

Wycherly, it is plain, was the original which our young poet admired and copied. Wycherly faithfully transcribed the manners of the times when the king and his courtiers, in conjunction with the poets, were the pimps to debauch the morals of the people. Dr. Johnson styles Wycherly a scribbler, from an honest indignation at the impurity of his writings; but surely the comedies of Dryden, Otway, and others, are not less exceptionable than his. He, like others, was borne down by the common current, which was rendered irresistible by royal patronage and protection. To this, Dryden himself ascribes the vicious writings of the poets:

> The poets, who must live by courts, or starve,
> Were proud so good a government to serve;
> And, mixing with buffoons and pimps profane,
> Tainted the stage for some small snip of gain;
> For they, like harlots under bawds profess'd,
> Took all th'ungodly pains and got the least.
> Thus did the thriving malady prevail;
> The court its head, the poets but the tail.
> Misses there were, but modestly conceal'd:
> Whitehall the naked Venus first reveal'd;
> Where, standing, as at Cyprus, in her shrine,
> The strumpet was ador'd with rites divine,* &c.

Few men were so admired, and beloved by his contemporaries, as Wycherly: he was esteemed the most accomplished gentleman of the age he lived in, and, as such, courted and caressed by his royal master.

Congreve was endowed with all the strong faculties of perception which enable the comic writer to describe the various characters of mankind. He seems to have known the foibles, passions, humours, and vices, of the world by intuition. His *Old*

Batchelor was acted when he was twenty-one; in his dedication, he tells Lord Clifford that it had lain by him almost four years. Dryden and Southern were astonished when they perused this play, and pronounced it a prodigy of early genius. In the *Old Batchelor*, we perceive, that, from Ben Jonson's Bobadil and Master Stephen, the author has formed his Captain Bluff and Sir Joseph Wittol. His gentlemen are partly his own and partly taken from Wycherly. Bellmour and Sharper are allied to Horner and Freeman, in the *Country Wife* and *Plain Dealer*. Vainlove, who loves no pleasure that is not to be obtained without difficulty, is a character of humour; and so, I think, is Heartwell, who resembles, in some of his features, Pinchwife in the *Country Wife*.

I cannot think, with Dr. Johnson, that Heartwell is a fictitious character. Many such may be seen, who, having, from spleen or positiveness of disposition, denied themselves, in early life, the pleasures of the conjugal union, growl out the remainder of their days in satirical reflections on the happiness they have rejected. The scene, between the Old Batchelor and Sylvia, in the third act, is a masterpiece.—The audience, in Congreve's time, were particularly fond of having a city-cuckold dressed out for their entertainment; and Fondlewife is served up with very poignant sauce, for the several incidents in the scene are extremely diverting. Lord Kaims finds fault with the dialogue, in the 1st act, between Bellmour, Sharper, and Heartwell, as if it was mere conversation, and that the business of the play stood still; but what business is more necessary than the knowledge of character? the manners of the personæ dramatis are by such dialogues unfolded to the audience. The same objection may be raised against some interviews of the Prince of Wales and Falstaff, in *Henry IV*.

The *Double Dealer* was acted a year after the *Old Batchelor*. This comedy was ushered into the world by a copy of verses, to his dear friend, Mr. Congreve, by Dryden. In this address, he freely acknowledges the superior genius of the old dramatic writers, with a fine compliment to the author of the *Double Dealer*, who alone supplies all those excellences which were deficient in the writers of Charles II's reign. The pathetic conclusion, every man of taste, though he has often read it, will be pleased to see inserted here:

[Quotes No. 10(a), ll. 64–77.]

In his dedication of the *Double Dealer*, to Montague, afterwards

275

E. of Halifax, the author, though he owns he failed in his attempt, says, he designed to have written a regular comedy. But he soon takes courage to assert, that he has not miscarried in the whole: he had resolved, he says, to preserve the three unities. Then, in a luscious style, he heaps abundance of nauseous flattery on his patron; and indeed I think Congreve as aukward a dedicator as any in our language. When he has finished his panegyric, he tells us, that he hearkened after objections; but, like his friend, Dryden, he can find none worth answering; yet he goes on answering several of them. At last he becomes humble, and begs the critic to re-consider his remarks. But what shocks our author most, is the offence he has given to the ladies; for he would rather offend all the critics in the world than one of the fair sex. And yet I think his defence is a very poor one, and amounts to little less than owning his fault; for surely, out of the whole sex, he might have chosen much better representatives of it than the ladies in the *Double Dealer*.

The manners of this play are more licentious than those of the *Old Batchelor.*—His cuckold, Fondlewife, in that comedy, pleased the town so greatly, that he determined to give the audience a leash of them in his *Double Dealer*; for he has presented them with no less than three. A father, talking obscenely to his daughter, is something monstrous, and almost incredible; and yet Sir Paul Pliant's instructions, to the only virtuous woman in the play, are of that kind.

Maskwell's character is partly taken from Syrus, in the *Heautontimorumenos* of Terence, who, by uttering truths, carries his point more covertly to deceive; and partly, I think, from the Timantus of Fletcher's *Cupid's Revenge*; as Lady Touchwood greatly resembles Bacha in the same play. Brisk's pertness is not unlike the petulance of Novel in the *Plain Dealer*, and Lord Froth's solemnity is an improvement of Lord Plausible's starch civility in the same play.

The plot is extremely intricate, and exacts from the spectator very deep attention; without it, he will not be able to see how it is unravelled in the catastrophe.

DOUBLE DEALER. ACT I. SCENE IV. [ll. 29–31]

LORD FROTH.

There is nothing more unbecoming a man of quality than to laugh;—it is such a vulgar expression of the passions!—Every body can laugh.

Of the same sentiment, with respect to laughter, was a late very accomplished nobleman, who, by his own example, justified the doctrine of Lord Froth. A genuine laugh is as difficult, I believe, to be had, as a generous tear.—Nature, by our frame, intended both for the purposes of humanity. There is certainly much hypocrisy in pretending to assume either; but the feigned laugh is less censurable than the vile imitation of the crocodile's tears. An assenting half-laugh, or smile, is as much expected from an acquaintance as a bow or a shake of the hand. From a Lord C. who wore a mask all his life-time, and taught his only son to do the same, nothing sincere, either in grief or mirth, was to be expected. The man, who strives to repress the natural impulse which ridicule excites, never knew the happiness which the tear of pity for the unfortunate bestows.

The *Guardian* has written an excellent paper, with much pleasantry and humour, on the several sorts of laughers, which he ranges under the following heads: the dimplers, the smilers, the laughers, the grinners, and the horse-laughers. Lord Froth and Lord C. are of the second species. The dimple, says this writer, was, by the antients, termed the Chian laugh;—and this he gives to the prudes. For my part, though I am not fond of the grin, which is generally practised by snarlers, or those who wish to shew their teeth, nor the Sardonic, which Steele says is the Greek and Roman horse-laugh, yet I am no enemy to what he calls the risus of the antients, which is the same as our hearty laugh. If the sect of dimplers and smilers prevail, we shall have no mirth but what the house of commons or the theatre can give. There we are certain to have a full chorus of laughers.

ACT. III. SCENE THE TENTH. [ll. 8–9]
LADY FROTH. BRISK.

BRISK.
Besides, your ladyship's coachman having a red face——

When this play was acted at Drury-lane, about five and twenty years since, an accidental or wilful blunder of Woodward, who acted Brisk in a lively and diverting manner, caused such repeated laughter in the theatre as I scarcely ever heard.—Mrs. Clive, who acted Lady Froth, had, by mistake, or in a hurry, laid on more rouge than usual; and Brisk, in his criticism on the lady's heroic poem, instead of saying, 'Your coachman having a red face,' said, *Your ladyship having a red face*. This was no sooner uttered, than peals of laughter were redoubled all over the theatre. Woodward affected to look abashed and confounded; Clive bore the incident heroically. When they retired to the green-room, from the stage, they were followed by the players, who expected a scene of violent altercation; but this inimitable actress disappointed them: 'Come, Mr. Woodward,' she gravely said, 'let us rehearse the next scene, lest more blunders should fall out.' Clive was, in Lady Froth, as in the rest of her comic characters, superior to all actresses. Happy was that author who could write a part equal to her abilities! she not only, in general, exceeded the writer's expectation, but all that the most enlightened spectator could conceive. By her encouragement and instructions, and her own industry, Miss Pope is become a valuable actress; but genius cannot be communicated. Mrs. Green, of all the female players, in comic humour came the nearest to this admirable comedian. It was Mrs. Green's misfortune to live at the same time with Clive. I shall as soon expect to see another Butler, Rabelais, or Swift, as a Clive.

By consent of all the critics, *Love for Love* is esteemed not only the most excellent of Congreve's plays, but one of the best in our language. His characters are drawn with such strength and comprehension, that his comedies are perpetual commentaries on the passions and humours of mankind. The punishment of an unnatural and hard-hearted parent is the moral aim of the poet; and in this he has, by a judicious conduct of his plot, fully succeeded.

Sir Samson Legend is a finished portrait of an ill-natured wit. Foresight is, I think, a character of humour; there were, it is true, in his time, many persons infected with judicial astrology; even the name of Dryden has enobled the insignificant sect; but Foresight is made up of dreams, nativities, and superstitions of every kind. A ridiculous dread of futurity goes through his whole life; and, as Bluff, in the *Old Batchelor*, says 'fighting is meat, drink, and cloth, to him,' so is omen-hunting to Foresight. But the number of the superstitious does not abate the humour of a character:—Cervantes wrote his *Don Quixote*, not with a view of curing one man infected with the spirit of knight-errantry, but a large number of Quixotes. A single character is a monster not worth a writer's aim.

There is surely an absurdity in making the son of a knight a common sailor or foremast-man; perhaps the author thought he could not raise so much mirth from the midshipman as a dealer in forecastle conversation. The character is well calculated to excite much laughter, and to carry on the fable with comic spirit; but Ben is not a humourist; he is, what Angelica terms him, an absolute sea-wit; his being a sailor is a matter of accident. The author, in his prologue, owns he took fire from the manly scenes of the *Plain Dealer*. Scandal is introduced, as a second Manly, to satirize the vices of the age: he performs his office with the true spirit of a reformer; for he absolutely forgets good manners, and, as to good-nature, that is not to be expected from a censor. Tattle is an original coxcomb, who, in the midst of his prattlings, brags of secrecy. Mr. Pope has questioned whether Congreve's fools are really such:

Tell me if Congreve's fools are fools indeed!

The mere fool is no object of comic satire. Though Congreve has given something like wit to his fops, on examination you will find that it is only the colour of it; it is the Bristol stone, but not the diamond. Brisk, in the *Double Dealer*, is so lively a coxcomb, that you are surprised into an opinion of his being something better than he is: Tattle is merely whipt syllabub and an empty phantom of liveliness.

The ladies in this play are Congreve's ladies, most of them vicious and abandoned. Mrs. Frail, a woman of the town, as he calls her in his dramatis personæ, is a main instrument to carry on the plot. Mrs. Foresight, *her sister every way*,[†] who is so generous as to forget, in the morning, the favours she grants her lovers overnight, is the much-boasted Doris of this writer. If the character were really original, I should not join the cry of its celebrators, for the thought is obvious; but, if the reader will turn to Otway's *Friendship in Fashion*, he will find Mrs. Foresight is only an improvement of Lady Squeamish.[‡] The author's favourite is Angelica, who at last rewards Valentine with her person and fortune: but that mistress is not an amiable character, who drives her lover to the brink of despair, and is satisfied with nothing less than his signing to his own ruin as a proof of his passion.

(III, pp. 312–28)

(ii)

The *Mourning Bride* of Congreve was originally acted in 1697. To see a tragedy, written by the best comic author of the age, drew together vast shoals of writers and critics by profession. It is traditionally said, that Dryden was present the first night of representation; that he was struck and surprised with the first act; but that, before the end of the second, he declared he was satisfied. It was, according to Downs, acted thirteen nights successively. It is still a very favourite play, especially with the ladies. The fable is not ill chosen, nor can I think the principal characters are weakly drawn. In the part of the King, the author has indeed mixed pompous phraseology with an outrageous vehemence of temper; yet still he is a character. Almeria is a fine picture of conjugal affection and persisting fidelity. Zara's noble and exalted mind, hurried away by ungovernable passions, renders her an excellent personage to excite pity and terror.—Osmyn is brave and generous, undismayed by adversity, and resigned to Providence.

The plot is intricate, and must be observed with the most scrupulous attention, or it will escape the spectator. That the contrivers of destruction ought to fall by their own arts, is the apparent moral of the *Mourning Bride*.

Dr. Johnson commends the following part of a scene, in the second act of this tragedy, as the most poetical paragraph in the whole mass of English poetry:

[Quotes Act II, iii, 1–17.]

The passage certainly deserves much praise; but I would beg leave to remark, that Almeria's taking notice of the architecture of the building,—

> By its own weight made steadfast and immoveable,
> Looking tranquillity,—
>
> > [ll. 10–11]

is a calm sentiment, and not of a piece with the rest. The fears of Almeria are raised by objects in her sight, which assist the fancy: but the successive images of terror, which Shakspeare gives his Juliet when she is about to drink the sleeping-potion given her by the frier, proceeding from a tender mind alarmed and apprehensive, are, in my opinion, equal, if not superior, to this boasted passage of Congreve:

[Quotes *Romeo and Juliet*, IV, iii, 20–58.]

The interview between Osmyn and Almeria, in the tombs, has

generally an aukward effect, from their both falling at the same time; and, while poor Leonora is endeavouring to support them, a new personage, Heli, arrives; and, his surprise not being generally well represented, a contemptuous laugh succeeds. I remember that Taswell, a comic actor of a particular cast, fancied he could speak tragedy as well as any man, and begged Mr. Fleetwood, the manager, to trust him with the part of Heli; but the player and the patentee both repented the frolic, for Taswell was born only to excite mirth; and surely a merrier audience, at his lisping out the lines of Heli, was never seen.

As this meeting of the husband and wife is lengthened out to tediousness, great part of it is curtailed by the prompter. Our author, who certainly felt the passion of love with energy, though he was not always very happy in expressing it, has thrown into this dialogue some very tender and affecting thoughts. Few of our play-writers were acquainted with the Greek dramatists: Congreve was a polite scholar; he was well read in them.—Several passages, in the admirable scene between Orestes and Electra, in the tragedy of that name, where he discovers himself to his sister, may be traced in the interview of Osmyn and Almeria. I mean that part of *Electra*, where the Greek player, Porus, in acting that character, bore in his arms an urn which contained the ashes of his own son, and melted, by the excess of his pathetic grief, all Athens into tears.

The prison-scene, in the third act, is made of consequence by the incident of Osmyn's finding a paper, written by his pious father, with a prayer for his son; and the reflections, on the word 'heaven' being torn from the petition, resulting from situation, are very natural. Osmyn's being roused to a sense of his people's wrongs, by his friend, Heli, is the effect of generous passion and nobly affecting. Garrick, through the whole part of Osmyn, was a skilful actor, but his inexhaustible fire had here room to operate to advantage.

In the prison dialogue, between Osmyn and Almeria, many expressions of the husband to the wife are extremely gross, and very disgraceful to the writer. The talking obscenely, in tragedy, is peculiar to the English dramatists; I do not remember to have read, in any of the French tragedies, a single line that intrenches upon good-manners. Dryden, Otway, and Lee, were continually offending against decency; and Congreve, whose fancy was warm and wanton, has imitated his licentious predecessors, nay, in one or two passages of this last scene, almost surpassed them:

Then Garcia shall lie panting on thy bosom, &c.

[III, vi, 112]

Zara's surprising Almeria and Osmyn in conference produces an incident, which, from situation and circumstance, is rather of the comic than the tragic strain. One princess jealous of another's superior charms may indeed be made a serious subject, as in the *Distressed Mother*,[1] but the expressions of anger and resentment, in the captive queen, seldom fail to excite laughter. Mrs. Porter, who was deservedly admired in Zara, and Mrs. Pritchard, her successor in that part, could not, with all their skill, prevent the risibility of the audience in this interview. Mrs. Siddons alone preserves the dignity and truth of character, unmixed with any incitement to mirth, from countenance, expression, or action.

If the composition of this tragedy, with respect to sentiment, passion, and diction, were equal to the well-studied œconomy of the fable, it might challenge a rank with our most frequented tragedies. But, notwithstanding we have, in some places, a false blaze of words and an exuberant swell of passion, blended with images far-fetched and unpleasing, there are scenes, in the *Mourning Bride*, which never fail to attract the attention and engage the heart of the spectator; the happy conclusion will for ever cause joy and exultation in the audience, who will continually dismiss the players with the loudest approbation.

The first characters of this play are generally disliked by the principal actors; their taste is too refined, it seems, to relish the language of it; and we seldom see Osmyn, Almeria, Zara, and the King, supported according to the strength of a company. But there is no discretion in being wiser than our customers, who are, at the same time, our judges. Booth, Oldfield, Porter, and Mills the elder, were long the favourites of the public in Congreve's pantomime, as Churchill terms it. Mr. Garrick did not, on account of turgid expression, reject the noble passion of Osmyn. At the same time, Miss Bellamy was a pleasing Almeria; Mrs. Pritchard and Berry supported Zara and the King.

When Oldfield, a few years before her death, resigned the *Mourning Bride*, Mrs. Thurmond, by the instructions of Booth in that part, became a favourite actress in tragedy. She was a rising performer at Lincoln's-inn fields, when, about the year 1724, Booth, Wilks, and Cibber, pleased with her manner of acting, engaged her at an advanced income. In 1733, she retired, in discontent, to Goodman's Fields, where honest Giffard gave her a kind reception.—Her first part, at his theatre, was the *Mourning Bride,* which she acted with applause several nights. In a year or two she returned to Drury-lane; and retired altogether from the theatre about forty years since.

For her own benefit, the comic Clive put on the royal robes of Zara; she found them too heavy, and, very wisely, never wore them afterwards.

The *Way of the World* was Mr. Congreve's next play. The moral intention of the author, in *Love for Love*, was the reward of constancy in the lover and the punishment of cruelty in the parent: in his last comedy, he proposes to guard mankind against matrimonial falsehood.—The plot is singularly intricate.

Mirabel, the fine gentleman of the play, is a successful lover of the Widow Languish, daughter of Lady Wishfor't, to whom he pays mock-addresses to cover his honourable courtship of Millamant, her niece, a lady of large fortune. To prevent the discovery of the expected consequences of his intrigue with the Widow Languish, he prevails on her to marry his acquaintance, Mr. Fainall; but, to guard the lady against the apprehended tyranny of her husband, Mirabel persuades her to make over to him her whole estate real in trust.—Mrs. Marwood, the friend and mistress of Fainall, secretly in love with Mirabel, discovers to the old lady his pretended courtship, which begets her irreconcileable hatred. To prevent Lady Wishfor't's entering into an improper match from resentment, Mirabel marries his servant, Waitwell, to Foible, her waiting-woman; and, by her assistance, hopes to impose him on the old lady for his uncle. By Marwood's overhearing the discourse, which passed between Wishfor't and Foible, and the latter's with Mrs. Fainall, the scheme of the sham marriage is discovered; the lady is in a rage with her attendant; and Waitwell, her husband, is arrested, and released on bail. Fainall, on his discovery that he was made a cuckold by anticipation, is enraged, and tries to oblige Lady Wishfor't to make over her estate to him, with several other hard conditions, from which she is unexpectedly delivered by the agency of Mirabel, who, by proving the infidelity of Fainall and Marwood and producing the deed of gift in trust, is rewarded with Millamant, which puts an end to the play.

Though this comedy does not present us with so glowing and so pleasing a picture of life and manners as *Love for Love*, yet the reader will be surprised at the great power and skill of the writer. To delineate the manners of a mere coxcomb is not so difficult; but to give the picture of a man who incurs ridicule from affectation of wit, one who says so many things like wit that the common observer mistakes them for it, is not a cheap business: Witwou'd cost the writer more pains than ten Tattles. Whether Petulant be a character of humour I am at some loss to determine. B. Jonson defines humour to be a quality of the mind which draws the passions and affections all one way. Congreve says, I believe truly, that humour is as hard to be defined as wit; and therefore declares he dares venture no farther than to tell us what it is not. Amongst his negatives he places habit and affectation. But how are they to be discriminated from true humour? There is, in my opinion, in that which is called humour, something of both these qualities. Morose, in Ben Jonson's *Silent Woman*, is quoted, by all critics on the subject, as a true character of humour: but how did he acquire that hatred to all speech and noise but his own, if not from an affectation of singularity? nor can I see how he could possibly arrive at that degree of moroseness but by long custom and habit. Dryden defines humour to be a ridiculous extravagance in conversation, wherein one man differs from another.—After having quoted Morose as a perfect character of humour, and more than insinuated that humour in itself is something uncommon, he soon after tells us, that there are no less than nine or ten parts of humour in the same comedy of the *Silent Woman*. If we subscribe to Locke's opinion, that we have no innate principles, we must likewise allow, that we have no innate humours. Much more depends on the construction of the body than we are, at all times, aware of. The organs of men, by which they receive outward impressions, are differently formed: from this alone the great variety of perceptions proceeds; and these, by degrees, produce distinction of humour and character. To make the reader amends for my presumption, in giving my opinion on this difficult subject, I will subjoin Mr. Congreve's opinion of humour, in his letter to Dennis, which he modestly says serves him for one: 'A singular and unavoidable manner of doing or saying any thing peculiar and natural to one man only, by which his speech and actions are distinguished from those of other men.' And this is certainly agreeable to Ben Jonson's definition of humour, though not expressed in the same words; and not very different from Dryden's.—Corbin Morris, in his Essay on Wit and Humour, though he assumes a superiority over Congreve, does not, in my opinion, vary from him or B. Jonson: 'A humourist is a person, in real life, obstinately attached to sensible peculiar oddities, of his own genuine growth, which appear in his temper and conduct.' Morris's man of humour is really the man of wit and pleasantry who can play with the foibles of another; and Foote says, in his Essay on the English Comedy, that the humourist is the food of the man of humour.

Sir Wilful Witwou'd is discriminated from any other fox-hunter by no peculiarity except his wilfulness: whether this will entitle him to a character of humour I leave to the critics.

Millamant is a most agreeable coquet, with a great share of sense and good-nature. She is, indeed, the most unexceptionable character in the play. The rest of the women are what I call Congreve's ladies. Strange! that a man, who conversed so much in the polite world, could scarcely find a female, amongst his acquaintance, of genuine worth and unblemished honour, fit to engraft in his comedies! In Lady Wishfor't's style, Mrs. Marwood and Mrs. Fainall had been *sophisticated*; a misfortune which the old lady would willingly incur in an honourable way. Foible is a go-between, or bawd; and Mincing is ready to swear to any thing, for *her ladyship's service*.

Congreve was so well assured of the success of the *Way of the World*, that, in his prologue, he seems to defy the critics; for he calls upon them to damn his play, if they do not approve it. With an affected modesty, he is entirely resigned to their pleasure:

> He owns with toil he wrought the following scenes;
> But, if they're naught, ne'er spare him for his pains.
> Damn him the more; have no commiseration
> For dulness on mature deliberation.
> He swears he'll not resent one hiss'd off scene;
> Nor like those peevish wits his play maintain,
> Who, to assert their sense, your taste arraign,
> In short,—one play shall, with your leave to shew it,
> Give you one instance of a passive poet,

Who to your judgement yields all resignation,
To save or damn after your own discretion.

[ll. 22–40]

Yet, after all this self-denial, we are told, in positive terms, by
Dennis, that this play 'was hissed by barbarous fools in the acting;
and this treatment justly raised so much indignation in the writer,
that he quitted the stage in disdain.' How is it possible to reconcile
this account with Congreve's own words, in his dedication of the
play to the Earl of Montague?—'That it succeeded on the stage was
almost beyond my expectation.' Several years after this he accepted
a share in one of the theatres: upon what account, except his
writing of plays, the share could be offered him, I am not
competent to guess. That this play was, very soon after its first
exhibition, in favour with the public, is certain. I long since heard,
indeed, that a particular scene, in the fifth act, between Lady
Wishfor't and Foible, was at first maltreated by the audience; and
perhaps for that very reason which the author would most value
himself upon, a close imitation of his great idol, Ben Jonson. Let
any body compare this dialogue, between the lady and her
waiting-woman, with the first scene of the *Alchemist*, between the
two sharpers, Face and Subtle, and he will find the reproaches of
the former to the latter, on the miserable state in which he found
him in St. Paul's, are strongly imitated; they are the closest
resemblances that can be found in any dramatic writings. This,
borrowing from old Ben, the critics, it seems, of those days, did
not approve; they thought Congreve rich enough in his own
treasures, without being obliged to have recourse to others.

It must not be to the condemnation of the whole, or any part, of
the *Way of the World*, that we must attribute this writer's quitting
the drama. A man, who, about ninety years since, when money
was at least twice the value it is now, enjoyed places to the amount
of 800l. per annum, could have little temptation to continue his
authorship. Besides, the warm sun of the Marlborough family, by
the elder branch of which he was particularly distinguished, in all
probability relaxed his poetical nerves. His patrons in vain complained of his indolence, after they had given him the means to be
idle.

The great skill of the poet, in conducting his plot, is no where
more conspicuous than in the second act of the play. Two artful

people, who, from satiety, are heartily tired of each other, and only from convenience and mutual interest keep up a correspondence, accidentally quarrel; and, from a collision of their passions, they not only unfold their own actions and characters, but open the preceding transactions necessary to be known by the audience. The scene between Marwood and Fainall I have always considered as a masterpiece of writing, which cannot be read or admired too much. It is indeed a happy imitation of Ben Jonson's manner of drawing the incidents of the fable, and explanation of characters by sudden altercation.

ACT III. [VII. 13–16]

MRS. MARWOOD, ALONE,
[After hearing the conversation of Lady Wishfor't and Foible, and Mrs. Fainall and Foible.]
O man, man! woman, woman!—the devil is an ass! If I were a painter, I would draw him like an idiot, a driveler, with a bib and bells.

This is a good commentary upon a passage, in Shakspeare's Timon, which puzzled his greatest commentators.

SERVANT TO TIMON, ALONE,
[After being denied money by Sempronius.]
The devil knew not what he did when he made man politic. He crossed himself by it; and *I cannot but think, in the end, the villanies of man will set him free.*
[*Timon of Athens*, III, iii, 28ff.]

In the fourth act of the *Way of the World*, the matrimonial articles, settled between Mirabel and Millamant, are so judiciously framed, that they will serve, with a little fashionable alteration, for a lasting model to all happy-marriage contractors.

ACT IV. SCENE V. [ll. 90–100]

MIRABEL.
No decoy-duck to wheedle you a fop-scrambling to the play in a mask.
(III, pp. 343–64)

(iii)
Of those comedians, who, within these fifty or sixty years, have distinguished themselves in Congreve's comedies, most of whom I have often seen act, something should be said. The *Old Batchelor* of Drury lane was Harper, a good low comedian, but whose

287

understanding was not of that size to give force to the sarcastic poignancy of expression, the whimsical struggles of amorous passion, or the violent rage on discovered folly, in Heartwell; all which Quin perfectly conceived, and justly represented many years at Lincoln's-inn fields and Covent-garden.—The Belmour of Wilks was the finished and polite libertine; that of Walker was the bold and manly rake. The Captain Bluffe of B. Jonson was as complete a piece of acting as I ever saw: his person was against him; for he was old and thin when I first saw him, which is now above fifty-two years since, and I remember I thought him ill chosen for a bully; but his exquisite performance soon cured me, and the whole audience, of any diffidence of his abilities. Colley Cibber's Fondlewife was much, and justly, admired and applauded, though some greatly preferred Dogget's portrait of old doting impotence to his. From a recollection of Cibber's manner, Foote acted a scene or two of Fondlewife better than any characters, except such as he wrote purposely for himself. Hippisley played Fondlewife in a manner original, and not much inferior to Cibber. Mrs. Horton, who was famous for coquets, was the Belinda of Drury-lane; and Mrs. Younger, the sister of Mrs. Bicknel, celebrated, in the Tatler and Spectator, for variety of humorous parts, was an actress much followed in this and many other comic characters, especially the Country Wife. But Mrs. Younger was a general actress, and sometimes appeared in tragedy, though, I think, not to advantage. Much about the time when she left the stage, she was married to the honourable Mr. Finch, who had, above twenty years before, been stabbed, in a quarrel, by the famous Sally Salisbury.

In *Love for Love*, I saw Wilks, in his old age, play the part of Valentine with all the spirit and fire of youth. Two years after, Colley Cibber, who had been long the finished Tattle of Drury-lane, acted Ben when he was past sixty: it was said that he copied Dogget, the original; but neither his voice nor look were suitable to the rough animation of a sailor.—His acting Ben was a piece of managers craft. Joe Miller, who was a lively comic actor, and a favourite of the town in Ben, and many other diverting characters, had, by some mean œconomy of the managers, been driven from Drury-lane to Goodman's Fields: when they were obliged to recal him to his old station, they imagined that Ben, acted first by Cibber, would bring several full houses; and that the public's being afterwards excited to see their friend, Joe Miller, in the same character, would double their profits. I believe they were disappointed in their expectations; for Cibber, though he acted Ben but two or three times, took off the edge of appetite to see Miller. Shepherd was a most spirited actor of the sarcastic Sir Sampson Legend. My old acquaintance, Jack Dunstall, for many years played this part, as well as several others in comedy, with truth and nature. Jack had, indeed, the fault of corresponding by looks, sometimes, with his acquaintance in the pit. His Hodge, John Moody, Lockit, Sir Jealous Traffic, Jobson, and many other characters of the same cast, will be remembered with pleasure by his old friends, whom he often delighted with many a jovial song, and especially that famous one on the sea-victory obtained by Admiral Russel over the French at La Hogue; this he sang harmoniously, and with a true English spirit. Dunstall was a member of several very respectable societies, and was valued, by all who knew him, for his honesty and good-nature.

Theophilus Cibber's first wife acted Miss Prue in an agreeable and lively manner. Clive gave such a romping spirit and humorous vivacity to the wild girl, that even Abington's childish simplicity and playful aukwardness cannot make us forget her.

The theatre of Covent-garden, in December, 1732, opened with the *Way of the World*. The scenes were new, and excellently well painted; all the decorations were suited to the grandeur and magnificence of the building. The boxes were, on this occasion, raised to half a guinea, the pit to five shillings, the galleries in proportion. The parts were thus distributed, as I remember:— Mirabel by Mr. Ryan; Quin, Fainall; Witwou'd, Chapman; Petulant, Neal; Sir Wilful Witwou'd, Hippisley; Waitwell, Pinketh- man, son of the famous Pinkey; Lady Wishfor't, Mrs. Eggleton; Millamant, Mrs. Younger; Marwood, Mrs. Hallam; Mrs. Fainall, Mrs. Buchanan; Foible, Mrs. Stephens, afterwards Mrs. Rich. Quin was a judicious speaker of Fainall's sentiments, but heavy in action and deportment; Walker, who succeeded him, understood and expressed the assumed spirit and real insolence of this artful character much better. Ryan was greatly inferior to the accom- plished Mirabel of Wilks; and Chapman's Witwou'd, though not so finished as that of Colley Cibber, was of his own drawing, and very comic. His quickness of speech resembled the articulate volubility of Mr. King, who is likewise a very pleasing representer of Witwou'd.

(III, pp. 366–71)

(iv)

Hippisley, who acted Sir Wilful Witwou'd, was not an auricular imitator of another's manner; he was solely directed by the force of his own genius. Though he did not, in Sir Wilful, present to the spectator such a laughable figure of a superannuated lubber as Harper, his rival at Drurylane, yet he pleased by dint of comic spirit and natural humour. Neal's Petulant was diverting, whimsical, and odd, though, I believe, not so critically just as Mr. Baddeley's.

Mrs. Younger's Millamant was spritely; but Oldfield's fine figure, attractive manner, harmonious voice, and elegance in dress, in which she excelled all her predecessors and successors except Mrs. Abington, left her without a rival. Mrs. Eggleton was a comic actress much admired by the best judges: John D. of Argyle, who was a frequenter of the theatre and a constant friend to the actors, took a particular pleasure in seeing Mrs. Eggleton on the stage. With a great share of merit, she was extremely diffident, and never attempted a new character but with the utmost apprehension of her failing to please the audience. Mrs. Eggleton, like another Ariadne, died enamoured of Bacchus, about the year 1734.

Though, after the *Way of the World*, Congreve wrote no plays, he brought on the stage a masque called the *Judgement of Paris*, and *Semele*, an opera. The music to the first was composed by Purcel, Eccles, Singer, and Weldon. It was revived at Drury-lane, about fifty years since, with fine scenes and decorations. 'This piece' the author of *Biographia Dramatica* says, 'is often performed to music by way of an oratorio.' The same author, speaking of *Semele*, says, 'that this short piece was performed, and printed in quarto, in 1707.'

The success of this opera is not mentioned by this or any other writer. The story is told by Ovid, in his Metamorphosis, l. 3. but the author has made an alteration in the fable, more conformable to the characters of the opera.—Congreve has shewn himself a scholar and a poet in this dramatic piece; and I should imagine, if revived, with proper music and good singers, it would please in representation. The fable of this opera, which is not, as the *Biographia Dramatica* says, a short poem, is well conducted. The measure of the airs is various, and suited to the situations of the personæ dramatis. The author accounts for having no regard to rime, or equality of measure, in that part of the dialogue designed for recitative, which, he says, is only a more tunable speaking and a kind of prose in music.—Mr. John Beard and Mr. Joseph Vernon excelled greatly in recitative, by giving uncommon force of expression to the passions of love, grief, and resentment.

Of almost all Congreve's poems, except his 'Ode on Mrs. Hunt', Dr. Johnson speaks with a marked contempt. The 'Birth of the Muse' he calls a wretched fiction. But Addison, in the dedication of his *Pax Gulielmi auspiciis Europæ reddita*, to Montague, bestows as much immoderate praise on the muse of Congreve as abuse on all the writers of his time who employed their pens on the subject of peace: *Quod si Congrevius ille tuus, divino quo solet furore correptus, materiam hanc non exornasset, vix tanti esset ipsa pax, ut illa lætaremur, tot perditissimis poetis tam misere decantata.*—This encomium is unworthy of Addison, and indeed is nothing less than absolute fustian; such it will appear, to every reader, in English as well as Latin: 'Had not your Congreve, seized with his usual fit of divine madness, condescended to celebrate the subject, *the peace itself would not have been of such importance to us, nor could we, indeed, have rejoiced in it,* considering how vilely it has been debased by the pens of despicable scribblers.'

Amongst the poems of Prior, on King William's military atchievements, Addison might, with ease, have selected a better subject for his panegyric than Congreve's 'Birth of the Muse'; but Prior was, I believe, in no part of his life, a favourite of Addison.

Before Congreve wrote his last comedy, he published a formal defence of the four plays he had then written; in which there is some wit, a good deal of learning, many unwilling concessions, and no small share of dissingenuity. Congreve's pride was hurt by Collier's attack on plays which all the world had admired and commended; and no hypocrite shewed more rancour and resentment, when unmasked, than this author, so greatly celebrated for sweetness of temper and elegance of manners. It must be confessed, that Collier, in his view of the stage, had gone too far; he had forgotten the old axiom of *Ab abusu ad usum non valet consequentia;* he would listen to nothing less than the entire abolition of stage-amusements and even of music itself; he resembled too much the root-and-branch men, in the days of Charles I. who, not satisfied with reforming abuses, determined to lay the axe to the root of monarchy, and destroy our constitution in church and state.

(III, pp. 373–7)

NOTES

* Dryden's epilogue to the Pilgrim [ll. 11–24].
† *Love for Love,* Act II.
‡ Tom Brown makes Mrs. Barry, the celebrated actress, a perfect Doris. He says, that she did not know the lover who gave her five guineas over-night, unless he brought the same sum in the morning. But Tom had an insuperable itch for scandal. Tom Brown's Works, vol. III, p. 36, 9th edn.
1 *The Distrest Mother* (1712), an adaption of Racine's *Andromaque* by Ambrose Philips.

77. Anon., review of *The Way of the World* in *The Public Advertiser*

1784

From *The Public Advertiser,* Friday 12 November 1784.

THEATRICAL INTELLIGENCE
COVENT GARDEN
MRS. ABINGTON—*and the Way of the World.*

MILLAMANT, the last and highest-finished character of Congreve's pen, 'whose follies (in the language of the poet) are so natural, or so artful, that they become her, and whose affectations, which in another woman would be odious, serve but to make her more agreeable,' would have lain on the shelf, or (what would be perhaps of more discredit to our taste) would be but *ill represented*, were it not for the peculiar talents of Mrs. Abington, who uniting her own experience of the manner of fashionable circles with the highest degree of merit in her profession, restores the character all its original value. To enter into the particulars of her performance would not be doing her justice.—Fine acting, like fine writing, should be felt by general impressions; and what these were throughout the Play, the warm applause of a very brilliant audience fully testified.

Witwou'd and Petulant, though drawn as foils, have more wit than half a dozen of our modern comedies can boast of. The first was very well hit off by Mr. Lewis; but we do not think the change was made for the better in substituting Bonnor in the room of Booth.

When Farren begins to *familiarize* his dialogue a little more, and speak less *declamatory*, he will do better in Fainall; but Mrs. Bates has only to hold her own to be more than respectable in Mrs. Marwood.

Though 'tis impossible not to recollect Yates in Sir Wilful to the disadvantage of his successor, yet we must do this justice to Wilson, that he is much more *chastised* in the part than when we saw him last. The same improvement lately appeared in his Justice Shallow; which, as it was *much wanted*, must be of use to himself as well as the Manager.

The rest of the characters were as well sustained as perhaps the strength of the Company would admit of:—but where is the whole of a *Dramatis Personae* that can do strict justice to the language of Congreve? An author who is in some respect getting obsolete, from our being so long used to *other kind of writers*.

78. Charles Este (?), reviews of *Love for Love* and *The Mourning Bride* in *The World*

1787

From (a) *The World: Fashionable Advertiser*, No. 40, Thursday 15 February 1787; (b) ibid., No. 121, Monday 21 May 1787.

These two reviews were probably written by Charles Este (1752–1829), an Anglican clergyman whose enthusiasm for the theatre led him to write dramatic reviews first for *The Public Advertiser*, and from 1787 to 1790 in his own paper *The World*. The unstinted praise of Kemble and Mrs Siddons is characteristic; so too, is the hostility towards *The Mourning Bride*.

(a)

THE PLAY—HOUSE
DRURY—LANE

Tho' it cannot easily be acknowledged with Addison, that *Love for Love* is the best play in the world,[1] and as such to be followed with equal eagerness, by those who have seen it, and those who have not, yet so many are its charms, in vivacity of dialogue, and strength of character, that the representation is amusing, tho' far from very safe.

With something more than abatement in the article of the moral praise, for the '*callida junctura*', and probability are no where visible. We sat this comedy with much contentment!

In the *acting* there is abundant merit. The Valentine of *Kemble*, is perfect in all its parts. The ease, the elegance, the strong sense, and feeling of the character came up, as Congreve would let them. *Parsons* in *Foresight*, is second to nothing, but *Parsons* in *Corbacchio*: he is the only player in this cast, who boasts as sure acceptance, and the same excessive applause, from the bottom, from the Stage Box to the Shilling Gallery!—*Dodd*, in spite of hoarseness, as every true *buff and blue* must be, was heard with pleasure. And *Ben*, never pleasant, and now wrong, as out of all probable date, yet forced into something better than sufferance, by the skill of *King*.

Miss *Farren's* comedy yields to none—her dress, one mass of *un*-relieved *white sattin*, did not aid her triumph. Miss *Pope* and Mrs. *Jordan* are not to be dismissed, but as the best representatives of Miss Prue and Mrs. Frail.

The *fall* of *Baddeley*, was a means to rise into laughter and applause—which, indeed, he deserved throughout.

(b)

THE PLAY—HOUSE
Mrs. Siddons

To enquire what beauty is—must be the question of a man who cannot see. He who can ask what dignity is, cannot have seen Zara by Mrs. Siddons!—The dignity of empire, and personal charms;—that is intrepid, and would be commanding.

And yet it is, in spite of all that astonishing acting can do for it, signifying nothing. Sound without cause, and fury without effect. If Zara's passions outstrip the wind, they neither interest the mind, nor impress the heart.

The play is very worthless. That it is a pantomime, is not its greatest fault.[2] Inasmuch as it offends manners no less than taste; and hurts with ribaldry more than nonsense.

And yet, such is the force of talents—that against this obstacle and others, with Farenheit at Summer heat, and all the acting about her, below freezing—such is the force of talents—there was a full house and much applause.—Lady Harcourt in one stage box—the St. John's in the other—Lord Harcourt, with Byng, in the orchestra—the Penns, Soames, Adairs—Sir Charles and Lady Dorothy, &c. &c.

The operation of the poison was very well. It would be better perhaps, if a *shudder* followed, upon the drinking of it.—The most finished scene, was that of scorn, and suppressed rage, with Osmyn, in act 3.

> As one hating to be obliged, &c.
> [I, vi, 31]

And,

> —Then 'twas a whisper spread by some, &c.
> [IV, v, 14]

These were brief passages, but very exquisite:
When Zara spoke this line,

> Thou hast a heart—tho' 'tis a *savage* one—
> [II, ix, 38]

A gentleman behind *Francis*, called out bravo! What could that mean?

NOTES

1 Addison makes a passing reference to *Love for Love* as 'one of the finest Comedies that ever appeared upon the *English* Stage' in *The Spectator*, No. 189, Saturday 6 October 1711.

2 On 7 January 1789, *The World* actually headed a brief review of a performance at Drury Lane, 'CONGREVE'S PANTOMIME'.

79. 'Censor Dramaticus' in *The Thespian Magazine*

1792

From *The Thespian Magazine and Literary Repository* (1792), 1: 163–6.

DRAMATIC CRITICISMS.
THE MOURNING BRIDE. *CONGREVE.*

A variety of opinion is so prevalent, amongst mankind, that it is not at all wonderful to find the same object considered by different persons in the opposite extremes of beauty and deformity; and if we attend to the many circumstances that conduce to form this variety of opinion, it will appear impossible that it should be otherwise: the prejudices of education, despotism, and situation in the world, these amongst many others, principally occasion it. It is universally acknowledged that the primary object to be considered in the works of art, is nature; and in this respect, we may be said to have a perfect standard; it requires not a superiority of intellect to perceive the likeness of a fine piece of mechanism to the object it is intended to represent; and this perception carries along with it an idea of perfection in proportion to the degree of resemblance: but by the prejudices above mentioned, even this knowledge is often rendered useless; and by a strange inclination in man to draw every thing within their own circumscribed circle of opinion, they are rendered incapable of judging between a real likeness and a false one. It must be evident that whilst these prejudices exist it will be impossible to form a complete standard of taste, such an one as might serve for a criterion of the works of art, yet we have certain rules laid down by which we are in some measure enabled to judge of their degrees of excellence; and by these rules we intend to conduct our criticisms.

There is not perhaps any piece on the stage that has caused more disputation than Congreve's *Mourning Bride.* It has been its fate to be extolled by its friends, and execrated by its enemies, beyond all probability; and they have both proceeded upon a false principle: the one party have converted its very errors into beauties, whilst the other will not allow it to be any other than a combination of absurdities. Regardless therefore of the praise of the many, and the censure of the few, we shall proceed to examine it by the rules of the Drama. The fable of this play is perfectly dramatic; it is the representation of one, entire, action, conducing to a single object, the happiness of Osmyn and Almeria; and out of which all the incidents naturally arise. It is in its nature implex, for the situation of the principal characters, is changed from misery to happiness, and that in the most perfect manner, for the expectation is contrary, and our surprise is concomitant with our wishes. With regard to the unities, this is one of the most perfect pieces in our language, in the fifth act only, the unity of place is broken by the prison scene. We shall next consider the characters in which we think the author has principally excelled: the character of Osmyn is eminently beautiful: in him all the conspicuous virtues are represented in thair utmost perfection; contrary to the generality of our writers, who make love the controling passion of their heroes, he has made the amor patriæ to predominate. How finely has he elucidated this in the speech of Osmyn to Kali, beginning,

By heav'n thou 'ast rous'd me from my lethargy.—

It is allowed that a perfect character is not suited to the Drama, and our author has very artfully avoided this: so we find the imprisonment of Osmyn, and his principal distresses, are brought on him by his own means; when after his shipwreck on the Moore's territories, he uses the love of Zara to prevail on her husband to undertake the war, in which he is defeated, imprisoned and obliged to endure her passionate importunity; yet though this sufficiently vindicates the appointment of providence, it does not prevent our pity for his sufferings, and satisfaction at their completion: since he was actuated by the most virtuous principles, the love of his country and desire to rescue his father. The rest of the characters are very happily drawn; the tenderness of Almeria, and the passion of Zara, in their different interviews with Osmyn, form an excellent contrast; and the effects of obstinate hatred, and unlawful ambition, are powerfully exemplified in the King and Gonsalez; the speech of the latter to his son, beginning, 'O my son,' is extremely beautiful and affecting. There is one circumstance in

297

this play which we regard as the utmost effort of human ability; it is that of Osmyn's finding the prayer of his father; had Anselmo been introduced in each act, we could not have formed a more adequate idea of his character than is presented to us in this beautiful incident. We come now to the sentiments and the diction which have been most reprehended, and not without some reason; the sentiments are often unappropriate or trivial, and the diction is sometimes too smooth for the language of passion; but these form but a small part of the whole, and lose all comparison when opposed to the number of beauties. The author particularly excelled in those bold strokes of art, that delineate a character in its utmost force, without seeming to intend it: we have already given two instances of this, and another just now occurs to us equally striking: it is in one of the interviews between Osmyn and Zara, when after upbraiding him with his ingratitude, she ends with, 'What then is Osmyn?' in his reply we behold the struggles of a great soul labouring under an imputation which it is impossible to refute till reflecting on his accumulated misfortunes he wonderfully exclaims.

> A fatal wretch!—a huge stupendous ruin,
> That tumbling on its prop, crush'd all beneath,
> And bore contiguous palaces to earth.
>
> [II, ix, 75–7]

This is surely something more than tuneful nonsense.*

We might enumerate many other exquisite passages, and likewise some defective ones, but as we have already exceeded our bounds, we shall close our remarks with an observation on the artful commencement of this piece. The melody of the first six lines is perhaps unequalled, and with the accompaniment of the music, awake the soul to a perfect sympathy with the woes of the tender Almeria.

We promised to say something of the performers in the Drama, but we have so far extended this article, that we shall be very brief. Mr. Kemble is undoubtedly the best Osmyn on the stage; the character is suited to his forte; that firmness of sentiment and action that characterises the unfortunate prince accords with the abilities of the actor, it is in such parts as these that he displays his principal excellence: we may say the same of Mrs. Siddons' Zara, her wonderful powers of declamation and feature in this cast of characters, is well known and felt.

CENSOR DRAMATICUS.

NOTE

* See Mr. Walpole's preface to the *Mysterious Mother*. [Horace Walpole had dismissed *The Mourning Bride* with this phrase in the preface to his own tragedy *The Mysterious Mother* (1768).]

1802–1913

80. Anon., reviews of *The Double-Dealer* and *The Mourning Bride* in *The Monthly Mirror*

1802–7

From (a) *The Monthly Mirror*, 1802 (March), 13:202; (b) ibid., 1807 (October), n.s., 2:288 (misnumbered 260) and 289.

(a)

DRURY-LANE

Feb. 27—*Double Dealer*—This is one of those comedies which, with the productions of Wycherly and many of the poets of King Charles's reign, ought never again to be revived. Its wit does not atone for its indecency, and even its admirable plot, perfect as it is, may be dispensed with, since it serves only to unfold scenes of grossness too shocking for exhibition on a moral stage. It is unnecessary to dwell on this subject, or to point out any of the offensive passages. It is not merely the dialogue that is objectionable—the whole mass is infectious, and defies any attempt at reform or qualification. Much to the credit of the times, the audience was not numerous, so that a repetition of this comedy is hardly to be apprehended. Should, however, another representation be hazarded, we hope the public, which with difficulty suppressed its indignation on this evening, will testify the most decided reprobation of a play to which no female can listen without emotions of shame, and which must excite the utmost abhorrence in every virtuous mind. We shall not even compliment the performers on this occasion, (for some of whom we felt more than we can adequately express) because, to play the scenes of the *Double Dealer*, with the effect intended by the author, requires a degree of effrontery which we will not impute to any actor, particularly to the females, by praising their performance.

(b)

Johnson has said that this single tragedy of Congreve contains '*the most poetical paragraph*' to be found in the whole mass of English poetry, and he finds it in the speech of *Almeria*, beginning—'*No, all is hush'd, and still as death.*'—Admitting this, we may also boldly claim admission to the fact, that the *Mourning Bride* displays as much inflated language, or what Aristophanes calls *prose on horseback*, as can be produced in any tragedy equally successful. The *Zara* of Mrs. Siddons was excellent throughout, but in the scene with *Osmyn*, in the prison, she was wonderfully fine. Mr. Kemble wore his Moorish dress with all its advantage, and played with great ability; but in tragedy Mrs. Siddons's star has so much the ascendant, as to eclipse every other within the sphere of its lustrous action. Her present bulk certainly makes her seem unfit to perform a lover's part, and for a time, leaves us without surprise that her overtures should be rejected; but we do not hear her long, before the defect is lost, and 'Pritchard is *genteel*'. Her very gaudy clothes seemed to us to trench on the privilege of *Queen Dolabella*, in the farce which succeeded; and her dying on a preparation of soft cushions, is only inferior in its whimsical effect, and perhaps in *softness*, to the temporary death of *King Arthur*, on the rump of his little queen. After her *Imogen*, we did not expect so much cleverness as Miss Norton exhibited in *Almeria*. For tragedy, however, she lacks dignity in her action, and expression in her countenance. *Manuel* and *Gonsalez*, were acted by Mr. Murray and Mr. Chapman. If these gentlemen would affect less ease, they would appear more easy. The latter in simply stabbing such a *good, easy* king as Mr. Murray, might be more seemly, and not return from the deed with both hands dyed, as if he had been shelling walnuts.

81. Anon., 'On the Character of Congreve as a Writer of Comedy'

1804

From *The Scots Magazine* (1804), 66: 9–14.

The general proposition, founded on the Philosophy of inductive reasoning, flattering to human nature, and consolatory or pleasing to the man of benevolence and the friend of truth; that mankind are constantly, gradually, and necessarily advancing in the extent and accuracy of their knowledge, in the soundness and comprehension of their judgment, and in the purity and correctness of their taste, must be granted, notwithstanding their progress is slow, and often imperceptible, and even though facts may be adduced, which prove an occasional temporary pause, or retrograde movement. Taste, which depends in a great degree upon feeling, and cannot therefore be regulated by any known and fixed standard, is more apt to continue stationary, or to relapse into its former vulgar and uncultivated state, than those mental improvements, which depend on the judgment exclusively, and can be referred to principles, simple, clear, and generally acknowledged. Whoever compares the productions of this nation, belonging to the province of taste, which are now poured from the press in almost daily succession, with those, which our ancestors, at the beginning of the 18th century received with admiration, will not hesitate to assert, that we have lost that relish for dramatic excellence at least, which distinguished that period. We could hardly have expected that any essential improvement should have been made, since the age of Beaumont and Fletcher, Farquhar, Congreve, and Cibber: the comedies of these celebrated writers were nearly perfect, in character, language, and plot: their defects and faults resulted, in general, from the manners of the age. But the writers of comedy of the present day seem, either from their own inability, or the corruption of the public taste, to have receded as far as possible from that path, which was clearly marked out to them, and had been previously trodden by the authors we have already mentioned. It is a curious and humiliating fact, that the public now prefer comedies, meagre in incident, insipid by their nothingness, or disgusting by their buffoonery; without any discrimination of character, except what arises from the fashion of the coat, the jargon of their language, or from ephemeral manners caricatured;—without any plot; or with a plot forced and unnatural;—written in incorrect and vulgar language; whose energy consists in oaths, and whose wit is confined to puns and quibbles.

It is perhaps equally difficult to account for this dereliction of judgment and taste, and to restore them to their former correctness and purity. No method seems more likely to revive the taste of our ancestors, than to hold up to the view of those, who countenance and admire the present comedy, those writers, who, most probably, were reciprocally the cause and effect of that taste. If comedy have no higher object than mere amusement, by the display of those incidents and characters, which are common and natural, and at the same time novel and interesting, and by the introduction of that language, which is correct and easy, pointed with wit and adorned with elegance, but at the same time characteristic; still for comedy, in this view of it, we must look back to the times that are past.

But if the object and design of comedy be of a higher and more important nature; if it be calculated, and therefore ought to be written, to give insight into human character,—to expose the follies and chastise the vices of mankind,—to be at once the school, in which the ignorant may gain knowledge, without the delays and the danger of experience, and the frivolous or abandoned may be reformed without the intervention of personal ridicule or chastisement; how ineffectual, and in most instances, how directly opposite to this object must the comedies of this age appear! At the same time it must be allowed, that the comedies written about the end of the 17th and beginning of the 18th centuries, are better calculated to answer the less important, though perhaps more proper, object of this species of dramatic writing. They are polluted by the most plain and unqualified grossness, both in the incidents which occur, and in the sentiments which are uttered; and the favourite and most highly-finished character is generally debauched, unprincipled, and lewd.

So far these authors are severely reprehensible; but there is no

303

danger that in the present day their faults would be committed, or tolerated if committed. Vice, now, if it be represented on the stage, must be stripped of its grossness: it must lose at least part of its deformity; thoughts, which border on obscenity, or indelicacy, must be rendered ambiguous by *double entendre*, or concealed in delicate and borrowed language. A Cynic might perhaps be inclined to consider these circumstances, as indicative, not of the superior purity of the public morals, and to ask whether the mode in which indelicate thoughts are now brought forward, be not necessary, to give a zest to the pallid appetites of a modern audience. It certainly must be said, respecting the present age, whether to its praise or discredit I shall not pretend to determine, that its modesty blushes and takes the alarm at expressions, which would have conveyed no indelicate ideas to the obtuse intellect, and less widely-extended associations of our ancestors.

We may therefore safely hold up for admiration and example the writers formerly mentioned; and if we can produce an imitation of their excellencies, and bring back to life the antient comedy, we need not be afraid that it will be accompanied with its gross obscenity.

In the following remarks I shall confine myself to Congreve:—a man to whom, when we consider at what an early period of his life the first and perhaps the best of his Comedies was produced, it would be difficult and unjust to deny the praise of great vigour of intellect; he was rapid, comprehensive, and clear in his views: striking and original, but at the same time natural and happy in the combination of his thoughts: and possessed the rare quality of infusing into the language, he used, the whole energy of his mind.

He who, for the first time, reads the Comedies of Congreve, especially if he begin with the *Old Bachelor*, will find himself unable, unless the eye of his mind be either very strong or very dull; to fix his attention on the progress and connection of the incidents; the discrimination and variety of the characters; or the gradual unfolding of the plot. He will be dazzled by the continued and incessant flashes of wit, which dart before his eyes: they will either entirely attract his notice and occupy his attention; or prevent him by their splendour from clearly perceiving the merits and defects of the play.

The wit of Congreve is poured forth in a rapid and copious

stream: it is never interrupted: it bursts forth on every occasion, and from every character. Pope has justly said,

Tell me, if Congreve's fools are fools indeed.

But his wit is not merely constant; it is also pure; unmixed with any play on words: it never borrows any assistance from ridicule: it is not indebted for its point to satire: it certainly is not unfrequently employed to set off a profligate or indelicate sentiment; but in these instances it gives and never receives. It is also brilliant without losing any of its solidity: it not only dazzles at the moment by its splendour; but retains all its peculiar qualities, when the eye views it more steadily and closely.

It may, however, be justly questioned, whether such wit is proper in comedy? Is it what we expect in the representation of characters, not selected for the occasion, but grouped and mixed as we find them in the world? Certainly not: in comedy we may allow a connection of incidents, and a catastrophe, which, tho' they seldom occur in real life, contain nothing unnatural or improbable: our knowledge of the various events of human life is more limited and more general than our acquaintance with the characters of mankind; the former may, under circumstances which we have never witnessed, excite our surprize, and baffle our conjectures; whereas the characters, which it is the business of comedy to represent, must all of them have been known to us in their great outline of sentiment, conduct, and language, and can be novel only in their lighter shades and more delicate features.

We are therefore surprized, and at first delighted; but on reflection, we are offended at the constant flow of wit in Congreve's comedies. In life we meet with few characters who can at all times, in the ease and freedom of conversation, pour forth pure and appropriate wit. The attempt is seldom made, and where it is made, the wit is frequently unnatural, languid or corrupt. But in Congreve, not only his principal and most accomplished characters are always witty, but they seem to have inspired no small portion of their wit into every person with whom they converse; into fools and waiting-maids:—into the gloomy puritan and the calculating usurer. Wit surrounds every personage, whom he introduces, as constantly, closely, and splendidly, as the Glory attaches itself to the head of the painter's favourite saint.

Hence, particularly in the *Old Bachelor*, the characters lose a great part of their individuality and distinction. Their wit, which strikes us first and most strongly, gives them such a general, mutual resemblance, that every other discriminating mark is greatly weakened, and often scarcely perceptible. The natural faces of his characters are indeed different in their contour, in their features, and in their general expression; but they are all hidden under masks of the same kind: and these are so seldom withdrawn, that it is difficult to distinguish exactly and fully one personage from another: when we do discover that they are actually and essentially distinct and different, the uniformity of their disguise appears unnatural and absurd.

Another disadvantage necessarily arises from these incessant and indiscriminate sallies of wit: the deception is destroyed; our thoughts and admiration are continually called off from the characters to the author. We naturally and constantly refer the wit to the quickness and fertility of his imagination, both from its copiousness and sameness; and think of the author in his closet, when we should be insensible of his existence, and believe in the reality of what we saw.

But, notwithstanding these objections to this striking characteristic of Congreve's comedies; even in regard to their wit, they may be held up as models to the present age: there is little likelihood that our present writers of comedy will attempt, or succeed if they do attempt, to imitate the prodigality of his wit.

Humour, if it be defined to consist 'in the representation of what is ridiculous in character, whether natural or artificial,' may justly be ascribed to Congreve. Indeed, a close and accurate examination of the comedies of Congreve, would serve better perhaps than any laboured or subtle disquisition, to fix exactly the boundaries between wit and humour, and to mark the peculiar and discriminating qualities of each.

Of the characters of Congreve it has been observed in general, that he did not draw much from common life. Dr Johnson, speaking of the *Old Bachelor*, observes, that 'the characters both of the men and women are either fictitious and artificial, as those of Heartwell and the ladies; or easy and common, as Wittol, a tame idiot; Bluffe, a swaggering coward; and Fondlewife, a jealous puritan.' It may be granted, without detracting from his merit, that his characters are not generally drawn from common life: the exhibition of such characters requires little skill, and excites little interest. In a comedy we do not expect that all the characters should be strongly marked and different from the mass of mankind; we expect, what we see in life, some that are common and undistinguished by any striking peculiarity: at the same time, we expect to find a few characters, which are not to be met with in the common and crowded walks of life. To create and pourtray these characters, a powerful and vivid imagination, furnished with materials, on which to work, from an accurate, profound, and extensive knowledge of human nature, is absolutely necessary. He who should borrow from common life all his characters, and his incidents, would produce an insipid and meagre comedy.

If we examine the character of Heartwell attentively, we shall not be inclined to pronounce it fictitious, or artificial. When considered in all its parts, it will be found to be natural, well supported, and uniformly consistent. He is a surly old bachelor, who, before the world at large, and his young and gay friends in particular, is severe and cynical in his remarks on the profligacy of the age, the folly of love, and the frailties and vices of women. He brands with indiscriminate and equal censure the purest and most rational love, and the caprice or thoughtlessness of youthful passion;—the naked lewdness of animal desire, and the forced and idiot fondness of advanced years. Love, in his opinion, is a passion, which admits of no excuse: it either proceeds from, or produces, imbecility of mind, dissoluteness of manners, and slavishness of disposition.

Shall we be surprised, when we find this man blindly and childishly attached to a woman, who makes him her dupe by the most barefaced artifices? when we perceive him the sport of her caprice, and the easy, unsuspecting instrument, of her designs? when we witness his mawkish fondness, and lavish prodigality?

Such is Heartwell; and many such there are in the world. Here is nothing artificial, or fictitious: nothing absurd or unnatural in his conduct; we expect that his violence and excess in one character should be proportionate to his violence and excess in the other.

Whoever contrasts the 4th scene of the 1st act, in which Heartwell is discoursing with Vainlove and Bellmour, with the 10th scene of the 3d act, in which he appears as the lover of Sylvia, will perceive the justness of these remarks, and acknowledge that the skill of the author is conspicuous in the natural and highly-finished consistency of the character. In the latter scene may also be distinguished another common result of such a character as

Heartwell's. Sylvia, in order the more certainly and closely to ensnare him, assumes the appearance, and borrows the language, of one who is ignorant of vice, and suspicious of man; but she misunderstands her assumed character:—in a man, not blinded by a doting passion, and the consciousness of superior discernment, her behaviour would create disgust, and excite suspicion. But Heartwell mistakes the stupid simplicity of ignorance for unsullied innocence of thought; and the affected coyness of overacted modesty, for the shrinking purity of real virtue.

It seemed proper to enter thus fully into the character of Heartwell, because it does not appear to have been fairly appreciated by Dr Johnson: it certainly is remarkably well drawn, and sufficient of itself to stamp the impression of superior merit on the play.

The characters of the ladies must be allowed, in some degree, to be artificial, and not sufficiently distinct. It is to be hoped, for the credit of the age in which Congreve wrote, that their exact resemblances in life were few; and that his females are rather the creation of his own dissolute fancy, than the pictures of such as were generally known; or even of those with whom he was so unfortunate as to have been acquainted.

The shades of difference between Bellmour and Vainlove are delicate; but, to the eye of the attentive and critical observer, they are never lost or confounded; they are both men of the world; they both pursue pleasure with equal eagerness, talent, and laxity of principle; but the desire of one of them to gratify his vanity, at the same time that he is indulging his sensual appetite, distinguishes their common motives; and to the same character variety seems necessary, in order to give a zest to those pleasures which the other expects to find in a constant attachment to a single object.

If the observations formerly made be true, it may be granted, that the characters of Bluffe, Wittol, and Fondlewife, are easy and common; they still discover the hand of a master. The characters of a tame idiot, a swaggering coward, and a jealous puritan, are easily drawn; the general outlines, and more striking features, may be traced by a painter of little skill, but only a proficient in the art could give those delicate and discriminating touches, which add personality to the characters, and distinguish them from the multitude of idiots, cowards, and fanatics.

If comedy be meant to please and instruct, common characters must always be introduced: the greatest talents must stoop to draw them; for, to many who read, and to most who see a comedy, only such characters can be intelligible, interesting, or useful. It may even be questioned, whether a man of talents, who has directed his observation and acuteness to the more complicated and subtle parts of human character, will not find it a difficult task to display characters of common occurrence and easy explanation.

Having examined the principal characters of the *Old Bachelor* with sufficient minuteness of analysis and scrupulosity of criticism, I shall merely observe further, that, however some characters may be thought artificial, and others mixed with inconsistency, yet all of them will be found striking and familiar, either to the superficial or to the intimate observer of mankind. They are never insipid or tame; they resemble mankind, not in the fluctuating, and superficial distinctions, which exist to-day, and are laid aside and forgotten to-morrow; but in those permanent and radical differences, which, however varied in their more trifling points, will always exist and be recognized, as the result of those immutable laws, which form the mind and character of man.

The incidents in the comedies of Congreve are striking and varied: they please, because they are at once natural, and rendered interesting by the novelty and closeness of their connection. Every incident seems to produce or include another: and yet our anticipation is not so correct and full, as to destroy that pleasure which arises from the union of that which is novel with that which is natural.

His plots are original; they are deeply laid, but not intricate; unexpected, but not improbable. Dr Johnson objects to the *Old Bachelor,* that the catastrophe arises from a mistake, not very probably produced, by marrying a woman in a mask. But when Congreve wrote, the improbability was much less, as masks were then very commonly and generally worn; and this circumstance, joined to the silliness of Wittol, would render the deception practised by Sylvia easy and unsuspected.

Such are the principal faults and merits of Congreve, as a writer of Comedy; and as it is not likely that any writer of the present age, however dissolute in his principles, would dare to imitate his grossness; or however adorned with wit, will possess so much of it, as to be equally indiscriminate and lavish in its use, he may be fairly held up as a model for those who write for the stage, and as a proper purifier of the public taste.

82. Elizabeth Inchbald on *Love for Love*
1808

From *The British Theatre*, 25 vols (London: 1808), xiii, pp. 5–6 (separately paginated).

A moderately successful actress, Elizabeth Inchbald (1753–1821) retired from the stage in 1789; but she had already begun a second career as a dramatist and novelist. Mrs Inchbald included two of Congreve's plays, *Love for Love* and *The Mourning Bride*, in her compendium *The British Theatre*. The following extract is taken from the 'Remarks' on the former play.

Were the characters in *Love for Love* as natural, and as edifying as they are witty, it would be a perfect composition: but the conversation of many of the persons of this drama is either so immoral, or so tinctured with their occupations or propensities, that no such people now exist, and it is to be supposed, never, at any period, existed.

The presiding quality of characters may be too closely adhered to, as well as too much neglected by an author. Men love, in general, to appear that, which they are not—but as their peculiar tempers or callings are no doubt, at times, discoverable either in their language or manners, such peculiarities, to appear natural in imitation, should only be resorted to occasionally.

It were indeed to be wished, that wicked men, like the men in this comedy, would hold discourse according to their evil natures; that the innocent and the unwary might know whom to shun—but to seem virtuous, is the usual design of people devoted to vice.

From the charge of conspicuous faults or singularities, the author has, however, exempted his two sincere lovers. For though Valentine and Angelica are both somewhat too gay to be good, yet compared with the company they keep, they are most respectable personages.

Dr. Johnson has so pointedly censured the improbability of a marriage contracted under a mask (an incident which occurs in most, if not all, of Congreve's plays), that any additional remark on that subject would be superfluous; and, when all the imperfections of *Love for Love* are summed up, there still remains a balance of entertainment so delectable, that it pleases at the present era as it did at the past, and will continue its attractions as long as wit, or a theatre shall charm.

Idolized as this author was for his dramatic genius, he retired from the pursuit of fame to a country life, instigated by a jealousy of Mrs. Centlivre's superior influence with the town as a dramatist.

83. William Hazlitt on Congreve
1816–19

From (a) *The Examiner*, No. 422, 28 January 1816, pp. 58–9; (b) *Lectures on the English Comic Writers* (London: 1819), pp. 135–46.

The first of the two pieces below is a review of a performance of *Love for Love* at Drury Lane. It first appeared in *The Examiner* for 28 January 1816, and was reprinted in 1818 in *A View of the Stage*, a collection of Hazlitt's theatrical reviews. The second is taken from 'On Wycherley, Congreve, Vanbrugh, and Farquhar', the fourth of the *Lectures on the English Comic Writers*.

THEATRICAL EXAMINER.
NO. 223.   *Drury-Lane.*

CONGREVE's Comedy of *Love for Love* is, in wit and elegance, perhaps inferior to the *Way of the World*: but it is unquestionably the best-acting of all his plays. It abounds in dramatic situation, in incident, in variety of character. Still (such is the power of good writing) we prefer reading it in the closet to seeing it on the stage.

As it was acted the other night, many of the finest traits of character were lost. Though *Love for Love* is much less a tissue of epigrams than his other plays, the author has not been able to keep his wit completely under. *Jeremy* is almost as witty and learned as his master.—The part which had the greatest effect in the acting was MUNDEN's *Foresight*. We hardly ever saw a richer or more powerful piece of comic acting. It was done to the life, and indeed somewhat over; but the effect was irresistible. His look was planet-struck, his dress and appearance like one of the signs of the Zodiac taken down. We never saw any thing more bewildered. PARSONS, if we remember right, gave more imbecility, more of the doating garrulity of age, to the part, and blundered on with a less determined air of stupidity.—Mr. DOWTON did not make much of *Sir Sampson Legend*. He looked well, like a hale, hearty old gentleman, with a close bob-wig, and bronze complexion;—but that was all.—We were very much amused with Mr. HARLEY's *Tattle*. His indifference in the scene where he breaks off his engagement with *Miss Prue* was very entertaining. In the scene in which he teaches her how to make love, he was less successful: he delivered his lessons to his fair disciple with the air of a person giving good advice, and did not seem to have a proper sense of his good fortune. 'Desire to please, and you will infallibly please,' is an old maxim, and Mr. HARLEY is an instance of the truth of it. This actor is always in the best humour possible with himself and the audience. He is as happy as if he had jumped into the very part which he liked the best of all others. Mr. RAE, on the contrary, apparently feels as little satisfaction as he communicates. He always acts with an air of injured excellence.—Mrs. MARDYN's *Miss Prue* was not one of her most successful characters. It was a little hard and coarse. It was not fond and yielding enough. *Miss Prue* is made of the most susceptible materials. She played the hoydening parts best, as where she cries out, 'School's up, school's up'—and she knocked off Mr. BARTLEY's hat with great good-will.—Mr. BARTLEY was *Ben*; and we confess we think *Miss Prue's* distaste to him very natural. We cannot make up our minds to like this actor; and yet we have no fault to find with him. For instance, he played the character of *Ben* very properly; that is, just like 'a great sea-porpoise.' There is an art of qualifying such a part in a manner to carry off its disagreableness, which Mr. BARTLEY wants.—Mrs. HARLOWE's *Mrs. Frail* was excellent: she appeared to be the identical

Mrs. Frail, with all her airs of mincing affectation, and want of principle. The character was seen quite in dishabille. The scene between her and her sister *Mrs. Foresight*, about the discovery of the pin—'And pray sister where did you find that pin?'—was managed with as much coolness as any thing of this sort that ever happened in real life.—Mrs. ORGER played *Mrs. Foresight* with much ease and natural propriety. She in general reposes too much on her person, and does not display all the animation of which the character is susceptible. She is also too much in female parts, what the *walking fine gentleman* of the stage used to be in male.—Mr. BARNARD played *Jeremy* with a smart shrug in his shoulders, and the trusty air of a valet in his situation.

(b)
Congreve is the most distinct from the others, and the most easily defined, both from what he possessed, and from what he wanted. He had by far the most wit and elegance, with less of other things, of humour, character, incident, &c. His style is inimitable, nay perfect. It is the highest model of comic dialogue. Every sentence is replete with sense and satire, conveyed in the most polished and pointed terms. Every page presents a shower of brilliant conceits, is a tissue of epigrams in prose, is a new triumph of wit, a new conquest over dulness. The fire of artful raillery is nowhere else so well kept up. This style, which he was almost the first to introduce, and which he carried to the utmost pitch of classical refinement, reminds one exactly of Collins's description of wit as opposed to humour,

> Whose jewels in his crisped hair
> Are placed each other's light to share.

Sheridan will not bear a comparison with him in the regular antithetical construction of his sentences, and in the mechanical artifices of his style, though so much later, and though style in general has been so much studied, and in the mechanical part so much improved since then. It bears every mark of being what he himself in the dedication of one of his plays tells us that it was, a spirited copy taken off and carefully revised from the most select society of his time, exhibiting all the sprightliness, ease, and animation of familiar conversation, with the correctness and delicacy of the most finished composition. His works are a singular treat to those who have cultivated a taste for the niceties of English style: there is a peculiar flavour in the very words, which is to be found in hardly any other writer. To the mere reader his writings would be an irreparable loss: to the stage they are already become a dead letter, with the exception of one of them, *Love for Love*. This play is as full of character, incident, and stage-effect, as almost any of those of his contemporaries, and fuller of wit than any of his own, except perhaps the *Way of the World*. It still acts, and is still acted well. The effect of it is prodigious on the well-informed spectator. In particular, Munden's Foresight, if it is not just the thing, is a wonderfully rich and powerful piece of comic acting. His look is planet-struck; his dress and appearance like one of the signs of the Zodiac taken down. Nothing can be more bewildered; and it only wants a little more helplessness, a little more of the doating querulous garrulity of age, to be all that one conceives of the superannuated, star-gazing original. The gay, unconcerned opening of this play, and the romantic generosity of the conclusion, where Valentine, when about to resign his mistress, declares—'I never valued fortune, but as it was subservient to my pleasure; and my only pleasure was to please this lady,'—are alike admirable. The peremptory bluntness and exaggerated descriptions of Sir Sampson Legend are in a vein truly oriental, with a Shakespearian cast of language, and form a striking contrast to the quaint credulity and senseless superstitions of Foresight. The remonstrance of his son to him, 'to divest him, along with his inheritance, of his reason, thoughts, passions, inclinations, affections, appetites, senses, and the huge train of attendants which he brought into the world with him,' with his valet's accompanying comments, is one of the most eloquent and spirited specimens of wit, pathos, and morality, that is to be found. The short scene with Trapland, the money-broker, is of the first water. What a picture is here drawn of Tattle! 'More misfortunes, Sir!' says Jeremy. *Valentine.* 'What, another dun?' *Jeremy.* 'No, Sir, but Mr. Tattle is come to wait upon you.' What an introduction to give of an honest gentleman in the shape of a misfortune! The scenes between him, Miss Prue, and Ben, are of a highly coloured description. Mrs. Frail and Mrs. Foresight are 'sisters every way;' and the bodkin which Mrs. Foresight brings as a proof of her sister's levity of conduct, and which is so convincingly turned against her as a demonstration of her own—'Nay, if you come to that, where did you find that bodkin?'—is one of the trophies of the moral justice of the comic drama. The *Old Bachelor* and *Double Dealer* are inferior to *Love for Love*, but one is never tired of reading them. The fault of the last is, that Lady Touchwood approaches, in the turbulent impetuosity of her character, and measured tone of her declamation, too near to the tragedy-queen; and that Maskwell's plots puzzle the brain by their intricacy, as they stagger our belief by their gratuitous villainy. Sir Paul and Lady Pliant, and my Lord and Lady Froth, are also scarcely credible in the extravagant insipidity and romantic vein of their follies, in which they are notably seconded by the lively Mr. Brisk and 'dying Ned Careless.'

The *Way of the World* was the author's last and most carefully finished performance. It is an essence almost too fine; and the sense of pleasure evaporates in an aspiration after something that seems too exquisite ever to have been realised. After inhaling the spirit of Congreve's wit, and tasting 'love's thrice reputed nectar' in his works, the head grows giddy in turning from the highest point of rapture to the ordinary business of life; and we can with difficulty recal the truant Fancy to those objects which we are fain to take up with here, *for better, for worse.* What can be more enchanting than Millamant and her morning thoughts, her *doux sommeils?* What more provoking than her reproach to her lover, who proposes to rise early, 'Ah! idle creature!' The meeting of these two lovers after the abrupt dismissal of Sir Wilful, is the height of careless and voluptuous elegance, as if they moved in air, and drank a finer spirit of humanity.

> *Millamant.* Like Phœbus sung the no less amorous boy.
> *Mirabell.* Like Daphne she, as lovely and as coy.
> [IV, iv, 70–v.1.]

Millamant is the perfect model of the accomplished fine lady:

> Come, then, the colours and the ground prepare,
> Dip in the rainbow, trick her off in air;
> Choose a firm cloud, before it falls, and in it
> Catch ere she change, the Cynthia of a minute.

She is the ideal heroine of the comedy of high life, who arrives at the height of indifference to every thing from the height of satisfaction; to whom pleasure is as familiar as the air she draws; elegance worn as a part of her dress; wit the habitual language which she hears and speaks; love, a matter of course; and who has nothing to hope or to fear, her own caprice being the only law to herself, and rule to those about her. Her words seem composed of amorous sighs—her looks are glanced at prostrate admirers or envious rivals.

> If there's delight in love, 'tis when I see
> That heart that others bleed for, bleed for me.
>
> [III, xii, 18–19]

She refines on her pleasures to satiety; and is almost stifled in the incense that is offered to her person, her wit, her beauty, and her fortune. Secure of triumph, her slaves tremble at her frown: her charms are so irresistible, that her conquests give her neither surprise nor concern. 'Beauty the lover's gift?' she exclaims, in answer to Mirabell—'Dear me, what is a lover that it can give? Why one makes lovers as fast as one pleases, and they live as long as one pleases, and they die as soon as one pleases; and then if one pleases, one makes more.' We are not sorry to see her tamed down at last, from her pride of love and beauty, into a wife. She is good-natured and generous, with all her temptations to the contrary; and her behaviour to Mirabell reconciles us to her treatment of Witwoud and Petulant, and of her country admirer, Sir Wilful.

Congreve has described all this in his character of Millamant, but he has done no more; and if he had, he would have done wrong. He has given us the finest idea of an artificial character of this kind; but it is still the reflection of an artificial character. The springs of nature, passion, or imagination are but feebly touched. The impressions appealed to, and with masterly address, are habitual, external, and conventional advantages: the ideas of birth, of fortune, of connexions, of dress, accomplishment, fashion, the opinion of the world, of crowds of admirers, continually come into play, flatter our vanity, bribe our interest, soothe our indolence, fall in with our prejudices;—it is these that support the goddess of our idolatry, with which she is every thing, and without which she would be nothing. The mere fine lady of comedy, compared with the heroine of romance or poetry, when stripped of her adventitious ornaments and advantages, is too much like the doll stripped of its finery. In thinking of Millamant, we think almost as much of her dress as of her person: it is not so with respect to Rosalind or Perdita. The poet has painted them differently; in colours which 'nature's own sweet and cunning hand laid on,' with health, with innocence, with gaiety, 'wild wit, invention ever new;' with pure red and white, like the wilding's blossoms; with warbled wood-notes, like the feathered choir's; with thoughts fluttering on the wings of imagination, and hearts panting and breathless with eager delight. The interest we feel is in themselves; the admiration they excite is for themselves. They do not depend upon the drapery of circumstances. It is nature that 'blazons herself' in them. Imogen is the same in a lonely cave as in a court; nay more, for she there seems something heavenly—a spirit or a vision; and, as it were, shames her destiny, brighter for the foil of circumstances. Millamant is nothing but a fine lady; and all her airs and affectation would be blown away with the first breath of misfortune. Enviable in drawing-rooms, adorable at her toilette, fashion, like a witch, has thrown its spell around her; but if that spell were broken, her power of fascination would be gone. For that reason I think the character better adapted for the stage: it is more artificial, more theatrical, more meretricious. I would rather have seen Mrs. Abington's Millamant, than any Rosalind that ever appeared on the stage. Some how, this sort of acquired elegance is more a thing of costume, of air and manner; and in comedy, or on the comic stage, the light and familiar, the trifling, superficial, and agreeable, bears, perhaps, rightful sway over that which touches the affections, or exhausts the fancy.—There is a callousness in the worst characters in the *Way of the World*, in Fainall, and his wife and Mrs. Marwood, not very pleasant; and a grossness in the absurd ones, such as Lady Wishfort and Sir Wilful, which is not a little amusing. Witwoud wishes to disclaim, as far as he can, his relationship to this last character, and says, 'he's but his half brother;' to which Mirabell makes answer—'Then, perhaps, he's but half a fool.' Peg is an admirable caricature of rustic awkwardness and simplicity, which is carried to excess without any offence, from a sense of contrast to the refinement of the chief characters in the play. The description of Lady Wishfort's face is a perfect piece of painting. The force of style in this author at times amounts to poetry. Waitwell, who personates Sir Rowland, and Foible, his accomplice in the matrimo-nial scheme upon her mistress, hang as a dead weight upon the plot. They are mere tools in the hands of Mirabell, and want life and interest. Congreve's characters can all of them speak well, they are mere machines when they come to act. Our author's superiority deserted him almost entirely with his wit. His serious and tragic poetry is frigid and jejune to an unaccountable degree. His *forte* was the description of actual manners, whether elegant or absurd; and when he could not deride the one or embellish the other, his attempts at romantic passion or imaginary enthusiasm are forced, abortive, and ridiculous, or common-place. The description of the ruins of a temple in the beginning of the *Mourning Bride*, was a great stretch of his poetic genius. It has, however, been over-rated, particularly by Dr. Johnson, who could have done nearly as well himself for a single passage in the same style of moralising and sentimental description. To justify this general censure, and to shew how the lightest and most graceful wit degenerates into the heaviest and most bombastic poetry, I will give one description out of his tragedy, which will be enough. It is the speech which Gonsalez addresses to Almeria:

[Quotes I, iii, 1–26.]

This passage seems, in part, an imitation of Bolingbroke's entry into London.[1] The style is as different from Shakspeare, as it is from that of Witwoud and Petulant. It is plain that the imagination of the author could not raise itself above the burlesque. His Mask of *Semele, Judgment of Paris*, and other occasional poems, are even worse. I would not advise any one to read them, or if I did, they would not.

Wycherley was before Congreve; and his *Country Wife* will last longer than any thing of Congreve's as a popular acting play. It is only a pity that it is not entirely his own; but it is enough so to do him never-ceasing honour, for the best things are his own. His humour is, in general, broader, his characters more natural, and his incidents more striking than Congreve's. It may be said of Congreve, that the workmanship overlays the materials: in Wycherley, the casting of the parts and the fable are alone sufficient to ensure success. We forget Congreve's characters, and only remember what they say: we remember Wycherley's characters, and the incidents they meet with, just as if they were real, and forget what they say, comparatively speaking.

NOTE

1 *Richard II*, V, ii, 7–21.

84. Richard Cumberland in *The British Drama*

1817

From *The British Drama, a Collection of the Most Esteemed Dramatic Productions, with Biography of the Respective Authors; and a Critique on Each Play*, 14 vols (London: 1817). (Each play is separately paginated.)

A prolific dramatist, Richard Cumberland (1732–1811) turned to the stage after being blocked in his political career. Cumberland is commonly considered a late writer of sentimental comedy, although his plays are not exclusively of that kind. Sheridan ridiculed him as Sir Fretful Plagiary in *The Critic*, and Goldsmith censured his sentimentalism in 'Retaliation', ll. 61–78; nevertheless Cumberland enjoyed the friendship and regard of Samuel Johnson. The following critiques were prefixed to three of Congreve's plays included in a collection edited by Cumberland and published posthumously.

(a) From the CRITIQUE on the *WAY OF THE WORLD*

Dr. South was reproved for being too witty in his sermons; Congreve suffered for being too witty in his comedies; I don't recollect any instance of a modern author falling into disgrace upon that account. Our critics will now and then damn an author to keep up their prerogative; but it is not because he wants wit, or that they themselves abound in it, but because they don't like to be insulted by pretended novelties that are not new; in which case, it must be acknowledged, nonsense loses all its charms, and becomes intolerable.

The plot of this comedy is not calculated to excite much interest; for it has no other object in view but to effect a marriage between Mirabell and Millamant, with the consent of Lady Wishfort, who has it in her power to hold back the half of the lady's fortune of twelve thousand pounds, if she marries without her consent.

Mirabell is not so disinterested as to be contented with less than the whole; and Millamant is so intent upon coquetry, that she seems very little disposed towards matrimony. How is it possible to have any interest for people of this description? And what object can it be to the audience, whether Mirabell gets a flippant woman with six thousand pounds only, or with twelve? Had the author given absolute power to Lady Wishfort over her niece, and taken any pains to recommend the lovers to the feelings of his audience, his fable might have kept our curiosity awake; but when five full acts are wholly occupied in mean and despicable contrivances how to save six thousand pounds (playhouse money), we may find some excuse for the neglect which this comedy experienced. I call Mirabell's contrivances by the hard names of despicable and mean, because I cannot consider the project of making a footman counterfeit a gentleman, for the purpose of entrapping the passions of an amorous old foolish woman, in any other light. This silly intrigue is traversed by Fainall, who is married to Lady Wishfort's infamous daughter, and by Mrs. Marwood, who is a kind of hanger-on upon the aforesaid old lady, and a *chere-amie* of Mr. Fainall. In short, the gentleman is a scoundrel, and the lady is a prostitute; but still the contesting parties are so nearly balanced, that if the matter in dispute could inspire a wish, it would be poised so indifferently between them, that we could feel neither pleasure nor disappointment by the issue. There are other idle gentlemen in the play, but by no means in the plot, viz. Messrs. Witwould and Petulant, who are brought in to talk, and they talk very pleasantly, especially the former; for Petulant, though far from devoid of humour, is flagrantly indebted for it to Shakspeare's Nym. There is also a Sir Wilful, half-brother to Witwould, whose vulgar rusticity is very amusing. Two waiting-women of the true playhouse stamp fill up the corps; amongst which there is wickedness in all its varieties to lower the human character, without one spark of virtue to uphold it.

Now if plot, character, and dialogue ought to combine in the construction of a comedy, it is plain they do not all combine in this; and I must therefore doubt if its author was entirely warranted to resent its treatment so heavily as he is said to have done, unless it were decided, that its dialogue alone ought to have borne it up, in spite of its defects in other properties. I am far from saying that his first audiences were totally inexcusable in slighting this fine specimen of comic style; but I am very ready to say I would not be one in the condemnation of such writing for any consideration. I am humbly of opinion, that Congreve has in this, and his other comedies, left the best model of dramatic style that the English language can afford; and they who can transfuse the spirit of it into their writings for the stage, will write the best; but let them recollect, that although this author had the happiest and the richest vein of wit, yet he was too apt to want discrimination, delicacy, and right judgment in the application of it. He had not always that self-denying sobriety, that could resist the impulse of saying a good thing, however out of character or out of place. I must also venture to remark, that there is occasionally a want of harmony in his periods, which, if his ear had been more perfect, could not have been: but upon the whole, I do not retract from what I have said of his style as a model for dramatic writing.

In the first act of this play Mirabell keeps the stage throughout; and the whole time is filled up with descriptions of characters, and alternate sallies of wit and raillery: and in these Witwould, who is Mirabell's butt, by no means seems to play the losing game, but in fact the hone bears as sharp an edge as the razor, which I apprehend is not commonly the case. The second act makes us acquainted with two ladies, Fainall and Marwood by name; and they make some confessions, which are neither wittily told, nor decently conceived. The married lady openly avows a detestation for her husband; and the unmarried lady says, 'If I could but find one, that loved me very well, and would be thoroughly sensible of ill-usage, I think I should do myself the violence of undergoing the ceremony,' viz. of marriage. These ladies are perfectly well-sorted in point of principle; but I should doubt if they were selected for the purpose of edification. They are useful to the author, however, in a double sense, as helping on the wickedness of his scenes, and throwing the gauntlet to Jeremy Collier, the arch-enemy of the immoral Muse.

It does not appear necessary that I should pursue my remarks upon this comedy any further. The enthusiastic admirers of Congreve will think I have said too much; but if I have said no more than in truth and conscience I am bound to say, I care little who may think that I have said too much.

(III, pp. iv–vii)

321

(b) CRITIQUE on *LOVE FOR LOVE*

WE read in the Arabian Tales of a certain prince of Balsora, Qeyn Alasnam by name, who, in digging for concealed treasures, discovered a subterranean chamber in which were eight beautiful statues, composed each of a single diamond, and standing upon golden pedestals. The lustre of these statues was such as to illuminate the whole room, and no doubt to dazzle the astonished spectator. There was, however, a ninth pedestal, for which no statue was yet found; and that statue, when found, was pronounced to be worth more than a thousand of these sparkling images:—The story informs us, that this ninth treasure was a living woman, or in other words—*Nature herself.*

Under the moral of this fable, I beg leave to insinuate (for I will not quite assert) my opinion of this brilliant comedy: there is plenty of bright and sparkling characters, rich as wit and imagination can make them; but there is wanting one pure and perfect model of simple nature, and that one, wherever it is to be found, is, like Alasnam's lady, worth them all.

I shall not be minute in my examination of this comedy, but dispatch it with what speed I can; for I am persuaded my remarks would not please my readers, nor profit my publisher, if I were compelled to give them. In fact, I wish it had not fallen in my way; for to assault a composition of such exquisite wit is a degree of poetical sacrilege, and to applaud what sets all decency at defiance is against all reason and morality. The prompter, it is true, has made deep cuts with his pruning knife; but the canker is incurable. The poet indeed has provided a very splendid and voluptuous entertainment; but he has invited too many guests for his table, where they have not elbow-room enough for their ease, nor opportunities sufficient for all to take a share in the conversation, and respectively to display their talents. Old Foresight breaks out upon us with a striking and extraordinary effect, but there is not business enough in the plot to supply the numerous parties that have claims upon it; and from the want of incidents to feed his humour, he becomes little better than the butt of Sir Sampson Legend, and the despicable wittol of a shameless barefaced profligate.

When sudden and abrupt expedients, such as Valentine's madness, are resorted to in a comedy, some allowances must be made, in consideration of the short compass within which the poet must compress his fable; but where the motive is so clear and obvious, why Valentine should counterfeit madness, and so totally out of all probability that it could be real, we can hardly find an apology for the absurd credulity of Sir Sampson Legend; for we may say with Pope—

Tell me if Congreve's fools are fools indeed—

They certainly are not, for though some of them may not *do a wise thing*, none ever *says a foolish thing*. It is not the *convenientia cuique* that Congreve studies; to every scene in the play we might prefix *poeta loquitur*. He is also a determined leveller, and distributes his favours, with democratic indifference, to the lacquey as liberally as to the lord; though, in justice, I must own he seems conscious of having been rather too bountiful to *Jeremy*, and apologizes for his partiality by giving him a kind of mock matriculation at the university of Cambridge. He serves out wit, however, as the purser serves out grog, to every individual his measur'd dole, without any regard to his occasions, or his capacity of disposing of it. He sets out a feast, like Aesop's feast of tongues, to every man his mess, and lets none sit down to his table without a full proportion of salt to his meat.

In what company Mr. Congreve liv'd whilst he was a writer of comedy, I cannot pretend to say; we all know with whom he consorted in his idle days: but if the ladies of fashion in his time talked the language which their representatives talk in his comedies, they were intolerably gross; and if they did not, he is unpardonably libellous.

Let the reader of this play examine what the directors of the stage have thought themselves obliged to expunge before they offered it to the audience, and what excuse will they find for a poet, whose Helicon is far from pure after such pains have been taken to filter it? Should the modest and chaste maiden be present at the play even now as it is represented? Can there be contamination and defilement more audaciously exemplified and set to view than in the characters of Mrs. Foresight, Mrs. Frail, and the impudent Miss Prue, (that household of infamy,) who, though kept afloat and buoyant on the corks of their poet's wit (the only life-boat that could have saved them from the fate they merit), are still such monsters of impurity as the curtain of a British theatre ought never to discover.

(V, pp. xviii–xxi)

(c) CRITIQUE of the *MOURNING BRIDE*

IT is to be regretted, that a writer of Mr. Congreve's eminence should have so totally misapplied his talents, as he appears to have done in this defective specimen, which is so far from possessing any of the properties essential to tragedy, that we may venture to presume he never could have succeeded in that department of the drama.

In his dedication of this tragedy to the Princess Ann, he describes it as 'a poem, constituted on a moral, whose end it is to recommend and to encourage virtue:' and he does not scruple to mark 'the licentious practice of the modern theatre;' which for one who was himself so great an adept in that *practice*, is a censure that might have come home to his own conscience, but if it did, it was a confession that wrought no amendment. His strain of flattery, in this dedication to the Princess, is profoundly abject, without the merit of being elegant. He tells her, that his poem, with all its moral zeal for the encouragement of virtue, 'aspires to cast itself beneath her feet, declining approbation till she shall condescend to own it, and vouchsafe to shine upon it, as on a creature of her influence.' How far her Royal Highness 'vouchsafed to shine' upon this poem, does not appear; but I am afraid the author's self-denial in 'declining approbation till she condescended to own it,' has not been recompensed by any fame, accruing or acquired under her patronage and protection.

In the character of Almeria (the Princess of Granada, and the Mourning Bride) we naturally expect to discover those sentiments which should mark the moral cast of this poem, so avowedly devoted to the cause of virtue; but in this expectation I confess myself disappointed, when I hear this lady, in the opening scene, with her attendant Leonora, thus venturing to expostulate with Providence:

> Why are all these things thus? Is it of force?
> Is there necessity I must be miserable?
> Is it of moment to the peace of Heav'n,

That I should be afflicted thus? If not,
Why is it thus contriv'd? Why are things laid
By some unseen hand, so, as of sure consequence,
They must to me bring curses, grief of heart,
The last distress of life, and sure despair?

[I, i, 53–60]

Sentiments like these are so very far from recommending virtue,
that I must doubt if the extreme folly of them can in any degree
apologize for their impiety. All the extenuation however that folly
can furnish, Almeria may with justice plead; for in that respect the
poet has been liberal to her without stint. Every speech in the scene
will testify to that; but the following, amongst numbers, would
nearly serve to save her life, if she had committed murder:

—Oh, no, thou know'st not half,
Know'st nothing of my sorrow—if thou didst—
If I should tell thee, wouldst thou pity me?
Tell me—I know thou wouldst; thou art compassionate.

[ibid., 83–6]

She wants to be told what she already knows; and the reason she
has for knowing that her attendant would pity her, is, because she
is naturally compassionate. Nothing can be more true than this; for
Leonora, who acquits herself of the arduous part of being
toad-eater to a driveller, is compassion personified, and instantly
cries out—

Witness these tears!—

She has them as Ulysses had the winds, and out they fly, for no
other purpose but to convince her mistress that she did not call her
compassionate without good cause; which is very considerate and
highly meritorious on the part of Leonora, who, though she did
not know a syllable of Almeria's sorrow, must have been most
perfectly convinced of her fatuity; and that indeed is pitiable
enough in all conscience.

Upon the sight of Leonora's tears, Almeria cannot do less than be
grateful, and accordingly replies—

I thank thee, Leonora.—

And to make it sure, she confirms it with an assertion, that puts it
out of doubt, not only as to fact, but also as to motive—

> Indeed I do, for pitying thy sad mistress:
> For 'tis, alas! the poor prerogative
> Of greatness, to be wretched and unpitied.
>
> [ibid., 88–90]

This is one of Almeria's discoveries, who, amongst the many 'poor prerogatives of greatness,' finds out that she ought to be wretched, with nobody to pity her; but seems to consider it as a privilege 'more honoured in the breach than in the observance.'

She then proceeds to recollect a promise she had never made—

> But I did promise I would tell thee—what?
> My miseries.—
>
> [ibid., 91–2]

And at the same time forgets what she had distinctly said—

> —Thou dost already know them;
> And when I told thee thou didst nothing know,
> It was because thou didst not know Alphonso.
>
> [ibid., 92–4]

To instance the absurdities of this scene would be to quote every line; and to expose the absurdities of the play, would be to instance every scene.

The lovers in this tragedy are the most unlucky personages that ever met together to perplex a plot. The king is in love with his captive Zara, who is in love with her slave Osmyn, who is in love with his wife Almeria, who is in love with him, and by no means disposed to obey her father by marrying Garcia, who is in love with her. In short, it is a complete game at cross purposes; and nothing short of a miracle could have brought it to a happy conclusion.

Zara is a lady of a remarkably high spirit, and of course has a right to her sublimities, though there may be neither modesty, morality, nor common sense in them. She is most outrageously in love; and being a great princess, and as savage as a tigress, she is entitled to at least as many prerogatives of greatness as Almeria found out, and has full authority to be 'wretched and unpitied.' She has had a few adventures also, which make no impression on her conscience, nor any abatement in her consequence; for, as she very properly observes to Osmyn—

> ——Is this then the return
> For fame, for honour, and for empire lost?

326

But what is loss of honour, fame, and empire?
Is this the recompence reserv'd for love?
Why dost thou leave my eyes, and fly my arms.
[II, ix, 4–8]

Surely this is a proper way of thinking for a great lady, who is above trifles; and this great lady is a very proper heroine of a play written professedly for the encouragement of virtue. There may be some small excuse for Osmyn's 'leaving her eyes,' forasmuch as she had thrown him into a dark prison; but for his 'flying her arms' there can be no apology, seeing they are so ready to receive him, and she so well reconciled to the loss of fame and honour.

She has a few claims upon him for past favours, amongst which saving his life was one; but for fear he should mistake her motive, and give her credit for one more virtue than she was entitled to, she candidly disavows compassion:

Compassion! scarce will 't own that name, so soon,
So quickly was it love: for thou wert godlike
Ev'n then.—
[ibid., 45–7]

Though the poor man was half-drowned, and full of salt-water, he was even then too *godlike* for her compassion, and she was overjoyed, for reasons of her own, when this *godlike* creature came to life again.

Oh, Heav'n! how did my heart rejoice and ake,
When I beheld the day-break of thine eyes,
And felt the balm of thy respiring lips.
[ibid., 51–3]

I should doubt if any lady, since the time of Potiphar's wife, was ever more explicit to the object of her desires. She always goes straight forward to her point; and though she is unwilling to be misunderstood in any case, she has not quite so much objection to the charge of madness, as to that of mercy:

——Wilt thou believe
So kindly of my fault to call it madness?
Oh, give that madness yet a milder name,
And call it passion—then be still more kind,
And call that passion love.—
[III, iv, 35–9]

327

As I humbly apprehend that Almeria is almost a perfect natural, I hope this lady is altogether out of nature: the fair sex will be no losers by her dismission. Though she murders the eunuch Selim with all possible dignity, yet there is a little want of female grace and delicacy in the manner of it:

Enter SELIM.

Sel. I've sought in vain, for no where can the king
Be found.—

[V, x, 1–2]

The poor man, because he can't find his master, concludes he is not to be found at all. The Princess Zara immediately strikes upon a ready method for convincing him of his mistake—

Get thee to hell, and seek him there!
Stabs him.

The eunuch makes a very good end, and I think I cannot do better than follow his example, and conclude.

(XII, pp. v–x)

85. George Gordon, Lord Byron in his letters to John Murray

1820–1

From *Letters and Journals*, ed. Leslie A. Marchand, 12 vols (London: John Murray, 1973–82).

The following passages in letters to his publisher are the most substantial of several references to Congreve in Byron's correspondence.

(a)

Ravenna. March 29th. 1820.

And in the next I differ from you about the 'refinement' which has banished the comedies of Congreve—are not the Comedies of

Sheridan acted to the thinnest houses?—I *know* (*as ex-Committed*) that the 'School for Scandal' was the *worst Stock piece* upon record.—I also know that Congreve gave up writing because Mrs. Centilevre's balderdash drove his comedies off—so it is not *decency* but Stupidity that does all this—for Sheridan is as *decent* a writer as need be—and Congreve no worse than Mrs. Centilevre—of whom Wilkes (the Actor) said—'not only her play would be damned but she too'—he alluded to a 'Bold Stroke for a Wife'.

(VII, p. 61)

(b)

Ravenna.—J[anuar]y 4th. 1821

Nothing so easy as intricate confusion of plot—and rant.—Mrs. Centilevre in comedy has *ten times the bustle* of Congreve—but are they to [be] Compared? & yet she drove Congreve from the theatre.—

(VIII, p. 57)

86. Charles Lamb in *The London Magazine*

1822

From *The London Magazine* (1822), 5: 305–7.

The following extract comes from the second of three essays on 'The Old Actors' contributed to *The London Magazine* under Lamb's usual pen name of 'Elia'. The essay appeared in the April number. When reprinted in the collection of 1823 it was given the title 'On the Artificial Comedy of the Last Century' to distinguish it from its predecessor.

THE OLD ACTORS.

The artificial Comedy, or Comedy of manners, is quite extinct on our stage. Congreve and Farquhar show their heads once in seven years only to be exploded and put down instantly. The times cannot bear them. Is it for a few wild speeches, an occasional licence of dialogue? I think not altogether. The business of their dramatic characters will not stand the moral test. We screw every thing up to that. Idle gallantry in a fiction, a dream, the passing pageant of an evening, startles us in the same way as the alarming indications of profligacy in a son or ward in real life should startle a parent or guardian. We have no such middle emotions as dramatic interests left. We see a stage libertine playing his loose pranks of two hours' duration, and of no after consequence, with the severe eyes which inspect real vices with their bearings upon two worlds. We are spectators to a plot or intrigue (not reducible in life to the point of strict morality) and take it all for truth. We substitute a real for a dramatic person, and judge him accordingly. We try him in our courts, from which there is no appeal to the *dramatis personæ*, his peers. We have been spoiled with—not sentimental comedy—but a tyrant far more pernicious to our pleasures which has succeeded to it,—the exclusive and all-devouring drama of common life; where the moral point is every thing; where, instead of the fictitious half-believed personages of the stage (the phantoms of old comedy) we recognise ourselves, our brothers, aunts, kinsfolk, allies, patrons, enemies,—the same as in life,—with an interest in what is going on so hearty and substantial, that we cannot afford our moral judgment, in its deepest and most vital results, to compromise or slumber for a moment. What is *there* transacting, by no modification is made to affect us in any other manner than the same events or characters would do in our relationships of life. We carry our fire-side concerns to the theatre with us. We do not go thither, like our ancestors, to escape from the pressure of reality, so much as to confirm our experience of it; to make assurance double, and take a bond of fate. We must live our toilsome lives twice over, as it was the mournful privilege of Ulysses to descend twice to the shades. All that neutral ground of character which stood between vice and virtue; or which, in fact, was indifferent to neither, where neither properly was called in question—that happy breathing-place from the burden of a perpetual moral questioning—the sanctuary and quiet Alsatia of hunted casuistry—is broken up and disfranchised as injurious to the interests of society. The privileges of the place are taken away by law. We dare not dally with images or names of wrong. We bark like foolish dogs at shadows. We dread infection from the scenic representation of disorder; and fear a painted pustule. In our anxiety that our morality should not take cold, we wrap it up in a great blanket surtout of precaution against the breeze and sunshine.

I confess for myself that (with no great delinquencies to answer for) I am glad for a season to take an airing beyond the diocese of the strict conscience,—not to live always in the precincts of the law courts,—but now and then, for a dream-while or so, to imagine a world with no meddling restrictions—to get into recesses, whither the hunter cannot follow me—

> —— Secret shades
> Of woody Ida's inmost grove,
> While yet there was no fear of Jove—

I come back to my cage and my restraint the fresher and more healthy for it. I wear my shackles more contentedly for having respired the breath of an imaginary freedom. I do not know how it is with others, but I feel the better always for the perusal of one of Congreve's—nay, why should I not add even of Wycherley's—comedies. I am the gayer at least for it; and I could never connect those sports of a witty fancy in any shape with any result to be drawn from them to imitation in real life. They are a world of themselves almost as much as fairy-land. Take one of their characters, male or female (with few exceptions they are alike), and place it in a modern play, and my virtuous indignation shall rise against the profligate wretch as warmly as the Catos of the pit could desire; because in a modern play I am to judge of right and wrong, and the standard of *police* is the measure of *poetical justice*. The atmosphere will blight it. It cannot thrive here. It is got into a moral world where it has no business; from which it must needs fall head-long; as dizzy and incapable of keeping its stand, as a Swedenborgian bad spirit that has wandered unawares within the sphere of one of his good men or angels.[1] But in its own world do we feel that the creature is so very bad?

The Fainalls and the Mirabels, the Dorimants, and Lady Touchwoods, in their own sphere do not offend my moral sense—or, in fact, appeal to it at all. They seem engaged in their proper element. They break through no laws, or conscientious restraints. They know of none. They have got out of Christendom into the land—what shall I call it?—of cuckoldry—the Utopia of gallantry, where pleasure is duty, and the manners perfect freedom.

It is altogether a speculative scene of things, which has no reference whatever to the world that is. No good person can be justly offended as a spectator, because no good person suffers on the stage. Judged morally, every character in these plays—the few exceptions only are *mistakes*—is alike essentially vain and worthless. The great art of Congreve is especially shown in this, that he has entirely excluded from his scenes,—some little generosities in the part of Angelica perhaps excepted,—not only any thing like a faultless character, but any pretensions to goodness or good feelings whatsoever. Whether he did this designedly, or instinctively, the effect is as happy, as the design (if design) was bold. I used to wonder at the strange power which his *Way of the World* in particular possesses of interesting you all along in the pursuits of characters, for whom you absolutely care nothing—for you neither hate nor love his personages—and I think it is owing to this very indifference for any, that you endure the whole. He has spread a privation of moral light, I will call it, rather than by the ugly name of palpable darkness, over his creations; and his shadows flit before you without distinction or preference. Had he introduced a good character, a single gush of moral feeling, a revulsion of the judgment to actual life and actual duties, the impertinent Goshen would have only lighted to the discovery of deformities, which now are none, because we think them none.

Translated into real life, the characters of his, and his friend Wycherley's dramas, are profligates and strumpets,—the business of their brief existence, the undivided pursuit of lawless gallantry. No other spring of action, or possible motive of conduct, is recognised; principles which universally acted upon must reduce this frame of things to a chaos. But we do them wrong in so translating them. No such effects are produced in *their* world. When we are among them, we are amongst a chaotic people. We are not to judge them by our usages. No reverend institutions are insulted by their proceedings,—for they have none among them. No peace of families is violated,—for no family ties exist among them. No purity of the marriage bed is stained,—for none is supposed to have a being. No deep affections are disquieted,—no holy wedlock bands are snapped asunder,—for affection's depth and wedded faith are not of the growth of that soil. There is neither right nor wrong,—gratitude or its opposite,—claim or duty,—paternity or sonship. Of what consequence is it to virtue, or how is she at all concerned about it, whether Sir Simon, or Dapperwit, steal away Miss Martha; or who is the father of Lord Froth's, or Sir Paul Pliant's children?

The whole is a passing pageant, where we should sit as unconcerned at the issues, for life or death, as at a battle of the frogs and mice. But, like Don Quixote, we take part against the puppets, and quite as impertinently. We dare not contemplate an Atlantis, a scheme, out of which our coxcombical moral sense is for a little transitory ease excluded. We have not the courage to imagine a state of things for which there is neither reward nor punishment. We cling to the painful necessities of shame and blame. We would indict our very dreams.

NOTE

1 Alluding to the spirit world described by the Swedish philosopher and mystic, Emanuel Swedenborg (1688–1722).

87. James Boaden on Congreve
1827–31

From (a) *Memoirs of Mrs. Siddons*, 2 vols (London: 1827); (b) *The Life of Mrs. Jordan*, 2 vols (London: 1831).

James Boaden (1762–1839) was a literary journalist and minor dramatist. He became editor of *The Oracle, or Bell's New World*, in 1789. In addition to his lives of Sarah Siddons and Dorothea Jordan, Boaden also wrote biographies of John Philip Kemble and Elizabeth Inchbald, and edited Garrick's correspondence.

(a) From *Memoirs of Mrs. Siddons*
I take the liberty to censure in this place a very mischievous tone of criticism, which began now to be prevalent in the daily press. Certain flimsy but authoritative writers, with a view, perhaps, at

best to recommend themselves to the leading performers of both houses, affected a sovereign contempt for the writings of men honoured by the ablest judgments; and the public were told that such stuff as the plays cited was only rendered bearable by the powers of the *reigning favourites*. The incense of such jargon fumed daily before Mrs. Siddons, as well as others—but I believe her own impressions of the poet's merit were little disturbed by these flights of impudence. She knew that, from Mrs. Elizabeth Barry to herself, their characters had always been great in the hands of adequate performers; and that, if they ever did fail in their effect, the cause of that failure was not in the author. One play in particular had been loaded with this despicable sort of commentary—I mean the *Mourning Bride* of Congreve—his *pantomime*, as it was styled in the cant of the times. This play, notwithstanding, Mrs. Siddons selected for her second benefit.

As the application of the term *pantomime* to this tragedy is intended for disparagement, it may be as well to look a little at its meaning, in order to judge how far it applies to the play in question. The pantomime is a dramatic entertainment, where *everything* is shewn in *action*. As a censure, therefore, it implies that the play, however aided by speech, retains too much of this character; that it is a *shew*, and little but a shew. If the critics mean, that this tragedy is more complex in its action than perhaps the French stage admits, this as an objection applies equally to the whole series of English authors, and to Shakspeare very particularly indeed. So picturesque and various are the situations of that great poet, so intelligent his dumb shew, abstracted from all speech, that he might be almost styled the PAINTER'S POET, and the *deaf* can never fail to comprehend the full scope of his exhibitions. It remains, therefore, to examine how Congreve stands with respect to the other nerves of the drama,—description, sentiment, and passion. As to verbal description, in the opinion of Dr. Johnson, he has the most expressive passage in English literature. It is given to his *Almeria*, the character from its gentleness best suited to the placid eloquence of description. It is the impression made by a gothic cathedral on the sensitive mind. *Decies repetita placebit:*—

[Quotes II, iii, 7–17.]

But Congreve, as a poet, has a seat the proudest that a poet can occupy; nor should we be indifferent to a sentiment, because from the hour it was first heard, it has flowed from the lips of every woman at all tinctured with letters. I allude to his eulogy on music:—

> Music has charms, &c.

His fancy and his sentiment, as Shakspeare says, 'mingle' frequently, their spurs together:

> The circling HOURS that gather all the woes,
> Which are diffus'd thro' the revolving year,
> Come heavy laden with th' oppressing weight
> To me; with me successively they leave
> The sighs, the tears, the groans, the restless cares,
> And all the damps of grief, that did retard their flight;
> They shake their downy wings, and scatter all
> The dire collected dews on my poor head;
> Then fly with joy and swiftness from me.
>
> [I, i, 145–53]

The fond astonishment of Osmyn bursts into language beyond measure beautiful:—

> Rivet and nail me where I stand, ye Powers,
> That motionless I may be still deceiv'd.
> Let me not *stir*, nor *breathe*, lest I dissolve
> That tender lovely form of *painted air*,
> So like Almeria.
>
> [II, vi, 10–14]

'But the reader in these passages is reminded of Shakspeare!' Need Congreve shrink from the competition?

For the glow of feminine transport was anything ever written with more sweetness, delicacy, and pathos, than the following?—

> O, how hast thou return'd? How hast thou charm'd
> The wildness of the waves and rocks to this?
> That thus relenting, they have giv'n thee back
> To earth, to light and life, to love and me!
>
> [II, vii, 26–9]

But Congreve added regularity of fable to all his other merits, and a truly excellent critic long since observed, that the usual censure upon our drama did not apply to him. 'From the foregoing censure must be excepted the *Mourning Bride* of Congreve, where

335

regularity concurs with the beauty of *sentiment* and *language* to make it one of the most complete pieces England has to boast of.'—*Ld. Kames E. of C.* vol. 3. p. 324, Edin. 1763.

I, therefore, call for an attentive reconsideration of this neglected tragedy. I do not mean as to the stage, for now we could not act it—but in the *closet*; to which I find his comedies have been condemned by the flippant school, on the pretence of their indecency. If the free passages in this author were expunged, would all comedy from his day to ours, equal the WIT *remaining*, even in *quantity*? But he was a first-rate genius in every thing, and perhaps few of my readers know that he has bestowed the utmost beauty upon a trifle such as the *candle*, burning before a lover contemplating the perfections of his mistress. The terms chosen will be found to apply equally to the *principal* and the *representative* subject. This is the character of HIS wit, and all true wit. But in a purely dramatic treatise, its place must be a note.*

Lest the reader should suspect my impartiality, I will point out one instance, where the imperfect expression of the author's idea renders even the solemnity of prayer itself ludicrous. It is in the first scene of his third act, where Osmyn reads a paper in the hand-writing of his father; which that graceless spouter Dick, the Apprentice, converts into a note of hand. The venerable man *would* pray that the *number* of mercies bestowed by heaven upon his son may *double* that of the hairs which sorrow rends from his own aged head. As the poet has left it, he invokes for him only a two-fold quantity of *hair*—e.g.:—

> Let every HAIR, which sorrow by the roots
> Tears from my hoary and devoted head,
> Be *doubled* in thy mercies to my son.
>
> [III, i, 14–16]

Another objection I make to a part of his catastrophe—It was necessary to Congreve that his king should be found *headless*; as Cloten decapitated is, in Shakspeare, mistaken for Posthumus:—but Congreve's king is *haggled* in a disgusting manner by the officious cunning of a creature of his favourite. In *Cymbeline* Guiderius, who had been assailed by Cloten drest like Posthumus, is told by him that he is the queen's son; but this circumstance, so far from alarming the young hero, he treats thus contemptuously:—

I have sent Cloten's clot-pole down the stream
In embassy to his mother; his body's hostage
For his return.

[*Cymbeline*, IV, ii, 185–7]

One is the result of a fair combat in times comparatively *barbarous*—In all other parts of Congreve's business the manners are refined. To *disgust* in tragedy is almost fatal. The very stratagem of a king's *hiding* himself, to surprise and reproach his mistress, is below the dignity of tragedy, though countenanced by Addison, as far as disguising Sempronius in the Numidian garb of Juba.

But even Congreve may detain us too long when Mrs. Siddons is waiting. I hasten to examine what his Zara and her representative reciprocally did for each other. The character is admirably described by its author, in the person of Osmyn. She has a soul of an intrepid and commanding cast, that challenges esteem even where she cannot be loved. Her personal are equal to her mental charms—but her passions are more furious than the winds, and uproot and scatter her virtues, as the hurricane plows the ocean and rears its waters into mountains of destruction. I can safely say that such a being Mrs. Siddons was on the first night of her Zara—but these are the mere outlines of the delineation; they were filled up as firmly as they were drawn.

On her entrance as a captive, the glance upon her chains, and the remark on captivity, expressed the quality of her mind admirably:—

But when I feel
These bonds, I look with *loathing* on myself.
[I, vi, 15–16]

Still more impressive, because steadier, was the ensuing acknowledgment.

Such thanks as one *hating to be oblig'd*—
Yet hating *more* INGRATITUDE, can pay,
I offer.
[ibid., ll. 30–3]

Her eagerness to cover the indiscretion of Osmyn, and explain favourably a rather ambiguous exclamation of his—Her throwing in the word Heli, in answer to the king, were skilful in the extreme—

337

The ninth scene, after Almeria has quitted Osmyn—her manner of coming in upon his meditation—

> See where he stands, folded and fix'd to earth,
> Stiff'ning in thought; a statue among statues.
>
> [II, ix, 1–2]

The tender expostulation, warming into reproach, and flaming into menace, with all the winning and alarming gradations of language, till the distinct proposal of herself to him is ultimately tried, and on his rejection of freedom and her love, she exclaims—

> Thou can'st not *mean* so poorly as thou talk'st–
>
> [ibid., l. 96]

were as truly displayed by the actress as they are suggested by the author. Nor was she less delightful when her self-love made her *detect* the passion of Osmyn, but mistake its *object,* till she settles in the conviction that HER charms have 'pierc'd his very soul,' but that his dastard nature recoils from the danger of becoming a rival to the king.

The following act shows a remission of her anger, and however he shall decide as to her love, she considers herself bound to restore to him that liberty of which her charge to the king had deprived him. How beautifully she extenuates her fault!—

> Can'st thou forgive me, then? wilt thou believe
> So *kindly* of my fault to call it MADNESS?
> O give that madness yet a milder name,
> And call it passion; then be still *more* kind,
> And call that passion, LOVE.
>
> [III, iv, 35–9]

But the *film,* that self-love has drawn over her eyes, is forcibly dispelled in the third act, when about to visit Osmyn, she is requested to suspend her entrance, until the Princess Almeria shall have retired. At first she dissembles with him, and then insults him coolly; but upon his exclaiming—

You do not come to mock my miseries?

She says fiercely—

I do:
> [III, viii, 14–15]

and loads him with the most opprobrious language. To her threat of procuring his death, Osmyn calmly replies, 'I thank you.' The points now come home in their altercation, and are admirably contrasted.

> —Thou LY'ST; for now I know for whom thou'dst *live*.
> Osm.—Then you may know for whom I'd die.
>
> [ibid., ll. 25–6]

Zara is now in the highest state of exasperation, and the actress looked the truism with which she concludes the act.

> Heav'n has no rage like love to hatred turn'd,
> Nor Hell a fury like a woman scorn'd.
>
> [ibid., ll. 42–3]

If the sorrows of Almeria had then moved in the majestic form and silver tones of Mrs. Yates, the perfect contrast of two women so accomplished, with even the Osmyn of Smith, would have carried imperial tragedy higher than it probably ever went in any age or nation.

The author has, however, avoided any scene of personal struggle between his heroines, though I think he would have left Rowe a model that might have saved him from the disgraceful ravings of Alicia. The plot now proceeds with great haste, and the ultimate feelings of Zara are consoling. She swallows the poison deliberately, which she supposes will unite her to Osmyn, and the actress was excellently 'studied in her death'—perhaps no performer ever threw so much variety into the close of dramatic existence.

Having now, I trust, shewn this *pantomime*, to be replete with description, sentiment, and passion, I turn to another class of objectors, who, admitting all these, contend we have too much of them, and find ourselves in consequence more pained than pleased. But the abundance of Congreve must not be supposed to diminish the lustre of his figures or sentiments; they are admirable, however numerous.

> Men doubt, because they stand so thick i' the sky,
> If those be STARS, which paint the galaxy.

But in all such cases, it is WE who should endeavour to rise to the affluence of the poet, rather than wish him brought down to the penury of our ideas. The crowded thoughts and splendid diction of Shakspeare must not, for vulgar apprehension, be lowered into the homely chat of Heywood.

(I, pp. 371–82)

(b) From *The Life of Mrs. Jordan*

Mrs. Jordan was more fortunate than her great rival—the getting up of *Love for Love* afforded her, in Miss Prue, a character exactly suitable to her style of acting, and which kept its hold upon the public mind. The first scene, where she enters with Tattle to Mrs. Foresight and her sister, was inimitably natural. The *scents*, of which the beau had been so liberal; the half check upon the *too plain* words which she blurted out with gay simplicity; and afterwards the apt scholar and the catechism of love, and the confirmation of its doctrines, were rich comedy indeed, for she had genius enough to keep it from offending. The courtship with Ben, with the sweet savours of Tattle all the time in her nostrils, afforded a striking contrast—the sullen aversion of her look—the 'I a'n't *deaf*,' with her skilful utterance of the word—the consolatory 'I'm too big to be whipped,'—her abuse of the 'sea calf'—and the 'tar barrel,'—and the passion of tears,—were all *truth* itself. Miss Prue has only one more scene, the first of the fifth act, where she exclaims, with indignation—'What! must I go to bed to nurse again, and be a *child* as long as she's an *old woman*?—Indeed, but I *won't*.' The last word, as she contrived to utter it, and the 'fiddle of a rod! I'll have a husband,' with the hint as to 'Robin the butler,' naturally enough produce the locking up of the young lady; whom the author unfortunately has *left* under lock and key, and neither involved in the catastrophe nor called in at the conclusion of the play.

Notwithstanding the eternal wit of Congreve's comedies, which is not approached even by Sheridan, it is not true that they have no *real* character. The present play abounds in characters admirably discriminated and preserved. Foresight and Sir Sampson Legend are perfectly in nature; so is Ben, though the lingo of the forecastle may vary from time to time; but he has the true *mind* of a sailor, and 'another trip' is his only remedy for disappointment. A sailor too always uses the terms of his *profession*, to which he is more heartily attached than any other man; and among his oddities, is more metaphorical in his brief vocabulary, than all the rhetoricians or even poets of the community.

Love for Love was first acted on the night of opening of the new theatre in Lincoln's Inn Fields. Hamlet considered himself entitled to a *whole share* among the players, for a few lines inserted into the play before his uncle. Congreve received that compliment on writing *Love for Love*; a whole share in the concern, for a single play per year. It is fatal to withdraw from an author the stimulus of *necessity*; the author of four such comedies as Congreve's, could easily persuade himself that he had done enough for fame. Plunging a wit into the *pipe-office*, or making him a licenser of either *coaches* or *wine*, is like marrying an actress, and taking her from the stage; the parties are no better than others in the new situations; to extend their attraction, and therefore happiness, they should be left to exert their genius in its proper sphere. To reward utility, without abridging it, is a problem of difficult solution. *We* may be apt to think such a poet disgraced by his preferments. Congreve, however, did not wish to be considered as an author, yet it is only as an author that he enjoys a name among the illustrious of his country.

Dr. Johnson has said of Congreve, 'that he was an original writer, who borrowed neither the models of his plot, nor the manner of his dialogue.' A mind so perspicacious as the doctor's, had he been acquainted with the writings of Ben Jonson, could not have failed to discern innumerable points of similitude between them; as to the *personages* of the drama, and the *manner* of the dialogue. The great Lord Camden was fond of displaying them.

(I, pp. 103–7)

NOTE

★
TO A CANDLE.
ELEGY.

THOU watchful TAPER, by whose silent light
I lonely pass the melancholy night;
Thou faithful witness of my secret pain,
To whom alone I venture to complain;
O learn with me my hopeless love to moan;
Commiserate a life so like thy own.
Like thine, my flames to my destruction turn,
Wasting that heart, by which supply'd they burn.
Like thine, my joy and suffering they display,

> At once, are signs of life, and symptoms of decay.
> And as thy fearful flames the day decline,
> And only during night presume to shine;
> Their humble rays not daring to aspire
> Before the sun, the fountain of their fire:
> So mine, with conscious shame, and equal awe,
> To shades obscure and solitude withdraw;
> Nor dare their light before her eyes disclose,
> From whose bright beams their being first arose.

Here we have none of the *perverse* ingenuity of the metaphysical poets. The points of *contact* seem obvious, and not to be missed; but such a parallel, so continued and so exact, was never made out before.

88. Hartley Coleridge in *Biographia Borealis*, with the annotations of Samuel Taylor Coleridge

1833

From *Biographia Borealis; or Lives of Distinguished Northerns* (London and Leeds: 1833); Samuel Taylor Coleridge's annotations from *Lives of the Northern Worthies*, new edition, ed. Derwent Coleridge, 3 vols (London: 1852).

Hartley Coleridge (1796–1849) was the eldest son of Samuel Taylor Coleridge. After failing first as an Oxford don and then as a schoolmaster, he undertook to write a series of lives of *The Worthies of Yorkshire and Lancashire* for the Leeds publisher F. E. Bingley. It was published in parts, beginning in October 1832, and reached the third number in the spring of 1833 before Bingley went bankrupt. The thirteen biographies which had appeared were republished as *Biographia Borealis*, a title dropped in subsequent editions. Samuel Taylor Coleridge's annotations were first published in a third edition prepared by Derwent Coleridge, Hartley's younger brother.

(i)

Although we cannot reckon the profusion of sinecures which rewarded the production of the *Old Bachelor* as one of the happiest signs of the times of Halifax, it was utterly unjust in Swift, Pope, and the other Tory wits, to represent that minister as regardless of the claims of genius, and only liberal to party virulence. Yet the Dean, in one of his minor poems, literally holds up Congreve as having been long neglected, and half-starved.—

> Thus Congreve spent, in writing plays,
> And one poor office, half his days;
> While Montague, who claimed the station
> To be Mæcenas of the nation,
> For poets open table kept,
> But ne'er considered where they slept;
> Himself, as rich as fifty Jews,
> Was easy, tho' they wanted shoes;
> And *crazy* Congreve scarce could spare
> A shilling to discharge his chair,
> Till prudence taught him to appeal
> From Pæan's fire to party zeal:
> Not owing to his happy vein
> The fortunes of his latter scene;
> Took proper principles to thrive,
> And so might any dunce alive.
> ['A Libel on Doctor Delany', ll. 33–48]

In this last line the Dean is deplorably in the wrong. Dunces never thrive but in the way of honesty. Had not Congreve been a splendid wit, he would not have been worth purchase. We cannot conjecture why he calls Congreve crazy. There is no madness in his writings,—neither the *fine madness* of poetry, nor the rant and fury of a disordered brain: and in his private conduct, whatever virtue he might want, he possessed an ample store of prudence. With so little of truth or reason could the man write, who, of all his contemporaries, *might* have been the greatest philosopher.*

Congreve's next play was the *Double Dealer*, produced in 1694. It seldom happens that a second work is received with an increase of applause. There is, independent of envy, a very strong tendency to

---

* That is if with equal genius he had *not* been Dean Swift, but almost the very contrary.—*S.T.C.*

suspect writers of falling below themselves. Homer himself has been accused of betraying senility in the *Odyssee*; and the more subdued interest necessarily arising from the plan and subject of *Paradise Regained*, has been ascribed, with little justice, to the increasing years of Milton. The *Double Dealer*, though the performance was honoured with the presence of Queen Mary, met with some opposition on the stage, and a good deal of severe criticism in the closet. Congreve had little difficulty in parrying the individual objections: of such criticism as was then current he was a dexterous master, and as he wrote with great care and forethought according to his own ideal of perfection, he probably anticipated every censure in his mind before it was uttered. But those who read his works in these days will be rather surprised to find him assuming the part of a censor and a moralist, and telling the *ladies* that he aims at their reformation and improvement.

[Quotes No. 9 above.]*

This is the common plea of satirists, but it is at best an afterthought. We are far from deeming the satirists among the most malicious of mankind: they are, at worst, splenetic, but for the most part rather vain than ill-natured. But it is much easier to shine in depicting a moral than an immoral character; and of all

* Genuine Comedy is, I fear, almost incompatible with Christianity, as it exists among the many, who neither can, nor will *abstract*. Now Comedy *is* an abstraction.—*S.T.C.*

This is, in effect, the defence set up with admirable skill, by Charles Lamb, in his apology for the Comic Dramatists of the Restoration, but it is not available *for them* as a moral justification. Comedy, it is true, enters not as such into the domain of the reason or conscience,—it deals with the senses, and with the sensuous understanding. It is an abstraction. So, in its own way, is Tragedy—so is all poetry, and all fine art. Its essence consists in a *restricted* imitation, observing a certain 'inward law,' as distinguished from a literal copy. The moral fault of Congreve's dramas is not that they imitate, it may be feared too faithfully, the manners and feelings of the readers or auditors for whom he wrote—that they show to that unhappy 'age and time his form and pressure,'—nor yet that the imitation is 'artificial,'—that for the purpose of comic effect, the spiritual part of man is left out of the representation; but that the *intention*, which in Shakspeare, and Molière, and even in Aristophanes, with all his grossness, is always good, and often serious, in Congreve and his compeers is almost always bad. There is no abstraction in the sense required. He represents positive relaxation of moral ties, not a mere absence, or conventional negation, and he does so approvingly.

Comedy, the pure abstraction exhibited by Aristophanes, has seldom if ever been produced in Christian times; but in the mixed and life-like drama to which we are accustomed, the comic element may very well carry with it its explanation and corrective even for the many.—*D.C.*

characters, the truly virtuous female is the most difficult to draw satisfactorily in a dramatic poem. It is easy enough to describe, for it is not unfrequently seen; it is very easy for a poet to praise, for he has little to do but to collect all the fine and savoury comparisons which Europe, Asia, Africa, and America, botany, mineralogy, zoology, and metaphysics supply, and attach them to a sylph-like figure, with black or auburn locks, as the case may require. But when the woman is to speak and act, when she is to shed the perfume of her goodness spontaneously, and shine by her own light, and yet not overstep the reserved duties of her sex—there is a task beneath which human genius is in danger of breaking down. We really cannot recal to memory a single dramatic female whom we should recommend for a wife, or for an example. Shakspeare's women are many of them exceedingly lovely, but from the small discretion he seems to have used in the choice of his stories, what they *do* is not always in unison with what they *are*. Their words and feelings are their nature; their actions are their destiny. The common run of tragedy queens are very unamiable; so much so, indeed, that it is pleasant to reflect that they have no resemblance to nature or reality. Comic females are much more entertaining; but with the exception of one or two specimens of prudent perfection, generally introduced, like Lady Grace, for the sake of contrast, and a few pieces of sentimental simplicity, such as Cicely Homespun, they are almost universally distinguished by a readiness of falsehood, a spirit of intrigue, and stratagem, which must make them very dangerous inmates or companions. Yet it would be next to impossible to write a comedy from which this sort of underplay was exiled. The choice seems to be, whether the interest shall turn mainly upon the bad characters, and the better sort of persons throughout be dupes and victims, consigned to happiness at last by some wonderful accident or discovery (the plan generally pursued by Fielding in his novels), or whether, as in Congreve, all shall play a game of delusion, at which all the *dramatis personæ* are playing, in which the best player is the winner. There is a strong tendency in the human mind to exult in the success of stratagem. There must, indeed, be some excuse invented for cheating; but love, revenge, self-defence, or the mere pleasure of witty contrivances, will answer the purpose very well with an audience, who are always glad to give their moral judgment a holyday.

But though the heroine of a comedy can hardly be a good

example to her sex, there is no necessity that she should be an offensive insult to it. Her faults should be such as a good woman might feel it possible for herself to have committed,—such as a moderate degree of self-delusion might pass off for virtues. The ladies were quite right in resenting the exhibition of Lady Touchwood. An innocent heart would require much and sad experience to convince it of the possibility of such a being. There are degrees of wickedness* too bad to laugh at, however they may be mingled with folly, affectation, or absurdity.

Towards the close of 1694 Queen Mary died. Few Queens have made fewer personal enemies, and perhaps few have been more sincerely regretted. But were we to judge of the quality of the national affliction by the sable flights of lugubrious verse that were devoted to the good Queen's memory, we should say that the English nation were the worst actors of royal woe in the world. Congreve committed a pastoral among the rest,—perhaps not the worst copy of verses produced on the occasion. It must be a very indifferent *Keen* that is not better than any of them. Such drivel might make the Muses join in the hyperbolical prayer of Flatman, that 'Kings should never die.'

Congreve's next play was *Love for Love*, produced in 1695. A new play, acted on a new stage, has every advantage which novelty can confer. Congreve advanced the higher claim of a service to an old favourite of the public. Betterton, who has left behind him a permanence of fame which some have denied that the actor can achieve, having reason to complain of his treatment by managers, was about to open a new theatre in Lincoln's Inn Fields. *Love for Love* was the first play acted on this stage. Its success was considerable, and it continued to be acted at intervals longer than any other of its author's comedies. But its charm as an acting play is gone; and perhaps it owed its occasional representation more to its containing those never-failing characters, a positive overbearing father, and a jack tar, than either to its wit or its licentiousness. It is said that Congreve, while engaged in composing this piece, paid a six weeks' visit to Portsmouth, in order to study sea manners from the life. Yet it has been objected, that the marine phraseology is not

---

* *Wickedness* is no subject for comedy. This was Congreve's great error, and almost peculiar to him. The Dramatis Personæ of Dryden, Wycherley, &c., are often *vicious*, obscene, &c., but not, like Congreve's, wicked.—*S.T.C.*

very accurate; and certainly, the character is so wide from the warm-hearted, gallant sailor of the modern stage, as to appear almost like a libel on the favourite profession. *Love for Love* is dedicated to Charles, Earl of Dorset and Middlesex, Lord Chamberlain of the King's Household, &c. One of Congreve's biographers commends this as containing '*no fulsome adulation.*' Pray what call you this?—'Whoever is King, is also the father of his country; and as nobody can dispute your Lordship's monarchy in poetry, so all that are concerned ought to acknowledge your universal patronage.' If this was meant to be believed, it was adulatory enough. But before we charge the authors of past days with universal sycophancy, we should duly consider, not merely what their words mean, but what sense they were intended to convey. The language of compliment was the only dialect in which a peer and a commoner could converse. The dedication was itself a real and sincere compliment; for it implied either gratitude for bounty, or a confidence in generosity. But the terms in which it was couched were merely conventional: to vary and adopt the topics of panegyric was a harmless exercise of ingenuity. Compliments, in ages past, were paid to sex or rank; in ours, they are directed to the person. Compliment, however, is not necessarily flattery. It is, at worst, but a foolish fashion, a misuse of words.

The experience of ages had not then convinced the poets that a battle fought last week is by no means a happy subject for a pindaric. The capture of Namur by Louis XIV. had been magnified by all the bards of Paris. The same fortress was unfortunate enough to give occasion to another volley of odes when recaptured by King William. Congreve's contribution was a series of irregular stanzas; a species of versification to which Cowley and his imitators had given a temporary eclat, confirmed and heightened by the success of Alexander's Feast. Congreve afterwards condemned these lawless measures; and, according to Johnson, had the merit of teaching the world, 'that Pindar's odes were regular,' a discovery which, we venture to affirm, an English ear, unassisted by eyes and fingers, would never have made. There seems to be no sufficient reason why a long ode should not occasionally vary its movement, if there be a corresponding variation in the feeling; but each system should certainly have a law, an ordonnance within itself, and there ought to be an equilibrium between the whole. But none but a great poet should be allowed to write irregular stanzas. Their tempting facility, which promises to give freedom to thought, does in reality save the trouble of thinking.

Congreve had produced three comedies in as many years, the only important results of that leisure and freedom from care which the Minister had bestowed upon him. Nearly two years elapsed between the representation of *Love for Love*, and that of the *Mourning Bride*, his single tragedy, which was more rapturously received than any product of his comic muse. The critics have not confirmed the sentence of the theatre. Yet the *Mourning Bride* is assuredly the effort of no common ability. It contains a passage which Johnson pronounced superior to any single speech in Shakspeare, and which appears to us more *poetical* than any thing in Rowe or Otway. But poetry seldom saves a new play, though it sometimes happens, that a *beauty*, which has become a common place, adds greatly to the reputation of an actor in an established piece.

Perhaps the great success of the *Mourning Bride* might be owing, in no small measure, to astonishment. Mankind are always pleased to wonder for a while, though they are soon tired of wondering. A tragedy by an author of so gay and comic a turn as Congreve, was something to wonder at. Moreover, tragedies are in general more favourably received than comedies in their first run. It is a rare thing for a serious drama to be hissed off the stage.* Truly has Terence spoken it:—

Tantum majus oneris habet comedia, quantum minus veniæ.
Comedy has so much the more of difficulty, as it has less of allowance.

Not long after the appearance of the *Mourning Bride*, Jeremy Collier produced his celebrated strictures on the *profaneness and immorality of the English stage*, and Congreve, among other and yet more grievous offenders, was severely handled for the licence of his pen. He would have done wisely had he, like Dryden, at once admitted the justice of the charge. But he was young, conscious of talent, elated with success, and probably unconscious of ill intent. He attempted an answer, which only brought upon him a fresh castigation. In truth, his defence was as feeble as his cause was indefensible.

While we gladly acknowledge the excellent scope and general

---

* No, only *silenced* and *thin-audienced* off.—*S.T.C.*

justice of Collier's reproofs, we may be allowed to doubt whether the effect of his admonitions was as great and sudden as some have supposed. He has been complimented as the purifier of comedy, and the great reformer of that stage which he purposed not to reform, but to overthrow. He certainly excited a great sensation, and gained both the King and the people to his side. William, educated in the strictness of Presbyterian discipline, and enured to the sobriety of Dutch manners, was so well pleased with the old non-juror's boldness, that he interfered to mitigate the severity of those laws which Collier's Jacobite principles had induced him to offend. Even the police were aroused by the crying scandal. Betterton and Mrs. Bracegirdle were fined for pronouncing profane and indecent words on the stage; and Colley Cibber tells us that comedy grew modest. The authors and actors might be upon their guard while public opinion, that Argus with a hundred drowsy eyes, was half awakened to their enormities; and many *well-meaning* people, roused by the indignant commentaries of Collier, blushed to find what they had not blushed at before. But, with few exceptions, the dramatists shewed as little amendment in their subsequent productions, as contrition in their angry replies. It was not in Collier's power to create a new idea of wit, or to erect a new standard of reputation; and while vice might be called wit without loss of reputation, it would never want auditors who stood well with the world. The worst of the old plays continued to be acted for many years after the date of Collier's diatribe; the new ones were a little more decent, but not a jot more moral.

Whatever refinement may have taken place in the public taste for diversion (and doubtless the improvement is considerable), is to be ascribed to other causes than the severity of satirists, or even the fulminations of the pulpit. The chief of these are, the general good education of females, the purifying influences of female society, the higher value set upon the domestic affections, the greater freedom of choice in marriage, and the more frequent intercourse between the religious and the fashionable world.[*]

It has been surmised, without much reason, that the reproof of Collier alienated Congreve from the stage. Yet he produced another comedy, written with infinite labour, but without any

---

[*] And more than all, the attendance of all classes on the theatres, except the gloomier sects; at least till of late.—S.T.C.

regard to the censor's admonitions. The reception of this play fell far below his expectations; and if we may credit the account given in the *Lives of the Poets*, published under the name of Theophilus Cibber, his disappointment betrayed him into a folly more ludicrous than any that he ridiculed on the scene. According to this incredible anecdote, he rushed upon the stage in a passion, and 'desired the audience to save themselves the trouble of shewing their dislike, for he never intended to write again for the theatre, nor submit his works again to the censure of impotent critics.' The audience must surely have concluded that he had undertaken to play the fool of the comedy himself, and that for once the fool *was* 'a fool indeed.' But Congreve had too much sense and too much pride to have acted thus, however keenly he might resent the stupidity of the many-headed monster. The tale may safely be set down as one of 'the weak inventions' which a poor slave of the ink-horn is ever ready to believe and promulgate of a rich, caressed, and pensioned author. Nothing disposes the humours so strongly to the acetic fermentation of envy, as the hopeless, heartless drudgery of the brain; and Envy is more credulous than Love, Fear, Superstition, even Vanity itself.

Congreve, however, was mortified at the dulness of his critics, and provoked that all the *labor limæ* had been thrown away. But no man should ever expect to profit in purse or reputation by superfluous painstaking. That very polish, that diligent selection and considerate collocation of words, that tight-lacing of sentences into symmetry, that exquisite propriety of each part and particle of the whole, which make *The Way of the World* so perfect a model of acuminated satire, detract more from scenic illusion than they add to histrionic effect. The dialogue of this play is no more akin to actual conversation, than the quick step of an opera dancer to the haste of pursuit or terror. No actor could give it the unpremeditated air of common speech. But there is another and more serious obstacle to the success of the *Way of the World* as an acting play. It has no moral interest. There is no one person in the *dramatis personæ* for whom it is possible to care. Vice may be, and too often has been, made interesting; but cold-hearted, unprincipled villainy never can.* The conduct of every character is so thoroughly and so

* Virtue and wickedness are *sub eodem genere*. The absence of *Virtue* is no deficiency in a genuine comedy, but the presence of wickedness a great defect.—S.T.C.

equally contemptible, that however you suspend the moral code of judgment, you cannot sympathise in the success, or exult in the defeat of any.

With all these abatements, it is impossible to read this comedy without wonder and admiration; but it is an admiration altogether intellectual, by which no man is made better.

(pp. 678–89)

(ii)

From a rapid survey of his life and character, he seems to have been one of those indifferent children of the earth 'whom the world cannot hate;' who are neither too good nor too bad for the present state of existence, and who may fairly expect their portion here. The darkest—at least the most enduring—stain on his memory, is the immorality of his writings; but this was the vice of the time, and his comedies are considerably more decorous than those of his predecessors. They are too cold to be mischievous; they keep the brain in too incessant inaction to allow the passions to kindle. For those who search into the powers of intellect, the combinations of thought which may be produced by volition, the plays of Congreve may form a profitable study. But their time is fled—on the stage they will be received no more; and of the devotees of light reading, such as could read them without disgust would probably peruse them with little pleasure.

(p. 693)

89. Leigh Hunt in the Introduction to *The Dramatic Works of Wycherley, Congreve, Vanbrugh, and Farquhar*

1840

From *The Dramatic Works of Wycherley, Congreve, Vanbrugh, and Farquhar* (London: 1840).

Leigh Hunt (1784–1859) had a long and productive career as a poet and literary journalist. *The Examiner*, a weekly established in 1808 by Hunt and his brother John, was noted for its radical but independent politics, and its generous championing of Keats and Shelley. The following extracts are taken from the 'Biographical and Critical Notices' which Hunt supplied for a one-volume edition of four Restoration dramatists by his current publisher Moxon.

(i)

On quitting the University, Congreve was entered of the Middle Temple; but he does not appear to have paid any attention to the law. Having family, as well as wit and scholarship, he was admitted into every kind of good company; and he probably soon discovered, that he could make way enough in life, without a profession, to suit the views of a man of no great affections, who saw little in the world superior to the union of wit and gentility. His first publication was a novel entitled *Incognita, or Love and Duty Reconciled*; which was said to have been written at the age of seventeen, but made its appearance at twenty-one. Johnson's convenient criticism upon it was, that he would 'rather praise it than read it.' Being of a less robust conscience on the reviewing side, it is our lot to have read it, without being able to praise. The author, though fresh from reading romances, already shows himself a man of the world, in the tone of his 'love,' and his notions of womankind. He was never young in that respect;—nor yet ever attained to years of poetical discretion. He aspires to be poetical nevertheless; and one of his fancies about his heroine is, that Cupid employs a quill out of his wings in 'picking her teeth!'

(p. xx)

(ii)

There is one evidence in Congreve, nevertheless, of the love of the highest aspirations, which has always puzzled us, and which, if it had not been for this bequest, would have forced us to give him credit for being superior, at heart, to his worldly tendencies. And indeed it is impossible to say, that such might not have been the case in his healthiest days, which are those in which the entire man is to be estimated. We allude to the power he had to write such verses as those on Lady Gethin, and such papers as the one he contributed to the *Tatler*, on the character of Lady Elizabeth Hastings,—an effusion so full of enthusiasm for the moral graces, and worded with an appearance of sincerity so cordial, that we can never read it without thinking it must have come from Steele. It is in this paper that he says one of the most elegant and truly loving things that were ever uttered by an unworldly passion:—'To *love* HER, is a *liberal education.*'[1] Alas! why does the faith in good and beauty sometimes light up the human bosom, as if only to show that every heart has a corner capable of reflecting it for a moment, but not strong enough to retain it!—And yet, let us be glad that even the temporary capability is there. Time, and healthier institutions, and then custom and convention itself, will bring the rest.

Meantime the plays of Congreve will not help the advancement, except inasmuch as their narrow views contradict worse bigotries, and serve to neutralize both. His love is spare and sorry; his belief in nothing, abundant; the whole set but a mass of wit, and sarcasm, and fine writing;—of brilliant exposures of hollowness, and of plots so over-ingenious as to become perplexing and tiresome. Speaking for ourselves, indeed, we can never attend sufficiently to the plots of Congreve. They soon puzzle us, and we cease to think of them. We see nothing but a set of heartless fine ladies and gentlemen, coming in and out, saying witty things at each other, and buzzing in some maze of intrigue. Yet incessant activity is there; the first demand of life, movement, is supplied; and no human beings are as bad as they sometimes *flatter themselves they are*, or as the gay comic writer amuses his activity by supposing them.

But above all, we must confess we find the 'wit' become tiresome. We love it heartily in its proper places, in Butler, Swift, and Addison, where it is serving some purpose greater than itself; and we love it still more, when it issues out of sheer animal spirits, and is happy as a child. But wit for wit's sake becomes a task and a trial; and in Congreve's days it was a cant, like the talk about 'sense' and 'reason;'—as if all sense, and reason, and wit, had been comprised in the substitution of the greater faculties of man for the less, and the critical for the unconscious. Everybody was to be 'witty.' Letters were to be full of 'wit,' and end in some 'witty turn'. Coffee-houses were to talk nothing but 'wit.' Ladies were to have 'wit and sweetness,' and gentlemen 'wit and fire;' not the old 'mother-wit' of Shakspeare and his fellows, which was a gift from the whole loving frame of Nature; but a trick of the fancy and of words, which you might almost acquire from the brother-wits of the tavern, and which dealt chiefly in simile, with a variation of antithesis. Every thing seemed to be of value, only inasmuch as it could be likened or opposed to something else; till at length simile and metaphor came to be taken for a 'reason;' and 'sense' itself was occupied, not in seeing into anything very deeply for its own sake, but in discovering how far it was capable of being split off into a couple of images. The great wits, to be sure, bantered the less, and affected to laugh at the affectation; but it was only for the purpose of guarding its rank and distinctions. This cant of wit, which affected 'manly Wycherley' himself a great deal more than it ought, came to its head in Congreve, and pretty well ceased with him. Vanbrugh was too robust and straightforward to care for it, and Farquhar too full of play.

From the artificial nature of Congreve's plays, partly owing to this wrong direction of his ingenuity, and partly to the sophisticate excesses of his men and women, and the riddles of his plots, we have scarcely retained an impression of them sufficiently distinct from one another to enable us to do justice to each, though we have just read them through for the express purpose, and marked them, and made notes besides. The *Old Bachelor* was thought astonishing for its knowledge of life, from an author not out of his teens; but the critics have long discovered that there was no such 'knowledge' in it as a youth so clever might not easily have attained. The wonderful thing was, the use he made of the knowledge, and the freedom from all appearance of immaturity. Dryden and Southerne, it is true, helped to fit it for the stage; but it is not likely that they made any great alteration in the main body and spirit of the thing, or the prevailing amount of its 'sense.' The characters of *Wittol, Bluffe*, and *Fondlewife*, are old stage property, as may be seen by their names; and the whole play, generally speaking, is but a wittier and less hearty re-fashionment of the style of Wycherley. Yet the reader, who has patience enough to watch the dialogue closely, will be rewarded with perpetual evidences of a quick observant mind, and of that conscious mastery over his pen and his sphere of action, which the new satirist of the circles appears to have felt the moment he entered them. The passage we call to mind with the greatest pleasure is the eighth scene of act the fourth, where Belinda sets her hair to rights, and describes the two girls from the country, whose dress she adjusted for them, and one of whom in gratitude gave her 'two apples, piping hot, out of an under-petticoat pocket.' *Pereant male qui ante nos,* &c. The '*fat* amber necklace' of the mother is a touch of genius.

The *Double Dealer*, with the solemn reciprocities of *Lord* and *Lady Froth*, and the capital character of *Lady Plyant*, 'insolent to her husband, and easy to every pretender,' is far superior to the *Old Bachelor*. Congreve excels in mixtures of impudence, hypocrisy, and self-delusion. The whole of the fifth scene of the second act, between *Lady Plyant* and *Mellefont*, is exquisite for the grossness of the overtures made under pretence of a delicacy in alarm. But it is no wonder a comedy did not succeed that has so black a villain in it as *Maskwell*, and an aunt who has a regularly installed gallant in her nephew. *Sir Paul Plyant* also says things to his daughter, which no decent person could hear with patience between father and child. The writer's object might have been a good one; but it is of doubtful and perilous use to attempt to do good by effrontery. It was on occasion of this play that Dryden addressed to Congreve his famous epistle, full of strength and good-nature, and almost as full of mistake. The dramatists of Charles the Second's age were described as superior in 'skill' to the 'giant race' their predecessors. Fletcher could 'move,' but had no power to 'raise;' Ben Jonson doubled Fletcher's 'force;' but all and everybody submitted to Congreve, except Shakspeare; and even he had but 'as much' in him; for Nature 'could not give him more!' But the panegyrics of this age, for want of that highest kind of truth on all sides, which only belongs to the highest genius, supplied defect of warmth with extravagance of attribution. There was generally a bargain in the matter: writers paid each other in kind, and lords paid dedicators in money. A natural excess of feeling on the part of the grateful, must be allowed to have had its share in the exaggeration. Flattery is not always insincere; and modesty itself may help to beguile gratitude into adulation, out of a doubt of its ability to render what is due.

Love for Love is the most amusing of all Congreve's plays, and the characters the least unpleasant. There are no revolting scoundrels; and the lovers really have some love. *Jeremy* is most improbably witty, for a servant; even though he once 'waited on a gentleman at Cambridge.' *Miss Prue* is not so naturally cunning as Wycherley's *Country Wife*, nor such a hearty bouncer as

Vanbrugh's *Hoyden*; but she is a very good variety of that genus.
The detection of one another by *Mrs. Frail* and *Mrs. Foresight*—
Where did you lose this gold bodkin? oh, sister, sister!—
Well, if you come to that, where did you *find* this bodkin? oh, sister! sister
every way!

[II, ix, 61–7]

is ever fresh and retributive. Mr. Hazlitt has noticed the startling
profundity of *Valentine's* request to his father, to disinherit him, not
simply of the family estate, but of the passions and appetites which
he begot in him. A less original, but like unconventional
intimation, is noticeable in the claim put in by the servant, to be
considered on a level in that respect with gentlemen:—

Sir Sampson, 'Oons, whose son are *you*? How were *you* engendered?
Jeremy. I am, by my father, the son of a chairman; my mother sold oysters
in winter, and cucumbers in summer; and I came upstairs into the world,
for I was born in a cellar.
Foresight. By your look you should go up stairs out of the world too,
friend.
Sir Sampson. And if this rogue were anatomised now, and dissected, he has
vessels of digestion and concoction, and so forth, large enough for the
inside of a cardinal, this son of a cucumber. These things are unaccountable
and unreasonable.

(II, vii, 122–33]

'The character of *Foresight*,' says Johnson, 'was then common.
Dryden calculated nativities; both Cromwell and King William had
their lucky days; and Shaftesbury himself, though he had no
religion, was said to regard prediction. The *Sailor* is not accounted
very natural, but he is very pleasant.' We know not why the *Sailor*
should have been accounted unnatural, except that he appears to be
a common sailor, and yet is the son of a man of fortune. It used to
be said that sailors do not talk like sailors, nor use a sea-jargon; but
they do. They talk, as other people do, within the limits of their
experience. As to Shaftesbury, it is far from surprising that they
who have no religion should yet be liable to superstition. They are
often but the more at mercy of it, from the want of any set limits to
belief. The demand for books of astrology is considerable at the
present moment; and perhaps has never failed. Mankind cannot get
rid of a sense of the unknown world, if it would; and till it takes to
it in the widest and most poetical sense, which is also the healthiest
and most natural,—such as a child instinctively has when it looks at

the stars,—it will dabble in the darkest borders of it, with a knowledge less than childish.

The *Mourning Bride* is not uninteresting in its story, nor so bad in its poetry as one might expect from the want of faith and passion natural to a town-wit of that age. Dr. Johnson, indeed, out of his amazing unacquaintance, or want of sympathy, (not to speak it irreverently) with poetry of the highest order, tells us, that if he were 'required to select from the whole mass of English poetry the most poetical *paragraph*,' (observe the instinct of that word!) 'he knows not what he could prefer to an *exclamation* in the *Mourning Bride*;' and then he quotes the passage in the third scene of act the second, where *Almeria* is so affected by the awful aspect of the interior of a cathedral. The passage indeed is a poetical one, and the best that Congreve wrote. The strong material presence of a cathedral-aisle, aided by the help of those thoughts of death which everybody experiences in looking at tombs, gave him a sufficient *knock on the head* to stir him to some emotion and attention, notwithstanding the neutralizing levity of his peruke. But a lover of the old poets will laugh as much at Johnson's unique notions of it, as the writer of the English ballad does at the irreparable loss which he supposes to be felt in Scotland at the death of a single hero:—

> I trust I have within my realm
> Five hundred as good as he.

As the love of the *Mourning Bride*, however, is defaced with the cant and sensuality of gallantry, so the style, for the most part, is poor, underbred (in a poetical sense), and instinctively prosaical; speaking neither with the richness nor the simplicity of passion, nor above the common-place of conventional metaphor. If the tragedy were revived now, the audience would laugh at the inflated sentences and unconscious prose. The revival of old English literature, and the tone of our best modern poets, have accustomed them to a higher and truer spirit. Yet some of the language of *Almeria*, as where, for instance, she again meets with *Osmyn*, is natural and affecting; and it is pleasing to catch a man of the world at these evidences of sympathy with what is serious. Nor are sensible and striking passages wanting. It is in this play, and the *Way of the World*, that are to be found some of those rhyming, sentious couplets which have become proverbial, and which their quoters are often at a loss in what author to find.

357

Heaven has no rage, like love to hatred turn'd,
Nor hell a fury, like a woman scorn'd.
                    Mourning Bride.—Close of Act III.
                                   [III, viii, 42–3]

For blessings ever wait on virtuous deeds,
And though a late, a sure reward succeeds.
                    Idem.—Close of the Play.

If there's delight in love, 'tis when I see
The heart which others bleed for, bleed for me.
            Way of the World.—Act III., Scene 12. [ll. 18–19]

The *Way of the World*, though not the most amusing, is assuredly the most complete, piquant, and observant of all the works of Congreve; full as an egg of some kind of wit or sense in almost every sentence, and a rich treat for the lover of this sort of writing, sitting in his easy-chair. *Millamant* pushes the confident playfulness of a coquet to the verge of what is pleasing; but her animal spirits and good-nature secure her. You feel that her airs will give way, by-and-by, to a genuine tenderness; and, meanwhile, some of them are exquisite in their affected superiority to circumstances.

Mrs. Fainall. You were dressed before I came abroad.
Millamant. Ay, that's true.—O, but then I had—*Mincing, what had I? Why was I so long?*
Mincing. O mem, your laship staid to peruse a pacquet of letters.
Millamant. O ay, *letters*—I had *letters*—I am persecuted with *letters*—I hate letters.—Nobody knows how to *write* letters; and yet one *has* 'em, one doesn't know why.—*They serve one to pin up one's hair.*
                                   [II, iv, 38–48]

And again:—

Beauty the lover's gift! Lord, what is a lover, *that it can give?* Why, one makes lovers as fast as one pleases, and they live as long as one pleases, and they die as soon as one pleases, and then, if one pleases, *one makes more.*
                                   [ibid., 95–9]

Mrs. Mincing, who pins hair up 'so pure and *crips*,' is the most *niminy-piminy* of attendants.—Act the fifth opens with one of Congreve's exquisite descriptions of common life:

Lady Wishfort. Out of my house, out of my house, thou viper, thou serpent, that I have fostered; thou bosom traitress, that I raised from nothing.—Begone, begone, begone, go, go.—That I took from washing

358

of old gauze and weaving of dead hair, with a black-blue nose over a
chafing-dish of starved embers, and dining behind a traverse rag, in a shop
no bigger than a bird-cage.   [V, i, 1–8]

This is certainly the *genius loci*;—the poetry of local description,
and narrow-minded contempt!

Very little poetry of any sort is there in the *Miscellanies* of
Congreve, and not much of his accustomed wit. To his scholarship, as Dr. Johnson observed, the public were indebted for the
discovery, that Cowley's irregular versification was not Pindaric;
though, in a directly critical sense, he can hardly be said to have
first taught the knowledge to 'English writers; ' for the example of
the true Pindaric (as far as metre goes) had been set with pedantic
nicety by Ben Jonson. Congreve professes not to be aware★ of the
existence of a precursor in this reformation; and most likely he had
forgotten Ben's miscellaneous poetry, though he had well studied
the dramas of the old scholar. He retained a better recollection of
Spenser; for in the 'Elegy on the Marquis of Blandford,' (the son of
his friend the Duchess of Marlborough,) the toiler through its
common-places is agreeably surprised at coming upon one or two
passages of real fancy and tenderness, evidently suggested by the
verses of the great poet on the 'Death of Sir Philip Sydney.' All his
other 'Mourning Muses,' and serious poems of any sort, with the
exception of a passage in his ode upon the singing of Arabella
Hunt, (for he had a real feeling for music,) are, for the most part, to
use a frank epithet applied to some of them by Johnson,
'despicable.' He sometimes follows Cowley so ill, that he may be
said to imitate Sprat!—as in the 'sigh' which Silence occupies by
way of 'throne,' and which has been 'purposely *annihilated*' to
oblige him with that accommodation! There is now and then a
strenuous couplet in his translations, caught from the tone of
Dryden. His art of 'Pleasing' consists in a freedom from affectation;
which though a necessary, is but a negative part of it. In his best
songs he is remarkable for the absence of everything that is inverted
in words, or superfluous to the thought; and here also his wit
returns; but he implies, as usual, little cordiality in his gallantry.
The following, however, is written in the spirit of a gentleman.

SONG.
False though she be to me and love,
I'll ne'er pursue revenge;

359

For still the charmer I approve,
    Though I deplore the change.

In hours of bliss we oft have met,
    They could not always last;
And though the present I regret,
    I'm grateful for the past.

The following is more characteristic of his writings in ordinary; as full of wit, and what was thought 'sense,' as it is deficient in sentiment. It is needless to add, that epicures of this sort are ignorant of half of what they think they know best, the very luxury of the senses.

SONG.

Tell me no more I am deceived,
    That Chloe's false and common;
I always knew, at least believed,
    She was a very woman.
As such I liked, as such caress'd;
She still was constant when possess'd
    She could do more for no man.

But oh! her thoughts on others ran,
    And that you think a hard thing;
Perhaps she fancied you the man,
    And what care I one farthing?
You think she's false, I'm sure she's kind,
I take her body, you her mind;
    Which has the better bargain?

The perplexed heroine of the next has been thought to be 'poor Mrs. Bracegirdle.'

SONG.

Pious Selinda goes to prayers,
    If I but ask the favour;
And yet the tender fool's in tears,
    When she believes I'll leave her.

Would I were free from this restraint,
    Or else had hopes to win her!
Would she could make of me a saint,
    Or I of her a sinner!

Congreve had an admiration of fair saints; which indeed is natural to a sinner of his sort. But 'Doris' was thought his master-piece.

The critics of the age, with good-natured Steele at their head, wanted words to express their admiration of 'Doris;'—Doris, which was the concatenation of everything new, and playful, and profound;—Doris, the 'inimitable Doris,' which, for aught that Greece or Rome had to show to the contrary, might have been written by Horace or Menander, or Virgil himself; nay, by Lord Dorset, or the Earl of Halifax. But we must not jest with a name like Steele, because we happen to live in an age which has been taught better. 'Doris' is, in truth, very acutely and pleasantly written, and, to this day, not a little startling; though the character was not a new one, even with Congreve. It shall be the last of our extracts in verse:—

[Quotes 'Doris' entire.]

(pp. xxix–xxxiv)

(iii)

Mr. Lamb, though a wide and subtle observer, was a sequestered liver. He was also one of an ultra-sensitive temperament, and so anxious to believe the best of everything, on more scores even than such as were healthy, that admitting as he did the utility and even joviality of some graver-looking perplexities in morals, which he was unable to be blind to, yet whenever he could not find what he thought a healthy or harmonious final reason for anything that was not so exactly within the limits of his experience, he was inclined either to doubt it altogether, or, for want of personal sympathy with the gaiety and robustness mixed up with it, and its possible convertibility into something better, to write as if he did. Perhaps he thought (surely not out of any presumption, but because his wisdom was of the best and most child-like sort itself,) that he could even play his readers a child's trick, and persuade them that Congreve's fine ladies and gentlemen, and the rakes of Vanbrugh and Farquhar, were doing nothing but 'making as if.' Most assuredly he was mistaken; and yet, with as equal certainty, most assuredly he need not have cared if he was. Nor would he, had the fact pressed itself upon him; even though he was without the additional comfort of such moralists as see a constant working and progression of society towards improvement. He could reconcile himself, some way or other, to anything which Nature in her energies brought about, or chose to go through. He hated to object to anything, except to objection; and to that too, when however passionate, it had a generosity and a health in it. But his idiosyncracies, and the possibilities of knowledge consequent upon them, were confined, though his heart was not; and even what he knew, he would not always choose to remember. Thus he speaks of a pedantic morality which finds nothing but evil in these plays, and which he represents as having come up in our own didactic times, and no longer enabling such plays to be acted. But every age has had a measure of the same kind of criticism, with regard to the one that preceded it. Shakspeare's Jew, Shylock, properly displaced (according to Mr. Lamb himself) the more malignant Jew of Marlowe. He does not complain that the age had found out the moral objection to the latter, or that a morality, no longer pedantic, made progression through the less inhuman nature of Shylock. Thus Dryden, who saw nothing to blame in Etherege, denounced the indecencies of Beaumont and Fletcher; while Steele, who recommended Congreve, thought Etherege not to be endured. Neither is it a fact that the comedies of the last age are no longer played or enjoyed. Whenever an actor comes up who is equal to them,—such as Mr. Farren, for instance,—they are always played and enjoyed; nor do the present audiences of Covent Garden object to them in the least, in the spirit of a pedantic morality. A critic here and there may do so; but it is neither the feeling of the press in general, nor of the play-going public; and if Congreve would not be liked now, neither was he in his own times, for what would now get him condemned. *Love for Love* is always liked when players can be got for it: so was the *Old Bachelor*, as far as Munden was concerned, even though astrology is gone out; but the villainous and tragical vices of some of the other of Congreve's plays hurt them in his own day, and were the cause in fact why he quitted the stage. In a word, there is more sympathy with real gaiety and spirits at all times, and greater instinctive allowance for the free drawing of nature and its healthy tendencies, than Mr. Lamb in this instance supposed; and unless there is a still more delicate inner doctrine in his essay than we seem warranted in supposing from some of the peremptory and final terms in it, we must believe it to be as unfounded in some conclusions, as it is admirable in every other respect, and useful for the enlargement of the understanding. Perhaps, after all, he intended nothing very different from what we do ourselves, though he took a different road for suggesting it. Certainly he intended nothing less innocent,—nor more so.

We cannot help thinking that Mr. Hazlitt's almost equally admirable essay on these writers (almost in point of style, and superior in hearty relish), leaves the far truer impression respecting them, as well as contains the best and most detailed criticism on their individual plays. We did not read either of these essays over again, till we had concluded our own remarks (for what we have here said of both is an insertion); but as we thought it would be an injustice to the reader to withhold from him what he has just seen, so we hold that it would be a still greater not to give him the benefit of the masterly criticism of Mr. Hazlitt. After we had again become acquainted with them, we found reason, generally speaking, to think nothing of our own, except inasmuch as we observed a prevailing similarity of opinion. Nor may the reader be sorry to hear a third lover of the drama speak on a subject so agreeable. What we hold ourselves to have contributed to this volume is a more pains-taking set of memoirs than, we believe, has yet appeared. Mr. Hazlitt's essay will complete, amplify, and abundantly enrich the criticism; and Mr. Lamb's will carry to its height a speculation more exquisitely artificial than its subject, and advantageous, some way or other, to all parties. But Hazlitt, it is to be observed, has none of the misgivings of Lamb. He does not even think it necessary to notice them. He takes the whole tribe, as nature and society (short of the exaggerations of art) threw them forward during the progress of civilization, neither doubting their reality, nor startled at it, nor forced to reconcile himself to the robustness of its levity.

(pp. lxix–lxx)

NOTES

1 The character of Lady Elizabeth Hastings appears in *The Tatler*, No. 42, but the phrase 'to love her, is a liberal Education' occurs in No. 49. Both these numbers are now attributed to Steele.

* See the *Discourse on the Pindarique Ode* prefixed to one of Congreve's poems on King William; and, in Ben Jonson's works, the 'Pindaric Ode' to the memory of Sir Lucius Cary and Sir H. Morison.

90. Thomas Babington Macaulay in 'Comic Dramatists of the Restoration'

1841

From *The Edinburgh Review* (1841), 72: 490–528.

Thomas Babington Macaulay (1800–59), Whig historian *par excellence*, had been writing for *The Edinburgh Review* since 1825. His review of Leigh Hunt's edition of the Restoration dramatists appeared in the issue for January 1841. Macaulay's contributions to the *Edinburgh* were collected, with some reluctance on his part, in *Critical and Historical Essays* in 1843.

(i) The immorality of Restoration comedy: a reply to Charles Lamb
We have said that we think the present publication perfectly justifiable. But we can by no means agree with Mr Leigh Hunt, who seems to hold that there is little or no ground for the charge of immorality so often brought against the literature of the Restoration. We do not blame him for not bringing to the judgment-seat the merciless rigour of Lord Angelo; but we really think that such flagitious and impudent offenders as those who are now at the bar, deserved at least the gentle rebuke of Escalus. Mr Leigh Hunt treats the whole matter a little too much in the easy style of Lucio, and perhaps his exceeding lenity disposes us to be somewhat too severe.

And yet, it is not easy to be too severe. For, in truth, this part of our literature is a disgrace to our language and our national character. It is clever, indeed, and very entertaining; but it is, in the most emphatic sense of the words, 'earthly, sensual, devilish.' Its indecency, though perpetually such as is condemned, not less by the rules of good taste than by those of morality, is not, in our opinion, so disgraceful a fault as its singularly inhuman spirit. We have here Belial, not as when he inspired Ovid and Ariosto, 'graceful and humane,' but with the iron eye and cruel sneer of Mephistopheles. We find ourselves in a world, in which the ladies are like very profligate, impudent, and unfeeling men, and in which the men are too bad for any place but Pandæmonium or Norfolk Island. We are surrounded by foreheads of bronze, hearts like the nether millstone, and tongues set on fire of hell.

Dryden defended or excused his own offences, and those of his contemporaries, by pleading the example of the earlier English dramatists; and Mr Leigh Hunt seems to think that there is force in the plea. We altogether differ from this opinion. The crime charged is not mere coarseness of expression. The terms which are delicate in one age, become gross in the next. The diction of the English version of the Pentateuch, is sometimes such as Addison would not have ventured to imitate; and Addison, the standard of purity in his own age, used many phrases which are now proscribed. Whether a thing shall be designated by a plain noun-substantive, or by a circumlocution, is mere matter of fashion. Morality is not at all interested in the question. But morality is deeply interested in this—that what is immoral shall not be presented to the imagination of the young and susceptible in constant connexion with what is attractive. For every person who has observed the operation of the law of association in his own mind, and in the minds of others, knows, that whatever is constantly presented to the imagination in connexion with what is attractive, will commonly itself become attractive. There is undoubtedly a great deal of indelicate writing in Fletcher and Massinger; and more than might be wished even in Ben Jonson and Shakspeare, who are comparatively pure. But it is impossible to trace in their plays any systematic attempt to associate vice with those things which men value most and desire most, and virtue with every thing ridiculous and degrading. And such a systematic attempt we find in the whole dramatic literature of the generation which followed the return of Charles the Second. We will take, as an instance of what we mean, a single subject of the highest importance to the happiness of mankind—conjugal fidelity. We can at present hardly call to mind a single English play, written before the civil war, in which the character of a seducer of married women is represented in a favourable light. We remember many plays in which such persons are baffled, exposed, covered with derision, and insulted by triumphant husbands. Such is the fate of Falstaff, with all his wit and knowledge of the world. Such is the fate of Brisac in Fletcher's *Elder Brother*—and of Ricardo and Ubaldo, in Massinger's *Picture*. Sometimes, as in the *Fatal Dowery*, and *Love's Cruelty*, the outraged honour of families is repaired by a bloody revenge. If now and then the lover is represented as an accomplished man, and the husband as a person of weak or odious character, this only makes the triumph of female virtue the more signal; as in Jonson's Celia and Mrs Fitzdottrel, and in Fletcher's Maria. In general, we will venture to say, that the dramatists of the age of Elizabeth and James the First, either treat the breach of the marriage-vow as a serious crime—or, if they treat it as matter for laughter, turn the laugh against the gallant.

On the contrary, during the forty years which followed the Restoration, the whole body of the dramatists invariably represent adultery—we do not say as a peccadillo—we do not say as an error which the violence of passion may excuse—but as the calling of a fine gentleman—as a grace without which his character would be imperfect. It is as essential to his breeding and to his place in society that he should make love to the wives of his neighbours, as that he should know French, or that he should have a sword at his side. In all this there is no passion, and scarcely any thing that can be called preference. The hero intrigues, just as he wears a wig; because, if he did not, he would be a queer fellow, a city prig, perhaps a Puritan. All the agreeable qualities are always given to the gallant. All the contempt and aversion are the portion of the unfortunate husband. Take Dryden for example; and compare Woodall with Brainsick, or Lorenzo with Gomez. Take Wycherley, and compare Horner with Pinchwife. Take Vanbrugh, and compare Constant with Sir John Brute. Take Farquhar, and compare Archer with Squire Sullen. Take Congreve, and compare Bellmour with Fondlewife, Careless with Sir Paul Plyant, or Scandal with Foresight. In all these cases, and in many more which might be named, the dramatist evidently does his best to make the person who commits the injury graceful, sensible, and spirited; and the person who suffers it a fool or a tyrant, or both.

Mr Charles Lamb, indeed, attempted to set up a defence for this way of writing. The dramatists of the latter part of the seventeenth century are not, according to him, to be tried by the standard of morality which exists, and ought to exist in real life. Their world is a conventional world. Their heroes and heroines belong, not to England, not to Christendom, but to an Utopia of gallantry, to a Fairyland, where the Bible and Burns's Justice are unknown— where a prank which on this earth would be rewarded with the pillory, is merely matter for a peal of elvish laughter. A real Horner, a real Careless would, it is admitted, be exceedingly bad men. But to predicate morality or immorality of the Horner of Wycherley, and the Careless of Congreve, is as absurd as it would be to arraign a sleeper for his dreams. They belong 'to the regions of pure comedy, where no cold moral reigns—when we are amongst them we are amongst a chaotic people. We are not to judge them by our usages. No reverend institutions are insulted by their proceedings, for they have none among them. No peace of families is violated, for no family ties exist among them. There is neither right nor wrong—gratitude or its opposite—claim or duty—paternity or sonship.'

This is, we believe, a fair summary of Mr Lamb's doctrine. We are sure that we do not wish to represent him unfairly. For we admire his genius; we love the kind nature which appears in all his writings; and we cherish his memory as much as if we had known him personally. But we must plainly say that his argument, though ingenious, is altogether sophistical.

Of course we perfectly understand that it is possible for a writer to create a conventional world in which things forbidden by the Decalogue and the Statute Book shall be lawful, and yet that the exhibition may be harmless, or even edifying. For example, we suppose that the most austere critics would not accuse Fenelon of impiety and immorality, on account of his *Telemachus* and his *Dialogues of the Dead*. In *Telemachus* and the *Dialogues of the Dead*, we have a false religion, and consequently a morality which is in some points incorrect. We have a right and a wrong, differing from the right and the wrong of real life. It is represented as the first duty of men to pay honour to Jove and Minerva. Philocles, who employs his leisure in making graven images of these deities, is extolled for his piety in a way which contrasts singularly with the expressions of Isaiah on the same subject. The dead are judged by Minos, and rewarded with lasting happiness for actions which Fenelon would have been the first to pronounce splendid sins. The same may be said of Mr Southey's Mahommedan and Hindoo heroes and heroines. In *Thalaba*, to speak in derogation of the Arabian impostor is blasphemy—to drink wine is a crime—to perform ablutions, and to pay honour to the holy cities, are works of merit. In the *Curse of Kehama*, Kailyal is commended for her devotion to the statue of Mariataly, the goddess of the poor. But certainly no person will accuse Mr Southey of having promoted or intended to promote either Islamism or Brahminism.

It is easy to see why the conventional worlds of Fenelon and Mr Southey are unobjectionable. In the first place, they are utterly unlike the real world in which we live. The state of society, the laws even of the physical world, are so different from those with which we are familiar, that we cannot be shocked at finding the morality also very different. But in truth, the morality of these conventional worlds differs from the morality of the real world, only in points where there is no danger that the real world will ever go wrong. The generosity and docility of Telemachus, the fortitude, the modesty, the filial tenderness of Kailyal, are virtues of all ages and nations. And there was very little danger that the Dauphin would worship Minerva, or that an English damsel would dance with a bucket on her head before the statue of Mariataly.

The case is widely different with what Mr Charles Lamb calls the conventional world of Wycherley and Congreve. Here the costume, the manners, the topics of conversation are those of the real town, and of the passing day. The hero is in all superficial accomplishments exactly the fine gentleman, whom every youth in the pit would gladly resemble. The heroine is the fine lady, whom every youth in the pit would gladly marry. The scene is laid in some place which is as well known to the audience as their own houses, in St James's Park, or Hyde Park, or Westminster Hall. The lawyer bustles about with his bag, between the Common Pleas and the Exchequer. The Peer calls for his carriage to go to the House of Lords on a private bill. A hundred little touches are employed to make the fictitious world appear like the actual world. And the immorality is of a sort which never can be out of date, and which all the force of religion, law, and public opinion united can but imperfectly restrain.

In the name of art, as well as in the name of virtue, we protest against the principle that the world of pure comedy is one into which no moral enters. If comedy be an imitation, under whatever conventions, of real life, how is it possible that it can have no reference to the great rule which directs life, and to feelings which are called forth by every incident of life? If what Mr Charles Lamb says were correct, the inference would be, that these dramatists did not in the least understand the very first principles of their craft.

Pure landscape painting into which no light or shade enters, pure portrait painting into which no expression enters, are phrases less at variance with sound criticism, than pure comedy into which no moral enters.

But it is not the fact, that the world of these dramatists is a world into which no moral enters. Morality constantly enters into that world, a sound morality, and an unsound morality; the sound morality to be insulted, derided, associated with every thing mean and hateful; the unsound morality to be set off to every advantage, and inculcated by all methods, direct and indirect. It is not the fact, that none of the inhabitants of this conventional world feel reverence for sacred institutions, and family ties. Fondlewife, Pinchwife, every person in short of narrow understanding, and disgusting manners, expresses that reverence strongly. The heroes and heroines too, have a moral code of their own, an exceedingly bad one; but not, as Mr Charles Lamb seems to think, a code existing only in the imagination of dramatists. It is, on the contrary, a code actually received, and obeyed by great numbers of people. We need not go to Utopia or Fairyland to find them. They are near at hand. Every night some of them play at the 'hells' in the Quadrant, and others pace the Piazza in Covent-Garden. Without flying to Nephelococcygia, or to the Court of Queen Mab, we can meet with sharpers, bullies, hard-hearted impudent debauchees, and women worthy of such paramours. The morality of the *Country Wife* and the *Old Bachelor*, is the morality, not, as Mr Charles Lamb maintains, of an unreal world, but of a world which is a great deal too real. It is the morality, not of a chaotic people, but of low town-rakes, and of those ladies whom the newspapers call 'dashing Cyprians.' And the question is simply, whether a man of genius, who constantly and systematically endeavours to make this sort of character attractive, by uniting it with beauty, grace, dignity, spirit, a high social position, popularity, literature, wit, taste, knowledge of the world, brilliant success in every undertaking, does or does not make an ill use of his powers. We own that we are unable to understand how this question can be answered in any way but one.

It must, indeed, be acknowledged, in justice to the writers of whom we have spoken thus severely, that they were, to a great extent, the creatures of their age. And if it be asked why that age encouraged immorality which no other age would have tolerated, we have no hesitation in answering that this great depravation of the national taste was the effect of the prevalence of Puritanism under the Commonwealth.

(pp. 492–7)

(ii) Congreve's career

His first work, a novel of no great value, he published under the assumed name of 'Cleophil.' His second was the *Old Bachelor*, acted in 1693, a play inferior indeed to his other comedies, but, in its own line, inferior to them alone. The plot is equally destitute of interest and of probability. The characters are either not distinguishable, or are distinguished only by peculiarities of the most glaring kind. But the dialogue is resplendent with wit and eloquence—which indeed are so abundant that the fools come in for an ample share—and yet preserves a certain colloquial air, a certain indescribable ease, of which Wycherley had given no example, and which Sheridan in vain attempted to imitate. The author, divided between pride and shame—pride at having written a good play, and shame at having done an ungentlemanlike thing—pretended that he had merely scribbled a few scenes for his own amusement, and affected to yield unwillingly to the importunities of those who pressed him to try his fortune on the stage. The *Old Bachelor* was seen in manuscript by Dryden; one of whose best qualities was a hearty and generous admiration for the talents of others. He declared that he had never seen such a first play; and lent his services to bring it into a form fit for representation. Nothing was wanting to the success of the piece. It was so cast as to bring into play all the comic talent, and to exhibit on the boards in one view all the beauty, which Drury-Lane Theatre, then the only theatre in London, could assemble. The result was a complete triumph; and the author was gratified with rewards more substantial than the applauses of the pit. Montagu, then a lord of the treasury, immediately gave him a place, and, in a short time, added the reversion of another place of much greater value, which, however, did not become vacant till many years had elapsed.

In 1694, Congreve brought out the *Double-Dealer*, a comedy in which all the powers which had produced the *Old Bachelor* show themselves, matured by time and improved by exercise. But the audience was shocked by the characters of Maskwell and Lady Touchwood. And, indeed, there is something strangely revolting in the way in which a group that seems to belong to the house of

370

Laius or of Pelops, is introduced into the midst of the Brisks, Froths, Carelesses, and Plyants. The play was unfavourably received. Yet, if the praise of distinguished men could compensate an author for the disapprobation of the multitude, Congreve had no reason to repine. Dryden, in one of the most ingenious, magnificent, and pathetic pieces that he ever wrote, extolled the author of the *Double-Dealer* in terms which now appear extravagantly hyperbolical. Till Congreve came forth—so ran this exquisite flattery—the superiority of the poets who preceded the civil wars was acknowledged.

> Theirs was the giant race before the flood.

Since the return of the Royal house, much art and ability had been exerted, but the old masters had been still unrivalled.

> Our builders were with want of genius curst,
> The second temple was not like the first.

At length a writer had arisen who, just emerging from boyhood, had surpassed the authors of the *Knight of the Burning Pestle* and the *Silent Woman*, and who had only one rival left to contend with.

> Heaven, that but once was prodigal before,
> To Shakspeare gave as much, he could not give him more.

Some lines near the end of the poem are singularly graceful and touching, and sank deep into the heart of Congreve.

> Already am I worn with cares and age,
> And just abandoning the ungrateful stage;
> But you, whom every Muse and Grace adorn,
> Whom I foresee to better fortune born,
> Be kind to my remains; and, oh, defend
> Against your judgment your departed friend;
> Let not the insulting foe my fame pursue,
> But guard those laurels which descend to you.

The crowd as usual gradually came over to the opinion of the men of note; and the *Double-Dealer* was before long quite as much admired, though perhaps never so much liked, as the *Old Bachelor*.

In 1695 appeared *Love for Love*, superior both in wit and in scenic effect to either of the preceding plays. It was performed at a new theatre which Betterton and some other actors, disgusted by the treatment which they received in Drury-Lane, had just opened in a tennis-court near Lincoln's Inn. Scarcely any comedy within the memory of the oldest man had been equally successful. The actors were so elated that they gave Congreve a share in their theatre, and he promised in return to furnish them with a play every year, if his health would permit. Two years passed, however, before he produced the *Mourning Bride*, a play which, paltry as it is when compared, we do not say with *Lear* or *Macbeth*, but with the best dramas of Massinger and Ford, stands very high among the tragedies of the age in which it was written. To find any thing so good we must go twelve years back to *Venice Preserved*, or six years forward to the *Fair Penitent*. The noble passage which Johnson, both in writing and in conversation, extolled above any other in the English drama, has suffered greatly in the public estimation from the extravagance of his praise. Had he contented himself with saying that it was finer than any thing in the tragedies of Dryden, Otway, Lee, Rowe, Southern, Hughes, and Addison—than any thing, in short, that had been written for the stage since the days of Charles the First—he would not have been in the wrong.

(pp. 515–17)

(iii) The Collier controversy

In 1698, Collier published his *Short View of the Profaneness and Immorality of the English Stage*, a book which threw the whole literary world into commotion, but which is now much less read than it deserves. The faults of the work, indeed, are neither few nor small. The dissertations on the Greek and Latin drama do not at all help the argument; and, whatever may have been thought of them by the generation which fancied that Christ Church had refuted Bentley, are such as, in the present day, a scholar of very humble pretensions may venture to pronounce boyish, or rather babyish. The censures are not sufficiently discriminating. The authors whom Collier accused had been guilty of such gross sins against decency, that he was certain to weaken, instead of strengthening his case, by introducing into his charge against them any matter about which there could be the smallest dispute. He was, however, so injudicious as to place among the outrageous offences, which he justly arraigned, some things which are really quite innocent; and some slight instances of levity which, though not perhaps strictly correct, could easily be paralleled from the works of writers who had rendered great services to morality and religion. Thus he blames Congreve, the number and gravity of whose real transgressions made it quite unnecessary to tax him with any that were not real, for using the words 'martyr' and 'inspiration' in a light sense; as if an archbishop might not say that a speech was inspired by claret, or that an alderman was a martyr to the gout. Sometimes, again, Collier does not sufficiently distinguish between the dramatist and the persons of the drama. Thus he blames Vanbrugh for putting into Lord Foppington's mouth some raillery on the Church service; though it is obvious that Vanbrugh could not better express reverence than by making Lord Foppington express contempt. There is also throughout the *Short View* too strong a display of professional feeling. Collier is not content with claiming for his order an immunity from insult and indiscriminate scurrility; he will not allow that, in any case, any word or act of a divine can be a proper subject for ridicule. Nor does he confine this benefit of clergy to the ministers of the Established Church; he extends the privilege to Catholic priests, and, what in him is more surprising, to Dissenting preachers. This, however, is a mere trifle. Imauns, Brahmins, priests of Jupiter, priests of Baal, are all to be held sacred. Dryden is blamed for making the Mufti in *Don Sebastian* talk nonsense. Lee is called to a severe account for his incivility to Tiresias. But the most curious passage is that in which Collier resents some uncivil reflections thrown by Cassandra, in *Cleomenes*, on the calf Apis and his hierophants. The words, 'grass-eating, foddered god,'—words which really are much in the style of several passages in the Old Testament, give as much offence to this Christian divine as they could have given to the priests at Memphis.

But, when all these deductions have been made, great merit must be allowed to this work. There is hardly any book of that time from which it would be possible to select specimens of writing so excellent and so various. To compare Collier with Pascal would indeed be absurd. Yet we hardly know where, except in the *Provincial Letters*, we can find mirth so harmoniously and becomingly blended with solemnity as in the *Short View*. In truth, all the modes of ridicule, from broad fun to polished and antithetical sarcasm, were at Collier's command. On the other hand, he was complete master of the rhetoric of honest indignation. We scarcely know any volume which contains so many bursts of that peculiar eloquence which comes from the heart, and goes to the heart. Indeed, the spirit of the book is truly heroic. In order fairly to appreciate it, we must remember the situation in which the writer stood. He was under the frown of power. His name was already a mark for the invectives of one half of the writers of the age; when, in the cause of good taste, good sense, and good morals, he gave battle to the other half. Strong as his political prejudices were, he seems on this occasion to have entirely laid them aside. He has forgotten that he is a Jacobite, and remembers only that he is a citizen and a Christian. Some of his sharpest censures are directed against poetry which had been hailed with delight by the Tory party, and had inflicted a deep wound on the Whigs. It is really inspiriting to see how gallantly the solitary outlaw advances to attack enemies, formidable separately, and, it might have been thought, irresistible when combined—distributes his swashing blows right and left among Wycherley, Congreve, and Vanbrugh—treads the wretched D'Urfey down in the dirt beneath his feet—and strikes with all his strength full at the towering crest of Dryden.

The effect produced by the *Short View* was immense. The nation was on the side of Collier. But it could not be doubted that, in the great host which he had defied, some champion would be found to lift the gauntlet. The general belief was, that Dryden would take the field; and all the wits anticipated a sharp contest between two well-paired combatants. The great poet had been singled out in the most marked manner. It was well known that he was deeply hurt, that much smaller provocations had formerly roused him to violent resentment, and that there was no literary weapon, offensive or defensive, of which he was not master. But his conscience smote him; he stood abashed, like the fallen archangel at the rebuke of Zephon,

> And felt how awful goodness is, and saw
> Virtue in her shape how lovely; saw and pined
> His loss.

At a later period he mentioned the *Short View* in the preface to his *Fables*. He complained, with some asperity, of the harshness with which he had been treated, and urged some matters in mitigation. But, on the whole, he frankly acknowledged that he had been justly reproved. 'If,' said he, 'Mr Collier be my enemy, let him triumph. If he be my friend, as I have given him no personal occasion to be otherwise, he will be glad of my repentance.'

It would have been wise in Congreve to follow his master's

example. He was precisely in that situation in which it is madness to attempt a vindication; for his guilt was so clear, that no address or eloquence could obtain an acquittal. On the other hand, there were, in his case, many extenuating circumstances, which, if he had acknowledged his error, and promised amendment, would have procured his pardon. The most rigid censor could not but make great allowances for the faults into which so young a man had been seduced by evil example, by the luxuriance of a vigorous fancy, and by the inebriating effect of popular applause. The esteem, as well as the admiration, of the public was still within his reach. He might easily have effaced all memory of his trangressions, and have shared with Addison the glory of showing that the most brilliant wit may be the ally of virtue. But in any case, prudence should have restrained him from encountering Collier. The nonjuror was a man thoroughly fitted by nature, education, and habit, for polemical dispute. Congreve's mind, though one of no common fertility and vigour, was of a different class. No man understood so well the art of polishing epigrams and repartees into the clearest effulgence, and setting them tastefully in easy and familiar dialogue. In this sort of jewellery he attained to a mastery unprecedented and inimitable. But he was altogether rude in the art of controversy, and he had a cause to defend which scarcely any art could have rendered victorious.

The event was such as might have been foreseen. Congreve's answer was a complete failure. He was angry, obscure, and dull. Even the Green Room and Will's Coffee-House were compelled to acknowledge, that in wit the parson had a decided advantage over the poet. Not only was Congreve unable to make any show of a case where he was in the wrong, but he succeeded in putting himself completely in the wrong where he was in the right. Collier had taxed him with profaneness for calling a clergyman Mr Prig, and for introducing a coachman named Jehu, in allusion to the King of Israel, who was known at a distance by his furious driving. Had there been nothing worse in the *Old Bachelor* and *Double Dealer*, Congreve might pass for as pure a writer as Cowper himself; who in poems revised by so austere a censor as John Newton, calls a fox-hunting squire Nimrod, and gives to a chaplain the disrespectful name of Smug. Congreve might with good effect have appealed to the public whether it might not be fairly presumed that, when such frivolous charges were made, there were no very serious charges to make. Instead of doing this, he pretended that he meant no allusion to the Bible by the name of Jehu, and no reflection by the name of Prig. Strange that a man of such parts should, in order to defend himself against imputations which nobody could regard as important, tell untruths which it was certain that nobody would believe.

One of the pleas which Congreve set up for himself and his brethren was, that, though they might be guilty of a little levity here and there, they were careful to inculcate a moral, packed close into two or three lines, at the end of every play. Had the fact been as he stated it, the defence would be worth very little. For no man acquainted with human nature could think that a sententious couplet would undo all the mischief that five profligate acts had done. But it would have been wise in Congreve to have looked again at his own comedies before he used this argument. Collier did so; and found that the moral of the *Old Bachelor*—the grave apophthegm which is to be a set-off against all the libertinism of the piece—is contained in the following triplet:—

> What rugged ways attend the noon of life!
> Our sun declines, and with what anxious strife,
> What pain, we tug that galling load—a wife.

'*Love for Love*,' says Collier, 'may have a somewhat better farewell, but it would do a man little service should he remember it to his dying day:'—

> The miracle to-day is, that we find
> A lover true, not that a woman's kind.

(pp. 520–3)

(iv) Congreve and Wycherley compared

We have said that Wycherley was a worse Congreve. There was, indeed, a remarkable analogy between the writings and lives of these two men. Both were gentlemen liberally educated. Both led town lives, and knew human nature only as it appears between Hyde Park and the Tower. Both were men of wit. Neither had much imagination. Both at an early age produced lively and profligate comedies. Both retired from the field while still in early manhood, and owed to their youthful achievements in literature the consideration which they enjoyed in later life. Both, after they had ceased to write for the stage, published volumes of miscellanies, which did little credit either to their talents or to their morals. Both, during their declining years, hung loose upon society; and both, in their last moments, made eccentric and unjustifiable dispositions respecting their estates.

But in every point Congreve maintained his superiority to Wycherley. Wycherley had wit; but the wit of Congreve far outshines that of every comic writer, except Sheridan, who has arisen within the last two centuries. Congreve had not, in a large measure, the poetical faculty; but compared with Wycherley he might be called a great poet. Wycherley had some knowledge of books; but Congreve was a man of real learning. Congreve's offences against decorum, though highly culpable, were not so gross as those of Wycherley; nor did Congreve, like Wycherley, exhibit to the world the deplorable spectacle of a licentious dotage. Congreve died in the enjoyment of high consideration; Wycherley forgotten or despised. Congreve's will was absurd and capricious; but Wycherley's last actions appeared to have been prompted by obdurate malignity.

(p. 528)

91. Reviews of *Love for Love* and *The Way of the World* in *The Times*

1842

From (a) *The Times*, Monday 21 November 1842, p. 5; (b) ibid., Monday 19 December 1842, p. 5.

(a)

DRURY-LANE THEATRE

William Congreve's *Love for Love* stands as a magnificent specimen of the second English drama—not the great national drama—but of that series of plays, written partly under a French influence, and commencing with the return of Charles II, when the stage ceased to be poetical and romantic, and wit and intrigue were considered the great qualifications for comedy. It is true that many of the plays of

Ben Jonson and his cotemporaries were written in prose, but these were rather the exception than the rule, and it does not seem that prose became the sole acknowledged vehicle for the comic drama till after the Restoration. Since that period it has maintained its dominion; prose is considered now the language of comedy; and if there be an instance in modern times of one written in blank verse, as in the *Honeymoon* or the plays of Mr. Knowles, they are rather deemed imitations of what was once called a comedy than of what is so in the present sense of the word. The change from verse to prose might at first sight seem only to affect the outward form of the dialogue, but this was not the case; on the contrary, the revolution was a more important one than might be imagined by the superficial thinker. Verse, by lifting the *dramatis personae* out of the ordinary language of life, was a great bar against mere 'naturalness', and as the characters were forced to be ideal in their language, they likewise became idealized altogether. The man, as a man, apart from conventionalities, is the subject of a metrical drama, while the prose play always has a tendency, by pulling him down into the real world, to involve him in all the customs and trifles of a particular period. The ideal and the real drama, though the former is of a higher order than the latter, may both be excellent, though their excellences will be of different kinds. The ideal dramatist will have to display his knowledge of those passions and feelings which belong to man universally, which must strike an audience; he must move by his pathos, he must astound by his sublimity; while the real dramatist will rather display what is included in the phrase 'knowledge of the world'—a phrase which, large as it sounds, means something infinitely less than knowledge of man. 'Knowledge of the world,' says Mr. Dickens in one of his novels, 'means the knowledge of every rascal in it,' and it was in that knowledge that Congreve, Wycherley, and Vanbrugh loved to display their proficiency.[1] Does the dramatist of reality attempt to touch the head alone of his audience, he will tread in the path of the dramatists of Charles II; does he attempt to touch their hearts, he will write such dramatic dramas as the *Road to Ruin* or the plays of Kotzebue. The faults of the ideal and the real dramatist will, like their excellencies, be of an opposite character. The former will have to check a tendency towards mere pompous lifelessness—the latter a decline into mere bald commonplace. It is, however, a misfortune, when the drama of a country has become exceedingly rich, that the mere commonplace may be easily adopted both in the poetical and prose play. So many characters are ready cut and dried in the *thesaurus* of English dramatic literature, that a skilful plagiarist may take them out, and construct at pleasure a drama of any kind, without having a natural calling for one rather than another. Hence the strange phenomenon, so common at the present day, of a mere abstraction forcing itself into a play that is, professedly, a picture of life.

But it is not in the works of Congreve that we must look for that mere 'naturalness' which has been the aim of more modern writers. Indeed, though his language approaches that of ordinary conversation, the omission of heart, as a dramatic ingredient, makes him appear even less natural than his Elizabethan predecessors. He revelled in his knowledge of the little world, but he displayed that knowledge rather by the apophthegms he put in the mouths of his characters, than by what they did and felt. His language could not sink into commonplace, for he felt a requisition to be witty, and by this one element of wit alone he created an atmosphere neither real nor ideal, but something between both, an artificial state of being in the midst of which he reigned as a monarch. His characters are broadly and hastily sketched, his plots are confused and miserably inartificial, he does not awaken a spark of interest for one of his people, and yet by this vast power of wit, which flows at his command like a never-ceasing fountain, he has produced dramas which, with all their deficiencies as dramas, stand a marvel for succeeding generations. He is not the perfect dramatist, having sacrificed every element of man to this one abstraction of wit; but in this wit he is unrivalled, and in this respect all the dramatists of his own, and of every other nation, must bow before him. Molière produced nothing of the kind, and the dialogue of the *School for Scandal*, brilliant though it be, is but as child's prattle compared with the cataract of wit that pours down in *Love for Love*. To the man of the world, who is familiar with the littlenesses of every-day life, to the lover of the repartee of the coffee-house or the club-room, the works of William Congreve remain a ceaseless source of admiration and delight. To the unsophisticated, to those who look for some one to like in a drama, his plays will appear purposeless and even heavy. They will see little to interest them in the tricks and contrivances of a number of vicious men and women, especially as the one virtuous woman of the piece

379

(Angelica) has even less heart than her profligate friends. As the old advice to the audience of an opera was that they should leave their heads at home, and employ their ears, so the audience of Congreve should be recommended to close their hearts and keep their heads as clear as possible.

The length of time that elapsed between the production of *Love for Love* on Saturday and its previous performance might justify us in giving an account of the plot. This, however, we shall not do for two reasons:— first, because the plot is the worst thing in the piece, and a description would give no notion of it whatever; and secondly, because if any one of our gentleman readers has not read the piece, the sooner he sets about it the better; as the Englishman who has not read *Love for Love* can scarcely know of what his own language is capable. We will merely say that in adapting comedy to modern delicacy the author of the version of Congreve produced on Saturday has shown himself a most rigid friend to propriety; so rigid, that if the Puritans of Cromwell's time had tolerated a drama at all, we believe this gentleman could have modified Ben Jonson's *Bartholomew Fair* so as to suit even the Barebones Parliament. The great alterations were the omission of Scandal's intrigue with Mrs. Foresight, of Angelica's coarse dialogue with her uncle in the second act, and a softening to the catastrophe of Miss Prue's love-scene with Tattle. In these alterations we heartily coincide with the adapter, whom we congratulate for having so well succeeded in turning a mass of licentiousness into a very proper sort of piece; but there are certain minor alterations of which we cannot approve. The same remarks which we made on the recent production of the *Tempest* at Covent-garden will apply here. Where the adapter consults the delicacy of his age he deserves commendation, but where he consults the merely *genteel* he is to blame. Hence such substitutions as that of 'gentlemen' for 'fellows', and indeed of a softer expression for one more nervous and characteristic, where no indecency is conveyed, is rather administering to a poor fastidiousness than to the good taste of an audience.

This admirable comedy was as successful as it deserved to be, though we must say that the audience showed a greater relish for the 'fun' that was introduced than for many of the most brilliant repartees. The smartest sarcasms in the mouths of Jeremy and Scandal missed fire, while the quarrel between the sisters Frail and Foresight, and the feigned madness of Valentine, produced roars of laughter. *Palmam qui* (or rather *quae*) *meruit, ferat,* and as far as the performers are concerned, it is just to state that the ladies had the best of it. Mrs. Nisbett seemed to be in the highest state of bliss while acting Mrs. Frail. A sense of enjoyment sparkled in her eye, while a repartee left her lips; nothing could have been more lively, more full of spirit, more thoroughly conceived than this character. The delight with which she gave the home-thrust to her sister, by asking her where she found the bodkin, was inimitable. Less striking, but scarcely less clever, was the Mrs. Foresight of Mrs. Stirling. If Mrs. Nisbett floated proudly along a sea of mirth, the more prudish mischief of Mrs. Foresight was completely represented in the subdued manner, the arch mouth, and the watchful eye of Mrs. Stirling. The Angelica of Miss H. Faucit was lady-like and delicate, and the actress had the merit of giving an interest to the unfeeling damsel, which we never feel on reading Congreve's play. Then, the Miss Prue of Mrs. Keeley was the drollest little vixen imaginable. The first bound on the stage was a burst of childish joy, and her subsequent quarrels the sublime of pettishness, which heightened into rage as she roared and screamed at her nurse for dragging her off the stage. Mrs. Keeley never appears a giantess, but she must by some magic or other have taken a couple of feet off her stature to become so diminutive as she looked in Miss Prue. Of the gentlemen we shall only mention Anderson, who played Valentine with great spirit, and by his tricks in the mad scene kept up the most violent laughter; and Keeley, who, though he did not realize the 'great sea-calf' in acting Ben, looked exceedingly comical in the old-fashioned sailor's dress, and displayed an easy *nonchalance* which was very amusing.

Amid loud applause Anderson announced *Love for Love* for repetition. Were all 'revivals' like this, there would be little cause of complaint; and we only hope that when we have another, whether it be at Drury-lane, Covent-garden, or the Haymarket, we shall find the manager, as on this occasion, dip deep into the collection of English dramas, instead of taking up the trumpery which a Colman or a Murphy may have left on the surface.

(b)

HAYMARKET THEATRE

There is a sort of rivalry among managers which is highly commendable, and if more prevalent might operate for the general good of the drama: this is the attempt, after the production of a piece excellent in its kind, to produce another that in the same kind is excellent also. The emulation works well for the amusement of the public, as its result will probably be the representation of a number of good pieces. All such rivalry as is shown by the production of the very same pieces with an inferior company as that performed or announced by another establishment, is pitiful in the last degree, as the public have nothing to do with the squabbles of managers, and the spirit of antagonism is more likely to damage both than to injure one alone of the combatants. Of the commendable sort of rivalry we have a specimen in the revival of Congreve's *Way of the World* on Saturday. Mr. Macready having been successful in producing *Love for Love*, Mr. Webster sets up against him not another *Love for Love*, but an equally celebrated comedy, the *Way of the World*. We are not quite sure that the selection is a wise one, but still, as we have said, the spirit is good.

The *Way of the World* is the last of the important dramatic works of Congreve. It has been erroneously called the last of all his works for the stage, and the error has arisen from overlooking two operas called *The Judgment of Paris* and *Semele*, which are published, indeed, in his works, and are scarcely ever thought of. The author had begun his career by the *Old Bachelor*, the success of which was most exhilarating, and he closed it (setting aside the two operas) with the *Way of the World*, which was the least successful of all his productions, and the indifferent reception of which caused him to retire disgusted with the stage, although it is now regarded as the most finished of his works. The old story goes, that on the first night of the *Way of the World* the author, at its conclusion, rushed upon the stage, and said to the audience, 'Ladies and gentlemen, you have d—d my comedy, but I can tell you, it will live when you are all dead and d—d!' This legend, we believe, is now generally thought apocryphal.

There is an immense difference between *Love for Love* and the *Way of the World*, the former a perpetual torrent of dashing repartee,—a representation of an artificial state of things; but nevertheless coarse and strong. The profligates of *Love for Love* are not ill-natured profligates; they rap out their good things with a thundering voice, and slap you on the back while they crack a joke. Male and female characters are altogether a roaring lot: without principle or chastity they kick the world before them like a foot-ball; and if they hit their neighbours on the shins, to be sure they are rather glad of it, but there was no very deep design in the mischief. Quite another set are the rogues and—ladies, whose predicate we suppress, who edify us by their very subtle contrivances and their very admirable dialogue in the *Way of the World*—the most artificial of artificial comedies. The men are quiet, smooth-spoken, well-behaved scoundrels, who say their good things cautiously, who glide about noiselessly in their laced coats and dress swords, and who having studied 'the way of the world', as they call it, are calmly resolved to make a practical use of their knowledge. Clear-headed villains are they, who having laid down sundry aphorisms of life hatch plots worthy of an Iago, and bide their time to carry them into effect. 'All is diamond cut diamond.' Certain it is, that your neighbour will make a thrust at you, if you are not sharp enough to anticipate the event by a thrust at him. We shall not trouble our readers with the full account of a plot, which is exceedingly intricate, and ought to be well known. Mirabell is a gay man of the town, who has married his friend Fainall to his (Mirabell's) mistress, and Fainall, also a profligate, would marry Mirabell to his own mistress, Marwood. Then there is an old Lady Wishfort, dying for a husband, mother to Mrs. Fainall, and aunt to Millamant, the lady with whom Mirabell is in love. This old lady is a mark for the plots both of Mirabell and Fainall, the latter wanting to make his own wife's dishonour a pretext for extortion from her family, while the former, by tricking the venerable dame into a sham marriage with a footman, would make the hand of Millamant the condition of releasing her from such a disadvantageous match. Mirabell at the end turns out to be the more clever scoundrel of the two, for he produces an ante-nuptial settlement, by which he is sole trustee of Mrs. Fainall's fortune, and thus destroys the power of Fainall, who was not aware of the existence of such a deed. The hand of Millamant, which he failed to obtain by the other device, is his reward. The underplot is formed of a country 'squire just come up to town, his brother, a small wit, something like Tattle, and who says really good things, and a character called Petulant, an illiterate man, who is half fop, half bully and serves as a butt to the witling.

There can, of course, be no interest, commonly so called, in the intrigues and dark designs of a set of men and women, who, with the single exception of Millamant, of whom anon, have not a single virtue. Yet is the *Way of the World* one of the greatest comedies that ever was written. A calm quiet knowledge of a state of society in which heart has no place, in which unclouded intellect reigns alone, is fully displayed in this wonderful production. That constant fire of epigrams which is kept up in *Love for Love* is not to be found here; indeed, by making Witwould, the utterer of epigrams, and those often good, a ridiculous character, by holding up to ridicule the construction of a repartee, it would almost seem as if Congreve had wished to discharge himself once for all of that kind of writing which is so great in *Love for Love*. Throughout the whole of the *Way of the World* the springs of a sophisticated life are inspected with the utmost acuteness; little truthful pictures find their way into it, which we may vainly seek for elsewhere; and in one dialogue, the celebrated treaty of marriage between Mirabell and Millamant, all the vices and foibles of the fair sex are condensed into a few speeches with wonderful fulness. Then, while we call the *Way of the World* the most artificial of comedies, we ought to define our meaning. *Love for Love* is artificial, because it is a thing of imagination. The characters are a set of impossible wits, who start full armed from the brain of their author, but he enjoys the joke, and halloos them on to the sport; so that they have a kind of spurious reality, from the manifest heartiness of their creator. On the other hand, the *Way of the World* gives a picture which is more true to life, but it is more artificial because the life represented is completely artificial, and the author has tamed himself down to the cool observer. The plot is improbable, but the characters are such as might have displayed themselves on the surface of society at the close of the 17th century. In the single speech, 'last night was one of the ladies' cabal nights; they have them three times a week, and meet by turns at one another's apartments, where they come together like the coroner's inquest, to sit upon the murdered reputations of the week'—in this single speech what a grasp of society is displayed. Lady Wishfort's enraged description of Foible is a masterly painting in miniature:—'I took her from washing of old gauze and weaving of dead hair, with a bleak blue nose over a chafing-dish of starved embers, and dining behind a traverse rag in a shop no bigger than a bird-cage.' These are two instances out of many of the accuracy displayed in the *Way of the World*.

Amid the herd of profligates of both sexes, one really charming creature springs up, from whom the predicate of heartlessness must be removed. This is Millamant, the reigning beauty; a spoiled child of the age, full of vanity and caprice, yet still uncorrupted, and without a particle of wickedness in her composition. To this one character would we not apply what we have said respecting the mere artificial tone of the *Way of the World.* Shining as she does in an artificial atmosphere, she is a beautiful reality, thoroughly organised. 'I love to give pain', says she, with all the petulance of a little tyrant; but there is no actual malice about her; she only feels a pleasure in contemplating her own power. 'When one parts with one's cruelty, one parts with one's power; and when one has parted with that, I fancy one's old and ugly.' The belief in the nothingness of her lovers is the prettiest vanity in the world:—'One makes lovers as fast as one pleases, and they die as soon as one pleases; and then, if one pleases, one makes more.' The rules she lays down for Mirabell's conduct, when a married man, the contemptuous love she has for poets, whose verses make such excellent curl-paper, all belong to the charming little despot's enurement to unlimited dominion; but the depth of Millamant speaks out when she says, 'If Mirabell should not love me, I am a lost thing, for I find I love him dearly.'

The comedy, as produced on Saturday, was adapted with, generally, a pretty strict adherence to the original, but the chief alterations that were made seemed to us most needless. In the first place, Mrs. Marwood, Fainall's mistress, was converted into a dull and heavy gentleman, who was assigned to Mr. Stuart, and the speeches intended for an indignant woman were made to croak harshly from the throat of a sort of heavy 'Snake'. Poor Mr. Stuart is really much to be pitied at finding such a dull personage thrust into Congreve's comedy for his special annoyance. The other alteration was made to preserve Mrs. Fainall's reputation, and render her merely the object of a wrongful persecution on the part of her husband. This change was no more felicitous than the other. Mrs. Fainall's intrigue does not introduce an offensive situation, like that of Mrs. Foresight in *Love for Love*. No one cares sixpence about her reputation; and we are convinced she must have appeared to all who were unacquainted with the original a singularly unmeaning personage. The comedy, on the whole, moved heavily. It has not the same material element for success as *Love for Love*, in which there is an amount of 'fun' that is an invaluable ingredient towards the acquisition of popularity. Of situations, in the accepted sense of the word, there is not one in the *Way of the World*, but the play depends on its dialogue and character, to give which with full force is above the capacity of the ladies and gentlemen who played it on Saturday, with the exception of Mrs. Glover and Farren. We should almost be inclined to except Madame Vestris, for there was something very pretty and amiable in her Millamant, but that is a character we cannot help measuring by a very high standard. Mrs. Glover was admirable. The opening of the third act, with her at her toilette, was the first appearance in the piece of any thing like full, vigorous impersonation. The audience, who, with the exception of a laugh or two at a few oddities of Mrs. F. Matthews, as the maid Mincing, had listlessly heard the beautiful dialogue of the first two acts, were shaken out of their lethargy by old Lady Wishfort. The severe scolding at her maid, her lusty demands for paint and cherry-brandy, produced quite a revolution in the aspect of affairs. Mrs. Glover was like a substantial body walking into a world of shadows. Farren, too, though a less perfect representation of the country squire, as Sir Wilful Witwould was another substantiality; there was force in his laugh and his drunkenness, something that was palpable to the audience. That many understood the plot, which is, even to the reader, a very intricate one, we do not believe; but are quite convinced that a great many perceived that something very direful was going on, without knowing what that was. *Love for Love* has an obscure plot, but still it will amuse, if we consider the scenes as isolated and leave plot out of our thoughts; whereas the *Way of the World* has much that, without a clear perception of the story, must be completely unintelligible and tedious. Hence we shall be justified in concluding, that the success of Saturday was almost entirely owing to Mrs. Glover and Farren, and to the dance at the end, which brought down the curtain with applause. Of the Mirabell of Holl, the Witwould of C. Mathews, the Petulant of Buckstone, the Fainall of Vining, we can only say that they were merely sketchy, though Mr. Mathews had, at least the merit of understanding the witling Witwould.

NOTE

1 The reviewer is remembering the last paragraph but one of ch 3 of *Nicholas Nickleby* (1839).

92. William Makepeace Thackeray in *The English Humourists of the Eighteenth Century*

1851

From *The English Humourists of the Eighteenth Century* (London: 1853), pp. 65–78.

The following extract is from 'Congreve and Addison', the second of the series of lectures which Thackeray first delivered between May and early July 1851. Such was their success that Thackeray took the course on a tour culminating in a visit to America in 1852. The lectures were published in 1853; the revised edition of the same year introduced only some slight changes. The footnotes were written for the most part by James Hannay (here omitted).

There is life and death going on in every thing: truth and lies always at battle. Pleasure is always warring against self-restraint. Doubt is always crying Psha, and sneering. A man in life, a humourist in writing about life, sways over to one principle or the other, and laughs with the reverence for right and the love of truth in his heart, or laughs at these from the other side. Didn't I tell you that dancing was a serious business to Harlequin? I have read two or three of Congreve's plays over before speaking of him; and my feelings were rather like those, which I daresay most of us here have had, at Pompeii, looking at Sallust's house and the relics of an orgy, a dried wine-jar or two, a charred supper-table, the breast of a dancing girl pressed against the ashes, the laughing skull of a jester, a perfect stillness round about, as the Cicerone twangs his moral, and the blue sky shines calmly over the ruin. The Congreve muse is dead, and her song choked in Time's ashes. We gaze at the skeleton, and wonder at the life which once revelled in its mad veins. We take the skull up, and muse over the frolic and daring, the wit, scorn, passion, hope, desire, with which that empty bowl once fermented. We think of the glances that allured, the tears that melted, of the bright eyes that shone in those vacant sockets; and of lips whispering love, and cheeks dimpling with smiles, that once covered yon ghastly yellow framework. They used to call those teeth pearls once. See! there's the cup she drank from, the gold-chain she wore on her neck, the vase which held the rouge for her cheeks, her looking-glass, and the harp she used to dance to. Instead of a feast we find a gravestone, and in place of a mistress, a few bones!

Reading in these plays now, is like shutting your ears and looking at people dancing. What does it mean? the measures, the grimaces, the bowing, shuffling and retreating, the cavalier seul advancing upon those ladies—those ladies and men twirling round at the end in a mad galop, after which everybody bows and the quaint rite is celebrated. Without the music we can't understand that comic dance of the last century—its strange gravity and gaiety, its decorum or its indecorum. It has a jargon of its own quite unlike life; a sort of moral of its own quite unlike life too. I'm afraid it's a Heathen mystery, symbolising a Pagan doctrine; protesting, as the Pompeians very likely were, assembled at their theatre and laughing at their games—as Sallust and his friends, and their mistresses protested—crowned with flowers, with cups in their hands, against the new, hard, ascetic pleasure-hating doctrine, whose gaunt disciples, lately passed over from the Asian shores of the Mediterranean were for breaking the fair images of Venus, and flinging the altars of Bacchus down.

I fancy poor Congreve's theatre is a temple of Pagan delights, and mysteries not permitted except among heathens. I fear the theatre carries down that ancient tradition and worship, as masons have carried their secret signs and rites from temple to temple. When the libertine hero carries off the beauty in the play, and the dotard is laughed to scorn for having the young wife: in the ballad, when the poet bid his mistress to gather roses while she may, and warns her that old Time is still a-flying: in the ballet, when honest Corydon courts Phillis under the treillage of the pasteboard cottage, and leers at her over the head of grandpapa in red stockings, who is opportunely asleep; and when seduced by the invitations of the rosy youth she comes forward to the footlights, and they perform on each other's tiptoes that *pas* which you all know and which is only interrupted by old grandpapa awaking from his doze at the pasteboard chalet (whither he returns to take another nap in case the young people get an encore): when Harlequin, splendid in youth, strength and agility, arrayed in gold and a thousand colours, springs over the heads of countless perils, leaps down the throat of bewildered giants, and, dauntless and splendid, dances danger down: when Mr. Punch, that godless old rebel, breaks every law and laughs at it with odious triumph, outwits his lawyer, bullies the beadle, knocks his wife about the head, and hangs the hangman,—don't you see in the comedy, in the song, in the dance, in the ragged little Punch's puppet-show,— the Pagan protest? Doesn't it seem as if Life puts in its plea and sings its comment? Look how the lovers walk and hold each other's hands and whisper! Sings the chorus—'There is nothing like love, there is nothing like youth, there is nothing like beauty of your spring time. Look! how old age tries to meddle with merry sport! Beat him with his own crutch, the wrinkled old dotard! There is nothing like youth, there is nothing like beauty, there is nothing like strength. Strength and valour win beauty and youth. Be brave and conquer. Be young and happy. Enjoy, enjoy, enjoy! Would you know the *Segreto per esser felice?* Here it is, in a smiling mistress and a cup of Falernian.' As the boy tosses the cup and sings his song. Hark! what is that chaunt coming nearer and nearer? What is that dirge which *will* disturb us? The lights of the festival burn dim—the cheeks turn pale—the voice quavers—and the cup drops on the floor. Who's there? Death and Fate are at the gate, and they *will* come in.

Congreve's comic feast flares with lights, and round the table, emptying their flaming bowls of drink, and exchanging the wildest jests and ribaldry, sit men and women, waited on by rascally valets and attendants as dissolute as their mistresses—perhaps the very worst company in the world. There doesn't seem to be a pretence of morals. At the head of the table sits Mirabel or Belmour (dressed in the French fashion and waited on by English imitators of Scapin and Frontin). Their calling is to be irresistible, and to conquer everywhere. Like the heroes of the chivalry story, whose long-winded loves and combats they were sending out of fashion; they are always splendid and triumphant—overcome all dangers, vanquish all enemies, and win the beauty at the end. Fathers, husbands, usurers are the foes these champions contend with. They are merciless in old age, invariably, and an old man plays the part in the dramas, which the wicked enchanter or the great blundering

389

giant performs in the chivalry tales, who threatens and grumbles and resists—a huge stupid obstacle always overcome by the knight. It is an old man with a money-box: Sir Belmour his son or nephew spends his money and laughs at him. It is an old man with a young wife whom he locks up: Sir Mirabel robs him of his wife, trips up his gouty old heels and leaves the old hunx—the old fool what business has he to hoard his money, or to lock up blushing eighteen? Money is for youth, love is for youth, away with the old people. When Millamant is sixty, having of course divorced the first Lady Millamant, and married his friend Doricourt's grand-daughter out of the nursery—it will be his turn; and young Belmour will make a fool of him. All this pretty morality you have in the comedies of William Congreve, Esq. They are full of wit. Such manners as he observes, he observes with great humour; but ah! it's a weary feast that banquet of wit where no love is. It palls very soon; sad indigestions follow it and lonely blank headaches in the morning.

I can't pretend to quote scenes from the splendid Congreve's plays—which are undeniably bright, witty, and daring,—any more than I could ask you to hear the dialogue of a witty bargeman and a brilliant fish-woman exchanging compliments at Billingsgate; but some of his verses,—they were amongst the most famous lyrics of the time, and pronounced equal to Horace by his contemporaries,—may give an idea of his power, of his grace, of his daring manner, his magnificence in compliment, and his polished sarcasm. He writes as if he was so accustomed to conquer, that he has a poor opinion of his victims. Nothing's new except their faces, says he, 'Every woman is the same.' He says this in his first comedy, which he wrote languidly in illness, when he was an 'excellent young man.' Richelieu at eighty could have hardly said a more excellent thing.

When he advances to make one of his conquests it is with a splendid gallantry, in full uniform and with the fiddles playing, like Grammont's French dandies attacking the breach of Lerida.

'Cease, cease to ask her name,' he writes of a young lady at the Wells at Tunbridge, whom he salutes with a magnificent compliment—

> Cease, cease to ask her name,
> The crowned Muse's noblest theme,
> Whose glory by immortal fame
>   Shall only sounded be.

But if you long to know,
Then look round yonder dazzling row,
Who most does like an angel show
    You may be sure 'tis she.

Here are lines about another beauty, who perhaps was not so
well pleased at the poet's manner of celebrating her—

When Lesbia first I saw, so heavenly fair,
With eyes so bright and with that awful air,
I thought my heart would durst so high aspire
As bold as his who snatched celestial fire.
But soon as e'er the beauteous idiot spoke,
Forth from her coral lips such folly broke;
Like balm the trickling nonsense heal'd my wound,
And what her eyes enthralled, her tongue unbound.

Amoret is a cleverer woman than the lovely Lesbia, but the poet
does not seem to respect one much more than the other; and
describes both with exquisite satirical humour—

Fair Amoret is gone astray,
    Pursue and seek her every lover;
I'll tell the signs by which you may
    The wandering shepherdess discover.

Coquet and coy at once her air,
    Both studied, though both seem neglected;
Careless she is with artful care,
    Affecting to be unaffected.

With skill her eyes dart every glance,
    Yet change so soon you'd ne'er suspect them;
For she'd persuade they wound by chance,
    Though certain aim and art direct them.

She likes herself, yet others hates
    For that which in herself she prizes;
And, while she laughs at them, forgets
    She is the thing which she despises.

What could Amoret have done to bring down such shafts of
ridicule upon her? Could she have resisted the irresistible Mr.
Congreve? Could anybody? Could Sabina, when she woke and
heard such a bard singing under her window. See, he writes—

See! see, she wakes—Sabina wakes!
   And now the sun begins to rise:
Less glorious is the morn, that breaks
   From his bright beams, than her fair eyes.
With light united day they give;
   But different fates ere night fulfil:
How many by his warmth will live!
   How many will her coldness kill!

Are you melted? Don't you think him a divine man? If not touched by the brilliant Sabina, hear the devout Selinda:—

Pious Selinda goes to prayers,
   If I but ask her favour;
And yet the silly fool's in tears,
   If she believes I'll leave her.
Would I were free from this restraint,
   Or else had hopes to win her:
Would she could make of me a saint,
   Or I of her a sinner!

What a conquering air there is about these! What an irresistible Mr. Congreve it is! Sinner! of course he will be a sinner, the delightful rascal! Win her; of course he will win her, the victorious rogue! He knows he will: he must—with such a grace, with such a fashion, with such a splendid embroidered suit—you see him with red-heeled shoes deliciously turned out, passing a fair jewelled hand through his dishevelled periwig and delivering a killing ogle along with his scented billet. And Sabina? What a comparison that is between the nymph and the sun! The sun gives Sabina the *pas*, and does not venture to rise before her ladyship: the morn's *bright beams* are less glorious than her *fair eyes*: but before night everybody will be frozen by her glances: everybody but one lucky rogue who shall be nameless: Louis Quatorze in all his glory is hardly more splendid than our Phœbus Apollo of the Mall and Spring Garden.

When Voltaire came to visit the great Congreve, the latter rather affected to despise his literary reputation, and in this perhaps the great Congreve was not far wrong. A touch of Steele's tenderness is worth all his finery—a flash of Swift's lightning—a beam of Addison's pure sunshine, and his tawdry play-house taper is invisible. But the ladies loved him and he was undoubtedly a pretty fellow.

93. Charles Cowden Clarke in 'Congreve and Wycherley'

1871

From *The Gentleman's Magazine* (1871), 229: 835–45.

Charles Cowden Clarke (1787–1877) was a childhood friend of Keats, a pupil at the school kept by Clarke's father. Their friendship is commemorated by Keats's 'Epistle to Charles Cowden Clarke'. As a young man Clarke was associated with Leigh Hunt, who introduced him to Hazlitt and Shelley. He had a successful career as a publisher, literary journalist, and especially as a lecturer. His essay on Congreve and Wycherley belongs to a series 'On the Comic Writers of England' which he contributed to *The Gentleman's Magazine* towards the end of his life.

With all this poor, hollow insincerity in the practical man, it were too much to expect any great promulgation of an exalted feeling from Congreve, or of faith in goodness, from the same being, when describing his species. Your thoroughly selfish men always entertain—and naturally—a low opinion of mankind. In the pages of Congreve therefore we meet with the very worst specimens of the artificial world of rank in society; it may be (and collateral history and biography sanction the idea) that his scenes and portraitures are faithful contemporary representations; if so, indeed 'The former times were not better than these;' neither is it to be believed for one moment that they were: but indeed, the intrigue—gross, coarse palpable intrigue—mistrust, scandal, treachery, scoundrelism of every description, so saturate his plots, that one becomes nauseated with the monotony of love swindling; and the only thing which keeps the mind buoyant upon the stream of his descriptions, is the uncommon force and brilliancy of the author's wit; and this really is out-pouring and unintermittent. But even this exquisitely pungent quality becomes in itself monotonous: all his gallants talk alike; all are equally witty; all are brethren with different names; the mere wittols, and such as the sea calf, Ben, are the exceptions. Even his very heroes and heroines appear to entertain the notion of matrimony only that they may be secure and free agents afterwards; and they appear to make no secret of their design; which, after all, is better than the *cant* of chastity; and that very loathsome sin—the hypocrisy of virtue.

For want of another word, which has been made too much of a stalking horse in our day, meaning the term 'morality;' I must say that, setting aside the single quality of his diamond-like wit, Congreve is a much less heart-to-heart writer, to my feelings, and far less moral than Wycherley, and this arises purely from his want of faith in single-mindedness and truth. This was the dead weight that kept Congreve's genius down. I bear to mind no one exalted character in all his comedies, meaning, a character to swear by and to set up as a beacon on the promontory of society, that men's eyes may gaze upon it, as on the brazen serpent, and be made whole of their moral leprosy. Are there then, no such characters in the world? Nay, does not every one of us, in our own little circles, know such a one, and did Mr. Congreve know none such? Or did he think that the only *true* thing in human nature was *un*truth? Why I prefer Wycherley to Congreve is, that although his scenes are protracted and diffuse, yet that they have a natural and conversational air about them; as a primitive-minded lady critic once observed, 'They are like things as might happen:' moreover, with all Wycherley's rough sketching, and his yet coarser verbiage, there is still a redemption about most of his characters; they are worth the trouble of being made better. Wycherley had by nature a generous and an honourable heart, and his real nature shone through his writings. As a wit, or as a writer (with regard to style), he is not to be compared with Congreve; but I like the native man better, and both men appear developed in their appreciation of human nature.

But let us turn to the comedies of Congreve, and first to his first production, *The Old Bachelor*. This was written, it should seem, when the author was under age, and a very extraordinary work of precocity it is. He started at once into a full knowledge of the world of artificial life: at eighteen his appreciation of his mother's sex was precisely that of a worn-out *roué* of fifty. How different from the glorious Jean Paul Richter's appreciation of women, who says: 'Oh worse than all is the man, for whom his own mother has not made all other mothers venerable!'

The principal character in the play, the Old Bachelor, is a disgusting wretch, and who, in the conclusion of the piece, is righteously hoaxed and tricked, and by men worthy to play such a game. He entertains the lowest opinion of women, and yet he would marry; he grants himself every licence, and yet is outrageous when he fancies his mistress assumes the same prerogative. He is a perfect specimen of what has been wittily styled, 'the *un*fair sex.'

As might be expected in the composition of one so young—and in a first attempt, too—we meet with one or two reflexes of anterior characters in other authors. Captain Bluff, for instance, is a close imitation, even to his being thrashed, of Ben Jonson's Bobadil. And the sparring between Belmour and Belinda reminds one of Benedict and Beatrice; but Belinda is more cat-like, and, moreover, she has neither the heart nor the cordial wit of Beatrice. But, oh! heaven, to talk of Shakespeare's women in the same breath with Congreve's! Here is a specimen of a cooled lover receiving a letter from his mistress. Silvia asks of her servant, Lucy, 'Tell me, for I would know, though to the anguish of my soul, how did he refuse? Tell me, how did he receive my letter—in anger or in scorn.'

Lucy. Neither; but what was ten times worse—with senseless indifference. By this light I could have spit in his face. Received it! why, he received it as I would one of your *lovers* that should come empty-handed; as a court lord does his mercer's bill; or a begging dedication: he received it as if it had been a letter from his wife.

[III, i, 20–7]

And here are the symptoms of love in one of Mr. Congreve's gallants, and which is an imitation (with his version of the passion) of Rosalind's, in *As You Like It*. Silvia says to Heartwell, the old bachelor, whom she is befooling—having been cast off by her former lover—'Indeed if I were well assured you loved; but how can I be well assured?'

Heart. Take the symptoms and ask all the tyrants of thy sex if their fools are not known by this party-coloured livery. I am melancholic when thou art absent; look like an ass when thou art present; wake for thee when I should sleep; and even dream of thee when I am awake; sigh much, drink little, eat less, court solitude, am grown very entertaining to myself, and, as I am informed, very troublesome to everybody else. If this be not love,

395

it is madness; and then it is pardonable. Nay, yet a more certain sign than all this—*I give thee my money*.

[III, x, 66–77]

A hopeful specimen of world-knowledge this, in a writer under twenty years of age! Here is a specimen of his wit in repartee. Belmour introduces himself to Letitia, wife to Fondlewife, in a clerical disguise, she having expected a visitor *in that habit*. Upon her starting at his appearance, she says, 'I may well be surprised at your person and impudence, they are both new to me. You are not what your first appearance promised. The *piety* of your habit was welcome, but not the hypocrisy.' He, knowing her mind, and whom she expected, answers, 'Rather the *hypocrisy* was welcome, but not the *hypocrite*.' This is a fair sample of the pointed character of Congreve's dialogue.

The *Double Dealer* is a far finer production than the *Old Bachelor*—more intricate and surprising in plot, more various in character, and displaying more relief in passion. Maskwell, the double dealer, is an unmitigated, unadulterated villain. He is even gratuitous in his wickedness. He is worse than Iago—which is saying much—for he has not even Iago's motive for revenge; and Shakespeare knew that every action which is a sane one must spring from a motive. Iago, therefore—whether truly to his own mind, or for an excuse—betrays both Othello and Cassio, because the latter was promoted over him, and because he suspected both had been too intimate with his wife, Emilia. But Maskwell is false to everybody, and most false to those from whom he had received the greatest kindness, having no apparent motive for such concentrated treachery. The whole paraphernalia of his schemes, manœuvres, excuses, hair-breadth escapes from detection, are detailed with uncommon skill; but it is not a natural plot—it is a melodrama of treachery. One wholesome moral is to be deduced from the play, and that is, that your plotters—your 'double-dealers'—give themselves ten times the labour of your 'plain-dealers;' and it is but justice that such should be the result.

Sheridan evidently took his screen-scene in the *School for Scandal* from the famous one in this play, and both scenes blow up the two hypocrites, Surface and Maskwell. Sheridan's, however, is by far the more plausible contrivance. Sir Peter Teazle, as a man of the world, might easily suppose that the moral Joseph would commit his peccadillos with the little French milliner, and he would think none the worse of him for it; but a wary villain like Maskwell never would have been betrayed into such a conversation as that which passes between him and Lady Touchwood, with a screen in the room, and neither of them to have taken the precaution to see if any eaves-dropper were behind it.

The most amusing characters in the play are, Sir Paul Plyant, a poor hen-pecked fool of a husband; Lord Froth, a solemn coxcomb; and Brisk, a pert coxcomb. The fourth scene in the play, where the whole party at Lord Touchwood's are after dinner to join the ladies, is a ludicrous picture of the flabby folly of high life in that day.

[Quotes I, iv entire.]

Love for Love was Congreve's third comedy; the heroine of which, Angelica, is his most estimable, if not his most showy female in point of talent, and certainly his most sensible one in point of conduct. In tact and matrimonial diplomacy she is a match for her lover, Valentine, who is a wanton spendthrift; and she will have nothing to say to him till she have substantial proofs of his reformation. He feigns madness to soften her obdurate heart; but she perceives his manœuvre, and listens to an offer of marriage from his father, who has determined to disinherit his sons. In the age of Congreve it should seem that the matrimonial 'black-leg' could scarcely have formed a distinctive class in the community, whether the character were male or female; for any manœuvre, however rascally, was lawful, and even laudable, that hooked a partner for life; and truly, to speak of such people, it was of little consequence how they became linked, or whether they pulled well or ill together afterwards. Their tricks are infinitely amusing, and we laugh at them in much the same spirit as at the impudent delinquencies of a pantomime clown. And as to the ribaldry of the dialogue—well, let us beware of the infection as we walk along our streets; the one scene is quite as likely to contaminate us as the other, if the mental constitution be not healthy and in good training. Who, for instance, is not simply entertained, and who but a born fool, after reading the scenes between Mrs. Frail and Mrs. Foresight, would take to a love of intrigue? It has been said that Schiller's play of *The Robbers* converted a whole set of university students into highwaymen—and an amazing herd of donkeys must those young gentlemen have been; for, without giving ourselves half their trouble, and with quite as much romance for adventure, we used at school to play at 'Watchmen and Thieves;' and yet I do not remember that in the staid realities of schoolboy life any one of our little highwaymen broke open a schoolfellow's box. Lying is said to be the root of all evil. If carefully investigated, I suspect that the tap-root—the origin, support and sustenance of *all* immoral, and therefore unjust, dealing, may be traced to selfishness, and no deeper. The principle and habit of respecting the feelings of others is *un*selfishness, and it is but a paraphrase of the command to do unto all men as you would all men should do unto you.

The character of old Foresight, the astrologer, is a favourite one in this play of *Love for Love*. That finest of all farce-actors, Munden, made it so some sixty odd years since; but one of the most entertaining, and the most natural, is Ben, the sailor, brother to Valentine. The blundering hard-headedness and yet instinctive truth in this fellow are delightful. How finely his straightforward conduct comes in relief against the manœuvring and insincerity of all the others. His father, Sir Samson Legend, designs him for Miss Prue; but he, having a spice of the paternal obstinacy, quarrels with her at their first interview. Mrs. Frail has hooked him. But Mrs. Frail finds afterwards that Ben is likely to be disinherited; she therefore determines to cut cables and let him drift. The scene between them is (so far as Ben is concerned) a good representation of straightforward 'end-on' honesty:—

[Quotes IV, xiii, 1–104.]

Of the last, and crowning comedy of Congreve's, *The Way of the World*, I do not think it too much to say in its praise, that it comprises the most quintessentialised combination of qualities requisite to compound an artificially legitimate comedy to be found in the whole range of our dramatic literature. I do not say, the comedy of *primitive* and *natural* life; but the comedy of the furbelows and flounces; of powder and essences; of paint and enamelling; of high-heels, hoops, and all hideous artificialities, concealments, intrigues, plots, and subterfuges. In reading the play, one's faculties are retained in a perpetual suspension of pleasure at the unabating and highly sustained succession of flights of wit, gaily tinctured imageries, flashing repartees, and skilfully contrasted characters on the scene. What can be more perfect in portraiture than Millamant—a genuine specimen of a lady of accomplishment and fashion; giddy, wayward, rallying and languishing; encouraging or repelling, according to the humour of the moment!—hovering in an atmosphere of duplicity, and on the brink of being singed,—like a moth round a candle; and yet, is saved by her excellent understanding, and naturally good heart. Nothing sure can be finer than her professed indifference to, and contempt of our sex prostrating themselves at the shrine of beauty: her having her curls pinned up in the poetical letters offered by her worshippers upon the altar of her loveliness.

[Quotes II, iv, 53–62.]

Then again, her retort to the rallying of her lover, Mirabel.

O, the vanity of these men!—Fainall, d'ye hear him? If *they* did not commend us, we were not handsome! Now, you must know, they could not commend one, if one *was not* handsome. Beauty the lover's gift! Lord, what is a lover that *it* can give? Why, one makes lovers as fast as one pleases; and they live as long as one pleases; and they die as soon as one pleases; and then, if one pleases, one makes more...... One no more owes one's beauty to a lover, then one's wit to an echo. They can but reflect what we look and say; vain empty things if we are silent, or unseen, and want a being.

[ibid., ll. 91–107]

This is the very climax of a spoiled and triumphant beauty; assured of her power, and running riot with it.

The celebrated scene in the 4th Act, where she makes her stipulations with Mirabel before their marriage, is unsurpassable for that pretty wanton wilfulness that a conscious and sweet-tempered beauty may indulge in, and be loved the better afterwards. Her affected regret at the thought of resigning her liberty is enchanting; and the more so because she is not the person either to resign at any time, or to afford a plea for her being disfranchised. When she says: 'Oh, I hate a lover that can dare to think he draws a moment's air, independent on the bounty of his mistress. There is not so impudent a thing in nature as the saucy look of an assured man, confident of success. The pedantic arrogance of a very husband has not so pragmatical an air. Ah! I'll never marry, unless I am first made sure of my will and pleasure.'

[Quotes IV, v, 33–61.]

This is but a small portion of a most delightful scene. Mirabel is not so agreeable a character as Millamant. Not less natural, however; but he has misgivings about his prerogative, and is more than tinged with coxcombry. That is a true picture of human nature and lover-resentment in the first scene of the play, where he and Fainall are discoursing of Millamant and her beauteous disdain, and he ends:—

I like her with all her faults; nay, like her *for* her faults. Her follies are so natural, or so artful, that they become her; and those affectations which in another woman would be odious serve but to make her more agreeable. I'll tell thee, Fainall, she once used me with such insolence that, in revenge, I took her to pieces, sifted her, and separated her failings. I studied 'em and got 'em by rote. The catalogue was so large that I was not without hopes one day or other to hate her heartily; to which end I so used myself to think of 'em that, at length, contrary to my design and expectation, they gave me every hour less and less disturbance; till, in a few days, it became habitual to me to remember 'em without being displeased. They are now grown as familiar to me as my own frailties; and, in all probability, in a little time longer, I shall like 'em as well.

[I, iii, 30–47]

The under-characters in the play—Mr. and Mrs. Fainall, Mrs. Marwood, Witwoud, Sir Wilful, &c.—are odious. Foible and Mincing are choice samples of rascally waiting-women, and Lady Wishfort is the farce-character in the piece. The scene in her boudoir, with Peg, the chamber-maid—the one in her fury wherein she is turning Foible out of her service— and that with Sir Wilful, when he is drunk, are all inimitable paintings. Like Mrs. Malaprop, she has a most choice 'derangement of epitaphs,' only that they are the dialect of a woman of society, with a vehement and glib tongue, with as slippery a conscience, and an equally inconsequent understanding.

Out upon't, out upon't! (she says to Sir Wilful, who is drunk.) At years of discretion, and comport yourself at this rantipole rate!
Sir Wilful. No offence, aunt.
Lady Wish. Offence! as I'm a person, I'm ashamed of you. Foh! how you stink of wine! D'ye think my niece will ever endure such a Borachio?—you're an absolute Borachio.

[IV, x, 1–8]

Millamant excuses herself from staying any longer.

Your pardon, madam,—Sir Wilful grows very powerful. Oh, how he smells! I shall be overcome if I stay.

Lady Wish. Smells! he would poison a tallow-chandler and his family. Beastly creature, I know not what to do with him.

[IV, x, 52–xi, 3]

The cause that this admirable collection of wit, raillery, sarcasm, and repartee was condemned on its first representation must have been the result of cabal and personal spite; for it is greatly the most polished of this author's compositions—the most natural in plot, and the least offensive in language and arrangement. The tradition exists, and probably is known to most readers, that the author leaned from the box where he had been witnessing its representation and condemnation, and addressed the audience with, 'Ladies and gentlemen, this play will live when you are all dead and—,' &c.

The stronghold of Congreve's genius was wit in its greatest brilliancy. His characters all talk in the superlative degree of correctness and gusto; but they are little better than machines for conversation. They come upon the scene and deliver themselves handsomely, but they have no movement, and no real sentiment or passion. The Cavalier, dare-devil age of the Restoration—with all its obscenity and coarseness of every kind—bad as that age was, carried with it, nevertheless, some soul of redemption, compared with the utter heartlessness and hoar-frost glitter of the age of William III. There is little doubt that Congreve was, indeed, a faithful and 'brief chronicler' of the spirit, morals, and manners of his contemporaries, a race of whom the Queen, Mary, used to say, despairingly, of their unprincipled recklessness with regard to every social tie, 'Can these dry bones live?'—a society wherein personal infidelity was considered the requisite accomplishment of a gentleman, and open adultery an exceedingly good jest. Throughout the whole of the three dozen dramas of Shakespeare— which people who have never read them call immodest—there is not one sentence so unsound, and not one principle so rotten, as are the foundation and main structure of the four comedies that accurately portray the aristocratic society of the boasted Revolution and 'Glorious Memory' of 1688.

94. George Meredith in 'On the Idea of Comedy, and of the Uses of the Comic Spirit'

1877

From the *New Quarterly Magazine* (1877), 8: 1–40 (12–14).

Meredith's essay on comedy was originally a lecture delivered at the London Institution on 1 February 1877. It was printed in Ford Madox Hueffer's *New Quarterly Magazine* in April of that year, and appeared in book form in 1897.

Congreve's *Way of the World* is an exception to our other comedies, his own among them, by virtue of the remarkable brilliancy of the writing, and the figure of Millamant. The comedy has no idea in it, beyond the stale one that so the world goes; and it concludes with the jaded discovery of a document at a convenient season for the descent of the curtain. A plot was an afterthought with Congreve. By the help of a wooden villain (Maskwell) marked Gallows to the flattest eye, he gets a sort of plot in *The Double Dealer*.* His *Way of the World* might be called *The Conquest of a Town Coquette*; and Millamant is a perfect portrait of a coquette, both in her resistance to Mirabel and the manner of her surrender, and also in her tongue. The wit here is not so salient as in certain passages of *Love for Love*, where Valentine feigns madness, or retorts on his father, or Mrs. Frail rejoices in the harmlessness of wounds to a woman's virtue, if she 'keeps them from air.' In *The Way of the World*, it appears less prepared in the smartness, and is more diffused in the more characteristic style of the speakers. Here, however, as elsewhere, his famous wit is like a bully-fencer, not ashamed to lay traps for its exhibition, transparently petulant for the train between certain ordinary words and the powder-magazine of the improprieties to be fired. Contrast the wit of Congreve with Molière's. That of the first is a Toledo blade, sharp, and wonderfully supple for steel; cast for duelling, restless in the scabbard, being so pretty when out of it. To shine, it must have an adversary. Molière's wit is like a running brook, with innumerable fresh lights on it at every turn of the wood through which its business is to find a way. It does not run in search of obstructions, to be noisy over them; but when dead leaves and viler substances are heaped along the course, its natural song is heightened. Without effort, and with no dazzling flashes of achievement, it is full of healing, the wit of good breeding, the wit of wisdom.

'Genuine humour and true wit,' says Landor,[†] 'require a sound and capacious mind, which is always a grave one. Rabelais and La Fontaine are recorded by their countrymen to have been rêveurs. Few men have been graver than Pascal. Few men have been wittier.'

To apply the citation of so great a brain as Pascal's to our countryman would be unfair. Congreve had a certain soundness of mind; of capacity, in the sense intended by Landor, he had little. Judging him by his wit, he performed some happy thrusts, and taking it for genuine, it is a surface wit, neither rising from a depth nor flowing from a spring.

On voit qu'il se travaille à dire de bons mots.

He drives the poor hack word, 'fool,' as cruelly to the market for wit as any of his competitors. Here is an example, that has been held up for eulogy:—

WITWOUD. He has brought me a letter from the fool my brother, etc., etc.
MIRABEL. A fool, and your brother, Witwoud?
WITWOUD. Ay, ay, my half-brother. My half-brother he is; no nearer, upon my honour.
MIRABEL. Then 'tis possible he may be but half a fool.
[*The Way of the World*, I, vi, 11–21]

Palpably, and by evident preparation. This is a sort of wit one remembers to have heard at school, of a brilliant outsider; perhaps to have been guilty of oneself, a trifle later. It was, no doubt, a blaze of intellectual fireworks to the bumpkin squire, who came to London to go to the theatre and learn manners.

Where Congreve excels all his English rivals is in his literary force, and a succinctness of style peculiar to him. He had correct judgment, a correct ear, and readiness of illustration within a narrow range, in snap-shots of the obvious at the obvious, and copious language. He hits the mean of a fine style and a natural in dialogue. He is at once precise and voluble. If you have ever thought upon style, you will acknowledge it to be a signal accomplishment. In this he is a classic, and is worthy of treading a measure with Molière. *The Way of the World* may be read out currently at a first glance, so sure are the accents of the emphatic meaning to strike the eye, perforce of the crispness and cunning polish of the sentences. You have not to look over them before you confide yourself to him; he will carry you safe. Sheridan imitated, but was far from surpassing him. The flow of boudoir Billingsgate in Lady Wishfort is unmatched for the vigour and pointedness of the tongue. It spins along with a final ring, like the voice of Nature in a fury, and is, indeed, racy eloquence of the elevated fishwife.

Millamant is an admirable, almost a loveable heroine. It is a piece of genius in a writer to make a woman's manner of speech portray her. You feel sensible of her presence in every line of her speaking. The stipulations with her lover in view of marriage, her fine lady's delicacy, and fine lady's easy evasions of indelicacy, coquettish airs, and playing with irresolution, which in a common maid would be bashfulness, until she submits to 'dwindle into a wife,' as she says, form a picture that lives in the frame, and is in harmony with Mirabel's description of her:—'Here she comes, i'faith, full sail, with her fan spread, and her streamers out, and a shoal of fools for tenders.' And, after an interview: 'Think of you! To think of a whirlwind, though 'twere in a whirlwind, were a case of more steady contemplation, a very tranquillity of mind and mansion.' There is a picturesqueness, as of Millamant and no other, in her voice, when she is encouraged to take Mirabel by Mrs. Fainall, who is 'sure she has a mind to him':—

MILLAMANT: Are you? I think I have—and the horrid man looks as if he thought so too, etc., etc.

[IV, vi, 1–12]

One hears the tones, and sees the sketch and colour of the whole scene in reading it.

Célimène is behind Millamant in vividness. An air of bewitching whimsicality hovers over the graces of this Comic heroine, like the lively conversational play of a beautiful mouth.

But in wit she is no rival of Célimène. What she utters adds to her personal witchery, and is not further memorable. She is a flashing portrait, and a type of the ladies who do not think, not of those who do. In representing a class, therefore, it is an inferior class, in the proportion that one of Gainsborough's full-length aristocratic women is below the permanent impressiveness of a fair Venetian head.

NOTES

* Maskwell seems to have been carved on the model of Iago, as by the hand of an enterprising urchin. He apostrophizes his 'invention' repeatedly. 'Thanks, my invention.' He hits on an invention, to say: 'Was it my brain or Providence? no matter which.' It is no matter which, but it was not his brain.

† IMAGINARY CONVERSATIONS: Alfieri and the Jew Salomon.

95. Algernon Charles Swinburne, 'Congreve'

1877

From *Encyclopaedia Britannica*, 9th edition, edited by T. S. Baynes and W. R. Smith, 24 vols (London: 1875–89), VI, pp. 271–2.

Swinburne's essay on Congreve was originally written as an entry in the *Encyclopaedia Britannica*. It was reprinted in his *Miscellanies* (London: 1886), pp. 50–5.

CONGREVE, WILLIAM (1670–1729), the greatest English master of pure comedy, was born, according to the latest and likeliest accounts, in 1670, according to the inscription on his monument, in 1672; and whether in England or in Ireland, at Bardsey near Leeds or at some place unknown beyond St George's Channel, has likewise been matter of doubt and dispute; but we may presumably accept the authority of Lord Macaulay, who decides against Dr Johnson in favour of the later date, and dismisses without notice the tradition of an Irish birthplace. To Ireland, at all events, is due the credit of his education,—as a schoolboy at Kilkenny, as an undergraduate at Dublin. From college he came to London, and was entered as a student of law at the Middle Temple. The first-fruits of his studies appeared under the boyish pseudonym of 'Cleophil,' in the form of a novel whose existence is now remembered only through the unabashed avowal of so austere a moralist as Dr Johnson, that he 'would rather praise it than read it.' In 1693 Congreve's real career began, and early enough by the latest computation, with the brilliant appearance and instant success of his first comedy, *The Old Bachelor*, under the generous auspices of Dryden, then as ever a living and immortal witness to the falsehood of the vulgar charge which taxes the greater among poets with jealousy or envy, the natural badge and brand of the smallest that would claim a place among their kind. The discrowned laureate had never, he said, seen such a first play; and indeed the graceless grace of the dialogue was as yet only to be matched by the last and best work of Etherege, standing as till then it had done alone among the barefaced brutalities of Wycherley and Shadwell. The types of Congreve's first work were the common conventional properties of stage tradition; but the fine and clear-cut style in which these types were reproduced was his own. The gift of one place and the reversion of another were the solid fruits of his splendid success. Next year a better play from the same hand met with worse fortune on the stage, and with yet higher honour from the first living poet of his nation. The noble verses, as faultless in the expression as reckless in the extravagance of their applause, prefixed by Dryden to *The Double Dealer*, must naturally have supported the younger poet, if indeed such support can have been required, against the momentary annoyance of assailants whose passing clamour left uninjured and secure the fame of his second comedy; for the following year witnessed the crowning triumph of his art and life, in the appearance of *Love for Love*. Two years later his ambition rather than his genius adventured on the foreign ground of tragedy, and *The Mourning Bride* began such a long career of good fortune as in earlier or later times would have been closed against a far better work. Next year he attempted, without his usual success, a reply to the attack of Jeremy Collier, the nonjuror, 'on the immorality and profaneness of the English stage,'—an attack for once not discreditable to the assailant, whose honesty and courage were evident enough to approve him incapable alike of the ignominious precaution which might have suppressed his own name, and of the dastardly mendacity which would have stolen the mask of a stranger's. Against this merit must be set the mistake of confounding in one indiscriminate indictment the levities of a writer like Congreve with the brutalities of a writer like Wycherley,—an error which ever since has more or less perverted the judgment of succeeding critics. The general case of comedy was then, however, as untenable by the argument as indefensible by the sarcasm of its most brilliant and comparatively blameless champion. Art itself, more than anything else, had been outraged and degraded by the recent school of the Restoration; and the comic work of Congreve, though different rather in kind than in degree from the bestial and blatant licence of his immediate precursors, was inevitably for a time involved in the sentence passed upon the comic work of men in all ways alike his inferiors. The true and triumphant answer to all possible attacks of honest men or liars, brave men or cowards, was then as ever to be given by the production of work unarraignable alike by fair means or foul, by frank impeachment or furtive imputation. In 1700 Congreve thus replied to Collier with the crowning work of his genius,—the unequalled and unapproached master-piece of English comedy. The one play in our language which may fairly claim a place beside or but just beneath the mightiest work of Molière is *The Way of the World*. On the stage which had recently acclaimed with uncritical applause the author's more questionable appearance in the field of tragedy, this final and flawless evidence of his incomparable powers met with a rejection then and ever since inexplicable on any ground of conjecture. During the twenty-eight years which remained to him, Congreve produced little beyond a volume of fugitive verses, published ten years after the miscarriage of his master-piece. His even course of good fortune under Whig and Tory Governments alike was counterweighed by the physical infirmities of gout and failing sight. He died, January 29, 1729, in consequence of an injury received on a journey to Bath by the upsetting of his carriage; was buried in Westminster Abbey, after lying in state in the Jerusalem Chamber; and bequeathed the bulk of his fortune to the chief friend of his last years, Henrietta, duchess of

Marlborough, daughter of the great duke, rather than to his family, which, according to Johnson, was then in difficulties, or to Mrs Bracegirdle, the actress, with whom he had lived longer on intimate terms than with any other mistress or friend, but who inherited by his will only £200. The one memorable incident of his later life was the visit of Voltaire, whom he astonished and repelled by his rejection of proffered praise and the expression of his wish to be considered merely as any other gentleman of no literary fame. The great master of well-nigh every province in the empire of letters, except the only one in which his host reigned supreme, replied that in that sad case Congreve would not have received his visit.

The fame of our greatest comic dramatist is founded wholly or mainly on but three of his five plays. His first comedy was little more than a brilliant study after such models as were eclipsed by this earliest effort of their imitator; and tragedy under his hands appears rouged and wrinkled, in the patches and powder of Lady Wishfort. But his three great comedies are more than enough to sustain a reputation as durable as our language. Were it not for these we should have no samples to show of comedy in its purest and highest form. Ben Jonson, who also attempted to introduce it by way of reform among the mixed work of a time when comedy and tragedy were as inextricably blended on the stage as in actual life, failed to give the requisite ease and the indispensable grace of comic life and movement to the action and passion of his elaborate and magnificent work. Of Congreve's immediate predecessors, whose aim had been to raise on French foundations a new English fabric of simple and unmixed comedy, Wycherley was of too base metal and Etherege was of metal too light to be weighed against him; and beside theirs no other or finer coin was current than the crude British ore of Shadwell's brutal and burly talent. Borrowing a metaphor from Landor, we may say that a limb of Molière would have sufficed to make a Congreve, a limb of Congreve would have sufficed to make a Sheridan. The broad and robust humour of Vanbrugh's admirable comedies gives him a place on the master's right hand; on the left stands Farquhar, whose bright light genius is to Congreve's as female is to male, or 'as moonlight unto sunlight.' No English writer, on the whole, has so nearly touched the skirts of Molière; but his splendid intelligence is wanting in the deepest and subtlest quality which has won for Molière from the greatest poet of his country and our age the tribute of exact and final definition conveyed in that perfect phrase which salutes at once and denotes him—'ce moqueur pensif comme un apôtre.'[1] Only perhaps in a single part has Congreve half consciously touched a note of almost tragic depth and suggestion; there is something well-nigh akin to the grotesque and piteous figure of Arnolphe himself in the unvenerable old age of Lady Wishfort, set off and relieved as it is, with grace and art worthy of the supreme French master, against the only figure on any stage which need not shun comparison even with that of Célimène.

NOTE

1 Victor Hugo, 'Les Pamphlétaires d'église', l. 98, from *L' Année terrible*, juillet.

96. Oswald Crawfurd in *English Comic Dramatists*

1883

From *English Comic Dramatists* (London: 1883), p. 130.

Oswald Crawfurd (1834–1909) was for many years the British consul at Oporto, where he passed his time writing novels, travel books, essays and verse dramas. The following is his introduction to some selected scenes from *The Double-Dealer* and *The Way of the World* included in a small drama anthology.

What makes CONGREVE hold so high a place among comic dramatists is not so much that naturalness which is the distinguishing characteristic of his school, nor his insight, nor his breadth; it is his style that gives him his pre-eminence, that 'subtle turn and heightening' which makes the sentences of his dialogue shine like well-faceted precious stones. The polish and elaboration he gives would be excessive were his wit less hard and pure and bright. Congreve has numerous obvious drawbacks, his outlook is not a broad one upon human nature, but upon 'the town' only—his sympathies are narrow, his morality on the wrong side of tolerable. A more technical objection to him as a playwright is that there is too much ingenuity, too much complexity, and too little true art in his plots; they do not move us, and they hardly interest us. Nevertheless, there are qualifications in Congreve for a great, almost the greatest, place in our literature as a comic dramatist besides this one of consummate wit and consummate style. One of these is his marvellous faculty of characterization. Mirabell, the fine gentleman lover, is not the mere 'walking gentleman' of most playwrights, but manly, lover-like, ready-spoken, and most witty on occasion. Lady Wishfort, Mincing, Foible, Lord Froth, the coxcomb, and that most entertaining of sots and country louts, Sir Wilfull Witwoud, are all personages with the stamp of humanity upon them, and Millamant is by common consent the most delightful of fine ladies that the world has ever known. Congreve's supremacy in the domain of comedy is to a great extent due to this, that he was an accomplished fine gentleman in the first place, and an accomplished *littérateur* in the second. Voltaire is said to have snubbed him for taking credit to himself in the first character only, and subsequent critics have approved the snub. Yet it may have been no coxcombry at all in Congreve, but only a true gentleman's modesty, and equivalent to saying, 'Do not praise me for my literary talent when I do but repeat in my plays the wit and manners of the society I live in, and in my verse I only reproduce the ease and epigrams of the wits, my friends.' Of course he did much more than this. No society talk was ever so clever as that of Congreve's *dramatis personae*: his very dullards are brighter in speech than most authors' wits, and no fine lady, even at the Court of Queen Anne, could ever have been so airy, so graceful, so wayward, so brilliant, and so charming as Millamant.

97. Edmund Gosse, in *The Life of William Congreve*

1888

From *The Life of William Congreve* (London: 1888).

Edmund Gosse (1849–1928) published his critical biography of Congreve during his tenure of the Clark Lectureship in English Literature at Trinity College, Cambridge. It belonged to the 'Great Writers' series, under the general editorship of E.S. Robertson. Gosse wrote several literary biographies, including that of his friend Swinburne. His autobiographical *Father and Son* appeared anonymously in 1907.

(i) On *The Double-Dealer*

The cast was a strong one; indeed, one would have supposed, even stronger than that of *The Old Bachelor*. Betterton gave the force of his robust genius to the detestable character of Maskwell, Doggett had a good opportunity for his farcical vivacity in Sir Paul Plyant, there were all the lovely ladies, the Bracegirdle, the Barry, the Mountfort, the Leigh. In addition to these, Kynaston, with his amazing beauty still unimpaired in old age, reminded the spectators by his Lord Touchwood of that charm and bloom of youth which had graced so many women's parts at the beginning of the reign of Charles II. But probably Williams was not quite strong enough to carry him well through the trying situations in which the hero,—if hero he be,—Mellefont, is constantly placed by his trusting disposition. From what we gather, it would seem to have been the incredulity of the audience in Mellefont which nearly wrecked the comedy.

But there was something worse than this. The ladies were angry, as Dryden told Walsh, and to see why they were angry needs no very great penetration. As is well known, ladies came in masks to the first night of Restoration and Orange comedies. They had good need to do so, since free as the discourse may have been at their own firesides, it was far outdone on the cynical and shameless stage. The dramatists had again and again drawn attention, especially in their prologues and epilogues, to the difficulty of distinguishing virtue from vice when each wore a vizard. But no one had carried his satire so far, or had pushed it home so keenly and so adroitly as Congreve in the third act of *The Double Dealer*. 'I find women,' his Careless had said, 'are not the same bare-faced and in masks, and a vizor disguises their inclinations as much as their faces.' And Mellefont, the man of virtue and honour, had replied, ''Tis a mistake, for women may most properly be said to be unmasked when they wear vizors, for that secures them from blushing, and being out of countenance, and next to being in the dark, or alone, they are most truly themselves in a vizor-mask.' The galleries 'where,' as Crowne puts it, 'roosting masques sat cackling for a mate,' must have thrilled with indignation at such audacity. The poet told them, when they complained, that they should no more expect to be complimented in a comedy than tickled by the surgeon when they went to be bled. The position was a bold one, and Congreve dared to sustain it. It probably accounts for his ultimate failure to please the public and the ladies, although he delighted the lettered world so constantly.

A third reason assigned for the want of success of *The Double Dealer* is of more literary interest. It is said that the audience resented the frequent soliloquies by which Maskwell explained to them his intentions and the progress of the intrigue. It is curious to find Congreve making use of this artifice, because it seems to take him back directly to the study of Molière. The English comic writers eschewed soliloquy very carefully. Wycherley never, so far as I remember, leaves a single character alone upon the stage, and the theatre of Shadwell habitually swarms like an ant-hill. On the other hand, in several of Molière's comedies, the central personage of the intrigue explains his purpose to the audience in an aside, exactly in Congreve's way. George Dandin is an example, and, in *L'Amour Médecin* Sganarelle. In *L'Étourdi*, and still more in *Le Dépit Amoureux* soliloquies of Mascarille may almost be said to tie the loose members of those plays together. Congreve thought it needful to excuse his return to this old conventional practice, and said, very justly, that 'we ought not to imagine that this man either talks to us, or to himself; he is only thinking, and thinking such matter as it were inexcusable folly in him to speak. But because we are concealed spectators of the plot in agitation, and the Poet finds it necessary to let us know the whole mystery of his contrivance, he is willing to inform us of this person's thoughts, and to that end is forced to make use of the expedient of speech, no other better way being yet invented for the communication of thought.' Notwithstanding these ingenious arguments, Congreve managed to do without soliloquy in his next comedy, though he was obliged to return to it in *The Way of the World*. His plays were never really well-made, in the modern sense, but no more are those of Molière or Shakespeare.

In his dedication to *The Double Dealer* Congreve rather rashly asserts that he does not know that he has 'borrowed one hint of it anywhere.' The general design, however, with its five acts' triumph of a social impostor, has some vague analogy with *Tartuffe*, and there are three prominent scenes in which Congreve certainly followed, perhaps with conscious rivalry, in the steps of his predecessors. The criticism of acquaintances in the third act is obviously reminiscent of the scene in Olivia's chamber in *The Plain Dealer*, but it is in every respect superior. The brutality and heartlessness of Wycherley's heroine are simply shocking, while Congreve retains our sympathies and shows his superior tact by making Cynthia disgusted at the spite of Brisk and Lord Froth. Sheridan, long afterwards, in essaying to produce the same effect, made no advance upon the wit of Congreve.

It will perhaps be less generally conceded that in competing with Molière in the absurd blue-stocking scene between Lady Froth and Brisk, and in the criticism of her ladyship's remarkable lyric, the English poet has the advantage. The conversation between Oronte and Philinte, with Alceste growling in the background, the fatuity of the 'petits vers doux, tendres et langoureux,' the insight into the vanity of the amateur,—these are delicious in the *Misanthrope* and of a very high order of writing. But Molière—dare we say it?—prolongs the scene a little too far; the episode threatens to become wearisome to all but literary spectators; whereas the brief and ludicrous exchange of compliments between Brisk and Lady Froth is soon over, the coachman-poem is in itself more funny than 'L'Espoir,' and the whole incident, as it seems to me, is treated in a more laughable, and dramatically in a more legitimate, way by Congreve than by Molière. It may be added that this central portion of the third act is unquestionably the best part of the play, some of which is not quite written up to its author's mark.

There is yet a third instance in which Congreve, in spite of his claim to originality, must be held to have undergone the influence of a predecessor. When Lady Plyant pays her monstrous attentions to Mellefont, it is impossible to avoid a comparison with the advances Bélise makes to Clitandre in the first act of *Les Femmes Savantes*. This is what reminded Macaulay of the house of Laius or of Pelops, and no one will deny its horror. But in sheer wit and intellectual daring, the English dialogue does not seem to me to be at all inferior to the French.

The Double Dealer contains some excellent characters. Sir Paul Plyant, with his night-cap made out of a piece of a scarlet petticoat, tied up in bed, out of harm's way, and looking, with his great beard, like a Russian bear upon a drift of snow, is wholly delightful; and Lady Froth, the charming young blue-stocking, with her wit and her pedantry, her affectation and her merry vitality, is one of the best and most complex characters that Congreve has created. Her doting affection for her child, 'poor little Sappho,' mingled with her interest in her own ridiculous verses, and set off by her genuine ability and power, combine to form a very life-like picture. Twenty years earlier she might have been supposed to be a study of Margaret, Duchess of Newcastle. Her astronomical experiments with Mr. Brisk are a concession on the poet's part to the worst instincts of his audience, and funny as they undeniably are, they spoil the part.

A fault in the construction of *The Double Dealer* is that Lord and Lady Froth are not sharply enough distinguished from Lord and Lady Touchwood. In Cynthia, Congreve produced one of those gracious and honest maidens whom he liked to preserve in the wild satiric garden of his drama, that his beloved Mrs. Bracegirdle might have a pure and impassioned part to play. We owe to this penchant the fortunate circumstance that, while in Etheredge, Wycherley, and Vanbrugh there is often not a single character that we can esteem or personally tolerate from the beginning of the play to the end, in Congreve there is always sure to be one lady of reputation, even if she be not quite of the crystalline order of that more famous Lady, who walked among apes and tigers in the boskages of *Comus*.

(pp. 50–6)

(ii) On *The Mourning Bride*

It has been the habit to quote *The Mourning Bride* as the very type of bad declamatory tragedy. No doubt Dr. Johnson did it harm by that extravagant eulogy in which he selected one fragment as unsurpassed in the poetry of all time. But if we compare it, not with those tragedies of the age of Elizabeth, studded with occasional naïve felicities, which it is just now the fashion to admire with some extravagance, but with what England and even France produced from 1650 to the revival of romantic taste, *The Mourning Bride* will probably take a place close after what is best in Otway and Racine. It will bear comparison, as I would venture to assert, with Southerne's *Fatal Marriage* or with Crébillon's *Rhadamiste et Zénobie*, and will not be pronounced inferior to these excellent and famous tragedies in dramatic interest, or genuine grandeur of sentiment, or beauty of language. It has done what no other of these special rivals has done, outside the theatre of Racine, it has contributed to the everyday fashion of its country several well-worn lines. But it is not every one who says that 'Music has charms to soothe a savage breast' or that 'Hell knows no fury like a woman scorn'd,' who would be able to tell where the familiar sentiment first occurs.

(pp. 87–8)

(iii) Versification of *The Mourning Bride*

The blank verse of *The Mourning Bride* deserves some consideration, because it seems to be the model on which most eighteenth-century unrhymed iambics were formed. It is the parent of Thomson's, as that is of Cowper's and of Wordsworth's blank verse. When the heroic tragedies went out of fashion, and dramatic blank verse was reverted to by Dryden and Otway, those writers took the easy versification of Shakespeare's later time, with the incessant extra syllable, as their model. Lee, who was influenced by Milton, is much more sparing of this redundancy, and Congreve follows Lee rather than any other dramatist. His real model is, however, Milton, and it is curious to trace in his tragic blank verse a respectful study of that impeccable master. There are few inversions of rhythm; the break or cæsura is very well managed, and when a variation of stress is admitted, it can almost always be justified in *Paradise Lost*. For instance—

My fáther's voíce! hóllow it sóunds, and cálls,
[IV, viii, 23]

with its inversion of the third stress, reminds us of Milton's

For óne restráint, lórds of the wórld besides;
[*PL*, I, 32]

and Congreve's

Crúel, crúel, o móre than kílling óbject
[V, ix, 8]

is paralleled in *Paradise Lost* by

Únivérsal reproách, far wórse to beár.
[*PL*, VI, 34]

The double inversion of stress, too, in Congreve's beautiful line—

Wás it the dóleful béll tólling for Déath?
[IV, viii, 16]

could no doubt be justified by Miltonic practice, though I doubt
whether in one single instance of a triple inversion Congreve does
not pass outside the record of any existing specimen of *Paradise Lost*.
The line is—

Óf a fáther's fóndness those ílls aróse.
[V, vi, 50]

These exceptions are worth noting, because they are introduced by
a poet—who thoroughly understood what he was doing—into a
system of blank verse more conservative than any which had been
seen since the beginning of the seventeenth century. The direct
influence of the verse of *The Mourning Bride* may be detected in the
tragedies of Young, and then in his *Night Thoughts*.

(pp. 92–3)

(iv) On *The Way of the World*

Successive critics, seeing, what we must all acknowledge, the
incomparable splendour of the dialogue in *The Way of the World*,
have not ceased to marvel at the caprice which should render
dubious the success of such a masterpiece on its first appearance.
But perhaps a closer examination of the play may help us to unravel
the apparent mystery. On certain sides, all the praise which has
been lavished on the play from Steele and Voltaire down to Mr.

Swinburne and Mr. George Meredith is thoroughly deserved. *The Way of the World* is the best-written, the most dazzling, the most intellectually accomplished of all English comedies, perhaps of all the comedies of the world. But it has the defects of the very qualities which make it so brilliant. A perfect comedy does not sparkle so much, is not so exquisitely written, because it needs to advance, to develop. To *The Way of the World* may be applied that very dubious compliment paid by Mrs. Browning to Landor's *Pentameron* that, 'were it not for the necessity of getting through a book, some of the pages are too delicious to turn over.' The beginning of the third act, the description of Mirabell's feelings in the opening scene, and many other parts of *The Way of the World,* are not to be turned over, but to be re-read until the psychological subtlety of the sentiment, the perfume of the delicately chosen phrases, the music of the sentences, have produced their full effect upon the nerves. But, meanwhile, what of the action? The reader dies of a rose in aromatic pain, but the spectator fidgets in his stall, and wishes that the actors and actresses would be doing something. In no play of Congreve's is the literature so consummate, in none is the human interest in movement and surprise so utterly neglected, as in *The Way of the World. The Old Bachelor,* itself, is theatrical in comparison. We have slow, elaborate dialogue, spread out like some beautiful endless tapestry, and no action whatever. Nothing happens, nothing moves, positively from one end of *The Way of the World* to the other, and the only reward of the mere spectator is the occasional scene of wittily contrasted dialogue, Millamant pitted against Sir Wilful, Witwoud against Petulant, Lady Wishfort against her maid. With an experienced audience, prepared for an intellectual pleasure, the wit of these polished fragments would no doubt encourage a cultivation of patience through less lively portions of the play, but to spectators coming perfectly fresh to the piece, and expecting rattle and movement, this series of still-life pictures may easily be conceived to be exasperating, especially as the satire contained in them was extremely sharp and direct.

Very slight record has been preserved of the manner in which *The Way of the World* was acted. The only part which seems to have been particularly distinguished was that of Mrs. Leigh in Lady Wishfort. Mrs. Bracegirdle, of course, was made for the part of Millamant, and her appearance in the second act, 'with her fan spread, and her streamers out, and a shoal of fools for tenders,' was carefully prepared; yet we hear nothing of the effect produced. Mrs. Barry took the disagreeable character of Mrs. Marwood, and Betterton had no special chance for showing his qualities in Fainall. Witwoud and Petulant, who keep some of the scenes alive with their sallies, were Bower and Bowman, and Underhill played Sir Wilful. It is very tantalizing, and quite unaccountable, that no one seems to have preserved any tradition of the acting of this magnificent piece.

In *The Way of the World*, as in *The Old Bachelor*, Congreve essayed a stratagem which Molière tried but once, in *Le Misanthrope*. It is one which is likely to please very much or greatly to annoy. It is the stimulation of curiosity all through the first act, without the introduction of one of the female characters who are described and, as it were, promised to the audience. It is probable that in the case of *The Way of the World* it was hardly a success. The analysis of character and delicate intellectual writing in the first act, devoid as it is of all stage-movement, may possibly have proved very tedious to auditors not subtle enough to enjoy Mirabell's account of the effect which Millamant's faults have upon him, or Witwoud's balanced depreciation of his friend Petulant. Even the mere reader discovers that the whole play brightens up after the entrance of Millamant, and probably that apparition is delayed too long. From this point, to the end of the second act, all scintillates and sparkles; and these are perhaps the most finished pages, for mere wit, in all existing comedy. The dialogue is a little metallic, but it is burnished to the highest perfection; and while one repartee rings against the other, the arena echoes as with shock after shock in a tilting-bout. In comparison with what we had had before Congreve's time that was best—with *The Man of Mode*, for instance, and with *The Country Wife*—the literary work in *The Way of the World* is altogether more polished, the wit more direct and effectual, the art of the comic poet more highly developed. There are fewer square inches of the canvas which the painter has roughly filled in, and neglected to finish; there is more that consciously demands critical admiration, less that can be, in Landor's phrase, pared away.

Why, then, did this marvellous comedy fail to please? Partly, no doubt, on account of its scholarly delicacy, too fine to hold the attention of the pit, and partly also, as we have seen, because of its too elaborate dialogue and absence of action. But there was more than this. Congreve was not merely a comedian, he was a satirist also—*asper jocum tentavit*. He did not spare the susceptibilities of his fine ladies. His Cabal-Night at Lady Wishfort's is the direct original of Sheridan's *School for Scandal*; but in some ways the earlier picture is the more biting, the more disdainful. Without posing as a Timon or a Diogenes, and so becoming himself an object of curious interest, Congreve adopted the cynical tone, and threads the brightly-coloured crowd of social figures with a contemptuous smile upon his lips. When we come to speak of his plays as a whole, we shall revert to this trait, which is highly characteristic of his genius; it is here enough to point out that this peculiar air of careless superiority, which is decidedly annoying to audiences, reaches its climax in the last of Congreve's comedies.

We have spoken with high praise of the end of the second act; but perhaps even this is surpassed in the third act by Lady Wishfort's unparalleled disorder at the sight of her complexion, 'an arrant ash-colour, as I'm a person,' and her voluble commands to her maid; or, in the fourth act, by the scene in which Millamant walks up and down the room reciting tags from the poets, not noticing Sir Wilful, the country clodpole squire, 'ruder than Gothic,' who takes the ejaculation, 'Natural easy Suckling!' as a description of himself. It is to be noticed, as a proof that this play, in spite of its misfortunes, has made a deep impression on generations of hearers and readers, that it is fuller than any other of Congreve's plays of quotations that have become part of the language. It is from *The Way of the World*, for instance, that we take—'To drink is a Christian diversion unknown to the Turk and the Persian'; while it would be interesting to know whether it is by a pure coincidence that Tennyson, in perhaps the most famous of all his phrases, comes so near to Congreve's "Tis better to have been left, than never to have been loved.'

(pp. 135–9)

98. W.E. Henley reviews Edmund Gosse's *William Congreve*

1888

From *The Athenaeum*, No. 3186, 17 November 1888, pp. 672–3.

William Ernest Henley (1849–1903) is now remembered mainly as the poet of 'Hospital Verses', first published in *The Cornhill*, and *London Voluntaries* (1893). But Henley's poetry was virtually a sideline in an extraordinarily busy life as art critic, literary editor, and reviewer. The following was reprinted with slight changes in *Views and Reviews: Essays in Appreciation*, a collection of Henley's reviews made in 1890.

DRAMA

GREAT WRITERS.—LIFE OF WILLIAM CONGREVE.
BY EDMUND GOSSE, M.A. (SCOTT.)

An American literary journal has just assured its readers that Congreve has a 'niche in the Valhalla of Ben Jonson.' The remark is injudicious, of course, even for a literary American, and there is no apparent reason why it should ever have got itself uttered. It is probably the unluckiest thing that ever was said of Congreve, who—with some unimportant exceptions—has been singularly fortunate in his critics and biographers. Dryden wrote of him with enthusiasm, and in doing so he may be said to have set a fashion of admiration which is vigorous and captivating even yet. Swift, Voltaire, Lamb, Hazlitt, Thackeray, Macaulay, to name but these, have dealt with him in their several ways, and of late he has been praised by such masters of the art of writing as Mr. Swinburne and Mr. George Meredith. Mr. Gosse, the last upon the list, surpasses most of his predecessors in admiration, and all, or nearly all, in knowledge. His book, indeed, is one of the best—if not actually *the* best—of the series to which it belongs. It sets forth with all possible propriety and a good deal of new material the facts of the poet's life;

420

it presents a complete account of his plays, with not a little sound criticism as to his place in art and his extraordinary and varied excellences as a writer; it includes what is certainly the fullest and the fairest history of the Jeremy Collier controversy which has yet been printed. In brief, it is good work, and Mr. Gosse is to be heartily congratulated on its achievement.

It is no fault of Mr. Gosse's that, with all his diligence, he has failed to give a complete and striking picture of the man, or to make more of what he describes as his 'smiling, faultless rotundity.' As he puts it a sentence or two before, 'there were no salient points about Congreve's character,' so that 'no vagaries, no escapades place him in a ludicrous or in a human light,' and 'he passes through the literary life of his time as if in felt slippers, noiseless, unupbraiding, without personal adventures.' That, we take it, is absolutely true. It is known that Congreve was cheerful, serviceable, and witty; that he was a man of many friends; that Pope dedicated his Iliad to him; that Dryden loved and admired him; that Collier attacked his work, and that his rejoinder to Collier was equally spiritless and ill-bred; that he was attached to Mrs. Bracegirdle, and left all his money to the Duchess of Marlborough; that he was a creditable Government official; and that, having written a certain number of plays, he suddenly at thirty ceased from production, lost his interest in life and art, and wrote no more. But that is about all that is known of him. Thackeray's picture of him may be, and probably is, as unveracious as his Fielding or his Dick Steele; but there is little or nothing to show how far we can depend upon it. The character of the man escapes us, and we have either to refrain from trying to see him, or to be content with mere hypothesis and speculation. So odd and abnormal is the mystery in which he is enshrouded that what in the case of other men would be notorious remains in his dubious and obscure, so that we cannot tell whether he was Bracegirdle's lover or only her friend, and the secret of his relations with the Duchess of Marlborough has yet to be discovered. If patience in research and skill in the arrangement of results were anything in this connexion, Mr. Gosse's work would be enough. But Mr. Gosse has failed, as we have said, with those who went before him. No more than they has he succeeded in plucking out the heart of Congreve's mystery. He was, and he remains, impersonal. At his most solid and substantial he is (as some one has said of him) but 'vagueness personified'; at his most luminous an appearance only, like the *Scin-laeca*, the shining, shadow adapted in a moment of peculiar inspiration by the late Lord Lytton.

It is otherguess work with the writer. We have the plays, and who runs may read and admire. We say advisedly, who runs may read, and not who will may see. Congreve's plays are, we can imagine, as dull to look at as they are entertaining to read. They have dropped out of the *répertoire*, and the truth is they are worthy of no better fate. They are only plays to the critic of style; to the actor and the average spectator they are merely so much weariness in print. To begin with, they are marked by such a deliberate and immitigable baseness of morality as makes them impossible to man. Wycherley has done more vilely; Vanbrugh has reached to higher altitudes of filthiness. But neither Wycherley nor Vanbrugh has any strain of the admirable intellectual quality of Congreve. Villainy comes natural to the one, and filthiness drops from the other as easily as honey from the comb; but in neither is there evident that admirable effort of the intelligence which is a distinguishing characteristic of Congreve, and with neither is the result at once so consummate and so tame. For the truth is both Wycherley and Vanbrugh are playwrights, and Congreve is not. Congreve is only an artist in style, writing for himself and half a dozen in the pit, while Wycherley and Vanbrugh (and for that matter Etheredge and Farquhar) are playwrights, producing for the whole theatre. Mr. Gosse has analyzed his Congreve with ever so much intelligence and care; but he has let his 'enthusiasm of biographer' run away with him, and has failed to recognize that Congreve's plays were only successful in proportion as they were less literary and 'Congrevian.' His first comedy was the talk of the town; his last, *The Way of the World*, that model of characterization (of a kind) and fine English, was only a 'success of esteem. The reason is not far to seek. Congreve's plays, as it appears to us, were too sordid in conception and too unamusing in effect even for the audiences to which they were produced; they were excellent literature, but they were bad theatre, and they were innately detestable to boot. Audiences are the same in all strata of time; and it is easy to see that Wycherley's Horner and Vanbrugh's Sir John and Lady Brute were amusing, when Lady Wishfort and Sir Sampson Legend and the illustrious and impossible Maskwell were found 'old, cold, withered, and of intolerable entrails.' An audience, whatever its epoch, wants action, and still action, and again (and for the last time) action; also it wants a point of departure that shall be something tainted with humanity, a touch of the human in the term of everything, and a 'sort of a kind of a strain' of humanity, at least, in the progress of events from the one point to the other. This, as it seems to us, it gets in Wycherley, brute as he is; it gets the same, with a far larger and more vigorous comic sense, in Vanbrugh; it gets it, with a difference, in the light-hearted indecencies of Farquhar. From the magnificent prose of Congreve it is absent. His it was to artificialize all that was most artificial in an artificial state of society; he was (in other words) the consummate artist of a phase that was merely transient, the laureate of a generation that was only alive for half an hour in the course of all the twenty-four. He is saved from oblivion by sheer strength of style. It is a bad dramatic style, as we know; it leaves the Witwoulds and the Plyants as admirable as the Mirabels and Millamants and Angelicas; it makes no distinction between the Mrs. Foresights and the Sir Sampson Legends; it presents an exemplar as in Lady Wishfort and an exemplar in Petulant; it is uneasy, self-conscious, intrusive, even offensive, the very reverse of dramatic; and in Congreve's hands it is irresistible, for, thanks to Congreve, it has been forced from the stage, and lives as literature alone. This, we are obliged to say, Mr. Gosse has not perceived. His enthusiasm is so large that he is able to criticize his author as though he were not one in the pit, but the whole house; to ignore the ineradicable turpitude of his author's view of life, and contrast Congreve with Molière, a little to Molière's disadvantage! Here, it is interesting to note, he is more 'advanced' than Mr. Meredith himself. Mr. Meredith has a sense of something better and more beautiful than mere epigram; and though Congreve is what he tries to be and cannot, and Molière is what he ought to be and will not, it is to Molière that he gives his vote. Mr. Gosse is lighter and less literary. He goes out of his way, indeed, to compare his author with Molière on grounds where comparison is impossible.

'His plays,' says he, with an engaging—and misleading—generosity of mind, 'were never really well made, in the modern sense, but no more are those of Molière or Shakspeare.' He should have reflected that, while Shakspeare and Molière both keep the stage, and Congreve has disappeared into the darkness of the closet, it is hardly fair in this connexion to compare Shakspeare with

Molière, much less to bracket Congreve with Molière and Shakspeare. Congreve was essentially a man of letters; his style (as Mr. Gosse has failed to note) is that of a pupil, not of Molière, but of the full, the rich, the excessive, the pedantic Ben Jonson; his Legends, his Wishforts, his Foresights are the lawful heirs—refined and sublimated, but still directly descended—of the Tuccas, and the Bobadils, and the Epicure Mammons of the great Elizabethan; they are (that is to say) more literary than theatrical—they are excellent reading, but they have long since fled the stage, and vanished into the night of mere scholarship. To compare an author of this type and descent with Shakspeare is, as it seems to us, a trifle unfair; to compare him with Molière is to misapprehend the differences between literature and drama. Congreve, as we have said, has disappeared from the boards, and is only tolerable, or even intelligible, to the ardent reader; while Shakspeare worked on so imperfect a convention that, though he keeps the stage and is known, indeed, for the poet of the most popular play ever written (for that, we take it, *Hamlet* is), he is yet the prey of every twopenny actor, or actor-manager, or actor-manager-editor, who is driven to deal with him. Molière, on the other hand, wrote as one who was primarily a great actor; who dealt not so much with what is transient in human life as with what is eternal in human nature; who addressed himself much more to an audience (Fénelon, who found fault with his style, is witness to the fact) than to a circle of readers. And the result is that Molière not only remains better reading (as Mr. Meredith has said) than Congreve, but is played at this time in the Rue de Richelieu line for line and word for word as he was played at the Palais Bourbon over two hundred years ago. This Mr. Gosse has not perceived, and for this he has not allowed. In that new edition of his book which must surely come to us, he will do well to make the correction and acknowledge the mistake.

99. Walter Raleigh in *The English Novel*

1894

From *The English Novel* (London: 1894), pp. 101–3.

Walter Raleigh (1861–1922) became the first Professor of English Literature at Oxford in 1904, having held in succession chairs at University College, Liverpool, and Glasgow. He was knighted in 1911, and made Merton Professor of English Literature at Oxford in 1914. *The English Novel* belongs to Raleigh's Liverpool years and appeared in the University Extension Manuals series; he defined its scope as 'studies of the work of the chief English novelists before Scott'.

Towards the close of the century a greater dramatist than Crowne followed Crowne's example, by preluding his dramatic work with a novel. In 1692 William Congreve, a young man then unknown to fame, produced a brief novel called *Incognita*. A novel he called it, for he is careful to distinguish it from the current school of romances, which bear the same relation to novels, he maintains, that tragedy bears to comedy. 'Romances,' he holds, and the description contains some good criticism, 'are generally composed of the constant loves and invincible courages of Heroes, Heroines, Kings and Queens, mortals of the first rank, and so forth; where lofty language, miraculous contingencies, and impossible performances elevate and surprise the reader into a giddy delight, which leaves him flat upon the ground whenever he leaves off.'

It is with no pretensions of this kind that Congreve, under the assumed name of 'Cleophil,' lays his first-born, a naked and shivering foundling, at the feet of Mrs. Katherine Leveson, and implores her 'that if it should want merit to challenge protection, yet, as an object of charity, it may move compassion.' After explaining, with the fashionable indifference that moved the scorn of Voltaire, that this piece of literature is the product of 'the idle hours of a fortnight's time,' Congreve claims for his novel that it is the first that observes dramatic laws. The action is comprised in three days, the scene is laid at Florence, the main design is the marrying of 'two couple so oddly engaged in an intricate amour.'

To any one sated with the masterpieces of the Grand Cyrus school, this little pamphlet must have come as a refreshment indeed, for here at last is a dramatist, and, what is more, a humourist, at work upon prose fiction. In the description of how Fabritio had 'vowed revenge upon Lorenzo if he survived, or, in case of his death, upon his next of kin, and so to descend lineally, like an English estate, to all the heirs males of his family,' there is a foretaste of the quality of Fielding. The development of the story, which deals with the fortunes of two friends who attend a masked ball at Florence, each taking the name of the other, and there fall in love, is pure drama, rapid and spirited. The picture of the two lovelorn youths, returned to their lodging, and sighing in company, each imagining that the other sighs out of complaisance, is pure humour. And Congreve displays something of the wit that was to make his name, both in the conversation, or polite 'raillery,' that he reports as taking place at the ball, and in the occasional introduction of himself to the reader,—the discussion, so dear to Fielding, of his own handling of the puppets of his story. Thus the author refuses to describe the dress of his heroine, lest he should err 'in some material pin or other in the sticking of which maybe the whole grace of the drapery depended.' But at the description of her beauty he will 'have a fling,' although he has 'prefaced it with an impossibility,' by the too liberal use of laudatory epithets,—and he writes half a page of delicate mock-heroic. There is great promise in this early work, and the history of Congreve's later literary production is only one more instance of how hardly the novel can maintain itself in a period of dramatic activity. Successful drama has generally offered higher rewards to the author, and has taken the bread out of the mouth of the novelist, by stealing the material of his stories. The heroic romances found their public in England during the failure of the drama, and availed themselves skilfully of the opportunity to foster a new taste in the reading public, a taste that the drama could never satisfy save imperfectly; a delight, namely, born of the fashionable leisure of a self-conscious society, in minute introspection and the analysis and portraiture of emotional states. In this particular development of fiction, which has since reached so high a pitch of perfection in England and France, the heroic romances are thus an important link.

100. G.S. Street in the Introduction to *The Comedies of William Congreve*

1895

From *The Comedies of William Congreve*, ed. G.S. Street, 2 vols (London: 1895).

George Slythe Street (1867–1936) combined a career in the civil service with that of theatre critic and man of letters. Apart from his edition of Congreve's comedies he published several volumes of essays, a play, and a novel. Rather curiously, considering his sensible defence of the morality of Restoration comedy, he became Joint-Reader of Plays for the Lord Chamberlain in 1914, and Reader in 1920.

(i)

Since Jeremy Collier let off his *Short View of the Immorality and Profaneness of the English Stage*, there has never lacked a critic to chastise or to deplore—the more effective and irritating course— not simply the coarseness but, the immorality of our old comedies, their attitude towards and their peculiar interests in life. Without affirming that we are now come to the Golden Age of criticism, one may rejoice that modern methods have taught quite humble critics to discriminate between issues, and to deal with such a matter as this with some mental detachment. The great primal fallacy comes from a habit of expecting everything in everything. Just as in a picture it is not enough for some people that it is well drawn and well painted, but they demand an interesting story, a fine sentiment, a great thought: so since our national glory is understood to be the happy home, the happy home must be triumphant everywhere, even in satiric comedy. The best expression of this fallacy is in Thackeray. Concluding a most eloquent, and a somewhat patronising examination of Congreve, 'Ah!' he exclaims, 'it's a weary feast, that banquet of wit where no love is.' The answer is plain: comedy of manners is comedy of manners, and satire is satire; introduce 'love'—an appeal, one supposes, to sympathy with strictly legitimate and common affection and a glorification of the happy home—and the rules of your art compel you to satirise affection and to make the happy home ridiculous: a truly deplorable work, which the incriminated dramatists were discreet enough for the most part to avoid. The remark brings us to the first of the half-truths, which cause the complexity of the subject. The dramatists whose withers the well-intentioned and disastrous Collier wrung seem to have thought their best answer was to pose as people with a mission—certainly Congreve so posed—to reform the world with an exhibition of its follies. An amusing answer, no doubt, of which the absurdity is obvious! It does, however, contain a half-truth. The idea of *The Way of the World's* reforming adulterers—observe the quotation from Horace on the title-page—is a little delicious; yet the exhibition in a ludicrous light of the thing satirised is surely an end of satiric comedy? The right of the matter is indicated in a sentence which occurs in the dedication of *The Double-Dealer* far more wisely than in Congreve's answer to Collier: 'I should be very glad of an opportunity to make my compliment to those ladies who are offended: but they can no more expect it in a comedy, than to be tickled by a surgeon, when he's letting 'em blood.' Something more than a half-truth is in Charles Lamb's theory, that the old comedy 'has no reference whatever to the world that is': that it is 'the Utopia of Gallantry' merely. Literally, historically, the theory is a fantasy. What the Restoration dramatists did not borrow from France was inspired directly by the court of Charles the Second, and nobody conversant with the memoirs of that court can have any difficulty in matching the fiction with reality. I imagine that Congreve in part accepted a tradition of the stage, but I am also perfectly well assured that he depicted what he saw. How far the virtues we should associate with the Charles the Second spirit may atone for its vices is a question which would take us far into moral philosophy. It is enough to remark that those vices are the exclusive possession of no period: so long as society is constituted in anything like its present order, there must be a section of it for which those vices are the main interest in life. But Charles Lamb's gay and engaging defiance of the kill-joys of his day has this value: it is most certainly just to say that, in appreciating satiric comedy, 'our coxcombical moral sense' must be 'for a little transitory ease excluded.'

For one may apprehend the whole truth to be somewhat thus. Satiric comedy, or comedy of manners, is the art of making ludicrous in dramatic form some phase of life. The writers of our old comedy thought that certain vices—gambling, adultery, and the like—formed a phase of life which for divers reasons, essential and accidental, lent itself best to their purpose. They may, or may not, have thought they were doing society a service: their real justification is that, as artists, they had to take for their art that material they could use best. They used it according to their lights: Wycherley with a coarse and heavy hand, so that it became nauseous; Etherege with a light touch and a gay perception; Congreve with an instinct of good-breeding, with a sure and extensive observation, and with an incomparable style. But all were justified in choosing for their material just what they chose. They sinned artistically, now here, now there; but to complain of this old comedy as a whole, that vice in it is crammed too closely, is to forget that a play is a picture, not a photograph, of life—is life arranged and coloured—and that comedy of manners is composed of foibles or vices condensed and relieved by one another. In so far as they overdid this work, the comic writers were artistically at fault, and Jeremy Collier was a good critic; but when he and his successors go beyond the artistic objection, one takes leave to say, they misapprehend the thing criticised. To complain that 'love' and common morality have no place in satiric comedy is either to contemplate ridicule of them or to ask comedy to be other than satiric. We know what happened when the dramatists gave way: there followed, Hazlitt says, 'those *do-me-good*, lack-a-daisical, whining, make-believe comedies in the next age, which are enough to set one to sleep, and where the author tries in vain to be merry and wise in the same breath.' These in place of 'the court, the gala day of wit and pleasure, of gallantry, and Charles the Second!' And all because people would not keep their functions distinct, and remember that at a comedy they were in a court of art and not in a court of law! The old comedy is dead, and its spirit gone from the stage: I have but endeavoured to show that no harm need come to our phylacteries, if a flame start from its ashes in the printed book.

(pp. viii–xi)

(ii)

It is not difficult to understand how it was that Dryden thought *The Old Bachelor* the best first play he had seen, and the town applauded to the echo. But it is a little hard to understand why later critics, with the three other comedies before them, have not more expressly marked the difference between the first and those. There is no new tune in *The Old Bachelor*: it is an old tune more finely played, and for that very reason it met with immediate acceptance. It is not likely that Dryden—a great poet and a great and generous critic, it may be, but an old man—would have bestowed such unhesitating approval on a play which ignored the conventions in which he had lived. As it was, he saw those conventions reverently followed, yet served by a master wit. The fact that Congreve allowed Dryden and others to 'polish' his play, by giving it an air of the stage and the town which it lacked, need not of course spoil it for us. The stamp of Congreve is clearly marked on the dialogue, though not on every page. You may see its essentials in two passages taken absolutely at random. 'Come, come,' says Bellmour in the very first scene, 'leave business to idlers and wisdom to fools; they have need of 'em: wit be my faculty and pleasure my occupation, and let Father Time shake his glass.' Or Fondlewife soliloquises: 'Tell me, Isaac, why art thee jealous? Why art thee distrustful of the wife of thy bosom? Because she is young and vigorous, and I am old and impotent. Then why didst thee marry, Isaac? Because she was beautiful and tempting, and because I was obstinate and doating. . . .' In the one passage is the gay and skilfully light paradox, in the other the clean, rhythmical, and balanced, yet dramatic and appropriate English that are elements of Congreve's style. It is in the conventions of its characterisation that *The Old Bachelor* belongs, not to true Congrevean comedy but, to that of the models from which he was to break away. The characterisation of *The Way of the World* is light and true, that of *The Old Bachelor* is heavy and yet vague. Vainlove indeed, the 'mumper in love,' who 'lies canting at the gate,' is individual and Congrevean. But Heartwell, the blustering fool, Bellmour, the impersonal rake, Wittol and Bluffe, the farcical sticks, Fondlewife, the immemorial city husband, and the troop of undistinguished women—what can be said of them but that they are glaring stage properties, speaking better English than the comic stage had before attracted? Germs, possibly, of better things to come, that is all, so far as characterisation goes. The Fondlewife episode, in particular, which doubtless was mightily popular—what is there more in it than the mutton fisted wit and brutality of Wycherley, with some of Congreve's

English? Such scenes as these, it may be hazarded, so contemptible in the light of Congreve's better work, are ineffective now because they fall between two stools: between the comedy (or tragedy) of a crude physical fact, naked and impossible, as in Rochester, and the comedy (or tragedy) of delicately-phrased intrigue. The latter was yet to come when this play was produced, and meantime such episodes went very well, and their popularity is intelligible. For the rest *The Old Bachelor*, though to us in these days its plot appear a somewhat uninspiring piece of fairyland, was a good acting play, fitted with great skill to its actual players. The part of Fondlewife, created by Dogget, was on a revival played (to his own immense satisfaction) by Colley Cibber. In Araminta Mrs. Bracegirdle began (in a faint outline as it were) the series of lively, sympathetic, intelligent heroines which Congreve wrote for her. Lord Falkland's Prologue is as funny as it is indecently suggestive, which is saying a great deal. The one actually spoken gave an opportunity of the merriest archness to Mrs. Bracegirdle, and was calculated to put the audience in the best of good humours.

The faults of *The Double-Dealer* are obvious on a first reading, and were very justly condemned on a first acting. The intrigue is wearisome: its involutions are ineffectively puzzling. Maskwell's villainy and Mellefont's folly are both unconvincing. The tragedy of Lady Touchwood, less tragic than that of Lady Wishfort in *The Way of the World*, is more obviously than that out of the picture. The play is, in fact, not pure comedy of manners: it is that *plus* tragedy, an element less offensive than the sentimentality which spoils *The School for Scandal*, but yet a notable fault. For while you can resolve the tragedy of Lady Wishfort into wicked and very grim comedy, you can do nothing with the tragedy of Lady Touchwood but try to ignore it. In his epistle dedicatory to Charles Montague, Congreve admits that his play has faults, but does not take in hand those adduced above, with the exception of the objections to Maskwell and Mellefont. 'They have mistaken cunning in one character for folly in another': an ineffectual answer, because the extremity of cunning is equally destructive of dramatic balance. He defends his use of soliloquy very warmly: of which it may be said that, so long as his rule—that no character may overhear the soliloquiser—is observed, it is a tolerable convention, but a confession of weakness in construction. He declares he 'would rather disoblige all the critics in the world than one of the fair sex,' and, having made his bow, he turns upon the ladies and rends them. An author campaigning against his critics is always a pleasant spectacle, but Congreve's defence of *The Double-Dealer* is rather amusing than convincing.

It needed no defence; for with all its faults, such as they are, upon it, there are in it scenes and characters which only Congreve could have made. Brisk is a worthy forerunner of Witwoud, Sir Paul Plyant a delicious old credulous fool; while the tyrannical and vain Lady Plyant is so drawn that you almost love her. But the triumph is Lady Froth, 'a great coquet, pretender to poetry, wit, and learning,' and one would almost as lief have seen Mrs. Mountfort in the part as the Bracegirdle's Millamant. Her serious folly and foolish wisdom, her poem and malice and compliments and babbling vivacity—set off, it is fair to remember, by a pretty face—are atonement for a dozen Maskwells. She is a female Witwoud, her author's first success in a sort of character he draws to perfection. The scene between Mellefont and Lady Plyant, where she insists on believing that the gallant, under cover of a marriage with her stepdaughter, purposes to lead her astray, and where she goes through a delightful farce of answering her scruples before the bewildered man—the scene that for some far-fetched reason led Macaulay's mind to the incest in the *Oedipus Rex*—is perhaps the best comedy of situation in the piece. But the scene of defamation between the Froths and Brisk is notable as (with the Cabal idea in *The Way of the World*) the inspiration of the Scandal Scenes in Sheridan's play. When we remember that less than two years were gone since the production of *The Old Bachelor*, the improvement in Congreve is remarkable. Almost his only concession to the groundlings is the star-gazing episode of Lady Froth and Brisk: a mistake, because it spoils her inconsequent folly, but a small matter. In his second play Congreve was himself, the wittiest and most polished writer of comedy in English. In the face of this fact 'the public' conducted itself characteristically: it more or less damned *The Double-Dealer* until the queen approved, when it applauded lustily. That occasion gave Colley Cibber his first chance as Kynaston's substitute in Lord Touchwood. When one remembers Dryden's long, struggling, cudgelling and cudgelled life, it is impossible to read without emotion his tribute to a very young and successful author in the verses prefixed to this play:

[Quotes No. 10 (a) ll. 17–19, 34 and 59–63.]

The tribute is indubitably sincere; in point of Congreve's wit and diction it is as indubitably true.

Love for Love was the most popular of Congreve's comedies: it held the stage so long that Hazlitt could say, 'it still acts and is still acted well.' Being wise after the event, one may give some obvious reasons. It is more human than any other of his plays, and at the same time more farcical. By 'more human' it is not meant that the characters are truer to life than those in *The Way of the World*, but that they are truer to average life, and therefore more easily recognisable by the average spectator. Tattle, for instance, is so gross a fool, that any fool in the pit could see his folly; Witwoud might deceive all but the elect. No familiarity—direct or indirect—with a particular mode of life and speech is necessary to the appreciation of *Love for Love*. Sir Sampson Legend is your unmistakable heavy father, cross-grained and bullying. Valentine is no ironical, fine gentleman like Mirabell, but a young rake from Cambridge, all debts and high spirits. Scandal is a plain railer at things, especially women; Ben Legend a sea-dog who cannot speak without a nautical metaphor; Jeremy an idealised comic servant; and Foresight grotesque farce. Angelica is a shrewd but hearty 'English girl,' and Miss Prue a veritable country Miss; while Mrs. Frail and Mrs. Foresight are broadly skittish matrons. There is nothing in the play to strain the attention or to puzzle the intellect, and it is full of laughter: no wonder it was a success. It is, intellectually, on an altogether different plane from *The Way of the World*, on a slightly lower one than *The Double-Dealer*. But in its own way it is irresistibly funny, and by reason of its diction it is never for a moment other than distinguished.

I imagine the bodkin scene will always take the palm in it for mere mirth. Delightful sisters!

I suppose you would not go alone to the World's End?
The World's End! What, do you mean to banter me?
Poor innocent! You don't know that there's a place called the World's End? I'll swear you can keep your countenance purely; you'd make an admirable player. ... But look you here, now—where did you lose this gold bodkin?—Oh, sister, sister!
My bodkin?
Nay, 'tis yours; look at it.

Well, if you go to that, where did you find this bodkin? Oh, sister, sister!—sister every way.

(II, ix, 38–67)

Broad, popular comedy, it is admirable; but it is not especially Congrevean. Tattle's love-lesson to Miss Prue and his boasting of his duchesses are in the same broad vein. Valentine's mad scene is more remarkable, in that Congreve gives rein to his fancy, and that his diction is at its very best. 'Hark'ee, I have a secret to tell you. Endymion and the Moon shall meet us upon Mount Latmos, and will be married in the dead of night. But say not a word. Hymen shall put his torch into a dark lanthorn, that it may be secret; and Juno shall give her peacock poppy-water, that he may fold his ogling tail, and Argus's hundred eyes be shut, ha? Nobody shall know, but Jeremy.'

TATTLE. Do you know me, Valentine?
VALENTINE. You? Who are you? No, I hope not.
TATTLE. I am Jack Tattle, your friend.
VALENTINE. My friend, what to do? I am no married man, and thou canst not lie with my wife. I am very poor, and thou canst not borrow money of me. Then, what employment have I for a friend?
ANGELICA. Do you know me, Valentine?
VALENTINE. Oh, very well.
ANGELICA. Who am I?
VALENTINE. You're a woman, one to whom Heaven gave beauty when it grafted roses on a briar. You are the reflection of Heaven in a pond, and he that leaps at you is sunk. You are all white, a sheet of lovely, spotless paper, when you first are born; but you are to be scrawled and blotted by every goose's quill. I know you; for I loved a woman, and loved her so long, that I found out a strange thing: I found out what a woman was good for.

(IV, xvi, 64–85)

Imagine Betterton, the greatest actor of his time, delivering that last speech, with its incomparable rhythm! I like to think that he gave the spectators an idea that Valentine's self-sacrifice for Angelica was nothing but a bold device, a calculated effect; otherwise the sacrifice is an excrescence in this comedy, which, popular and broad though it be, is cynical in Congreve's manner throughout. One is consoled, however, by the pleasant fate of the ingenious Mr. Tattle and the intriguing Mrs. Frail, who are left tied for life against their will. The trick, by the way, of a tricked

434

marriage is constant in Congreve, and reveals his poverty of construction. He can devise you comic situations unflaggingly, but when he approaches the end of a play his *deus ex machinâ* is invariably this flattest and most battered old deity in fairyland.

The dedication to Lord Dorset contains nothing of interest beyond the confession that the play is too long, and the information that part of it was omitted in the playing. A line in the prologue, 'We grieve One falling Adam and one tempted Eve,' is explained by Colley Cibber to refer to Mrs. Mountford, who, having cast her lot with Betterton and migrated to Lincoln's Inn Fields, threw up her part on a question of cash, and to Williams, an actor who 'loved his bottle better than his business,' who deserted at the same time. It serves to show the interest the town took in the players, that the fact was referred to on the stage. The lady's part was taken by Mrs. Ayliff; Mrs. Leigh played the nurse—a very poor part after Lady Plyant; Dogget's success as Ben Legend has been noted. Mrs. Bracegirdle's Angelica was doubtless ravishing: a 'virtuous young woman,' as our ancestors phrased it, but quite relieved from insipidity.

It would need a greater presumption than the writer is gifted withal to add his contribution to the praises critics have lavished on *The Way of the World*. It is better to quote Mr. Swinburne. 'In 1700 Congreve replied to Collier with the crowning work of his genius—the unequalled and unapproached masterpiece of English comedy. The one play in our language which may fairly claim a place beside, or but just beneath, the mightiest work of Molière, is *The Way of the World*.' But he continues: 'On the stage, which had recently acclaimed with uncritical applause the author's more questionable appearance in the field of tragedy,'—*The Mourning Bride*,—'this final and flawless evidence of his incomparable powers met with a rejection then and ever since inexplicable on any ground of conjecture.' There the critics are not unanimous. Mr. Gosse, for instance, has his explanation: that the spectators must have fidgeted, and wished 'that the actors and actresses would be doing something.' Very like, indeed: the spectators, then as now, would no doubt have preferred 'knock-about farce.' But, I venture to think, the explanation is not complete. The construction of the play is weak, certainly, but the actors and actresses do a great deal after all. For that matter, audiences will stand scenes of still wit—but they like to comprehend it; and the characters in *The Way of the*

World, or most of them, represent a society whose attitude and speech are entirely ironical and paradoxical, a society of necessity but a small fraction of any community. Some sort of study or some special experience is necessary to the enjoyment of such a set. It is not the case of a few witticisms and paradoxes firing off at intervals, like crackers, from the mouths of one or two actors with whom the audience is taught to laugh as a matter of course: the vein is unbroken. Now, literalness and common sense are the qualities of the average uninstructed spectator, and *The Way of the World* was high over the heads of its audience.

To come to details. The tragedy of Lady Wishfort has often been remarked—the veritable tragedy of a lovesick old woman. All the grotesque touches, her credulity, her vanity, her admirable dialect ('as I'm a person!'), but serve to make the tragedy the more pitiable. Either, therefore, our appreciation of satiric comedy is defective, or Congreve made a mistake. To regard this poor old soul as mere comedy is to attain to an almost satanic height of contempt: the comedy is more than grim, it is savagely cruel. To be pitiless, on the other hand, is a satirist's virtue. On the whole, we may reasonably say that the tragedy is not too keen in itself, but that it is too obviously indicated. Witwoud is surely a great character? The stage is alive with mirth when he is on it. His entrance in the very first part of the play is delightful. 'Afford me your compassion, my dears; pity me, Fainall; Mirabell, pity me. ... Fainall, how does your lady? Gad, I say anything in the world to get this fellow out of my head. I beg pardon that I should ask a man of pleasure, and the town, a question at once so foreign and domestic. But I talk like an old maid at a marriage, I don't know what I say.' But one might quote for ever. Witwoud, almost as much as Millamant herself, is an eternal type. His little exclamations, his assurance of sympathy, his terror of the commonplace—surely one knows them well? His tolerance of any impertinence, lest he should be thought to have misunderstood a jest, is a great distinction. But Congreve's gibe in the dedication at the critics, who failed 'to distinguish betwixt the character of a Witwoud and a Truewit,' is hardly fair: as Dryden said of Etherege's Sir Fopling, he is 'a fool so nicely writ, The ladies might mistake him for a wit.' Then, Millamant is the ultimate expression of those who, having all the material goods which nature and civilisation can give, live on paradoxes and artifices. Her insolence is the inoffensive insolence only possible to the well-bred.

'O ay, letters,—I had letters,—I am persecuted with letters,—I hate letters,—nobody knows how to write letters; and yet one has 'em, one does not know why,—they serve one to pin up one's hair.' 'Beauty the lover's gift!—Lord, what is a lover, that it can give? Why one makes lovers as fast as one pleases, and they live as long as one pleases, and they die as soon as one pleases; and then if one pleases one makes more.'

In parts of its characterisation *The Way of the World* is extremely bold in observation, extremely careless of literary types and traditions. Mrs. Fainall, a woman who is the friend, and assists in the intrigues, of a man who has ceased to be her lover, is most unconventionally human. Of all the inimitable scenes, that in which Millamant and Mirabell make their conditions of marriage is perhaps the most unquestionable triumph. 'Let us never visit together, nor go to a play together, but let us be very strange and well-bred'—there is its keynote. The dialogue is as sure and perfect in diction, in balance of phrases, and in musical effectiveness as can be conceived, and for all its care is absolutely free in its gaiety. It is the ultimate expression of the joys of the artificial. As for the prologue, it is an invitation to the dullards to damn the play, and is anything but serenely confident. The dedication, to 'Ralph, Earl of Mountague,' has an interesting fact: it tells us that the comedy was written immediately after staying with him, 'in your retirement last summer from the town,' and pays a tribute to the influence of the society the dramatist met there. 'Vous y voyez partout,' said Voltaire of Congreve, 'le langage des honnêtes gens avec des actions de fripon; ce qui prouve qu'il connaissait bien son monde, et qu'il vivait dans ce qu'on appelle la bonne compagnie.'

The want of dramatic skill which has been alleged against Congreve is simply a question of construction—of the construction of his plays as a whole. His plots hang fire, are difficult to follow, and are not worth remembering. But many things besides go to the making of good plays, and few playwrights have had all the theatrical virtues. Do we not pardon a lack of incident in a novel of character? In this connexion it is worth while to contrast Congreve with Sheridan, who in the matter of construction was a far abler craftsman. But is there not in the elder poet enough to turn the scale, even the theatrical scale, ten times over? Compare the petty indignation, with which the dramatist of *The School for Scandal* deals with his scandalmongers, and the amused indifference of

Congreve towards the cabalists in *The Way of the World*. Or take any hero of Congreve's and contrast him with that glorification of vulgar lavishness and canting generosity, that very barmaid's hero, Charles Surface. It is all very well to say that Joseph is the real hero; but Sheridan made it natural for the stupid sentimentality of later days to make him the villain, and Congreve would have made it impossible. Of wit (of course) there is more in a scene of Congreve than in a play of Sheridan. Moreover, faulty in construction as his main plots are, in detail his construction is often admirable: as in play of character upon character, in countless opportunities for delightful archness and cruelty in the women, for the display of every comic emotion in the men. He lived in the playhouse, and his characters, true to life though they be, have about them as it were an ideal essence of the boards. With Hazlitt, 'I would rather have seen Mrs. Abington's Millamant than any Rosalind that ever appeared on the stage.' A lover and a constant frequenter of the theatre—albeit the plays he sees bore him to death—cannot, in reading Congreve, choose but see the glances and hear the intonations of imaginary players.

(pp. xviii–xxix)

101. Sir Leslie Stephen in *English Literature and Society in the Eighteenth Century*

1904

From *English Literature and Society in the Eighteenth Century* (London: 1904), pp. 59–67.

Sir Leslie Stephen (1832–1904), father of Virginia Woolf and Vanessa Bell, abandoned his career as clergyman and Cambridge don after the loss of his religious faith. He became editor of the *Cornhill Magazine* in 1871, where he first published the series of essays known as 'Hours in a Library'. He was the original editor of the *Dictionary of National Biography*, and initiated the 'English Men of Letters' series with a study of Samuel Johnson in 1878. *English Literature and Society in the Eighteenth Century* was his Ford lectures, delivered at Oxford in 1903.

The comedy, as it appears to us, must have been written by blackguards for blackguards. When Congreve became Dryden's heir he inherited the established tradition. Under the new order the 'town' had become supreme; and Congreve wrote to meet the taste of the class which was gaining in self-respect and independence. He tells us in the dedication of his best play, *The Way of the World*, that his taste had been refined in the company of the Earl of Montagu. The claim is no doubt justifiable. So Horace Walpole remarks that Vanbrugh wrote so well because he was familiar with the conversation of the best circles. The social influences were favourable to the undeniable literary merits, to the force and point in which Congreve's dialogue is still superior to that of any English rival, the vigour of Vanbrugh and the vivacity of their chief ally, Farquhar. Moreover, although their moral code is anything but strict, these writers did not descend to some of the depths often sounded by Dryden and Wycherly. The new spirit might seem to be passing on with more literary vitality into the old forms. And yet the consequence, or certainly the sequel to Collier's attack, was the decay of the stage in every sense, from which there was no recovery till the time of Goldsmith and Sheridan.

This is the phenomenon which we have to consider;—let us listen for a moment to the 'distinguished critics' who have denounced or defended the comedy of the time. Macaulay gives as a test of the morality of the Restoration stage that on it, for the first time, marriage becomes the topic of ridicule. We are supposed to sympathise with the adulterer, not with the deceived husband—a fault, he says, which stains no play written before the Civil War. Addison had already suggested this test in the *Spectator*, and proceeds to lament that 'the multitudes are shut out from this noble "diversion" by the immorality of the lessons inculcated.' Lamb, indulging in ingenious paradox, admires Congreve for 'excluding from his scenes (with one exception) any pretensions to goodness or good feeling whatever.' Congreve, he says, spreads a 'privation of moral light' over his characters, and therefore we can admire them without compunction. We are in an artificial world where we can drop our moral prejudices for the time being. Hazlitt more daringly takes a different position and asserts that one of Wycherly's coarsest plays is 'worth ten sermons'—which perhaps does not imply with him any high estimate of moral efficacy. There is, however, this much of truth, I take it, in Hazlitt's contention. Lamb's theory of the non-morality of the dramatic world will not stand examination. The comedy was in one sense thoroughly 'realistic'; and I am inclined to say, that in that lay its chief merit. There is some value in any truthful representation, even of vice and brutality. There would certainly be no difficulty in finding flesh and blood originals for the rakes and the fine ladies in the memoirs of Grammont or the diaries of Pepys. The moral atmosphere is precisely that of the dissolute court of Charles II., and the 'privation of moral light' required is a delicate way of expressing its characteristic feeling. In the worst performances we have not got to any unreal region, but are breathing for the time the atmosphere of the lowest resorts, where reference to pure or generous sentiment would undoubtedly have been received with a guffaw, and coarse cynicism be regarded as the only form of comic insight. At any rate the audiences for which Congreve wrote had just so much of the old leaven that we can quite understand why they were regarded as wicked by a majority of the middle classes. The doctrine that all playgoing was wicked was naturally confirmed, and the dramatists retorted by ridiculing all that their enemies thought respectable. Congreve was, I fancy, a man of better morality than his characters, only forced to pander to the tastes of the rake who had composed the dominant element of his audience. He writes not for mere blackguards, but for the fine gentleman, who affects premature knowledge of the world, professes to be more cynical than he really is, and shows his acuteness by deriding hypocrisy and pharisaic humbug in every claim to virtue. He dwells upon the seamy side of life, and if critics, attracted by his undeniable brilliance, have found his heroines charming, to me it seems that they are the kind of young women whom, if I adopted his moral code, I should think most desirable wives—for my friends.

Though realistic in one sense, we may grant to Lamb that such comedy becomes 'artificial,' and so far Lamb is right, because it supposes a state of things such as happily was abnormal except in a small circle. The plots have to be made up of impossible intrigues, and imply a distorted theory of life. Marriage after all is not really ridiculous, and to see it continuously from this point of view is to have a false picture of realities. Life is not made up of dodges worthy of cardsharpers—and the whole mechanism becomes silly and disgusting. If comedy is to represent a full and fair portrait of life, the dramatist ought surely, in spite of Lamb, to find some space for generous and refined feeling. There, indeed, is a difficulty. The easiest way to be witty is to be cynical. It is difficult, though desirable, to combine good feeling with the comic spirit. The humourist has to expose the contrasts of life, to unmask hypocrisy, and to show selfishness lurking under multitudinous disguises. That, on Hazlitt's showing, was the preaching of Wycherly. I can't think that it was the impression made upon Wycherly's readers. Such comedy may be taken as satire; which was the excuse that Fielding afterwards made for his own performances. But I cannot believe that the actual audiences went to see vice exposed, or used Lamb's ingenious device of dis-believing in the reality. They simply liked brutal and immoral sentiment, spiced, if possible, with art. We may inquire whether there may not be a comedy which is enjoyable by the refined and virtuous, and in which the intrusion of good feeling does not jar upon us as a discord. An answer may be suggested by pointing to Molière, and has been admirably set forth in Mr. George Meredith's essay on the 'Comic Spirit.' There are, after all, ridiculous things in the world, even from the refined and virtuous point of view. The saint, it is true, is apt to lose his temper and become too serious for such a treatment of life-problems. Still the sane intellect which sees things as they are can find a sphere within which it is fair and possible to apply ridicule to affectation and even to vice, and without simply taking the seat of the scorner or substituting a coarse laugh for a delicate smile. A hearty laugh, let us hope, is possible even for a fairly good man. Mr. Meredith's essay indicates the conditions under which the artist may appeal to such a cultivated and refined humour. The higher comedy, he says, can only be the fruit of a polished society which can supply both the model and the audience. Where the art of social intercourse has been carried to a high pitch, where men have learned to be at once courteous and incisive, to admire urbanity, and therefore really good feeling, and to take a true estimate of the real values of life, a high comedy which can produce irony without coarseness, expose shams without advocating brutality, becomes for the first time possible. It must be admitted that the condition is also very rarely fulfilled.

This, I take it, is the real difficulty. The desirable thing, one may say, would have been to introduce a more refined and human art and to get rid of the coarser elements. The excellent Steele tried the experiment. But he had still to work upon the old lines, which would not lend themselves to the new purpose. His passages of moral exhortation would not supply the salt of the old cynical brutalities; they had a painful tendency to become insipid and sentimental, if not maudlin; and only illustrated the difficulty of using a literary tradition which developed spontaneously for one purpose to adapt itself to a wholly different aim. He produced at best not a new genus but an awkward hybrid. But behind this was the greater difficulty that a superior literature would have required a social elaboration, the growth of a class which could appreciate and present appropriate types. Now even the good society for which Congreve wrote had its merits, but certainly its refinement left much to be desired. One condition, as Mr. Meredith again remarks, of the finer comedy is such an equality of the sexes as may admit the refining influence of women. The women of the Restoration time hardly exerted a refining influence. They adopted the ingenious compromise of going to the play, but going in masks. That is, they tacitly implied that the brutality was necessary, and they submitted to what they could not openly approve. Throughout the eighteenth century a contempt for women was still too characteristic of the aristocratic character. Nor was there any marked improvement in the tastes of the playgoing classes. The plays denounced by Collier continued to hold the stage, though more or less expurgated, throughout the century. Comedy did not become decent. In 1729 Arthur Bedford carried on Collier's assault in a 'Remonstrance against the horrid blasphemies and improprieties which are still used in the English playhouses,' and collected seven thousand immoral sentiments from the plays (chiefly) of the last four years. I have not verified his statements. The inference, however, seems to be clear. Collier's attack could not reform the stage. The evolution took the form of degeneration. He could, indeed, give utterance to the disapproval of the stage in general, which we call Puritanical, though it was by no means confined to Puritans or even to Protestants. Bossuet could denounce the stage as well as Collier. Collier was himself a Tory and a High Churchman, as was William Law, of the *Serious Call*, who also denounced the stage. The sentiment was, in fact, that of the respectable middle classes in general. The effect was to strengthen the prejudice which held that playgoing was immoral in itself, and that an actor deserved to be treated as a 'vagrant'—the class to which he legally belonged. During the next half-century, at least, that was the prevailing opinion among the solid middle-class section of society.

102. A. B. Walkley, review of *The Way of the World* in the *Times Literary Supplement*

1904

From the *Times Literary Supplement*, 22 April 1904, pp. 125–6.

Arthur Bingham Walkley (1855–1926) spent his working life as a Post Office official, simultaneously writing dramatic reviews for *The Times* and other newspapers. His early criticism was influenced by his friend William Archer, and he welcomed the appearance of Ibsen's plays on the London stage; but his later views became conservative and conventional. Walkley's review of the Mermaid Society production of *The Way of the World* at the Court Theatre, London, was reprinted with slight changes in his *Drama and Life* in 1907.

'THE WAY OF THE WORLD'

Pleasure-seekers ought to be grateful to the Mermaid Society for reviving *The Way of the World*. We say pleasure-seekers advisedly.

443

For it is the primary business of dramatic entertainments, old or new, to entertain. A classic is a classic not because it is old, not (as Stendhal petulantly said) because it pleased our grandfathers, but because it pleases us. When it ceases to please it is only a *ci-devant* classic. It may still have its proper place on the museum shelf, but the theatre has no use for it. The Mermaid Society has demonstrated *The Way of the World* to be still a live classic. Lady Wishfort and Mrs. Millamant and Sir Wilfull Witwoud are brimming over with life. Congreve is still capable of giving you a vivid sense of reality. You may have suspected that as likely; but it is only through the Mermaid Society that you know it for certain. And how have they enabled you to know it? Through the quite straightforward and familiar, yet magical and inscrutable, influence of flesh and blood.

It is, we suggest, just because this influence is so familiar that its importance in the theatre is commonly under-estimated. What are the elements of an acted drama? Apart from the costumes and scenery, there is the contribution of the dramatist and the contribution of the players. The dramatist 'invents' the story and characters and dialogue. The players contribute their skill; the propriety with which they speak the words set down for them and the art with which they assume their imaginary character. But they also contribute something infinitely more important—something which marks off an acted drama from every other work of art, and something with which art has nothing to do—flesh and blood, their bodies, gestures, glance and voices. It is, probably, because this element has nothing to do with art that we hear so little about it from the artists. They hardly like to admit, or even to think, that they owe so much of their effect to the brute forces of nature, to the simple fact that they are what Lady Wishfort would call 'persons'. Yet there is nothing more certain. The fascination of what is vaguely called 'temperament'—which, whatever else it may mean, means something physical and innate—is supreme in the theatre. A player who has it may warp and maim his part to suit it and yet give the spectator greater pleasure than the merely skilful 'mime' who has it not. Eleonora Duse is a case in point. So, it is evident, was Edmund Kean. The curious psychical influence of bodily presence, the invisible currents that pass between one human being and another, are now the subject of a scientific research still only in its first beginnings. When more is known about them, then more will be known about the peculiar energies of the acted drama. But, though the causes are as yet obscure, the effects are plain enough. There is all the difference in the world between certain lines of printed dialogue headed 'Millamant,' supplemented by the reader's imagination, and the same words spoken by a real woman, with a certain smile, a certain toss of the head, a certain gait. It is a difference not of degree but of kind. What Congreve has done for an imaginary woman called Millamant suddenly springs into life through everything that nature has done for a real woman called Ethel Irving. Of course this flesh-and-blood element, so enormous an aid to the dramatist, may also turn and rend him. Many a speech or action will pass muster in print but stand forth as false or inadequate when actually uttered or performed before us. The character must hold together before, so to speak, the human body is put into it. Congreve's characters stand this test. Therefore *The Way of the World* is still a 'live' classic.

Pursue this analysis a little further and you find the flesh-and-blood element contributing to the total effect in two rather different ways. An old play will present permanent features of human nature—scenes of love and jealousy and hate, or, it may be, a coquette's airs, or, perhaps, an old matron's vain affectations—and temporary transitory features, manners, or language now obsolete. A reader would mentally distinguish between them as the 'actual' and the 'historical' features. What happens, precisely, when they are presented on the stage by means of flesh and blood? The 'actual' features merely become more actual. Their effect of reality is deepened. Such a scene, for instance, as that between Fainall and Mrs. Marwood in the Mall, when the guilty lovers fall out, taste something of the bitterness of a clandestine *amour* with its eternal hovering on the edge of hate, and then kiss again with tears, gains enormously in reality, though it was real enough in the printed page. It was real enough, but now it becomes 'modern'; its close resemblance to sides of life that we know or divine positively startles us. To see a beautiful, highly-strung woman, in the person of Miss Edyth Olive, before our eyes in this plight is a much more poignant thing than to read about the same situation in the book as concerning an imaginary Mrs. Fainall. Still, the difference of impression is only one of degree. So with Millamant's scenes and Lady Wishfort's scenes. These women are eternally true; Miss Ethel Irving and Mrs. Theodore Wright only come in to reinforce the author. Now turn to the 'historical' features—as, for example, Sir Wilfull's tipsy scene or the dialogue between Witwoud and Petulant—and you find the flesh-and-blood element not deepening the impression, but transforming it. What was 'historical' now becomes 'actual'. The things said and done are strange, but the fact that they are said and done by real people makes them credible. While you laughed at Sir Wilfull in the printed page, you scarcely believed in him; it is impossible not to believe in Mr. Lennox Pawle. *Could* there have been such a creature as Witwoud? the reader asks himself. Yes, answers the spectator, for there the fellow really *is*, with the voice and strut and grin of Mr. Nigel Playfair. About Petulant, perhaps, you may still have a lingering doubt; he is an untractable character, and Mr. Ian Maclaren hardly succeeds in dragging him out of the 'historical' limbo. But of one thing this revival has quite convinced us. It has knocked the bottom out of Lamb's plea for Congreve's immoral world as something conventional and fantastic. So soon as the characters are put solidly before you by living men and women you are absolutely appalled by their grim reality. To say that you are appalled is only another way of saying that you are pleased; you snatch a fearful joy.

We have dwelt on the impression of reality given by the revival of this play and the causes of it because we are tired of the nonsense talked about Congreve as now fit only for the 'closet'. We need not examine the reasons why his *Way of the World* is so weak in plot. It is customary to say that Congreve could not invent a plot; it would be much more accurate to say that, given the existing conditions of the 'platform' stage at the time, there was no particular need for him to try. More than once in these columns the reasons have been given for the fact that the Congrevean stage was not a stage of plots, but a stage of 'turns'. This is the very feature which sends Londoners of to-day flocking to 'musical comedy'; why, then, complain of it in Congreve? By the way, it was an actress hitherto associated with 'musical comedy' who played Millamant. Miss Ethel Irving affords another illustration of what we were saying about the supremacy of 'temperament.' She did not quite harmonize with our preconceived notions of Congreve's *grande coquette*, who is majestic, almost awe-inspiring. Miss Irving was rather the 'dainty rogue,' but so dainty a rogue, so 'magnetic', so real a piece of womanhood, such a delight to ear and eye, that it would be affectation to profess any disappointment over her failure in exact coincidence with the ideal character. Mrs. Theodore Wright obviously revelled in the part of Lady Wishfort, yet carefully refrained from over-acting a part which offers strong temptations to exaggeration; in every detail an admirable performance. Mr. Arthur Eckersley was weirdly grotesque as Waitwell, an animated gurgoyle; the Fainall of Mr. Frank Lascelles was good, and the Mrs. Fainall of Miss Ada Potter not bad; but Mr. C. M. Hallard made an unexpectedly embarrassed and occasionally inaudible Mirabell. Both his embarrassment and his inaudibility were now and then shared by the other actors, when some queer words had to be uttered in the presence of ladies. They reminded us of the 'reduced gentlewoman' in the anecdote, who cried 'matches' and then hoped to goodness nobody would hear her.

103. William Archer in the Introduction to *William Congreve*

1912

From *William Congreve* (New York: 1912).

William Archer (1856–1924), a Scot, entered journalism while still a student in Edinburgh and went on to become an influential drama critic for several newspapers. He was the friend of George Bernard Shaw and Harley Granville Barker, and his translations of Ibsen were for long the standard version. Hence there is a special point to his use of the term 'well-made play' below. Archer's edition of Congreve belonged to a series of 'Masterpieces of English Drama'. The opening and concluding sections of the introduction had already appeared in *The Forum* (1910), 43(3) (March): 276–82 and (4) (April): 343–6.

(i) The well-made play
The fate of Congreve's plays in their novelty was, on the face of it, paradoxical, and calculated to beget in him a contempt for the public judgement. He very well knew that *The Double-Dealer* was

a far maturer effort than *The Old Bachelor*, and that *The Way of the World* was a much finer piece of work than *Love for Love*. Yet *The Old Bachelor* and *Love for Love* were triumphantly successful, while *The Double-Dealer* and *The Way of the World* were comparative failures. Whether he actually formed such a resolve or not, it would certainly not have been surprising if, after the cool acceptance of the play illumined by the exquisite creation of Millamant, he had vowed, as Genest says, 'to commit his quiet and his fame no more to the caprices of an audience.'

Yet, had he been able to look into the matter with dispassionate penetration, he might have found the public judgement not so very capricious after all. Many theories have from time to time been advanced to explain why the curve of success ran so directly counter (it would seem) to the curve of merit; but the main and sufficient reason, I think, was a purely technical one. For the immediate success of a new play, the one thing absolutely needful is clearness of construction. An audience cannot endure to have its attention overtaxed in a futile effort to follow the windings of a labyrinthine intrigue; and that was precisely the task which, in *The Double-Dealer*, and to a less degree in *The Way of the World*, Congreve had imposed upon his public. In both cases he rashly essayed to write a 'well-made play,' without possessing the rudiments of what was then an undiscovered, or at any rate an unimported, art. Now there is nothing more irritating than a play which sets forth to be well-made, but is, in fact, helplessly ill-made; so that it need not at all surprise us to find that *The Double-Dealer* and *The Way of the World* had to live down the confused and fatiguing impression which they at first produced, whereas the comparatively simple and perspicuous action of *The Old Bachelor* and *Love for Love* offered no obstacles to instant appreciation.

We must not forget, of course, that the accepted dramatic formula or ideal of that age was widely different from that which is now dominant. Unity of action, or at any rate of theme, is to our mind indispensable in any play which pretends to rank as a work of art. The dramatist seizes upon a crisis in the lives of his characters, states its conditions, and follows its evolution to an end, comic or tragic, ironic or sentimental, as the case may be. We start from a state of calm which contains in it the elements of a dramatic conflict; we see these elements rush together and effervesce; and we watch the effervescence die back again into calm, whether it be that of triumph or disaster, of serenity or despair. No dramatist of the smallest skill will introduce a character that is wholly unnecessary to the advancement of the action, or a conversation that has no bearing on the theme. In a second-rate order of plays, indeed, a certain amount of 'comic' (or sentimental) 'relief' may be admitted; but even if, for instance, a pair of young lovers is suffered to lighten the gloom of a tragic story, an effort is always made to weave them into the main fabric and give them an efficient part in it. This conception of a play as the logical working-out of a given subject has had for its necessary consequence the total abandonment of the old five-act convention. The main crisis of which the action consists falls naturally and almost inevitably into a series of sub-crises, to each of which an act is devoted. Five acts are still the limit which can scarcely be exceeded in the three hours to which a representation is confined; but a four-act distribution of the subject is far commoner, while three acts—a beginning, middle, and end—may almost be called the normal and logical modern form.

In Congreve's day, on the other hand, the dramatist's problem was, not to give his action an organic unity, but to fill a predetermined mould, so large that one action seldom or never sufficed for it. The underplot, therefore, was an established institution; and sometimes a play would consist of two or three loosely interwoven actions, so nearly equal in extent and import-ance that it was hard to say which was the main plot and which the underplots. The result of this mingling of heterogeneous matters was to render doubly difficult the manipulation of a complex intrigue. Audiences, indeed, were not so exacting on the score of probability as they now are. But though they would accept a good deal that we should now reject as extravagant, they wanted to understand what they were accepting; and that they could not do when a chain of events demanding close and continuous attention was being constantly interrupted by the humours and intrigues of subsidiary characters. Both from internal and external evidence, we can see that Congreve's keen intellect was dissatisfied with the loosely-knit patchwork play of the period. In the preface to *The Double-Dealer* he says: 'I made the plot as strong as I could, because it was single; and I made it single, because I would avoid confusion, and was resolved to preserve the three unities of the drama.' In the preface to *The Way of the World*, again, he complains of the spectators 'who come with expectation to laugh at the last act of a play, and are better entertained with two or three unseasonable jests, than with the artful solution of the *fable*.' These remarks show a technical ideal far in advance of his time; but whenever he essayed to realize that ideal, he met with misfortune; partly because his manipulative skill was inadequate to the tasks he set himself, partly because the five-act form, forbidding continuity and concentration, unduly handicapped what skill he possessed.

Such, at least, is my solution of the seeming paradox presented by the success of his less elaborate, and the comparative failure of his more elaborate, comedies.

(pp. 9–13)

(ii) Ill-made and well-made plays by Congreve
The character of his next play was as different as its fate; and the difference is so full of instruction, even for the modern playwright, that I must beg the reader's indulgence if I analyze *The Double-Dealer* at some length.

This remarkable melodrama—for a comedy it can scarcely be called—might serve as a typical specimen of an ill-made 'well-made play'; or, in other words, a standing example of the dangers of misdirected ingenuity. Its title-character, Maskwell, the Double-Dealer, is its ruin. The incredible daring of his turpitude he shares with Iago and with a thousand villains of melodrama. But Iago's intrigues are perfectly clear and comprehensible; whereas Maskwell's are so involved and obscure that it is almost impossible to unravel their tangled skein. I propose, however, to make the attempt.

First, the reader (or the audience) has to master a complex set of relationships—always a defect in drama. Lord Touchwood, an elderly nobleman, has married the sister (the much younger sister, we must assume) of one Sir Paul Plyant. Sir Paul by his first wife has had a daughter named Cynthia, now grown up; and he has married a second wife, the Lady Plyant of the play. Now Lord Touchwood has a nephew and heir presumptive named Mellefont, who is betrothed to Cynthia Plyant. The 'writings' are to be 'settled' on the very day on which the action passes, and the marriage is 'appointed' for the morrow.

Mellefont, however, knows that his uncle's wife, Lady Touchwood, will do all she can to prevent his marriage with Cynthia, because she is herself frantically in love with him and fiercely

450

resentful of his rejection of her advances. He has a friend, Jack Maskwell, whom he has introduced into Lord Touchwood's household, it does not appear in what capacity; and this friend he has commissioned to watch Lady Touchwood narrowly, and give him notice if she attempts any move to his disadvantage. But in a scene between Maskwell and Lady Touchwood we very soon learn that she is his (Maskwell's) mistress—he has caught her on the rebound from her rejection by Mellefont—and that he is plotting with her to prevent Mellefont's marriage with Cynthia. As yet—that is to say, in Act I—they have hit on nothing better than to persuade Lady Plyant, Cynthia's foolish and affected step-mother, that Mellefont's addresses to her stepdaughter mask a passion for herself. Lady Touchwood justly observes that this is 'a trifling design; for her first conversing with Mellefont will convince her of the contrary'; to which Maskwell replies: 'I know it.—I don't depend upon it.—But it will prepare something else; and gain us leisure to lay a stronger plot.'

Here, manifestly, is a grave technical error. The conspirators have only a few hours at their command, for it is already afternoon, and the signing of the settlement is to take place that evening; yet they waste energy on a plot which they know must fail, in order to 'gain leisure' for a stronger contrivance. It is true, no doubt, that the law of economy which prevails in our stricter forms of drama had not the same force in the patchwork plays of that period. Yet it can never have been otherwise than dangerous to demand the attention of an audience for an intrigue confessedly foredoomed to failure, at a time when the whole hopes of the intriguers depended upon prompt and effective action.

The device, however, is temporarily successful, thanks to the voluble vanity of Lady Plyant and the unbounded credulity of Sir Paul. It furnishes a couple of good comedy scenes, the main substance of the second act. Towards the close of the act, Maskwell meets the distracted Mellefont and reassures him (oddly enough!) by the information that he has wormed himself into the confidence of Lady Touchwood by pretending to be her confederate against Mellefont, and even 'encouraging' her, for Mellefont's 'diversion,' in slandering him to Lady Plyant. He tells him, moreover, that to convince Lady Touchwood that he really shares her hatred of Mellefont, he has told her that he (Maskwell) has 'been long secretly in love with Cynthia,' and hopes to succeed to her hand

and fortune when Mellefont is ruined. All this is supposed in some way to console Mellefont mightily; but Maskwell does not show how Mellefont's cause has been in any practical way advanced by his elaborate duplicity. Then, when Mellefont is gone, he lets us see, in a soliloquy, that he is really in love with Cynthia, and that this is the ultimate motive of his whole policy.

These scenes are injudicious in the extreme. It is their smallest fault, perhaps, that they make Mellefont's credulity seem excessive and contemptible. He has been warned by his true friend, Careless, not to put too much trust in Maskwell; yet it never occurs to him to wonder whether the man who makes such a boast of duping Lady Touchwood (and to such small apparent purpose) may not be duping other people as well. Still more unfortunate, from the technical point of view, is the impossibility of distinguishing truth from falsehood in Maskwell's statements. He tells Mellefont that in order to hoodwink Lady Touchwood he has affected to be in love with Cynthia; whereas the truth is that he loves her without any affectation, and has breathed no word of it to Lady Touchwood.

So stated, the matter seems tolerably simple; but it is only in the light of after events that all this is ascertained. At the point we have reached, the audience has no means of knowing what to believe or what to disbelieve, and has merely a sense of being lost in a maze of duplicity. Congreve was partly led astray by the desire to draw an original type of villain whose method should be to deceive people by telling them the truth.* The notion was ingenious; but it demanded the inventive craftsmanship of a Scribe to carry it out successfully; and this Congreve was far from possessing.

At the beginning of Act III, Lady Touchwood, apparently acting on her own initiative, accuses Mellefont to Lord Touchwood of having persecuted her with his addresses. This is, of course, the master card in her ladyship's hand, and ought to have been played with all possible care and deliberation; yet an hour or so before, when she and Maskwell adopted a 'trifling design' in order to 'gain leisure to lay a stronger plot,' this obvious piece of villainy does not seem to have occurred to either of them. No skilful dramatist would have discounted his great effect by thus giving it the air of a fortuitous afterthought. Lord Touchwood believes his wife's story, and determines to disown and disinherit Mellefont; whereupon she, in elation at her success, arranges an amorous rendezvous with Maskwell at eight o'clock in her bedchamber. Mellefont then

entering, Maskwell (true to his system) tells him of this arrangement, and suggests that he (Mellefont) should come upon the scene
of the assignation and thus ever afterwards have his aunt at his
mercy. Mellefont agrees with enthusiasm, and calls down blessings
on the head of his friend and 'better genius.'

Though there are many improbabilities in this combination, it is
plausible enough according to the accepted conventions of that day,
and it holds out promise of a strong situation. But what does
Congreve do? He suffers the interest of the audience to evaporate
while he carries forward the two underplots—the amours of
Careless and Lady Plyant, Brisk and Lady Froth—in a series of
scenes which fill forty-two pages of the edition of 1710, and must
have taken at least an hour in the acting. Then, towards the close of
Act IV, the main intrigue is resumed, Mellefont surprises Maskwell and Lady Touchwood together, Maskwell escapes, Lady
Touchwood grovels at Mellefont's feet, until Lord Touchwood,
brought thither by Maskwell, appears upon the scene, when she
turns the tables by accusing Mellefont of an infamous attempt upon
her. This is undoubtedly a strong scene of what we should now call
emotional drama, and might have made the success of the play had
it been followed by a brief and effective last act. Unfortunately the
last act merely carried to a pitch of extravagance the imbecile
audacity of Maskwell's double-dealing, and proved Congreve
incapable of attaining that clearness-in-complexity which is indispensable in a play of intrigue.

At the very beginning of Act V, we find a touch which betrays
the weakness of the author's method. Maskwell congratulates Lady
Touchwood on her triumph over Mellefont, but says nothing to
show that it was he himself, and not chance, that brought Lord
Touchwood on the scene. Then in a soliloquy he says, 'I durst not
own my introducing my lord, ... for she would have suspected a
design which I should have been puzzled to excuse.'

Now it is and must ever remain an enigma what Maskwell here
has in mind. There are two or three possible solutions, but none
convincing; and none, certainly, that would come home to the
instant apprehension of a spectator in the theatre. Even if one could
produce an argument to show that the policy of silence was
certainly the right one from Maskwell's point of view, or certainly
the one which Maskwell would have adopted, the very fact that
such an argument was needed would prove the author to have

become involved in a tangle of circumstance which could only baffle and fatigue the mind of an audience. Moreover, the best conceivable reasons for Maskwell's silence to Lady Touchwood are cancelled by the fact that a chance word from Lord Touchwood to his wife might, and in all probability would, upset his calculations. The husband and wife could not but discuss the incident; and it is a hundred chances to one that something would be said to reveal the fact of Maskwell's intervention. Lady Touchwood would then say to herself, 'Why did he conceal this from me?'—and she would necessarily conclude that he was playing some double game with her. I dwell upon this trifling matter because it affords a characteristic instance of the dangers of over-complexity. .

Having explained, or rather failed to explain, in soliloquy, why he kept Lady Touchwood in the dark, Maskwell sees Lord Touchwood approaching, and holds this a good opportunity to keep on soliloquizing and let his Lordship overhear a confession of his love for Cynthia. We know from Congreve's Epistle Dedicatory that one of the features of his play on which criticism fastened was his use of soliloquy; and Mr. Gosse represents that this was a 'return to an old conventional practice' which 'the English comic writers had carefully eschewed.' As a matter of fact, there are a good many soliloquies in Etheredge, in Wycherley, and in Shadwell. Still, the tendency of the past thirty years had no doubt been to adopt the French device of the confidant in preference to the Elizabethan convention of the soliloquy; so that, in making Maskwell unpack his heart like Iago or Richard III, Congreve was, unconsciously it would seem,[†] reverting to a somewhat antiquated form of technic.

We need not dwell on his arguments in its defence: they are commonplaces whose force depends upon the question whether we do or do not aim at a complete illusion of reality; and, indeed, it is hard to see why audiences who habitually accepted the 'aside' (a far more crying sin against illusion) should have boggled at the soliloquy, as such. But Congreve oddly omits to notice a very obvious distinction: the difference between the soliloquy pure and simple and the overheard soliloquy. The gist of his defence is that 'we ought not to imagine that this man either talks to us or to himself; he is only thinking.' Very well; but how comes it, then, that Lord Touchwood overhears Maskwell's thoughts? It may be said that Maskwell intends that he should do so, and deliberately speaks for that purpose. But this plea is of no avail; for if we admit, as Congreve starts by admitting, that 'for a man to talk to himself appears absurd and unnatural,' how comes it that the absurdity and unnaturalness do not strike Lord Touchwood? The truth is that the overheard soliloquy, whether the speaker be, or be not, aware of the listener's presence, is an outrage on probability of a wholly different order from the soliloquy proper, if I may so distinguish it. The true defence of the soliloquy is that which Congreve alleges: the character is not supposed to be really speaking: it is the audience which becomes, for the nonce, a company of thought-readers, to whom his brain is supernormally transparent. But when another person on the stage hears him, the assumption that he is merely thinking breaks down, and all plausibility at once vanishes. The convention, in short, is tolerable only as between the actor and the audience. When another actor overhears the imaginary utterance, it becomes no longer imaginary, but actual—and impossible.

We may pretty fairly conclude, I think, that even if the first-night audience did not clearly realize it, their objection was much less to Maskwell's soliloquies in general than to his overheard soliloquy in particular. The device might be passable enough in such a purely comic scene as that between Sharper and Sir Joseph Wittol in *The Old Bachelor*; but as a serious expedient at a critical point in a serious play it was certainly very dangerous.

To resume our analysis: Maskwell, having disclosed to Lord Touchwood his love for Cynthia, and secured that nobleman's enthusiastic support for his suit, points out to us, in another soliloquy, that he has got himself into an extremely precarious situation; for if Lady Touchwood should learn of his design 'Her fury would spare nothing, though she involved herself in ruin.' This is a very just apprehension, and might have occurred to him earlier; but it is one of the constant characteristics of the melodramatic villain to be at once the most calculating and the most foolhardy of men.

As a matter of fact, the first thing Lord Touchwood does is (quite naturally) to tell Lady Touchwood of Maskwell's design upon Cynthia; and it is one of the innumerable constructive errors of the play that, though her Ladyship is duly incensed, her fury is not the main factor in Maskwell's final discomfiture. From this point onward, indeed, the plot becomes so incredibly complicated that one despairs of making it comprehensible. Maskwell tells Mellefont that Lord Touchwood, at Lady Touchwood's suggestion, is planning his (Maskwell's) marriage with Cynthia, so that Mellefont's only chance is promptly to elope with her. But they cannot elope (it would appear) save in Lord Touchwood's coach and six; and how are they to obtain the use of it? For this, too, Maskwell has his scheme. He will tell Lord Touchwood of the proposed elopement, declaring that, at the last moment, by an ultimate masterpiece of subtlety, he proposes to substitute himself for Mellefont, and marry Cynthia in spite of herself. This is, of course, his real design, though to Mellefont he represents it as a plan for hoodwinking Lord Touchwood. To prevent all danger of discovery, Mellefont is to disguise himself as the Touchwoods' domestic chaplain; and Maskwell contrives that Mellefont shall be hindered in putting on his disguise, and that the real 'Levite,' Mr. Saygrace, shall drive away with him (Maskwell) and Cynthia, who shall take Saygrace for Mellefont in clerical costume.

Is it possible to imagine a more inextricable tangle? No human brain can keep the threads clear for two consecutive minutes. And, after all, even if the plot should succeed, one does not see how Maskwell is to make Cynthia marry him. To do her justice, she is not a young lady who is likely to be terrorized into consent. In point of fact, the whole intrigue comes to nothing, not through its inherent impossibility, but through the chance that Lord Touchwood happens to overhear a violent scene between Lady Touchwood and Maskwell, which opens his eyes to their relations and to the villain's character. It is worth noting that even at this last moment Maskwell succeeds in throwing dust in Lady Touchwood's eyes by pretending that all his plotting has really been directed to the advancement of her designs upon Mellefont.

What wonder if audiences were at first baffled and fatigued by the effort to follow the outs and ins of this labyrinthine plot! Well may Lord Touchwood say (Act V, Scene iv): 'I am confounded when I look back, and want a clue to guide me through the various mazes of unheard-of treachery.' The public no doubt echoed his sentiment; and it was, I cannot but think, this sense of bewilderment that was mainly accountable for the cold reception of the comedy. There was no professional criticism in those days; which means that playgoers were not accustomed to attempt any clear analysis of the effect produced upon them by a given work of art.

Doubtless, then, they were even more apt than playgoers of to-day to mistake, or remain unconscious of, the true grounds of their sensations and judgements.

But, while conventions, prejudices, and ideals change, the psychological conditions of attention and comprehension remain much the same from age to age; wherefore we are justified in arguing, on the purely technical plane, from the sensations of an audience of to-day to those of an audience of two centuries ago. Other than purely technical considerations may have affected the fortunes of the play; perhaps the character of Lady Touchwood was felt to be too tragic for a play that was nominally a comedy; perhaps, even in the days before Collier's *Short View*, the ladies did not much like to see three women of quality (not mere citizens' wives) represented as so many adulteresses. But we may feel pretty confident, I think, that the main reason of the public coolness was the inextricable complexity of Maskwell's machinations, combined with the total lack of skill displayed in laying down the lines and marking the rhythm, so to speak, of the action. Congreve had no idea how to seize the attention and sustain the interest of his audience.

Yet there was much that was attractive in the play. Lady Touchwood was a splendidly vivid creation, and the other two ladies were amusing and nicely differentiated studies. Cynthia was a pleasant and unaffected young woman, and Brisk an agreeably diverting fribble. The dialogue of the lighter passages, too, had all Congreve's brilliancy; so that it is not surprising that after the first few performances the comedy (as Dryden said) 'gained ground daily.' The approval of Queen Mary came to its aid, and it soon established itself as a stock piece.

Experience has shown again and again that if a play has sufficient general vitality to survive technical defects of the kind I have pointed out, they are less and less felt as time goes on, until they come to be accepted as matters of course. The perceptions of later audiences are never quite so alert, or their nerves so highly strung, as those of the public which sees a play in its novelty. When it has once established its position, people come to it prepared to enjoy what is good and endure or ignore the rest. Excellence of character-drawing, in particular, will often enable a play to live down very grave defects of plot. It is not surprising, then, that *The*

457

Double-Dealer should have held the stage during the whole of the eighteenth century. Fourteen revivals are indexed in Genest, the last in 1802.

When we pass to *Love for Love*, we find an action far better knit than that of *The Old Bachelor* and infinitely less involved than that of *The Double-Dealer*. Put to the test of narration, the story appears, not very probable indeed, but fairly simple and coherent. Valentine Legend is deeply in love with an heiress named Angelica, who, out of sheer contrariety as it would seem, affects indifference towards him. In his depression he runs into extravagance, and incurs the resentment of his father, Sir Sampson Legend, who offers to pay his debts on condition that he will sign a deed enabling Sir Sampson to leave all his property to his younger son Ben, a sailor. Valentine agrees, and receives the four thousand pounds which his father has promised him; but when it comes to carrying out his promise of breaking the entail, he pretends to be insane, and unfit to execute any legal document.

Meanwhile, Ben has come home from sea, and Sir Sampson has arranged for him a marriage with Miss Prue, Angelica's cousin, the ignorant, hoydenish daughter of old Foresight, an astrological monomaniac. Prue, however, is so enraptured with a scented fop, Tattle, that she will have nothing to say to the rough and boisterous tarpaulin, Ben; while Mrs. Foresight's sister, the too aptly named Mrs. Frail, throws herself at Ben's head and almost carries him off. When she learns, however, that, owing to Valentine's madness, it is doubtful whether Ben will be his father's heir, she at once cools towards him, and plots with Valentine's man, Jeremy, to induce his crazy master to marry her, mistaking her for Angelica. Tattle, meanwhile, sees in Valentine's affliction an opportunity to make love to Angelica; and Jeremy arranges one of those amazing masked marriages, so dear to playwrights and audiences of the period, whereby Tattle marries Frail, mistaking her for Angelica, and Frail marries Tattle, mistaking him for Valentine. Sir Sampson, baffled by Valentine's madness and Ben's refusal to marry Prue, thinks of marrying Angelica himself, and she feigns to consent. On learning this Valentine returns to his senses, and offers to fulfil his promise of signing away his inheritance; whereupon Angelica at last confesses her love for him, and the comedy is at an end.

This is a very trivial and poorly invented story, running into sheer conventional extravagance in the marriage of Tattle and Mrs. Frail. But, such as it is, it possesses some approach to unity. All the parts are interdependent, except one slight episode which I have not mentioned: the inevitable adultery, between Valentine's friend Scandal and Mrs. Foresight. It is, then, much more of an ordered structure than the plot of *The Old Bachelor*, and much less of a bewildering tangle than the plot of *The Double-Dealer*. But its merit is mainly extrinsic, in that it affords ample and unencumbered scope for the character-drawing and dialogue wherein lay Congreve's real strength. In *The Double-Dealer* a large part of the scanty time at the playwright's command was given up to the mere mechanism of the intrigue; in *Love for Love* there is no more intrigue than is necessary to keep the personages in motion, and exhibit their characters in divers aspects. And the characters themselves have the merit (from the point of view of popular acceptance) of being familiar and readily comprehensible, yet drawn with a vividness which imparts to them an air of novelty.

We have, first, the indispensable two wits and the butt (or half-wit) who form the nucleus of almost every comedy of the period. In *The Old Bachelor*, the wits are Vainlove and Belmour, and the butt (of a somewhat unusual type) is Heartwell; in *The Double-Dealer*, the wits are Mellefont and Careless, the butt Brisk; in *The Way of the World*, the wits are Mirabell and Fainall, the butt Witwoud (with Petulant as his understudy); here the wits are Valentine and Scandal, the butt Tattle. One knows not which to admire the most: the delicate differentiation of such characters as Vainlove, Valentine, and Mirabell, Brisk, Tattle, and Witwoud, or the patience of the audiences who did not find such established types, however subtly differentiated, intolerably monotonous. In the present instance, however, Valentine's assumed madness gave his character a certain external novelty which was no doubt appreciated. Then we have in Sir Sampson Legend an extremely spirited variant of the 'heavy father' type, which was, perhaps, less hackneyed in Congreve's time than one is apt to imagine. It descended, indeed, from the classic comedy, and is familiar in Molière; but I do not find that it had hitherto been much employed on the Restoration stage. Sir Sampson is the ancestor of a long line, but does not seem to have had many noted predecessors in the plays of his own period. Foresight, again, is a strongly-drawn eccentric, who might have walked out of a play of Jonson's. The sailor, Ben, was at once the most novel character in the play and its greatest attraction. The trait on which Lamb commented—his forgetfulness of the death of 'brother Dick'—is a touch of nature worth a score of brilliant repartees. Mrs. Foresight and Mrs. Frail are commonplace types of middle-class femininity, as the comedy of the day was pleased to represent it; Miss Prue is one of the horribly debased descendants of Molière's Agnès, through Wycherley's Margery, who are popular to this day with a certain order of playwrights and audiences; and Angelica is a character, not without a certain chilly charm, but so enigmatic that no two critics interpret her in quite the same way. Add to these a witty valet and a coarsely comic nurse, and we have such a gallery, if not of great characters, at any rate of strongly-marked acting parts, as could not but ensure the success of the play, in the absence of any good reason to the contrary. As we have seen, then, that the plot was clear and simple, the action coherent and continuous, there is nothing to surprise us in the instantaneous triumph of *Love for Love*.

The comparative failure of *The Way of the World* may seem to present a far more difficult problem; but here, too, I think that technical considerations amply account for the initial coolness it had to overcome. Undeterred by his experience in *The Double-Dealer*, Congreve once more embarked on a complicated plot; and once more he put a fatiguing strain on the attention of the audience.

Here again we have to master a complex set of relationships, legal and illicit. Millamant is Lady Wishfort's niece, and half her fortune is dependent on her aunt's consent to her marriage. Mrs. Fainall is Lady Wishfort's daughter, was a widow before she married Fainall, and is Mirabell's ex-mistress. Mrs. Marwood is Fainall's present mistress, and is in love with Mirabell. Sir Wilfull Witwoud is Lady Wishfort's nephew, and half-brother to Tony Witwoud; Mirabell has an uncle, Sir Rowland,‡ personated by his valet Waitwell; and Waitwell is secretly married to Lady Wishfort's maid, Foible. This marriage, by way of keeping the audience in something of a fog from the first, is announced in the scene between Mirabell and the footman in Act I, when we do not in the least know who are the parties referred to, and is not explained until we come to the scene between Mirabell and Mrs. Fainall in the middle of Act II.

That, however, is a trifle; the real weakness of the play lies in the extreme difficulty of bearing in mind, from moment to moment, the motives of all concerned. Mirabell's plot is, it would seem, to cover Lady Wishfort with ridicule through her acceptance of the false Sir Rowland, and then, as a condition of keeping the affair secret, to insist on her consenting to his marriage with Millamant. It is a hazardous experiment at best; one would think it probable that resentment might only make her doubly resolute to oppose the marriage. But, assuming that 'Sir Rowland's' success would mean Mirabell's success, why does not Mrs. Marwood, when she overhears the plot in Act III, instantly put Lady Wishfort on her guard? She knows that her lover, Fainall, is bent on having his wife's fortune augmented by the six thousand pounds of Millamant's fortune which will be forfeited if Millamant marries without Lady Wishfort's consent; yet she (Marwood) holds her peace until the 'Sir Rowland' plot is on the verge of success, and then clumsily discloses it in a written denunciation which Foible's resourcefulness parries and turns to the advantage of the plotters!

There is really no good reason for this tardiness; Mrs. Marwood suffers the plot to proceed simply because, if she did not, the author would be balked of his most effective scenes; and that was not a good reason for an audience of 1700, any more than for an audience of to-day. The event, indeed, shows the emptiness of Mirabell's machination; for if fear of ridicule was to bring Lady Wishfort to terms, she might surely have been brought to terms at the end of Act IV—greater ridicule she could not well have incurred. As it is (and this is a fault of art), she learns the truth in the interval after Act IV, and is disclosed to us, in the first scene of Act V, at the height of exasperation.

The scenes that ensue probably determined the ill-fortune of the play, for they are involved, melodramatic, and tedious.§ Indeed, it is practically a new intrigue on which our attention is centred. Fainall's bullying attempt to levy blackmail on his wife and her mother, by the threat of publishing his own dishonour, is at once displeasing and uninteresting; and when he is baffled by the production of a deed conveying the whole of Mrs. Fainall's fortune to Mirabell in trust, we feel that, even if the device be defensible from the legal point of view, it is dramatically of the feeblest. The tangle of intrigues is not by any means so inextricable as that of the last Act of *The Double-Dealer*; but it is mechanical, sordid, and open to criticism at a dozen points. Though the audiences of that day did not rebel against cynicism, they preferred

461

it with a smack of sensuality; whereas in this case it was merely intellectual and arid. Once more, in fact, Congreve had tried, and failed, to construct a well-made play.

But once more, and much more decisively than in the case of *The Double-Dealer*, the abounding merits of the play gradually outweighed its defects, and established it as a classic of the stage. Millamant was by far the most delightful and vital creation of the whole school of comedy; and Lady Wishfort was the consummate and incomparable incarnation of the amorous old woman—a hideous type, but always popular with audiences of somewhat crass sensibilities. It has been suggested, as a reason for the initial failure of the play, that Lady Wishfort was thought a too 'tragic' character. This I cannot for a moment believe. It is a reading of modern fastidiousness into the eighteenth-century public, and a fastidiousness, too, which many modern audiences do not exhibit. Witwoud was the pleasantest of Congreve's fribbles, and Sir Wilfull by no means the least pleasant of the country squires who abounded in the comedy of the day. Petulant I cannot but think somewhat of an anachronism—an Elizabethan or Jacobean survival—and one wonders whether the audience may not have felt that one drunken man was enough for a single evening's entertainment. The servants, on the other hand, are all brilliant acting parts. Mrs. Fainall is the only colourless character in the play. Fainall, though preternaturally odious, is at least more human than Maskwell; and in Mrs. Marwood we have a rather effective suggestion of a dark, passionate, sinister nature. The comedy held its own on the stage until 1800, and has been revived in recent years (1904) by Mr. Philip Carr's Mermaid Company of players. *Love for Love*, on the other hand, was currently acted as late as 1825, and was revived by Macready at Drury Lane in 1842.

(pp. 15–34)

NOTES

* Maskwell says in Act V: 'I must deceive Mellefont once more.... Now will I, in my old way, discover the whole and real truth of the matter to him, that he may not suspect one word on't.' See also the motto from Terence on the title-page of the play.

† He says that the objection to the soliloquy 'does not relate in particular

to this play, but to all or most that ever have been written.'
‡ It is not quite clear whether Mirabell really possesses such a relative or whether he is invented for the nonce.
§ I speak of their effect not on speculation alone, for I saw the play acted in London in 1904.

104. Charles Whibley in *The Cambridge History of English Literature*

1912

From 'The Restoration Drama II', in *The Cambridge History of English Literature*, eds A.W. Ward and A. R. Waller, 15 vols (Cambridge: 1912), VIII, *The Age of Dryden*, pp. 147–57.

Charles Whibley (1859–1930) collaborated with W. E. Henley on the *Scots Observer* (later the *National Observer*) and on 'The Tudor Translations' series of reprints. On his return from Paris in 1897 after three years as correspondent of the *Pall Mall Gazette*, he began regular contributions to *Blackwood's Magazine* which continued over twenty-five years. Besides his literary and political journalism, Whibley supplied introductions to a variety of texts. The chapter from which the following extract is taken was reprinted in Whibley's *Literary Studies* (1919).

In his preface to the published play [*The Old Bachelor*], Congreve pleaded in extenuation an ignorance of the town and stage. No plea was necessary; and, if his ignorance of the town were confessed, the stage had left him no lessons to learn. With him, indeed, the craft of the stage was instinctive. From the very first he translated whatever he saw and heard in terms of the theatre. The comedy, which beguiled 'a slow recovery,' displays all the technical adroitness of an old hand. The dialogue is polished to an even surface; the play of wit flashes like sunlight upon water; of the writing no more need be said than that it is Congreve's own. For the rest, *The Old*

Bachelor wears upon it every sign of youth and inexperience. Neither of the two stories which are interlaced, none too closely, in its plot is fresh or original. Though none of Congreve's contemporaries could have written the play, any one of them might have devised its fable. In other words, Congreve is playing supremely well the tune of the time. Heartfree and Silvia are but counters of artificial comedy. The marriage of the lady in the mask, which unties the knot of the play, is no better than an accepted convention of the stage. Bluffe, Sharper, and Wittol, who conduct the underplot, are stock characters of a still older fashion. They might have stepped out from Ben Jonson's comedy of humours. When Bluffe says: 'Sir, I honour you; I understand you love fighting, I reverence a man that loves fighting, sir, I kiss your hilts,' you recognise the authentic accent of Bobadill. Even Fondlewife, that 'kind of mongrel zealot' owes less to life than to Zeal-of-the-land Busy. In the scene where Lucy, Silvia's maid, altercates with Setter, the pimp, the language is marked by all the bombast of youth, which Congreve presently laid aside. Says Setter: 'Thou art some forsaken Abigail we have dallied with heretofore, and art come to tickle thy imagination with remembrance of iniquity past.' And Lucy replies: 'No, thou pitiful flatterer of thy master's imperfections! thou maukin, made up of the shreds and parings of his superfluous fopperies!' This is the language neither of life nor of comedy, and it was doubtless acceptable to the audience by its mere expectedness.

But if we put aside the youthful extravagance of some passages and the too frequent reliance upon familiar types, we may discern in *The Old Bachelor* the true germs of Congreve's comedy. Not merely is the style already his own; his purpose and sense of character are evident on every page. Belinda, an affected lady, who 'never speaks well of Bellmour herself, nor suffers anybody else to rail at him,' might be a first, rough outline of Millamant. And Bellmour sketches, in a single speech, the whole philosophy of the poet: 'Come, come,' says he, 'leave business to idlers, and wisdom to fools: they have need of 'em: wit be my faculty, and pleasure my occupation, and let father Time shake his glass.' Henceforth, wit was Congreve's faculty, pleasure his occupation; and he succeeded so well that time still shakes his glass at him in vain.

In the same year (1693), *The Double-Dealer* was played at Drury lane, and Congreve's reputation, great already, was vastly enhanced. In character, style and construction, *The Double-Dealer* is far above its predecessor. The one fault commonly imputed to it is that it has too grave a motive for a comedy of manners. Lady Touchwood is in love with Millefont, to whom Cynthia is promised. Maskwell, lady Touchwood's gallant, knows her secret, and attempts to use it for Millefont's discomfiture and his own conquest of Cynthia. Such is the simple story, told with a simplicity of purpose in which Congreve himself took a proper pride.

'The mechanical part of it,' said he, in the dedication addressed to Charles Montague, 'is regular. . . . I designed the moral first, and to that moral I invented the fable, and do not know that I have borrowed one part of it anywhere. I made the plot as strong as I could, because it is single, because I would avoid confusion, and was resolved to preserve the three unities of the drama.'

That he succeeded in his design none will deny. *The Double-Dealer* is sternly classical in construction, and moves, from the rise of the curtain in the first act to the fall of the curtain in the fifth, to a settled end and with a settled purpose. The machinery of the play is still conventional. A wrong letter given to Sir Paul by lady Plyant, the villain surprised from behind a screen—these are the keys which unlock the plot. We might forget their simple artifice, were it not for the conscious villainy of Maskwell. That surpasses pretence and belief. Maskwell, indeed, is the familiar villain of melodrama. He is the ancestor in a direct line of Blifil and Joseph Surface, 'a sedate, a thinking villain,' as lady Touchwood calls him, 'whose black blood runs temperately bad.' The violence of his scenes with this lady exceeds the proper limit of comedy, and his discovery by lord Touchwood verges upon the tragic:

'Astonishment,' he exclaims, 'binds up my rage! Villainy upon villainy! Heavens what a long track of dark deceit has this discovered! I am confounded when I look back, and want a clue to guide me through the various mazes of unheard-of treachery. My wife! damnation! my hell!'
[V, xix, 2–8]

But there is no anticlimax. Congreve, with characteristic restraint, permits Maskwell after his unmasking to say no word.

Indeed, were it not for Maskwell's inveterate habit of soliloquy, he might trick us almost as easily as he tricks Millefont.

'Why let me see,' he murmurs, 'I have the same force, the same words and accents, when I speak what I do think, and when I speak what I do not think—the very same—and dear dissimulation is the only art not to be known from nature.'

[II, vii, 26–31]

And, again, 'I will deceive 'em all and yet secure myself: 'twas a lucky thought! Well, this double-dealing is a jewel.' Here Congreve resolutely parts company with nature, and relies upon an artifice of the stage, an artifice which he defends with considerable ingenuity. 'A man in a soliloquy,' he argues, 'is only thinking, and thinking such matter as were inexcusable folly in him to speak.' In other words,

because we are concealed spectators of the plot in agitation, and the poet finds it necessary to let us know the whole mystery of his contrivance, he is willing to inform us of this person's thoughts; and to that end is forced to make use of the expedient of speech, no other better way yet being invented for the communication of thought.

That is as good a defence of soliloquy as may be made, and, employed by Congreve, soliloquy had this advantage: it gave the author an opportunity, which he was quick to seize, of Sophoclean irony. None of the personages of the drama, except lady Touchwood, knows what is evident to the audience, that Maskwell is a villain. When Millefont says, 'Maskwell, welcome! thy presence is a view of land appearing to my ship-wrecked hopes,' the sense of irony is complete, and Congreve plays upon this note with the highest skill.

But it is not for its fable or for its Sophoclean irony that *The Double-Dealer* is chiefly admirable. Rather, we wonder today, as the town wondered then, at its well drawn characters and its scenes of brilliant comedy. Lord and lady Froth, who might have been inspired by the duke and duchess of Newcastle, are masterpieces of witty invention. The scene is never dull when her ladyship, a true *précieuse*, counters the gallantry and *bel air* of Mr Brisk, the most highly finished of coxcombs, with her coquettish pedantry. And is not Sir Paul Plyant, a kind of Fondlewife in a higher sphere, an excellent creature? And is not the vanity of his lady touched with a light and vivid hand? When she accepts Millefont's addresses to Cynthia as an assault upon her own honour, bidding him 'not to hope, and not to despair neither,' the true spirit of comedy breathes upon us. That the play was ill received, until it won the approval of the queen, is surprising. Dryden, the omnipotent dispenser of reputations, had no doubt of its merit. He wrote such a set of commendatory verses as might have put a seal upon the highest fame. He pictured himself as worn with cares and age, 'unprofitably kept at Heaven's expense,' and living 'a rent-charge on his providence.' He implored Congreve to be kind to his remains, to defend his departed friend, and 'to shade those laurels, which descend to him.' Meanwhile, he lavished the most generous praises upon him whom he looked upon as his inevitable successor:

[Quotes No. 10(a) above, ll. 20–7 and 61–3.]

This, of course, is the hyperbole of friendship. Congreve was supreme in his own realm; it was not for him to match his prowess against greater monarchs.

With all good faith, Dryden adjured Congreve to maintain his post: 'that's all the fame you need.' In *Love for Love*, his next comedy, Congreve did far more than maintain his post. He travelled one stage further towards the final triumph of *The Way of the World*. In 1695, Betterton and the best of his colleagues, having a just quarrel with the patentees of Drury lane, and being empowered by the king's licence to act in a separate theatre for themselves, opened the famous house in Lincoln's inn fields with *Love for Love*. The success of the play was without precedent and well merited. At each step, Congreve approached nearer to life as to the summit of his art. It is true that the pure comedy of *Love for Love* is intricated with a farce, in which Prue and Young Ben play their parts. It is true, also, that the hoyden's nurse had been a convention upon the stage ever since the performance of *Romeo and Juliet*. But she affords a relief to the brilliant flash of Congreve's wit, and, as for the sailor, if he be not 'accounted very natural,' he is 'very pleasant,' as Dr Johnson observed long ago. For the rest, it may be said that at last Congreve has entered into his kingdom. In every scene, he shows himself a perfect master of his craft. The exposition of the plot is perfect. Jeremy, although he speaks with Congreve's voice, is the best servant in the whole range of comedy. You will search in vain for a truer picture of a curmudgeon than Sir Sampson Legend, compact of humour and ill nature, whose 'blunt vivacity,' as Cibber calls it, was marvellously portrayed by Underhill. Foresight, that 'peevish and positive' old fellow, with an absurd pretence to understand palmistry, astrology, physiognomy, dreams and omens, was familiar to all frequenters of the theatre in those days of occult and half understood superstitions. When the two meet to discuss the marriage of Ben and Angelica, they vaunt their excellence in alternate strains.

'But I tell you,' brags Foresight, 'I have travelled, and travelled in the celestial spheres, know the signs and the planets, and their houses...know whether life shall be long or short, happy or unhappy, whether diseases are curable or incurable. If journeys shall be prosperous, undertakings successful; or goods stolen recovered, I know—'

[II, v, 46–55]

Sir Sampson's *riposte* is magnificent:

'I know,' thus he interrupts, 'the length of the Emperor of China's foot; have kissed the great Mogul's slipper, and rid a hunting upon an elephant with the Cham of Tartary.—Body o' me, I have made a cuckold of a king, and the present Majesty of Bantam is the issue of these loins,'

[II, v, 56–61]

a valiant boast, the repartee to which,— 'thou modern Mandeville! Ferdinand Mendez Pinto was but a type of thee, thou liar of the first magnitude!'—seems singularly ineffective.

But it was upon Valentine, the lover of Angelica, that Congreve lavished all the resources of his art. There is a nobility of phrase and thought in Valentine's encounters with his father, Sir Sampson, which may be called Shakespearean in no mere spirit of adulation. In these passages, Congreve rises to a height of eloquent argument, which gives a tragic force to his work.

'Why, sirrah,' asks Sir Sampson, 'mayn't I do what I please? are you not my slave? did I not beget you? and might not I have chosen whether I would have begot you or not? 'Oons, who are you? whence come you?...Come, uncase, strip, and go naked out of the world, as you came into 't.' 'My clothes are soon put off,' replies Valentine; 'but you must also divest me of reason, thought, passions, inclinations, affections, appetites, senses, and the huge train of attendants that you begot along with me.'

[II, vii, 61–83]

Still better, as diction or invention, are the speeches of the mad Valentine, who speaks with the very voice of Hamlet.

Alas, poor man! his eyes are shrunk, and his hands shrivelled; his legs dwindled, and his back bowed, pray, pray for a metamorphosis. Change thy shape, and shake off age; get thee Medea's kittle and be boiled anew;

come forth with labouring callous hands, a chine of steel, and Atlas
shoulders.

[IV, xv, 44–50]

But all is not on this high plane. Ben and Prue, Tattle and Scandal
carry us away to the lower slopes of farce, and when Mrs Frail
meets her sister, Mrs Foresight, it is a contest always of gaiety. No
scene in Congreve's plays is touched with a lighter hand than that
in which Mrs Foresight asks Mrs Frail where she lost her gold
bodkin: 'O Sister, Sister!' And Mrs Frail demands in answer, 'if
you go to that where did you find this bodkin? O Sister, Sister!
Sister every way.'

After the triumph of *Love for Love* at the theatre in Lincoln's inn
fields, Congreve agreed to give the managers a new play every
year, if his health permitted, in exchange for a 'full share.' In 1697,
he produced, not another comedy, but *The Mourning Bride*, a rash
experiment in the later Elizabethan drama. To a modern ear *The
Mourning Bride* is sad fustian. The action, such as it is, is enwrapped
in impenetrable gloom. Prisons and burial-vaults are its sombre
background. The artifice—disguise—upon which its plot turns is
borrowed from comedy, with the simple difference that the wrong
man is not married but murdered. In other words, Manuel, king of
Granada, personates Alphonso for jealousy of Zara:

> There with his bombast, and his robe arrayed,
> And laid along as he now lies supine,
> I shall convict her to her face of falsehood.

Were it not that Manuel is decapitated by his favourite, we might
be assisting at captain Bluffe's marriage with the masked Lucy. But
the taste of the time hailed it as a masterpiece. It was heard with
enthusiasm, and held the stage for many years. Stranger still is it
that Dr Johnson pronounced the description of the temple in the
second act 'the finest poetical passage he had ever read.' It is idle to
discuss the vagaries of criticism, though few will be found now to
mistake the pompous platitude of Congreve for poetry. For the
rest, the play opens with one of the oftenest quoted lines in
English—'Music hath charms to soothe a savage breast'; its third
act concludes on a famous tag, the sense of which is borrowed from
Cibber:

> Heaven has no rage, like love to hatred turned,
> Nor hell a fury, like a woman scorned;

and its production was but an interlude in the career of Congreve.

Three years later, in 1700, Congreve's masterpiece, *The Way of the World*, was played at the theatre in Lincoln's inn fields. That it was a failure on the stage is not remarkable. It was written to please its author's fastidious taste not to chime with the humour of the age. It was, in brief, a new invention in English literature. It is deformed neither by realism nor by farce. The comic spirit breathes freely through its ample spaces. 'That it succeeded on the stage,' says Congreve, 'was almost beyond my expectation.' There is no hint of grossness in the characters. They are not of the common sort, 'rather objects of charity than contempt,' which were then popular on the stage. In brief, it was Congreve's purpose

to design some characters, which should appear ridiculous, not so much through a natural folly (which is incorrigible, and therefore not proper to the stage) as through an affected wit, a wit, which at the same time that it is affected is also false.

And so, he set upon the boards a set of men and women of quick brains and cynical humours, who talked with the brilliance and rapidity wherewith the finished swordsman fences. They are not at the pains to do much. What Congreve calls the fable is of small account. It is difficult to put faith in the document which unravels the tangle and counteracts the villainy of Fainall. The trick played upon lady Wishfort, that most desperate of all creatures, a lady fighting an unequal battle with time, does no more than interrupt the raillery, which, with a vivid characterisation, is the play's excuse. The cabal nights, on which they come together, and sit like a coroner's inquest on the murdered reputations of the week, and of which Sheridan's imitation fell far below the original, demonstrate at once what manner of men and women are the persons of the drama. Witwoud, indeed, is the very triumph of coxcombry, with Petulant for his engaging foil. He never opens his lips without an epigram, and in his extravagant chatter climbs to the topmost height of folly. 'Fainall,' says he, 'how's your lady... I beg pardon that I should ask a man of pleasure and the town, a question at once so foreign and domestic.' And again: 'A wit should be no more sincere than a woman constant; one argues a decay of parts, as t'other of beauty.' How light, and cynical, and wellbred it all is, in spite of its purposed affectation! And the other characters, Mrs Marwood and the Fainalls, though the deeper seriousness of intrigue inspires them, are drawn with a perfect surety of skill and knowledge.

But Mrs Millamant and Mirabell overtop them all. The warfare of their wits and hearts is the very essence of the drama. George Meredith has said with justice that the play might be called 'The Conquest of a Town Coquette'; and, when the enchanting Millamant and her lover are on the stage, our interest in the others fades to nothingness. By a happy stroke, Millamant does not appear until the second scene of the second act, but Mirabell has discoursed of her qualities, and you are all expectancy. And nobly does the love-sick Mirabell hail her approach. 'Here she comes, i'faith, full sail, with her fan spread and her streamers out, and a shoal of fools for tenders; ha, no, I cry her mercy!' It is impossible to think of anything save the apparition of Dalila, in *Samson Agonistes*,

> That so bedeckt, ornate, and gay,
> Comes this way sailing
> Like a stately Ship
> Of Tarsus, bound for th'Isles
> Of Javan or Gadier
> With all her bravery on and tackle trim,
> Sails fill'd, and streamers waving.

And Mrs Millamant reveals herself at once as a woman of fashion, sated with life. Instantly she strikes the note of nonchalance in her famous comment upon letters. 'Nobody knows how to write letters and yet one has 'em, one does not know why. They serve one to pin up one's hair.' Then, she and Mirabell fall bravely to the encounter. 'Nay, 'tis true,' says he, 'you are no longer handsome when you've lost your lover; your beauty dies upon the instant; for beauty is the lover's gift.' 'Lord, what is a lover, that it can give,' asks Millamant. 'Why, one makes lovers as fast as one pleases, and they live as long as one pleases, and they die as soon as one pleases; and then, if one pleases, one makes more.' Whenever Millamant is upon the stage, Congreve is at his best. The speeches which he puts in her mouth are all delicately turned and finely edged. She is a personage by and of herself. She comes before you visibly and audibly. She is no profile, painted upon paper, and fitted with tags. Her creator has made her in three dimensions; and, as she always differs from those about her, so she is always consistent with herself. Mirabell knows her when he says that 'her true vanity is in her power of pleasing.' She is, indeed, a kind of Beatrice, who strives with a willing Benedick. But, though she loves her Mirabell, yet will she not submit. When he, lacking humour as a lover would in the circumstances, complains that 'a man may as soon make a friend by his wit, or a fortune by his honesty, as win a woman by plain-dealing and sincerity,' how deftly she turns his gravity aside! 'Sententious Mirabell!' And it is to Mrs Fainall, not to her lover, that at last she acknowledges, 'well, if Mirabell should not make a good husband, I am a lost thing—for I find I love him violently.'

But, before the end, there is many a battle to be fought. In her contest with Mrs Marwood, the spurned beauty, she hides her passion behind a veil of malicious merriment. 'I detest him, hate him, madam,' declares Mrs Marwood. 'O madam, why so do I,' answers the defiant Millamant, 'and yet the creature loves me, ha! ha! ha! how can one forbear laughing to think of it.' Nor will she dwindle into marriage without an exaction at every step. She'll be solicited to the very last, nay, and afterwards. It is not for her to endure 'the saucy looks of an assured man.' And so she makes terms with Mirabell, and he, in turn, offers conditions of matrimony, in a scene which for phrase and diction Congreve himself has never surpassed. Even at the last, she will yield only with an impertinence. 'Why does not the man take me? would you have me give myself to you over and over again?' And Mirabell replies, 'Ay, and over and over again.' Thus, they share the victory; and, as you lay down the play, in which incense has been offered to the muse of comedy, you feel that *The Way of the World*, for all its malice, all its irony, all its merriment, is as austere as tragedy, as rarefied as thought itself.

Congreve, then, carried to its highest perfection what is known as the artificial comedy or comedy of manners. He regarded himself as the legitimate heir of Terence and Menander, and claimed with perfect justice to paint the world in which he lived. Something, of course, he owed to his predecessors, and to the noble traditions of the English stage. Shakespeare, as has been hinted, was ever an example to him, and at the beginning of his career he worked under the domination of Ben Jonson. Of those nearer to his own time, he was most deeply indebted to the lighthearted Etherege. But, being himself a true master of comedy, he took for his material the life about him, a life which still reflected the gaiety of king Charles's court. The thirty years which had passed since the restoration, when Congreve began to write, had not availed to darken 'the gala day of wit and pleasure.' A passage, in which he describes the composition of *The Way of the World*, reveals in a flash his aim and ambition.

'If it has happened,' he writes in a dedication addressed to Ralph earl Montague, 'in any part of this comedy, that I have gained a turn of style or expression more correct, or at least more corrigible, than in those that I have formerly written, I must with equal pride and gratitude ascribe it to the honour of your Lordship's admitting me into your conversation, and that of a society where everybody else was so well worthy of you, in your retirement last summer from the town.'

When due allowance is made for the terms of a dedication, in which accuracy is asked of no man, it is easy to believe that, in lord Montague's country house, he found that wit and sparkle of life which he transferred to his scene, 'as upon a canvas of Watteau'—a Watteau, whose gaiety and elegance are tempered by malice.

But the life which he painted was not the life of common day. It was a life of pleasure and gallantry, which had a code and speech of its own. No man ever selected from the vast world of experience what served his purpose more rigorously than Congreve. He never cared for seeing things that forced him to entertain low thoughts of his nature. 'I don't know how it is with others,' said he, 'but I confess freely to you, I could never look long upon a monkey, without mortifying reflections.' Nor was he one who saw life whole. His sympathy was for 'persons of quality,' and he lived in a world situate on the confines of cynicism and merriment. Had he ever descended to realism his comedies might have been open to reproach. But the scene, in which his Plyants and Froths, his Mira-bells and Millefonts, his Millamants and Angelicas, his Brisks and Tattles, play their parts, is, like their names, fantastic enough half to justify the famous paradox of Charles Lamb. Even while we admit that Congreve painted what he chose to see, we may yet acknowledge that the persons of his drama 'have got out of Christendom into the land of—what shall I call it?—of cuckoldry—the Utopia of gallantry, whose pleasure is duty, and the manners perfect freedom.'★

It is in the interpretation of this gallantry that Congreve displayed his true genius. He was, above and before all, a man of

473

letters. It was not enough for him, as for most of his contemporaries, to devise an ingenious situation or to excite the laughter of the pit by the voice of boisterous fun. He had a natural love and respect for the English tongue. He cared supremely for the making of his sentences. His nice scholarship had taught him the burden of association which time had laid upon this word or that. He used the language of his own day like a master, because he was anchored securely to a knowledge of the past. In point and concision, his style is still unmatched in the literature of England. There is never in his writing a word too much, or an epithet that is superfluous. He disdains the stale artifices wherewith the journeyman ties his poor sentences together. As a stern castigator of prose, he goes far beyond the example of his master, Molière. And this sternly chastened prose, with its haunting memories of Shakespeare and Jonson, its flashing irony, and its quick allusiveness, is a clear mirror of Congreve's mind. The poet's phrase is penetrated and informed by the wit and raillery of the poet's thought.

In nothing does Congreve prove his art more abundantly than in the rhythm and cadence of his speech. His language appeals always to the ear rather than to the eye. So fine a master of comic diction was he, that, in every line he wrote, you may mark the rise and fall of the actor's voice. His words, in brief, were written to be spoken; he sternly excludes whatever is harsh or tasteless; and we in our studies may still charm our ears with the exquisite poise of his lines, because the accent still falls where he meant that it should fall, the stage effect may still be recovered in the printed page. He arranges his vowels with the same care which a musician gives to the arrangement of his notes. He avoids the clashing of uncongenial consonants, as a maker of harmonies refrains from discord. Open *Love for Love* or *The Way of the World*, where you will, and you will find passages which, by the precision wherewith they fit the voice, would give you pleasure, were they deprived of meaning.

NOTE

* See Lamb's eassy *On the Artificial Comedy of the Last Century*.

105. John Palmer in *The Comedy of Manners*

1913

From *The Comedy of Manners* (London: 1913).

John Leslie Palmer (1885–1944) wrote his study of Restoration comedy while dramatic critic and assistant editor of *The Saturday Review*. After the First World War he worked for the League of Nations, but continued to produce books on English drama at frequent intervals.

(i)

Congreve's first comedy *The Old Bachelor* was produced at Drury Lane in 1693. It is said to have been revised for the stage by Southerne, with Dryden's help; but we need not suffer ourselves to be disturbed into detecting the consequences of this revision. The writing is plainly Congreve. The play, as we have already seen, was immediately successful. The spectators might feel that happiest of sensations—the sensation of meeting with something new, but at the same time, familiar. Here was the vein they had welcomed in Etherege more surely and firmly pursued; together with the vivid, voluble buoyancy and keen touches of character they had applauded in Wycherley. The play was brilliantly acted by Mrs. Bracegirdle, Mrs. Barry, Mrs. Mountfort, Betterton and Dogget. It ran for fourteen nights. Southerne was expressing the general view:

[Quotes No. 3 (a), ll. 18–39.]

Is it entirely an accident that the opening lines of Congreve's first comedy are a manifesto?

BELLMOUR *and* VAINLOVE *meeting.*

Bell. Vainlove, and abroad so early! good morrow. I thought a contemplative lover could no more have parted with his bed in a morning, than he could have slept in't.

Vain. Bellmour, good morrow—Why, truth on't is, these early sallies are not usual to me, but business, as you see, sir—[*Showing letters.*] And business must be followed or be lost.

Bell. Business!—and so must time, my friend, be close pursued, or lost. Business is the rub of life, perverts our aim, casts off the bias, and leaves us wide and short of the intended mark.

Vain. Pleasure, I guess, you mean.

Bell. Ay, what else has meaning?

Vain. Oh, the wise will tell you—

Bell. More than they believe—or understand.

Vain. How, how, Ned, a wise man say more than he understands?

Bell. Ay ay; wisdom's nothing but a pretending to know and believe more than we really do. You read of but one wise man, and all that he knew was, that he knew nothing. Come, come, leave business to idlers, and wisdom to fools: they have need of 'em: wit, be my faculty, and pleasure my occupation; and let father Time shake his glass.

[I, i, 1–27]

If this be not malice aforethought, it is at any rate no accident that Bellmour and Vainlove are soon talking as if they had walked out of the last comedy of Etherege into the first comedy of his successor.

Bell. Why, faith, I think it will do well enough, if the husband be out of the way, for the wife to show her fondness and impatience of his absence by choosing a lover as like him as she can; and what is unlike, she may help out with her own fancy.

Vain. But is it not an abuse to the lover to be made a blind of?

Bell. As you say, the abuse is to the lover, not the husband: for 'tis an argument of her great zeal towards him, that she will enjoy him in effigy.

[I, i, 58–68]

Etherege continually recurs in passages which irresistibly appeal to be quoted. The following short passage between Bellmour and Belinda is Sir Frederick Frollick and his widow in transmutation to something finer. The spirit is Etherege. The manner begins to be Congreve:

Belin. Prithee, hold thy tongue!—Lard, he has so pestered me with flames and stuff, I think I shan't endure the sight of a fire this twelvemonth!

Bell. Yet all can't melt that cruel frozen heart.

Belin. O gad, I hate your hideous fancy! you said that once before.—If you must talk impertinently, for Heaven's sake let it be with variety; don't come always, like the devil, wrapped in flames.—I'll not hear a sentence more, that begins with an 'I burn'—or an 'I beseech you, madam.'

Bell. But tell me how you would be adored; I am very tractable.

Belin. Then know, I would be adored in silence.

Bell. Humph! I thought so, that you might have all the talk to yourself.

[II, viii, 4–20]

Wycherley recurs in scenes less susceptible of quotation. We detect him in the rough-and-tumble of the Fondlewife passages, and in the implicit satire of Heartwell's Comedy of Courtship. But Congreve has refined upon his model. There is less rapidity of merriment and less vigour of thrust, but a more deliberate expression. The satire is calculated, tolerant, delivered with the irritating superiority of an even temper. In the scene where Heartwell, the surly bachelor, hovers before the door of his enchantress, Congreve owes much to the models of his predecessor. But even as we recognise the debt, we feel how differently Wycherley would have used—or misused—the opportunities of Heartwell's misogamy.

[Quotes III, ii entire.]

In later scenes Congreve stands almost unsupported, a little too consciously aware, perhaps, that Wycherley was young ambition's ladder.

Belin. [*To* BELLMOUR.] O' my conscience, I could find in my heart to marry thee, purely to be rid of thee: at least thou art so troublesome a lover, there's hopes thou'lt make a more than ordinary quiet husband.

Bell. Say you so? is that a maxim among you?

Belin. Yes; you fluttering men of the mode have made marriage a mere French dish.... You are so curious in the preparation, that is, your courtship, one would think you meant a noble entertainment; but when we come to feed, 'tis all froth, and poor, but in show; nay, often only remains which have been I know not how many times warmed for other company, and at last served up cold to the wife.

Bell. That were a miserable wretch indeed, who could not afford one warm dish for the wife of his bosom.—But you timorous virgins form a dreadful chimera of a husband, as of a creature contrary to that soft, humble, pliant, easy thing, a lover; so guess at plagues in matrimony, in opposition to the pleasures of courtship. Alas! courtship to marriage, is but as the music in the playhouse till the curtain's drawn; but that once up, then opens the scene of pleasure.

Belin. Oh, foh! no; rather courtship to marriage, is as a very witty prologue to a very dull play.

[V, x, 15–39]

Finally, in a bravura passage, entirely dissociated from the rest of the play, Congreve definitely announces himself. We no longer detect the faintest accent of another voice. Belinda is describing to Araminta how in the Royal Exchange she had encountered a countryman come up to town with his wife and daughters:

[Quotes IV, viii, 1–57.]

(pp. 170–8)

(ii)

The Double Dealer is a masterpiece—with reservations. Congreve definitely appears. The play's defects are not, as were those of *The Old Bachelor*, a consequence of the incomplete assimilation of his models. The lighter scenes are as perfect Congreve as any in *The Way of the World*. But the play fails in equability. The tempestuous wickedness of Lady Touchwood, and the deliberate villainy of Maskwell are out of the picture. Save that he seldom neglects to speak exquisite prose, Maskwell is anybody's property. Only occasionally he belongs to Congreve. 'For your honest man, as I take it, is that nice, scrupulous, conscientious person who will cheat nobody but himself: such another coxcomb as your wise man, who is too hard for all the world, and will be made a fool of by nobody but himself.' This is obviously a personage of Congreve. But for the most part, Maskwell walks through the play disguised in heavy eyebrows and a scowl.

We at once appreciate the immense advance in maturity of style between the first and second of Congreve's comedies. No longer are we disconcerted with memories, as in *The Old Bachelor*. Congreve, of course, accepted precedents. He is still the heir of his predecessors. Etherege continues to be the model of his style; and the invocation of his comic mood. Wycherley continues to furnish him with many of his comic figures and situations. All this holds as definitely of *The Double Dealer* as of *The Old Bachelor*. But the difference is immense. The Fondlewife passages of *The Old Bachelor* were an absolute echo of Wycherley's lively, impudent and breathless theatre. Compare with these either of the passages where my lady Plyant, the familiar false prude of Wycherley's aversion, is so entertainingly divided between her honour and her necessity.

'Etherege, his courtship,' has fused with the 'satire, wit and strength of manly Wycherley'; and the fusion is chemical, not mechanical, the compound being quite unlike either of its constituents.

The Double Dealer is, of all Congreve's plays, the fullest of quotations. The few here selected are chosen not alone for their merit. They are a necessary preface to a general criticism of Congreve's work.

Mellefont's dialogue with Cynthia in the Second Act is the germ of that more brilliant scene between Mirabell and Millamant in *The Way of the World*—perhaps the most perfect scene in English comedy. This earlier scene is but a shadow; but the delicate superiority of Congreve's attitude towards the chapters of life which are commonly regarded as of some importance to mankind is already conspicuous:

Mel. You're thoughtful, Cynthia?

Cyn. I'm thinking, though marriage make man and wife one flesh, it leaves them still two fools; and they become more conspicuous by setting off one another.

Mel. That's only when two fools meet, and their follies are opposed.

Cyn. Nay, I have known two wits meet, and by the opposition of their wit render themselves as ridiculous as fools. 'Tis an odd game we're going to play at; what think you of drawing stakes, and giving over in time?

Mel. No, hang't, that's not endeavouring to win, because it's possible we may lose; since we have shuffled and cut, let's e'en turn up trump now.

Cyn. Then I find it's like cards: if either of us have a good hand, it is an accident of fortune.

Mel. No, marriage is rather like a game at bowls; Fortune indeed makes the match, and the two nearest, and sometimes the two farthest, are together; but the game depends entirely upon judgment.

Cyn. Still it is a game, and consequently one of us must be a loser.

Mel. Not at all; only a friendly trial of skill, and the winnings to be laid out in an entertainment.

[II, iii, 1–27]

Since we are very gravely to consider the objections which many of Congreve's critics have scored against him on moral grounds, it may be well to choose for our text, where it is possible, passages that have actually offended, especially where these passages are diverting, easily lifted from their context, and characteristic of their author. Two such passages of *The Double Dealer* at once suggest themselves. Mr. Brisk is Sparkish of *The Country Wife*. It has been objected that Congreve has spoiled the encounters between Mr. Brisk and my Lady Froth by allowing them to misconduct themselves in the prevailing fashion of the comedy. Let us very solemnly reflect that the loves of Mr. Brisk and my Lady Froth have very solemnly been censured. Then let us read the passage wherein they are discovered:

Lady Froth. O Parnassus! who would have thought Mr. Brisk could have been in love, ha! ha! ha! O Heavens, I thought you could have had no mistress but the nine Muses.

Brisk. No more I have, egad, for I adore 'em all in your ladyship. Let me perish, I don't know whether to be splenetic or airy upon 't; the deuce take me if I can tell whether I'm glad or sorry that your ladyship has made the discovery.

Lady Froth. O be merry by all means! Prince Volscius in love! ha! ha! ha!

Brisk. O barbarous, to turn me into ridicule! Yet, ha! ha! ha!—the deuce take me, I can't help laughing myself, ha! ha! ha!—yet by Heavens! I have a violent passion for your ladyship, seriously.

Lady Froth. Seriously? ha! ha! ha!

Brisk. Seriously, ha! ha! ha! Gad, I have, for all I laugh.

Lady Froth. Ha! ha! ha! What d'ye think I laugh at? ha! ha! ha!

Brisk. Me, egad, ha! ha!

Lady Froth. No, the deuce take me if I don't laugh at myself; for, hang me! if I have not a violent passion for Mr. Brisk, ha! ha! ha!

Brisk. Seriously?

Lady Froth. Seriously, ha! ha! ha!

[IV, vi, 30–56]

It is a grave text indeed.

Another passage, which seems painfully to have disturbed Sir Richard Steele, is a duologue between Sir Paul Plyant and his daughter Cynthia. Sir Paul has been censured for indelicately assuming that a possible result of his daughter's marriage will be an heir:

Sir Paul. [*To* CYNTHIA.] He! and wilt thou bring a grandson at nine months' end, he!—a brave chopping boy? I'll settle a thousand pound a year upon the rogue, as soon as he looks me in the face; I will, gadsbud! I'm overjoyed to think I have any of my family that will bring children into the world. For I would fain have some resemblance of myself in my posterity, hey, Thy? Can't you contrive that affair, girl? do, gadsbud, think on thy old father, he? make the young rogue as like as you can.

Cyn. I'm glad to see you so merry, sir.

Sir Paul. Merry! gadsbud, I'm serious; I'll give thee five hundred pounds for every inch of him that resembles me; ah, this eye, this left eye! a thousand pound for this left eye. This has done execution in its time, girl; why thou hast my leer, hussy, just thy father's leer:—let it be transmitted to the young rogue by the help of imagination; why 'tis the mark of our family, Thy; our house is distinguished by a languishing eye, as the house of Austria is by a thick lip.—Ah! when I was of your age, hussy, I would have held fifty to one I could have drawn my own picture.—Gadsbud! I could have done—not so much as you neither,—but—nay, don't blush—

Cyn. I don't blush, sir, for I vow I don't understand—

Sir Paul. Pshaw! pshaw! you fib, you baggage; you do understand, and you shall understand.

[IV, iii, 109–38]

This passage, transcribed *literatim*, is not precisely in late nineteenth century phrase or taste; but the old gentleman who jokes at the marriage feast about a christening is encountered outside the licentious comedies of the Restoration.

In many scenes of *The Double Dealer* 'manners' alone are the theme. Of these, two at least may profitably be cited here. The first is a dialogue on laughter between Lord Froth, Brisk, Careless and Mellefont:

Lord Froth. I assure you, Sir Paul, I laugh at nobody's jest but my own or a lady's: I assure you, Sir Paul.

Brisk. How? how, my lord? what, affront my wit! let me perish, do I never say anything worthy to be laughed at?

Lord Froth. O foy! don't misapprehend me: I don't say so, for I often smile at your conceptions. But there is nothing more unbecoming a man of quality than to laugh; 'tis such a vulgar expression of the passion! everybody can laugh. Then, especially to laugh at the jest of an inferior person, or when anybody else of the same quality does not laugh with one; ridiculous! To be pleased with what pleases the crowd! Now when I laugh, I always laugh alone.

Mel. But does your lordship never see comedies?

Lord Froth. O yes, sometimes;—but I never laugh.

Mel. No?

Lord Froth. O no;—never laugh indeed, sir.

Care. No? why, what d'ye go there for?

Lord Froth. To distinguish myself from the commonalty, and mortify the poets.

[I, iv, 22–v, 9]

The second is a dialogue wherein is devised between Mr. Brisk

481

and my Lady Froth the celebrated heroic poem of Jehu, formerly a hackney-coachman. It recalls, certainly not to its disadvantage, a classic passage of Molière.

[Quotes III, x, 1–58.]

Congreve's next play, *Love for Love*, was his most successful comedy. It held the stage to the time of Hazlitt, who has eloquently described Munden in the part of Foresight. Its success upon the stage is easily understood. It has a better plot; and a better selection of what, in slang of the theatre, are called 'character' parts than any other comedy of the period. Ben, 'the absolute sea-wit;' Foresight, the astrologer; Sir Sampson, the travelled ass; Tattle, who kept his secrets so mysteriously that all the town had wind of them; Miss Prue, the rustic ingénue, as forward as she is innocent—all are admirably of the stage. It is characteristic of *Love for Love* that one remembers the persons and story of the play, which is neither possible nor necessary in the majority of Restoration comedies.

Nevertheless, *Love for Love*, as Congreve knew, is infinitely less admirable than *The Double Dealer* or *The Way of the World*. It may reasonably be urged that comedies are built for the stage, and that if *Love for Love* acts better than *The Way of the World*, it is therefore a better play. But this argument begs the question. Whether a play *acts* better or worse than another, entirely depends upon the audience, and the particular qualities in a play which the audience is expecting. Every audience to-day expects in a play the qualities in which *Love for Love* is stronger than *The Way of the World*. They expect an intelligible story, characters strongly marked, and diverting situations, not too elaborately prepared. But the audiences of the Restoration period were being educated into expecting a different sort of merit. The tendency from Etherege to Congreve was to encourage the qualities in which *The Way of the World* excels every English comedy. Plot counts hardly at all; characters are finely shaded; manners are the principal theme; style is the necessary excellence. This type of comedy has never succeeded in England with a popular audience. Undoubtedly it would have done so, had the Restoration influence survived; but causes, hereafter to be examined, were already at work, which damned the current of English comedy.

In *Love for Love*, Congreve turned aside from the natural development of his style. It is the most loosely written of his comedies. The best scenes are a bright effervescence of that style of which the full body is Millamant and Mirabell. In one or two scenes—notably the scene where Miss Prue receives a first lesson in love from Mr. Tattle—Congreve goes negligently back to the tumbling comedy of Wycherley. The whole play is so obviously a backwater of the authentic stream, that it scarcely pays to dwell upon it very particularly. As a specimen of the light running style of its dialogue—written, as it seems, joyously, *currente calamo*—we may with advantage read the celebrated passage between Mrs. Foresight and Mrs. Frail:

> *Mrs. Fore.* You never were at the World's-End?
> *Mrs. Frail.* No.
> *Mrs. Fore.* You deny it positively to my face?
> *Mrs. Frail.* Your face! what's your face?
> *Mrs. Fore.* No matter for that, it's as good a face as yours.
> *Mrs. Frail.* Not by a dozen years' wearing.—But I do deny it positively to your face then.
> *Mrs. Fore.* I'll allow you now to find fault with my face; for I'll swear your impudence has put me out of countenance:—but look you here now—where did you lose this gold bodkin?—O sister, sister!
> *Mrs. Frail.* My bodkin?
> *Mrs. Fore.* Nay, 'tis yours, look at it.
> *Mrs. Frail.* Well, if you go to that, where did you find this bodkin?—O sister, sister!—sister every way.

[II, ix, 50–67]

The Way of the World was produced in 1700. Betterton, Mrs. Barry, Mrs. Bracegirdle, and Mrs. Leigh were in the cast; and Congreve wrote a prologue, in which the verdict of his audience was asked, with a confession that the play had cost him dear. The respectful irony of this appeal was too fine to be resented, even had it been perceived. But the verdict was against him.

The Comedy of Manners, as we have followed it from Etherege through Wycherley, to Congreve, has been a reflexion of contemporary life. Congreve has left, in his dedication of *The Way of the World* to Montague, unmistakable evidence of his intention.

'If,' says Congreve, 'it has happened in any part of this comedy, that I have gained a turn of style or expression more correct, or at least, more corrigible, than in those which I have formerly written, I must, with equal pride and gratitude, ascribe it to honour of your Lordship's admitting me into your conversation, and that of a society where everybody else was so well worthy of you, in your retirement last summer from the town; for it was immediately after that this comedy was written.'

We are now upon the summit of our theme. *The Way of the World* is a perfect expression of the temperament whose origins we have studied in the letters and plays of Sir George Etherege. Life is accepted and observed—not as a problem, but a pageant. The earlier author's impudent and bustling hedonism has, in his successor, grown to a calm and finished superiority to all that life can offer of good or bad. Etherege accepted life as the raw material of good manners. He asked no questions of Fate; life should minister to him occasions which he would improve as became a gentleman. He was the cheerful philosopher, as yet unthinking, innocent of a system, obeying his appetite for the day, keeping no account of himself for the satisfaction of an imaginary creditor. In Congreve, this life of the superficies has grown into a principle. Existence is an agreeable pageant. Microcosm and macrocosm are justified in that they are plain to the senses. The whole duty of man is to talk, when he can, like Mirabell. The cheerful wickedness of Etherege has given place to a more rounded and systematic iniquity; Congreve's characters are epicures in pleasure, exquisites in villainy. Their morality is as smoothly asserted in conduct and precept as the philosophy of Pope, which confines the universe in a couplet, and dismisses its ruler in an epigram. Congreve's muse is the full-blooded jade of Etherege and Wycherley come to discretion. Coleridge was right. Congreve's theme is often but simple wickedness, empty of pleasure or lust. There is an equable finality about the morality of *The Way of the World*—a dead level of conscience against which is vividly thrown a brilliant variety of manners and habits. It is a final assertion of that noble laziness of the mind which began with Etherege, in accepting and enjoying the vicissitudes of fortune, and ended, with Congreve, in despising them. Congreve seems ever to be passing his creatures in review with faint, expressive smiles of disdain.

Congreve's finished wickedness, of a world that has refined upon its worldliness, is admirably sampled in the opening scene of our comedy:

[MIRABELL *and* FAINALL, *rising from cards.*]
Mir. You are a fortunate man, Mr. Fainall!
Fain. Have we done?
Mir. What you please: I'll play on to entertain you.

Fain. I'll give you your revenge another time, when you are not so indifferent; you are thinking of something else now, and play too negligently; the coldness of a losing gamester lessens the pleasure of the winner. I'd no more play with a man that slighted his illfortune than I'd make love to a woman who undervalued the loss of her reputation.

Mir. You have a taste extremely delicate, and are for refining on your pleasures.

[I, i, 1–14]

Even more significant is the dialogue between Mirabell and his cast mistress in the Second Act.

Mrs. Fain. While I only hated my husband, I could bear to see him; but since I have despised him, he's too offensive.

Mir. Oh, you should hate with prudence.

Mrs. Fain. Yes, for I have loved with indiscretion.

Mir. You should have just so much disgust for your husband, as may be sufficient to make you relish your lover.

Mrs. Fain. You have been the cause that I have loved without bounds, and would you set limits to that aversion of which you have been the occasion? Why did you make me marry this man?

Mir. Why do we daily commit disagreeable and dangerous actions? to save that idol, reputation. If the familiarities of our loves had produced that consequence of which you were apprehensive, where could you have fixed a father's name with credit, but on a husband? I knew Fainall to be a man lavish of his morals, an interested and professing friend, a false and a designing lover; yet one whose wit and outward fair behaviour have gained a reputation with the town enough to make that woman stand excused who has suffered herself to be won by his addresses. A better man ought not to have been sacrificed to the occasion; a worse had not answered to the purpose. When you are weary of him you know your remedy.

[II, iii, 3–32]

Mirabell here justifies himself by the code, striking in cold blood a profit-and-loss account of what, if we invoke the moral values of a later period, is inexcusable, perfidious villainy.

Lady Wishfort, Mirabell, and Millamant of *The Way of the World* are the three most brilliant and equably sustained comic figures of the Restoration theatre. Lady Wishfort is presented as a portrait; but she is in every stroke impressed with the style of her master. It is not easy to recover the mood in which Congreve conceived her. We are persistently troubled with intrusions of pity or disgust, equally remote from the contemptuous ironical detachment of her author:

485

Mrs. Fain. Female frailty! we must all come to it, if we live to be old, and feel the craving of a false appetite when the true is decayed.

Mir. An old woman's appetite is depraved like that of a girl—'tis the green sickness of a second childhood; and, like the faint offer of a latter spring, serves but to usher in the fall, and withers an affected bloom.

[ibid., ll. 76–83]

Mirabell and Millamant are gallantry upon the heights. Millamant makes love with the tips of her fingers; Mirabell with the finished decorum of the man who has in this world nothing to learn or to lose. In the last encounter of Mirabell and Millamant, Congreve's comedy reaches a full close. 'Here,' in the words of Mirabell, 'the chase must end,' though Millamant would be followed to the last:

[Quotes IV, v, 8–149.]

The Way of the World but rarely falls beneath the level of this passage. It is equally brilliantly, monotonously fine. Comic dialogue can no further go.

(pp. 180–98)

Index

The following index is not a comprehensive index of names. In particular it rarely covers names in the footnotes. All the authors here constituting the critical heritage of Congreve are included, however, not now in the chronological order of the Contents but in wider alphabetical order. (Where the contribution is anonymous, the item is represented by the name of the periodical or work in which it first appeared.) There is an entry for each of Congreve's works formally mentioned in the primary material. The names of actors and actresses cited as having played in Congreve are included, though it has not always been possible to discover the full name. In addition, a series of thematic sub-headings, after the list of Congreve's works, is intended to help the reader with more general concerns.